Social Psychology

The Theory and Application
of Symbolic Interactionism

SOCIAL

PSYCHOLOGY

Robert H. Lauer & Warren H. Handel

Southern Illinois University at Edwardsville

THE THEORY AND

APPLICATION

OF SYMBOLIC

INTERACTIONISM

HOUGHTON MIFFLIN COMPANY • BOSTON

Atlanta Dallas Geneva, Illinois Hopewell, New Jersey

Palo Alto London

Printed in the U.S.A.

Library of Congress Catalog Card Number: 76–10895

ISBN: 0–395–24333–5

TO   Frances Lauer

Clinton Pentecost

and

Sam and Clara Handel

Contents

Preface

It is an "extraordinary blindness," wrote Pascal, "to live without investigating what we are." Long before Pascal penned those words, Confucius had said that one who "learns but does not think, is lost" while one who "thinks but does not learn is in great danger." These two quotes from two very different civilizations sum up our intention in this book. We want to provide a work that not only gives the student materials for understanding human behavior but also stimulates the student to use those materials in making his or her own analyses. Thus, in investigating "what we are" the student must both learn and think, which means learning what materials to use and learning to use those materials. To achieve this, we have emphasized both theory and application, both a perspective for understanding and the way in which the perspective has been used.

One of the initial decisions in putting together a specialized textbook of this kind was what to include and how to organize it. We were aiming at a work that is accessible to the beginning student. But we also wanted to include materials for upper-level and graduate students, for many students do not plunge deeply into symbolic interactionism until they are advanced.

We therefore organized the work so that both beginning and advanced students of social psychology could profit from it. Chapter 4 in particular is directed at the advanced student. The beginning student may read the entire book (with the possible exception of Chapter 4) for a comprehensive study of symbolic interactionism, or may read Chapters 1 through 3 and selected chapters from Parts 2 and 3 for an abbreviated course of study.

Throughout this book, social life is conceived as an ongoing process rather than a static structure. We have chosen to organize our statement of the theory around the interaction process. The interaction process is regarded by symbolic interactionists as the crucial forum of human social life, the primary occasion for communication, and the origin of both social structure and the individual human identity. By reviewing in Chapter 2 the major concepts of symbolic interactionism, and considerable research related to them, we have avoided becoming too narrow by our concentration on the interaction process. Further, we have tried to emphasize, in our discussion of interaction, those aspects of the process which contribute to the maintenance and change of broader aspects of the social structure.

We have characterized social interaction as essentially a socialization episode in which beliefs are tested, acted upon, and modified in response to ongoing events. In our view, socialization is continuous. In addition to the socialization of the infant from a creature that is only potentially social into a competent member of society, adults are continuously confronted with new information that alters their beliefs and the patterns of action based upon them. These changes may be transitory or they may have profound effects on the life of the individual involved and on the social structure as well. Our reviews of studies of deviance and of self-conceptions and the in-depth analyses in Part 3 will support these ideas. Finally, socialization may continue even when one is alone through one's ability to anticipate the responses of others in one's imagination.

In our view, human life is best conceived as a continuous learning process. Patterns of behavior may alter; the meanings attributed to events may alter; one's image in one's own and others' eyes may alter. Through it all, the process continues through which humans socialize one another and interpret their world. In a sense, human beings are never complete. So long as they live, they respond creatively and actively to their environment, changing themselves and it in the process.

With respect to structure, the book is divided into three major parts. The first part contains a systematic presentation of the theoretical position of symbolic interaction. Chapter 1 has been devoted to the assumptions underlying the work of symbolic interactionists and their historic roots in George Herbert Mead's thought. Chapter 2 defines the major terms and concepts employed in symbolic interaction and presents research in support of those concepts. Chapter 3 presents a statement of symbolic interaction theory focused on the interaction process. Chapter 4 considers some of the criticism raised against symbolic interaction and responds to it with reference to recent developments in several fields of study. Together these four chapters provide a comprehensive view of symbolic interactionism.

Theoretical positions are not the end of research, but the beginning. In the second section of the book we have examined how the theory of symbolic interactionism has been applied to a variety of substantive areas of sociological interest. Chapter 5 reviews the research on the self-concept, particularly as that research intersects with the theoretical position of symbolic interactionism. Chapter 6 examines the extensive body of research and theorizing about deviant behavior that is based on the symbolic interaction perspective. Chapter 7 examines a number of diverse phenomena that relate to everyday life experiences and which have been studied by symbolic interactionists, though not intensively for the most part. Chapter 8 is somewhat of a departure. It considers the position of the ethnomethodologists, who are not properly in the symbolic interactionist tradition. Despite this, the two address similar topics and an introduction to the issues raised by ethnomethodology are important for an understanding of social interaction. These four chapters obviously do not exhaust the application of symbolic interactionist theory. Taken together, however, they do provide insight into the way in which the general theoretical position can be brought to bear on specific substantive problems.

In Part 1 we have treated symbolic interactionism as a consensual body of theory. In fact, it is a body of ideas in flux, some more generally accepted than others. In the third section of the book, recognizing this fact, we review important, coherent variants of the basic symbolic interactionist position. We have done this by systematically presenting the distinctive views of four important contributors to the tradition: Herbert Blumer, Tamotsu Shibutani, Anselm Strauss, and Erving Goffman. In their work we can see the development of selective aspects of symbolic interaction theory and their applications to a variety of substantive topics. We hope, in these chapters, to give at least the flavor of the clash of ideas that characterizes sociology, but which is often omitted from texts.

The above materials and their organization achieve at least three purposes: (1) a systematic presentation of symbolic interactionism; (2) a broadened understanding of social life and human behavior; and (3) a set of tools with which the student can continue his or her education and expand his or her understanding. The student is carried through a logical sequence of first being grounded in the theory, then shown the application of the theory to various social phenomena, and then introduced in a systematic fashion to some of the major contributors. We have attempted throughout the book to facilitate understanding by the use of concrete examples from empirical research and by providing suggested readings at the end of each chapter for those who wish to pursue particular topics further.

Many people were important in completing this book. The senior author is indebted to Paul Campisi, who taught him symbolic interactionism and supported his professional aspirations. Nancy Stephens typed and retyped the seemingly endless pages, and kept a watchful eye for ambiguities and awkwardness. She has made our task easier and we deeply appreciate her contribution. Finally, we are grateful to those who read various chapters and offered helpful comments: Herbert Blumer, University of California at Berkeley; Joseph F. Zygmunt, University of Connecticut; Edward Z. Dager, University of Maryland; David C. Lundgren, University of Cincinnati; Raymond L. Schmitt, Illinois State University; Judith Handel, University of Missouri at St. Louis; Martha Becker, Andrew Bova, Stephanie Sanford, Nancy Yoffie, and Susan Zonia. The final work may not measure up to what they would have liked, but it would have been much poorer without their contributions.

Social Psychology

The Theory and Application
of Symbolic Interactionism

PART 1

THE THEORY

OF SYMBOLIC

INTERACTIONISM

Do you believe there is life on other planets? In response to that question, a wit said, "Of course. And the proof is, they're using earth for their insane asylum." The answer reflects a feeling that most of us have at some point—that human life can be perplexing, irrational, and even outrageous. At such times we may ponder the questions of why people are what they are and why they behave as they do. And those are questions that are the central concern of social psychologists.

It is, of course, not only the "insane" facets of human existence that interest us. Rather, we want to understand all that is true about humans because they live in relationships with others—we want to understand the nature and behavior of the social creature called man. Social psychology is an effort to gain such understanding, and symbolic interactionism is a particular approach in social psychology.[1]

In this first part, then, we examine symbolic interactionist theory. We begin with the basic assumptions and central concerns of symbolic interactionism. We will then examine ten key concepts. These concepts will be followed by an explication of the interaction process and, finally, by a brief discussion of theoretical and methodological problems.

We might pause at the outset, however, and ask the question, why theory? Why not simply study the world and let the facts "speak for themselves"? With respect to the first question, there is nothing esoteric or difficult about theory. Put in simplest, perhaps crudest, terms, a theory is simply a way of making sense out of the world. Thus, we all use theories to understand the world in which we live. For example, the theory may involve a negative view of human nature. From this it could be deduced that societies must exercise strong control over the behavior of individuals (we must be tough and maintain law and order); that individuals are foolish to engage in trusting relationships (it's a dog-eat-dog world); and that everyone would do well to watch out for themselves and get what they can (do unto others before they do it to you). One who held to such a theory about the world would behave in certain ways that reflected the theory; one would also analyze the behavior of others and events in the world in terms of that theory. Theories, then, may be accurate or inaccurate with respect to their explanations of the world, but we all use theories to make sense out of our world.

Symbolic interactionism is a theory that makes sense out of the world in a particular way. If you accept it as valid, you will be led to behave in certain ways and to analyze the behavior of others and events in the world in particular ways. The kind of understanding afforded by symbolic interactionism will be clear in the chapters in this part; here we simply want to stress the point that in offering a theory we are more likely offering an alternative mode of understanding rather than a first insight into the many phenomena discussed.

With respect to the second question raised above, the facts never speak for themselves. As the above discussion implies, "facts" are always interpreted, and interpretation always takes place within some theoretical framework. Human beings are cognitive creatures who always strive to make sense out of the world. But the world does not force any particular

---

[1] Space limitations prohibit a discussion of various social psychological approaches. To fully understand symbolic interactionism, however, the student should have some knowledge of other perspectives. Two helpful sources are Morton Deutsch and Robert M. Krauss, *Theories in Social Psychology,* Basic Books, New York, 1965, and John W. McDavid and Herbert Harari, *Social Psychology: Individuals, Groups, Societies,* Harper & Row, New York, 1968, pp. 20–38.

understanding on them. This may be seen in the fact that different individuals interpret the same objective situation in quite differing ways. For example, experiments in which subjects are given pictures to interpret show that the situations portrayed in the pictures may be interpreted in radically different ways by different individuals. A picture of an impoverished family may be interpreted by one individual as an illustration of people who are oppressed by an unjust social order and neglected by the government, while another individual may interpret it as a clear case of people who lack ambition and enjoy living in their own dirt. And a third individual may deny that the family is even impoverished. What are the "facts" of the situation portrayed? Again, so-called facts do not speak for themselves. Each of us interprets the world in which we live in accord with our theoretical perspectives. The following chapters offer the theory of symbolic interactionism as a unique and fruitful mode of understanding.

Chapter 1

Foundations: The Assumptions of Symbolic Interactionism

"Social psychology"—even the name suggests its interdisciplinary character. Nevertheless, social psychology is not simply a combination or synthesis of sociology and psychology. In the first place, many other fields have contributed to social psychology. Concepts, techniques, and information from over a dozen disciplines are typically incorporated in social psychological thought. Several of those disciplines, such as genetics, neurophysiology, and biochemistry, are relatively obscure to most social scientists. However, as the understanding of the organic bases of human behavior increases, the importance of these disciplines to social psychology increases. For example, a recent development is the technique of bio-feedback, in which an individual can learn to control such bodily processes as brain waves and blood pressure. The technique has obvious importance for mental and physical health, and it also illustrates the point that humans can be treated neither as mindless organisms nor as pure minds. Human life is bound up with both cognitive and bodily processes, and bio-feedback has opened up anew the important question of the relationship between the two.

Second, social psychology is not a distinctive discipline. Rather, it is found in several disciplines under a variety of names. The discipline within which it is practiced greatly influences the choice of problems and methods. Thus, the social psychology practiced in sociology is quite different from that practiced in psychology, and both differ from the study of "culture and personality" in anthropology. In the following paragraphs, therefore, we will outline a sociological approach to social psychology.

Social Psychology from a Sociological Perspective

Sociology is concerned with the study of social systems. The social system is conceived to have emergent characteristics which cannot be explained in terms of the characteristics of the people that make it up. Typically, structural regularities are defined and attempts are made to analyze the consequences of those regularities, the conditions under which they arose, the conditions under which they change, and the processes that maintain and alter them.

An illustration of a structural regularity is the "rush hour" in our society. Every workday morning a predictable number of cars drive in predictable directions over predictable routes to predictable central locations. And every workday evening they return. The rush hour is like a human tide in which the central location, ordinarily a city, is the shoreline. Like the tide, the rush hour is something different from its parts—molecules of water and carloads of people, respectively. Every morning, some people do not drive during the rush hour as they usually do. They are sick, on vacation, laid off, or AWOL. But although we cannot predict accurately who will be absent, we can predict accurately how many will be absent. The rush hour goes on without the presence of its absentees and is, in fact, defined by their predictable absence as well as by the presence of others. It is in this predictability that the rush hour has its own existence.

This structural regularity has consequences that cannot be reduced to the contributions of individuals. For example, rush hours create smog—

concentrations of pollutants—that are the result of the heavy concentration of traffic, not of individual exhaust systems. From the hills overlooking Los Angeles, one can see the smog grow daily as the air over more and more of the city becomes brown, and then shrink as the concentration of traffic diminishes each evening. The processes that maintain and alter the rush hour are also distinguished from those affecting the lives of its individual participants. For example, each driver in the rush hour is responding to a unique set of practical considerations. For the sake of simplicity, let us limit our consideration to the most common concern— the need to get to work on time. If workers were given different times to start work, each would continue to respond to his or her own situation as before. However, the rush hour would be altered or eliminated because those individual life conditions would no longer lead so many people to drive at the same time.

Two considerations suggest the importance of social psychology to sociologists. First, although the social structure cannot be reduced to the activities of individuals, it does emerge from them. To understand fully how the social structure operates or how it can be altered we must know about the processes affecting the individuals involved. The rush hour is a misleadingly simple example. We know that the rush hour emerges from the need of people to drive to a central location at the same time and we also know that getting to work is the predominant concern. Thus we are able to see easily that the rush hour, as a social structure, could be eliminated if people did not need to drive at the same time. The means of changing the structural arrangement, in this case, requires only a minimal understanding of the conditions under which individuals live and the processes involved in their behavior. However, the regular occurrence of murder, rape, suicide, changes in fashion, and preferences for certain types of television shows emerge from individual life situations in the same way as the rush hour. To understand these structural phenomena fully we would need, once again, to understand how individuals respond to their unique life situations. However, neither the crucial conditions nor the processes that lead to the behavior involved and that result in stable, predictable rates of their occurrence are well understood. That is one task for social psychologists—to understand how individual behavior occurs in a larger social context so that social regularities in behavior can be understood.

Second, we must recognize that social systems come in various sizes and exist for various lengths of time. At one extreme we have nations and institutions whose structure involves millions of people and which must be analyzed on a historical or evolutionary time scale. At the other extreme, we have the social interaction, the coming together of a few individuals in a situation for time spans that may sometimes be measured in seconds. An interaction may be simply two people who greet one another in passing. Even this situation has emergent structural characteristics, as we will see, but their scale makes the conduct of each individual much more crucial to understanding the situation as a whole. In these small systems, in fact, the individual and structural concerns are so closely intertwined that their study often becomes differentiated from the rest of sociology—social psychological rather than purely sociological. Thus, there is a group of social systems that cannot be analyzed without consideration of the processes of individual conduct.

These two considerations converge on social interaction as the major focus of social psychological interest. First, in dealing with small social systems the importance of the individual is increased and the analysis must take that into account. And second, the individual life situations from which larger systems emerge are primarily those of social interaction. People live their lives in the presence of others, influence and are influenced by them, understand their problems in terms of the others who are involved, and so on. All of this occurs in interaction, from the time of infancy until death. As we shall see, human symbolizing ability is social, and even when alone, the thinking person exists in a *social* symbolic world.

Both of these reasons for the study of social interaction are reflected in our treatment of the phenomenon. First, social interaction is a phenomenon that is interesting and important in itself. To understand it is to understand how humans make their way through the social world. Also, to understand larger-scale phenomena completely, social interaction must be understood as well. Thus, we will analyze social interaction in detail. In addition, we emphasize as much as possible the implications of the social interaction process for larger-scale phenomena and the insights that the study of social interaction lend to those phenomena. Social psychology, then, is the study of social interaction as a phenomenon in its own right and as a component of larger social systems.

General Assumptions of Symbolic Interaction

The social psychological perspective developed in this book falls within the tradition known as symbolic interaction. In addition to their sociological approach to social psychology, the research and theory in this tradition (as in any other) rest on a number of assumptions about the nature of the subject matter and the most appropriate ways in which to study it. These assumptions constitute an important part of the body of knowledge. They shape inquiry by suggesting what topics are fruitful to explore and the appropriate way to explore them. In so doing, they also suggest what topics may be ignored.

Differences between their assumptions link each specialized discipline to others. The assumptions made in one discipline are often the core subject matter of other disciplines. For example, symbolic interactionists assume that the processes of human communication and social life are different from those underlying the conduct of other species. This assumption discourages the study of other species. However, other species are studied in several other disciplines and the information gathered is crucial to the evaluation of our own assumptions. While the assumptions made by different disciplines may be different, none of them should contradict established knowledge. By discussing our assumptions we hope to indicate that they are congruent with the best factual information currently available and also that we will change them (and our approach) if future information contradicts them.

Such linkages forge the various specialized disciplines of modern science into a collective enterprise to which each discipline or specialty contributes in the effort to solve the enormously complex puzzle presented by human beings and nature. Still, the disciplines remain distinctive, and assumptions of each are important because of the fervor and depth of people's commitment to them. In fact, assumptions are often so profoundly believed within a discipline that they are considered beyond proof and challenge. Campbell, for example, notes that there are issues raised by philosophers as a matter of course that physicists greet not only with disinterest but with outright hostility. For philosophers may challenge the existence of the world itself as a step in their analysis of how knowledge is justified. Such philosophical debates concern matters that physicists insist upon taking for granted.[1] Thus, the challenge of basic assumptions is likely to produce an emotional reaction greater than that produced by a challenge of either empirical findings or theories. For the student, assumptions may be encountered as a "blind spot" in the discipline, a place where a probe may produce hostility but no clear answer. Understanding a theory is understanding what is *not* asked, as well as understanding the answers to what *is* asked.

In our view, the assumptions of a discipline resemble a shared culture more than a set of logical premises. For, they cannot be listed in a complete and precise way, nor is the connection between them and the research based upon them clearly defined. Rather, like cultural axioms, they are vague, difficult to apply to specific situations, and often understood differently by colleagues. Often we are unaware of our assumptions and are surprised when we realize that we have beliefs that have gone unchallenged, but for which alternatives exist. Also, assumptions are not static, but emerge from the very social processes which we will be discussing.

[1] Norman Campbell, *Physics: The Elements,* University Press, Cambridge, 1920, p. 9.

While the subject matter of theory may become highly explicit and formalized, the vagueness of assumptions is a stubborn fact of intellectual life. The problem is not that we cannot focus on our assumptions and be more precise about them. Rather, the problem is that in studying assumptions we must move into a new discipline. For example, we may gain insight into the assumptions that underlie the study of humans by moving into an analysis of animal communication. But such a move is made at the expense of no longer studying humans, and of adopting some new set of assumptions which can only be studied by changing focus once again.

The fact of intellectual specialization, then, implies a kind of vagueness concerning the assumptions of each speciality. The boundaries of the discipline are defined by which matters are discussed as clearly and precisely as possible and which are not. Thus, our treatment of assumptions will employ the empirical studies made in other disciplines. Those studies do not share our assumptions, but they do allow us to indicate that our assumptions are realistic, congruent with the known empirical facts. The discussion also provides a sense of our orientation or starting point, a sense that puts our detailed discussion of social processes in a broader context.

PHILOSOPHICAL ORIGINS: THE WORK OF GEORGE HERBERT MEAD

The social psychological approach that is now called symbolic interaction has its roots in the pragmatic school of philosophy that developed, and had its greatest influence, during the first quarter of this century. The pragmatists believed that many philosophical problems should be reformulated in the context of the rapid growth of scientific knowledge, especially evolutionary theory. The philosophical tradition, they argued, had become fundamentally isolated from both the practice of science and the world of practical problems. The pragmatists attempted to lessen this isolation.

The core issue in the isolation of philosophy was the increasingly radical approach to the study of the bases of knowledge. It had become common for philosophers to question the foundations of knowledge and to cast all knowledge into doubt. If knowledge is questioned in a sufficiently radical way, one is led to the conclusion that all tests of knowledge ultimately involve our subjective experience or perception. How, for example, do we know that a book exists? We can feel it, see it, smell it, even taste it. However, each test results only in additional subjective experiences. The existence of the experiences themselves cannot be denied, but the existence of the book independent of that subjective experience, its existence as an existing object in the world, *can* be doubted. Following this reasoning, yet interested in certainty, philosophers had come to doubt the existence of the world and to turn to an analysis of subjective experience as the only basis for certain knowledge.

The pragmatists rejected this radical approach. As an alternative, they proposed that philosophical analysis should proceed from the same assumption as empirical science. George Herbert Mead argued that scientists never question the existence of the world in a radical way, nor do they open all knowledge to doubt. Rather, their methodology *assumes* the existence of the world and gives this assumed world priority over both theory and subjective experience. The priority of the world over theory is shown in the fact that when scientists face a contradiction between theory and evidence gathered in a methodologically sound way, they alter the theory.[2] That is, conditions are imposed by the world to which theory must be responsive. The existence of real objects of perception is also assumed in explaining our subjective experience. Given the assumption of a real world, we must explain the objective conditions under which a particular subjective experience arises.[3] (For further discussion, see the distinction between the attitudes of common sense and scientific theorizing in Chapter 8.)

Another distinctive characteristic of the pragmatists was their belief in the priority of behavior over subjective experience. Meaning and consciousness of meaning were conceived to emerge from behavior. As William James put it, we do not run because we are afraid, rather, we experience fear because we run. This reversed the common view that the human ability to think was a prior condition for the development of our social life. This view was shared, of course, with the behavioral psychologists of the period. The behaviorists, however, were involved primarily with the study of infrahuman animals and their approach was less sophisticated than the behaviorism suggested by the pragmatists. Several pragmatists criticized the concepts of animal behaviorism, especially those developed by John Watson, as too simplistic to be generalized to humans.

A final distinguishing characteristic of pragmatism is its concern for bringing philosophical analysis to bear upon practical, social issues. The kind of certain knowledge sought by other philosophers was from the pragmatic perspective useless, and certainty was not considered to be as important as usefulness. The pragmatists were quite successful in influencing social movements. John Dewey, the best known pragmatist, was especially concerned with the process of education and his work still exerts a strong influence on our educational system.

Within social psychology, George Herbert Mead is clearly the most

[2] George Herbert Mead, *The Philosophy of the Present,* edited by Arthur Murphy with Prefatory Remarks by John Dewey, Open Court, La Salle, Ill., 1932, pp. 93–118.
[3] George Herbert Mead, *The Philosophy of the Act,* edited, with an introduction by Charles Morris, The University of Chicago Press, Chicago, 1938, pp. 8–9.

influential of the pragmatists. This influence has been achieved and maintained since his death in 1931 despite the peculiar character of his available, published work. Mead published several dozen short papers in a variety of scholarly journals. However, he never presented a systematic discussion of his views in a longer format. The only books published under his name were actually assembled by his students and colleagues, posthumously, in an attempt to systematize his thought.[4] They utilized class notes, recollections of conversations, a series of lectures that Mead intended to revise for publication, and unpublished notes found among Mead's effects. The resulting volumes reflect the creative efforts of several men, in addition to Mead, but they have had the effect of presenting Mead's views in a systematic form to an audience that could not be reached by the scholarly papers alone.

In the general philosophical dispute concerning whether a radical philosophical or scientific approach to knowledge should be taken, Mead's special concern was the application of the issues to social psychology. Mead believed that the strength and success of the physical sciences virtually forced the reality of their objects upon philosophy. The social sciences, however, did not have such well-defined objects and were not compelling in the same way. The success of physics, for example, forces the belief in electrons upon us in a way that sociology cannot force the belief in social structure upon us. In lieu of that compelling force, Mead undertook to demonstrate in terms of subjective experience itself, that the existence of a social world, independent of that experience, was a necessary condition for our experience of it.[5] In other words, Mead adopted the techniques of the radical philosophers, the analysis of experience through introspection, and showed that our experience of selves could not arise unless the selves existed. In so doing, Mead addressed the very issues that are still crucial to social psychology—the interrelationhips among thought, action, and social organization.

Mead holds a double status in social psychology. He is a historical figure whose work is part of the development of our current thought. At the same time, many of his ideas are still in use. Many of them will be discussed throughout the book in the relevant contexts. Two of his specific

---

[4] Mead's most influential work, published posthumously, is George Herbert Mead, *Mind, Self, and Society,* edited, with an introduction by Charles Morris, The University of Chicago Press, Chicago, 1934. Many of Mead's papers are collected in two volumes. George Herbert Mead, *Selected Writings,* edited, with an introduction by Andrew J. Reck, Bobbs-Merrill, Indianapolis, 1964. George Herbret Mead, *Essays on His Social Philosophy,* edited by John Petras, Teachers College Press, New York, 1968.

[5] George Herbert Mead, "What Social Objects Must Psychology Presuppose?" in George Herbert Mead, *Selected Writings,* ed. Andrew Reck, Bobbs-Merrill, Indianapolis, 1964, pp. 105–113.

contributions, however, constitute part of the fundamentals of our approach and will be discussed briefly as part of this introduction. These are Mead's definition of "meaning" and his analysis of "the act."

Meaning. Meaning is a relationship between an individual and events in the environment. Environmental events confront the individual as a set of conditions within and in response to which he or she must act. The meaning of the event to the individual is the response he or she makes to it or the readiness to respond to it in a particular way. Consider, for example, a door. The meaning of the door as we approach it is "an object to open" and then "an opening to walk through" and then "an object to close." Each of these responses is a meaning of the door and complex definitions are syntheses of our various possible responses. The door exists independent of its meaning to us. Its meaning is all of the responses we make to it, all of the ways in which we act toward it. Insofar as different people respond to the door differently, it has different meanings for them. But clearly many meanings can be shared.

Environmental events have meaning for any acting individual, human or nonhuman, insofar as the individual responds to them. The meaning of the object may be expressed in conduct without consciousness of it. The meaning of a speck of dust or pollen as "an object to be flushed from the body by a running nose and tearing eyes" may not be conscious. Rather, we respond to the object and learn of the object's meaning by observing our own response. In this case, we will probably not even be aware of the presence of the object until the response has begun, indicating that the object, although not otherwise noticed, must be there. In general, the meaning of an object arises from our response to it. That is, in defining an object we must first react to it, and then, through observing the consequences of our action, discover the meaning of the object.

Mead argued that as the selection of an appropriate response to an object becomes less problematic, the tendency to be conscious of its meaning diminishes. If the current situation closely matches our past experience and if a desirable response is already clearly defined by that experience we respond automatically to events without consciousness. Mead argued that these automatic responses, without consciousness, are essential for efficient responses. On the other hand, the utility of consciousness in problem-solving situations is suggested. Otherwise, he argues, consciousness would not have survived in the evolutionary process.

Two conditions contribute to the consciousness of meaning. First, the situation may be an unfamiliar one for which our experience suggests no appropriate response. Second, while the experience with such situations may be extensive, it may also be ambiguous, suggesting several possible responses. In such a case, the meaning of the event in the new situation is problematic since only one of the possible responses can be actualized. Even simple objects such as a door may create such problematic situations if, for example, we are unsure of whether to push or pull it open.[6]

The act. Although Mead's analysis of the act is behavioristic, it stands in sharp contrast to the relatively simple version of action suggested by animal behaviorists during the same period. At that time the process now known as "operant conditioning" was beginning to be described and to be suggested as the process underlying all behavior, including that of humans. In that view, learning occurred only as a result of experience. The organism, confronted with a novel situation, was conceived to behave in an essentially random fashion and to experience the consequences of his action. When favorable consequences resulted, the tendency to repeat the action in similar future situations was enhanced. On those future occasions, the appearance of a familiar stimulus would automatically lead to the repetition of the previously successful act. When unfavorable consequences resulted, the organism would avoid the response in the future and continue to behave randomly in future similar situations, excluding those responses with negative consequences until positive consequences were achieved. Thus, learning was conceived to be the result of trial and error. And orderly behavior was conceived to be the mechanical repetition of acts in response to stimuli and based on prior experience.

For Mead, the mechanical repetition of previously successful acts represents only a small part of human activity. Smooth, mechanical repetition of responses occurred, according to Mead, only in acts "made perfect in habit." In situations that very closely resemble prior experiences there will be little difference between our memories of prior experience and the actual experience of the ongoing act. In these cases, action proceeds automatically, without consciousness of meaning. Only if some difficulty arises in the course of the act does the inhibition of the act lead to consciousness of meaning, thought, and a disruption of mechanical repetition.[7] Tying one's shoes is an example of an act made perfect in habit. It is done automatically and without awareness, except on those occasions when the act is interrupted by, for instance, a broken shoelace.

The recognition that consciousness of meaning emerges among humans in some situations is part of Mead's addition to the simpler behavioristic model. His analysis of the function of that consciousness led him to believe that humans could learn new responses, new meanings, without

[6] George Herbert Mead, "Social Consciousness and Consciousness of Meaning," in George Herbert Mead, *Selected Writings,* ed. Andrew Reck, Bobbs-Merrill, Indianapolis, 1964, pp. 125–127.
[7] *Ibid.,* pp. 128–129.

actual trials and without the actual experience of their consequences. Consider a problematic situation in which several meanings are suggested for an object, only one of which can be actualized in conduct. The readiness to act in several ways inhibits the response—each possible response being blocked by the alternatives to it. If we become conscious of those various meanings, we can review our past experience with each type of response and *imagine* the consequences of actualizing each alternative. At the same time, we can examine the present situation in more detail to determine if unnoticed details favor one response over the others. In short, we can, in some circumstances, conduct our trials in imagination, learning from the image of what would happen to us if we acted in a certain way rather than from actual experience.

Consider the fact that our shoelaces always seem to break when we are already late. Does one replace the broken shoelace with the one in the hall closet? Or was that the upper left drawer in the kitchen? Or were shoelaces bought at the last shopping? Or is there a perfectly good shoelace in another shoe? Does one search for a shoelace or make do with the one in another shoe? Does a search mean being late for work? If one begins the search, how long can one continue it before it is necessary to stop and improvise with the broken shoelace or be late?

For Mead, thought is always the solution of problems. And although this example is simple, it reflects the role of thought, of being conscious of meanings, in the act. Mead's analysis of the act is a more complete statement of that role, and it supplements rather than replaces the analysis of the effects of trial and error on subsequent behavior.

Mead analyzed the act into four stages: impulse, perception, manipulation, and consummation. These four stages occur only in acts not made perfect in habit. The impulse, in Mead's definition, is not confined to needs or desires. The impulse is the consciousness of meaning, which occurs only in problematic situations. In the act made perfect in habit, the stimulus has power over the organism in the sense that it dictates automatically, without consciousness, a particular response. When that response does not have the expected results, the object becomes undefined and loses that power.[8] Harmony with the environment, the success of actions based on existing definitions, then, does not lead to consciousness of meaning or thought. The human being in perfect harmony with his or her environment would never think. Like any other animal, a human would respond automatically. But when the harmony is disrupted, thinking occurs and is the mechanism by which harmony is regained. Our ability to think, then, makes it possible for us to re-establish harmonious relationships with our environment, with fewer risks than actual trials.

[8] Mead, *Philosophy of the Act,* pp. 6–8.

Perception is an active response to the problematic situation. It involves consciousness of the stimuli presented by the immediate situation. In addition, memory images of past experience are part of the percept or image. These memory images are compared with the stimuli arising from the situation and our ongoing action in it. The comparison allows us to anticipate the consequences of our ongoing action, based on our memories of past experience with similar objects. Thus, the image is not a static representation of the external world. It is a representation of a complete act which is compared with the immediate situation.[9] By altering the memories with which the present situation is compared, we are able to imagine a variety of possible consequences and learn from them.

During the manipulatory stage of the act, the individual acts in the immediate situation and experiences the actual consequences of his action. During this phase, the meaning of events is still problematic, even if thinking has resulted in a new tentative definition. The meaning of events remains problematic, and consciousness continues, until the actual consequences of action are experienced and found to be in harmony with our definition. The emergence of a new, proven definition and the recession of meaning from consciousness is the consummation of the act.

We can summarize the functions of meaning and consciousness of meaning in the act. Meaning is originally our response to an act. That is, in order for an event to have meaning for us, we must first respond to it. The meaning is not in the event per se, but in the response we make to the event. Subsequently, we may be ready to respond in the same way again. This readiness to respond, then, becomes a further condition in our environment and guides our action. If our response is unsuccessful, we become consciously concerned with meaning until a satisfactory meaning is achieved. Consciousness of meaning is always a consequence of interrupted action. And the complete act is the mechanism through which the human brings his or her meaning into harmony with nature.

HUMANS RESPOND TO MEANINGS

A first, fundamental assumption of symbolic interaction, then, is that humans live in a world of meanings. They respond to events and objects in terms of meanings they have attributed to them. Stated in this general form, there is virtually no disagreement on this characterization of humans by any student of social life. Consider the condition that would prevail if this were not true: any human being confronted with a situation would respond to it in the same way as any other human being. The events themselves would dictate the response, independent of the previous learning and experiences of the individual. This situation obviously does not

[9] *Ibid.,* pp. 3–6.

exist. Instead, we find the world populated with many cultural groups, each recognizably human, and each responding to events in characteristic and unique ways. Furthermore, within each culture we find, instead of unanimity, a variety of subcultures, sharing some ways of responding to the world with the larger group, but unique in others. Finally, even within the most tightly knit subcultures, we find individual differences in how people respond to the world. Two crucial topics are suggested immediately by this view: the study of culture and subculture as systems of meanings that shape the world for the individual, and the study of individual definitions of the situation which produce individual meanings and idiosyncratic responses to the situation. These topics are addressed by many groups of specialists who share these general assumptions, including symbolic interactionists.

The meanings of events are not static and inflexible. If they were, social change and response to new situations would be impossible. Further, they are not simply given to the individual and learned by rote for later application. If they were, creativity would be impossible and there would be absolute conformity to the meanings and preferred patterns of response to events of the culture. None of these conditions prevails. Rather, the meanings of events can be changed by the creative actions of individuals and the individual may influence the complex of meanings that comprise his or her culture as well as being influenced by it.

The above suggests the characteristic approach of symbolic interactionists to culture and to the response to meanings. Meanings, whether they are collectively or individually held, are not viewed as an inflexible inventory or dictionary that can be listed with finality. Rather, they are looked upon as the product of a continuous interpretive process which is at least as interesting to study as the meanings it produces.

To point out that culturally shared meanings arise from an interpretive process is to highlight the collective character of the process. Individuals can, of course, engage in this interpretive process alone, through thinking. But individual thought is not the origin of socially shared definitions nor the basis of human social organization. Rather, thinking is made possible through participation in interaction. Thinking can be regarded as "talking to oneself," a special kind of conversation, but still, ultimately, a social activity. The meanings of objects are shared not only in the sense that they are beliefs held by many people, but also in the sense that they are created by many people cooperatively.

Obviously, the socialization process through which meanings are acquired is crucial to this view of meaning and social life. A theory of socialization must account for two phenomena: first, human infants and adults are reliably taught many meanings that are already common in the group; second, and equally important, each individual remains flexible and capable of developing and communicating new meanings when the established ones are inappropriate. The interpretive process provides the basis for such a theory of socialization. Through this process, existing meanings are utilized to interpret events and events are simultaneously utilized to evaluate the adequacy of those meanings. Whenever existing meanings are inappropriate or inadequate to explain and respond to events, new meanings are sought that will be more useful. Thus, the interpretive process is ongoing, continuing even when the existing meanings survive scrutiny for long periods of time. Thus, it is not paradoxical that we view humans as creative and flexible in their response to their environment and, at the same time, recognize the stability of institutions and meanings in human societies. People are capable of change through this process but they are not frivolous in changing. They reserve the search for new meanings and institutions for those occasions when the old ones are unsatisfactory.

There is a final aspect to the symbolic interactionist view of these issues. The creation of meanings and appropriate responses to objects based on them is, in fact, the creation of a behavioral environment. Human beings do not have complete freedom in this regard. Define as we will, we cannot wish away what we might call "facts of nature." Humans can be killed by eating certain mushrooms, even if they persist until the time of death to define them as harmless. While the environment is not created entirely by the application of meanings, one does have considerable liberty in one's assignment of meanings to events, and each successful assignment creates features of the behavioral environment. Put simply, humans with different meanings for events live in different worlds or environments. For example, the environment of the American Indian did not include petroleum although later it was discovered to have been present in some physical sense. This meaning was not in their culture and petroleum, as an object to which to respond, simply did not exist in their world. Until quite recently, in fact, this continent itself did not exist for Europeans. By "creating an environment" we obviously do not mean to imply that events come into existence in the physical sense only when they are defined; rather individuals create responses or uses for those existent events. It is in terms of possibilities for human behavior that the environment is created by meanings.

HUMAN INFANTS ARE PLASTIC

The view of the human as a symbol-manipulating animal, responding to events in terms of their individually and collectively attributed meanings implies a high degree of plasticity on the part of the human infant. The normal human infant must be regarded as capable of being socialized into any human society or subculture. This in turn suggests, at the least, that the genetically given behavior patterns of the human infant are few and sufficiently modifiable and general in form to allow the learning of any of the divergent behavior patterns that characterize any human society. The human infant is an active and potentially social organism, but one whose impulses are unspecific. Unsocialized human nature is amorphous and lacks organization.

Even in this extreme form, this view that the human infant is almost totally plastic, or flexible, is shared by many both within and without symbolic interaction. Williams treats this position not as an assumption, but as a warranted conclusion drawn from a large variety of studies. There are a few species-characteristic behaviors observed in human infants but these are diffuse, not triggered by particular stimuli, and modifiable by the socialization process into the patterns characteristic of the child's culture. Human cultural behavior is learned and will not appear if the socialization process is deficient.[10] When the socialization process is deficient, as in the case of feral or severely neglected children, the child will be strikingly different from "human" in the normal sense of that term. Humanness is potential, not given, and achieved only through an adequate socialization experience.[11]

The recognition of human plasticity is not limited to social scientific or behavioral dimensions. It has long been known that the brain undergoes functional changes in its operation through experience. These functional changes are neurophysiological evidence of learning. Recent studies have shown that anatomical changes occur in the nervous system as a result of experience and that different types of experience produce different changes.[12] The idea of humanness as a "potential" of the infant is in no way metaphorical. The conceptual apparatus itself, the nervous system, appears to be, in part, a product of experience.

This extreme flexibility does not mean that the human infant is completely unorganized in its behavior or completely unlimited by its genetic inheritance. First, and most obviously, we cannot ignore the fact that we have many limitations imposed upon us by our genetically given bodily structure. None of us can fly unaided, breathe under water unaided, grow feathers, perceive ultraviolet light frequencies as do some bees, or sonar frequencies as do bats and dolphins; furthermore, none of us can survive without oxygen, and so on. In addition, there are a number of genetically programmed behaviors that are general throughout our species.

---

[10] Thomas Williams, *Introduction to Socialization,* Mosby, St. Louis, 1972, pp. 23–39.

[11] *Ibid.,* p. 114.

[12] For example, see the following: Ralph Freeman and Larry Thibos, "Electrophysiological Evidence that Abnormal Early Visual Experience Can Modify the Human Brain," *Science,* 180 (25 May, 1973), 876–878; Mark Rosenzweig et al., "Brain Changes in Response to Experience," *Scientific American,* 226 (February 1972), 22–29.

Human infants make gross random movements of the torso, arms, and legs, and make babbling sounds. These "unorganized" behaviors are refined into culturally accepted forms through socialization.

Genetic inheritance also has an effect at the individual level by influencing individual differences among people. There is little disagreement with the assertion that many physical characteristics are determined or greatly influenced by genetic inheritance. Height, eye, hair and skin color, and facial characteristics are obvious examples. Controversy rages, however, over the degree to which genetic inheritance influences individual differences in social and conceptual abilities. The nature of the roles of both hereditary and environmental factors is in doubt, and the problems are compounded by methodological problems inherent in the current measures of these skills. IQ test scores are a good example of the problem. Many studies of genetically identical monozygotic twins separated and raised apart indicate that environmental differences during childhood significantly influence IQ scores.[13] But the nature of these environmental influences is apparently complex and is certainly little understood. For example, so long as minimal conditions are met, differences in early environment have relatively little importance for early intellectual development. However, early environmental differences do seem to affect later intellectual capacities.[14] While heredity is commonly believed by researchers to have an influence on IQ, others argue that methodological problems make it impossible to estimate the nature or extent of that influence.[15]

For all the difficulties of assessing its determinants, IQ is one of the more reliably defined social or conceptual skills. While current information is inconclusive, it appears likely that genetic inheritance as well as environment influence these skills. This implies genetic limits to human plasticity, but also recognizes extensive influences from the socialization environment.

Innate perceptual organization as a limit to human plasticity. Recent studies suggest that the conception of the infant as unorganized and as behaving in an essentially random fashion may require qualification. Both behaviorally and conceptually the human infant appears to be more organized than was formerly believed. First, we must reconsider the conceptual world of the infant. Clearly, a newborn human is not symbolically organized and clearly the infant does not evince knowledge of specific information about its surroundings immediately following birth. On the other hand, it is now clear that the infant's world is not completely formless.

---

[13] Many of these studies are reviewed by Williams.

[14] Ronald Wilson, "Twins' Early Mental Development," *Science,* 175 (25 February, 1972), 914–917.

[15] David Layzer, "Heritability Analyses of IQ Scores: Science or Numerology?" *Science,* 183 (29 March, 1974), 1259–1266.

One important characteristic of the adult's conceptual world is that information from the various senses is integrated. Information from each sensory mode can be corrected by contrary information from the others. For example, when we tilt our heads the image on our retinas cast by objects is also tilted. But by coordinating this tilted image with the feedback from the muscular systems involved in tilting the head we can compensate for the displaced visual image and perceive the object as upright. In adults, all of the sensory systems have been shown to be integrated and mutually corrective in this way. Now it is known that human infants organize the world in the same way, at least as far as the auditory and visual senses are concerned.

The voices of infants' mothers were recorded in one experiment. While the mother was visible to the infant, the apparent source of the voice was altered by manipulating the balance between stereo speakers. Infants as young as thirty days old exhibit agitation and distress when the source of the voice and visual location of the mother are not the same.[16] The child must, of course, learn the specific fact that a particular voice and a particular person go together, but this learning is apparently based on consistency among the sensory modes, grounded in neural structure, and precedes exposure to specific instances. At least for these two sensory modes, and probably for the others, the human infant is apparently genetically programmed to assume consistency among the input from its various senses. This asumption leads the human infant to correlate the input from various senses so that it automatically perceives an integrated environment. The alternative would be to learn sights, sounds, feeling, smell, and so forth separately, without perceiving that they come from the same sources in the environment. This programmed integration challenges the concept of an unorganized infant, but not its plasticity. The infant so programmed will integrate whatever appears in his environment and the assumption of consistency cannot help but make many kinds of learning easier, thus contributing to plasticity and responsiveness to the features of the infant's environment.

Of course, once particular events are encountered frequently enough to become associated, new relationships between them will be disorienting. This is shown by infants' responses to the displacement of their mothers' voices. Having integrated an environment in which voices and visually perceived locations are correlated, a disruption of the pattern is disturbing. If an infant were confronted with an environment in which voices were always located some distance from the visual location of the speaker, a change in *that* arrangement would be disorienting. This is demonstrated

16 Eric Aronson and Shelley Rosenbloom, "Space Perception in Early Infancy: Perception Within a Common Auditory and Visual Space," *Science,* 172 (11 June, 1971), 1161–1163.

in studies of adults who wear goggles that are designed to invert the visual world or to reverse the right and left halves of the visual field. Initially, attempts to walk or to grasp objects are unsuccsessful—the hand is guided to the wrong place by the eye. However, soon this environment becomes integrated and can be negotiated with ease. When the goggles are removed, the subject is disoriented, for a time, in the "normal world" because it presents a challenge to newly learned assumptions about the relationships among information in the sensory modes. Thus, we are apparently programmed to integrate our sensory input, but can integrate whatever is encountered.

Innate behavioral sequences as a limit to human plasticity. Infants also exhibit some well-coordinated behavior patterns, distinct from the random bodily movements described before. The infant's bodily movements are closely synchronized with adult speech as early as the first day of life. The infant does not start and stop its motions to accompany sounds, but while already moving it will change the direction of its motion as the sounds of adult speech change. With these movements, the infant must be recognized as an active participant in interaction from birth and certainly long before it is able to vocalize in a meaningful way. These motions are timed to the rhythm of the speech around the infant and they constitute practice and learning experience in many aspects of language.[17]

The newborn infant also exhibits a complex, well-coordinated reflex that closely resembles the movements of adult walking. If the infant is held under its arms so that its feet touch a flat surface, the walking movements will occur although the infant is not yet capable of supporting its own weight or actually walking. As this procedure is repeated, the motions change from reflexive to instrumental. This walking response disappears after several weeks, but those infants who have exercised the reflex begin to walk earlier than those who have not.[18]

These two well-coordinated behavioral patterns again challenge the conception of an unorganized infant, but, as with the conceptual organization, they do not challenge the view that it is extremely flexible. Neither of these genetically given behavior patterns is a fully developed adult behavior form. Rather, each seems to serve the function of facilitating learning of adult forms of behavior. In these two cases the infant appears to be genetically programmed to provide itself with important and necessary information for its own development. If further reflexes of this kind are dis-

[17] William Condon and Louis Sander, "Neonate Movement is Synchronized with Adult Speech: Interactional Participation and Language Acquisition," *Science,* 183 (11 January, 1974), 99–101.

[18] Phillip Zelazo, Nancy Zelazo, and Sarah Kolb, " 'Walking' in the Newborn," *Science,* 176 (21 April, 1972), 314–315.

covered, we are presented with the possibility that human infants are genetically programmed, not to behave inflexibly in certain ways, but rather to systematically gather certain kinds of experiential information that form the basis for mature patterns of conduct. Thus, although the infant may be less unorganized than was previously believed, there is no indication that it is less flexible or that learning is less important to the development of mature social behavior.

HUMANS ARE UNIQUE IN THEIR USE OF SYMBOLS

Social behavior of varying degrees of complexity is found throughout the animal kingdom. In fact, virtually any animal species that exhibits *any* behavior has some capacity for social behavior. In addition, virtually all behavior has aspects of social causation or social consequeces connected with it. Among highly social animals, of whatever species, interdependence of behavior is almost always present.[19] Recognizing this, symbolic interactionists maintain that human social life is unique in that the use of symbols has emerged within it. On the evolutionary scale, physiological and social evolution are believed to have led to the appearance of the symbol as a communicative tool among humans. On an individual scale, each child develops the capacity to use symbols through interaction with other humans.

This assumption is extremely important in a number of ways. First, it is a statement about the nature of evolution and of the nature of the differences between species. At least in the case of humans, it asserts the emergence of qualitative differences between species. Further, it states a relationship between many of the disciplines studying social life. It asserts that so long as symbolizing behavior is at issue, the study of humans cannot be aided by the study of other species. It implies that studies of other animals are irrelevant to the study of human symbolizing.

This last implication of the view is unfortunate, if true, because it makes comparative research on symbolizing impossible. As D. O. Hebb and W. R. Thompson point out, comparison between man and other species must be made carefully and pragmatically on an issue-by-issue basis: comparisons are only relevant if they clarify questions encountered in the study of humans.[20] Comparative research on many topics may clarify questions, if for no other reason because we are able to treat members of other species much more harshly than members of our own. For example, hepatitis,

---

[19] J. P. Scott, "The Social Psychology of Infrahuman Animals," in *Handbook of Social Psychology,* ed. Gardner Lindzey and Elliott Aronson, 2d ed., Addison-Wesley, Reading, Mass., 1968, IV, 611.

[20] D. O. Hebb and W. R. Thompson, "The Social Significance of Animal Studies," in *Handbook of Social Psychology,* ed. Gardner Lindzey and Elliott Aronson, 2d ed., II, 732.

fatty liver, and cirrhosis have recently been induced in baboons who were fed excessive alcohol in an otherwise sound diet.[21] This similarity to the human response to excessive alcohol promises a program of medical experimentation on the effects of alcohol and their treatment that will be useful in human medicine.

Differences among species also contribute to useful comparisons. As the number of vasectomies has increased, sexual problems have arisen for vasectomized males. From studies of humans alone it is difficult to determine whether these difficulties are organic or psychosomatic in origin. Rhesus monkeys were subjected to both sham and actual vasectomies and their sexual performance was monitored both before and after the surgery. Neither group suffered in sexual performance as a result of surgery, nor did their postsurgical performance differ from each other. Because these monkeys are *not* likely to be experiencing guilt, anxiety, or other human emotions, the human sexual problems can be identified as psychosomatic.[22] Neither of these experiments, nor many like them, could have been performed on human subjects. Similarly, we are not willing to subject children to deficient socialization environments to determine what damage this will cause to their social skills. Thus, while it is somewhat depressing to have our uniqueness as a symbolizing species challenged, it would be useful, as a practical matter, to find species upon which we could experiment in that area as well.

In considering the uniqueness of human symbolizing, two comparisons will be made. First, because their social structure is the most intricate and complex, except for our own, we will consider the dynamics of insect social life. Second, because they are our closest relatives in the animal kingdom, we will consider the dynamics of primate social life.

Insect social dynamics. Because of the complexity of their division of labor, their apparently high degree of cooperation, and the apparent complexity of their communication, insect society is often compared to human society. However, the similarities to human society are superficial. Although the social arrangements of insects are the most complex aside from those found in human societies, the dynamics underlying them are dramatically different. Insect society is based on inflexible, instinctual response to specific stimuli while the basis of human society is ideational.[23]

Certain wasps lay their eggs in a nest along with a cricket paralyzed by the female wasp's sting. When the eggs hatch, the paralyzed but alive and

---

[21] Emanuel Rubin and Charles Lieber, "Experimental Alcoholic Hepatitis: A New Primate Model," *Science,* 182 (16 November, 1973), 712–713.

[22] Charles Phoenix, "Sexual Behavior in Rhesus Monkeys After Vasectomy," *Science,* 179 (2 February, 1973), 493–494.

[23] Hebb and Thompson, p. 733.

undecayed cricket serves as food for the wasp grubs. This is an apparent display of concern for the young, preparation for the future, and shows elaborate organization and planning. These interpretations evaporate, however, when the activity is examined in more detail. After bringing the cricket to the opening of the burrow, the female wasp leaves it on the threshold and enters the burrow to make a final inspection. Only then does she emerge and drag the cricket into the burrow. If the cricket is moved a few inches away while the wasp is in the burrow the wasp will retrieve it and drag it back to the burrow entrance but will not take it in. Rather, she will re-enter and recheck the burrow. The wasp will repeat this behavior as many times as the cricket is moved. In one experiment the procedure was repeated forty times. Rather than a purposive action, the wasp's behavior appears to be an inflexible routine, triggered by a specific stimulus and not variable in response to unusual contingencies. Apparently, dragging the cricket to the burrow entrance will be followed by a check of the burrow's interior, regardless of how many times the burrow has already been examined. We must conclude that it is the stimulus situation, including perhaps the act of dragging the cricket, *not* concern for the conditions in the burrow that is the impetus for the search. The wasp cannot do anything but search the burrow in that situation.

This automatic, inflexible pattern appears to characterize insect behavior. Consider some of the highly structured social behavior of the nest insects. Worker ants fiercely defend their nest by attacking intruders. This "defense," however, is an inflexible reaction to the unusual scent of the invader. If the invader is protected in the nest until that scent disappears and it acquires that of the nest, it will be ignored by the workers even while it disrupts the nest and feeds on its inhabitants.[24] Chemicals have recently been isolated that elicit this alarm behavior in ants. The ants attack the source of the odor, including members of their own nest who have become contaminated by the chemical.[25]

The dance performed by bees when they return to the nest helps others locate sources of nectar. However, if the nest is empty when the bee returns, it will perform the dance anyway. It can hardly be regarded as a purposeful attempt to communicate.

The attention of drone termites to their queen, often characterized as grooming, is also a stereotyped response to specific chemical stimuli. The queen termite exudes a chemical over the surface of her body which is eaten by the other termites and is, in fact, necessary for their survival. Their "grooming" is self-serving and often so vigorous that it tears the

[24] Dean Wooldridge, *The Machinery of the Brain,* McGraw-Hill, New York, 1963, pp. 82–83.
[25] James Wheeler and Murray Blum, "Alkylpyrazine Alarm Pheromones in Ponerine Ants," *Science,* 182 (2 November, 1973), 501–503.

queen's skin.[26] Again, the social appearance of the behavior is created by stereotyped and rigid response to a specific stimulus.

Among insects, as among other invertebrates and lower vertebrates, the communication involved in social behavior is typically stereotyped. As in the examples we have already considered, it is characteristic for insects to exhibit very few responses to a given signal, to emit relatively few signals, and to exhibit the same signal/response combinations throughout the species.[27] A variety of signals are utilized besides those mentioned already—including other chemical emissions and mating songs.[28] The difference between our main communication and that of insects can be grasped more fully by considering chemical communication among insects carried on by means of pheromones. Pheromones are "chemical compounds . . . which are secreted by an animal and elicit a specific kind of behavior in animals of the same species."[29]

The control exerted over insect behavior by these chemicals, of which the grooming of termite queens and the attack of invaders to the nest by ants are examples, can be strikingly illlustrated by considering the increasingly well-documented mating behavior of moths. (Moths are destructive animals and interruption of their mating is expected to provide an ecologically sound way to control their destructiveness without affecting other species.) The female moth has glands that excrete chemicals that attract the male moth. The male's antennae are responsive to even one molecule of the sex attractant and when the concentration of the attractant becomes great enough, the male moth moves upwind toward its source. The idea of a sexual attractant does not seem particularly alien until we realize that it is any source of the smell, not necessarily a female moth, that is the sexual object for the male. When a female moth is picked up and put under glass, leaving her visible but blocking the odor, male moths ignore her and congregate at the place from which she was removed.[30] Furthermore, the male's interest in the female is ended by the removal of his sensory antennae. With these removed, the male not only cannot find the distant female, but if placed near her will not mate. Finally, if the female's glands are removed and placed with her in a cage, the male will ignore the female and attempt to mate with the scent glands.[31]

[26] Wooldridge, pp. 83–84.

[27] Edward Wilson, "Animal Communication," *Scientific American,* 227 (September 1972), 54.

[28] S. M. Ulgaraj and Thomas Walker, "Phonotaxis of Crickets in Flight: Attraction of Male and Female Crickets to Male Calling Songs," *Science,* 182 (23 July, 1973), 1278–1279.

[29] Dietrich Schneider, "The Sex-Attractant Receptor of Moths," *Scientific American,* 231 (July 1974), 28.

[30] Ibid.

[31] Wooldridge, p. 84.

Insect social structure and insect communication in general, then, are maintained by rigidly inflexible instinctive responses to specific stimuli. The societies are viable because the specific stimuli usually occur in a context in which the stereotyped response to them is adaptive. However, when this context is disrupted—by protecting an invader until his scent is camouflaged, by providing an unusual source for the sex attractant, by copying mating calls, by moving a wasp's paralyzed prey slightly—the responses become futile, but continue. Insect behavior is shown to be unresponsive to novelty and to lack purposiveness. Despite their apparently complex social structure, therefore, the insects provide little, if any, comparative insight into human social life.

Primate social dynamics. In contrast to the complex social structure often exhibited by insects, our close relatives among the primates display relatively simple social organization. Paradoxically, despite this simplicity, the underlying dynamics of primate social life are quite similar, although distinguishable from, those underlying human social life. We will consider the abilities of primates in three broad areas, each extremely important to social life—ability to cooperate, cognitive organization, and language abilities. In each case we will attempt to indicate the maximum abilities shown by primates in each area rather than attempt a review of their typical behavior. This strategy is dictated by our interest in our fellow primates as a possible source of comparative information that will aid in the study of human communication and symbolizing.

Among the primates many forms of social cooperation occur. Interestingly, not all instances of cooperation are dependent on mutual reward, but show evidence of what, at a human level, we would call altruism and friendship. Two chimpanzees in a cage were confronted with a "bold" man, one who retaliated to their attacks in kind. One of the chimpanzees learned from the first attack by the human to stay safely out of his reach, but the other responded by continuing to attempt attacks against him at every opportunity. While staying out of reach herself, the more discrete chimpanzee often pulled her more aggressive companion's hands away from the cage wire and out of reach of the aggressive human. This behavior was clearly purposive and clearly oriented to the protection of another as a goal in itself. On other occasions, a chimpanzee would purposely instigate a fight with one in a neighboring cage to distract him so that an accomplice could steal food by reaching through the bars. These, and other similar types of behavior are common and occur spontaneously, but only in "dramatic episodes that are infrequent and cannot be repeated at will for study." [32] They represent the most advanced form of cooperative behavior among the chimpanzees, not the workaday norm.

[32] Hebb and Thompson, p. 747.

It is among chimpanzees that the highest level of cooperation, other than that achieved by humans, has been experimentally observed. But, as in the spontaneous behavior, it exhibits "only the barest beginning of teamwork as we know it in man . . . even this was achieved in an artificial experimental setting which needed the planning of the human experimenter." [33] In this regard, experiments on cooperative tool use are relevant. Two chimpanzees were taught separately to pull a weighted box with food in it to within their reach by means of an attached rope. The box was then made too heavy for either one to move by its individual efforts. Two ropes were attached and the two chimps were placed in the same cage. At first the two chimpanzees pulled without reference to one another, and did not learn to cooperate even when occasional simultaneous pulls resulted in moving the box. The experimenter was able to induce cooperation by giving a signal that each had separately learned as a cue to pull the rope. After coordination was established, the signal was no longer needed to achieve cooperative efforts. In fact, altruistic cooperation was requested and obtained by one of the chimpanzees. A hungry chimp could encounrage a satiated one to pull the box within reach by begging gestures. The hungry chimpanzee ate all of the food without protest from his partner.

The ability for chimpanzees to request and direct the nature of cooperation is further supported by another experiment. One chimpanzee was trained to push four colored plaques in a particular sequence to obtain food while another chimpanzee was taught only to press the plaques; the latter did not know the correct sequence. The two were then placed in adjacent cages with the first and third plaques in the sequence in one cage, the second and fourth in the other. The chimpanzee who knew the correct sequence was able to conceive of pressing the plaques as a cooperative venture and to instruct the other chimpanzee in the correct sequence by using begging gestures directed at the appropriate plaque.[34] Note that this chimpanzee was able to plan a sequence of integrated actions involving two participants and to instruct the other participant in the correct completion of its part in the sequence as well as performing its own part at the appropriate time.

Chimpanzees are not the only primates who exhibit cooperative tool use. A large male baboon was confined in a cage from which he could see but not reach food. Previously, he had learned to reach this food using a tool. A similar tool was out of his reach in an adjoining cage holding two smaller males and a smaller female. These smaller baboons could pass through a conecting door but the large male could not. Occasionally the

[33] Ibid, p. 742.
[34] Ibid, pp. 741–742.

tool would be dropped within his reach through the bars, but the smaller males would attack him and remove the tool from his reach when the larger male attempted to reach it. The larger male and the female then engaged in mutual grooming, and after some time the female went back to her own cage, brought the tool back through the door, and set it down. After waiting for a while the male took the tool, reached the food with it, and shared the food with the female. This cooperative activity became common between the two.[35]

These studies allow some conclusions about the limits of cooperation among our fellow primates. Under some circumstances they are able to cooperate quite effectively, requesting cooperation from one another, and even instructing one another in correct performance. They can apparently conceive of sequences of integrated actions of more than one participant. While not unusual, however, such instances are infrequent, are quite simple, and are in no way equivalent to the cooperative efforts of which human beings are capable.

Human cognitive organization is most often studied through linguistic communication—humans tell one another what they are thinking. This procedure is impossible with other primates and cognitive structure must be studied through other forms of behavior. We have already noted, for example, that certain kinds of cooperative activity imply the chimpanzee's ability to cognitively organize collective plans of action. Other forms of action, cooperative and individual, reveal additional information about primate cognitive organization. Hebb reported the occurrence of deceitful attacks by chimpanzees upon humans in the laboratory. The chimpanzees encourage the human to approach the cage by making affectionate gestures. The arm of the victim is held, cuddled, caressed, and pulled through the bars into the cage and a firm grasp of it is secured. Only then, when the arm cannot be quickly or easily withdrawn, does the chimpanzee attack, often viciously.[36] In a later experiment, Hebb reported a similar, if less dangerous form of spontaneous, planned, and deceitful behavior by the chimpanzees. A visitor enters the laboratory area. The chimpanzee goes to the faucet, fills its mouth with water, but does not swallow. It then moves to the front of the cage, nearest to where the tour will pass. When the visitor is within range, the chimpanzee drenches him or her with the patiently held water. These behaviors show planning and the ability to be deceptive, a complex ability requiring the animal to maintain one type of action while planning another.[37] In addition, the chimpanzee must be

[35] Benjamin Beck, "Cooperative Tool Use by Captive Hamadryas Baboons," *Science,* 182 (9 November, 1973), 594–597.

[36] D. O. Hebb, "Emotion in Man and Animal: An Analysis of the Intuitive Process of Recognition," *Psychological Review,* 53 (March 1946), 88–106.

[37] Hebb and Thompson, pp. 740–741.

able to anticipate the course of the human's action and to disguise its own so that the human cannot anticipate it. If perceived in a human child, we would have no hesitation in identifying the practical joke as an instance of role-taking. (Role-taking is defined in Chapter 2.)

Hebb and Thompson express discomfort with this sort of inference, however, because the evidence includes reports of interpretation as well as of observable facts.[38] While these naturalistic observations are suggestive, more systematic research is required to establish with more precision the degree of complexity and nature of primate cognitive organization. Some experimental evidence already exists concerning chimpanzee cognitive organization. Chimpanzees were carried around a field and allowed to watch as eighteen pieces of food were concealed. Because they did not walk from place to place or get motor referents for the hiding places, their ability to efficiently locate the food must rest on visual memory, and the efficiency of their search for it must rest on the cognitive organization of this memory and its use in planning. The chimpanzees were returned to a cage along with several others who had not seen the food hidden. All the chimpanzees were then released into the field and observed. Those who had not seen the hiding of the food wandered aimlessly around the field and found food only when they came close enough to smell or see it. In contrast, the animals who had seen the food hidden went directly and quickly from hiding place to hiding place and found an average of 12.5 of the 18 hidden items. Considering the fact that some food was found by the ignorant chimpanzees, we can see that the chimps could remember at least two-thirds of the hiding places after one exposure to them. Moreover, instances of sudden recall occurred. After a resting period of up to thirty minutes, chimpanzees would suddenly jump and run directly to a hiding place. The chimpanzees almost never returned to recheck a hiding place they had emptied, indicating their recall of their own actions. The organization of their search pattern was similar to that of humans in its efficiency. The chimpanzees took both the closeness of sources of food to their present location and the location of closely spaced hiding places into account in choosing the sequence of their search. That is, they went to areas of the field containing several food sources and then went along a path, from source to source, that minimized the amount of walking.[39] This experiment indicates, under more controlled conditions, that many of the inferences from less systematic observation are correct.

For humans, language is clearly the predominant form of conceptual organization. Our consideration of primate cognitive organization must

---

[38] *Ibid.,* p. 747.

[39] Emil Menzel, "Chimpanzee Spatial Memory Organization," *Science,* 182 (30 November, 1973), 943–945.

include an estimation of their language skills. It is the symbolic aspects of language that are regarded as uniquely human by many, yet recent studies of chimpanzees indicate that their abilities are much greater in this area than had been previously believed. Using plastic symbols, Ann and David Premack have demonstrated that chimpanzees can be taught a wide range of conceptual and language skills. Using such symbols, the chimpanzee can sort items into classes. This is more than recognizing differences between specific items—the same item can be symbolically grouped in various classes depending on the choices offered. The chimpanzees can also be taught to give and take items from one another when instructed to do so symbolically. To differentiate between these two commands, the chimpanzee must be able to distinguish between itself and the other by name. The Premacks' chimpanzees learned how to answer questions symbolically, and also to ask them. This latter requires them to initiate linguistic contacts. Furthermore, they proved able to comprehend the conditional mode and to choose the most favorable of two choices when the consequences of each were explained to them linguistically. Told to choose, for example, the symbol for apple or that for banana, and told that if they chose the apple they would receive chocolate but if they chose the banana they would not, the chimpanzees could reliably choose the symbol for apple. Further the chimps could learn about objects linguistically by being told about them. The chimpanzee was first confronted with the color word "brown" in a sentence stating that brown is the color of chocolate. Later, the chimp was able to select the brown item from among four of various colors. Chocolate was not present at either time. The chimpanzee was apparently able to generalize the color from a known to an unknown object and to know which feature of the object is its color without immediate contact with the object. The chimpanzee clearly distinguished between the symbol and its referent. Asked to describe an apple, the chimpanzee gave features of the apple itself, not those of the plastic symbol for it. Finally, the chimpanzee was able to follow commands given in a complex sentence. When told to place two objects in different places in a compound sentence, the chimp was able to recognize which place was appropriate for each object.[40]

The Premacks are not alone in their success in teaching language ability to chimpanzees. Chimpanzees have been trained to read sentence beginnings and to recognize whether they are grammatically correct. If the sentence beginnings are ungrammatical, the chimpanzees interrupt them, but if they are grammatical, the sentence is correctly completed. This illustrates an ability not only to follow simple grammatical and

[40] Ann Premack and David Premack, "Teaching Language to an Ape," *Scientific American,* 227 (October 1972), 92–99.

syntactical rules but to evaluate sentences of others and recognize whether they are grammatically sound or not.[41] Similar results are being generated in studies in a variety of laboratories.

There seems to be little doubt that chimpanzees can learn many specific language skills and that they utilize symbols, although their most complex efforts are clearly not equivalent to the symbolic manipulation of humans. Still, these studies, and others, suggest that the nature of the distinction between human communication and that used by other primates may require reconsideration. The Premacks assert that the performance of their chimpanzee is equivalent to that of a two-year-old child.[42] Jolly denies that there are any "absolute differences" between ourselves and our primate relatives. She suggests that our emotions and some aspects of our logic originate in our primate past.[43] Wilson, referring specifically to the Premacks' chimp, asserts a large difference between its performance and that of a human, but considers that *the difference may be quantitative rather than qualitative.* [44] Hebb and Thompson also imply that the differences between man and the other primates are quantitative and feel that the chimpanzee is close to a "liminal level" necessary for full-fledged language.[45] While acknowledging the impressive results of their experiments, however, we would still argue for qualitative differences. Chimpanzees can do far more than we previously believed, but they are incapable, nevertheless, of functioning like adult humans.

To date, the research on chimpanzees and other primates has not been truly comparative. Rather, experiments have concentrated on establishing the abilities of primates, hopefully in preparation for later comparative studies that will be relevant to the study of human beings. If the current evaluations of species differences between humans and the other primates are sustained, the prospects for the use of primates to study human socialization and symbolizing are more promising than anyone hoped until quite recently. Clearly, many aspects of adult human performance are exhibited only by humans and can be studied only directly on human subjects. On the other hand, depending on the limits of chimpanzee development, the study of early human socialization may soon be profiting from studies of chimpanzees and, perhaps, other primates. Also, as long as generalization is cautious, we may soon be able to use primate subjects to study aspects of cooperation, altruism, and other social abilities

---

[41] Duane Rumbaugh, Timothy Gill, and E. C. von Glasersfeld, "Reading and Sentence Completion by a Chimpanzee (Pan)," *Science,* 182 (16 November, 1973), 731–733.

[42] Premack and Premack, p. 99.

[43] Allison Jolly, *The Evolution of Primate Behavior,* Macmillan, New York, 1972, p. 1.

[44] Edward Wilson, p. 60.

[45] Hebb and Thompson, p. 740.

shared with the primates. Thus, although their typical social structure is quite simple, the underlying dynamics of primate cooperation and communication are sufficiently similar to those of humans to allow some comparative study, even of human symbolizing.

Suggested Reading

The characteristics of the human infant and the processes by which it becomes socialized were touched upon in this chapter. David Goslin's collection, *The Handbook of Socialization Theory and Research* (Rand McNally, Chicago, 1971), is an excellent reference volume that summarizes the important areas of research and theory on the topic and provides excellent bibliographies for further study. D. O. Hebb and W. R. Thompson provide a broad, well-integrated overview of studies of infrahuman species and their relevance for understanding human behavior ("The Social Significance of Animal Studies," in *Handbook of Social Psychology,* ed. Gardner Lindzey and Elliott Aronson, 2d ed., Addison-Wesley, Reading, Mass., 1968, II). *Scientific American* frequently publishes summaries in relatively nontechnical language of the most recent developments in this area. These can be used to keep up-to-date with developments in the field that are too recent to have appeared in books and beyond the scope of the sociology journals. A more detailed interest in the seminal philosophy of G. H. Mead is easily served. G. H. Mead, *Mind, Self, and Society* (ed. C. Morris, The University of Chicago Press, Chicago, 1934) is regarded as a classic in sociology. Many of Mead's papers from professional journals, reflecting the broad scope of his interests, have been collected by Andrew Reck (G. H. Mead, *Selected Writings,* ed. Andrew Reck, Bobbs-Merrill, Indianapolis, 1964).

Chapter 2

The Conceptual Apparatus: Tools of Analysis

"What a chimera then is man! What a novelty! What a monster, what a chaos, what a contradiction, what a prodigy!" [1] Pascal's dramatic description reflects his awareness of the enormous complexity of human beings and human behavior. That complexity confronts the social psycho-

[1] Blaise Pascal, *Pensées,* trans. W. F. Trotter, Modern Library, New York, 1941, p. 143.

logists as a challenge, and they are committed to the task of understanding and explaining human behavior. As with all sciences, the task requires tools; for the social psychologist, concepts are fundamental tools of analysis.

A concept is an abstraction—"A term or symbol that represents the similarities in otherwise diverse phenomena." [2] For example, all humans may be grouped together under the concept of mammal; males and females may be distinguished from each other by the concept of sex role; and, finally, young people whose behavior reflects the values of their peers may be distinguished from those whose behavior reflects parental values by the concept of reference group. Thus, a concept is a useful device for conveying information and for grouping various phenomena.

Concepts are also the building blocks of theory. Simply put, a theory is an explanation. Thus, we may use concepts to explain relationships, combine a number of those relationships, and arrive at a theory which enables us to understand and explain human behavior. Some key concepts which are used by symbolic interactionists will be presented in this chapter; the integration of those concepts into a theory of human behavior will be elaborated in the following chapter.

In the following pages, then, we will explore the meaning of ten selected, but key, concepts: symbol, interaction, attitude, socialization, role, role-taking, self, generalized other/reference group, and definition of the situation. They are key in the sense that they are integral to the theory and/or in the sense that they have been an important part of research. Some of them are shared by other social psychological perspectives; taken together, however, they form a distinctive set of analytical tools.

Symbol

HUMAN LIFE AS SYMBOLIC

A human is a symbolic creature. It is, in fact, the unique capacity for functioning in a symbolic environment that distinguishes humans from the lower animals. For no other creature has the capacity to create, manipulate, and employ symbols to direct his own behavior and influence the behavior of others. As White put it, the symbol "transformed our anthropoid ancestors into men and made them human." [3] White argues that an infant is not even human until it attains the ability to grasp and use symbols.

---

[2] Sanford Labovitz and Robert Hagedorn, *Introduction to Social Research,* McGraw-Hill, New York, 1971, p. 18.

[3] Leslie A. White, *The Science of Culture,* Farrar, Straus & Giroux, New York, 1941, p. 22.

In order to understand the distinctiveness of symbolic behavior, we must distinguish between natural signs and symbols. The former are cues or stimuli that are associated with something particular. The glow of hot metal, the smell of perfume, the red cross on a hospital ship, and the frown of anger on another's face all serve as signs that indicate something particular. Animals also respond to signs—various sounds, odors, and objects that elicit particular kinds of behavior. Thus, the sign of a stranger elicits barking from a dog and the sign of odorous food elicits saliva and tail wagging. Both humans and animals learn to respond in particular ways to natural signs.

Natural signs are similar to Mead's notion of gestures: behavior which acts as stimuli for responses. All animals, including humans, employ both vocal and nonvocal gestures. Thus in the cooing process among pigeons, says Mead, a vocal gesture from one calls forth a vocal gesture from another such that we get a "conversation of gestures." [4] This is not merely a process of imitation, for the vocal gestures differ somewhat from each other (a difference even more apparent in the conversation of gestures in a dogfight).

All animals, then, engage in communication. But only human beings communicate with symbols, which are particular kinds of vocal gestures. Mead defined symbols in terms of meaning. A system of symbols, or a language, "is the means whereby individuals can indicate to one another what their responses to objects will be, and hence what the meanings of objects are." [5] Symbols therefore are shared meanings, and any individual symbol has meaning only in the context of a symbolic system. Consider, for example, a man. To a dog, the man may be an object to be barked at, a natural sign. But to various humans, that man may be a "pigeon," a "mark," a customer, an enemy, a friend, and so forth. Each symbolic definition of the man will indicate to particular people how they are to respond to his presence (note that some definitions are irrelevant or even meaningless to those not making them or not a part of the system in which the symbols are used).

Mead called those vocal gestures which reach the stage of language "significant symbols." The gestures in a dogfight call forth appropriate responses, but significant symbols both reflect a certain meaning in the experience of the speaker and also elicit that same meaning in the audience. [6] An animal does not respond to its own vocal gesture in the same way as another animal responds. In the human, however, all participants in the interaction respond in the same way to the stimulus of the significant

[4] George H. Mead, *Mind, Self and Society,* ed. Charles W. Morris, The University of Chicago Press, Chicago, 1934, p. 61.
[5] *Ibid.,* p. 122.
[6] *Ibid.,* p. 46.

symbol.[7] In other words, the human is a cognitive creature who functions in a context of shared meanings which are communicated through language.

An important characteristic of symbols is their utility in the absence of objects or events to which they refer. Symbols, unlike natural signs, do not depend upon the presence of external stimuli for their use, a fact which differentiates human from infrahuman behavior in important ways. For example, symbolic behavior is enormously superior for solving problems. In some early experiments with chimpanzees, the experimenter placed food in one of four boxes placed in the four corners of the room. The chimp was allowed to watch him, was taken out of the room, and was brought back a few minutes later. As long as the food was in the same corner of the room, the chimp would retrieve it. But if the food were kept in the same box and exchanged with a different colored box in another corner, the chimp was helpless. The experimenter concluded that in spite of the chimp's excellent color-discrimination ability, it failed to find the food because it "lacked a symbol or representative process comparable with our word 'green.' " [8]

Similarly, in an experiment with children aged two to seven, three different sets of papier-maché objects were to be identified. The first set contained five unnamed shapes, the second set contained five shapes with nonsense names, and the third set was composed of five well-known animals. The subjects were to find the object in each set that would give them a reward. When they chose that object on four successive trials they were considered to have solved the problem of identifying the rewarding object. The median number of trials for success was 69 for the unnamed shapes, 37 for the shapes with nonsense names, and 5 for the animals. Language facilitated the success, and familiar symbols were particularly facilitative.[9]

At a more general level, symbolic behavior is the basis for civilization. "Symbols enable man to escape the narrow confines of the immediate natural world and to participate in the artistic, religious, moral, and scientific worlds created by his contemporaries and ancestors." [10] Man has been called the only "time-binding" animal. Both humans and animals have the capacity for "space-binding," but only man is capable of ordering his existence so that "the past lives in the present and the present for the

---

[7] *Ibid.*, p. 67.

[8] Quoted in O. Hobart Mowrer, *Learning Theory and Personality Dynamics,* Ronald, New York, 1950, p. 441.

[9] Reported in Denis Lawton, *Social Class, Language and Education,* Routledge, London, 1968, p. 59.

[10] Alfred R. Lindesmith and Anselm L. Strauss, *Social Psychology,* 3d ed., Holt, New York, 1968, p. 49.

future." [11] In other words, humans can order their present behavior on the basis of an anticipated future or a distant past. They are not confined to the present and the immediate past as are animals. This time-binding capacity is fundamental to the creation of civilization, and it is the human's symbolic capacity which enables him or her to be a time-binding creature. Without symbols, men and women, like infants and animals, would live only in the present.

VARIATIONS IN SYMBOL SYSTEMS

There are enormous variations among symbol systems. Symbols derive from the social context, so that each social world has its own distinctive system. In other words, quite different meanings may be attached to the same words, both within the same language and between languages. An interesting illustration of this contextual basis for meaning is a study of bilingual students in which it was found that the greatest variation in meaning attributed to equivalent words occurred in those students who had learned their two languages in very different social contexts.[12]

Similarly, Dennis studied cultural differences in the meaning of various simple objects among groups of Lebanese, Sudanese, and American children. The children were asked such questions as, "What is sand for?" The American children thought about sand in terms of playing, while the Lebanese and Sudanese children thought about the functional uses of sand. Significant differences were also found in the meaning of words like "cat," "dog," "bird," and "gold." [13]

Even within the same language, we find important differences in meaning when the language is used by diverse groups. Meanings are derived from interaction experiences, and interaction varies considerably. In the United States, for example, numerous studies have shown that, compared with middle- and upper-class children, the lower-class child grows up in a world where the emphasis is on action, the concrete, and the sensory rather than on thought, reflection, and the abstract.[14] The lower-class child, then, will have quite different interaction experiences from those of middle- and upper-class children. When an individual attempts to interact in diverse groups, to function in diverse symbolic en-

[11] Alfred Korzybski, *Manhood of Humanity,* New York, 1921, p. 60.

[12] W. E. Lambert, J. Havelka, and C. Crosby, "The Influence of Language Acquisition Context on Bilingualism," *Journal of Abnormal and Social Psychology,* 56 (1958), 239–244.

[13] W. Dennis, "Uses of Common Objects as Indicators of Cultural Orientations," *Journal of Abnormal and Social Psychology,* 55 (1957), 21–28.

[14] Not everyone would accept this characterization. For an argument that ghetto children are *not* verbally deprived see W. Labov, "The Logic of Nonstandard English," in *Language and Social Context,* ed. Pier Paolo Giglioli, Penguin, Middlesex, England, 1972, pp. 179–215.

vironments, he or she may have difficulty. As William Foote Whyte says in his classic study of street-corner life among Boston's Italian youths:

> When John Howard first came down from Harvard to join me in the Cornerville study, he noticed at once that I talked in Cornerville in a manner far different from that which I used at Harvard. This was not a matter of the use of profanity or obscenity, nor did I affect the use of ungrammatical expressions. I talked in the way that seemed natural to me, but what was natural in Cornerville was different from what was natural at Harvard. In Cornerville, I found myself putting much more animation into my speech, dropping terminal g's, and using gestures much more actively. (There was also, of course, the difference in the vocabulary that I used. When I was most deeply involved in Cornerville, I found myself rather tongue-tied in my visits to Harvard. I simply could not keep up with the discussions of international relations, of the nature of science, and so on, in which I had once been more or less at home.)[15]

FUNCTIONS OF SYMBOL SYSTEMS

Symbols, then, are stimuli with learned meanings. They are the foundation not only of everyday social life, but of human civilization. They derive from specific social contexts in the course of interaction. As this suggests, symbols form the basis for our understanding of reality, for our cognitive processes generally, and for our overt behavior.

First, with respect to our understanding of reality, we live in a symbolic environment: our responses are to symbols and our relationships with the external world are symbolically mediated.[16] As Mead put it: "Language does not simply symbolize a situation or object which is already there in advance; it makes possible the existence or the appearance of that situation or object, for it is a part of the mechanism whereby that situation or object is created."[17] We can only understand the world in terms of the symbols that are available to us or in terms of symbols which we create to explain the world. The latter is rare, however. For the most part, people accept the world in terms of the language they learn.

Both vocabulary and phonological differences in languages are related to different ways of understanding the world.[18] Some people perceive

---

[15] William Foote Whyte, *Street Corner Society*, 2d ed., The University of Chicago Press, Chicago, 1955, p. 304.

[16] Lindesmith and Strauss, p. 53.

[17] Mead, *Mind, Self and Society*, p. 78.

[18] Some of the research that supports these ideas is discussed in *Basic Studies in Social Psychology*, ed. Harold Proshansky and Bernard Seidenberg, Holt, New York, 1965, pp. 236–237.

colors differently from others because of differing degrees to which their languages discriminate among colors. Eskimos perceive snow differently from Americans because of the various symbols available to the former that attach to differing kinds of snow. An Arab surely sees something more than an American does when he or she looks at a camel, for an Arab has roughly six thousand words related in some way to camels.[19] This does not mean, of course, that the lack of certain distinctions in a language makes the individual *incapable* of perceiving those distinctions. The American could perceive and learn the same distinguishing features of the camel as the Arab, and could create new symbols to identify those distinctions. Once the new symbols were created, Americans would perceive camels differently from their forebears. Our language leads us in general to see the world in particular ways, but it does not make us incapable of creating new perspectives.

New interaction experiences and the acquisition of new symbols or new meanings, then, will change our understanding of the world. We will "see" the world differently as our symbol system is modified through interaction. An interesting example is provided by an experiment with police administration students.[20] The study employed a stereoscope to present the subjects a series of figures. In earlier studies, slightly different photographs of the same face were shown to subjects; each eye saw one of the photographs, but the subject saw a single face. That is, the subject would accomplish binocular fusion, creating a single picture out of two slightly disparate ones.

In the present study the two figures on each stereogram were similar in size, outline, and in the area of the visual field which they covered. But the figure exposed to one eye was related to violence or crime (murder, suicide, theft, prisoner, and policeman) while the figure exposed to the other eye was neutral (farmer, drill press operator, radio announcer, mailman, two women). Three different groups participated in the experiment—a class of psychology students, a set of first-year students in police administration, and a set of advanced students in police administration. The subjects were asked to identify the objects shown them, and they perceived a single picture for each stereogram as expected. But the picture perceived differed considerably. The psychology students and first-year police administration students were similar in their responses; the former saw an average of 4.03 violent figures in 9 stereograms, while the latter saw an average of 4.69 violent figures. The advanced police administration students, however, saw an average of 9.37 violent figures. Clearly,

[19] Lindesmith and Strauss, p. 28.

[20] Hans H. Toch and Richard Schulte, "Readiness to Perceive Violence as a Result of Police Training," in *Social Perception,* ed. Hans Toch and Henry Clay Smith, Van Nostrand, Princeton, N.J., 1968, pp. 152–158.

people may look at the same reality and yet perceive a quite different reality because of differing symbol systems.

Second, not only our understanding of reality but all of our cognitive processes depend upon the symbol system we use. What we call "mind" or thought is not possible without language, and the latter must have begun to develop before the former.[21] It has been suggested, in fact, that the primary reason for our inability to remember much of childhood is in the relationship between the acquisition and development of language use on the one hand, and our cognitive functioning on the other. The "universal amnesia for childhood" can be explained in terms of the inextricable relationship between language and cognition (including memory).[22]

The important relationship between symbols and thought can be illustrated by examining any group's language and ideas. The Chinese language, for example is rich in words relating to concrete entities but poor in verbs that convey the notion of change. It is not surprising, therefore, "that Chinese thinking has tended to concreteness of expression." [23] The language makes the expression of abstract ideas an awkward procedure at best. Thus, the Chinese did not formulate many universal laws, and developed scientific thought only through contact with the West. Furthermore, the Chinese never pursued the study of logic; Indian logic was brought to China, but it "exerted no significant influence" and "soon declined and disappeared as a branch of study." [24] Clearly, cognition is closely dependent upon symbol systems. At the same time, symbol systems change and develop; the Chinese language had to change in order to facilitate new modes of understanding, but the people were not prevented from that change by a language that prevented creative thinking.

Third, symbols form the basis for our overt behavior. We are led to act by the stimulus of symbols. This includes both the symbols of others and our own symbolization. For before a response is made to any situation, that situation must be defined; the individual strives to make sense of it by representing it to him- or herself symbolically so that he or she can make an appropriate response. It is for this reason that different individuals may act quite differently in the same situation. Individuals arriving at a party where there is heavy drinking may react with pleasure, disgust, or disappointment depending upon whether they define such drinking as fun, sinful, or boring.

[21] Mead, *Mind, Self and Society,* p. 192.

[22] Jerome S. Bruner, Rose R. Olver, and Patricia M. Greenfield, eds., *Studies in Cognitive Growth,* Wiley, New York, 1966, p. 64.

[23] Hajime Nakamura, *Ways of Thinking of Eastern Peoples,* ed. Philip P. Wiener, East-West Center Press, Honolulu, 1964, p. 177.

[24] *Ibid.,* p. 191.

In sum, then symbols are learned, shared meanings, distinguishing human from infrahuman behavior. Symbols enable us to transcend the immediate situation, the present. And symbol systems are the basis for our understanding of reality, our cognitive processes, and our overt behavior.

Interaction

THE MEANING OF INTERACTION

We have already indicated the importance of the concept of interaction in pointing out that symbols emerge from human interaction, and that the same words may receive quite different meaning content because of differing interaction experiences. Interaction, then, is one of the pillars of the theory of symbolic interactionism. Neither human beings nor their social life can be comprehended apart from an understanding and analysis of human interaction.

Interaction refers to reciprocally influenced behavior on the part of two or more people. That is, when two people interact, each influences the behavior of the other, and each directs one's own behavior on the basis of the other's behavior towards one. This means that individuals are viewed in a distinctive way. The individual is neither the product of impinging stimuli, nor a reflection of an overarching and overwhelming cultural system, nor an organism driven by and essentially determined by internal mechanisms like the Freudian instincts. Rather, what a human being *is* depends upon interaction with others. And what a human being *does* depends not simply upon what kind of person he or she is (personality), but upon the person's interaction with others. At the same time, the individual is part of the interaction, acting and not merely reacting, creating and not merely being formed or controlled. Consequently, a basic unit of analysis is what Mead called "the social act," a process that includes at least two individuals who must take each other into account in satisfying their own impulses.[25]

MAINTENANCE FUNCTIONS OF INTERACTION

Our very humanity is linked up with ongoing interaction. That is not a new insight. Aristotle pointed out that man is a social animal. In China, Confucianism stressed the social nature of man: "Only unnatural and abnormal people live outside the communities . . . it is only in society that men reach their fullest development and realize their potentialities." [26]

---

[25] Mead, *Mind, Self and Society*, p. 6n.
[26] Paul Thomas Welty, *The Asians: Their Heritage and Their Destiny*, 3d ed., Lippincott, Philadelphia, 1970, p. 149.

And the pioneer American psychologist, William James, wrote in 1890 that "no more fiendish punishment" could be conceived for a human being than to be in society and yet be treated as nonexistent:

> If no one turned round when we entered, answered when we spoke, or minded what we did, but if every person "cut us dead," and acted as if we were nonexisting things, a kind of rage and impotent despair would ere long well up in us, from which the cruellest bodily tortures would be a relief; for these would make us feel that, however bad might be our plight, we had not sunk to such a depth as to be unworthy of attention at all.[27]

The validity of these insights is supported by a variety of evidence. The feral children—those who survived isolation in early childhood (whether raised by animals or not is a matter of debate)—did not function in a human fashion when found, and were generally never fully capable of behaving in what we consider a human way.[28] A study of members of Parents without Partners concluded that we all have needs "which can only be met within relationships, that relationships tend to become relatively specialized in the needs for which they provide, and as a result individuals require a number of different relationships for well-being." [29]

Apart from interaction, then, we neither develop nor maintain those qualities which we call human. As a contemporary psychiatrist tersely puts it, "It isn't quite human constantly to prefer one's own company." [30] But in addition to the individual's physical and emotional well-being, interaction is important in the maintenance of attitudes and beliefs. Voluntary associations such as unions and churches recognize this principle in providing various social activities for their members. Union members who otherwise might have little ideological sensitivity are kept sensitive through their participation in union social activities (as opposed to activities specifically involving union matters).[31] Religious commitment is likewise dependent upon interaction. Pentecostals are notably intense in their beliefs, and stress the individualism of their religion—that is, that commitment is a matter between the individual and God. But Pentecostals also acknowledge that such commitment cannot be maintained without

[27] William James, *The Principles of Psychology,* Dover, New York, 1950, I, 293–294.

[28] See Tamotsu Shibutani, *Society and Personality,* Prentice-Hall, Englewood Cliffs, N.J., 1961, pp. 475–478.

[29] Robert S. Weiss, "The Fund of Sociability," *Trans-Action,* 6 (July/August 1969), 38.

[30] Karl A. Menninger, *The Human Mind,* Knopf, New York, 1961, p. 81.

[31] Seymour Martin Lipset, Martin Trow, and James Coleman, *Union Democracy,* Anchor Books, Garden City, N.Y., 1956, p. 379.

interacting with others who are equally committed, whether that interaction occurs in a church or in informal gatherings.[32]

Contrary to the American myth of autonomous man, then, interaction is crucial to the individual's well-being and to the maintenance of his or her attitudes and beliefs. The individual who stands alone against the tide of opinion and forges his or her own way in the midst of skepticism and opposition is a myth. No one stands totally alone unless one is mentally ill. We may indeed stand against a strong majority, but we are sustained in that stand because of interaction with others who are also not with the majority. Human beings are social animals.

FORMATIVE FUNCTIONS OF INTERACTION

Behavior is created by interaction rather than merely occurring during the course of interaction. We can never understand human behavior by studying the individual in isolation; we can never predict human behavior by apprehending all of the psychological qualities of an individual. For behavior is a function of the interaction itself and not merely of those qualities which individuals bring into the interaction.

A series of experiments dating back into the nineteenth century have shown that even the presence of another human being tends to alter behavior. Two types of alteration occur: audience effects and co-action effects.[33] The former involves the effects of spectators upon the individual's behavior. In general, it appears that learning is impeded by an audience but that performance of a learned task or skill is facilitated. Co-action effects are distinguished from audience effects in that the former occur when everyone is engaged in a joint task rather than some being engaged and some comprising an audience. Co-action effects have been observed in animals and insects as well as humans. For example, animals generally eat more when other animals are eating with them; ants work more when other ants are present. Humans have been found to perform better at a variety of tasks when working in groups rather than individually.

In the 1960s psychologists were stimulated by incidents of violence and murder in which many bystanders were present, but unresponsive to victims, to investigate the causes of bystander "apathy." Again, the fact that there were bystanders rather than a bystander made a significant difference. In one experiment male students were brought into a room which began to fill with smoke. When two passive confederates of the

[32] Luther P. Gerlach and Virginia H. Hine, *People, Power, Change: Movements of Social Transformation,* Bobbs-Merrill, Indianapolis, 1970, p. 113.

[33] See Robert B. Zajonc, "Social Facilitation," in *Current Perspectives in Social Psychology,* ed. Edwin P. Hollander and Raymond G. Hunt, 2d ed., Oxford, New York, 1967, pp. 9–14.

experimenter were also present, only 10 percent of the subjects reported the smoke. When three subjects were brought in together, 38 percent of the groups reported. But when subjects were alone, 75 percent of them reported the smoke! The experimenters concluded that among the groups the situation was defined by observing the behavior of other members of the group; if others remained passive, the smoke was defined as not dangerous.[34] The conclusion of the group could have been quite wrong, of course. Individuals do not necessarily make better decisions when in a group, but their behavior is likely to be altered by the very fact of interacting with others.

The formative aspect of interaction and its significance vis-à-vis personality and social background variables is well demonstrated in another set of experiments involving the signing of petitions.[35] The experimenters secured a number of student subjects and asked them to arrive at a particular room at a particular time. Presumably, the subject was to wait there until asked to go into another room where the experiment would take place. Another student (a confederate of the experimenter) was also waiting in the room. A third student (also a confederate) came into the room to ask the two to sign a petition. The subject was more or less willing to sign the petition depending upon whether the confederate signed it. But in addition, the probability of signing remained the same independently of background variables such as personality traits of the subject and the content of the petition. The major influence on the subject was the behavior of the other.

Clearly, then, interaction is a creative process. As Blumer rightly argues, many social scientists have failed to recognize the significance of interaction by treating it as "a mere forum through which sociological or psychological determinants" result in certain behavior.[36] On the contrary, he points out, interaction "*forms* human conduct instead of being merely a means or a setting for the expression or release of human conduct." [37]

The formative aspect of interaction has been observed in field settings as well as in the experimental situation. In his study of French bureaucracies, Crozier found three different shop organization patterns.[38] In one, each maintenance man worked with twelve pairs of women machine oper-

---

[34] B. Latane and J. M. Darley, "Group Inhibition of Bystander Intervention in Emergencies," *Journal of Personality and Social Psychology,* 10 (1968), 215–221.

[35] P. Himelstein and J. C. Moore, "Racial Attitudes and the Action of Negro-and-White Background Figures as Factors in Petition-Signing," *Journal of Social Psychology,* 61 (December 1963), 267–272.

[36] Herbert Blumer, *Symbolic Interactionism: Perspective and Method,* Prentice-Hall, Englewood Cliffs, N.J., 1969, p. 7.

[37] *Ibid.,* p. 8.

[38] Michel Crozier, *The Bureaucratic Phenomenon,* The University of Chicago Press, Chicago, 1963, pp. 95–100.

ators; the man maintained the six machines upon which pairs of women worked as equals. In a second pattern, each maintenance man cared for three machines, and a woman operator and product receiver worked at each machine. In the third pattern, each maintenance man also cared for three machines; a woman operator, two women packagers, and a male laborer worked at each machine. In all three patterns, the maintenance men worked directly only with the machine operators. This meant that they had direct contact with all other workers in the first pattern, but with half or less in the other two patterns.

In other words, we have three different patterns of interaction in the three shops. And Crozier found interesting consequences of those differing patterns. The greatest frequency of complaints about maintenance men occurred in the second pattern and the least in the first pattern. Maintenance men were regarded with less suspicion when they worked directly with others. And among the workers themselves, 46 percent complained about not getting along well with fellow workers in the third pattern, while the figure rose to 70 percent for the second pattern and 75 percent for the first pattern.

Thus, interaction is a formative process, and differing patterns of interaction will have differential consequences for behavior. It should be emphasized, however, that we are not saying that personality and social background variables are unimportant or irrelevant. For if the interaction itself were the only causal variable, we would not find individual differences. That is, we would expect 100 percent complaints in two of the patterns above and no complaints in the other. And in the experiment on reporting smoke, none of the subjects should have reported the smoke when two passive confederates were with them.

Human behavior is extraordinarily complex, and we are not advocating simplistic explanations. If we have emphasized the importance of interaction and interaction patterns in this section, it is simply because the formative aspect of interaction, as Blumer pointed out, has been grossly neglected by social psychologists.

Attitude

DEFINITION OF ATTITUDE

The concept of "attitude" is one which is shared by symbolic interactionists with other social psychologists. In fact, Gordon Allport called attitude "the most distinctive and indispensable concept in contemporary American social psychology." [39] Nevertheless, attitude has been variously

[39] G. W. Allport, "Attitudes in the History of Social Psychology," in *Attitudes,* ed. Marie Jahoda and Neil Warren, Penguin, Baltimore, 1966, p. 15.

defined. Mead defined attitudes primarily in behavioral terms, as the "beginnings of acts." [40] We shall, however, adopt a more common definition in accord with the prevailing use of the concept: "attitude" "refers to certain regularities of an individual's feelings, thoughts, and predispositions to act toward some aspect of his environment." [41] As typically pointed out, then, attitudes have affective, cognitive, and behavioral components. One's attitude toward rock music, for example, includes one's "love" of it, one's belief that such music is gratifying and expressive of youth's values, and one's propensity for attending rock concerts and buying records.

SOURCES OF ATTITUDES

Attitudes arise through interaction. Because interaction experiences are diverse, differing and, from an observer's point of view, contrary attitudes develop and are maintained within the individual. For example, in the previously cited study of French bureaucracies, individuals were found to have both liberal and conservative attitudes. Directors and assistant directors were conservative with respect to the larger society, but fought "with great passion for technical change and modernization within the bureaucracy," while the technical engineers were committed to change in the larger society and were "very conservative about technical matters." [42] Differing kinds of interaction experiences within the larger society and within the bureaucracy led to quite different attitudes about the two entities. This may mean that the individual can maintain contradictory attitudes, or that the contradiction is only apparent to the observer and that the individual is consistent from his own point of view (a position in accord with the bulk of social psychological theory). But the point is one to be explored in more advanced study; our interest is in demonstrating the way in which an individual can hold diverse attitudes on the basis of differing interaction experiences.

Furthermore, because interaction is a formative process, there is ongoing change in attitudes. Some attitudes, which Mead called "fundamental," change slowly, while others may be in continual and relatively rapid flux. But by the very nature of interaction, attitudes tend to change; the individual continually brings up "the attitudes of the group toward himself, responds to it, and through that response changes the attitude of the group." [43]

[40] Mead, *Mind, Self and Society*, p. 5.
[41] Paul F. Secord and Carl W. Backman, *Social Psychology*, McGraw-Hill, New York, 1964, p. 97.
[42] Crozier, p. 156.
[43] Mead, *Mind, Self and Society*, p. 180.

ATTITUDES AND BEHAVIOR

The nature of attitudes, their interrelationships, and their relationship to behavior are all complex factors; this complexity, in turn, underlies one of the more perplexing problems in social psychology—the *apparent disparity* between attitudes and overt behavior which has been identified by a number of researchers. As noted above, one of the components of attitudes is behavioral: an attitude means that an individual has a predisposition to act in some way. Yet studies of attitudes and behavior have rather consistently concluded that the former are poor predictors of the latter. Thus various researchers have found that attitudes of prejudice do not predict discriminatory behavior. In a classic study, LaPiere noted that West Coast hotel and restaurant personnel served his Chinese friends, but over 90 percent indicated some months later on a questionnaire that they would *not* serve the Chinese.[44] Subsequent investigations confirm these results, typically showing that the prejudicial attitudes people express on paper are not consistent with the way they behave in a concrete situation.

How can we account for this discrepancy? We will outline the complex characteristics of attitudes and show the various functions of attitudes below. The discussion will show that the problem is rooted in inadequacies in research rather than a lack of relationship between attitudes and behavior; attitudes are complex phenomena which have important functions in human life.[45]

With respect to the complex characteristics of attitudes, we need to keep in mind the following:

(1) *Attitudes are interdependent.* In much of the research, a specific attitude has been posited as the independent variable and overt behavior that appears to be logically derived from that attitude has been offered as the dependent variable. However, overt behavior normally involves a number of attitudes rather than a single one. It may be impossible to isolate a single attitude for experimental purposes. As Mead argued, our attitudes toward any object include alternative responses, since any attitude object comprises diverse meanings for us. It is, therefore, unrealistic

[44] LaPiere's article, along with an extended discussion of the problem, may be found in Irwin Deutscher, *What We Say/What We Do,* Scott, Foresman, Glenview, Ill., 1973. See also Howard J. Ehrlich, "Attitudes, Behavior, and the Intervening Variables," *The American Sociologist,* 4 (February 1969), 29–34.

[45] The remainder of this section is a somewhat modified version of Robert H. Lauer, "The Problem and Values of Attitude Research," *The Sociological Quarterly,* 12 (Spring 1971), 247–252.

to expect to isolate a single attitude that will invariably result in a specific behavior. Furthermore, an attitude to a specific action is not necessarily the same as an attitude toward an issue with which that action is related. For example, an individual may possess a strongly negative attitude toward capitalism but also be opposed to a general strike designed to disrupt capitalistic enterprise. Unfortunately, many studies have neglected to obtain attitudes toward action as well as toward issues; when the two are combined, better predictions of behavior are obtained.[46]

Thus, behavior is always organized in terms of a plurality of attitudes. For example, in a study of attraction, Byrne and McGraw concluded that individuals low in prejudice will respond similarly to both black and white strangers. Individuals high in prejudice, on the other hand, will respond positively to a black stranger only when they share similar attitudes with the black toward a large number of subjects; otherwise, they will respond negatively.[47] The differing responses make sense only when we know the various attitudes involved—the attitude of prejudice alone does not account for the behavior.

(2) *Attitudes are multidimensional.* As noted before, there are three components of attitudes—the affective, cognitive, and behavioral.[48] While social psychologists generally hold that both the affective and cognitive components are present in all attitudes, most would agree that the behavioral component may be lacking. If one accepts, then, the multidimensional nature of attitudes, a behavioral manifestation of every attitude is not expected.

There are other reasons for not expecting a behavioral manifestation of every attitude. The particular attitude may be a peripheral one (see number 4 below). Or the behavioral tendency may be inhibited by situational factors (see number 6 below). Or the behavioral tendency of an attitude may be inhibited by other attitudes with which it is interdependent and which are also related to the situation. Finally, behavior may be present but different from that which the researcher expected. For example, an individual may show strong racial prejudice in his or her responses to a questionnaire. Later, in another facet of the experiment, he or she may be asked to treat someone of another race as an equal in

---

[46] A. G. Weinstein, "Predicting Behavior from Attitudes," *Public Opinion Quarterly*, 36 (Fall 1972), 355–360.

[47] Donn Byrne and Carl McGraw, "Interpersonal Attraction toward Negroes," in *Contemporary Research in Social Psychology*, ed. Henry Clay Lindgren, Wiley, New York, 1969, pp. 85–101.

[48] See Daniel Katz and Ezra Stotland, "A Preliminary Statement to a Theory of Attitude Structure and Change," in *Psychology: A Study of Science*, ed. Sigmund Koch, McGraw-Hill, New York, 1959, III, 423–475, for an early statement.

a particular situation. If the subject does so, how can the attitude and the behavior be reconciled? We suggest the following as one possibility. The cognitive and affective components of the attitude result in a contradiction between preferred and requested behavior. The preferred behavior is inhibited by other factors such as social norms. The individual complies with the norms, but the behavioral component of the attitude is still functioning; that behavioral component results in aggression, but aggression towards the self rather than the other. Because the aggressive behavior is self-directed, psychosomatic symptoms develop in the subject. Thus, the subject has behaved in a manner congruent with his or her attitude; but the behavior was not that which the experimenter hoped to observe.

(3) *Extrapolated attitudes must be distinguished from existential attitudes.* Extrapolated attitudes refer to those which are projected into an imaginary situation; existential attitudes are those which are operative in and arise out of an actual situation. The presumed failure of attitudes to correlate with behavior is based upon studies of extrapolated attitudes. But the value of such attitudes is a function both of the skill of the researcher in replicating the actual situation and of the ability of the subject to apprehend the actual situation in his imagination.

In other words, an extrapolated attitude is the way one imagines that one will feel, believe, and act toward something; an existential attitude is one's actual feelings, beliefs and behavior in the concrete situation. Even though the extrapolated attitude (as measured by a questionnaire) is prejudicial and negative towards those of another race, the existential attitude may differ because of social norms or other factors which the individual failed to consider, or because the actual interaction process modifies the attitude (many people who are required to interact with those of another race find their prejudice diminished or negated by the experience, stressing once again the formative nature of interaction).

(4) *Attitudes may be central or peripheral.* The organization of attitudes may be conceived in terms of a network of interlocking attitudes. Any single attitude is more or less central or peripheral in this system. The more central the attitude, the greater the number of other attitudes with which it is linked, and, consequently, the more likely it is to influence behavior. Attitudes with fewer linkages to other attitudes, on the other hand, are more likely to be subservient to situational factors.

Attitudes may be central or peripheral in another sense—in the strength of their development in the individual. Those which are strongly developed will be more significant for overt behavior than those which are weak. In their study of voting behavior during an undergraduate student election, Sample and Warland not only measured attitudes towards student government, but also secured a measure of the certainty of the responses —in other words, a measure of how strongly developed the attitudes were. As a result, they found that attitude was a major predictor of both intention to vote and actual voting behavior among high-certainty respondents; among low-certainty respondents, other variables were more important in predicting voting intentions and behavior.[49]

(5) *Attitudes may be primary or secondary.* Primary attitudes are those which are crucial to the individual's selfhood. They may be either attitudes about one's self or about other matters that directly bear upon one's self. For example, prejudice towards those of another race may be rooted in distrust based on lack of contact and information about the others; but in some cases, prejudice against another race may maintain the individual's self-esteem—those whom one despises as inferior and undesirable also assure one that he or she is better than some others in the society. In the former case the attitude is secondary, while in the latter case it is primary.

It is important to know whether attitudes are primary or secondary, for Jones has presented experimental evidence suggesting that subjects may be incapable of making accurate judgments in matters that bear upon their self-concepts.[50] We may anticipate, therefore, considerably greater difficulty in tapping the primary attitudes. In particular, any effort to measure primary attitudes from simple paper and pencil tests that purport to derive those attitudes from anticipated behavior in hypothetical situations is suspect. To the extent that such methods are useful, attitudes must be inferred from both the test and the actual behavior. In any case, since attitudes have diverse functions for individuals, the primary attitudes, which have the crucial function of maintaining the self-concept, are not only the most difficult to measure but also the most significant for understanding behavior.

(6) *Attitudes become factors in behavior in specific social context,* interacting with the other variables in that context. That is, behavior is always a function of both attitudes and situations, and the situation includes interaction with its formative potential. Moreover, there are likely to be inconsistent factors in any complex, real-life situation, so that the indi-

[49] J. Sample and R. Warland, "Attitude and Prediction of Behavior," *Social Forces,* 51 (March 1973), 292–304.

[50] Edward E. Jones, *Ingratiation: A Social Psychological Analysis,* Appleton-Century-Crofts, New York, 1964, pp. 77–79.

vidual must reconcile these inconsistencies or choose from among them as he acts.[51]

Thus, in striving to understand the role of attitudes in behavior we must take account of the fact that attitudes interact with other variables in complex situations. In the case of the employees of the French bureaucracies cited above, the situation was one of an ongoing struggle for power among various employee groups. We may infer that the generalized attitudes toward change which, as noted above, were inverted within the organization, were displaced by other and stronger attitudes—namely, those towards the acquisition and exercise of power.

FUNCTIONS OF ATTITUDES

Attitudes affect behavior in diverse and sometimes indirect ways. We may identify at least six significant functions of attitudes in this respect:

(1) *Attitudes influence various psychological processes.* Various modern studies have shown attitudes to affect both perception and learning.[52] For example, a study was made of student perceptions of a Dartmouth-Princeton football game. A movie of the game was shown to groups of students from each school after postgame accusations by both sides of deliberate and extreme roughness on the part of the other side. The Princeton students saw twice as many cases of rule breaking by Dartmouth as Dartmouth students saw. Attitudes about the game and the other side clearly influenced perception.

Attitudes are part of the selective mechanisms that govern perception, so that perception of any phenomenon tends to be congruent with existing attitudes. In like manner, material that is discordant with existing attitudes is less likely to be learned and/or retained. Mead put it more strongly than this however. He argued not simply that attitudes affect perception, but that they determine it in the sense of defining the nature of the perceptual object. Objects are defined in terms of their meaning; meaning is the individual's behavior toward the object; and behavior is the consequence of attitudes. "I see the object as I may later respond to it . . . What I see will depend upon what I am going to do later." [53] Thus, a piece of aged wood from an old barn may be seen as ugly scrap by a gardener, as useful firewood by a suburbanite, and as beautiful material for creative work by an artist.

[51] H. Schuman, "Attitudes vs. Actions *Versus* Attitudes vs. Attitudes," *Public Opinion Quarterly,* 36 (Fall 1972), 347–354.

[52] Theodore M. Newcomb, Ralph H. Turner, and Philip E. Converse, *Social Psychology,* Holt, New York, 1965, pp. 73–77.

[53] George Herbert Mead, *The Philosophy of the Act,* ed. Charles W. Morris, The University of Chicago Press, Chicago, 1938, p. 131.

(2) *Attitudes may function as an ecological variable.* Shibutani has argued that three factors must be grasped in order to understand an individual's behavior: how the situation is defined, the individual's self-concept, and reference groups. The latter is "the audience before which he tries to maintain his self-respect" and may be conceptualized in terms of a particular set of attitudes.[54] That is, the individual functions within the context of prevailing community attitudes, and his understanding of the attitudes of those significant others who comprise his reference groups will bear directly upon his behavior. Thus, in spite of the rhetoric during the 1960s about waging war on poverty, official failure to adequately cope with the problem is understandable in the face of the dominant tendency to define the poor as in some sense "disreputable." [55]

(3) *Attitudes function as selective mechanisms in interaction patterns.* Other things being equal, individuals tend to choose to interact with those who have attitudes similar to their own.[56] Furthermore, individuals will choose to interact with others on the basis of attitudes toward the group of which the others are a part. For example, an individual may choose friends who have political and religious attitudes similar to his or her own. And he or she may select a physician on the basis of the ethnic background of the various physicians available to him. Newcomb's study of the "acquaintance process" illustrates the way in which attitudes act as selective mechanisms. Seventeen male students who were strangers to each other were invited to live together in a house on campus. A year later, a second set of seventeen strangers occupied the house. A series of measurements were made of attitudes, including economic, aesthetic, and social concerns. Newcomb found that as the group interacted and learned about each other, each would prefer to associate with others who held similar attitudes about important matters (including the others' feeling about him). Because of the preference for others with similar attitudes, preferred associations changed over time; those with whom an individual initially preferred to associate were not necessarily the same as those preferred later when more was learned about attitudes.

(4) *Attitudes act as inhibitory factors on certain behavior.* A concern with relating attitudes to behavior may completely overlook the signifi-

---

[54] Shibutani, p. 279.

[55] David Matza, "The Disreputable Poor," in *Class, Status, and Power,* ed. Reinhard Bendix and Seymour Martin Lipset, 2d ed., Free Press, New York, 1966, pp. 289–302.

[56] J. A. Precker, "Similarity of Valuings as a Factor in Selections of Peers and Near-Authority Figures," *Journal of Abnormal and Social Psychology,* 47 (April 1952), 406–414; Theodore M. Newcomb, *The Acquaintance Process,* Holt, New York, 1961.

cance of attitudes in inhibiting behavior. That is, attitudes not only mean that we feel and think and tend to act in a particular way, but that we tend *not* to feel and think and act in other ways. Thus, in his survey of Asian problems, Myrdal points out that attitudes and institutions comprise the main barriers to social change.[57] Included in the former are negative attitudes relating to work habits, to material gain, and to change itself. These attitudes are supported by the social structure, and together they serve to inhibit the kinds of behavior necessary for modernization.

(5) *Attitudes affect the behavior of those who are the objects of the attitudes.* A great deal of the concern with attitudes and behavior has focused on the behavior of the individual holding the attitudes. But attitudes of one individual affect the behavior of others with whom he or she interacts and who are the objects of his or her attitudes. The debilitating effects of white attitudes on the black personality and behavior[58] and the effects of teacher attitudes on pupil performance[59] are but two examples of the importance of attitudes on overt behavior—in this case, not the overt behavior of the subject but of the objects of the attitudes. Self-concepts are also shaped, in part, by the attitudes of others as we shall discuss below.

(6) *Attitudes function to legitimate change and to influence, in turn, the subsequent direction of change.* A number of studies have shown that attitudes are changed as a result of other kinds of change. For example, it has been found that a change of roles effects attitudinal change; that changing discriminatory practices leads to a change of discriminatory attitudes; that attitudes may shift as a result of participating in various task groups; and that legislation may change attitudes even before behavior changes.[60] Thus, a sample of New York physicians opposed a governmental hospitalization plan for the elderly before Medicare was passed, but indicated approval after the program became law. The passage of the law itself, even before it was officially implemented, was sufficient to change a great number of attitudes. The changed attitudes made the new

[57] Gunnar Myrdal, *Asian Drama,* Pantheon, New York, 1968, III, 1873.

[58] Thomas Pettigrew, *A Profile of the Negro American,* Van Nostrand, Princeton, N.J., 1964.

[59] Robert Rosenthal and Lenore Jacobson, *Pygmalion in the Classroom: Teacher Expectation and Pupjls' Intellectual Development,* Holt, New York, 1968.

[60] See, respectively: S. Lieberman, "The Effects of Changes in Roles on the Attitudes of Role Occupants," *Human Relations,* 9, No. 4 (1956), 385–402; H. H. Hyman and P. B. Sheatsley, "Attitudes on Desegregation," *Scientific American,* 211 (July 1964), 16–23; Paul E. Breer and Edwin A. Locke, *Task Experience as a Source of Attitudes,* Dorsey, Homewood, Ill., 1965; and J. Colombotos, "Physicians and Medicare: A Before-After Study of the Effects of Legislation on Attitudes," *American Sociological Review* 34 (June 1969), 318–334.

law legitimate for the physicians. For humans are cognitive creatures. They strive to make sense out of life, to explain and justify their existence. Attitudes help in this by legitimating the existential situation.

The emergence of the attitude serves not only to legitimate change, but also to influence subsequent interaction. And just as the discordance between prior attitudes and change led to a change of attitude, the new attitude will interact in discordance with future situations, leading to further change in interaction patterns or attitudes or both.

Socialization

THE MEANING OF SOCIALIZATION

Socialization has been defined as "those processes whereby newcomers learn to participate effectively in social groups." [61] This brief definition is preferable to those which define socialization as essentially a childhood process. For one of the implications of symbolic interaction theory is the lifelong nature of socialization. Through socialization, the biological infant acquires human characteristics. But socialization continues beyond the infant stage. Effective participation in any social group—whether children, adults, or both—depends upon an understanding of the symbolic environment in the group and an ability to function within the symbol system of the group. Socialization, therefore, is an interaction process that involves the acquisition of shared meanings; such meanings are manifested in the symbol system of a group and in the attitudes that prevail among group members.

CHILDHOOD AND ADULTHOOD SOCIALIZATION

This is not to say that there are no important differences between child and adult socialization. A most important difference is that the adult comes to the socializing situation with a background of numerous and diverse prior socialization experiences. Childhood socialization is therefore a unique process. Arnold Rose has described three phases of that process; the phases demonstrate not only the nature of the process but also its uniqueness. [62]

The first phase of childhood socialization, according to Rose, occurs in the life of the infant when learning takes place through a psychogenic process of the kind found in other animals. This process may be one of

---

[61] Shibutani, p. 473.

[62] Arnold M. Rose, "A Systematic Summary of Symbolic Interaction Theory," in *Human Behavior and Social Processes,* ed. Arnold M. Rose, Houghton Mifflin, Boston, 1962, pp. 15–16.

conditioning or trial and error; through it, the infant acquires a habitual "sequence of behaviors and events." [63]

In the second phase, the habitual sequence is interrupted. For example, the infant experiences hunger but the mother does not appear with food. The infant completes the act of being fed in its imagination, however, and is able to reconstruct that completed act in the future whether or not blockage occurs. In other words, the infant has begun to endow certain objects (mother) in its environment with meaning and to associate those objects with its own gestures (overt manifestation of hunger such as crying). Others in the environment behave in accord with the meaning which the infant's gesture has to them, and thereby make a meaningful symbol out of the gesture for the infant.

In the third phase, the child acquires an increasing number of symbols and he or she employs them to indicate both to him- or herself and to others the meaning of his or her behavior. This does not mean that nonverbal behavior completely disappears. Some psychogenic learning may occur in the growing child and adult. But socialization involves a development into a world that is essentially understood in symbolic terms; as a result of socialization, the individual functions within and responds to a symbolic environment.

Rose's analysis accords with the pattern of cognitive development outlined by the noted psychologist Jerome Bruner, who has argued that cognitive growth proceeds by "a series of technological advances in the use of the mind. Growth depends upon the mastery of techniques." [64] One of the most important of the techniques is language. But the individual is able to represent the world to himself in other ways and these others are particularly important in infancy. Bruner identifies three basic modes of understanding the world or ways in which the individual represents the world to himself. The first is the "enactive" mode, which involves motor responses; the individual's understanding of the world is based upon his or her own motor activity. The second is the "iconic" mode, which involves the organization of percepts and images; the individual understands the world through the construction of nonverbal images. The third mode is the symbolic, involving language and making possible intellectual activities significantly beyond those available in either of the other modes. For when language is employed to translate experience, there results a "progressive release from immediacy." [65] Thus, the infant's imaginative construction of the completion of the act is qualitatively different when it begins to employ verbal symbols.

[63] *Ibid.*, p. 15.

[64] J. S. Bruner, "The Course of Cognitive Growth," *American Psychologist,* 19 (1964), 1–15.

[65] *Ibid.*, p. 14.

There is no question but that the childhood socialization experience is of critical importance for the individual. Nevertheless, symbolic interactionists reject the determinism of Freudian thought, and stress the fact that socialization is a lifelong process. Groups within a society are quite diverse; since socialization is the process of learning to participate effectively in groups, we are socialized anew each time we enter a new group or a situation involving those of a different group. The individual hired by a business who learns to be a "good member of the team," the young person who only knows politics from high school civics and who becomes an involved member of the local political club, the individual who experiences a religious conversion and becomes a member of a church, the individual who moves to a new region of the country—all are examples of experiences involving socialization and, therefore, changes in the individual. Each organization, each group, and each individual coming into an interaction situation has a unique set of meanings; the construction of a set of shared meanings for those participating in the organizations, the groups, and the interaction is a socialization process. This means that socialization is a reciprocal process; any individual is both a socializing agent and one who is being socialized. Such reciprocity is most likely to occur in small groups; in organizations, the individual is more likely to be overwhelmed by number and to be socialized far more than he socializes.

THE DIVERSITY OF SOCIALIZATION

This latter point, combined with the explanation of childhood socialization, may suggest a greater degree of determinism than we would accept. While it is true that the infant is socialized by others whose power is massive compared to its own, and that the individual entering an organization is subjected to overwhelming forces of socialization, there are a number of reasons why the individual is not merely a helpless object shaped into a particular form by external forces over which he or she has no control.[66]

One important reason why the individual remains an actor and not merely a reactor is the diversity of any complex society. The way in which this diversity can have differential consequences for various individuals is illustrated in a study of Chinese in urban Thailand.[67] The study emphasizes both the importance of adult socialization and the consequences of diversity. Three different Chinese groups were included. The three groups were chosen on the basis of similar patterns of childhood socialization and diverse patterns of adult socialization, the latter being rooted in various

[66] These reasons have been briefly noted by Rose, pp. 14–15.
[67] B. Punyodyana, "Later-life Socialization and Differential Social Assimilation of the Chinese in Urban Thailand," *Social Forces,* 50 (December 1971), 232–238.

patterns of interaction with the Thai. The first group was composed of those who did not work for the Thai government and who were less educated in the Thai system than the other groups. A second group was composed of those who did not work for the Thai government but who had more education in the Thai system and a higher average income than those in the first group. And the third group contained employees of the Thai Government Civil Service.

The Chinese individuals in each of the groups differed significantly from those in the other groups in both attitudes and behavior. The government employees were most assimilated into Thai society, as measured by such things as number of Thai versus Chinese friends, language spoken at home, and preference for Thai versus Chinese marriage partner. The less-educated Chinese who did not work for the Thai government were the least assimilated of the three groups. Thus, in spite of initial socialization experiences which were similar, adult socialization processes resulted in important differences between the groups—the individuals in the groups developed different attitudes and behavior as a result of diverse interaction patterns and differential participation in organizations.

Diversity, then, gives one at least some choice, some alternative ways by which one can satisfy one's own impulses. Diversity also means that one is likely to be confronted with conflicting forces of socialization. And, again, one will have alternative ways of dealing with the conflict. In some cases, the conflict may be internalized; a woman might struggle with guilt and anxiety when she opts for college later in life because of the conflict between her own expectations of herself as a family member and the socializing forces of school. In other cases, the individual may choose between contrary alternatives; a student might opt for peer group values with respect to drinking and abandon the parental value of total abstinence. Finally, in some cases one may be so committed to those patterns derived from prior socialization experiences that one may opt for the role of maverick. In spite of the great pressures toward conformity, every organization and virtually every group has its "deviant" members. Even a tightly knit group such as a community based on utopian principles will have individuals within it who find it necessary to deviate from the group norms in order to satisfy their own impulses.[68] In other words, after childhood every individual enters each new interaction situation with a background of socialization experiences; because of the complexity of the attitudes which he or she has acquired from those experiences, the individual will not be wholly shaped by the new interaction situation but will, on the contrary, have alternative courses to choose from and will have some degree of influence over the situation.

[68] See Benjamin Zablocki, *The Joyful Community,* Penguin, Baltimore, 1971.

AGENTS OF SOCIALIZATION

All interaction serves to socialize to a greater or lesser degree. We have already mentioned the extreme importance of the family as the initial context for socialization. Families differ, however, both across and within societies. One well-known study of socialization investigated child-rearing practices in six different cultures: northern India, Okinawa, Mexico, Africa, the Philippines, and the northeastern United States. Among the findings were seven different ways in which family settings vary:[69]

1. the extent to which children are expected to be responsible for fulfilling various tasks;
2. the extent to which mothers feel and express positive emotions such as praise and warmth;
3. the extent to which aggression toward peers is condoned;
4. the extent to which aggression and disobedience toward parents is controlled;
5. the extent to which the mother cares for the babies (as opposed to a surrogate mother);
6. the extent to which mothers care for older children;
7. the extent to which mothers are emotionally stable.

Obviously, fundamental attitudes and behavioral patterns are involved in these differences. It is not surprising, then, that some researchers have posited that notion of a "national character," a modal personality type that may be found in a particular society. But there are also considerable differences within a particular society, such as difference by religion, by social class, and even by region. For example, on the basis of numerous studies, Kerckhoff has argued that "greater moral development, a higher level of achievement motivation, a clearer and more favorable self-image, and greater role-taking and role-playing ability are associated with the kind of parent-child relationship more frequently found in middle-class families." [70] Moral development here refers not to the researcher's judgment, but to the child's acquisition of values that lead him or her to define the behavior of him- or herself and others as right or wrong.

In addition to the family and other primary relationships such as kin and close friends, organizations are important socializing agents. Schools and churches are among the first organizations that have an impact on the individual's life. One piece of research relating to each of these organizations will illustrate the socialization process. With respect to schools,

[69] William W. Lambert and Wallace E. Lambert, *Social Psychology,* 2d ed., Prentice-Hall, Englewood Cliffs, N.J., 1973, p. 18.

[70] Alan C. Kerckhoff, *Socialization and Social Class,* Prentice-Hall, Englewood Cliffs, N.J., 1972, pp. 58–59.

some extensive research was carried out by Henry in elementary school classes. He found that teachers manipulated the emotions of the children in order to instill values and produce behavior that accord with adult standards. Specifically, the children were rewarded for such things as "carping criticism" which reflected individualistic competition.[71] Presumably, this prepared them to function in the adult world; the classroom had become a microcosm of the competitive capitalistic system, and the attitudes and interaction patterns necessary for functioning within that system were being developed by teacher manipulation of the children.

With respect to churches, Johnson's study of Holiness groups yielded similar results—that is, the groups were also socializing their members into those attitudes and behavior congruent with the values of the larger society. The Holiness groups emphasized much the same kind of attitudes and behavior described by Weber in *The Protestant Ethic*. That is, the Holiness perspective was found to be otherworldly while at the same time stressing devotion to God in the present life. Such devotion demands diligence, achievement, and a certain degree of asceticism. As one of Johnson's respondents put it: "If you had a call to the grocery business, then you ought to be ambitious for the glory of God . . . I'm trying to think of some Scripture. One that comes to mind is, 'Be not slothful in business.' " [72]

Although both of the above examples involve socialization into the dominant values of the larger society, some organizations—including some schools and some churches—socialize members into attitudes and behavior that are contrary to those values. For example, the American draft resistance movement that emerged in the late 1960s socialized its members into new attitudes. The socialization was necessitated by a comparatively large number of new recruits; such recruits always pose a potentially undermining force for a movement unless they are socialized into the movement's symbol system. Interviews with one hundred of the recruits showed that those who had had no previous association with radical movements experienced considerable change in beliefs and attitudes; they became much more radical in their attitude toward American society, becoming thereby less adjusted to the larger society but more capable of participating in the movement.[73]

Thus, some groups strive to socialize in accord with dominant values and some seek to socialize in terms of values which are contrary to the

[71] Reported in Charles E. Bidwell, "The School as a Formal Organization," in *Handbook of Organizations,* ed. James G. March, Rand McNally, Chicago, 1965, p. 986.

[72] B. Johnson, "Do Holiness Sects Socialize in Dominant Values?" *Social Forces,* 39 (May 1961), 309–316.

[73] M. Useem, "Ideological and Interpersonal Change in the Radical Protest Movement," *Social Problems,* 19 (Spring 1972), 451–469.

dominant ones. In either case, we should note that the socialization process may proceed both through interaction with group members and through such mechanisms as books, games, and the mass media. Consider, for example, what is happening to children who play the game of Monopoly; they are being socialized into attitudes that are necessary for the functioning of a capitalist economy. Or consider the way that preschool picture books present life to young children. One study of such books concluded that females are portrayed in rather dull terms: "little girls receive attention and praise for their attractiveness, while boys are admired for their achievements and cleverness . . . Through picture books, girls are taught to have low aspirations because there are so few opportunities portrayed as available to them." [74] Socialization into sex roles occurs in very early childhood. We could provide countless similar illustrations with respect to the mass media. But the point is clear: socialization is a pervasive process. Diverse and sometimes contrary socializing forces impinge upon the individual continually through both interaction experiences and the varied facets of the individual's culture.

Role-Taking

DEFINITION OF ROLE-TAKING

"Role-taking" is a central concept in the social psychology of Mead, but perhaps none of the concepts has suffered any greater confusion of meaning. Most often, role-taking is confused with role-playing. It has also been used as synonymous with empathy and with identification. [75] But none of these terms are interchangeable with role-taking, although role-playing, empathy, and identification are all related to the process of role-taking.

In essence "role-taking" is "the process whereby an individual imaginatively constructs the attitudes of the other, and thus anticipates the behavior of the other." [76] Thus, when a young woman takes the role of her father, she imaginatively constructs his attitudes so that she can anticipate his behavior. Knowing his attitudes, she also knows how he will probably react to a particular young man she might invite for dinner, or to her college grade report, or to her desire to move into an apartment, and so forth. This knowledge enables the young woman to map out her own

[74] L. J. Weitzman, D. Eifler, E. Hokada, and C. Ross, "Sex-Role Socialization in Picture Books for Preschool Children," *American Journal of Sociology,* 77 (May 1972), 1125–1150.

[75] See Walter Coutu, "Role-Playing vs. Role-Taking: An Appeal for Clarification," *American Sociological Review,* 16 (April 1951), 180–187, for some illustrations.

[76] Robert H. Lauer and Linda Boardman, "Role-Taking: Theory, Typology, and Propositions," *Sociology and Social Research,* 55 (January 1971), 137. A good part of the discussion in this section follows this paper.

behavior with respect to her father—she knows when to confront him, when to argue, when to "get around" him, when to request and when to assert, how to please and how to displease him. She does not know all this perfectly, of course, because we never are able to perfectly take the role of the other.

ROLE-TAKING AS BASIC TO HUMAN LIFE

Perfectly accomplished or not, role-taking is an essential process of human life. As noted before, human interaction always involves behavior in which individuals are taking account of each other. Role-taking enables such mutual taking-account to occur before overt behavior; that is, an individual takes account of the behavior of the other *before* it occurs by taking the role of the other. Because of this characteristic of role-taking, Mead asserted, it is of the essence of human, as opposed to infrahuman, society. In contrast to the beehive or the ant nest, the human capacity for role-taking is the creator of "the duties, rights, the customs, the laws, and the various institutions in human society." [77]

Mead argued, then, that role-taking is basic to the development of the self and of human society. As the individual develops, role-taking includes an increasingly wider range of his or her behavior. But individuals do not share the same capacity for role-taking, so that we will find variations in that capacity within any group. Nevertheless, all human life involves role-taking, and human society is only possible because of the role-taking capacity of the individuals comprising the society.

Role-taking is the basis for a society because cooperative processes are necessary for the maintenance of an organized community, and cooperative processes can only occur to the extent that individual members are able to apprehend the general attitude and, therefore, predict the behavior of other members of the society. In the ideal human society, all individuals are capable of entering into the attitudes of all others whom they are affecting in the course of performing their own functions.[78]

Mead also viewed role-taking as the "essence" of intelligence. For intelligence involves one putting oneself in the place of others, that is, taking the role of others, so that one can be sensitive to the attitudes of others toward oneself and toward all others during the course of inter-action. As one does this, one apprehends the meaning of the symbols or gestures which express the attitudes of others. And as one grasps the meaning of symbols one is able to carry on an internal conversation with oneself by employing those symbols. Such an internal conversation is a process of thinking.

[77] Mead, *Philosophy of the Act,* p. 625.
[78] Mead, *Mind, Self and Society,* p. 327.

THE DEVELOPMENT OF ROLE-TAKING

Thus far, we have assumed the existence of a role-taking capacity. How can we account for the appearance of that capacity in humans? Mead identified language as the mechanism of role-taking. Until the individual acquires language, role-taking is elemental. Incipient role-taking may be first seen within the context of the significant gesture. For example, when a mother and infant communicate through the use of significant symbols, role-taking has begun for the infant. The mother and infant are employing symbols which have the same meaning for each of them so that the infant, in understanding the symbol, is also apprehending the attitudes of its mother. Attitudes are expressed in behavior, and language is a form of behavior. When the infant begins to communicate symbolically, therefore, it is at the same time constructing the attitudes of the other.

In brief, language is a system of shared meanings and a form of human behavior. It is therefore an overt expression of the attitudes of the individual. To the extent that it is a system of *shared* meanings, that is, to the extent that individuals are engaging in the use of significant symbols, each interactant is constructing the attitudes of the other and thereby anticipating the behavior of the other. Thus, a conversation of significant gestures is also a process of role-taking.

The child's capacity to role-take develops through play and through participation in games. Gradually, he or she is able to take the roles of many others simultaneously, to take the role of the "generalized other" (see page 71). All adult interaction proceeds by virtue of this capacity for taking the role of the generalized other.

In sum, when Mead talks about role-taking capacity developing in humans, he is talking about a phenomenon that is integrally tied up with the development of the self, the mind, the generalized other, and the capacity for social interaction.

TYPES OF ROLE-TAKING

The concept can be sharpened and made more useful if we recognize the various kinds of role-taking: basic, reflexive, appropriative, or synesic. "Basic role-taking" conforms to the definition given above of the process of imaginatively constructing the attitudes of the other so as to anticipate the behavior of the other.

"Reflexive role-taking" is related to the reflexive nature of the self, that which can be both subject and object (see the discussion below). It is that process described by Turner in which "the role of the other is employed as a mirror, reflecting the expectations or evaluations of the self as seen in the other-role." [79] For example, in an experiment in which students believed that they were being evaluated in their reading performance by an expert, they tended to change their self-evaluation to accord with that of the presumed expert.[80] The students changed their attitudes toward their abilities as they saw those abilities mirrored in the evaluations of a significant other (it should be noted, however, that they were much more ready to accept evaluations which were more positive than their self-evaluations than those which were more negative).

"Appropriative role-taking" refers to the process of imaginatively constructing the attitudes of the other and internalizing them into the self. The attitudes of the other are not only apprehended, but incorporated into the structure of the self. These attitudes are not necessarily evaluative; reflexive role-taking may or may not be associated with appropriative role-taking. The German youth who began to believe and act like Hitler were engaging in appropriative, but not necessarily reflexive, role-taking. Furthermore, the other whose attitudes are appropriated may be an individual or a group, real or imaginary. Finally, appropriative role-taking is selective; normally, one or a few of the attitudes of the other, not all of them, are internalized. In some cases, however, a group might demand that the attitudes of the individual conform in toto with those of the group. As a Nazi prosecutor expressed it to a defendant in a court: "Christianity and we National Socialists have one thing in common, and one thing only: we claim the whole man." [81]

"Synesic role-taking" is a process of apprehending the feelings and the perceptions of the other. It is a more inclusive process than basic role-taking, for it is an effort to apprehend everything necessary to an understanding of the behavior of the other. It is the kind of role-taking which occurs in the work of the psychiatrist and of the novelist who carefully creates and shapes his characters.

These various kinds of role-taking enable us to distinguish the process from those related concepts with which it has been confused. Playing at a role, for example, presupposes the capacity to role-take. A child plays at being a mother or a friend, but it can only do that because it has the capacity to take the roles of those others. The child imaginatively constructs the attitudes of the other such that it can anticipate and, therefore, imitate the appropriate behavior.

Such playing at roles is an important part of the child's development, for he or she must put a series of roles to the test in order to appropriate those which the child ultimately defines as conducive to her or his own

---

[79] Ralph H. Turner, "Role-Taking, Role Standpoint, and Reference Group Behavior," *American Journal of Sociology*, 61 (January 1956), 321.

[80] R. Videbeck, "Self-Conception and the Reactions of Others," *Sociometry*, 23 (December 1960), 351–359.

[81] Quoted in Helmut Gollwitzer, Kathe Kuhn, and Reinhold Schneider, eds., *Dying We Live: The Final Messages and Records of Some Germans Who Defied Hitler*, Fontana Books, London, 1956, p. 121.

growth. But playing at roles occurs throughout life. The adult plays at a role when she or he tests a new social position to ascertain whether he or she will appropriate the attitudes and behavioral pattern associated with it, or when the adult deliberately seeks to project an image of him- or herself which he or she deems false but necessary to a particular situation.

"Role-playing," as distinguished from playing at roles, refers to the fulfillment of a behavioral pattern associated with a social position. It is the result of reflexive-appropriative role-taking, through which the individual develops a self-concept and appropriates certain attitudes consistent with that self-concept. After the child has played at a particular role, he or she either rejects or appropriates various attitudes associated with the role; the appropriated attitudes become the basis for role-playing.

Another related process is "identification," which is basically appropriative role-taking. To "identify" with an other is to appropriate for oneself certain attitudes of the other, thus becoming more like the other than before the appropriation. Identification may also involve reflexive role-taking; a perceived evaluation of the self that is enhancing may be the basis for subsequent appropriation of attitudes of the other who has been a source of gratification. A student, for example, who receives strong encouragement with respect to his or her intellectual abilities from a professor may subsequently internalize some of the professor's attitudes toward man, work, society, and so forth. Finally, in extreme cases, identification may involve synesic role-taking: an effort at total identification with the other.

"Empathy" is one other concept with which role-taking has been confused. "Empathy" is a process based upon synesic role-taking; empathy adds the element of feeling, so that the other's experience is not only understood but, to some extent, shared.

The way in which these various processes are interrelated but distinct can be illustrated by reference to studies that investigate the influence of role-playing (what we have called "playing at roles") to opinion change. Early experiments in social psychology indicated that playing at roles can induce marked opinion change under certain conditions.[82] This principle is used in so-called "role reversal," in which two individuals with contrary attitudes must each present the other's attitudes to the satisfaction of the other. For instance, role reversal can be used in labor-management disputes. Each side would have to express the other side's position to the satisfaction of the other, and when this is done there is a tendency for the attitudes of each to be altered. In terms of our discussion, the following sequence occurs: role-taking ability underlies the actual playing at a role;

[82] Irving L. Janis and Bert T. King, "The Influence of Role Playing on Opinion Change," in *Readings in Social Psychology*, ed. Eleanor E. Maccoby, Theodore M. Newcomb, and Eugene L. Hartley, 3d ed., Holt, New York, 1958, pp. 472–482.

playing at the role leads to appropriative role-taking, and the latter involves an opinion change. That is, playing at a role presupposes role-taking capacity. The individual imaginatively constructs the attitudes of the other and thereby plays at the other's role. In the course of playing at the role, of acting out the attitudes of the other, the individual internalizes some of these attitudes. The individual has constructed the attitudes of the other, acted them out, found them to be appealing, and appropriated them as his or her own.

THE SOCIAL CONTEXT OF ROLE-TAKING

Role-taking of all types is situational. That is, the kind of role-taking in which an individual actually engages is, in part, a function of the social context. We can identify certain structural conditions that tend to be associated with greater or lesser amounts of role-taking and also with certain types of role-taking.

With respect to amount of role-taking, for example, the structure of power is an important variable. Those who are in the higher positions of a power structure may have less reason to take the roles of others in the situation than those in lower positions. Tht latter may be engaged in an effort to gain more power or at least to prevent a greater degree of oppression by the powerful. Consequently, apprehending the attitudes and anticipating the behavior of others is more important to those with lesser power. A study of role-taking in families supports this line of reasoning; it was found that role-taking was most accurate among children, less accurate among mothers, and least accurate among fathers.[83]

With respect to situational variations in types of role-taking, the individual will be pressured to engage in certain kinds of role-taking in particular situations. For example, Davis has described the way handicapped people strive to establish a pattern of social interaction that removes their handicap from the focus of attention. A part of what is involved is a "redefinitional process in which the handicapped person projects images, attitudes and concepts of self which encourage the normal to identify with him (i.e., 'take his role') in terms other than those associated with imputations of deviance."[84] In other words, the handicapped person attempts to get the other to engage in synesic role-taking in order that the latter may redefine the situation in accord with the wishes of the former.

[83] D. L. Thomas, D. D. Franks, and J. M. Calonico, "Role-Taking and Power in Social Psychology," *American Sociological Review,* 37 (October 1972), 605–614.

[84] Fred Davis, "Deviance Disavowal: The Management of Strained Interaction by the Visibly Handicapped," in *Symbolic Interaction,* ed. Jerome G. Manis and Bernard N. Meltzer, Allyn and Bacon, Boston, 1967, p. 198.

Finally, the effort to get someone to "see himself as others see him" is an example of pressure to engage in reflexive role-taking. This occurs in marriage counseling and labor-management arbitration. Pressure to engage in appropriative role-taking will occur whenever conformity is defined as necessary to preserve the social order; bureaucracies, totalitarian systems, and religious orthodoxies are examples of settings where we would expect to find pressures towards appropriative role-taking.

Self

NATURE OF THE SELF

In his 1947 presidential address to the American Psychological Association, Carl Rogers noted that the "self" had come back into psychology. The concept of "self" had fallen into disrepute in psychology but was coming back as a legitimate research concern by the late 1940s. One reason the concept had been pushed to the periphery lies in the dominance of behaviorism, which proposes to understand human behavior without reference to any mentalistic or subjective concepts. Another reason has been pointed out by Allport, who says that the central objection has been that the concept begs the question. Ever since the time of Wundt, notes Allport, psychologists have objected to an explanation that involves "a mysterious central agency" which "performs in such a way as to unify the personality and maintain its integrity." [85]

Undoubtedly the concept had been abused by serving as an easy explanation for the otherwise inexplicable. But abuse is no reason for discarding it, and, in fact, the notion that humans have a self is of central importance in the social psychology of symbolic interactionists.

What, then, is this "self" about which psychologists have had ambivalent thoughts and which is of central import to symbolic interactionists? Mead's ideas are rather complex, but, in simplest terms, to have a self is to have the capacity to observe, respond to, and direct one's own behavior. One can behave towards oneself as one can towards any other social object. One can evaluate, blame, encourage, and despair about oneself; one can alter one's behavior. And in the process of observing, responding to, and directing one's behavior, one's structure of attitudes is changing (keep in mind that behavior towards the self does not occur in a vacuum—one is behaving toward oneself in the context of interaction with others). We will elaborate these ideas in terms of four characteristics of the self.

First, the self is not an entity, but a process. Mead further defined the self in terms of two phases of the process—the "I" and the "me." The

[85] Gordon W. Allport, *Becoming,* Yale, New Haven, 1955, p. 36.

"I" is the unpredictable, the novel, the driving impulses which comprise one phase of the self. The "me" is the organized community within one as reflected in one's attitudes. The self, then, is a dialectical process, with the "I" calling out the "me" and then responding to the "me." The "I" is never predictable, but the "me" reflects the generalized expectations of the social environment. In the ongoing dialectic between these two phases, we have the process which is the "self." In this process, the "I" is roughly equivalent to the Freudian id, while the "me" acts as a Freudian censor.[86] The "me" sets the limits within which the "I" can act.

The notion of self as process means that one's behavior is a process that includes: carving out a line of action that mediates between one's impulses and the expectations of the social environment; observing and responding to one's own and others' behavior; adjusting and directing one's subsequent behavior on these two bases. One takes into account both the way in which one's impulses accord with community attitudes— the norms and values which one has internalized or at least recognizes— and also the meanings that emerge in a specific situation of interaction. For example, a man may stifle his impulse to speak to an attractive female stranger because community attitudes define that behavior as inappropriate. But subsequent glances and gestures on the part of both of them may convey to him that she desires him to initiate a conversation. He will not only now follow his initial impulse, but his attitude about such behavior and about community standards may change.

The self as process also means that the individual changes; the particular structure of attitudes that comprise the self at a particular time is not permanent. There is perhaps no better illustration of this than for a person to reflect back upon what she or he was a few years previously; he or she might observe altered political orientations, religious beliefs, evaluations of various abilities, feelings about social problems, or any number of other changes.

A second characteristic of the self is that it is reflexive. This means that the individual can be an object to her- or himself. He or she can observe, evaluate, respond to, and direct his or her own behavior. As Blumer put it, the possession of a self *means* that the individual can be an object of his or her own behavior, that he or she is aware of various qualities he or she has and of roles he or she plays. "In all such instances he is an object to himself; and he acts toward himself and guides himself in his actions toward others on the basis of the kind of object he is to himself."[87] A student will act differently toward a professor than will a book salesperson, and a student who defines him- or herself as of mediocre intellect will act

---

[86] Mead, *Mind, Self and Society,* p. 210.
[87] Blumer, p. 12.

differently than one who defines him- or herself as superior. In each case, one defines the kind of person one is and directs one's behavior on that basis; and one can do this because the self is an object which one can observe and evaluate.

A third characteristic of the self, as noted above, is that it is comprised of attitudes. As Mead explained it, the self is an organization of shared attitudes. It is this structure of attitudes, rather than a group of habits, which comprises the self.[88] Every individual has a group of habits—certain typical ways of speech intonation and emotional expressions, for example. But these do not constitute the self. Humans are cognitive creatures, not mere creatures of habit and reflex actions. The self, then, involves a set of attitudes which are aroused in both the individual and in others who compose the social milieu.

The structure of attitudes means that all those individuals who comprise a community share a common framework. Each individual is different also—the self is an "I" as well as a "me." But Mead insisted that there is no self apart from membership in a group such that a community of attitudes exists within each member and controls the attitudes of all members. To be a symbolic creature and live in a symbolic environment means to function through shared meanings. Those meanings will change over time, of course, but if we take a cross-sectional slice of life we should find a framework which is common to all individuals participating in a community as well as differences among all those individuals. Without the shared attitudes, there could be no self and no viable communal life; without the differences, there could be no novelty and no individuality.

A final characteristic of the self follows directly from the above: the self is the means whereby social control becomes self-control. That is, to have a self is to internalize the attitudes of the community and thereby to control one's own behavior in terms of those attitudes. Mead identified social control as the dominance of the "me" over the "I," which is a way of saying that the individual's behavior conforms to community expectations. From one's own viewpoint, the attitudes are one's own: one prefers monogamous marriages, or believes that they are "natural" or morally right. But in another social context, one would have held the same attitudes about polygamous marriages. From the community's standpoint one's behavior is controlled because one has internalized the attitudes which prevail in the community and therefore directs one's behavior in accord with community standards.

This is not a static and deterministic position, however. Community attitudes change over time, in part because of the dialectic between individual and society. The individual must take the attitudes of others in

[88] Mead, *Mind, Self and Society*, p. 163.

order to belong to the community and possess a self. But the individual does more than internalize those attitudes; he or she reacts to them, thereby changing to some extent the community. The change in any particular case may be quite small, but the individual and the social milieu are engaged in an ongoing process of reciprocal influence that involves a degree of change in each.

ORIGIN OF THE SELF

The self arises out of interaction. Mead pointed out that the self is the result of a social process, which implies both interaction among individuals and the prior existence of the group in which the self arises.[89] In other words, the self arises in the course of interaction in a pre-existing symbolic environment; it is the most significant product of early socialization. Again, this is not to say that the self which arises out of early socialization and which is modified through subsequent interaction is nothing more than a reflection of social forces. Mead argued that the social process involves ongoing change so that "there is a social process out of which selves arise and within which further differentiation, further evolution, further organization, take place." [90]

Mead identified a certain sequence in the development of the self out of the social process.[91] Initially, the infant engages in imitative but meaningless (to it) behavior. Soon, however, the conversation of gestures in which the infant engages includes significant symbols, arousing in itself and the other the same responses. This conversation of gestures with significant symbols is an indispensable basis for the genesis of the self. For the self can arise only as the infant can be an object to itself. And it can only understand itself as an object as it sees itself in terms of the attitudes of others. And, finally, the infant can only understand the attitudes of others through language. The ability to employ language in order to take the standpoint of others occurs early. Some recent research indicates that the child has this capacity as early as one year of age.[92]

Once the child has begun to function symbolically, play activities become important in the development of the self. The child plays at various roles—mother or father, a policeman, a teacher, and so forth. For example, a girl might play at being her mother. She has a doll and behaves toward the doll as her mother behaves toward her; she apprehends her mother's behavior toward herself and applies it to the doll. She may speak to the doll, love it, feed it, and discipline it. In doing so, she is achieving

---

[89] *Ibid.,* p. 164.
[90] *Ibid.*
[91] *Ibid.,* pp. 144–158.
[92] Norman K. Denzin, "The Genesis of Self in Early Childhood," *Sociological Quarterly,* 13 (Summer 1972), 291–314.

two important things: first, she is "taking the role" of her mother, apprehending her mother's attitudes; second, she is becoming an object to herself, placing her own behavior outside herself (in the form of the doll) where she can understand and evaluate it.

The next phase of self-development is the organized game. It differs from the play phase in two respects: the child must now take the role of all others who are engaged in the game and the various roles must be related to each other in a definite way. In the game situation, one must see oneself as all the others in the situation see one; one must generalize the expectations of the others and act on that basis. This represents a decided advance over the play phase because the latter involves only a series of responses following each other in sequence whereas the game phase demands the complex organization of stimuli. In the game the child has advanced from the phase of being able to take the role of others in play to the phase in which she or he organizes many roles into a generalized set of expectations. In the play phase, the child can take the role of particular others; he or she can understand their attitudes toward him- or herself and toward each other. But in the game, the child organizes the attitudes of all those engaged and also organizes the attitudes of the social group to which he or she belongs. The child is thereby becoming an organic member of the group and is at the same time achieving full self-consciousness: "After all, what we mean by self-consciousness is an awakening in ourselves of the group of attitudes which we are arousing in others, especially when it is an important set of responses which go to make up the members of the community." [93]

Discussion of the development of the self must also include the views of Charles Horton Cooley. His views differ significantly from those of Mead, although they are often treated as variants of the same basic perspective. In some ways Cooley provides a corrective to Mead, as Mead provides a corrective to Cooley. Both insisted on the social nature of the self, but Mead viewed the self as essentially rational and the result of the objective factor of interaction in a symbolic environment; Cooley viewed the self as having an important affective component and as the result essentially of subjective processes of the individual.

According to Cooley, we must always keep in mind that the self "is any idea or system of ideas with which is associated the appropriate attitude we call self-feeling." [94] The self, he argued, is what we mean whenever we use the personal pronouns "I," "me," "my," "mine," and "myself." That self is the result of the individual's imaginative processes and emotions as he or she interacts with others; it is a reflected or looking-glass

[93] Mead, *Mind, Self and Society*, p. 163.
[94] Charles Horton Cooley, *Human Nature and the Social Order,* Scribner, New York, 1902, p. 224.

self composed of three principal elements: "the imagination of our appearance to the other person; the imagination of his judgment of that appearance, and some sort of self-feeling, such as pride or mortification." [95]

If we follow Cooley, then, we must acknowledge that the self is not necessarily the consequence of how we actually appear to others, nor of how they actually judge our appearance, but only of how we imagine those processes. It is possible, of course, that our imagination could be fairly accurate, but it is also possible that it could be quite wrong. Thus, whereas Mead stressed the apprehension and appropriation of the actual attitudes of others, Cooley stressed the importance of how we imagine those attitudes to be. Both men make valid and important points; perhaps future researchers will synthesize their insights in a useful way.

Generalized Other/Reference Group

MEANING OF THE GENERALIZED OTHER

The concepts of "generalized other" and "reference group" are so similar that they must be treated together. The generalized other was a most significant concept for Mead, but subsequent social psychologists have pretty well abandoned it—except for theoretical discussions—and employed the concept of reference group. As we shall note below, the two concepts are not synonymous, though they are sufficiently similar to warrant their treatment together.

We have already encountered the generalized other in discussing the development of the self and the process of role-taking. Mead identified the "generalized other" as the "organized community or social group which gives to the individual his unity of self. . . ." [96] The self, as noted above, is a structure of attitudes which are derived from the social milieu of the individual. That organized structure of attitudes which are appropriated from the social milieu is the "generalized other"; it is that to which the individual responds in all of his or her social behavior.

The generalized other is an integral part of thinking. We pointed out above that thinking is an internal conversation which employs symbols. The conversation can be carried on because of the individual's capacity for role-taking; in taking the role of many others, and incorporating the attitudes of those others into the self, the individual has internalized a generalized other with whom the internal conversation takes place. That is, the conversation which one carries on with oneself is carried on from the perspective of the generalized other; it is an "inner conversation going on

---

[95] *Ibid.*, p. 152.
[96] Mead, *Mind, Self and Society*, p. 154.

between this generalized other and the individual." [97]   To think is to interact with oneself from the standpoint of all possible observers.

Thus, the generalized other is involved in all human behavior, including communication and thinking, for the generalized other is that to which the individual responds in all his or her behavior. This is a way of stressing the fact that humans are social creatures whose total behavior is a function of their interaction with others.

At first, this might appear to severely limit the range of responses which any individual can make. And the concept has been criticized as failing to allow for the multiplicity of perspectives in any complex social order. Thus, Mead has been said to assume "a single, universal generalized other for the members of each society—rather than a variety of generalized others (even for the same individuals), at different levels of generality." [98] This misrepresents the concept.

Mead pointed out that there are indeed diverse groups which comprise the generalized other for various kinds of behavior. In playing on a ball team, for example, the team is the generalized other for each individual player. With respect to politics, the party becomes the generalized other as the individual takes the organized attitudes of the party toward the community and the social problems of that community. Furthermore, the generalized other may be considerably removed from particular individuals or groups. In abstract thinking, for example, the individual carries on his or her internal conversation with a generalized other which is far removed from any particular individuals. The generalized other always arises out of social interaction, and because interaction is diverse, the generalized other is a complex rather than a homogeneous phenomenon. That complexity is manifest in the fact that, depending upon the situation and the kind of behavior involved, the generalized other may range from a small group like a team to an unidentifiable other which is a perspective rather than a particular group.

The generalized other, then, links the individual with the social structure. For it is through the generalized other that individual behavior is influenced by the social process and the community exerts its control over the individual. We have already referred to this idea in our discussion of the "me" which is one phase of the self. But, as may be evident, the "me" is simply the internal manifestation of the generalized other; the latter is the organized attitudes of social groups while the former is the internalization of those organized attitudes.

Consider, for example, attitudes related to sex roles. Every society distinguishes between males and females in terms of what is considered

[97] Mead, *The Philosophy of the Act,* p. 152.
[98] Bernard N. Meltzer, "Mead's Social Psychology," in *Symbolic Interaction,* ed. Jerome G. Manis and Bernard N. Meltzer, Allyn and Bacon, Boston, 1967, p. 21.

normal and appropriate behavior. In the United States, men are generally viewed as less expressive than women in their emotional behavior. This attitude about "normal" differences between male and female behavior forms a part of the generalized other; to the extent that individual males and females appropriate this attitude, it becomes a part of the "me" of each of them. Thus, it has been found that women report a greater number of psychiatric symptoms than do men, who have the same number of physical illnesses.[99] There is no biological basis for women being more expressive about their emotions, but obviously both women and men have appropriated for themselves an attitude which formed part of the structure of attitudes of a generalized other—in this case a generalized other which comprised an entire society.

MEANING OF REFERENCE GROUP

The "reference group" concept was first used by Hyman in 1942 in a study of the groups people use for purposes of comparison and evaluating themselves, but perhaps the greatest impetus to the use of the concept came from the work of Merton and Kitt in 1950.[100] Again the concept was employed to analyze behavior that involved comparison. For example, studies of the American soldier during World War Two uncovered, among other things, the fact that better-educated inductees were less likely to feel deprived by being drafted than were lesser-educated inductees. This can be understood in terms of the basis of comparison used for the two types of soldiers. Lesser-educated men were more likely to be working in factories at the outset of the war, and their jobs were therefore likely to be declared as essential (draft-exempt) when the factories were converted into the production of war materials. Better-educated men were more likely to have white collar jobs, which were nonessential, and therefore subject to the draft. Thus, the lesser-educated man who was drafted knew that many of his friends had not been drafted, while the better-educated man knew that he shared a similar fate with his friends.

In other words, the reference group for men of each educational level was men of their same level and not men of other educational levels. The lesser-educated man who was drafted compared himself with his friends and acquaintances, many of whom were deferred, and felt deprived; the better-educated man who was drafted compared himself with his friends and acquaintances, many of whom were drafted, and was less likely to feel deprived.

[99] D. L. Phillips and B. F. Segal, "Sexual Status and Psychiatric Symptoms," *American Sociological Review,* 34 (February 1969), 58–72.

[100] H. H. Hyman, "The Psychology of Status," *Archives of Psychology,* No. 269 (1942); Robert K. Merton, *Social Theory and Social Structure,* rev. ed., Free Press, New York, 1965, pp. 225–280.

When used in this way, "reference group" is a comparative concept; it refers to a group which is used as a basis for comparison of some sort. A second common definition of reference group has been the normative one. Kelley first distinguished between the two types, defining a "comparative reference group" as one used by the individual in making evaluations of her- or himself or others and the "normative reference group" as one that establishes and enforces standards for the individual.[101] The normative sense has been used more commonly than the comparative, although some social psychologists argue for both meanings.

The concept of normative reference groups has been used to account for a variety of phenomena. A number of studies have focused on changed attitudes among students, including political attitudes and racial prejudice. One of the latter, conducted by Pearlin in a southern women's college, showed that the least prejudiced students were those whose normative reference group had shifted from their more prejudiced precollege relationships to their less prejudiced college groups. With respect to political attitudes, Newcomb's study of Bennington College students showed that most came from very conservative political backgrounds but were often liberalized by their experience at the college. The liberalized students adopted the college as a reference group, while those who remained conservative retained their precollege relationships as a reference group.[102]

In addition to the normative and comparison distinction, a more recent refinement of the concept has been worked out by Schmitt.[103] He argues that we should use the term "reference other" rather than "reference group" because the phenomenon is more complex than the latter term suggests. Schmitt proposes that we need to consider three components of the individual-other relationship: the reference other, the reference relationship, and the individual. The "reference other" is the "other" that is influencing the individual; that "other" may be real (another individual), quasi-real (a group, a norm, an object), or even something imaginary (imaginary playmates or supernatural beings). The reference relationship may be normative, comparative, or "identification-object" (the latter occurs when the sentiments of the individual towards the other are suffi-

[101] Harold H. Kelley, "Two Functions of Reference Groups," in *Readings in Social Psychology,* ed. Guy E. Swanson, Theodore M. Newcomb, and Eugene L. Hartley, Henry Holt, New York, 1952, pp. 410–414.

[102] L. I. Pearlin, "Shifting Group Attachments and Attitudes toward Negroes," *Social Forces,* 33 (October 1954), 47–50; T. M. Newcomb, "Attitude Development as a Function of Reference Groups," in *Readings in Social Psychology,* ed. Eleanor E. Maccoby, Theodore M. Newcomb, and Eugene L. Hartley, 3d ed., Holt, New York, 1958, pp. 265–275.

[103] Raymond L. Schmitt, *The Reference Other Orientation,* Southern Illinois University Press, Carbondale, Ill., 1972. Schmitt has made an exhaustive study of the history, use, and problems of the concept; his work should be consulted by anyone interested in a more detailed analysis.

ciently strong to elicit behavior towards the other—Schmitt gives the example of a young man who desires to marry his girl friend). This approach stresses the complexity of the concept in terms of both the diverse nature of "others" and the differing kinds of relationships that may exist between an individual and his or her reference others.

How, then, does this differ from Mead's concept of the generalized other? Contrary to some criticisms, the generalized other allows as much diversity, as many differing perspectives, to influence individual behavior as does the reference group concept. Both concepts indicate that the individual acts within the context of a multiplicity of perspectives, that the individual has the capacity to take the role of the groups represented by these perspectives, and that the consequence of role-taking will be the appropriation of elements of those perspectives into the individual's own frame of reference. The major difference is that the generalized other always implies the process of role-taking, whereas the reference group or reference other concept does not (one need not take the role of a group, for example, in order to use the group as a basis for comparison).

THE REFERENCE OTHER, SOCIALIZATION, AND SELF-CONCEPTS

The reference other is intimately linked up with the other concepts we are discussing. We will show this by relating it to socialization and the self-concept. First, to adopt the standpoint of an other as one's own frame of reference is to be socialized by that other. In the infant this occurs with a limited number of others. Initially parents and siblings are the reference other who socialize the infant. As the child grows, other primary relationships—friends and kin—add a dimension; the child is beginning to confront a multiplicity of perspectives which offer her or him some degree of diversity.

Among adults there are a great diversity of potential reference others. These are not necessarily membership groups. In some cases, they may be anticipated membership groups and anticipatory socialization occurs. An individual may, for example, anticipate membership in the legal profession. In this case he or she takes the role of lawyers and adopts the perspective of lawyers (appropriative role-taking) before he or she has actually entered the profession. In a study pursuing this line of reasoning, it was found that students in a school of law who planned to practice law had the legal profession as a reference other, while those who were in the school but planning on entering another area such as politics or business had different reference others. Those with the legal profession as a reference other differed along a number of lines: they were more likely to interact with others primarily within the law school, evaluate the profession and the school more highly, and to associate more closely with faculty members.[104] In other words, those who had the profession as a reference other had already been socialized into it, and were a more integral part of it than their fellow law students who had other careers in mind.

In other cases of nonmembership reference others, there may be no anticipation of future membership. For example, an individual might accurately apprehend the prevailing attitudes of a political party, appropriate them as his or her own, but have no intention of becoming a member of the party. There are also nonmembership groups which are closed to the individual, yet serve effectively as a reference other. This can be seen wherever an individual or group accepts the perspective of another group regarding her- or himself or itself. An individual or a minority group may accurately apprehend attitudes of negative evaluation by the other, adopt those attitudes, and develop a destructive self-hatred. For instance, the Burakumin of Japan are physically and ethnohistorically indistinguishable from most other Japanese. But they have suffered segregation and discrimination for centuries, a consequence of having engaged in ritually unclean occupations earlier in Japanese history. The majority holds them to be inferior and many of the Burakumin, particularly those in the lower strata of the Burakumin, have accepted this perspective toward themselves and regard themselves as actually inferior. As one member of the group put it, "We are bad people, and we are dirty." When asked if he thought that the judgment of some outsiders that the Burakumin are not even human was a correct one, he replied after a pause, "I don't know." [105] Like many others, this respondent had correctly taken the role of the larger society, appropriated it to himself, and developed a self-hatred that mirrored that of his reference other.

Thus, the reference other is intimately related to the individual's self-concept as well as to the process of socialization. An experiment carried out by Reeder, Donohue, and Biblarz demonstrates rather effectively the dependence of the self-concept upon the reference other.[106] The researchers administered a questionnaire to groups of military personnel, obtaining self-evaluations, perceived evaluations of other members of the group, and actual evaluations of other members of the group on leadership ability and work performance for each individual. They found a significant relationship between perceived evaluations of others and self-evaluations, supporting the thesis that self-conceptions are primarily based

[104] S. E. Wallace, "Reference Group Behavior in Occupational Role Socialization," *The Sociological Quarterly,* 7 (Summer 1966), 366–372.

[105] John Donoghue, "The Social Persistence of an Outcaste Group," in *Comparative Perspectives on Race Relations,* ed. Melvin M. Tumin, Little, Brown, Boston, 1969, p. 121.

[106] L. G. Reeder, G. A. Donohue, and A. Biblarz, "Conceptions of Self and Others," *American Journal of Sociology,* 66 (September 1960), 153–159.

upon perceptions of the evaluations of one's reference other(s). There was also a significant relationship between actual evaluations of others and self-evaluations for those who were at lower levels of evaluation, but not for those at higher levels. The researchers offer evidence that suggests that those whose self-evaluations disagreed with the actual evaluations of their work group had a greater number of reference others, and were basing their self-evaluations as well as their (mis)perceived evaluations of their work group upon one of their many other reference others. In any case, the reference other is clearly an integral part of the development and maintenance of self-conceptions.

In sum, the reference other is an integral part of the individual's life process. Through apprehending and appropriating the organized attitudes of those others, the individual is socialized into various groups throughout his or her life. The process of thinking, and the development of the self and of self-conceptions occurs by interaction between the individual and the reference others. Human beings are social creatures; the nature of their existence and the directions of their development are a direct consequence of their interaction with reference others.

Role

THE MEANING OF ROLE

Like attitude, "role" is a concept that is widely shared among social psychologists. But, as with other concepts, a somewhat different emphasis is given to it by symbolic interactionists.

The role concept was initially formulated in two different disciplines—anthropology and social psychology. One of the earliest formulations, which became a classic definition, was that of the anthropologist Ralph Linton, who distinguished role from status. "Status," said Linton, "is simply a collection of rights and duties," while "role" "represents the dynamic aspect of status." [107] In other words, when the individual effects the rights and duties attached to a particular status, he or she is performing the role. The two concepts therefore are really inseparable. Thus "student" is a status, while "attending class," "studying," "taking tests," and so forth are all part of the role. "Physician" is a status, while "the diagnosis and treatment of patients" is part of the role. The various statuses in any society come from the division of labor; workers and managers, parents and children, husbands and wives, physicians and patients—all have differing tasks which are defined as appropriate for those statuses and as necessary for the functioning of the society. Further-

[107] Ralph Linton, *The Study of Man*, Appleton-Century, New York, 1964, pp. 113–114.

more, these statuses and roles are part of the social system itself. They exist independently of the particular people who occupy them, so that the status and role of physician, for instance, will continue when all present physicians are dead.

A somewhat different approach to the concept emerged from the social psychological perspective represented by Mead. For while the anthopological approach stressed the functioning of the social structure, Mead was interested in describing "the processes of cooperative behavior and of communication." [108] The difference is quite significant. The structural approach emphasizes the performance of a set of behaviors which are prescribed for any individual who might assume a particular status, while the Meadian approach emphasizes the interaction among roles and consequent modifications of behavior. We shall discuss these two approaches further.

All perspectives agree that role refers to behavior. They agree also that behavior is interrelated with other behaviors; that is, roles can only be understood vis-à-vis other roles. The concept of "role-set" has been created to describe this phenomenon. For example, the role-set of "teacher" would include students, other teachers, school administrators, and perhaps parents. The behavior of the teacher only makes sense in terms of the behavior of the other roles with which that of teacher is integrally linked.

ROLES AS PRIOR TO INDIVIDUALS

The definition of role-set leads to another aspect of the concept of role that all social psychologists would accept: roles exist prior to individuals. This means that individuals, as role performers, may be replaced without necessarily changing the social expectations regarding a role. In the extreme case this would mean, for instance, that it makes no difference who is President of the United States, that the role itself demands and elicits behavior regardless of the particular person involved. Obviously this overstates the case. For the total behavior of a particular status is never prescribed for the individual. There is always an ongoing process of interaction and modification. Nevertheless, the role is not a tabula rasa whose content must be supplied by the individual. There are social expectations relating to all roles which exist prior to any individual who assumes the role. (The only exception to this is the interpersonal roles discussed below.)

The extent to which these prior expectations affect individuals is well illustrated by sex roles. Although anthropologists have demonstrated

---

[108] Lindesmith and Strauss, p. 277.

that the meaning of masculinity and femininity varies widely throughout the world, there is likely to be considerable conformity in any particular society, and that conformity is rooted in social expectations rather than in human biology. At least as early as five years of age, American children have decided notions about the meaning of sex roles, a meaning which has nothing to do with biological differences. In a study of children in kindergarten and the sixth grade, two researchers found decided notions of appropriate and inappropriate careers for the two sexes.[109] The children were shown pictures of various work settings and asked whether a man could do the job or a woman could do the job. They were also asked about their own aspirations. Some of the work settings were traditionally female (schoolrooms), while others were traditionally male (doctors' offices). The children not only assigned the traditionally proper sex to the traditionally proper job, but were likely to see men as able to perform most of the traditionally female jobs and women as unable to perform most of the traditionally male jobs. Furthermore, 97 percent of the boys and 83 percent of the girls had aspirations congruent with traditional expectations.

ROLES AND THE VARIABILITY OF BEHAVIOR

Thus whatever the role involved—sex, occupational, political, and so forth—there are social expectations about appropriate behavior, and these expectations exist prior to any individual who assumes a particular role. Nevertheless, as illustrated by the point made above about the role of President of the United States, roles do not result in rigidly standardized behavior. Rather, there is both standardized and variable behavior. The variability is rooted in a number of factors. First, the behavioral expectations virtually always involve some flexibility. Second, roles may be conventional or interpersonal. Third, roles involve interaction, processes of cooperative behavior, and ongoing modifications. Fourth, the relationship between the role and the individual who assumes the role varies. Finally, there is the problem of role conflict. We shall examine each of these points briefly.

With respect to the flexibility of the behavioral expectations, we may note that while there are appropriate and inappropriate kinds of behavior for any role, expectations also include certain alternatives. For example, it is expected that a teacher behave in a manner congruent with student learning. At the same time, there are alternatives such as lecturing, discussion, and learning by doing. In a study of judges, Smith and Blumberg concluded that any particular judge may perform his role in a variety of

---

[109] N. K. Schlossberg and J. Goodman, "A Woman's Place: Children's Sex Stereotyping of Occupations," *Vocational Guidance Quarterly,* 20 (June 1972), 266–270.

acceptable ways.[110]   They examined the behavior of nine judges of a criminal court and found that all had similar backgrounds in terms of education and political experience.   Yet at least six variants of the role of judge could be observed in the men, which the authors termed the "intellectual-scholar," the "routineer-hack," the "political adventurer-careerist," the "judicial pensioner," "hatchet-man," and the "tyrant-showboat-benevolent despot."   These represent, respectively, men who: have a scholarly bent but also a need to be in the limelight and who therefore work passionately hard; work exceptionally hard but in a routine, conventional manner; have a basic concern with their own aspirations, which do not focus on a judicial career; do minimal work while waiting for retirement; handle special cases that, for purposes of public relations, should give the impression of swift, sure justice being meted out; and terrorize the courtroom because of frustrated career aspirations.

While some of these variants of the role of judge may be defined as outrageous by a legal purist or a defendant or complainant, all are acceptable or at least tolerable in terms of the legal profession's expectations. Indeed any role could be analyzed in similar terms, and we would find flexibility in the expectations.   Thus one reason that behavior is variable is that a certain variability is built into social expectations regarding the roles.

The second basis for variability is the distinction between "conventional" and "interpersonal roles" which Shibutani has made.   The former are "standardized and impersonal; the rights and duties remain the same regardless of who plays the part." [111]   The latter, however, depend upon personal characteristics and refer to interpersonal relationships involving love, friendship, hatred, and so forth.   Obviously, the behavior which is demanded by a conventional role can be modified by interpersonal roles. For example, the expectation that a teacher can be impartial in grading students can be modified by interpersonal relationships which have developed, resulting in a higher grade for a liked student and a lower one for a disliked student.   In fact, impartiality, which is a central characteristic of bureaucratic organization, is violated in any number of contexts because of the intervening variable of interpersonal roles.   An individual does not often relate to a close friend in a "standardized and impersonal" manner, even if the relationship involves the roles of, say, sales clerk and customer or teacher and student.

The third basis for variability is the fact that roles involve interaction, an ongoing process of reciprocal modification between individuals engaged in various roles.   This has been stressed by Ralph Turner in his notion of

---

[110] A. B. Smith and A. S. Blumberg, "The Problem of Objectivity in Judicial Decision-Making," *Social Forces,* 46 (September 1967), 96–105.

[111] Shibutani, p. 326.

"role-making." [112] Turner argues that roles vary in the extent to which they are concrete and consistent, even though individuals commonly behave as though role expectations are quite explicit. In the course of acting, therefore, and of striving to make the role explicit, the actor creates and modifies the role. We do not merely assume roles, but make them. It is for this reason, in part, that we may trace out the change in any role over time. Individuals who engage in roles are in a continuing process of modifying those roles through interaction with others. Roles may be influenced by a long tradition, such as that of priest; or related to fundamental, continuing biological differences, such as that of male and female; or appear to be quite explicit and narrow because of stereotypes, such as that of college professor; but all will be found to differ from the same role at a previous point in time. The priest of 1970 could conduct a marriage service jointly with a Protestant minister, while the priest of 1950 would have viewed such behavior as intolerable. A female in the 1970s could decide to be a jockey, while females in the 1950s would have viewed such a decision as bizarre. A college professor in the 1970s might appear in class in anything from shorts to jeans, while the professor of 1950 would consider the removal of his suit coat in class as highly inappropriate. Numberless priests, women, and college professors interacting with numberless others modified their roles over time, and, as the examples are designed to show, over a short period of time.

The fourth factor we noted for variability is the relationship between the individual and the roles he or she assumes. Newcomb was one of the first social psychologists to point out that individual role behavior and social expectations regarding that role behavior are not necessarily congruent.[113] Newcomb distinguished between prescribed role and role behavior, the former referring to social expectations and the latter to the actual behavior of an individual assuming the role.

An important reason for a discrepancy between role prescriptions and role behavior is the extent to which various individuals are committed to the role. That is, the relationship between the individual and the role is one of greater or lesser "distance," as Goffman put it. Goffman defined "role distance" as the gap between the obligations of the role and the individual's performance. He interpreted the gap in terms of the individual disavowing certain aspects of a situation as sources of definition of the individual's self. The individual is not denying the role "but the virtual self that is implied in the role for all accepting performers." [114] Thus, a

[112] Ralph H. Turner, "Role-Taking: Process Versus Conformity," in *Human Behavior and Social Processes,* ed. Arnold M. Rose, Houghton Mifflin, Boston, 1962, pp. 20–40.

[113] See Brian Morris, "Reflections on Role Analysis," *British Journal of Sociology,* 22 (December 1971), 397.

[114] Erving Goffman, *Encounters,* Bobbs-Merrill, Indianapolis, 1961, p. 108.

surgical junior may not be willing to accept fully his or her subordinate position and may behave in various ways which are incongruous with the role of surgeon—such as leaning on the patient—in order to deny that his or her selfhood is wholly defined by the subordinate position. The surgical junior maintains a certain role distance, a less-than-wholehearted commitment to the role of surgical junior.

An earlier formulation of this idea was offered by Theodore Sarbin, who spoke of various degrees of "organismic involvement" with roles.[115] At one extreme is the level of casual roles, where the individual strongly differentiates between himself and the role, has minimal involvement with the role, and exerts little effort in assuming the role. An example is the role of customer in a supermarket. At the other extreme is the level of the role of the dying person; the individual makes no distinction between the role and himself, has maximal involvement, and expends considerable effort in behaving in accord with role expectations. An example of this is voodoo death, or similar cases where an individual dies in accord with social expectations without exhibiting any organic pathology. Between these extremes, Sarbin identifies five additional levels, covering every imaginable role. The point is, again, that there are variations in the extent to which individuals are committed to roles (and in the extent to which they are expected to be committed), and this is one reason for variations in role performance.

The final reason for the variability of behavior is the problem of role conflict, in which the various roles of an individual are in some way incompatible with each other. An individual may occupy two statuses which are both relevant to a particular situation but whose roles are incompatible. The policeman or woman who must arrest his or her brother, the woman who struggles with the conflicting demands of being a wife, mother, and having a career, and the physician who is harried by the contradictory expectations of his or her patients and his or her family are all examples of role conflict. In a particular situation, then, the individual may act somewhat differently from what was expected because he or she is struggling with role conflict. The physician may express feelings that differ from those of the normal father or mother, and admit that he or she is eager for the children to grow up and leave home so that he or she will no longer feel guilty about not spending time with them. Behavior will vary among people as they are working out differing kinds of role conflicts.

THE FUNCTIONS OF ROLES

There are a number of important functions of roles for social life. In the first place, roles provide an initial framework for interaction. To insist on

[115] Theodore R. Sarbin, "Role Enactment," in *Role Theory: Concepts and Research,* ed. Bruce J. Biddle and Edwin J. Thomas, Wiley, New York, 1966, pp. 195–200.

the variability of role behavior should not obscure the fact that certain relatively stable expectations are associated with all roles. These expectations provide the basis for interaction; they form an initial framework within which interaction occurs. Once begun, however, the interaction becomes a modifying factor. For example, a sick woman who goes to a male physician can properly expect that the physician will not make sexual advances toward her, or mock her illness, or send her to a faith healer. But as the two interact over a period of time, any of the three forms of behavior might occur as the conventional roles intersect with interpersonal roles modifying the former. And as the behavior of a particular physician and patient alters and becomes known to others, that behavior might diffuse and ultimately cause changes in the social expectations regarding the roles.

Thus there are expectations which are relatively stable (in the sense that they do not change from moment to moment nor day to day) and which form the basis for interaction. A sick woman knows what to expect from a male physician and how to relate to him initially even though she has never seen the man before. There is a set of shared meanings attached to the roles of physician and patient that facilitates the initial interaction. Indeed without such shared meanings social life would be chaotic and precarious. If a patient had no prior notion of whether a physician would assault him, scorn him, or try to heal him, he might prefer sickness to the uncertainties of visiting the physician.

Roles are important, then, in providing this initial framework for interaction between people who have no knowledge of each other except the roles each has assumed. Roles are also important in assessing behavior. Although modifications occur through interaction, some kinds of behavior are unacceptable for any role. Even though many people expect politicians to be somewhat less than honest, no one will accept the politician who is caught redhanded in corruption. The physician who deliberately kills suffering patients rather than prolonging their lives is likely to be condemned and perhaps to lose his license to practice. Behavior which is acceptable for some roles is unacceptable for others: the executioner may kill, the physician may not; the parent may strike the child, but the child should not strike the parent; the male is applauded for aggressiveness, but the female may be derided. Roles provide the basis for assessing behavior, and the same behavior may be defined as proper for one person and improper for another, depending upon their roles.

A third way in which roles are significant is in their effects upon the individual's selfhood. We noted above that when an individual plays at a role he or she may appropriate aspects of that role (certain attitudes), with the result that his or her opinion about something changes. Playing at a role, and appropriating that role or aspects of it, has more profound effects than mere opinion change however. For whenever one appropriates attitudes of the other for oneself, one is modifying one's "self" (which is, it will be recalled, a structure of attitudes).

Thus, depending upon the extent of role involvement (or conversely of role distance), the individual who assumes a particular role is at the same time opting for alterations in his or her selfhood. The effects of assuming new roles may be seen even when the roles are known to be temporary. Actors, for example, assume multiple but temporary roles throughout their careers. Typically, however, their involvement with a particular role is intensive. As a result, whether amateurs or professionals, there is a tendency for actors to appropriate aspects of their stage roles such that their offstage life manifests an altered self that reflects the stage role.[116]

Conversely, to disengage oneself or to be disengaged from a role also alters the self. This process occurs in the student who decides to drop out of school, the older person who is compelled to retire from his job,[117] the individual whose spouse dies, and the individual who leaves a particular occupation to pursue a new career. As the examples suggest, disengagement can be either enhancing or debilitating to the individual's self-conception. The same is true of assuming a new role. Neither the process of disengagement from nor the process of assuming roles is inherently enhancing or debilitating, but both processes inevitably involve changes in the self.

Definition of the Situation

THE MEANING OF THE CONCEPT

The classic formulation for "definition of the situation" was provided by W. I. Thomas: "Preliminary to any self-determined act of behavior there is always a stage of examination and deliberation which we may call the definition of the situation." [118] Thomas pointed out that this process was one of the "most important powers" that man gained during the course of evolution; the infrahuman world acts on the basis of external forces but humans make decisions. And behavior based on decisions involves the prior process of examination and deliberation known as "the definition of the situation."

To "define a situation" is to represent it to the self symbolically so that a response can be made. As noted earlier, the human lives in a symbolic environment; he or she responds to situations indirectly through symbolic

---

[116] Kenneth J. Gergen, *The Concept of Self,* Holt, New York, 1971, p. 55.

[117] Ruth Shonle Cavan, "Self and Role in Adjustment During Old Age," *Human Behavior and Social Processes,* ed. Arnold M. Rose, Houghton Mifflin, Boston, 1962, pp. 526–536.

[118] William I. Thomas, *The Unadjusted Girl,* Little, Brown, Boston, 1937, p. 42.

mediation. Thus, the individual's response in any particular situation is a function of how he or she defines that situation, rather than how the situation is objectively presented to him or her. This is not to say that the objective factors in the situation are unimportant, but only that they are insufficient in terms of understanding the behavior of any individual in that situation.

OBJECTIVE REALITY, DEFINED REALITY, AND BEHAVIOR

The importance of the individual's definition of the situation is demonstrated in an experiment that measured the effects of objective and perceived rates of change on anxiety level in individuals.[119] Based upon a questionnaire administered to a random sample of classes at a midwestern university, the study found that perceived rate of change was more important than objective rate as a predictor of anxiety in life circumstances for respondents over the previous year; these changes included those occurring in family relationships, occupation, financial affairs, health, education, and religion. The perceived rate was measured by the extent of agreement with three statements: "the world we live in is changing so fast it leaves me breathless at times"; "there is so much information accumulating that I can't keep up with everything I need to know"; and "generally, it seems to me that the passage of time is more like a rushing river than a slowly trickling stream." The more the individual agreed with the three statements, the higher his or her anxiety level tended to be, and the relationship was stronger than that between anxiety level and number of changes in life circumstances. Furthermore, the anxiety level was moderated when the changes were defined by the subject as generally desirable.

In other words, the way the respondents defined the situation was more crucial than the situation as objectively measured. Moreover, there was no significant relationship between objective rate of change and perceived rate; that is, the respondents did not have a generalized sense of rapid change in their world simply because of numerous changes in their personal life circumstances. Rather some individuals *defined* the world they live in as changing rapidly and, depending upon the extent to which they defined those changes as desirable or undesirable, they exhibited more or less anxiety.

To understand how people define situations, then, is to understand the meaning that the situation has for them and thereby to understand why they behave as they do in the situation. Much behavior that is otherwise perplexing can be understood when we know the definition of the situation

[119] R. H. Lauer, "Rate of Change and Stress: A Test of the 'Future Shock' Thesis," *Social Forces,* 52 (June 1974), 510–516.

which the actor holds. Furthermore, to know how people define situations is to understand why they behave differently in the same situation. For example, a part of American ideology holds that all work is honorable. Anyone who has any kind of job should therefore experience satisfaction in fulfilling the responsibilities of that job. As a professional man said to one of the authors: "When I was in college, I worked as a janitor. It wasn't too good for me, and it isn't too good for anyone else." But that, of course, ignores the fact that the meaning of being a janitor is quite different when one is upwardly mobile than it is when one can expect nothing more for the rest of his life. Doing the same job is really doing something quite different when it is defined, on the one hand, as a temporary step on the way to a highly rewarding career or, on the other hand, as the highest level one will attain in his life.

The definition of the situation, then, is a most important part of all interaction. For if people define situations as real, they are real in their consequences. To define the world in which one lives as changing very rapidly, as in the above study, means that one is likely to exhibit a rather high anxiety level, whether or not the world is really changing rapidly as measured in some objective fashion. In fact, the situation may even be wrongly defined in terms of an objective appraisal, but the consequences will be real nonetheless. For example, Pentecostals in Haiti define the world as a place inhabited by voodoo spirits who can be mobilized to bring misfortune, disease, or even death to people. This belief helps them to maintain a strong commitment to their Christian faith, since the fact that they do not die or become ill is proof of the power of Christ to overcome the voodoo spirits.[120] A skeptic might argue that the lack of illness or death is proof that the spirits are only illusions. But the Haitians define them as real, and that has consequences for their beliefs and behavior.

Similarly, a situation was apparently wrongly defined in 1962 in a small factory in the United States.[121] Forty of the two hundred employees at the factory became extremely ill as a result, supposedly, of insect bites. Public health officials investigated the case but could find no insects which would have caused the illness. The symptoms were not contrived; there was no question about the reality of the illness. Nevertheless, there was no insect that caused it. Some analysts labeled it as hysterical contagion, but the employees were no less sick because the insect did not exist. In other words, they defined the insect as real, and they became quite ill as a result. The situation was wrongly defined, but the consequences were quite real.

---

[120] Gerlach and Hine, p. 186.
[121] Alan C. Kerckhoff and Kurt W. Back, *The June Bug: A Study of Hysterical Contagion,* Appleton-Century-Crofts, New York, 1968.

The consequences of wrongly defining a situation are not always visited upon those doing the defining. In Jamaica the lower classes have been defined by those above them in the stratification system as being hostile.[122] This definition of hostility was maintained both by shared attitudes among the middle and upper classes and by the press. In a survey of 120 lower-class, urban Jamaicans, however, only 20 percent expressed hostility toward the higher strata, while 56 percent wanted to emulate the privileged. In other words, the privileged people defined the situation wrongly; the lower classes were not predominantly hostile towards them. Nevertheless, the definition had unfortunate consequences for the lower-class Jamaicans, who were on various occasions suppressed with a harshness that was disproportionate with their attitudes and with any threat offered by those attitudes.

CHANGES IN MODES OF DEFINING SITUATIONS

It is important to note that, as with other concepts, the definition of the situation is processual in the sense of being more or less fluid. That is, one does not continue to define situations in a similar fashion throughout one's life and may not do so throughout a specific situation. Modes of defining situations will change in two ways. First, one will alter the way in which one defines situations as one changes, that is, in accord with the process of one's self. And secondly, one may alter one's definition within the course of a particular interaction process.

Definitions change in the course of interaction both by design and as an unanticipated consequence of the interaction. When we say "by design" we mean that one or more of the interactants strives to change the definition maintained by one or more of the other interactants. For example, in a marital dispute the two partners may each try to get the other to redefine the situation. They may argue about the woman's flirtation with another man; the husband may define it as an attempt at seduction, while the wife may define it as nothing more than a normal friendliness, and each may try to get the other to redefine it as he or she defines it.

This process of changing a definition by design may often occur in an organizational context as illustrated in a study by Fred Davis of polio patients.[123] Davis investigated children who were stricken with paralytic poliomyelitis, and found that hospital personnel had to alter both the children's and their parents' definitions of time and of recovery progress.

---

[122] James A. Mau, *Social Change and Images of the Future*, Schenkman, Cambridge, 1968, pp. 98–102.

[123] Fred Davis, "Definitions of Time and Recovery in Paralytic Polio Convalescence," in *Readings in Social Psychology*, ed. Alfred R. Lindesmith and Anselm L. Strauss, Holt, New York, 1969, pp. 148–155.

Initially both children and parents tended to define the illness as one requiring short-term hospitalization and involving rapid recovery. Soon they changed their definition to one of long-term hospitalization and ambiguity about recovery.

This change of definition is accomplished through certain mechanisms. For one, a doctor has the status and power of an expert, and his or her judgments are not contradicted by other hospital personnel or patients or outsiders. A second mechanism is the "gradient approach" to recovery employed by the hospital. There is a decided sequence of treatment procedures. Included in this is a restriction on parental visitation to once or twice a week, which lengthens the parents' time perspective (particularly as they note only slight change from one visit to another). This mode of treatment also serves to lengthen the child's time perspective by loosening his or her ties with the home and making the hospital a surrogate home.

By such means both children and parents alter their definition of the nature of recovery and the time required for recovery. They redefine the illness in a way that facilitates the work of the hospital. The mechanisms employed by personnel to effect this redefinition normally work quickly and effectively. It is an excellent example of an organization efficiently leading individuals to redefine a situation.

Not all redefinitions of situations are by design, however. Some are emergent phenomena in particular interaction processes. For example, Deutsch and Krauss set up an experiment in which two people had to each guide a truck to a particular destination.[124] Each was given a reward for completing the trip, but a deduction was taken from the reward according to the amount of time taken for the trip. That is, players were given maximum rewards for completing the trip in minimum time. Each player could choose one of two routes to the destination, but one of the routes was 56 percent longer than the other so that the player would actually lose money by taking it. If the player took the shorter route, he or she could encounter the truck of the other player on a one-lane road.. In fact, the only time one player would know the position of the other was if they met on the road. There were two gates at either entrance to the one-lane road, each controlled by one of the two players. The object was to try to earn as much money as possible.

Obviously, the players would normally choose the route that led along the one-lane road, and when they confronted each other they would have to bargain in order to continue their journeys. The longer it took them to come to an agreement, the costlier it was for each of them. The experimenters found some interesting things occurring in the course of the bar-

[124] M. Deutsch and R. M. Krauss, "Studies of Interpersonal Bargaining," *Journal of Conflict Resolution,* 6 (March 1962), 52–76.

gaining. For the meaning of the amount of time consumed in the task changed when two players failed to reach agreement. When the two trucks initially met, the players were pressured to come to a quick agreement so that their costs for the trip did not eradicate their profits. But as time passed and they failed to reach an agreement, their increasing losses seemed to intensify their determination not to yield to each other. Some players got to a point of refusing to yield regardless of the losses incurred. Among other things, time was redefined. Initially, the situation was defined as one in which time was a challenge, and the time for the trip was to be minimized. But during the course of interacting with the other, the situation was redefined to be one in which time became a means of punishing the other and manifesting one's own determination not to give in.

REFERENCE GROUPS AS THE BASIS FOR DEFINING SITUATIONS

The way in which situations are defined is a crucial aspect of human behavior. Since it is so important, we need to know the basis for defining situations; that is, why do people define situations as they do? When we ask the question, we are led back to reference groups for the answer. A reference group, as noted above, is a group which provides the actor with a frame of reference. It is within the context of this frame of reference (or rather within the frame of reference constructed out of the many reference others which are salient for the individual) that the individual defines situations. The reference group, however, provides the individual with an initial basis for defining the situation. As the experiment we have just described demonstrates, the definition may be altered in the course of interaction.

The importance of the reference group in the individual's mode of defining situations is underscored in a study of varied responses to pain. Zborowski studied patients at a veterans hospital in New York to ascertain various cultural responses to pain.[125] Groups in the study included Jewish, Italian, and Old American (English, Scandinavian, and other) patients. Zborowski also interviewed a number of members of each group who were healthy.

The Jewish and Italian patients had similar overt reactions to pain. In both cases they freely expressed their feelings in verbal reports of suffering, groans, and crying. In addition, they did not hesitate to admit that they complained and that they expected sympathy from others. But in spite of these similar overt reactions, the two groups had quite different attitudes about pain. The Italians were essentially concerned with the immediate experience of pain, whereas the Jewish patients were primarily concerned

[125] M. Zborowski, "Cultural Components in Responses to Pain," *Journal of Social Issues,* 8, No. 4 (1952), 16–30.

with the long-range meaning of the pain. Thus, when the Italians were given medication that alleviated the pain, they were able to act in a normal fashion. But the Jewish patient was reluctant to receive the medication in the first place, and once having received it, continued to be worried and depressed about the meaning of pain.

Old American patients, on the other hand, were rather stoic in terms of their overt reactions. They indicated that there was little point in complaining or crying aloud; they preferred to suffer in silence or at least to reserve groaning or crying for times when they were alone. The Old Americans, like the Jewish patients, were concerned with the long-range implications of their pain. But unlike the Jewish patients, they tended to be optimistic about the future.

Thus the three groups each defined pain in quite different terms. Pain is a basic physiological phenomenon; nevertheless, the experience of pain, the meaning of pain, varies considerably depending upon how it is defined. Italian, Jewish, and Old American patients each defined it differently, because each defined it within the framework of a different reference group. The same pain in terms of physiology is not the same pain in terms of diverse modes of defining it.

The role of reference groups in the individual's mode of defining situations further clarifies a point made above, namely, that different individuals may respond quite differently in the same situation. They respond differently because they define it differently, and they define it differently because their reference groups are diverse. Consider the following report.[126] A prison inmate was walking along a corridor when he happened upon another inmate lying on the floor and bleeding from the head. His first impulse was to help the other; instead, he quickly went to his cell.

Other prisoners discussed the situation with the prison psychiatrist and agreed that the behavior was correct—they too would have said nothing and gone to their cells. For if the first inmate had called a guard, he would have opened himself to accusations or at least to intensive interrogation. Furthermore, other inmates who saw him call the guard would have considered him a stool pigeon, and the prisoner who administered the beating to the man on the floor would have likely beat the one who informed the guard. And, finally, such concern would have suggested the possibility of a homosexual relationship with the victim.

Obviously, the first inmate's reference group was the other prisoners, who defined the situation as he defined it—an invitation to trouble and various undesirable consequences for anyone trying to help. Conceivably, a different inmate might have helped anyway. For instance, an inmate who was being considered for parole, or one whose release was imminent, might

---

[126] "The Code of the Convict," *St. Louis Post-Dispatch,* August 5, 1969, p. 1B.

be in the process of disengaging himself from the inmate role and from the structure of attitudes that comprise the frame of reference of other prisoners. He would then have had other reference groups more significant to him than other prisoners. Moreover, the first inmate's own later report of the situation indicated an initial impulse to help; in a different context, he too would likely have helped a hurt individual. Thus, the same individual might respond differently to a similar problem depending upon the context and the reference groups that are operative for him or her, and different individuals might also respond differently to the same problem in the same context depending upon their reference groups. Situations must be defined for people to act in them, and definitions of situations are made on the basis of reference groups.

Suggested Readings

A brief, readable explanation of concepts and their place in theory may be found in Nicholas C. Mullins, *The Art of Theory* (Harper & Row, New York, 1971, pp. 7–11). Note, however, Blumer's critique of typical sociological uses of concepts in Chapter 9 of this book. Some of the concepts as formulated by Mead, and Mead's philosophical connections, are given in Don Martindale, *The Nature and Types of Sociological Theory* (Houghton Mifflin, Boston, 1960, pp. 353–359). The concepts and theory of interactionism in general, and symbolic interactionism in particular, are also briefly discussed in Jonathan H. Turner, *The Structure of Sociological Theory* (The Dorsey Press, Homewood, Ill., 1974, pp. 151–192). All of these are works of theorists. For excellent though short statements of the theory and some of its major concepts as understood by social psychologists, see Sheldon Stryker, "Symbolic Interaction as an Approach to Family Research" [*Marriage and Family Living,* 21 (1959), 111–119], and Arnold Rose, *Human Behavior and Social Processes* (Houghton Mifflin, Boston, 1962, pp. 3–19).

Chapter 3

The Interaction Process

Social interaction, as we are using the term, occurs whenever two people communicate. Episodes of interaction occur with great frequency and the unfolding of each episode is affected by many aspects of the social context in which it occurs. Are the people involved in a lasting or temporary relationship? Does the situation require cooperation, conflict, competition, or some combination of these? Is the interaction official activity of a larger organization, informal activity in an organizational context, or activity outside of an organizational context? How many people are involved? Is there a joint task to be accomplished and, if so, how well defined is it? These questions, and many more, reflect the conditions involved in episodes of interaction.

A thorough investigation of these many factors would require a vast improvement of our current knowledge and would fill a library of volumes, not a single essay. The contribution of the symbolic interactionist perspective to the study of social interaction involves the approach people take to the expectations that guide their participation in interaction, and the creative process through which the network of social obligations is defined and redefined in the course of interaction. While these processes do not provide a complete understanding of interaction, they are fundamental in the sense that they occur in all types of interaction (although the content and the degree to which they influence the course of particular episodes varies).

Social Interaction as a Phenomenon

Three considerations have prompted this approach to the discussion of interaction. First, regardless of the substantive content, symbolic interactionists tend to concentrate on the interaction among the people they study. For example, Shibutani presents a theory of the development of shared perspectives through the interaction of those facing the crisis.[1] Becker, in studying the development of identification with the deviant subculture of jazz musicians emphasizes the socialization of the musicians through interaction with one another to a common set of values, opinions, and so forth.[2] Second, the interaction process has been considered an important substantive topic in its own right throughout the development of symbolic interactionism. And third, social control is conceived to be exercised in interaction and the interaction serves as the arena in which important social processses occur.

Each episode of interaction has its own history. The people involved begin with a set of attitudes and goals and a general understanding of the situation. Communication begins and the interpretation of evidence that is received allows existing expectations to be reconsidered and perhaps changed. Where dissensus is discovered, cooperative efforts can be made to reach some mutually satisfactory definition of events and obligations. In a sense, the reception and interpretation of evidence and the reconsideration of expectations in light of new discoveries is continuous. We continu-

[1] Tamotsu Shibutani, *Improvised News,* Bobbs-Merrill, New York, 1966.
[2] Howard Becker, *Outsiders,* Free Press, New York, 1963.

ally receive information and act upon it. However, if we consider a particular interaction, a particular sequence of communication with particular other people, we can isolate a sequence of events that can be discussed in historical order as if they occurred in a discrete series of steps. This historical approach to particular episodes of interaction provides a relatively straightforward way to analyze the processes involved. Our discussion, therefore, deals with a person's expectations upon entering the interaction; how those expectations are modified by first impressions of the actual situation; the response to dissensus, if it is encountered; and finally some of the broader consequences and implications of this view of interaction. Before addressing the interaction process in more detail, it may be helpful to comment on the second and third points made above.

THE INDIVIDUAL SOCIAL INTERACTION AS A UNIT

From the beginning symbolic interactionists have defined their approach in critical contrast to those of others. As we have seen, Mead in his seminal writings contrasted his social behaviorism with the inadequate behaviorism of Watson.[3] Later, Blumer, who coined the term "symbolic interaction," contrasted the perspective with behaviorism and with other dominant theoretical and methodological approaches in sociology.[4] Mead placed considerable emphasis on the interaction between humans both as a topic of interest in its own right and as the setting in which human abilities were developed. Blumer, for his part, continues this interest. He argues that human group life is made possible in and indeed consists of the interpretive process occurring in interaction. He criticizes much of sociology for ignoring this process. It is in the context of this history of concern for the interaction process that we define the distinctive contribution of symbolic ineractionism.

Our approach is derived from the view that man responds creatively to the environment through an interpretative process. Humans do not respond mechanically to the intrinsic qualities of situations. Rather they assign meanings to the situations and respond in terms of those meanings.[5] This tendency to respond in terms of meanings is expressed in overt behavior. Mead makes it clear that the very perception of objects is accomplished through the assignment of meanings.[6]

---

[3] George H. Mead, *Mind, Self, and Society,* ed. with an introduction by Charles Morris, The University of Chicago Press, Chicago, 1934, pp. 1–33.

[4] Herbert Blumer, "The Methodological Position of Symbolic Interactionism," in *Symbolic Interactionism: Perspective and Method,* ed. Herbert Blumer, Prentice-Hall, Englewood Cliffs, N.J., 1969, pp. 1–60.

[5] *Ibid.*

[6] George H. Mead, "The Genesis of the Self and Social Control," in *Selected Writings: George Herbert Mead,* ed. Andrew H. Reck, Bobbs-Merrill, Indianapolis, 1964, pp. 267–293.

Interpretation is not merely an individual process, in the sense that it occurs in the minds of individuals. The individual's ability to assign meaning to events is learned in interaction with others. In some cases people may learn to assign meanings which are repugnant to outsiders. Thus most of us would find the notion of wrapping rattlesnakes around our necks to be thoroughly repulsive. But members of snake-handling cults in some parts of the South define this activity as an affirmation of their faith in God.

One's ability to correctly assign meaning to events is under constant scrutiny by others. Since each person will respond to events in terms of the meanings he or she assigns to them, each person's action is comprehensible and predictable to others only to the degree that the underlying meanings are known. To operate successfully in the social world one must take the role of others. That is, one must predict the likely behavior of others with whom one deals and upon whom one depends. Hence there is mutual scrutiny of the ongoing interpretive process. Only through achieving some consensus concerning how events are to be interpreted, and from that the correct response to them, can individuals coordinate their activities with those of others. To achieve this consensus, people correct and supplement each other's interpretation of events. Minimally, then, the interpretative process in interaction is crucial to the understanding of human social life. It is the means by which individuals coordinate their actions with those of others as they attempt to achieve their individual and collective goals. One cannot play ball if the rules of the game are unknown; and we cannot engage in social life generally unless we have shared understandings.

SOCIAL INTERACTION AND BROADER SOCIAL PROCESSES

Although we are addressing the symbolic interactionist perspective in terms of its approach to the interaction process, its implications are much broader. Blumer's consistent concern with the role of interaction in the "fitting together of lines of action," [7] the coordination of the activities of individuals with different goals and abilities, links the study of the interaction process to the broader concerns of sociology. With the possible exception of an occasional hermit, human beings are not self-sufficient. We are virtually helpless at birth, our very survival depending on others for several years. As adults we become specialized, and hence limited, in our abilities. We remain dependent on others in the social group who have different specialized skills to fill many of our needs. Thus the coordination of activities does not relate only to cooperation in face-to-face groups during interaction. It refers as well to the coordination of activities of people who may never meet, who need not even know of each other's existence, but who are involved in specialized aspects of the overall social

[7] Blumer, "Methodological Position."

system. For example, the availability of packaged food in stores, a taken-for-granted feature of our society, is achieved through the coordinated activities of farmers, fertilizer manufacturers, teamsters, salespeople of various kinds, advertising executives, corporation lawyers, crop dusters, tractor repairers and many others. Somehow these activities must be coordinated, even though the various specialists need not deal directly with one another, know much about one another's part in the overall system, nor even know with any accuracy what sorts of specialized activities are involved.

Mead used the term "social acts" to refer to the acts of individuals that contribute to such cooperative systems. Social acts are defined by two characteristics. First, social acts are initiated by one person in response to the conduct of another. Second, the products of the social act are generated by the cooperative efforts of many people, not the specialized efforts of one.[8] This second characteristic of social acts imparts a peculiar character to individual efforts: taken by themselves they are often incomplete and ineffective. They have meaning only in terms of the entire cooperative system. Unless others are performing their specialized parts of the overall process, and unless those specialized parts are well integrated, the actions of each individual would be futile. An appropriate image, perhaps, is that a social system resembles a complex assembly line to which we all contribute. Its products are diverse, ranging from physical objects to a characteristic value system to social relationships. As on an assembly line, the contribution of one individual is ineffective without the contributions of others.

Under certain circumstances the coordination of activities—even in such a complex system as a society—could pose no problems. If the role of each participant were explicitly defined in great detail, and if the roles were perfectly integrated so that no conflict occurred, and if no unforseen problems arose, coordination could be maintained mechanically and without effort. Each participant could be taught his or her role once and continue to perform it repeatedly without creative thought. Coordination would then be an automatic consequence of individual action.

Eugene Weinstein has argued that sociologists often assume conditions similar to these—that people learn a set of purposes that correspond to the needs of maintaining an integrated social system and a set of rules for pursuing those purposes legitimately. But real life situations, he notes, often contrast with these assumptions. Roles may be incompletely defined and what is expected of a person may not correspond to his or her needs. Further, role reciprocity may not be automatic but may depend on negoti-

---

[8] Mead, "The Genesis of the Self," pp. 279–280.

ations among the participants.[9] In addition, conditions change, often in unexpected ways. As a consequence roles must often be altered, often on an ad hoc basis, to meet them. In short, coordination of activities in social systems is a constant problem that is not solved by the repetition of cut-and-dried routines of behavior.

The coordination of activities throughout a social system, as well as co-ordinaton in face-to-face groups, is achieved through the interaction process. As we will show, social interaction occurs in such a way that the needs of others who are in the social system, but not present, are among the factors that guide and constrain ongoing behavior. In addition, the interaction includes mechanisms that can provide controlled social change, either in response to new conditions in the environment or simply because some segment of the society wants to initiate change. Controlled social change means that the interaction allows for both the innovation necessary for change and for limits to acceptable change.

Entering the Interaction

THE PRELIMINARY DEFINITION OF THE SITUATION

In a concrete sense an interaction has a clearly marked beginning and end for its participants: it begins when they come into one another's physical presence or perceptual range and ends when they leave it. As Goffman points out, the mere copresence of individuals, allowing each to perceive and be perceived by the other, constitutes social interaction, if of a limited sort. Even before a person enters the interaction situation and is able to observe and define the actions of others, he or she has constructed a pre-liminary definition of the situation by which to guide his or her conduct. This definition, although it is not based on evidence gathered in the par-ticular interaction, is not fanciful. It is based on information that is avail-able before the interaction starts.

Interactions do not occur in a social vacuum. Their content is con-strained by a variety of factors that are more or less known to the individ-uals involved. Goffman points out that the type of social occasion or affair in which an interaction occurs may oblige the participants to accept a certain definition of the situation.[10] For example, people attending a fu-neral may be obliged to treat the occasion as a solemn one, to refrain from cheerful socializing or discussing business matters, and so forth. Where the nature of the occasion is known in advance, such constraints can be incor-

[9] Eugene Weinstein, "The Development of Interpersonal Competence," in *Hand-book of Socialization Theory and Research,* ed. David Goslin, Rand McNally, Chicago, 1969, p. 753.

[10] Erving Goffman, *Encounters,* Bobbs-Merrill, Indianapolis, 1961, pp. 7–19.

porated into the definition of the situation before the situation is entered. McCall observes that role relationships, while they do not rigidly define the content of an interaction, do constrain its form.[11] A person entering a store, doctor's office, court, classroom, or any setting in which the role relationships with others can be anticipated, will have generally accurate information about what will happen to him or her and how to conduct him- or herself. In addition, one person may have had prior experience with the particular people one is about to interact with or in the particular setting one is about to enter. In such cases, one will be able to anticipate in more detail the sort of events with which one will be confronted. Knowledge of the kind of setting one is entering, of the role relationships in which one will be involved, and of the detailed characteristics of the setting and people one will deal with varies from person to person and from situation to situation. The preliminary definition of the situation will also vary, then, in terms of its completeness and accuracy.

GOALS AND THE DEFINITION OF OBJECTS

In addition to a person's expectations concerning what he or she will find in an interaction, the individual has goals that he or she intends to accomplish during the interaction. In fact, from the individual's perspective, interaction is the procedure for pursuing his or her personal goals in the social context.[12] By referring to goals as personal, we highlight the fact that they are not necessarily congruent with the institutionally approved goals for one's role, nor are they necessarily well integrated with the goals of one's fellow interactants. As does the preliminary definition of the situation, one's goals vary in terms of their explicitness and completeness.

Much of what occurs in interaction is mysterious until we recognize the intimate connection between goals and the definition of the situation. According to Mead, the environment of the living organism is defined in large part by its goals. Objects are defined by the organism orienting itself to their use in some project. He states explicitly, in fact, that "objects are plans of action." [13] He does not question the physical existence of things. But he insists that they become objects in our environment only through our perception of them. We perceive them in terms of their relevance to our plans. Mead illustrates this process of creating objects by pointing out that food exists as such only as a result of the selection by an organism of things to eat. The same physical matter appears as different objects on different occasions, each object corresponding to a plan of action that includes its use. For example, the same pie may be food or

[11] George McCall, "The Social Organization of Relationships," in *Social Relationships,* George McCall et al., Aldine, Chicago, 1970, p. 5.
[12] *Ibid.,* p. 24.
[13] Mead, "The Genesis of the Self," p. 276.

a plaything, depending on whether one plans to eat it or to throw it in someone's face. At the same time, the continuity of the thing—in this example the pie— is recognized. By a process of association the various plans of action associated with it are recognized as implicit possibilities even though only one plan is relevant at a given time.

At least with respect to physical objects, the preliminary definition of the situation is dependent upon the goal or plan of action of the actor. The things he or she encounters will be defined in terms of their relevance to his or her plans, while at the same time other possible definitions of these things will be recognized to exist. It is not merely that one's view of the situation is altered or distorted by the plan or goal one is trying to achieve. Rather, in a fundamental sense, the situation cannot be defined without reference to those plans.

DEFINING PEOPLE AS OBJECTS

Perhaps the most important aspect of our preliminary definition of the situation is our definition of the others with whom we are to interact. This is achieved through role-taking. This process is very similar to the process of defining nonhuman objects. Mead, in fact, states explicitly that we define the object's characteristics by "taking the attitude of the object." [14] That is, we anticipate the response of the object which our projected action will call out from it. For example, we take the attitude of a heavy object and anticipate that it will respond to us by resisting our efforts to move it. The similarity between the processes of defining people and objects suggests that there will be significant parallels between the ways in which we define people and objects. Exploring such parallels should provide insight into how we relate to the other people with whom we interact. We will discuss three such parallels: the definition of people as undimensional objects relevant in a specific way to our plans; the recognition of other possible definitions of people and their continuity across definitions; and the definition of people in terms of our plans, that is, as manipulable.

Defining others as unidimensional objects: the role. First, there is a clear parallel between our perception of other people and the physical object when each is narrowly defined by a single plan of action. With respect to people, this means defining the other person in terms of a single role he or she assumes in the interaction. A role constitutes one unified, predictable way in which a person's actions can be defined in a situation. Just as a pie can sometimes be defined as food, a person can sometimes be defined solely in terms of a single role—store clerk, doctor, gas station attendant,

[14] George H. Mead, *The Philosophy of the Act,* The University of Chicago Press, Chicago, 1938, pp. 151–152.

traveling companion, hitchhiker—and nothing else. As such, the person relates to our plans in a particular way, and his or her other possibilities may not necessarily be interesting. Moreover, this person can be replaced in our planning by any other person who could be defined as performing the same role. We can fill our cars with gasoline without learning anything about the attendant if we wish, and we can patronize a different station and deal with other attendants.

Defining others as multidimensional objects: situated identity. A second parallel in our definitions involves continuity; we recognize in both physical objects and people other potential definitions which are beyond our immediate plans for their use. The term "situated identity" refers to the stereotyped self imputed to others on the basis of the role they are currently performing.[15] One fundamental observation that recurs throughout Erving Goffman's work is that people tend to impute entire selves to others on the basis of their role performance and appearance in interaction. He observes that we have stereotyped conceptions about the kind of person who will be an incumbent of a particular role, a person with a certain kind of personal history, attitudes, personal characteristics, and other role obligations. The stereotypical character of situated identities allows one to define them, as one defines other aspects of a situation, before direct evidence is available. In a sense, the participants find that identities are tailor-made and waiting for them when they first enter an interaction, at least in the expectations of the others involved. Goffman points out that formal organizations do not merely expect job-performing activities of their members but also expect them to be certain kinds of people. The organization defines for its members appropriate values, applicable rewards and penalties, and so on. In this way the organization provides an overall identity for each member as a person who accepts these values, responds to the rewards and punishments, and so forth. By cooperating in the organization, the member accepts this definition of her- or himself and his or her membership becomes an obligation not only to contribute work, but also to be a certain kind of person.[16]

Although Goffman is most emphatic about this process occuring in formal organizations, it occurs in interactions in other settings as well; of course, the identities associated with less-structured role relationships are anticipated in less detail. But the phenomenon does appear in more loosely structured situations, for all social relationships are forms of social organization and share many characteristics in common.[17]

---

[15] Weinstein, p. 756.
[16] Erving Goffman, *Asylums,* Doubleday, Garden City, N.Y., 1961, pp. 179–188.
[17] McCall, p. 5.

The situated identity has an interesting characteristic that differentiates it from the self: whereas the self is a relatively stable organization, built up in a variety of situations, the situated identity changes along with the role the individual is performing. Situated identity is a stereotyped version of other people's selves, associated more with the role than the particular person performing it. In the absence of information to the contrary, any person occupying a role would be considered to have a situated identity that is similar to those of other persons performing that role. Further, when one changes the role one is performing or when others redefine that role, other people's conception of one's identity will also change. Paradoxically, the situated identity is an attempt to define a whole person, but the definition is by its very nature transitory. It changes as the role relationship between people changes and is, therefore, appropriate only in the situation in which it is framed.

Despite their transitory nature, defining situated identities is important in guiding our behavior in interactions. As Weinstein points out, the situated identity we assign to others affects our expectations concerning what roles they will assume beyond the interaction context and the level of performance we can expect.[18] By inferring a situated identity from the role relationships in which a person is involved, we anticipate information about his or her performance in other situations and with other people. This may be extremely important in trying to estimate a person's commitment to his or her role relationship with us, his or her competence to perform it properly, and his or her personal priorities among the roles the person must perform.

Defining others manipulatively. The third parallel to be observed between the definition of people and physical objects is the manipulative attitude involved in the definitions. Of the roles that a person may routinely perform, our preliminary definition will be concerned with those that relate to his or her involvement in our plans. It is in relation to these plans that we are interested in predicting and understanding other people's actions. The situated identity we anticipate for a person is our attempt to estimate how the part of his or her actions that are involved with us and our plans fit into the overall structure of this person's life.

Roles and situated identities are well suited to the goal of manipulating others or, in less strategic terms, involving them to our advantage in our plans. Two characteristics of these ways of defining people are involved. First, both allow prediction of others' activities. This is an essential condition for successfully including others in our plans. Second, roles and situated identities have a normative character. By accepting a certain

18 Weinstein, p. 756.

role or identity, a person obligates himself to perform in the expected way. This provides a guarantee, although an imperfect one, that the expected actions will be performed and performed at least as well as is normatively enforced. The sanctions associated with proper and improper role performance make the assignment of roles manipulative in a literal sense. In applying a role to a person, assuming this role is socially ratified, one is assigning obligations to that person and makinig him liable to sanctions based on his performance.

It is essential to remember that simply defining a person as having a certain role or identity does not have this characteristic. The definition of another person must be accepted by people involved in the interaction, and, often, by the person himself. In the preliminary definition of the situation, we try to anticipate roles that will both be convenient in terms of our plans and acceptable to the other people involved. We are interested in predicting what will occur and what will be normatively guaranteed. Our anticipations of a person's role and character may be simply inappropriate—we may define a person in terms of roles that are not part of his or her repertoire. For example, we may enter a store and, mistaking a customer for a salesperson, attempt to deal with her or him on that basis. At other times we may attempt to deal with a person in terms of a role which he or she accepts occasionally but will not accept at the particular time that we want him or her to. For example, a friend who is usually willing to act as a counselor may have problems of her own or may be too busy to accept that role on some occasions. Success in implementing our original plans, then, depends on defining the situation in a way that is appropriate and acceptable to the others involved. Thus, even though we attempt to define people in terms of categories that relate them favorably to our plans, we must also be realistic and define tasks for them that they are willing and able to perform.

Elements of self-control also influence the ways in which we will define other people, even in our imagination. In many situations, certain identities could be assigned to people and ratified socially, but are not used. For in addition to anticipating the responses of those involved in an interaction, each person is able to take the role of the generalized other and to be constrained by the perspective it represents. Other reference groups may also provide perspectives which preclude certain definitions of others. For example, the perspectives of the generalized other or reference group may lead a married person to never define members of the opposite sex as sexual objects even though they would accept that definition and others immediately involved would also accept it.

We can, then, summarize the attitude and knowledge of a person entering an interaction. The interaction is entered with a more or less well-defined goal and plan of action for accomplishing it. The actor constructs a definition of the situation which anticipates what he or she will encounter in the interaction in terms of that goal. The social context of the interaction, the role relationships that are expected to prevail, and experience with the setting and people involved all contribute to the person's ability to accurately anticipate the situation. The people with whom one expects to interact will typically be defined in terms of the roles they are expected to perform and in terms of stereotyped situated identities that define their more personal characteristics. The person seeks, in this preliminary definition of the situation, to anticipate roles and identities that are relevant to his or her plans and that will also be acceptable to the people involved. Through acceptance of these definitions, the others become normatively obligated to perform certain roles and with certain levels of involvement and competence.

Presenting and Evaluating First Impressions

We have suggested that each person enters the interaction setting with a preliminary definition of the situation, a crucial part of which is the normatively sanctioned obligations that he or she hopes will be accepted more or less willingly by the others present. Each person also has a plan of action that he or she hopes to initiate and which he or she hopes will be acceptable to the others involved. Of course the question of how the others' definitions of the situation, especially their plans for him or her and for themselves, compare to his or her own is a factual one. It cannot be known until the interaction is under way and other people's plans become apparent. The primary mechanism involved is, again, taking the role of the other. But once the interaction begins this can be done on the basis of people's actual behavior, not merely one's general expectations regarding the situation. This sets one task for the participants that must be accomplished regardless of the other purposes one brings to the interaction: each participant must evaluate the actions of the others and, by taking their roles, compare their intended courses of action with those he or she had hoped they would take.

At the same time, one must determine how the others will respond to one if one implements one's original plan of action. This can only be accomplished if one indicates to the others, through one's own actions, what that intended course of action is. Each individual, then, begins to act in the situation in accord with his or her preliminary definition. This indicates to the others, through their ability to take the person's role, how he or she intends to act as the interaction continues. At the same time, the individual monitors their actions with two especially important concerns in mind. First, he or she is interested in how their plans for their own action compare to his or her anticipations of what they would do. Second, he or she is concerned with their response to his or her intended action.

Taken together, these various concerns allow one to evaluate whether one's initial plans can be successfully carried out. For one's own practical interests, it is important that this judgment be accurate. Before entering the interaction, one is somewhat constrained in one's planning by the social context of the interaction, unavoidable role obligations, and so on. Still, one has discretion in the performance of one's roles, although the amount of discretion may vary. During the interaction one must pursue some course of action and the course of action one elects to follow will commit one to performances that may extend far beyond this interaction situation. Commitments can be made explicitly as promises or contracts to do things. They can also be made implicitly by accepting certain roles. Especially if one takes one's own commitments seriously, one will be interested in assurances from others that they will fulfill their obligations as well. Briefly, when the achievement of one's goals depends on the cooperation of others, one will want to be sure that their cooperation can be counted on before one commits oneself in terms of time and resources. Where this dependence is mutual, each participant will want assurances that the others will contribute to his or her own plans before committing him- or herself to contribute to theirs.

The difficulties of deciding what sort of commitment to make are compounded by the temporal sequence involved. Frequently a commitment must be made before other people's performances can be evaluated directly. For example, when contracting to have an appliance repaired we usually are committed to pay before the quality of the work can be judged. If the commitment is made unwisely, we may be forced to fulfill our part of the bargain by paying, although others have not fulfilled their part of the bargain satisfactorily. This same temporal sequence occurs when the exchanges involved are less concrete. For example, we often have to show gratitude for a favor before the favor is actually done. Not only must commitments be made before compensating obligations are fulfilled, but somebody must act first. In many situations one of the parties must make his or her contribution to a cooperative effort on the basis of the other's commitment. For example, either the employer must pay on the basis of an employee's commitment to work or the employee must work on the basis of the employer's commitment to pay. One friend or the other, before a pattern is established, must be the first to lend clothes or records or money, on the assumption that similar privileges will be allowed them.

We have already observed that it is the standardization of action, insured by the normative character of roles that allows reasonably accurate implications for future action to be drawn. Further, it is the roles in terms of which behavior is defined, not the behavior itself, that provide the sense of obligation and commitment to a course of action. Turner has suggested in fact that the defining of behavior in terms of roles is prerequisite to making sense of that behavior.[19] (As we noted before the term "role" is often used in an extremely broad sense to include any socially patterned and comprehensible course of action.)

Several bases for determining what roles are being performed are known even before interaction begins and continues to provide important input to the defining process. But in the interaction another source of information becomes available: the appearances of the situation and of the people present in it. The term "appearances" refers to an extremely varied group of factors. It refers generically to anything that is perceptible about the situation or the people in it. It includes behavior but extends beyond it to personal appearance, clothes, perceptible signs of cleanliness, sound of the voice, racial or ethnic characteristics, steadiness and direction of the gaze, and so on. It is on the basis of these appearances of the situation and the people in it that individuals decide what roles are being performed. From the categorization of appearances into roles inferences are made concerning the commitments of other people, their personal characteristics, attitudes, and a host of other matters summarily called the "situated identity."

This reliance on appearances for so many crucial judgments about other people elevates appearances to a position of importance in one's plans for dealing with others. We are all more or less aware that our appearance is being judged by others and taken seriously by them in a number of ways. We also know that everyone else is more or less aware of this. In many circumstances, as a result, appearance is not left to chance but planned and controlled carefully as part of our overall strategy. "Getting ready" for a social event, dressing up for a job interview, or dressing down for a picnic or athletic event are common situations in which we consciously plan our appearances to achieve some effect. Even at other times, when we are less aware of the planning, our appearance is hardly a matter of chance. Decisions are constantly being made that produce an appearance that is characteristic of us—we choose which clothes to buy, which to wear every day and which on special occasions we choose a hairstyle and perhaps color, we shave or don't, use perfume or don't, and so forth. Thus even when an overall plan is not involved, many decisions are.

The planning of appearance is possible because we can anticipate the kind of responses different appearances will call forth from others and we can contrive, if we desire to, an appearance that will lead us to be treated how we would like to be treated. Others are able to do this as well.

[19] Ralph Turner, "Role-Taking: Process Versus Conformity," in *Human Behavior and Social Processes,* ed. Arnold Rose, Houghton Mifflin, Boston, 1962, p. 24.

Thus, while we may be interested in contriving our own appearances to lead others to treat us in a desirable way, we will also be interested in seeing through others' contrivances so that we can know what they are "really like" before we respond to them. From the beginning of the interaction, then, and continuing throughout its duration, the participants will be trying to control their own appearances and the implications drawn from them by others and, at the same time, trying to see through the efforts of others to control their appearances. The procedures involved in this dual task are crucial to the interaction process. In a sense they are a more detailed account of role-taking.

SELF-PRESENTATION

By "self-presentation" [20] we mean the establishment of a situated identity through the appearance one presents in an interaction. The situated identity includes the roles that others will understand one to be performing in the interaction as well as personal characteristics and other role obligations. Although self-presentation can be strategically contrived, it is important to realize that people are not necessarily involved in contriving their appearances. They may simply be acting naturally, doing what they think is expected of them, and their appearance may be uncontrolled and natural. Even when contrivance is involved, deceit may neither be intended nor achieved.

Honest appearances may be contrived. Difficult planning and control of appearances may be necessary for appearance to be congruent with the individual's self-conception. This is strikingly illustrated by Goffman's study of the ways in which mental patients establish an identity for themselves that is more than the institutionally prescribed role under the difficult conditions of institutionalized life.[21] The mental hospital is characterized by a number of conditions that severely limit personal expressions: there is extensive, legitimate surveillance by authorities; there is a great deal of regimentation, including detailed rules and sanctions; physical facilities are limited; what physical facilities exist are not owned by patients and subject to personal embellishment, but used by them and subject to organizational attempts to regulate which patients will have access to them and to standardize the use to which they are put; and finally, the acquisition of personal possessions to supplement those supplied by the institution may be severely restricted both in terms of limiting the amount of money that can be spent and the kinds of items that can be bought.

[20] The discussion that follows is indebted to Goffman's discussions in a variety of sources.
[21] Erving Goffman, "The Underlife of a Public Institution," in Goffman, *Asylums.*

Under such conditions even so simple a matter as establishing one's own standard of cleanliness for clothes, if it differs from that of the institution, can be a difficult task. Goffman reports that patients laundered their own clothes by hand and dried them on radiators or bribed laundry workers with candy or cigarettes to have them laundered more often than the hospital routine called for. In a similar way, maintaining an adequate supply of cigarettes might involve such steps as performing services for which one could be bribed or rewarded with cigarettes and saving the butts and rerolling the tobacco into usable cigarettes. Most of us do not face such extreme problems in our attempts to look and act as we would like. But still the efforts involved in maintaining a supply of properly clean and pressed, or faded and patched, clothes to suit our tastes can make our appearance more contrived than accidental, even when we are expressing our real tastes.

The pressures to contrive one's appearance, whether honestly or deceitfully, are strong. By our appearance we indicate to others the line of action we intend to pursue and the kind of person we are. These factors are important in their determination of how we should be treated. To be treated in the ways we would like to be treated, both in terms of cooperation in joint action and in terms of personal deference, we must appear to be the kind of person who deserves such treatment. Being that kind of person is not enough—we must communicate to others, through our appearance, that we are that kind of person. Thus the success of our plans, the respect and deference we receive from others, and the tone of our relationships with them all depend to a considerable extent on the appearance we present to people while we interact with them. To the extent that we care about such matters, which is typically a great deal, it is important that we be sure that our appearances reflect a reality about ourselves that we would like others to use as basis for their action.

Goffman presents considerable evidence, based on observations in natural settings, of control of appearances by individuals. Simply observing one's actions, it is difficult for the observer to know whether they are controlled or whether they are spontaneous and natural. The observations of behavior as the person moves from one region to another, especially between frontstage and backstage regions suggest that control is widespread. In Goffman's terms a "region" is an area that is bounded by barriers to perceptions. A "front region," using any performance or interaction as the point of reference, is that region in which the performance is actually presented to others. In the front region each performer typically exerts efforts to maintain the appearance that his or her activities meet appropriate standards. Relative to the same performance, a "backstage region" is one in which the impression maintained in the front region is routinely and knowingly violated.[22] The barriers to perception that define the region make it difficult or impossible for the audience to observe these contradictions to the impression they receive. Concretely, one observes that in these different regions the same individual will routinely express different situated identities. A person will appear to be two different kinds of people. Moreover, when people are observed as they cross the boundary between two regions, their behavior is observed to change dramatically to anticipate the demands of the situation they are entering. For example, waiters passing from the kitchen to the customers' dining room change the terms of address by which they refer to each other and to other staff members, add and subtract aprons, display different standards for the neatness of their uniforms, change their posture, change the tones and volume of their voices, express different attitudes about the customers and help, and so forth. The abruptness of the changes involved and the fact that those changing their appearances anticipate entrance into a new situation suggest that the changes are controlled rather than spontaneous or natural expressions.

Behavior may be chosen for its identity implications. Some experimental evidence also suggests that many aspects of our behavior are affected by our attempts to establish a particular situated identity in interaction. Alexander and Weil have shown that the strategy selected in certain games and the way in which a successful outcome is defined are related to the kind of situational identity the players wish to establish for themselves. In mixed-motive games, including the so-called prisoner's dilemma, two players each make one of two choices. They each then receive a payoff that varies according to the combination of their choices. For example, if both players choose black each may receive a small payoff; if both choose red each may receive a larger payoff; but if one chooses red and the other chooses black, the player choosing black may get a very large payoff while the player choosing red gets a penalty. Thus the payoff for any choice depends upon what the other player chooses. Successful play in such a situation can only be defined if the goals of the participants are known. To achieve the maximum total payoff for both players, a cooperative goal, each player should always choose red. However, if one player wanted to maximize his or her own score, even at the other's expense, the best strategy would be to establish the pattern of choosing red and then switch occasionally to black for the larger payoff combined with a penalty to the other. This line of play would "win" in a competitive situation. The selection of a goal, and hence the success of a strategy is not dictated by the game rules, but by

[22] Erving Goffman, *Presentation of Self in Everyday Life,* Doubleday, Garden City, N.Y., 1959, pp. 106–112.

providing experimental subjects with incentives to choose a particular situated identity for themselves. Alexander and Weil were able to predict the strategy that would be adopted. If, for example, cooperation were stressed as a valuable trait, cooperative game-playing occurred.[23]

Friedman shows that experimenters, even when they have a supposedly complete script, vary in their treatment of subjects in an experiment.[24] Variations include such things as variations in the greeting, insertion of questions into the information-gathering process, frequency of smiles, amount of eye contact, displays of interest, and differences in posture. These variations in the experimenters' routines appear to be related to role relationships between the experimenter and the subject that transcend the official experimental one. For example, male experimenters treat female subjects differently than they treat male subjects. Further, these differences of treatment are correlated with the performance of the subjects in the experimental task. In Friedman's analysis we find both that situated identities are expressed in appearances and that the response of others is affected by them.

Obvious contrivance may be a virtue. Preparation for self-presentation may begin, as we noted in regard to mental patients, before the interaction begins and may be conducted in privacy from the other participants. Goffman notes that such preparation is one of the important uses of the backstage region. Appearing well dressed in an interaction, by whatever standards, may involve such preparations as washing and pressing clothes, replacing buttons, sewing on patches, polishing shoes, matching clothes into an outfit, remaining aware of changes in "fashion," and so on. The preparations are not directly observed in the interaction—only the final result is—but the fact that they have occurred is known. Many aspects of appearance then can serve as a sign that one has a commitment to the obligations of the interaction that extends beyond those times when one is under direct surveillance. This may serve as the basis for concluding that other obligations that involve activities not directly observable will also be performed satisfactorily.

Clothing and grooming may seem to be trivial dimensions to use in evaluating another person's competence. However, these aspects of appearance are often directly related to competence; for example, when one's role requires one to gain other people's confidence in one's judgment and financial abilities. Who would entrust their money to a threadbare financial adviser? Other aspects of a person's appearance are related to interper-

---

[23] C. Alexander and Harrison Weil, "Players, Persons, and Purposes: Situational Meaning and the Prisoner's Dilemma Game," *Sociometry,* 32 (June 1969), 121–144.

[24] Neil Friedman, *The Social Nature of Psychological Research,* Basic Books, New York, 1967.

sonal skills. The ability to speak smoothly and convincingly, to think quickly, to handle people and manipulate them, or to intimidate people with an imposing manner may be just the qualities one seeks when employing a lawyer to negotiate on one's behalf.

In addition, these preparations may involve the help of other people both within the interaction and in preparation for it. People who are color-blind, for example, often prevent garish combinations of colors in their clothes by having someone else, a salesperson for example, match their clothes into outfits. Often it requires the cooperative efforts of teams of people working on a regular, institutionalized basis to maintain an appearance. For example cleaning and maintenance crews, linen services, interior decorators, receptionists, telephone-answering services, and nurses may all contribute services that are essential for a doctor to present the appearance he or she desires to patients.

UNMASKING

Whether or not one makes any efforts to control or contrive it, a person must make *some* appearance in an interaction. By responding to others on the basis of the appearances they present, people exert pressure on each other to make their appearances consistent with the kind of treatment they would like to receive. As the intentional control of appearances increases, a paradoxical situation arises: as appearances become more contrived and standardized they also become less valuable to the observer as a means to evaluate other people and differentiate them from others who might perform the same role.

This difficulty is countered by observers through an attempt to distinguish between the controlled and uncontrolled aspects of the appearances with which they are confronted. Once this distinction is made, judgments can be more confidently based on the relatively uncontrolled, natural, and revealing aspects of appearance. This distinction between uncontrolled and controlled aspects of appearance corresponds to the difference between the identity the person would like to establish through his or her appearance and the identity to which he or she is rightfully entitled. The two identities, even in situations that include contrived performances, may be the same—close analysis may reveal that the person has worked hard to contrive an appearance that is in accord with his or her actual role and other characteristics. In such cases the controlled and uncontrolled aspects of the appearances should be in agreement. For example, a person may receive a telephone call during a business meeting, interact differently with the caller than with his or her clients, perhaps less formally, but still reveal the same personal characteristics. The fact that the same characteristics are revealed by actions that are not part of the regular performance increases one's confidence that these characteristics are accurate reflections of the other's real identity. Consistency in the characteristics revealed in different performances, and relative to different audiences, if such information is available, also serves to increase our confidence that we have recognized true identity. In this context minor details of behavior and appearance become extremely important because the observer feels that the planning could not be extended to them.

Appearances include unintended communications. Just as uncontrived aspects of appearance may be major sources of information about a person, so can obvious signs of contrivance. The amount of information revealed by unmasked contrivance will, of course, vary. Ekman and Friesen distinguish between deception clues and leakage in this regard.[25] "Deception clues" indicate to the observer that some deception has occurred but do not reveal the nature of the true information. A person may be evasive, indicating that some secret exists, without revealing its content. "Leakage" reveals the nature of the information the person was attempting to conceal. Goffman, in his discussion of "passing" by stigmatized individuals, illustrates ways in which the very actions that conceal a stigma from some observers reveal its presence and nature to other, more sophisticated ones.[26] People with hearing difficulties, for example, have characteristic ways of getting through conversations without revealing that they have problems with their hearing. To others with similar problems or to others who have dealt extensively with those problems, these "passing behaviors," attempts to deceive, are easily recognized for what they are. Thus the sophistication of the observer is a crucial variable in determining the extent to which contrivance can go undetected.

Ekman and Friesen suggest that different parts of the body vary in the extent to which they can be used to transmit information and also to the extent that they provide deception clues and leakage. As the length of time required for a meaningful expression by some part of the body decreases; as the number of discriminable expressions increases, and as the visibility increases, the part of the body increases its ability to express meaning. Thus the face, which is highly visible, which changes expression rapidly, and which admits of an extremely large number of discriminable expressions, is the most important transmitter of both contrived and uncontrolled information. The face is the major source of nonverbal gestures in interaction. The feet and legs, on the other hand, provide relatively little information. The face is under considerable control, and facial ex-

[25] Paul Ekman and Wallace Friesen, "Non-Verbal Leakage and Clues to Deception," in *Social Encounters,* ed. Michael Argyle, Aldine, Chicago, 1973, p. 134.

[26] Erving Goffman, *Stigma,* Prentice-Hall, Englewood Cliffs, N.J.; 1963, pp. 85–86.

pressions can be contrived to express unfelt emotions, but, at the same time, it responds rapidly and is very expressive and under great surveillance. "In a sense the face is equipped to lie the most and leak the most, and thus can be a confusing source of information during deception." Leakage occurs through the presence of easily discriminated but uncontrolled micro-displays and in "rough edges" in simulated displays. Most people will be misled by a skillful person's use of facial expression but good observers are able to notice and interpret contradictions. What is most interesting is that although the face is the most easily controlled body part by people attempting to contrive an appearance, it is also the most easily available to observers in uncovering deception. Legs, feet, and hands, although they are under less control and therefore more "truthful," are not as closely attended by observers. Still, information is derived from observing the hands—nervous gestures, handling objects, tapping, picking at things—and the legs and feet—tense leg positions, restless movement, frequent shifts of posture.[27]

Information can be drawn from many other sources. Argyle and Dean review experimental evidence that the amount of eye contact and the topics of discussion under which eye contact is maintained are signs of intimacy.[28] Further, eye contact was shown to vary to balance other signs of intimacy. Eye contact is reduced, for example, when the topic verbally discussed is an intimate one, or when the distance between the parties decreases. Thus, on balance, the different signs of intimacy work together to present a uniform impression. Mehrabian notes that closeness of the speaker to the listener indicates a positive attitude towards him or her.[29] He also shows that attention can be communicated by a forward lean of the body, withdrawal by leaning back or turning away, pride or disdain by a characteristic posture, warmth by the openness of arms, and relaxation by forward leaning and closeness. Scheflen provides clinical evidence that posture, facial expression, distance, touching, and other nonverbal actions can convey detailed and complicated information about one's self and one's opinion of others.[30]

Hall further documents the importance of the distance between people and the general use of space as means to communicate attitudes. Hall observed that different kinds of activities and different interpersonal rela-

[27] Ekman and Friesen, pp. 136–141.

[28] Michael Argyle and Janet Dean, "Eye Contact, Distance and Affiliation," in *Social Encounters,* ed. Michael Argyle, Aldine, Chicago, 1973, pp. 173–187.

[29] Albert Mehrabian, "Inference of Attitudes from the Posture, Orientation and Distance of a Communicator," in *Social Encounters,* ed. Michael Argyle, Aldine, Chicago, 1973, pp. 103–118.

[30] Albert Scheflen, *Body Language and the Social Order,* Prentice-Hall, Englewood Cliffs, N.J., 1972. This volume is especially recommended for its many photographs that illustrate the topics being discussed.

tionships are accompanied by the maintenance of different physical distances between people when they interact. The distances vary from culture to culture. In our culture four zones have been observed: intimate distance (contact to eighteen inches), personal distance (eighteen inches to four feet), social distance (four to twelve feet), and public distance (twelve feet or more). The distance chosen communicates a great deal about the nature of the content of the interaction, what the people are doing, and the degree of intimacy between them. Thus, for example, sexual advances can be initiated by moving closer and rejected by withdrawing. Personal anger can also be communicated by moving closer, indicating its intimate character.[31]

Birdwhistell, a pioneer in the study of nonverbal, or "kinesic" communication, argues that the immense detail of various studies can be organized into a nonverbal communicative system that is as orderly and regulated as the verbal one.[32] Although the processes involved are not well understood at this time, the number and variety of studies available make it clear that people have many sources of information about each other available to them and that our knowledge about them is not limited to impressionistic information. Although Mead stressed the importance of verbal gesture, recent studies such as those above underscore the importance of nonverbal gestures in establishing the meaning of interaction.

Control of appearances does not escalate. With strong pressures to contrive appearances, and with the variety of sources of information available to attempt to see through contrived performances, one might expect that people would become involved in an ever increasing attention to detail in appearance. Control would be exerted over ever more aspects of appearance and efforts to unmask this control and see through it would involve ever more minute details that seem to be natural. At least two factors prevent this from happening. First, most people are not sophisticated enough to unmask well-arranged contrivances, nor even to discover that contrivance is taking place. The regular performers of roles, such as waiters, become more sophisticated at contrivance than their customers who have relatively less experience in the role relationship. Overall the sophistication of customers should remain relatively constant, although particular customers will increase their sophistication. Thus, while some customers may be very sophisticated, the level of contrivance need not be constantly escalated. In many social relationships it is the regular performers of roles who are both more sophisticated about the role relationships involved and also under greater surveillance. This coincidence

---

[31] Edward Hall, *The Hidden Dimension,* Doubleday, New York, 1966.

[32] Ray Birdwhistell, "Kinesics," in *Social Encounters,* ed. Michael Argyle, Aldine, Chicago, 1973, pp. 93–102.

makes it unnecessary for the regular performer of a role to constantly increase his efforts to contrive a proper appearance.

The second factor is that the arts of unmasking contrivance are, when levels of sophistication are held constant, better developed than the arts of contrivance. This means that as one becomes sophisticated in performance of a role relationship, one becomes better at avoiding being deceived than at deceiving others. This view is implied by Goffman and by Ekman and Friesen in their discussion of leakage. The result is that even one is confronted by sophisticates, the need to contrive is balanced by the futility of contrivance.

ALTERCASTING

The roles and identities of people in an interaction must be integrated. They cannot be developed in disregard for the roles and identities assumed by others. In general, "a role cannot exist without one or more relevant other-roles toward which it is oriented." [33] A person cannot adopt the doctor role without someone to adopt the patient role; cannot adopt the role of leader without someone to adopt the role of follower; cannot adopt the husband role without someone to adopt the wife role, and so forth. Thus, as Turner points out, defining one's role by setting the boundaries of its obligations limits the choices open to others in defining their own roles. In expressing one's own role, one is expressing at the same time the roles one expects others to adopt. Weinstein refers to this process of assigning complementary roles to others by adopting one's own role as "altercasting." [34]

Thus the initial appearance one makes in an interaction has a dual character because it expresses others' roles as well as one's own. On the one hand, in expressing one's own role, one makes implicit promises about how one will perform in the interaction and in related ones; on the other hand, in defining the others' roles, one is making demands upon them. These demands on others are extremely important because, if accepted, they are normative in character: they are enforced with sanctions. The demands, then, whatever their character, constitute an attempt to subject others to normative control that will insure their cooperation in joint projects.

SUMMARY OF INITIAL PROCESSES IN INTERACTION

Although the processes involved continue throughout the interaction, we are now concerned primarily with the presentation and analysis of appearances that are presented early in an interaction. Entering the inter-

[33] Turner, p. 23.
[34] Weinstein, p. 756.

action, each person must present *some* appearance, whether it is contrived or natural, honest or deceitful. Others, through the process of role-taking, assign a situated identity to each person on the basis of this appearance. Thus, there is pressure on each person to make an appearance that will lead people to treat him or her as he or she would like to be treated—in a way that conforms to his or her plans for the interaction. Each person, then, begins to act in accord with his or her own plans and definition of the situation. Such acting presents the appropriate appearances to others. At the same time each person observes the appearances presented by others in an attempt to unmask or see through any deception they may be attempting. Each is interested in responding to the others' true character, rather than to contrived, undeserved ones. All of this activity must be begun early in interaction because commitments must be made for later action. These commitments must often be honored, even if one has been deceived by the other. In defining one's own role and accepting the normative controls that accompany it, one is at the same time defining the roles of others. Thus, through his or her appearance, each person provides, and attempts to impose on the others, not only an identity for her- or himself, but a definition of the identities and socially enforced obligations of all the participants—a version of the nature of the entire interaction and related activities, or a definition of the situation.

Confronting Multiple Definitions of the Situation: The Working Consensus

As each actor acts on the basis of his or her definition of the situation, he or she becomes aware through his or her interpretations of others' actions of their definitions of the situation. The degree of consensus among these definitions is important to each person involved and must be determined in each interaction. In many cases the mutual scrutiny of the people involved uncovers no difficulties for any of them in continuing with their planned lines of action. Each may observe (1) that the roles and attitudes displayed in the appearances of others are compatible with the roles and attitudes he or she had hoped and expected the others would display; and (2) that the others have accorded him or her the identity he or she wanted to establish. In such cases, the various definitions of the situation are compatible and each may proceed with the line of action as planned. The compatibility of definitions of the situation is possible when the expectations, upon which each person based his preliminary definitions of the situation, are an accurate predictor of the situation he or she encounters.

The degree to which this occurs is of course variable. Situations in which expectations are highly correlated are considered to be highly institutionalized. As Blumer points out, even in the most highly institutionalized situations, those in which action is repetitive and predictably correlated with expectations, the interpretive processes we have been discussing must continue to operate.[35] The people involved must know, on an immediate basis, that this institutionalized character prevails. They must maintain their attention to the appearances of others to be sure that the implications of earlier actions are being actualized. They must maintain their own appearances so that they can withstand the scrutiny of others.

CONSENSUS AS A PRODUCT OF INTERACTION

It is in less-institutionalized situations that problems arise for the people involved in an interaction. Problems arise when people discover that their definitions of the situation and therefore the lines of action they had planned to pursue are not compatible with those of others. Each person discovers that others are not willing to accept the identities that would allow smooth cooperation in his or her plans; that others are not willing to treat him or her in terms of the identity he or she had chosen for him- or herself. In such situations, the options open to the actor are limited.

First, one may terminate the interaction. If one does so, however, one forfeits the ability to accomplish the goals that brought one to the interaction in the first place. Two variables are likely to affect the decision to terminate the interaction: the importance of one's goals to oneself and the availability of alternate ways to achieve them. A person finding a surly or disrespectful bank teller at the end of a long line will probably continue the interaction rather than repeat the wait to deal with another teller. On the other hand, if one were treated disrespectfully by a casual acquaintance at a party, one would probably talk to someone else.

Second, the person may simply accept the definition of the situation preferred by the other people involved. Sometimes others' definitions of the situation will be an improvement on one's own.[36]   Others may treat one with more respect, show more affection, or offer compliments that one did not anticipate. In these cases there will be no hesitation on a person's part in accepting others' version of events and of his or her role in them. A person may also decide to go along with others even when she or he is disappointed with the definition of the situation they prefer. The disappointment may not be great enough from his or her point of view to warrant either discontinuing the interaction or attempting to change the

[35] Herbert Blumer, "Society as Symbolic Interaction," in *Symbolic Interaction,* ed. Jerome Manis and Bernard Meltzer, Allyn and Bacon, Boston, 1972, pp. 145–154.
[36] Erving Goffman, "On Face Work," in *Interaction Ritual,* Erving Goffman, Doubleday, Garden City, N.Y., 1967, pp. 5–46.

conditions under which it proceeds. Situations in which we are disappointed by the treatment of people with whom we have limited relationships are often of this character. It may be too much trouble to do anything but ignore the apparent attitudes of people who are nonetheless performing some service for us—disrespectful waiters, impolite clerks, and so on.

Third, the person may attempt to impose his or her definition of the situation on the other participants. If they have already decided to either accept this individual's definition of the situation or to terminate the interaction, the outcome of this strategy is clear. But if they too have decided to persist and to try to impose their own definitions of the situation, the outcome becomes quite problematic. Each person would be expressing a commitment to continue the interaction. But, at the same time, each would be proposing different conditions for the continuation—different versions of what each participant should do and be in the interaction. The outcome of this situation is likely to be a compromise definition of the situation, acceptable to, if not preferred by, the participants. Much of the interaction, regardless of the other goals of the participants, should be devoted to achieving this compromise.

Goffman observes that the collective definition of the situation is a compromise that does not necessarily reflect the true feelings of the participants. Rather than expressing his or her immediate feelings, each participant suppresses them in favor of giving lip service to policies and ideals that will be at least marginally acceptable to those involved. The result is tacit agreement that open conflict should be avoided, that the interaction should continue on some compromise version, and that certain people will have their way on certain issues.[37] Goffman gives the name "working consensus" to this practical agreement concerning the nature of the reality to be accepted by interactants. One important implication of the surface character of this consensus, the ability to act expediently in contradiction to one's real beliefs, is that people are able to adapt to the demands made upon them by others on a temporary basis. Thus the conseusus achieved in interaction can be discarded if it becomes too burdensome and the participants can adopt beliefs as a basis of action without corresponding changes in their "real" beliefs.

The development of a working consensus over the course of an interaction suggests that the relationship between a person's definition of the situation, especially the nature of the normative constraints on interaction, and his or her action is quite complex. On the one hand people have expectations about these constraints and about the social reality they will confront in interaction. These expectations are a major factor in planning their actions in a situation. On the other hand people are able to adapt

[37] Goffman, *Presentation of Self,* pp. 9–10.

their plans to situations in which their expectations are not fulfilled. That is, they are able to interact even when the normative order and social reality they anticipated is proved to be inoperative, and they are able to cooperatively design a new social reality and normative order in terms of which to plan action at the same time as they are initiating that action. This complex view of social reality and of normative constraints in particular is the heart of the characteristic approach of symbolic interaction to these phenomena. As Turner points out:

> An initial distinction must be made between taking the existence of distinct and identifiable roles as the starting point in role theory, and postulating a tendency to create and modify conceptions of self- and other-roles as the orienting process in interactive behavior. The latter approach has less interest in determining the exact roles in a group and the specific content of each role than in observing the basic tendency for actors to behave as if there were roles. Role in the latter sense is a sort of ideal conception which constrains people to render any action situation into more or less explicit collection of interacting roles.[38]

That is, people are constrained to provide a working consensus that defines the basis of joint action by specifying the nature of the normatively sanctioned role relationships, among other things, relevant to the interaction. In this context, Blumer's equation of joint action with an interpretive process seems well taken. This view contrasts sharply to the conception that a complex of roles, normative sanctions, and values, all more or less well defined and known by members of society, exists prior to interaction and governs its courses. In this view, joint action is possible through individual conformity to pre-established and integrated rules. In the symbolic interactionist view, joint action is possible through cooperative efforts to define social reality in a mutually acceptable way during interaction so that people can use the definition as a basis of joint action.

Before discussing the interpretive process through which a working consensus, or jointly accepted definition of the situation, is achieved in detail, three general topics must be considered. These serve as an introduction to the more detailed discussion to follow. First, we would like to briefly discuss the characterization of the interpretive process as one that involves bargaining among the participants. Second, we would like to indicate the scope of the issues that are included in the working consensus governing an interaction. Third, we would like to indicate how the development of the working consensus is an important instrument of social change.

[38] Turner, pp. 21–22.

NEGOTIATING REALITY

The achievement of a working consensus requires negotiation, not merely as a metaphor, but in the full, literal sense of that term. Why negotiations occur can be understood in terms of the conditions under which the working consensus is problematic. First, the participants must each have concluded that his or her goals are worth pursuing in the interaction even though their expectations concerning the nature of the interaction have been proved false by the actions of others. Each must revise his or her plans for achieving those goals to a form that is acceptable to the others. For each, the changes that must be made are disappointing, rather than pleasant, and must be too disappointing to simply accept the preference of others involved.

Under these conditions some of the participants, and very probably all of them, will find that the compromise they reach, called the working consensus, will be less favorable to them than their own original plans. On the positive side, the working consensus will probably be an improvement, from each person's point of view, over the plans of the others. Each participant, then, can be expected to minimize the degree to which the working consensus disappoints him or her relative to his or her original plans. In this task, each participant is at cross-purposes with the others who are trying to minimize the differences of the working consensus from their own plans.

As we have pointed out, there are tangible gains and losses associated with variations in the definition of the situation. These include, but are not limited to, differences in the obligations imposed on each participant and the compensating contributions they can expect from others. The participants can be expected to try to make as few concessions to others as they can manage and to avoid compromising their plans more than is necessary. With each participant acting from this sort of concern, the result must be bargaining or negotiating in the full sense of those words. It is in accord with this general characterization of interaction that such terms as negotiating reality and role-bargaining are employed.

Negotiations may appear to be a harsh model of human relationships, yet even our most intimate relationships may involve negotiations over tangible matters, especially when institutionalized arrangements are disrupted. Until approximately ten years ago, for example, the distribution of household chores between men and women was strongly institutionalized. Women did them all, by and large, even in addition to nondomestic employment. This arrangement is still very common, of course, but it is also increasingly common for men to share in domestic chores. Discussions about who will wash dishes, carry garbage, cut the lawn, do household repairs, do laundry, or sweep floors are all negotiations in a very concrete sense. So are discussions of how often these chores are to be done and how carefully. These discussions have caused more excitement than one might expect over apparently trivial issues such as washing dishes. What is at stake, however, is the definition of masculinity and femininity in our culture, and the identity implications for those who do these chores.

What seems to be occurring in our society is the dissociation of many commonplace activities, of which chores are an obvious example, from the definition of sex roles. For the time being, many men are embarrassed by engaging in "women's work" and many women are frightened by the loss of traditional "protections." These facts perhaps account for the degree of excitement that can be generated by seemingly trivial issues— those issues are defined as important to identity. Negotiations need not be so emotional or have such far-reaching implications however. Groups of male roommates are able to divide household chores with much less excitement, even if they would object to doing the work with a woman available.

Several points can be made about the negotiating model. Negotiation may explicitly be concerned with very tangible and seemingly trivial issues. However, as noted above, such issues may conceal broader concerns. The identities of the participants may define what will be considered an important issue, as illustrated by the relative willingness of even "traditional" men to do household chores when women are not available for the task. The importance of the matters being discussed may be drastically altered, as suggested by the possibility of redefining sex roles so that many matters that were once crucial to a masculine or feminine identity become unimportant or irrelevant. If that occurs, negotiations over those matters can become as routine as discussions of what television show to watch. Finally, we can see that the negotiating model provides insight into how relationships are sustained through periods of stress and change and how issues affecting society can be experienced and resolved in interaction.

WHAT IS NEGOTIATED?

Most immediately, the participants in an interaction are concerned with establishing their relationships to each other as they affect the interaction. These relationships, although they are important because they relate to the interaction, define activities that extend beyond the particular interaction situation. They may also have implications for many individuals that are not parties to the interaction. Much of the need to accurately take the roles of others derives exactly from the fact that obligations are fulfilled when those people cannot be observed. By defining role relationships during an interaction we are typically defining obligations that must be fulfilled at other times and in other situations, often when we will not be present. For example, in reaching an agreement with a repairperson we will be concerned with his or her performance in actually doing the repairs as well as with how he or she acts during the interaction with us.

It is not merely that some actions prescribed by the role relationships defined in an interaction occur outside the interaction. In addition, the sanctions that accompany the role performance may also be applied outside the interaction and by people who are not present in the interaction. For example, the obligations incurred by writing a check or using a credit card rather than money are not usually enforced by the person to whom the check is given. Rather, all those concerned with the transaction are aware that sanctions can be applied at later times by bank officials, credit card companies, credit-rating bureaus, the police, bill collection agencies, and so forth. Similarly, the products or services paid for may be delivered at a later time and by people not present at the interaction during which the arrangements are made. It is not that people are unable to use sanctions immediately during an interaction—for example we may not be able to define ourselves successfully as a person who is trustworthy enough to pay by check. Rather, by defining a role relationship with others in an interaction, we are often, at the same time, defining role relationships with others outside the interaction, relying on their competence and accepting their ability to sanction our performance, even though they are not present when these relationships are defined.

It is also clear that role relationships between the parties to an interaction and others not present in the interaction are defined by the working consensus. They are not defined in detail, to be sure, but constraints are placed on them. In the simple act of accepting a check in payment from another person we are accepting a definition of his or her relationships with his or her bank, employers, and so on, at least as they relate to the value of the check. At the same time we are defining a relationship between ourselves and all those involved in converting that check into money or other commodities at a later time.

The working consensus, then, extends to issues well beyond the limits of the particular interaction in which it develops. It defines activities of the participants that occur outside the interaction but relates to the relationships defined in the interaction. It defines role relationships between the participants in the interaction and others who are not present as they relate to performing the roles defined in the interaction. It brings participants in the interaction under the control of others who have the ability to sanction those aspects of role performance that occur outside the interaction. In short, the working consensus defines a social reality that extends beyond the interaction, but defines it in terms of its relevance to the interaction.

This closely parallels the kind of information that is involved in the definition of situated identities that are one part of the working consensus. As with situated identities, a reality extending beyond the interaction is defined but the details of that reality can be expected to change from interaction to interaction as the concerns of the participants change. As for the scope of the definition, we can say the following: social relationships in the society at large are defined in as much breadth and detail as is necessary to sustain the relationships defined in the interaction. The relevant aspects of society, then, are defined. As with the situated identity, the significance of the definition is related to the belief that it is an accurate reflection of a stable reality, and the definition will vary from interaction to interaction. Gouldner's concept of mock bureaucracy illustrates the sorts of elements that are included in the definition of the situation. In the industrial setting many rules exist, along with the appropriate penalties for disobeying them, "on paper" only. In fact although the rules are known to exist, they are disregarded openly by those involved, including those officially responsible for enforcing them. An example is the no-smoking rule: signs are visible which forbid smoking but under ordinary circumstances the rule is ignored by management as well as by the laborers who work in the areas to which it applies. To all concerned, the reason for leaving the rule on the books is obvious: it is a condition placed on management by an outside agency, the insurance company. When representatives of the insurance company are present, workers are warned in advance by management and are told not to smoke. The workers are glad to comply on those occasions and even react hostilely to "troublemakers" who continue to smoke when the inspectors are present.[39]

The pattern of mock bureaucracy is maintained as a complex bargain between the workers and the management. The workers want to smoke on the job. Management must have a no-smoking rule on the books and they must have no smoking while insurance inspectors are on the premises. Because both workers and management recognize that the no-smoking rule is a concession to a third party they are able to reach a compromise in which both are partially satisfied. Among other things, this pattern of ignoring rules indicates the ability to bargain for the "real expectations" in the presence of written rules. The bargain takes into account more than just the immediate setting however. It recognizes the responsibilities of management to the insurance companies and allows those to be met to the satisfaction of the inspectors. By recognizing the pressure from the insurance company as part of the definition of the situation (rather than being limited to only immediate concerns), the extremes of fully enforcing

[39] Alvin Gouldner, *Patterns of Industrial Bureaucracy,* Free Press, Glencoe, 1964, pp. 184–186.

the smoking rule or jeopardizing the insurability of the firm and its employees are avoided. In order to make the compromise successful, the publicly acknowledged definition of the situation must be varied, depending on the presence or absence of the insurance inspectors. The underlying attitudes of both workers and management may not change, but their display of respect for the no-smoking rule is sometimes part of the working consensus and sometimes not. This illustrates the distinction between the real feelings of the participants and the working consensus and the fact that the working consensus can be altered from situation to situation for strategic reasons without affecting those real feelings.

SOURCE OF SOCIAL CHANGE

Differences between people's preliminary definitions of the situation and the working consensus that develops in an interaction, and those differences between definitions of social reality in different interactions, may be transitory and inconsequential. People may cooperatively modify the role relationships between them in developing a working consensus, but may not continue to employ this definition of the relationships in future situations. For example, a person who accepts impolite treatment on one occasion is not bound to continue to accept it in the future. Even if the working consensus achieves some stability in the group, and comes to represent a new definition of their relationships on a regular, more or less permanent, basis, it may not be adopted by others in similar situations. For example, a group of office workers who regularly interact can develop a system of expected favors, unofficially assigned duties, and personal relationships, that has no influence on the actions of other groups of workers in similar situations.

On the other hand, such redefinitions of the situation may become widely accepted throughout a social system (of course, these mechanisms for instituting social change are much more likely to be effective in relatively small social systems than in larger systems such as an institution or a nation). When this occurs, the social reality which is perceived by the group and upon which it bases its actions becomes altered. Thus, when the working consensus in interactions differs from the original expectations of the participants, the consensus may become the source of innovations for social change. Also, the compromise nature of the working consensus suggests that such changes would occur over issues that are the source of conflict between individuals and groups and that the changes would tend to mitigate the conflict.

Social change originating in such a way requires both individual and social influences in generating innovation. Certainly definitions of the situation vary among individuals. The working consensus, however, is a product of the interaction. It is achieved through negotiations and need not have existed in the minds of any of the participants in advance. Thus it is the interaction process itself, and not just the creative abilities of individuals, that provides the innovations that may become the basis of social change.

Factors Constraining the Working Consensus

People in an interaction are not free to arrive at any bargain they prefer as their working consensus. The involvement of others not party to the interaction but affected by the working consensus precludes unreasonable arrangements. For the working consensus developed in interaction suggests preliminary definitions of the situation for others.

As we have seen, the preliminary definition of the situation is not automatically accepted as a basis for action. Each individual, as a result, must consider many factors while deciding whether a working consensus is an acceptable one for him or her to use as a basis for his or her action. Many of these factors are taken into account in developing a preliminary definition of the situation as well. However, we are now concerned with their influence on the working consensus, especially where it differs from the preliminary definition of the situation. The factors fall into two general groups. First are those that are physically present during the interaction itself. These are not available for consideration as factors in the preliminary definition of the situation. Although they are physically present, they must be symbolically mediated through the ongoing interpretative process to affect the working consensus. Second are those that are symbolically represented in the interaction but not physically present. Some of these factors, such as the reference group and generalized other, have no physical embodiment at any time. Others, such as the responses of third parties to the role bargain, are physically observable at certain times. These factors are relevant to the development of the preliminary definition of the situation and are involved in that process in the same way that they are involved in bargaining for a favorable working consensus.

FACTORS PHYSICALLY PRESENT IN INTERACTION

Both the physical setting and facilities available for an interaction and the actions of other people present will influence each person's evaluation of whether a definition of the situation is acceptable. These factors serve to notify each person that a redefinition of the situation is necessary if they do not meet expectations for the interaction. In addition, these factors inform each person what is possible in the situation and thereby set limits on what can be sought, even as an ideal goal, in negotiating a working consensus.

Physical setting as a constraint on action. The role of the physical setting is obvious but nonetheless important. Simply put, facilities that are not available cannot be used. All participants must accept the fact that a working consensus cannot require facilities that are not available. If a working consensus cannot be achieved that restricts itself to available facilities, the interaction must be terminated.

One's preliminary definition of the situation may have included expectations that certain facilities would be available. One may attend a party expecting that someone has arranged for music; one may enter a waiting room expecting to find something to read while one waits, or one may enter a restaurant expecting to find all the menu items available. If these expectations are not met, one's definition of the situation must be altered to exclude the missing items from one's plans. Concretely, if the restaurant is out of apple pie there is nothing to be done except to make do with something else or to leave.

Actions of others as a constraint on action. The actions of the others in an interaction, especially when they indicate the degree of flexibility in the others' plans, also serve to set limits on what one can hope to include in the working consensus. First, people are able to sanction one another during interaction. The sanctions applied by others set a price for actions, and as they become more severe the sanctions may effectively preclude certain lines of action. An enormous variety of actions can serve as sanctions.

In an ingenious experiment, Rosenfeld and Baer created a situation in which the repetition of nervous gestures by the experimenter served as reinforcers for certain aspects of the subject's speech.[40] They created a situation in which the subject was eager to see those gestures and in which the experimenter did not perform them unless the subject first used certain expressions. Two graduate students were used, each thinking he was the experimenter and the other was the subject. An open-ended interview was conducted, with one student acting as the interviewer and the other acting as the interviewee. The interviewer was told to watch for a nervous habit that was spontaneously expressed by the other student while talking—rubbing his chin—and to reinforce that habit by making affirmative remarks when it appeared. The other, acting as the interviewee, only performed his gesture when the interviewer used a particular, prechosen affirmative word—either "yes" or "hmm." The eagerness of the interviewer to see the gesture transformed it into a reinforcer and the frequency with which he chose the two words was successfully manipulated by using the gesture only in response to the "correct" word. What is important here is

[40] Howard Rosenfeld and Donald Baer, "Unnoticed Verbal Conditioning of an Aware Experimenter by a More Aware Subject," *Psychological Review,* 76 (July 1969), 425–432.

the illustration that extremely unlikely actions can serve as sanctions and be effective in changing others' actions.

Application of institutional sanctions as a constraint on action. More commonly the expression of attitudes and emotions through one's appearance functions to sanction others' actions, both positively and negatively. We have already discussed this process of communication in the contexts of self-presentation and unmasking. Once people have begun to present themselves in interaction, the actions of others can serve as sanctions, both approving and disapproving, of that presentation. Thus, expressions of intimacy, approval, respect, liking, arrogance, and others serve to provide information about the person who expresses them, and at the same time to sanction the performance of others.

In addition to the expression of personal reactions, individuals often have officially based sanctions at their disposal. Gouldner points out that bureaucratic rules allow individuals to mobilize the resources of the organization in sanctioning others.[41] In fact, holders of some bureaucratic positions are specifically required to do so. He points out that frequently the individual has considerable discretion in applying these sanctions. Individuals violating the same rules, for example, may be treated quite differently. The real reason for the application of a sanction may have little to do with the violation of the rule that serves as the justification for applying it. He points out that those who have dangerous, difficult jobs that call for independent problem-solving may be allowed considerably more freedom to be absent from work, disrespectful to superiors, and so forth, than those in more mundane jobs. Thus the availability of discretion in applying official sanctions can be used as a bargaining tool in imposing conditions on the working consensus.

Dalton reports that the mobilization of the desirable resources of the organization may also be contingent upon the personal relationships maintained between the members of the organization. Such presumably automatic services as the maintenance of machinery, supply of materials for manufacturing processes, and cleaning of work areas may be distributed by those with discretion over them on the basis of friendship, reciprocal favors, and so forth. In addition, positive sanctions of an organization, such as promotions, may be contingent upon religious affiliation, membership in the appropriate social groups, or locus of residence in the community. The ability to provide or withhold these services and sanctions can also be used to enforce conditions on interactions with others in the organization.[42]

[41] Gouldner, pp. 168–174.
[42] Melville Dalton, *Men Who Manage,* Wiley, New York, 1959.

In a similar vein, Egon Bittner describes the peace-keeping activities of policemen on skid row beats. Bittner points out that the police rely on detailed information concerning the habits and needs of the people on their beat, the routines of the neighborhood, and their own needs in evaluating what must be done in response to the situations they confront. He reports that policemen feel that they need to control the situation if they are to avoid more serious troubles in the future. Accordingly they insist that their authority not be challenged by the residents of the neighborhood. This is enforced by utilizing the available legal option, such as the vagrancy laws, as an ever present threat that imposes their immediate authority over interactions with people who could be legitimately arrested but who will not be unless they challenge police authority. In such situations the law is employed, as are other bureaucratic rules and sanctions, as a tool to deal with problems that are unrelated to the law violation itself. The law, Bittner points out, can also be used to protect individuals from severe, if only potential, danger. He reports occasions in which a person is charged with some violation as a form of protective custody. For example, one skid row inhabitant was known to have received a disability check and to be drinking heavily. When drunk he was known to seek the company of rough, dangerous types, probably with some vaguely homosexual intent. The combination of being drunk and having money put him in special danger of being robbed and beaten. As a protective measure he was arrested.[43]

People control one another's actions during interaction in ways that do not involve sanctions in the usual sense of the term. Scheff reports that the power to control the way information is presented aids in imposing a definition of the situation.[44] Specifically he shows that by the questions chosen and the answers accepted as final without further probing, an interrogator can guide others to a favored definition of the situation.

Kendon argues that the flow of the interaction itself, especially the change from speaker to speaker, is controlled to a large extent by mutually guiding actions of the participants. Speakers tend to avoid eye contact with others while they are formulaing their thoughts. While talking they survey others only sporadically to monitor their responses. Extended eye contact is renewed shortly before the speaker has finished and serves to warn others that he or she will soon be expecting some verbal response from them.[45]

---

[43] Egon Bittner, "The Police on Skid Row," *American Sociological Review,* 32 (October 1967), 699–715.

[44] Thomas Scheff, "Negotiating Reality," in *Social Psychology and Everyday Life,* ed. Billy Franklin and Frank Kohout, McKay, New York, 1973, pp. 55–72.

[45] Adam Kendon, "Some Functions of Gaze-Direction in Social Interaction," in *Social Encounters,* ed. Michael Argyle, Aldine, Chicago, 1973, pp. 76–92.

In addition to sanctions, threats of sanctions, and actions that guide the content or sequence of interaction, each person may also indicate to others the absolute limit beyond which his or her participation is not available. In a sense, this is analogous to the absolute limits imposed by physical facilities. One is indicating the limits of how one will allow oneself to be used in others' plans. Schelling points out that convincing others that a line of action is your "best offer," that you are committed to it irrevocably, is a useful strategic ploy.[46] It places others in the position of accepting that line of action or terminating the interaction. This kind of commitment can be communicated in a number of ways. One can indicate one's intention to pursue the course of action and then close oneself off from further communication. This makes it impossible for others to suggest alternatives or compromises. Bureaucrats who explain a complicated process and then return to their paperwork, thus preventing personal attention or suggestion of short cuts, are practicing this technique. Alternately, one can demonstrate to the satisfaction of others that one is subject to severe sanctions, positive or negative, contingent on one's performance of the plan of action. However it is accomplished, committing oneself to a line of action presents others with a take-it-or-leave it option which they must consider in their own attempts to control the situation.

FACTORS NOT PHYSICALLY PRESENT IN INTERACTION

Each interaction, no matter how important, is only part of the social life of each person in it. The obligations defined by the roles relevant in any interaction are only part of the total obligations of each person. The demands made by others in an interaction and the sanctions they use to enforce them are only part of the sanctions and demands to which each person is subject. The ability to represent such matters symbolically, even when they are not physically present, allows the participant to orient his or her action to these other contingencies as well as to those physically present ones.

Anticipated responses of particular others. People orient their actions to the anticipated responses of particular others with whom they will have to deal on the basis of relationships defined in an interaction. As the working consensus develops, implications will arise for other situations in which each of the participants will be involved. Each person can anticipate how that interaction will be affected and how others who will be involved in it will respond to the relationships he or she will have to try to carry through. In essence, each participant is constructing preliminary definitions of rele-

---

[46] Thomas Schelling, *The Strategy of Conflict,* Oxford, New York, 1963.

vant situations so that he or she can evaluate the impact of his or her present actions on them.

Bittner reports evidence that such considerations are in fact made by professional policemen in performing their duties. Frequently, policemen are called in to handle situations in which a person is apparently mentally ill and cannot be controlled by his or her family or friends. Such apparently mentally ill people may indeed have long been recognized as such but may suddenly present an especially difficult control problem by becoming violent, suicidal, and so forth. On the other hand, they may be people displaying bizarre behavior for the first time. One option the policeman has in such situations is to remove these people to a hospital for observation. Among the other options are restoring calm in an immediate sense and returning the person to the care of his or her family, especially if they have been able to cope with the behavior in the past. Obviously among the concerns of the policeman in deciding what to do, the welfare of the patient and of others who might be affected by future outbursts are very important. Bittner reports however that the anticipated response of superiors and colleagues to the action chosen, in terms of its quality as professional police work, is also very imporant. Dealing with psychiatric hospitals is time consuming and takes the policeman away from other, more important duties. The policeman takes this into account in his determination of what to do with an apparently mentally ill person.[47]

William Goode provides a useful theoretical framework for discussing this aspect of people's concerns in evaluating a role bargain. Goode points out that, for a variety of reasons, the demands made upon an individual by his or her role obligations may be contradictory, burdensome, and beyond his or her resources. Typically, he argues, the individual experiences some strain in his or her attempt to fulfill these various obligations. The strain is not a property of an individual role relationship but of the whole network of role relationships in which one is involved. Accordingly, the strain is reduced by achieving a satisfactory arrangement, not for one interaction or role relationship, but for the whole group of them in which one is involved. Each person attempts to manipulate each set of obligations, not to achieve the best results for his or her overall situation. In one's role bargains, then, one is constrained by self-interest to sometimes accept more obligations than one has to in a given situation in order to avoid more onerous consequences in other ones.[48]

Each individual is also constrained, according to Goode, by the influence of third parties to any bargain he or she makes. Goode observes that

[47] Egon Bittner, "Police Discretion in Emergency Apprehension of Mentally Ill Persons," *Social Problems,* 14 (Winter 1967), 278–292.

[48] William Goode, "A Theory of Role Strain," in *Problems in Social Psychology,* ed. Carl Backman and Paul Secord, McGraw Hill, St. Louis, 1966, pp. 372–382.

a person may be sanctioned by others with whom he or she interacts for his or her conduct in interactions in which they are not directly involved. These sanctions may be the result of standards of fair play, or commitment to existing arrangements. Thus, even when the role bargain is acceptable to those immediately involved and does not cause inconvenience to third parties, these third parties may exert pressure against the bargain.[49] Third parties may also object to obligations imposed on them by the bargain struck in an interaction in which they are not present. For example, an agreement between a customer and a salesperson may impose a difficult schedule on production personnel or delivery people.

This concern for the reaction of third parties is part of the process by which people in interactions are able to coordinate the activities throughout a social system. From the perspective of each individual, what is accomplished is the balancing and integration of the influences of the various people with whom he or she interacts. One places oneself, at least in one's anticipations, under the control of the whole complement of role others in each interaction rather than responding to each only when they are face to face. If each person does this an additional effect is achieved. The compromise reached in an interaction will reflect the anticipated responses of the third parties of everyone involved. This effect can be introduced without all the people involved in the interaction knowing why others insist on certain features in the working consensus. In effect each person in the interaction serves to represent the responses of his or her own set of third parties, and this representation serves to integrate the activities of all those in the interaction with the needs of all the sets of third parties involved. For example, a customer accepting a later date for the delivery of a purchase than she or he would have preferred is, although he or she deals only with a salesperson, orienting his or her action to the realities of delivery schedules, warehouse problems, and vacation schedules, of which he or she need not even be aware. Thus, each person by taking his or her network of role relationships into account when making a role bargain serves to integrate the activities of many people in many situations, some of which he or she is not even aware of, into a coordinated system of activities.

Anticipated responses based on shared organized perspectives. At a more abstract level, the individual may respond to a generalized other, rather than or in addition to, the specific others with whom he or she must deal. By adopting this general, organized perspective, the individual can put the demands of others with whom he or she deals into perspective.

[49] William Goode, "Norm Commitment and Conformity to Role-Status Obligation," *American Journal of Sociology,* 66 (November 1960), 246–258.

This allows one to evaluate each demand made upon one, not only in terms of other demands, but also in terms of the general context in which they are all organized. The use of the generalized other as an organized perspective enhances the social integrating effects of interaction. It allows group activities as organized systems and the effect of one's action on the system as a whole to be considered as a factor in deciding on the acceptability of a course of action.

Reference groups, as noted earlier, are distinguished from the generalized other in that the former need not be composed of individulals with whom one interacts, nor even of individuals who really exist.[50] Thus, while reference groups provide a socially organized perspective in terms of which to evaluate events, this perspective also reflects, through the ability of the individual to select his or her reference group, the values of the individual involved. Regardless of whether they correspond to the people with whom one actually interacts, the existence of the reference group allows the individual to assess any course of action in terms of the anticipated response of people about whom he or she really cares. These anticipated responses may differ from the actual responses of those in the interaction, from the anticipated responses of particular role others, or from the perspective suggested by the generalized other. The reference group provides a socially organized basis for a person's values in a form that allows their use as a tool for evaluating possible courses of action and definitions of the situation. It also provides social support, although this may be imaginary, for values that may not be supported by the people with whom one actually interacts. Through the selection of a reference group each person can avoid standing alone in his value judgments, thus providing a countering force against the responses of others.

These various factors considered by a person in determining what he or she will accept as a definition of the situation and as a course of action must be integrated and a decision must be based on them. This integrative function is served by the self. In this view, the self has an active role in each activity undertaken by the person. It is not merely a hypothetical construct used to summarize the various perspectives and roles taken by the individual. Rather, the self actively assigns weights to the various influences upon the person, integrates them, and determines a course of action that reflects both these influences and the person's unique organization of them.

We have noted that the nature of people's concerns as they decide upon a course of action serves to integrate each interaction with others in the social system and to coordinate activities throughout the system. At the

[50] Tamotsu Shibutani, "Reference Groups as Perspectives," in *Symbolic Interaction,* ed. Jerome Manis and Bernard Meltzer, Allyn and Bacon, Boston, 1972, p. 165.

same time these concerns constrain role-bargaining which often results in redefinitions of the role relationships throughout the system. If a person considers all of these factors in the role bargains he or she makes, the effect will be that changes in the definitions of role relationships will not be accepted unless, in sum, they seem to be acceptable in terms of his or her overall considerations. The same factors that allow one to integrate one's activities with those of others control the amount and kinds of change one will accept in the role bargain. The social control represented by the consideration of third parties, of the generalized other, and of the reference group has its influence on change as well as on maintaining stability.

Socialization as a Consequence of Interaction

Consider what happens to an individual in an interaction. One enters the interaction with a definition of the situation and of related social realities. Included in this are a plan of action and a set of expectations for the actions of others. During the interaction one is confronted with the actions of others, including sanctions and other attempts to control one's behavior. In light of these, along with a consideration of anticipated responses of relevant third parties, the generalized other, and one's reference groups, one revises the definition of the situation to compromise with others on at least a temporary basis. That is, one is taught to accept and act upon a new definition of the immediate situation and of the related social realities. One is socialized—and all of this can occur over the span of a few minutes during interaction.

The actor makes, or creates, his or her role in concert with others. He or she is able to act on the basis of obligations that he or she has negotiated during the course of the interaction to which they apply. As Turner notes, "Interaction is always a *tentative* process, a process of continuously testing the conception one has of the role of the other." [51]

The tentative character of interaction and the recognition that socialization occurs over such a short time span and must be successful in guiding action as the bases for action are being learned suggest that interaction has some unique characteristics. We are led to the conclusion that until the role bargaining or working consensus is finalized, the actors must perform satisfactorily in a role that they have not yet learned and that may not even exist yet. Related to this, the people involved must perform a second task: they must be able to redefine early actions, initiated under discarded definitions of the situation, in terms of the working consensus that develops later.

[51] Turner, p. 23.

SMOOTHING OVER DISCREPANCIES

Goffman discusses several cooperative facework processes that allow individuals to smooth over discrepancies between their initial actions and the ones occurring later in the interaction. He focuses especially on the differences between the situated identities implied in the discrepant actions. When a discrepancy is recognized to have occurred, all those involved in the interaction may cooperate to smooth over the difficulty. Often the discrepancy may be treated jokingly. Alternately, the person may apologize or otherwise indicate that he or she is aware of the discrepancy and its seriousness. Or in some cases the discrepancy may be ignored, as if it had never occurred. The common theme underlying these reactions to discrepancy is that the individual re-establishes others' belief that he or she is a responsible person who can fulfill the obligations he or she assumes. This belief can be shaken by the appearance of contradictory identities.[52]

This theme is repeated in Mills' discussion of the vocabulary of motives.[53] Mills points out that standardized forms exist which can be employed by people to explain and excuse their actions in a situation. Social control is exerted over the excuses offered for improper actions as well as over the definition of what will be regarded as improper. For example, social norms define missing work as an improper action. Additional norms define illness as a reasonable explanation for absence, one that will remove or mitigate the negative consequences, while defining the desire to spend the day at the zoo as an unreasonable one. The vocabulary of motives is the collection of socially acceptable reasons for doing things that are unacceptable unless a reasonable explanation is offered. Improper actions, which might include discrepancies in one's standard identity, have the effect of calling one's competence into question. The use of a vocabulary of motives for improper action reasserts one's commitment to the standards of the group in the face of apparent deviation from it.

Thus mechanisms exist that allow people to smooth over discrepancies between early and later activities in an interaction while retaining a sense that the discrepancies do not indicate inability or unwillingness of the participants to meet obligations in a consistent way. Verbal expressions that reduce one's responsibility for unacceptable action and express one's allegiance to group values may be made after the action or may anticipate the action (apologizing in advance). These verbal expressions can of course take a variety of forms. For example, a person may deny that the act harmed anyone while admitting that it was committed. Such pleas

[52] Goffman, "On Face Work."

[53] C. Wright Mills, "Situated Actions and Vocabularies of Motive," in *Symbolic Interaction,* ed. Jerome Manis and Bernard Meltzer, Allyn and Bacon, Boston, 1972, pp. 393–404.

are common when financial dealings with the telephone company, internal revenue service, or other large impersonal bureaucracies are challenged. Alternately, a person may deny full responsibility for an act, while admitting the harm it caused. Blaming an automobile accident on defective brakes is an instance.[54]

LEARNING WHILE DOING

The paradoxical fact that actors are able to begin the performance of roles before the role has been defined has also received some attention. Garfinkel and Sacks describe an ingenious but easily performed experiment to illustrate this phenomenon. For example, a man walking or driving through an area which he has never seen before acts as though he is closely studying its appearance. He then comments to those he is with that the neighborhood has changed substantially since he last saw it. From the response of the others he discovers what the neighborhood was like and how and when the changes occurred. In a sense he learns from their response what his own comment really meant. Clearly, meaning is being treated not as a private experience but in terms of its expression in action. Even if the others do not respond, and the person never discovers anything about the neighborhood, he gives the appearance to others that he already knows the neighborhood. This experiment can be applied to other situations as well. One could make a similar remark about the furniture in a house, the service in a restaurant, the routine in an organization, the personality of a person, and so on. Garfinkel and Sacks suggest that the pattern of appearing knowledgeable and acquiring knowledge subsequently is a common one.[55]

Garfinkel documents an extreme but informative instance of this process: the successful passing of a transsexual person as a normal woman. Her major handicaps in this venture were a fully developed penis that accompanied feminine secondary sex characteristics and the fact that she had been raised as a male. When she decided after high school that she was properly a woman, she was forced to pass as a woman while she learned the appropriate behavior for the role. The need to begin performing a role while one is still learning it is not unusual. What is extraordinary in this case is that she was able to begin to perform as a woman with little preparatory time and in contrast to her early experiences as a male. She was able, once she had her hair styled and bought appropriate clothes, to

---

[54] Marvin Scott and Stanford Lyman, "Accounts," *American Sociological Review,* 33 (February 1968), 46–64. For a related discussion, see John Hewitt and Randall Stokes, "Disclaimers," *American Sociological Review,* 40 (February 1975), 1–11.

[55] Harold Garfinkel and Harvey Sacks, "On Formal Structures of Practical Actions," in *Theoretical Sociology,* ed. John McKinney and Edward Tiryakian, Appleton-Century-Crofts, New York, 1970, pp. 337–366.

begin to work, appear in public, make friends, share an apartment, and date almost immediately. In doing all these activities she was able to appear as a woman and to be treated as such by others. In addition to the learning of the skills associated with the new sex role she adopted, she had to make special arrangements to conceal her unusual physical characteristics, while still appearing to be a more or less normal person. Even with severe handicaps, people are able to perform in a role while they are still learning it.[56]

Goffman suggests one mechanism that permits this sort of activity to occur: there are standards of decorum that are applicable in a wide variety of situations.[57] By maintaining these standards, one is able to appear generally competent and to learn the details to support this competent appearance as the interaction progresses. Goffman also suggests that those more sophisticated in a role relationship, especially regular performers of a role who deal with a changing population of others, will guide those who are less sophisticated.[58] He cites as an example that waitresses must control the interactions between them and their customers to get all the information they need in a brief time and to keep their work flowing smoothly. Similarly, customers allow barbers to manipulate their position either physically or through instructions. The person who knows in detail what needs to be done in the interaction guides others through it. Ideally this is done in a way that does not reflect on anyone's competence, but on occasion people can be sanctioned for their ignorance in such situations.

DIFFERENCES FROM CHILDHOOD SOCIALIZATION

The socialization process that occurs in an interaction differs from the long-term process of childhood and adult socialization. First, the learning involved in the role bargain may be transitory and of little consequence, either to the individual or to social arrangements. We have noted that the working consensus is often a shallow, expedient agreement. Thus, while individuals may teach one another a basis for action during an interaction, they may discard that basis quickly. When the working consensus becomes recognized as a new, stable reality, however, it may serve as the basis for adult socialization or social change.

Second, the socialization process occurring in interaction is constrained by forces that have less impact on the long-term process of childhood socialization. We have noted that consideration of third parties who are

---

[56] Harold Garfinkel, "Passing and the Management of Sex Status in an Intersexed Person," in *Studies in Ethnomethodology*, Harold Garfinkel, Prentice-Hall, Englewood Cliffs, N.J., 1967, pp. 116–185.

[57] Erving Goffman, *Behavior in Public Places*, Free Press, New York, 1963.

[58] Goffman, *Presentation of Self*, pp. 11–12.

not present, the generalized other, and reference groups are important in constraining the definition of the situation that will be acceptable to a person in an interaction. We also noted that all of these concerns are integrated by a relatively well-formed self. Especially in early childhood, these forces are extremely weak. The child's self is not fully formed and he or she has little experience on which to base estimations of the responses of others. Thus the learning of the child is more highly responsive to the immediate situation. In fact, the long-term process of socialization results in, among other things, the development of the self and of the related abilities that constrain adult interaction and role learning.

Finally, particular role bargains do not necessarily have the impact on the self of the adult as they do on the self of a child. The weight of past experience and the presence of already organized perspectives allows a context in which one can change one's role relationships, at least temporarily, with relatively little impact on one's self or future development. Profound changes in one's self continue to occur throughout one's life. Socialization on the large scale is thus continued. At the same time, however, we must recognize that transitory changes in role relationships occur on a regular basis that are tangential to long-term development and ephemeral in their effects.

Altruism as a Consequence of Interaction

The symbolic interactionist analysis of the way in which social control operates in the interaction setting helps to clarify an issue that has disturbed sociologists for many years. Most views of human nature place a heavy emphasis on the role of sanctions (rewards and punishments, reinforcement) in controlling human behavior. The implication of this emphasis is that humans are basically economic creatures, calculating, more or less consciously, the benefits and debits of any line of action. With this essentially selfish basis for behavior it becomes difficult to explain the frequent altruistic behavior displayed by humans, behavior which involves sacrifice for the benefit of others.

This altruistic bent has been discussed under a variety of names and from several theoretical perspectives. George Homans, in his extension of the principles of behavioristic psychology to humans, suggests that there is a norm of distributive justice. Rather than seeking to maximize his or her own rewards, the individual, using others as a point of reference, seeks only a fair or just reward. By "just," Homans means that the amount of reward is proportional to the costs—people making a large commitment of resources are expected by all concerned to receive a proportionally larger reward than those who are less involved. Homans suggests that people adopt this standard of distributive justice because the condition of fair exchange is, in itself, a reward,[59] apparently one that is more valuable than the rewards to be gained by selfishness. At best, proposing fair exchange as a reward is a temporizing answer. Is there a human instinct toward altruism? Is it learned? If it is learned, what reinforcements underlie the emergence of fairness as a secondary reward?

Gouldner proposes a similar solution to this issue. He suggests that there is a norm of reciprocity that transcends the norms governing specific social relationships. This norm requires that a person receiving benefits from another must reciprocate by providing benefits in return. Gouldner's analysis does not assume that the returns are equal or even proportional—rather, he leaves this as an empirical matter. He argues that the reciprocation may be unequal, giving rise to the sorts of institutions that do not seem to be justified by their contributions to the society. While his analysis seems to intend large-scale institutions, it appears applicable to smaller-scale ones, social relationships, as well. The norm of reciprocity serves several functions, among them to provide an additional incentive to fulfill obligations and establish trust. By trust we mean that this norm provides a guarantee that others with whom we deal will reciprocate our services. This allows interaction to proceed without the crippling problem of who will make a commitment based only on the promises or assurances of others.[60] As we have noted before, the social sanctions accompanying norms provide a basis for us to estimate with some confidence that others' behavior will conform to these norms. In short, they allow us to trust the other.

Although Gouldner's analysis introduces a fully sociological concept of norms to this problem and although he does seem concerned with exchange, he too does not address the problem of how this norm is enforced and by whom. In his analysis we can see that this question is crucial. If such a norm is operative, and if its effect is to build trust, deviation from this norm should be very disruptive. In addition to the failure of obligations to be met, those involved should feel disillusioned—that is they should feel that the fairness (distributive justice, reciprocity) of the system has broken down and that their trust is unfounded. While deviance from this norm is especially troublesome for a social system, the nature of the norm makes it a tempting one to break. The trust of others, based on their expectation that reciprocity will be maintained, makes them easy marks. That is, they are led to trust you by the norm and this makes it easy to deceive them. Gouldner's discussion of reciprocity adds much to clarify

[59] George Homans, *Social Behavior: Its Elementary Forms,* Harcourt, Brace & World, New York, 1974, pp. 68–78.

[60] Alvin Gouldner, "The Norm of Reciprocity: A Preliminary Statement," *American Sociological Review,* 25 (April 1960), 169–177.

the problem, but it suggests that the temptation to violate these norms of reciprocity should be great and it does not provide an answer as to how this norm is maintained.

Extensive work has been done on this problem by psychologists who refer to the problem as one of equity. Research has shown that the maintenance of equity is not continuous but breaks down under at least three conditions. First, the punishments of behaving inequitably may not outweigh the rewards for doing it. Second, unless one occasionally acts inequitably, one cannot be sure that the sanctions associated with the norm are still operative. That is, one may be making sacrifices that are no longer normatively expected of one. Thus occasional tests of the rules are a necessary mechanism for discovering and adapting to social change. Third, the inequity may be in the favor of others, as when a person who cannot reciprocate is nonetheless treated well. In such cases, no negative sanctions may be involved. The research reviewed supports Gouldner's analysis in one important respect. When inequity is perceived, it is the occasion for distress and the distress is greater when the inequity is seen as intentional rather than accidental. This is in accord with the special disillusioning characteristics of the norms involved.

In the review of equity theory, it is explicit that the sanctions supporting this norm are not the responsibility of the affected individuals. Rather, the group is responsible for the distribution of sanctions.[61] The location of the sanctions in the group is the beginning of the missing explanation of how these norms are maintained. In all of the approaches to the problem outlined above, the exchange of benefits is conceived as occurring between two people and in one role relationship. The incentives to behavior are conceived as two-party exchanges and the fairness of the exchange is evaluated in terms of the contributions of the individuals directly involved. Our discussion of interaction, however, suggests a more complex model for exchange. In our view, the individual is guided in the interaction not only by the sanctions applied by the others directly involved but also by the anticipated responses of third parties, reference groups, and parties involved in the implications of the bargain. The bargain one strikes in the interaction is not struck merely with the particular individuals with whom one interacts, but also with the various others with whom one must interact. Thus, the benefits and costs of an interaction may include those applied by others not directly involved in the interaction. And, whether the exchange is just will depend on its effects on all of these others. We are proposing that the analysis of the interaction or exchange between in-

---

[61] Elaine Walster, Ellen Bersheid, and G. Willian Walster, "New Directions in Equity Research," *Journal of Personality and Social Psychology*, 25 (February 1973), 151–176. This article provides a review of current theory and research in this area and many references to other sources.

dividuals cannot be made without consideration of the broader social context in which it occurs. The influence of the network of social obligations on each interaction provides the mechanism by which the norms governing fairness are maintained.

The development of fairness, reciprocity, or equity as rewarding in themselves can also be explained in this way. Among the influences on action and interaction are reference groups and the generalized other. Reference groups need not include people with whom we interact, nor even people who exist. Nonetheless, we utilize their perceived values as a standard of perspective. Similarly, the generalized other is an organization of views and attitudes. Compliance with these perspectives is continued even when there is no tangible sanction associated with them. That is, these organized perspectives become ideals to be followed for their own sake. The perspectives may develop in the context of concrete sanctions, but once developed they take on a life of their own and serve as a mechanism of self-control. It is important to recognize the sense in which even an imaginary group can apply sanctions to violators of its norms. In imagined future discourse with a group, its disapproval may be repeatedly expressed and experienced as guilt or remorse. We may do things that we think would disappoint others, about whom we care deeply, if they became aware of them. We think about these people and are reminded of how they would respond to our act. This form of sanction can be applied by a group that exists only in our imagination as well as by a real group. For example, our concern for the response of our parents may continue very strongly after they have died and therefore continue to exist only in our imagination. Although such sanctions are not tangible in a narrow sense, they can be effective and can be applied by even imaginary groups like "posterity," the "judgment of history," or deceased loved ones. In effect, the attitudes and perspectives become values or rewards in themselves.

Conclusion

Our discussion has concentrated on the interpretive processes that occur in interaction rather than on the behavior associated with particular role performances. The particular roles being performed in an interaction do, of course, greatly affect the activities of the participant. These vary from situation to situation, however, while the interpretive process remains substantially the same regardless of the context in which the interaction occurs.

The interpretive process allows preparation for interaction and is begun by each person before he or she enters the interaction situation. Each person, through his or her ability to take the role of the other, constructs a preliminary definition of the situation he or she is about to enter. Based on both general knowledge about the type of social setting and the type of people who frequent it and on his or her knowledge about the specific setting and people he or she will encounter, an individual defines the nature of the situation and the role relationships he or she anticipates will be accepted by him- or herself and others during interaction. By considering likely third parties to the interaction, and the perspectives provided by the reference group and by the generalized other, a person is able to relate this preliminary definition to the broader social context. The preliminary definition of the situation is related to the goals a person intends to achieve in the interaction and is the basis for the person's plans for how to act in the situation.

Once the interaction begins, the actions of each person indicate to the others the nature of his or her definition of the situation. Both the role relationships defined in an interaction and the more general situated identity each person is perceived to have define normatively sanctioned obligations for each participant. These affect both what a person will be expected to do and how he or she will be treated by others, and are of considerable strategic importance. Each person will try to determine the attitude and intentions of the others. At the same time an individual will attempt to control his or her own actions so that they communicate a favorable definition of him- or herself to others. Often, the preliminary definitions of the situation held by the various people in an interaction are similar enough so that no difficulties arise. Each person is able to proceed with his or her original plans, receiving the anticipated cooperation from others. In other situations, the preliminary definitions held by the various people are not compatible. Sometimes the interaction is simply terminated. Alternatively, the people involved may negotiate a compromise definition of the situation, or working consensus. The role relationships defined by the working consensus often include people who are not present in the interaction. Thus the working consensus is a definition of a broad social reality, not merely of the interaction. In the negotiations, each person will consider the perspectives of the likely third parties to the interaction, the reference group, and the generalized other in evaluating whether the compromise is acceptable. These broader social considerations provide a mechanism through which the interaction can be coordinated with other activities in the social system. At the same time, when the working consensus is a modification of original expectations, these considerations exert social control over the process of social change. Only those changes are accepted which, in the beliefs of those involved, will be compatible with social arrangements beyond the immediate interaction.

In this view the interpretive process, and especially negotiating the social reality, make each interaction the occasion for the socialization of its participants. Each person learns what is expected of him or her and what he or she can expect from others during the interaction at the same time as the person begins to perform those obligations.

Suggested Readings

Drawing on theatrical performances as a metaphor, discussions of how meanings are negotiated in social interaction are frequently cast in terms of a dramaturgical model. Many interesting studies have been collected under the title *Life as Theater* (ed. D. Brissett and C. Edgley, Aldine, Chicago, 1975). A less-focused collection by J. Manis and B. Meltzer includes a variety of excellent studies from interactionist perspectives. This book (*Symbolic Interaction,* Allyn and Bacon, Boston, 1972) is suitable for browsing in or as a starting point for research on many specific topics addressed from an interactionist perspective. Erving Goffman's *Presentation of Self in Everyday Life* (Anchor, Garden City, N.Y., 1959) is already recognized as a classic study. It is beautifully written, not too long, and has obvious relevance to everyday situations. Two theoretical resources were especially influential in this chapter, and deserve reading by students who wish to pursue this approach further. Robert Merton's "The Role Set: Problems in Sociological Theory," [*British Journal of Sociology,* 8 (June 1957), 106–120] is not often associated with interactionist approaches to social psychology, nonetheless it has been utilized by many interactionists, and very explicitly by William Goode, "A Theory of Role Strain," [*American Sociological Review,* 25 (1960), 483–496]. In this chapter we discussed the bargain struck by the multiple interested parties to an interaction. A concrete description of a factory setting [J. Bensman and I. Gerver, "Crime and Punishment in the Factory," *American Sociological Review,* 28 (August 1963), 588–598] provides an illustration of treating role bargains in terms of the diverse interests of many interested parties.

Chapter 4

Some Problems of
Theory and Method

Traditionally, science means "the advancement of our understanding of
the way in which the observable world works, the development of logical,
integrated and self-consistent descriptions of why and how such and such
individual happenings occur, why apples fall from trees, why they are
coloured red and green, why they are good to eat." [1] Science has greatly

[1] Hilary Rose and Steven Rose, *Science and Society,* Penguin, Baltimore, 1969, p. 1.

enlarged our understanding of our world, but there is a great deal more to learn. We may know a lot about apples, but we still have not resolved a host of problems, ranging from the nature of the universe to the nature of material being to why a rattlesnake can detect temperature differentials as small as 0.001° C. Moreover, there are disagreements among scientists on a number of points; astronomers differ over the nature of the universe and physicists differ over the nature of matter. In other words, to call a discipline a "science" does not mean that all the questions have been answered and all the problems resolved.

In like manner, social science seeks to advance our understanding of social life and individual behavior. And while we have learned a great deal, there are many remaining questions and problems. All science—physical and social—is a developing enterprise, and our understanding grows only through persistent efforts in the face of trial and error. In this chapter we want to look at some of the questions and problems that pertain to social psychology. They are applicable to all social psychological perspectives, but we shall address them primarily from the point of view of symbolic interactionism. They involve both theory and method, and they reflect both debates between differing social psychological perspectives and questions raised by students.

Theoretical Problems

CONCEPTUAL CLARITY

Are the concepts used in the perspective precise and clear? If concepts are to be useful, their meaning must not be clouded by ambiguities. Thus, in Chapter 2 we gave considerable attention to the definition of concepts. But why was such a chapter necessary? Why is there lack of clarity after over half a century of work? Ambiguities can arise in a number of ways, and there are at least four reasons why the concepts of symbolic interactionism may not be clear: the concepts may be imprecisely defined by researchers or theoreticians; there may be a lack of consensus, with various definitions being offered by differing scholars; the perspective may be contrary to common sense thinking; and a certain amount of imprecision may be intentional.

Imprecise definitions. Mead has been faulted at this point. Meltzer, for example, argues that concepts such as "impulse," "meaning," "mind," the "I," "self," and others are "somewhat vague and 'fuzzy,' necessitating an 'intuitive' grasp of their meaning."[2] Mead's imprecision is not as

[2] Bernard N. Meltzer, "Mead's Social Psychology," in *Symbolic Interaction,* ed. Jerome G. Manis and Bernard N. Meltzer, Allyn and Bacon, Boston, 1967, pp. 20–22.

troublesome as it might first appear, since concepts are necessarily refined through research and further theoretical work. The very imprecision of the initial formulator can be a stimulus to research, to additional thought by other minds, to varied kinds of research, and to subsequent conceptual refinements. Indeed, it would have been remarkable if such a novel and complex set of ideas had been more precise when they were initially formulated.

An imprecise concept catches a portion of a terribly complex world and allows us to think a bit more about, and perhaps to research somewhat, that world. This is not merely an apology for our inability to be more precise. As noted above, in the physical sciences there is also ambiguity and conflict of perspectives. Dalton quotes a theoretical physicist: "My own pet notion is that in the world of human thought, and in physical science particularly, the most important and most fruitful concepts are those to which it is impossible to attach a well-defined meaning." [3] The concept of "energy" is an example; though the concept has never been defined with any precision, it has proven most useful and is amenable to measurement.

Thus, imprecise definitions of concepts may reflect the state of our knowledge of a complex world rather than careless work. Furthermore, concepts are sharpened as they are used for research. If Mead was imprecise, it was in part because his contribution was a theoretical perspective rather than a body of research. The imprecision does not negate the value of his contribution, any more than the imprecise nature of the concept of energy negates the conclusion of theoretical physicists.

Differing definitions.   A more serious problem is the lack of clarity due to varied definitions by differing scholars. The lack of consensus about conceptual definitions can leave us in a fragmented and confused state. Undeniably, symbolic interactionism has suffered from this problem. For example, as pointed out in Chapter 2, the important concept of role-taking has been used to mean role-playing, empathy, and identification. We will briefly note two pieces of research that employed role-taking to mean something other than what Mead meant by it.

First, an experiment in "role-taking" that involved boys and girls acting out situations actually dealt with playing at roles rather than role-taking.[4]

---

[3] H. A. Kramera, as quoted by Melville Dalton, "Preconceptions and Methods in Men Who Manage," in *Sociologists At Work,* ed. Phillip E. Hammon, Anchor Books, Garden City, N.Y., 1967, p. 67.

[4] James C. Brown, "An Experiment in Role-Taking," *American Sociological Review,* 17 (November 1952), 587–597. It will be recalled that in Chapter 2 we defined "role-taking" as "the process whereby an individual imaginatively constructs the attitudes of the other, and thus anticipates the behavior of the other." Playing at roles requires role-taking ability but is an attempt to actually simulate the behavior of the other rather than to anticipate it in order to construct one's own behavior.

In the experiment boys and girls were asked to act out situations such as the following: four boys and girls are taking a car trip when a tire blows out. What happens? Who does what? Clearly, the experiment focuses on playing at roles, although role-taking capacity is a prerequisite for the ability to play at roles.

A second example is an experiment on "couple role-taking" in which husbands and wives were exposed to a series of contrived situations involving conflict.[5] Four alternatives were offered for resolving the dilemma faced by the couples; these alternatives presumably required each subject to either take the role of the other or to refrain from role-taking. For example, in a situation in which a new baby wakes up a number of times during the night, the husband was offered the following four alternatives: (1) it is the wife's responsibility to get up; (2) although the wife is tired, it's more important for the husband to get his sleep; (3) although the husband needs the sleep badly, the wife is also tired, so each should get up half of the time; and (4) the husband would get up half of the times because he wants to help his wife as much as possible. Such a test measures empathy rather than role-taking per se; it could be utilized to measure what we have called synesic role-taking, but it is not strictly a measure of basic role-taking. Again, role-taking was undoubtedly involved in deciding among alternatives. But if a husband decided that it was his wife's responsibility to get up, we cannot conclude that he failed to take the role of his wife. He may have correctly taken her role, but still have given priority to his own needs.

These examples point up a serious problem—the lack of consensus regarding the meaning of important concepts. Nevertheless, it is not a problem unique to symbolic interactionism. In social psychology generally there has been, and is, considerable diversity of definitions. Long ago Strauss pointed out that while the concept of attitude was widely acknowledged to be significant and useful, the definitions varied considerably.[6] He cited definitions which referred to attitudes as overt behavior of a particular kind, as a type of neurological action, as a combination of neurological action and behavior involving meaning, and as a process of individual consciousness. More recently, the important and widely used concept of "role" was noted to have three somewhat differing meanings.[7] In one, called "prescribed role," the concept refers to a set of social expectations. In another, called "subjective role," the concept refers to the individual's

[5] Jack V. Buerkle and Robin F. Badgley, "Couple Role-Taking: The Yale Marital Interaction Battery," *Marriage and Family Living,* 21 (February 1959), 53–58.

[6] Anselm Strauss, "The Concept of Attitude in Social Psychology," *The Journal of Psychology,* 19 (April 1945), 329–339.

[7] Morton Deutsch and Robert M. Krauss, *Theories in Social Psychology,* Basic Books, New York, 1965, p. 175.

perception of expectations related to his position. In the third, called "enacted role," the concept means overt behavior which occurs during interaction. These are useful refinements of the concept, of course, but unfortunately various authors still merely use the term "role" to refer to one or more of the three meanings. Even in the relatively concrete and explicitly experimental branch of social psychology, similar problems arise. "Cognitive dissonance," one of the more prominent concepts in the field, has been defined as a drive to reduce disagreement among contradictory ideas; as a behavioral response to perceived inconsistency in one's own behavior; and as the result of certain kinds of reinforcement schedules that occur at the infrahuman as well as the human level.[8]

Such variations in conceptualization can be problematic for a developing social science. They make comparison of studies difficult, and may lead to the conclusion that different researchers are coming to contradictory conclusions when they are only using diverse definitions of the same concept.

Concepts and common sense.   A third reason for the lack of clarity in symbolic interactionist concepts is that much of the perspective is contrary to common sense notions and common sense modes of thinking. Westerners tend to think in terms of what Whitehead called "simple location," viewing all phenomena as more or less fixed entities in time and space. In this perspective, each entity—whether a human, a group, or a physical object—has its own distinguishing properties independently of any other entity. But symbolic interactionism shares with process and dialectical philosophy the notion that entities must be understood in terms of their relationships. Thus, for example, we cannot understand why an individual behaves as he or she does if we consider only his or her personal characteristics ("intelligent," "shy," "ambitious," and so forth). As the last chapters amply illustrate, individuals behave as they do because of their relationships with others and because of their interaction with others in specific situations.

Intentional imprecision.   While at least some precise definitions may be ultimately desirable, they can also be an impediment to fruitful research. Thus, Blumer has argued that the insistence on definitive concepts and "the quest for exact data and their relations is to turn away from the problems of the field." [9] What we need is a "working relation" between concepts and

---

[8] See, respectively: Leon Festinger, *A Theory of Cognitive Dissonance,* University Press, Stanford, 1957; Daryl J. Bem, "Self-Perception: An Alternative Interpretation of Cognitive Dissonance Phenomena," *Psychological Review,* 74 (May 1967), 183–200; and Douglas H. Lawrence and Leon Festinger, *Deterrents and Reinforcement,* University Press, Stanford, 1962.

[9] Herbert Blumer, "The Problem of the Concept in Social Psychology," *American Journal of Sociology,* 45 (March 1940), 709.

empirical observations such that the concepts are checked by the empirical observations while the latter are "ordered anew" by the former. The reason that concepts are vague, Blumer asserts, is that many of our observations of human behavior are matters of judgment and inference. The study of the empirical social world demands therefore an approach that is flexible. This is achieved by the use of "sensitizing concepts," which do not aim at precise definition but which provide us with "a general sense of reference and guidance in approaching empirical instances." [10] Precise concepts are "prescriptions" of what we are to observe, while sensitizing concepts merely offer directions along which we are to look. Through the use of such sensitizing concepts, there is an ongoing modification of theory and a sharpening of the conceptualizations, along with a growing understanding of the empirical world.

In sum, we need to strike a middle ground between offering concepts which are so precise as to rigidly channel research and the interpretations of research, and those which are so imprecise as to offer no directives at all. Concepts should be our tools, not our masters. They should provide directives without blinding us to alternatives or suppressing creativity in empirical research.

ACCOUNTING FOR STRUCTURAL VARIABLES

A second question which must be answered by any social psychological perspective is, how is the social structure handled? Are there not such things as group differences in power and property which are significant for human behavior? Symbolic interactionists have acknowledged "society" as important for our understanding; nevertheless, minimal attention has been paid to structural variables. In part, this is rooted in the nature of the perspective. Unlike Marx and other structuralists, Mead did not begin with a model of social order and identify the consequences of that order for behavior. Rather, he began at the level of interaction and tried to show how social order emerges from that interaction. Can, then, both micro and macro processes be accounted for? Can any social psychological perspective do justice both to the impact of the social structure and to the importance of interaction? Certainly both are important, but the former is difficult to incorporate into social psychology. Perhaps future theoretical developments will more satisfactorily link together the various levels of human existence; at present, structural variables tend to be neglected in social psychology generally and symbolic interactionism in particular.

Having said all of the above, we must qualify the notion of inadequate treatment of structural variables. Specifically, structural variables are to

[10] Herbert Blumer, "What Is Wrong With Social Theory?" *American Sociological Review,* 19 (February 1954), 7.

some extent accounted for both in the theory of symbolic interactionism and in the work of symbolic interactionists. The accounting is less than satisfactory to structuralists, but it is present.

Theory and structure. First, with respect to the theory itself, symbolic interactionism takes the structure as problematic rather than as given. The structure is continually being modified through interaction as well as continually providing the context in which that interaction occurs. In other words, there is a dialectical process involving structure and interactants, with each being influenced by the other, and with the outcome being an altered structure and changed modes of interaction. For example, the power structure in the United States once set a specific context for black-white interaction, namely, one in which blacks were required to be subservient. Over time, an increasing number of blacks defined such interaction as illegitimate. Various interaction experiences supported their new definition and also helped alter the self-concepts of blacks. These changes, in turn, legitimated new modes of interaction, in which blacks were equal to whites. Meantime, certain structural changes were also occurring, including a number of important legal changes (largely the result of work by the NAACP). The power structure still sets the context for interaction, but the structure is much different from what it was and therefore sets a quite different context.

The process has been more complex than the above brief description would indicate, of course. But the point is that modes of interaction between the races and the power structure of the society have been characterized over time by reciprocal influence and by change. The structure is problematic in another sense—there is no uniform and automatic impact of structural variables upon individual behavior. Individuals always define situations, and definitions will vary in the same situation. Thus, while some blacks in earlier years defined the white power dominance as both proper and unassailable, others defined it as illegitimate. Had this not been true, the structure would have remained unchanged, and black-white modes of interaction would still be characterized by the subservience of the former. But, as Blumer has emphasized (see Chapter 9), the power structure was altered through the emergence of a collective definition of racism as illegitimate.

A second way in which attention is directed to the social structure is the symbolic interactionist view of social control. Consider the following hypothetical analysis.[11] A coal miner in Appalachia is impoverished be-

---

[11] Shibutani's discussion of the conditions under which rumors flourish, the ways in which they develop, and the uses to which they are put supports this hypothetical analysis. See Tamotsu Shibutani, *Improvised News,* Bobbs-Merrill, Indianapolis, 1966.

cause the coal mine shut down and no other kind of work is available in the area. There are a number of conceivable responses he might make to this situation. He might adapt to it by accepting his poverty as in some sense legitimate and continuing to eke out an existence in the area. Or he might leave the area to seek employment. Or he might attempt to create opportunities in his area by developing local crafts or by exploiting local resources. Or he might become part of a radical movement designed to change the political and economic system of the nation, by revolution if necessary. Social control means that, whatever else he does, he will not choose the latter, for the latter alternative would mean that the social order no longer constrained his behavior in a way that helped maintain the order. At the same time, social control is not a deterministic notion; one of the implications is that certain *logically* possible alternatives will likely be rejected.

But how does the community exercise such control? Let us assume that the man initially defines his situation of deprivation as one that oppresses but perplexes him. He sees himself as powerless, yet is unwilling to acquiesce to the situation. In part, his sense of powerlessness stems from his inability to understand why the mine closed, why other kinds of industry cannot be developed, and what if any alternatives he has. His initial response then is likely to be a discussion of the situation with others who are similarly affected. In the course of their interaction, the definition of the situation is sharpened. The man now understands that a competitive economic system required the shutdown of the mine; that the demands of the market make it unlikely that any new industry will be established; and that his basic alternatives are to seek employment elsewhere or to remain in his home, endure his impoverishment, and cling to the meager hope that some unforeseen events will alter his situation.

The man does not seriously consider the alternative of a radical movement for a number of reasons. First, he conceives of himself as a loyal American, who will not turn against his country simply because he has come upon hard times. Second, neither he nor his fellow sufferers fault the economic system or the government for their plight; they define the situation in terms of bad luck, the breaks of a game which is essentially a sound game. Third, this definition is corroborated by all those with whom the man interacts and those whom he considers important for assessing the situation. His family agrees with the general community viewpoint of the basic soundness of the system. The newspapers reflect the fact that other players in the game are coming out ahead, and that both individuals and groups are concerned about the plight of the poor. The minister assures him that God knows and understands the situation and will give them all the grace to endure their tribulation. Even the mine owners show the man their sense of solidarity with him and their commitment to fair play in the game, by allowing him to continue to live in the company-owned shack that he calls his home.

In other words, the man may ultimately leave the community or may vainly spend his days in squalor, hoping for something to happen that will rescue him. But he will probably not become a rebel. For the way he thinks of himself, the way in which he and his associates have collectively defined their situation, and the response to his situation from individuals and groups whom he defines as significant all combine to minimize the possibility of rebellion.

A structuralist might look at this same situation and analyze it in terms of a capitalistic system that exploits the many for the benefit of the few and that maintains the power of the few by the imposition of an ideology that legitimates the system. He or she might deny the importance of self-concepts or definitions of the situation or reference groups, arguing that the crux of the matter is the structure of the system in which human beings are systematically oppressed. But as we have tried to show, it is precisely such structural variables which are incorporated into the individual and which become controls over his or her behavior. We have identified the social psychological processes through which the social structure is articulated in individuals and in community life. Thus, social control in the People's Republic of China would lead to quite different consequences for the miner. The man might conceive of himself as one who loyally carries on revolution. He and his fellows would define a situation in which some members of the society lived in squalor as an intolerable social aberration. And his community, the mass media, and his country's leaders would applaud his efforts to carry on the revolution so that poverty is eliminated.

In both cases, the same social psychological processes are at work, though the outcomes would be quite different because of the diverse structural contexts in which they occur. As we pointed out in Chapter 3, there are variations from situation to situation, though the interpretive process remains substantially the same. In like manner, there are variations from society to society, though the social psychological processes remain the same. If symbolic interactionists have been remiss in failing to identify the structural contexts and to note the significance of those contexts, they are nevertheless not negated by the perspective, and a full understanding of social life cannot be gained without them.[12]

---

[12] A partial exception to this failure is Goffman's lengthy discussion of the nature of the structural arrangements characteristic of total institutions and their effects on the self-perceptions of the inmates, on the opportunities for and nature of self-presentation within them, and on the professional activities of the staff. See Erving Goffman, *Asylums,* Garden City, N.Y., Anchor Books, 1961. Goffman has consistently maintained that the nature of the occasion is a crucial variable in the definitions

Analysis and social structure.   Symbolic interactionists have used social structural variables as both independent and dependent variables. Examples of the former are provided by Blumer's analysis of prejudice and by Schatzman and Strauss' analysis of class variations in modes of communication. We will look briefly at each of these. First, as noted above, some critics have alleged that the perspective is incapable of adequately dealing with structural variables. Zeitlin has made this charge with specific reference to Blumer, arguing that the latter's interpretation of Mead "denies altogether social relationships, social structure, and social organization. Society, from this standpoint, becomes a plurality of disembodied, unconstrained selves floating about in amorphous situations." [13] But an examination of Blumer's work shows this charge to be false, and his analysis of prejudice is one good example.

In analyzing the question of racial prejudice, Blumer stressed the fact that such prejudice cannot be understood as simply as a set of feelings possessed by members of one group towards members of another group, but rather as rooted in a sense of group position.[14] Prejudice is a group rather than individual phenomenon, arising out of a collective process in which various racial groups develop images of themselves and of other racial groups. Prejudicial images will develop and will be most serious in a situation where two groups are part of the same society, one of the groups has a subordinate status, and the subordinate group is defined as threatening by the dominant group. The greater the threat is perceived to be, the greater the prejudice likely to develop.[15]

Furthermore, racial prejudice must be understood as the outcome of a historical process. Interaction between the two groups occurs in the context of "claims, opportunities and advantages" which help to shape the developing images. As members of the two groups struggle for prestige, power, and other desired goals, the sense of group position emerges. Depending upon the particular opportunities and other factors involved, the sense of group position may become acute or may atrophy, may become deeply rooted or tenuous, may become sharply clear or remain vague. In

---

of the situation that will develop within it. Nevertheless, Goffman does not go beyond the organizational structure and relate his analysis to the larger societal structure. This, of course, was not his purpose, and, as we have tried to stress, further analysis would not negate the work that Goffman has done, it would simply complete the analysis by showing the significance of all of the levels from the interpersonal to the societal.

[13] Irving M. Zeitlin, *Rethinking Sociology: A Critique of Contemporary Theory,* Appleton-Century-Crofts, New York, 1973, p. 218.

[14] Herbert Blumer, "Race Prejudice as a Sense of Group Position," *The Pacific Sociological Review,* 1 (Spring 1958), 3–7.

[15] Herbert Blumer, "The Nature of Race Prejudice," *Social Process in Hawaii,* 5 (1939), 11–20.

any case, it is the outcome of "a running process in which the dominant racial group is led to define and redefine the subordinate racial group and the relations between them." [16] While Blumer has not himself analyzed empirical situations of prejudice along the lines he suggests, his theoretical analysis clearly demands a structural and historical approach to the problem of prejudice. The distribution of power, the struggle for desired goods, and the structure of opportunities are, among others, factors which enter into the development of the sense of group position.

A second example of social structural variables being used as independent factors is Schatzman and Strauss' analysis of class variations in modes of communication. [17] The researchers interviewed individuals in a number of communities which had been struck by tornadoes. Using income and education as measures of social class, significant class differences were noted in ability to communicate with interviewers. The differences were more than variations in intelligibility or grammatical correctness or extensiveness of vocabulary. For example, there were differences in respondents' ability to take the listener's role, with lower-class respondents typically offering descriptions as seen through their own eyes; the lower-class respondents did not "assume the role of another toward still others, except occasionally in an implicit fashion." [18] Additional important class differentials were observed; the point of importance here is that a structural variable was used as the independent variable in a symbolic interactionist analysis.

Aspects of the social structure can also serve as dependent variables in symbolic interactionist analyses. Hall has shown how the perspective can be fruitfully employed to analyze politics. [19] In particular, he examines one of the most important facets of any political analysis—the processes of power. Among the important mechanisms of power are the control of the flow of information and the symbolic mobilization of support. These are forms of "political impression management," the former referring to "backstage behaviors involving insulation, concealment, secrecy, structuring and planning" and the latter involving "public performances of persuasion." [20]

Again, our purpose is not to examine in detail these efforts, but to indicate that symbolic interactionism does not negate the importance of structural variables. Both the theory itself and the studies pursued by

[16] Blumer, "Race Prejudice as a Sense of Group Position," p. 5.
[17] Leonard Schatzman and Anselm Strauss, "Social Class and Modes of Communication," *American Journal of Sociology,* 60 (January 1955), 329–338.
[18] *Ibid.,* p. 331.
[19] Peter M. Hall, "A Symbolic Interactionist Analysis of Politics," *Sociological Inquiry,* 42, No. 3–4 (1972), 35–75.
[20] *Ibid.,* p. 54.

symbolic interactionists have taken aspects of the social structure into account, treating those aspects both as independent and dependent variables.

ARTICULATION WITH EMPIRICAL EVIDENCE

There are two problems that arise with respect to empirical evidence. One concerns the testability of the theory: any theory is worthless if it cannot be subjected to empirical testing. The second problem relates to empirical evidence: how does the theory square with the evidence of empirical studies (including those based on other theories)? We will examine each of these problems in turn.

Testability. As texts on theory construction and methods will point out, theories may be evaluated by, among other things, the extent to which they yield testable hypotheses. It does no good to assert that the self arises out of the process of interaction if there is no way to test that proposition. The most common criticism of symbolic interactionism in this respect involves concepts such as the "I" that are by definition untestable. But the "I" is an important concept which cannot be rejected in spite of its untestability. For it emphasizes a certain indeterminacy, the fact that any statements we make about human behavior are probabilistic rather than deterministic. The interaction process, as we have stressed, is formative; human behavior cannot be totally predictable.

This is not to say that interaction is capricious, or that the "I" can result in infinite variations. Indeed, we may confidently make certain predictions about human behavior as long as we keep in mind that our predictions are probabilistic. For there are structural constraints and culture tendencies such that an individual is likely to define situations in particular ways, act on the basis of consensual values, and so forth. The fact that a theory incorporates indeterminacy does not make it useless for anticipating human behavior or the course of social life. This is well illustrated by Blumer's work on race relations. As Killian points out, Blumer's 1956 article on desegregation "foresaw that efforts to bring about desegregation would lead to a tremendous power struggle, not to a gradual diminution of rapid prejudice." [21] In 1965, when considerable progress appeared to have been made in breaking down southern desegregation, Blumer again predicted accurately the course of subsequent events. He observed that more rather than less intense struggles would result as blacks sought to penetrate deeper and deeper into the "series of ramparts"

---

[21] Lewis M. Killian, "Herbert Blumer's Contributions to Race Relations," in *Human Nature and Collective Behavior,* ed. Tamotsu Shibutani, Prentice-Hall, Englewood Cliffs, N.J., 1970, p. 188.

that comprise the "color line." [22]   This, incidentally, is another example of the way in which the insights of symbolic interactionism may be applied to macro-sociological phenomena. We shall discuss Blumer's ideas about the race problem in more detail in Chapter 9; the point here is that adherence to a theory that incorporates indeterminacy does not negate one's ability to correctly anticipate the probable course of human behavior.

Thus, a theory's value is not dependent upon deterministic propositions. And the fact that a theory contains untestable elements does not prevent us from utilizing the testable notions, keeping in mind that we are always testing probabilistic rather than deterministic propositions. Can symbolic interaction, then, generate testable hypotheses? Can its conceptual apparatus be utilized for fruitful empirical research? A considerable amount of work shows that the theory is capable of generating both numerous and highly interesting hypotheses which incorporate its concepts and which can be empirically tested.

For example, in an effort to clarify the concept of role-taking and demonstrate its empirical utility, Lauer and Boardman suggest twenty-three testable propositions involving various relationships. [23]   Among others, they hypothesize that the greater the range of the symbol system, the greater the role-taking capacity; the more accurate the role-taking in a common-goal situation, the greater the consensus in that situation; and the more accurate the role-taking, the greater the potential for manipulation. Earlier, two experiments designed to test the concept of role-taking were reported by O'Toole and Dubin. [24]   In one experiment mothers were observed while feeding their babies. The researchers point out that mothers often may be seen opening their mouths as they put the spoon up to the baby's mouth. If this is role-taking behavior, a mother is responding to her own gestures from the perspective of the baby—she is taking the baby's role. An alternative explanation is based upon imitation —either the mother is trying to induce the baby to imitate her or she is imitating the baby's gesture. In either case, there should be a definite sequence observed; in the former instance the mother would open her mouth first, and in the latter the baby would open its mouth first. On the basis of 1,013 feeding sequences, the researchers concluded that 55 percent of the feeding episodes involved role-taking rather than imitation.

[22] Herbert Blumer, "The Future of the Color Line," in *The South in Continuity and Change,* ed. John C. McKinney and Edgar T. Thompson, Duke, Durham, 1965, p. 323.

[23] Robert H. Lauer and Linda Boardman, "Role-Taking: Theory, Typology, and Propositions," *Sociology and Social Research,* 55 (January 1971), 137–148.

[24] Richard O'Toole and Robert Dubin, "Baby Feeding and Body Sway: An Experiment in George Herbert Mead's 'Taking the Role of the Other,'" *Journal of Personality and Social Psychology,* 10 (September 1968), 59–65.

The role-taking explanation accounted for a majority of the observed behavior and was a more powerful explanation than the imitation model.

The second experiment involved body sway. The subjects watched an actor bend over a table and reach for a package of cigarettes that were just beyond his grasp. The actor performed this movement from each side of the table. If the observing subject took the role of the actor, he or she would tend to bend forward himself each time. If the subject imitated the actor, he or she would bend forward, backward, to the left, and to the right on successive episodes. In other words, role-taking would involve the subject in making the same movements as the actor, while imitation would involve the subject in mirror-image movements of those of the actor. Once again, role-taking explained most of the behavior, accounting for 52 to 56 percent of all body sway. Only 2.5 to 17.9 percent of the subjects' movements could be explained on the basis of the imitation model.

A final example of the way in which symbolic interactionism can stimulate useful research is provided by the work of Stryker in the area of the family. In one study, Stryker hypothesized that "the adjustment of the individual is a function of the accuracy with which he can take the role of the other(s) implicated with him in some social situation." [25] The hypothesis was tested by measuring role-taking and adjustment between parents and their children. The hypothesis was rejected on the basis of the evidence; in fact, parents who were poorer role-takers were better adjusted with their children. As Stryker noted, this does not negate Mead's point that role-taking is basic to the process of adapting one's behavior with others, but it does raise the question of the extent to which role-taking leads to more satisfaction or happiness. Thus, some important findings about family processes were uncovered through an effort to apply the symbolic interactionist perspective to the analysis.

Empirical challenges. Just as symbolic interactionism challenges other perspectives, the work of others may appear to challenge or invalidate symbolic interactionism at various points. We will look at two such pieces of work. The first is Rheingold's claim that the infant is a social creature. [26] This, of course, challenges not only symbolic interactionism but a good many other social psychological perspectives. The statements that the infant "begins life as a social organism," that he or she "behaves in a

[25] Sheldon Stryker, "Role-Taking Accuracy and Adjustment," in *Symbolic Interaction,* ed. Jerome G. Manis and Bernard N. Meltzer, Allyn and Bacon, Boston, 1967, p. 482.

[26] Harriet L. Rheingold, "The Social and Socializing Infant," in *Handbook of Socialization Theory and Research,* ed. David A. Goslin, Rand McNally, Chicago, 1969, pp. 779–790.

social fashion" during the first year of life, and that he or she "socializes others more than he is socialized" [27] is contrary to much of the assumptions and the work done in the area of socialization. A closer examination of Rheingold's argument, however, shows that it does not conflict as much with others as it first appears to do.

In the first place, she argues that the newborn infant is a social organism because it is born into and can only survive in a social environment. In other words, at this point she is using "social" in a somewhat different fashion from that in which symbolic interactionists employ it; we would in no way disagree that the newborn infant is immediately a part of a social environment and that its very existence depends upon that environment. Nevertheless, that does not justify the assertion that the infant is social, for the latter term implies meaningful participation in the environment. That is, Rheingold employs the term "social" to mean existing in and affecting a social environment. Symbolic interactionists employ the term to mean symbolic participation in a social environment.

This difference is accentuated by Rheingold's treatment of the infant's "social" behavior. The infant, she points out, responds to the stimuli presented by others, may prolong such stimulation from others, and may even initiate interaction through such mechanisms as crying. But again, this is not symbolic behavior; it is little more than animals do in their ininteraction with humans. The same point may be made with respect to the way in which infants socialize their parents. Through crying and smiling, the infant "modulates, tempers, regulates, and refines" the parents' behavior.[28] A pet may do the same thing through its own demands for eating, drinking, going outside to relieve itself or search the neighborhood, and caressing.

In sum, we would not disagree with the fact that the infant is an important part of its social environment, affecting others by its very presence. Our claim that the infant is asocial, and becomes capable of participating in its environment only through the process of socialization, simply means that we define "social" differently from Rheingold. To say that the infant *becomes* rather than *is* a social creature is to say that being social means carrying on symbolic interaction.

The second type of empirical work that appears to challenge symbolic interaction is that involving the training of chimpanzees to use language. We have argued previously that symbolic interactionism views language as a significant differentiating factor, clearly making human existence qualitatively different from the infrahuman world. Some recent experi-

---

[27] *Ibid.,* p. 780.
[28] *Ibid.,* p. 785.

ments with chimpanzees have produced striking results, however, that may appear to make the human-infrahuman gap less significant than we have maintained.

For example, one set of experiments with a two-and-one-half-year-old chimp by the name of Lana concluded that the animal was able to effectively read word-characters which constituted the beginnings of sentences and to finish the sentence in order to receive a reward or to reject the sentence.[29] In the first experiment, Lana pressed certain keys on a console in order to receive various rewards; she then learned to precede each request with "please" and complete it with "period"; then she learned increasingly complex procedures until she could select and depress the proper keys in the proper order even with the keys randomly placed among others on a console. Further experiments employed variations in procedure, but taken together they show that the chimp "accurately perceives Yerkish words, reads their serial order, and discriminates whether they can or cannot be completed in order to obtain the various incentives."[30] Furthermore, claim the authors, if we define typewriting as the succesful completion of the start of a valid sentence, then the chimp can be said to have learned to both read and write.

To what extent do such experiments deny the significant differences which we have posited between human and infrahuman behavior? It should be immediately evident that the chimpanzees are still not dealing with abstractions; even the series of word-characters used by the chimp has a single, concrete referent. Chimpanzees can learn to use human words, but not in the same sense that humans use them. Chimpanzees can even learn the rudiments of syntax and can invent short sentences of their own. But they cannot employ words as symbols; the word-characters they use do not comprise a set of shared meanings, and they do not enable the animal to incorporate the distant past and future into its behavior. As one study of animal communication (including that of the chimpanzees) concludes, there is an "enormous gulf" that still separates human and animal use of words; for the chimpanzee's words "are given to her, and she must use them in a rigid and artificial context. No chimpanzee has demonstrated anything close to the capacity and drive to experiment with language that is possessed by a normal human child."[31] This, we think, succinctly sums up the difference that still exists in spite of the impressive

---

[29] Duane M. Rumbaugh, Timothy V. Gill, and E. C. von Glaserfeld, "Reading and Sentence Completion by a Chimpanzee (Pan)," *Science,* 182 (November 16, 1973), 731–733.

[30] *Ibid.,* p. 733.

[31] Edward O. Wilson, "Animal Communication," *Scientific American,* 227 (September 1972), 60.

achievements of the chimpanzees. Human behavior, we must insist, is qualitatively different from animal behavior, and that qualitative difference is due to the fact that humans are creatures who live in a symbolic world.

ACCOUNTING FOR AFFECTS AND IGNORANCE

There are texts in social psychology which make little or no mention of emotions or affects. Humans are treated as though they acted almost exclusively as cognitive creatures. In fact, Mead gives us an overrational image of man. He tends to minimize the emotional element by noting that for the most part we do not feel the emotions which we arouse in others; our language stimuli call out in ourselves the same cognitive response which we are calling out in others, but we do not normally use those stimuli to call out the same emotional response.[32] To put it explicitly and succinctly: "The essence of the self . . . is cognitive." [33]

Mead's emphasis was on the rational rather than the emotional or the nonrational. This emphasis has been continued by many symbolic interactionists. Blumer points out that there are three lines of meaning in gestures. The gestures: (1) indicates to the other what he or she is expected to do; (2) indicates what the person making it plans to do; and (3) "signifies the joint action that is to arise by the articulation of the acts of both." [34] If there is any breakdown along these three lines of meaning, argues Blumer, "communication is ineffective, interaction is impeded, and the formation of joint action is blocked." [35] This fails to account for that interaction which can continue in what has been called a situation of "pluralistic ignorance"; that is, individuals may continue to interact over time even though there is considerable misunderstanding and/or ignorance about the beliefs and the meaning of the interaction to others. Thus, there is a need to more adequately account for the role of emotions and of ignorance in human behavior.

Emotions and behavior. There have been some efforts to incorporate emotions into symbolic interactionism. In fact, in an early article Blumer examined the role of emotions, though he did not follow up in later works on his initial formulation.[36] In his 1936 article, Blumer remarked that the "affective nature" of social attitudes is normally ignored or minimized.

---

[32] George Herbert Mead, *Mind, Self and Society,* ed.. with an introduction by Charles W. Morris, The University of Chicago Press, Chicago, 1934, pp. 148–149.

[33] *Ibid.,* p. 173.

[34] Herbert Blumer, *Symbolic Interactionism: Perspective and Method,* Prentice-Hall, Englewood Cliffs, N.J., 1969, p. 9.

[35] *Ibid.*

[36] Herbert Blumer, "Social Attitudes and Non-Symbolic Interaction," *Journal of Educational Sociology,* 9 (1936), 515–523.

But feelings cannot be ignored, since they are "intrinsic" to all of our attitudes, and perform important functions: "it is the affective element which ensures the attitude of its vigor, sustains it in the face of attack, and preserves it from change." [37] Another function which such affective components fulfill is to gain attention and create impressions. For they comprise what may be called our expressive behavior, and such behavior exerts influence over the behavior of others. Humans do not react to each other solely on the basis of verbal interchange, but on perceived emotional interchange and various other nonverbal forms of interaction.

Cooley, in fact, argued that a purely cognitive approach to life is rare. "Rationality, in the sense of a patient and open-minded attempt to think out the general problems of life, is, and perhaps always must be, confined to a small minority even of the most intelligent populations." [38] He noted that the creation of imaginary playmates by children reflects their need for something more than muscular or sensory activities; children need to experience personal emotions and sentiments which are released through communication.

Cooley did not, of course, neglect the cognitive aspects of human interaction. In fact, he argued that the imaginations which we have of each other are the "solid facts" of society, and that the observation and interpretation of those imaginations comprise the chief work of sociology. But feeling is inextricably a part, and a most important part, of social life, and Cooley discussed in some detail a number of human emotions such as hostility. "It must always be borne in mind that the self is any idea or system of ideas with which is associated the peculiar appropriative attitude we call self-feeling." [39]

Another effort to deal with the affective component of social life is that of Shibutani, who discusses the role of emotions in interpersonal relations. One point at which emotions enter is when one encounters some kind of blockage to one's goal-oriented behavior.[40] Emotional reactions are one form of tension release when ongoing activity has been interrupted; thus, they enable one to adapt to one's situation.

Emotions are also important in interaction in the form of sentiments. For we do many things that can hardly be considered as strictly rational. Sentiments may alter our rational pursuit of self-interests and may moderate our conformity to group norms. Indeed, the more intimate our knowledge of each other as "unique individuals," according to Shibutani,

---

[37] *Ibid.*, p. 517.

[38] Charles Horton Cooley, *Human Nature and the Social Order,* Scribner, New York, 1902, p. 44.

[39] *Ibid.*, p. 224.

[40] Tamotsu Shibutani, *Society and Personality,* Prentice-Hall, Englewood Cliffs, N.J., 1961, pp. 71–73.

the more we are likely to "make allowances" for each other.[41] For personal obligations develop and interfere with relationships based upon mere duty. As a result, group life is typically characterized by norms which govern sentiments; some kinds of sentiments are encouraged by group norms, while others are discouraged or even prohibited. Such norms illustrate the fact that groups recognize the significance of sentiments in the behavior of group members. The interesting conclusion of this observation is that, if social psychologists have underestimated the importance of feelings in social life, no group or society has! For all social groups have developed norms that regulate, or at least try to regulate, human sentiments.

Some of Goffman's analyses suggest a general procedure for analyzing emotion as, in part, a product of social factors. In several of his studies, emotions are treated as the result of social structural conditions and of definitions of the situation rather than as causes of behavior. For instance, embarrassment is the result of inconsistencies among the individual's roles becoming public in a particular situation.[42] Emotions, both the conjunctive and the disjunctive kinds, result from the contrast between the individual's self-image and the expressed opinion of others in interaction.

The important point here is not to try to synthesize these views or to develop and incorporate a theory of emotions into symbolic interactionism, but to point out that the theory does not preclude such a development in spite of its neglect. We might follow Blumer's lead and show how the affective component of interaction is a parallel phenomenon to symbolic interaction and a buttress to the cognitive component of attitudes. We might try to develop Cooley's insights into the inherent feeling aspect of the self and, therefore, of all human interaction. We might further Shibutani's notions about the ways in which emotions alter interaction. Or we might follow Goffman's lead and explore the social functions of emotions and the way in which emotions reflect structural conditions and the process of interaction. But in any case, the theory is well able to incorporate the emotional component of human life and social interaction.

Ignorance in social life. As noted above, social psychologists have tended to view humans as though they were almost exclusively cognitive creatures. This not only neglects the importance of emotions; it also neglects the importance of nonrational behavior. In symbolic interactionism, for example, it is generally assumed that there is shared understanding

[41] *Ibid.,* p. 400.

[42] Erving Goffman, *Interaction Ritual,* Anchor Books, Garden City, N.Y., 1967, pp. 97–112.

among interactants. This assumption is shared by other social psychologists. Until at least the 1950s, most role theorists assumed that actors in any situation agreed on the expectations attached to each of their roles. It was also assumed that the stability of the social order is dependent upon the accuracy with which roles are perceived; roles themselves were viewed simply as a set of behavioral expectations attached to particular social positions, so that not only the incumbent of the role but others with whom he or she interacted shared a common understanding regarding expected behavior.

But this notion of shared understandings has been challenged by a number of empirical studies which indicate that deception, ignorance, and partial information may characterize certain social relationships. Furthermore, such ignorance may be necessary or desirable for the individuals interacting.[43] For example, a study by Gross and his associates showed that both intra- and interposition consensus may be far less than many role theorists have assumed.[44] Intraposition consensus was defined as agreement among the incumbents of a particular position on the expectations attached to that position. Interposition consensus was defined as agreement between incumbents and others in their role-set on the expectations attached to each of the positions. The particular roles studied were that of school superintendent and school board members. There was more disagreement than agreement on both the intra- and the interposition responses regarding role expectations. Thus, a particular social situation was quite viable in spite of the lack of consensus, the lack of shared understandings, on the part of participants.

Another example is provided by a study of teacher roles conducted by Bruce Biddle and his associates.[45] The researchers found that pupils and parents were often in error about the norms of teachers and school officials, while school officials were often in error about the norms of people in general. Following the suggestion of Robert Merton, this was called a "situation of pluralistic ignorance," and Biddle observed that it may have both positive and negative consequences for social life.[46] We do not yet

[43] Bruce J. Biddle, Howard A. Rosencranz, Edward Tomich, and J. Paschal Twyman, "Shared Inaccuracies in the Role of the Teacher," in *Role Theory: Concepts and Research,* ed. Bruce J. Biddle and Edwin J. Thomas, Wiley, New York, 1966, p. 302.

[44] Neal Gross, Ward S. Mason, and Alexander W. McEachern, *Explorations in Role Analysis: Studies of the School Superintendency Role,* Wiley, New York, 1957.

[45] Biddle, Rosencranz, Tomich, and Twyman, "Shared Inaccuracies in the Role of the Teacher," pp. 302–310.

[46] Bruce J. Biddle, "Roles, Goals, and Value Structures in Organizations," in *New Perspectives in Organization Research,* ed. W. W. Cooper, H. J. Leavitt, and M. W. Shelly II, Wiley, New York, 1964, pp. 169–170.

have sufficient studies nor an adequate theoretical framework, however, for making sound conclusions about the overall consequences of pluralistic ignorance.

Can symbolic interactionism accommodate this phenomenon? We should first point out that the notion of a lack of understanding is not in itself antagonistic to the theory. For instance, in his analysis of fashion, Blumer argues that there is virtually always a lack of awareness on the part of those caught up in the operation of fashion: "What may be primarily response to fashion is seen and interpreted in other ways—chiefly as doing what is believed to be superior practice. The prevalence of such unwitting deception can be considerable." [47] Thus, fashion is one area of social life that generally proceeds apart from utilitarian or rational judgments.

Others have also incorporated ignorance in some manner into their analyses. Goffman's notion of the "back region" is a prime example; in the back region there are obvious contradictions of the impressions fostered by the performers.[48] The audience is kept ignorant of certain aspects of the performance, and this ignorance is an integral part of that performance. Glaser and Strauss bring in the notion of ignorance in their discussion of "awareness contexts." [49] There are four types of such contexts. In the open type, each participant is aware of both the identity of the other and of the way the other views his or her identity. In the closed type, one participant does not know either the other's identity or the other's understanding of his or her identity. In the suspicion type, one of the participants *suspects* the identity of the other or the way the other views his or her identity, or both. In the pretense type, both participants are aware of the identities involved but both pretend to be unaware. These notions are used to analyze interaction between dying patients on the one hand and the family and hospital personnel on the other. Various consequences result depending upon which type of awareness context is maintained in the interaction.

In spite of these efforts, the theory still contains the basic formulation of interaction as outlined by Blumer above—the three lines of meaning which are crucial to interaction and which presuppose shared understandings. Again, our point is not to resolve the issue, but to identify it and to note that various symbolic interactionists have incorporated the notion of ignorance into their work. Thus, the theory can accommodate

[47] Herbert Blumer, "Fashion: From Class Differentiation to Collective Selection," *The Sociological Quarterly,* 10 (Summer 1969), 286.

[48] Erving Goffman, *The Presentation of Self in Everyday Life,* Anchor Books, Garden City, N.Y., 1959, p. 112.

[49] Barney G. Glaser and Anselm L. Strauss, "Awareness Contexts and Social Interaction," *American Sociological Review,* 29 (October 1964), 669–679.

the important phenomenon of ignorance, but the role of ignorance has not yet been systematically worked out.

Problems of Method

There is a saying that one does not try to open clams with a crowbar. In other words, the tools must be appropriate to the task. The chemist must use the test tube, not his or her hand or a wash tub. But what tools are appropriate for the social psychologist? And what methods does he or she employ along with those tools? In this section we shall discuss some of the complex issues and problems regarding social psychological methods of research.

METHOD AND THEORY

First, problems of method are related to the theory. That is, symbolic interactionism makes certain assumptions about the nature of social reality —that reality is process; that social life proceeds in accord with the way in which situations are defined rather than the way in which they are in some sense objectively constituted; and so forth. Whatever problems of method arise, they are related to these assumptions.

Like other researchers, then, symbolic interactionists must employ methods which are congruent with their theoretical perspective. They must also attend to the problems of validity, the extent to which the methods employed are really "getting at" the social reality they are studying.[50] This is one of the major criticisms leveled by Huber, who has argued that symbolic interactionism yields results which reflect the researcher's perspective and the distribution of power among the subjects and in the setting the researcher is studying.[51] In other words, the research is inherently biased by its very nature; it does not give us a valid picture of social reality.

Huber's real concern is with establishing a deductive approach as the proper sociological method. She argues that "the prior construction of logically related propositions is important in science because it gives the researcher a chance to lose the game."[52] On the other hand, in the absence of a "theoretical formulation" the researcher can't lose; any outcome of the research is acceptable.

[50] The question of validity is discussed in somewhat more detail in Norman K. Denzin, "The Methodologies of Symbolic Interaction: A Critical Review of Research Techniques," in *Social Psychology Through Symbolic Interaction*, ed. Gregory P. Stone and Harvey A. Farberman, Ginn-Blaisdell, Waltham, Mass., 1970, pp. 451–452.

[51] Joan Huber, "Symbolic Interaction as a Pragmatic Perspective: The Bias of Emergent Theory," *American Sociological Review*, 38 (April 1973), 274–284.

[52] *Ibid.*, p. 282.

This is a curious argument. Obviously, symbolic interactionists do not begin research without any theoretical formulation. What they sometimes do, as we shall discuss more below, is to begin research without rigidly defined concepts or explicitly formulated hypotheses. But the theory itself provides directives for this approach. Huber's charge of a lack of theoretical formulation apparently means only the lack of precisely defined concepts embedded in explicitly formulated hypotheses. We must point out, however, that such formulation does not guarantee that the results will be unbiased. On the contrary, a considerable amount of social psychological research demonstrates any number of sources of bias even when the researcher begins with carefully constructed hypotheses. We will discuss some of these sources of bias, for they apply to all social psychological research, not merely that of symbolic interactionists; furthermore, they emphasize the point that one does not escape bias simply because one begins research with carefully formulated hypotheses.

BIAS IN RESEARCH

One source of bias is the so-called "Hawthorne effect," which was discovered as a result of research at the Hawthorne plant of Western Electric.[53] The researchers were striving to uncover the conditions that would maximize productivity of factory workers. But every change they tried—increasing or reducing the light, increasing or reducing the wage scale, and so forth—increased group productivity; they had expected the productivity to alternately increase and diminish as they varied the conditions. Ultimately, the researchers concluded that the cause of the increasing productivity was the attention they were paying to the workers rather than the external conditions which they were manipulating. This effect—subjects responding to the mere fact of being the objects of attention rather than to variables manipulated by the researcher—has been called the Hawthorne effect. Thus, one type of bias that can enter research is the presence of the researcher, which may have effects upon the subjects that are hard to differentiate from other effects.

A second type of bias involves "demand characteristics," an effect noted by Martin Orne.[54] Briefly, Orne says that the "totality of cues which convey an experimental hypothesis to the subject become significant de-

---

[53] The Hawthorne studies are described in John Madge, *The Origins of Scientific Sociology,* Free Press, New York, 1962, pp. 162–209; for a methodological discussion of this problem see John Ross and Perry Smith, "Orthodox Experimental Designs," in *Methodology in Social Research,* ed. Hubert M. Blalock, Jr., and Ann B. Blalock, McGraw-Hill, New York, 1968, pp. 340–343.

[54] Martin T. Orne, "On the Social Psychology of the Psychological Experiment: With Particular Reference to Demand Characteristics," *American Psychologist,* 17 (November 1962), 776–783.

terminants of subjects' behavior." Orne calls such cues the "demand characteristics" of the experimental situation. Here again, we have variables which are presumably extraneous to the situation entering in as independent variables. As a result, subjects may respond to perceived cues rather than to experimental variables. Orne suggests that it might profit us to analyze social psychological experiments as a special form of social interaction. Thus, the notion of demand characteristics indicates that in any experiment the subject will ascribe purpose and meaning and will behave on that basis rather than on the basis of the experimental conditions as set by the researcher. This, of course, is precisely the symbolic interactionist view of human behavior; it is interesting that a psychologist concludes that people behave in an experimental situation in the same way that symbolic interactionists claim that people behave generally.

A third source of bias is the so-called "Rosenthal effect." [55] The basic idea of this effect has been known in sociology as the "self-fulfilling prophecy." Actually the phenomena addressed by Robert Rosenthal and his coworkers fall into two categories: experimenter effects and experimenter bias. The "experimenter effect" refers to the fact that different experimenters obtain different results from experiments using comparable subjects. "Experimenter bias" refers to the fact that when an experimenter has an expectation concerning the performance of the subjects, their performance will be influenced in the direction of that expectation. In the laboratory, these effects have been established for both human and infrahuman subjects.

Although both effects are usually studied in the experimental setting, and are usually treated as methodological problems, each has been shown to have social significance as well. The experimenter bias effect was studied in a classroom setting by Rosenthal and Jacobson. [56] Their study showed that the expectations of schoolteachers concerning the intellectual abilities of their students was reflected in the students' measured IQ scores. That is, the performance of the students on tests was influenced by the expectations that the teachers had of that performance. A student who was expected to do poorly tended to get low scores and vice versa. Thus, the experimenter bias effect resembles the commonly observed self-fulfilling prophecy in which our actions bring about the conditions we believed would occur. The experimenter effect has also been demonstrated to influence IQ test scores. Neil Friedman [57] briefly reviews studies con-

[55] Robert Rosenthal, *Experimenter Effects in Behavior Research,* Appleton-Century-Crofts, New York, 1966.

[56] Robert Rosenthal and Lenore Jacobson, *Pygmalion in the Classroom: Teacher Expectations and Pupils' Intellectual Development,* Holt, New York, 1968.

[57] Neil Friedman, *The Social Nature of Psychological Research,* Basic Books, New York, 1967, pp. 114–119.

ducted by a number of researchers over a span of approximately thirty years. These studies show that the race of the examiner is an important factor in the child's IQ test score. Specifically, black children perform better on IQ tests when the examiner is also black. Some of the results also indicate that some phenomenon akin to rapport between the teacher and the child, built up during the interaction in which the test is embedded, is crucial. That is, the effect of race is a reflection of the differences between the way in which black children interact with black and white adults. Work by William Labov on the language abilities of black children supports the interpretation that the character of the interaction is a critical factor in test scores and other measures of intellectual and verbal ability. He documents the position that the interaction between the white adult and black child is perceived as threatening by the child and that the child withdraws from interaction as a strategic device.[58]

Despite the existence of suggestive experimental results, Friedman recognized that there has been little work that attempts to systematically describe how these various results are produced.[59] He himself has applied Goffman's theoretical perspective, starting with the social nature of the experiment, the fact that it is, regardless of the variables involved, a social interaction. Friedman conducted an experiment similar to those of Rosenthal, but, in addition, videotaped the interaction between the experimenters and subjects. This procedure allowed detailed later study of the actual events that occurred during the experiment.

Examination of the videotapes justified a sharp contrast between the methodological ideal of experimentation, called by Friedman the "standardization myth," and the actual conduct of the experimenters and subjects in the experiment. The ideal requires that the experimenter say exactly the same things to each subject, in the same order, and in the same way. Thus, the subjects would be exposed to the same stimulus. In fact, the experimenters do not behave as automatons but rather introduce variations into the experimental routine—both by improvising content not included in the experimental script and by varying the nonverbal aspects of their presentation.[60] These variations are not merely present in the experiment, but also are correlated with variations in experimental results. Friedman's study shows that such diverse factors as the time spent on each segment of the experiment, the number of glances exchanged between the experimenter and the subject, whether the experimenter wears glasses, and the formality of the experimenter's clothes all affect the subjects' perform-

---

[58] William Labov, "The Logic of Nonstandard English," in *The Myth of Cultural Deprivation,* ed. Nell Keddie, Penguin, Baltimore, 1973, pp. 21–66.

[59] Friedman, p. 32.

[60] *Ibid.,* pp. 71–109.

ance in the experiment.[61] These results are not peculiar to Friedman's study; similar findings have subsequently been reported by Rosenthal.[62]

These findings indicate that the appearance of the experimenter and the content and manner of his or her communications with the subjects affects their responses to the questions. Friedman's analysis goes further. He observed that the variations are not random, but are rather related to relationships between the experimenter and subject other than that officially prescribed by the experiment. For example, terms of address are used that emphasize age differences between the subject and experimenter.[63] The single male experimenter may express interest in female subjects, and vice versa, by inserting unprogrammed remarks into the discussion or by the nonverbal reaction to discovering her marital status. Friedman observes that these variations sacrificing perfect performance of one role in favor of the influence of other roles is an excellent example of role distance.[64]

Friedman adopts the view that the experimenter and the subject must be conceived as creative interactants. Each assesses the appearance and communication of the other and fashions his or her own line of action accordingly. The experimenter does this by embroidering the programmed experimental role to suit the occasion, the subject by being "biased." In so doing, each responds to the other in terms of multiple role relationships between them and creates expectancies as the interaction progresses.

Two final comments about the studies of the experimental situation are in order. First, we see that close examination of the experimental situation supports the symbolic interactionist perspective. Empirically, this means that the phenomena which are thought to characterize human conduct generally are also present in the experimental setting. This is especially significant since they are regarded as nuisances, as methodological difficulties, and attempts are made to remove them by writing scripts, training experimenters, and so on. Nonetheless they survive. Second, we are confronted with irony. Symbolic interactionists are often criticized on methodological grounds. Yet in the work of Orne, Rosenthal, Friedman, and others, we find experimenters using their insights to understand what occurs in their own experiments and to raise a challenge to the adequacy of the experimental method as it is currently conceived for the study of human behavior.

Undeniably, then, there are sources of bias in any social psychological

---

[61] *Ibid.*, pp. 46–51.

[62] Robert Rosenthal, "Covert Communication in the Psychological Experiment," *Psychological Bulletin,* 67 (1967), 356–368; and Robert Rosenthal and Ralph Rosnow, eds., *Artifact in Behavioral Research,* Academic Press, New York, 1969.

[63] Friedman, p. 75.

[64] *Ibid.*, pp. 105–109.

work which cannot be negated simply by formulating hypotheses prior to the research. Symbolic interactionism, however, may have an advantage over other perspectives in dealing with such sources of bias. Its flexibility, its insistence upon really getting at the meaning of situations to participants, and its focus on history and process allow analyses to emerge out of involvement with social reality rather than out of the imposition of a rigid framework on that reality.[65]

THE METHODS OF SYMBOLIC INTERACTIONISM

To return to our initial point, the methods employed by symbolic interactionists reflect the basic assumptions of the theory. One such assumption is that reality is process. How can we research processual phenomena? Any adequate research demands participation in an ongoing investigation of the subjects of the research. This is, in part, the basis of Blumer's criticism of much sociological research—such research tends to pluck out a piece of social reality from its context and from its place in the ongoing social process. Norman Denzin has similarly criticized survey research because of its tendency to "dichotomize all process into past or present" and thereby miss the basic point that "human conduct reflects a world of past, present, and future simultaneously playing upon man's behavior." [66]

Furthermore, because reality is process, because social life is constructed out of the matrix of interaction, there is rich variety to social reality. This fact has also been the basis of much criticism of conventional sociological methods. Blumer argues that the practice of depending upon operational definitions of concepts neglects the rich complexity of social life by making our approach to the empirical world too structured and too rigid. As discussed above, he advocates the use of sensitizing concepts instead.

In addition to the notion of reality as process, symbolic interactionists have been guided by the assumption that social life can only be understood through an understanding of the perspectives of the actors. Any method which gets at subjective meanings may be used, and quite a variety of methods have been defined as useful for this purpose.[67] Included in these methods are those employed by researchers who have been criticized for failing to adequately grasp social reality. For example, Denzin includes the social survey as one method, even though in the above quote he criticized the common use of such a method. But to criticize the common

---

[65] Compare Gregory P. Stone et al., "On Methodology and Craftmanship in the Criticism of Sociological Perspectives," *American Sociological Review,* 39 (June 1974), 459–460.

[66] Denzin, p. 454.

[67] *Ibid.,* pp. 456–464.

use is not to say that the method is worthless. The survey is quite appropriate for stable forms of interaction. It is only when it is used to study more fluid forms of interaction that it misleads us into thinking that we have adequately analyzed that interaction.

Perhaps one of the commonest methods of symbolic interactionists is participant observation. As defined by McGill and Simmons, participant observation is more than a single method, however, for it "involves some amount of genuinely social interaction in the field with the subjects of the study, some direct observation of relevant events, some formal and a great deal of informal interviewing, some systematic counting, some collection of documents and artifacts, and open-endedness in the directions the study takes." [68] Thus, the researcher directly participates in and observes the social entity he or she is studying; ideally, the researcher is at once both a part of it and detached from it.

The nature of this method is well illustrated by the study of medical students conducted by Howard Becker and his associates. [69] The aim of the researchers was to study matters important to the subjects rather than to themselves, and those matters generating conflict or tension between students and others involved in the students' lives. The researchers participated in the daily activities of the students, attending classes, and following students from class to labs to hospital wards. In studying students in their clinical years they merged with one of the subgroups of the class which was assigned to a particular section of the hospital and remained with that group through the day's activities. With students in their first two years, the researchers skipped from one group to another in the class instead of staying with a single group.

Sometimes participant observers elect to remain covert with respect to their identity. But Becker and his associates were identified to students, teachers, and patients alike as researchers rather than as medical students (the specific purpose of the study was covert, however, for the researchers were ostensibly gathering materials for a book on medical education). Since the students were the focus of the study, the researchers participated with that group; thus, after a class, they would leave with the students and not with the teacher. This participation was comprehensive; a particular group would be observed more or less daily for a period ranging from a week to two months; and the totality of the day's activities would be observed rather than certain segments.

Observations were written down as soon as possible, with minimal

[68] George J. McCall and J. L. Simmons, eds., *Issues in Participant Observation: A Text and Reader,* Addison-Wesley, Reading, Mass., 1969, p. 1.
[69] Howard S. Becker, Blanche Geer, Everett C. Hughes, and Anselm Strauss, *Boys in White: Student Culture in Medical School,* The University of Chicago Press, Chicago, 1961.

selectivity in the recording (as shown by the fact that the final collection of notes and interviews comprised some five thousand single-spaced, typewritten pages). Two kinds of interviews were also employed: casual and informal interviews and formal, structured interviews with both students and faculty. But the interviews were of little utility in the final analysis, serving primarily as material on student backgrounds and students' views of their professional futures.

The researchers made a number of initial assumptions. They worked within the framework of symbolic interactionism, assuming that behavior is symbolic, processual, and an emergent from interaction. They also accepted the notion of methodological flexibility, assuming that the data gathered would provide an adequate guide to analytic procedures (rather than imposing a set of procedures on the research). Finally, they assumed their own ignorance—ignorance both of the perspectives that doctors need in order to function effectively in practice and of the perspectives acquired in medical school. This led them to adopt a stance of conceptual openness; they would allow their findings to identify the important variables as well as the relationships between those variables.

This kind of procedure has been charged with providing no reliable method of proof, and the researchers were concerned with the problem of the validity of their findings. They responded to the problem by indexing their field notes so that all materials bearing on a particular topic were readily available. In addition, they offered a specific innovation, namely, the presentation of the data in tabular form, showing both frequencies and appropriate percentages as follows:

		Volunteered	Directed by observer	Total
Statements	To observer alone			
	To others			
Activities	Individual			
	Group			
Total				

In other words, Becker and his associates took great pains to insure that their final analysis was not biased by such things as selective perception on the part of observers and directed influence by the research participants. In addition, the fact that the research was done by a team rather than a single participant-observer increases our confidence in the validity of the results.

The above considerations do not answer all the questions which may be raised about participant observation as a method—nor are they meant to. They are meant to illustrate the way the method can be used to study a particular social phenomenon.

Symbolic interactionists, as pointed out above, employ many different kinds of methods. To some extent, the diverse methods used reflect the divergence between the Chicago and Iowa schools of symbolic interactionism.[70] The Chicago school bears the mark of Blumer's influence, and has continued to stress the processual nature of reality and emergence in school life. The Iowa school, on the other hand, reflects the influence of Manford Kuhn, and has emphasized the utility of conventional sociological methods for the study of social life—including the operationalization of variables, against which Blumer has argued.

While there are some fundamental differences in the two approaches, they are not necessarily contradictory. For process does not mean total fluidity. There are some continuities and some stable features of social life. As Denzin points out with respect to the use of survey research, stable forms of interaction are to be found and are amenable to conventional methods of research. Whether a particular phenomenon is stable or fluid depends in part upon one's perspective. Thus a chair is a stable entity and can be studied as such by a physicist. But for a process philosopher like Alfred North Whitehead, a chair is in process like everything else in the universe. The chair is simply changing at a much slower rate than certain other entities.

In other words, to speak of stable forms of social interaction is not to say that such forms are changeless. It is rather to argue that they are stable over a sufficiently long period of time that they may be studied by different methods than those forms which change more rapidly. Symbolic interactionists, like process philosophers, argue that all social reality is process. But we do not argue that all processes proceed at the same rate. Some processes may be studied through the so-called positivistic methods of social science. Others must be studied through participant observation. Still others can only be fully understood when we have explicated their history as well as their present characteristics. In all cases, methods should be guided by theoretical considerations and by the results of ongoing empirical studies. That is, we must employ those methods which will allow us to explore processes and to get at the meaning of situations to participants.

[70] Bernard N. Meltzer and John W. Petras, "The Chicago and Iowa Schools of Symbolic Interactionism," in *Human Nature and Collective Behavior,* ed. Tamotsu Shibutani, Prentice-Hall, Englewood Cliffs, N.J., 1970, pp. 3–17.

Suggested Readings

Symbolic interactionism has been criticized by both opponents and advocates. For the former, see Irving M. Zeitlin, *Rethinking Sociology* (Prentice-Hall, Englewood Cliffs, N.J., 1973, pp. 191–256). For a brief exposition and critique of Mead, see Bernard N. Meltzer, "Mead's Social Psychology" (in *Symbolic Interaction,* ed. Jerome G. Manis and Bernard N. Meltzer, Allyn and Bacon, Boston, 1967, pp. 5–24). The best way to understand problems of theory and method is to compare various approaches. For an overview and comparison of differing social psychological perspectives, see Morton Deutsch and Robert M. Krauss, *Theories in Social Psychology* (Basic Books, New York, 1965) and Wiliam Gamson and André Modigliani, *Conceptions of Social Life* (Little, Brown, Boston, 1974).

PART 2

SOME MAJOR THEORETICAL AND RESEARCH DEVELOPMENTS

Symbolic interactionism has often been accused of being primarily a theoretical enterprise, with little in the way of empirical research directed by the theory. Actually, the perspective has given birth to a considerable amount of empirical research and, in addition, has served as a point of departure for new theoretical developments. In this part, we will explore some of these developments.

Chapter 5 examines the self-concept. An enormous amount of research has been conducted on self-concepts, much of it by social psychologists of other theoretical perspectives. Nevertheless, the results of the research can be used to support basic symbolic interactionist propositions. In addition, this chapter picks up on the work of the so-called Iowa school of symbolic interactionism. The Twenty Statements Test, the hallmark of the work of this school, simply and neatly demonstrates the social nature of the self, and in addition has been used in various ways as an effective research tool.

Chapter 6 explores an approach to a major area of sociological study: deviance. The approach is labeling theory, and it extends the concepts and insights of symbolic interaction to deviant behavior. The theory and the attendant research stress the importance of symbols ("labels") in directing the responses of others, in the formation of the self and the self-concept in deviant roles, and in the development of deviant subcultures.

In Chapter 7 we delve into a number of areas which we call "everyday life." These areas are part of our common experiences, and range from very personal experiences such as embarrassment to large-scale collective experiences, such as the women's liberation movement, that are included under the rubric of "collective behavior." This chapter demonstrates that symbolic interactionism is useful for the analysis of the broad range of human experiences and behavior. Symbolic interactionism can illuminate not only dyadic interaction but behavior in large-scale organizations and among masses of people.

Finally, Chapter 8 is an explication of a major line of development in contemporary sociology—ethnomethodology. Symbolic interactionism and ethnomethodology both stress the importance of the actor's ability to negotiate reality in the service of practical interests. But there are some fundamental differences, including the nature of common understanding, the nature of symbols and the way symbols are used in interaction, and the relationship between social structure and particular interactions. Both the similarities and the differences are noted in this chapter.

The materials in this part demonstrate two things. First, the empirical application of symbolic interactionism is still in its infancy, and numerous exciting possibilities are open. Second, the theory is a general one and can be applied to virtually any interest in human phenomena from personal experiences to large-scale social phenomena. Whether the researcher's interest is human emotions, small-scale interaction like friendships, behavior in organizations, or large-scale social processes such as social movements, symbolic interactionism offers a theoretical perspective that will provide directives for research.

Chapter 5

The Self-Concept

"Know thyself," advised the ancient Greeks. And the precept was considered so important, it is said, that it was inscribed in gold letters on the temple at Delphi. Like all of the great precepts of human history, however, this one is easier said than realized in practice. In modern times the effort to know oneself has led many individuals to the office of the psychotherapist. Others have wrestled with the question of their identity through a good part of their lives. The question to be addressed in this chapter, therefore—the question of what kind of person am I—is intimately bound up with our aspirations, our struggles, and our well-being.

Definition and History of the Self-Concept

Because the self is reflexive, because the individual can be an object to him- or herself, each individual has some kind of conception of him- or herself. The self-concept and self are not therefore equivalent; the former is an aspect of the latter. As Chad Gordon has put it, the "self"

> is a complex *process* of continuing interpretive activity—simultaneously the person's located subjective stream of *consciousness* (both reflexive and nonreflexive, including perceiving, thinking, planning, evaluating, choosing, etc.) *and* the resultant accruing *structure of self-conceptions* (the special system of self-referential meanings available to this active consciousness).[1]

This definition both maintains the processual nature of the self and also allows us to speak of a relatively stable aspect of the self—the "self-concept." Thus we are able to reconcile the processual emphasis of Mead and Blumer with the more static, content approach of the Iowa school (which we will discuss below).

In addition, we will follow Argyle's suggestion that the literature allows us to distinguish between the "self-image" and "self-esteem." "Self-image" is "the descriptive part, what sort of person P thinks he is," while "self-esteem" is "how favourably P regards himself."[2] Self-esteem is an aspect of the self-concept, for the way in which one evaluates oneself is inseparably tied to the kind of person one thinks one is. Since, however, a great many studies have focused specifically on self-esteem, we will consider it separately (remembering that it is an aspect of the self-concept and also keeping in mind that many researchers have not carefully distinguished the two terms). Finally, we will consider the ideal self, which is, as Argyle notes, the result of "imagination and fantasy." The "ideal self" is the individual's imaginative construction of the kind of person he or she wants, or ought, to be.

The self-concept is both general and situationally specific. For example, one might conceive of oneself as generally intelligent, but also define oneself as quite inept in mastering a foreign language. In other words, the fact that a person has a generalized conception of him- or herself as intel-

---

[1] Chad Gordon, "Self-Conceptions: Configurations of Content," in *The Self in Social Interaction,* ed. Chad Gordon and Kenneth J. Gergen, Wiley, New York, 1968, p. 116.

[2] Michael Argyle, *Social Interaction,* Aldine, Chicago, 1969, p. 356.

ligent does not mean that he or she believes him- or herself capable of mastering anything. Nevertheless, the general concept that one has of oneself provides an initial behavioral tendency in any situation—people generally act, or strive to act, in ways that are consistent with their self-concepts.

As this suggests, self-concepts both arise out of interaction and influence the course of interaction. In this chapter we shall look at some of the empirical research that has been conducted and that bears upon the sources and the consequences of the self-concept. We shall have to be quite selective in our examination, for an enormous amount of research has been conducted; there are literally thousands of studies available. Social, developmental, clinical, and personality psychologists have all investigated the self-concept. In fact, a count in *Psychological Abstracts* for the single year 1973 shows 383 articles on the self-concept; in addition, there were articles on self-esteem, self-evaluation, self-perception, and articles not included under any of those because they were published in sociology journals. Furthermore, there are literally hundreds of different scales which have been developed to measure self-concepts, including self-esteem scales.

This extensive interest in the self has a long history. Experimental work was carried on at least as early as 1903, when J. McKean Cattell used a self-rating technique to study American scientists. And as early as 1915 experimentalists compared self-evaluations on a number of traits with the evaluations of others.[3] But theoretical interest in the self and the self-concept has a longer history yet, for the notion of the self can be traced back to the ancient Greeks. The formulations by Mead and Cooley provided a fruitful basis for empirical work; nevertheless, the notion of the "self-concept" did not become a common research concern until the 1940s.

Among the most influential works in stimulating research on the self-concept was the text of Snygg and Combs.[4] They presented a method of predicting behavior in specific situations, and their method assumed that an individual's personal frame of reference is a crucial factor in his or her behavior. In particular, they declared that the "phenomenal field" is the cause of individual behavior; the phenomenal self is a part of that phenomenal field, that part which the individual experiences as "characteristic of himself." All behavior is directed towards the goal of preserving and enhancing the phenomenal self. Finally, the self-concept is a part of the phenomenal self, that part which the individual perceives as a set of specific and relatively stable self-characteristics.

---

[3] These two experiments are reported in Linda Viney, "Self: The History of a Concept," *Journal of the History of the Behavioral Sciences,* 5 (October 1969), 349–359.

[4] Donald Snygg and Arthur W. Combs, *Individual Behavior,* Harper, New York, 1949.

In 1961, a critical review of the growing body of literature on the self-concept was published by Ruth Wylie.[5] Her critique was primarily aimed at the methods, although she also criticized the theory, and her conclusions were rather dismal. There is minimal value in the over-four-hundred papers examined, Wylie argued, because the theories are "vague, incomplete, and overlapping," while the methods are deficient because of lack of attention to problems of validity, reliability, and to safeguards against spurious correlations.

Despite her criticism, Wylie did offer some conclusions from the literature. We shall include these, and offer additional conclusions based primarily on materials published after Wylie's review. First, however, we need to discuss the problems of measuring the self-concept. Following that we shall look at the sources and behavioral consequences of the self-concept as these have been identified in empirical studies.

Measurement of the Self-Concept

PROCESS AND MEASUREMENT

To what extent is the self-concept a stable phenomenon subject to measurement? We have pointed out that the self is a process, but that self-concepts are relatively stable. The stability is only relative, however. Because the self is processual, the conceptions we have of ourselves are also processual to some extent. But process does not mean total fluidity. There is continuity as well as change, and the rate of change varies considerably. Thus studies have shown that some elements of the self-concept remain stable even while other elements may change. Engel measured the self-concepts of a group of adolescents in 1954 and again in 1956. Those whose self-concepts were positive (high self-esteem) were more stable than those whose self-concepts were negative (lower self-esteem). But there was both stability and change, with the change tending towards more positive self-concepts.[6] These findings were supported and illuminated by Backman, Secord, and Pierce some years later, although a different method of measuring the self-concept was used in their study. They found that the aspects of the self-concept most resistant to change are those perceived to be supported by significant others. When subjects perceived a low degree of consensus among significant others with respect to some aspect of the self, they were more likely to alter that aspect in response to feedback.[7]

[5] Ruth C. Wylie, *The Self Concept,* University of Nebraska Press, Lincoln, 1961.
[6] Mary Engel, "The Stability of the Self-Concept in Adolescence," *Journal of Abnormal and Social Psychology,* 58 (March 1959), 211–215.
[7] Carl W. Backman, Paul F. Secord, and Jerry R. Pierce, "Resistance to Change in the Self-Concept as a Function of Consensus among Significant Others," *Sociometry,* 26 (March 1963), 102–111. See also E. R. Mahoney, "The Processual

Again, both continuity and change were evident in the self-concept when it was measured at different points in time. Thus, while new situations and developing action will effect changes, there is a core which is sufficiently stable to make measurement useful.

How then can we measure the self-concept? As Wylie noted there is a "bewildering array" of instruments available. We will look at a few of the more widely used out of the hundreds available.[8] The scales we shall describe have each been shown to be reliable and valid.

THE Q SORT TECHNIQUE

In the Q Sort method, subjects are given a set of cards which are to be placed in piles along some dimension such as "like me" and "unlike me." This technique lends itself particularly well to measuring discrepancies between the individual's perception of his or her real and ideal selves. For example, the individual might be asked to rate statements like "I never put on a false front." The subject would indicate the extent to which he or she believed the statement to apply to him- or herself, and also the extent to which he or she would like it to apply to him- or herself. Or an individual might be given cards with adjectives—"honest," "aggressive," "anxious," and so forth—and asked to put them into a series of piles, with the pile at one end representing "most like me" and the pile at the other end representing "most unlike me."

THE SEMANTIC DIFFERENTIAL

This technique was created to measure the meaning of various phenomena to an individual. Subjects are given a series of polar adjectives, separated by seven spaces. For example, the following might be among those used:

I am:

Good ____ ____ ____ ____ ____ ____ ____ Bad

Smart ____ ____ ____ ____ ____ ____ ____ Stupid

Kind ____ ____ ____ ____ ____ ____ ____ Cruel

Each subject is to place a check in one of the seven spaces for each dimension according to which of the paired adjectives is closer to his or her self-concept. The scales can be used to measure both the "real" and "ideal" self. Osgood and his associates, who developed the semantic differential, found that three dimensions of meaning emerge: evaluative,

Characteristics of Self-Conception," *The Sociological Quarterly,* 14 (Autumn 1973), 517–533.

[8] These scales are described in John P. Robinson and Phillip R. Shaver, *Measures of Social Psychological Attitudes,* Institute for Social Research, Ann Arbor, 1969, pp. 53–142.

potency, and activity. Different sets of adjectives, of course, measure these three differing dimensions. Thus "good-bad" would be evaluative, while "strong-weak" would measure potency, and "excitable-calm" would measure activity. Some studies have only used the evaluative dimension, while others have employed all three to measure self-concept, ideal self, or both.

LIKERT-TYPE SCALES

In tests using Likert-type scales, subjects are given a set of statements and asked to rate them on a five- or seven-point scale such as "seldom, occasionally, about half the time, a good deal of the time, most of the time." The scale may also involve terms like "very unlike me" and "very much like me." The statements on the test might look as follows:

	very much like me	like me	unlike me	very unlike me
I don't doubt my worth as an individual even if others do.	____	____	____	____
I prefer to be by myself rather than to maintain close friendships with others.	____	____	____	____

CHECK LISTS

A fourth method employs check lists of statements or adjectives. Subjects are asked to check those which apply to them or to their ideal self. This differs from the above in that an individual cannot indicate partial agreement or disagreement; the subject must either accept or reject each item totally. The Adjective Check List includes three hundred words, ranging from "absent-minded" through "ingenious" to "zany." The Self-Esteem Inventory developed by Coopersmith offers fifty-eight statements which are to be checked as either "like me" or "unlike me." The statements are of the following type: "I spend a lot of time daydreaming"; "I get upset easily when I'm scolded"; and so forth.

PROJECTIVE AND OPEN-ENDED TECHNIQUES

A number of projective and open-ended techniques have been employed to study the self, including the Thematic Apperception and Rorschach tests. The former involves ambiguous pictures about which subjects are to write stories while the latter employs ten standard inkblots in which subjects see various things. Training is required to properly interpret the responses. Obviously, such measures require considerable time on the part of the researcher.

A test which is relatively easy to administer, which requires relatively little time, and which lends itself to larger as well as smaller groups of subjects is the Twenty-Statements Test (TST), sometimes called the "Who Am I?" test. This measure was designed by sociologists in the symbolic interactionist tradition. We will look at it in somewhat more detail.

The TST was developed by Manford Kuhn and first systematically tested by Kuhn and Thomas McPartland.[9] Subjects are asked to provide twenty answers to the question "Who Am I?" and to write them in the order that they occur to them. In an initial test of 288 undergraduate students, the number of responses ranged from 1 to 20, with a median of 17. The responses were categorized into "consensual" and "subconsensual." The former refers to "groups and classes whose limits and conditions of membership are matters of common knowledge," while the latter refers to matters requiring interpretation in order to be understood. For example, the consensual answers include such things as "student," "girl," "daughter," "Methodist," and so forth. The subconsensual category includes such things as "happy," "intelligent," "attractive," and so forth. An example of the way in which people respond is provided by a female student of one of the authors. Her twenty responses to "Who am I?" were:

1. Debbie
2. my parents' daughter
3. Jean's best friend
4. alive—sometimes
5. in love most of the time
6. alone even in a crowd
7. scared and bold
8. mixed-up
9. different in my thoughts
10. deep
11. happy and unhappy
12. a student who wants to learn
13. a thinker, not a doer
14. a poem reader
15. a music listener
16. insane
17. curious
18. without Jack

[9] Manford H. Kuhn and Thomas S. McPartland, "An Empirical Investigation of Self-Attitudes," *American Sociological Review,* 19 (February 1954), 68–76.

19. a caller on God
20. a child mostly

The theoretical basis for the TST lies in the basic notion that the self is an object as well as a subject. And we must "know what kinds of objects we ourselves are before we can control and direct our own activity." [10] Furthermore, in determining what kind of objects we are, we use the commonly used symbols of the groups of which we are a part. Thus, just as the symbol "apple" indicates to us the meaning of a particular, edible object, the symbols "Methodist," "father," "lover," and so forth, indicate that the individual is a particular kind of object and that particular kinds of activity are therefore appropriate. In sum, the self consists of "the individual's attitudes (plans of action) toward his own mind and body, viewed as an object. We may think of it as consisting of all the answers the individual might make to the question 'Who am I?' " [11]

On this basis, Kuhn developed a measure of the individual's self attitudes. Such a measure had to deal with a number of problems.[12] First, we must decide what items to include, what attitudes to tap. How can we be sure that we have covered all the appropriate attitudes? The open-ended TST, which "leaves the formulation of relevant items up to the respondent," solves this problem. Second, we must avoid suggesting responses to the subjects; they may accept suggestions that are of little pertinence to their self-attitudes. Again, the open-ended TST avoids this problem by letting the subjects formulate the responses rather than respond to the researcher's suggestions. Third, the measure must tap general attitudes, not merely those which are relevant only to specific situations (in particular, to the test situation). The TST minimizes this by having no situational referents. Thus, Kuhn argued, we have a measure of self-attitudes that will enable us to understand the bases for organizing and directing behavior.

The TST was given to a sample of 1,213 adults in Iowa.[13] The most frequent responses were the consensual categories of family, occupation, marital status, and religion. Some differences were found between male and female answers, but in both cases the tendency was to respond first in terms of consensual categories and, in particular, the four categories noted. This supports a point we shall make below—that the self is social. For when people respond to the question "Who am I?" they tend first of all to think of themselves in terms of social roles such as plumber, student, father, daughter, or Methodist.

[10] C. Addison Hickman and Manford H. Kuhn, *Individuals, Groups, and Economic Behavior,* The Dryden Press, New York, 1956, p. 43.

[11] *Ibid.*

[12] *Ibid.,* pp. 242–243.

[13] Harold A. Mulford and Winfield W. Salisbury II, "Self-Conceptions in a General Population," *The Sociological Quarterly,* 5 (Winter 1964), 35–46.

A more sophisticated use of the TST has been offered by Gordon.[14] He suggests a number of lines to follow that could be very fruitful. For one, he points out the importance of the "tenses of self." The individual's responses may be categorized as past-continuing ("I am female"), completed past ("I am no longer single"), current ("I am depressed"), or future ("I hope to be a doctor"). These can give us insight into the way in which past, present, and future are incorporated into self-concepts. Such insight is important. For example, temporal orientations reflect the state of the individual's mental health. In a study of adolescents in a psychiatric hospital, tests of the time perspectives were analyzed and revealed that the adolescents were ready to leave the hospital after reorganizing a deficient time perspective. Adolescents who were able to utilize the "psychiatric moratorium" offered by the hospital in order to think more in terms of the future were prepared to return to their homes.[15]

Gordon also suggests that the TST may be used for longitudinal studies. He gives the example of a seventeen-year-old girl who took the test twice, six months apart. The two tests show a change in selfhood. The girl pointed out, for example, on the second test that she was no longer a virgin, that she was "now" eighteen years old (she had not mentioned age the first time), and that she was "now" very depressed. This changing selfhood or transformation of identity, as Strauss called it, is a most important aspect of human life, and it has not received the attention it merits.

Finally, Gordon suggests a more complex scheme for analyzing the responses. He suggests eight categories. The eight, along with a few examples of the content of each, are as follows: ascribed characteristics (sex, age, name, race, religion); roles and memberships (kinship roles, occupation, and group memberships such as teams, clubs, and friends); abstract identifications (ideological identifications such as liberal or conservative and reference to the self as a "person" or "human"); interests and activities (likes and dislikes with respect to music, art, sports, and literature); material references (owner of car or clothes and references to the body as tall or short, good-looking, or homely); major sense of self (the sense of moral worth, of self-determination, of unity, and of competence); personal characteristics (typical ways of acting, such as friendly, and of thinking and feeling, such as happy); and external meanings (the way others think about the individual, situational references such as hungry or tired, and uncodable responses such as "superman").

This scheme was developed on the basis of actual responses to the TST. It attempts to analyze more accurately and in more detail the kinds of responses people make and the complexity of self-conceptions. Gordon

14 Gordon, pp. 115–136.
15 A. E. Rizzo, "The Time Moratorium," *Adolescence,* 2 (1967-68), 469–480.

still found that the most frequent responses were the first two types, the consensual categories that most clearly demonstrate the social nature of the self. But there were responses in all other categories as well—self-concepts are complex phenomena and in spite of the massive amount of research already done, we are far short of a satisfactory understanding.

MEASUREMENT AND INTERPRETATION

All of the above methods of measuring the self-concept have been used in the studies that form the basis for the following sections. This is not as problematic as it might appear, for when various methods yield the same results it gives us greater confidence in the validity of those results. Thus, although the results reported below were arrived at through various methods, they form a consistent and logical coherent portrait of the self-concept.

Sources of the Self-Concept

THE SELF-CONCEPT AS SOCIAL

To say that the self-concept is social is to say that we all think of ourselves in terms that we learn from and share with others—the consensual categories on the TST. These are not the only categories of course; we also think of ourselves in the diverse other terms identified by Gordon, but the former are the most salient and the latter are also social in the sense that they arise in the course of interaction. The salience of the consensual categories is seen in the fact that they tend to be listed first in the TST. And the social nature of the other categories is demonstrated in numerous experiments that show the changes in self-evaluation that occur in interaction.

More specifically, the self-concept arises in, and changes in, interaction through the mechanism of the perceived reactions of others. As Cooley emphasized in his concept of the looking-glass self, it is the *imagined* reactions of others that are crucial. This has been shown in a number of studies. In 1955, Melvin Manis measured the self-concepts of 101 university freshmen who were living in a dormitory. The self-concepts were measured at two different times, six weeks apart. He found that the individual's self-concept tended to converge with the conception held of him by others; that the convergence was due primarily to changes in his conception of himself rather than in the conception of him held by others; that changed self-concepts were more likely to occur in a favorable rather than an unfavorable direction; and that changed self-concepts were more likely to converge with conceptions held by friends than those held by nonfriends.[16]

[16] Melvin Manis, "Social Interaction and the Self-Concept," *Journal of Abnormal and Social Psychology,* 51 (November 1955), 362–370.

Manis did not measure the perceived reactions of others; a 1956 study by Miyamoto and Dornbusch did though.[17] Using a Likert-type measure of the self-concept, they tested 195 subjects. The subjects comprised ten different groups. For each subject the following were measured: self-concept; actual response of others (each subject was rated by others in his group); perceived response of others (each rated how he thought the others in his group would evaluate him); and the generalized other (each rated the way he perceived most people as viewing him). The authors found that the self-concepts of individuals were closer to the perceived reactions of others than to the actual reaction of others. They also found that self-concepts were closer to the perceived generalized other than to the perceived responses of group members.

This latter finding was not supported by the 1966 study of Quarantelli and Cooper, though they also found support for the hypothesis that self-concepts are closer to the perceived than to the actual responses of others.[18] The contradictory findings about the generalized other is due, in part, to two different kinds of measurement; Quarantelli and Cooper defined it as the aggregate of the individual's perceptions of the ratings of particular others, whereas Miyamoto and Dornbusch measured it in terms of the perception of the rating of "most people." In any case, it is clear that self-concepts derive from interaction and, in particular, from the perceived responses of others that occur during interaction.

This raises the question of the relationship between the perceived and actual responses of others. Could an individual be quite wrong about the actual way others view him or her, so that his or her self-concept is totally incongruous with the evaluations of others? Actually, in the studies cited there is a significant relationship between self-concepts and actual responses of others, but that relationship is not as close as the one between self-concepts and perceived responses of others. How are these variables related? We suggest two factors, which have been stressed previously, and which account for the relationships which have been found: the processual nature of reality and the definition of the situation. The actual responses of others never operate directly upon the individual; they are always interpreted. Furthermore, "actual responses" do not consist of a written summary of evaluations that are handed to the individual by the other, but include words, facial expressions, gestures of various sorts—in other words, those things which not only require interpretation but which are subject to diverse interpretations. In addition, the actual responses of

[17] S. Frank Miyamoto and Sanford M. Dornbusch, "A Test of Interactionist Hypotheses of Self-Conception," *American Journal of Sociology,* 61 (March 1956), 399–403.

[18] E. L. Quarantelli and Joseph Cooper, "Self-Conceptions and Others: A Further Test of Meadian Hypotheses," *The Sociological Quarterly,* 7 (Summer 1966), 281–297.

others are not static; they fluctuate over time and in various interaction situations. Finally, as the latter suggests, the actual responses may include contrary evaluations as the individual interacts with different groups. Thus, the perceived responses of others are correlated with, but never perfectly reflect, the actual responses of others. And the self-concept is more closely related to the perceived responses, because the latter represent the individual's interpretation of the actual responses.

The relationships are still more complex, however. For the responses of others are affected by the individual's behavior, which is in turn related to his or her self-concept. Clearly this is a circular process, and it has been well summarized by Kinch as follows.[19] First the individual's self-concept is based on his perception of the responses of others. The self-concept, in turn, directs the individual's behavior. The behavior influences the actual responses of others. And, finally, the actual responses of others influence the individual's perceptions. This circular process is illustrated in a study of 220 male-female dyads made by Robert Coombs.[20] The subjects were studied over time, beginning with their first date. Coombs found, in accord with his hypothesis, that interpersonal success results in a more favorable self-concept, which leads to a greater amount of social participation, which in turn tends to promote more interpersonal success.

In sum, the self-concept is a social phenomenon. It arises out of interaction and is modified in the course of further interaction. It is based upon the individual's interpretation of the responses of others, and influences the individual's behavior. Since the individual's behavior affects the actual responses of others, the process becomes a circular one. Self-concepts, responses of others, and the individual's own behavior comprise an ongoing process, a process of fitting together developing lines of action.

THE SELF-CONCEPT AND SIGNIFICANT OTHERS

Not all interaction is equally important in terms of the development of the self-concept. That is, a store clerk will not affect the self-concept as a friend will, and some friends will be more influential than other friends. In this section, then, we will identify those others who are significant for our self-concepts.

In general, primary relationships, particularly family relationships, are crucial for our self-concepts. Self-concepts first emerge in the context of the family as the growing child learns to view him- or herself as his or her parents view him or her. Moreover, there is evidence that the importance of parents for self-concepts continues through adolescence rather

---

[19] John W. Kinch, "A Formalized Theory of the Self-Concept," *American Journal of Sociology,* 68 (January 1963), 481–486.

[20] Robert H. Coombs, "Social Participation, Self-Concept and Interpersonal Valuation," *Sociometry,* 32 (September 1969), 273–286.

than declining markedly as has been commonly believed.[21] Other kinds of family relationships are also important. As noted above, family statuses and roles are among the most frequent responses on the TST. In the Mulford-Salisbury survey of Iowa residents, 29 percent of the men and 41 percent of the women referred in some way to their roles as husbands and wives. And when other relationships in the nuclear family are considered, 49 percent of the men and 81 percent of the women included such relationships in their responses.

Friends are also important in self-concepts. Recall in the Manis study that changes in self-concepts were much more likely to be influenced by friends than by nonfriends. In a later study by Dorothy Kipnis, the importance of friends is again stressed.[22] Kipnis tested eighty-seven students living in a dormitory and found that those who perceived their best friends to be relatively unlike themselves tended to change their self-evaluations during the six weeks of the study so that the differences between themselves and their friends were smaller.

Various experiences in school comprise a third important influence on self-concepts. Teacher-student interaction, of course, is of prime importance. Significant correlations have been found between the self-concepts of children and their perceptions of their teachers' feelings toward them.[23] A correlation does not tell us about the direction of causation (the students could have perceived positive feelings because of their positive self-concept rather than vice versa). But it is reasonable to argue that teachers' feelings and students' self-concepts mutually support each other. Furthermore, other studies indicate that even if a child comes to school with a positive self-concept, he or she may change in a negative direction if his or her teacher reacts negatively to him or her.[24]

A positive correlation between teacher ratings and self-ratings has also been found among educable mentally retarded children.[25] A total of one hundred such children, between the ages of nine and fifteen, were tested on a measure of self-esteem. The children's self-images were positively correlated with the teachers' rating of their academic ability. Such

[21] W. W. Purkey, *Self-Concept and School Achievement,* Prentice-Hall, Englewood Cliffs, N.J., 1970.

[22] Dorothy M. Kipnis, "Changes in Self Concepts in Relation to Perceptions of Others," *Journal of Personality,* 29 (December 1961), 449–465.

[23] Helen H. Davidson and Gerhard Lang, "Children's Perceptions of Their Teachers' Feelings Toward Them Related to Self Perception, School Achievement, and Behavior," *Journal of Experimental Education,* 29 (December 1960), 107–118.

[24] See, for example, Richard Videbeck, "Self-Conception and the Reaction of Others," *Sociometry,* 23 (December 1960), 351–359, and Robert Rosenthal and Lenore Jacobson, *Pygmalion in the Classroom: Teacher Expectation and Pupils' Intellectual Development,* Holt, New York, 1968.

[25] Bert O. Richmond and J. Leon Dalton, "Teacher Ratings and Self Concept Reports of Retarded Pupils," *Exceptional Children,* 20 (November 1973), 178–183.

findings suggest that teachers are important in children's self-concepts, and not only in their self-concepts of ability but also in their conceptions of their worth as persons.

A fourth influence on our self-concepts is our reference groups. It will be recalled that a reference group is not necessarily a membership group. This point was underscored in a study by Bilha Mannheim of 103 male college students living in a dormitory.[26] Mannheim administered a semantic differential type questionnaire on two different occasions to measure self-concepts. In addition, information was obtained on reference groups (subjects were told to list four "groups most important to you and by whom you want to be accepted"); on "reference group self" (subjects were asked to describe themselves in the same terms as they thought those in their reference group would use); on "membership group self" (subjects were asked to describe themselves as "others in the building probably see you"); and on whether they were members of the reference groups they named. Among the results of the experiment were the following:

1. Subjects tended to alter their self-concepts in accord with that of the "reference group self";
2. The relationship between self-concept and reference group self was unaffected by whether or not the subject was a member of the reference group;
3. When membership group was also a reference group, there was greater agreement between self-concept and membership group self than when the membership group was not listed as a reference group.

Thus, although we all belong to groups, our membership alone does not mean that the group will influence our self-concepts. Some group memberships are involuntary and some are matters of expediency (an individual may go to college simply to get a good job or join a church because he or she thinks it will improve his or her business). On the other hand, groups may be reference groups even though we are not members of them, and reference groups are always important in self-concepts. This is true even when the reference group is imaginary. The artist who paints for "posterity" may have a positive self-concept of his or her ability even though his or her work receives little acclaim.

This emphasizes a point which we have made repeatedly and which is of fundamental importance to the symbolic interactionist position: we cannot understand human behavior unless we get at the actor's point of view. An individual's self-concept may make no sense to us as we make an

[26] Bilha F. Mannheim, "Reference Groups, Membership Groups and the Self Image," *Sociometry,* 29 (September 1966), 265–279.

appraisal of his or her situation, but may become quite understandable when we discover his or her reference groups and his or her definition of the situation.

The significance of reference groups for self-concepts raises another point: the others who are influential are not merely those with whom we are directly interacting. We are all part of particular social contexts, and we learn to take the attitude of the community and incorporate it into ourselves and our self-concepts. This is clearly evident in the effects of roles on self-concepts, for roles reflect shared social expectations.

Roles of course can be learned and accepted in direct, forceful ways. This is illustrated in the reasons given by a seventeen-year-old delinquent boy for getting into serious trouble shortly after returning home from a reformatory:

> Man, I wanted to do good—I tried, but even my grandfather wouldn't hardly talk to me. Some of the parents in the neighborhood —some with kids in more trouble than me—wouldn't even let their kids talk to me . . . They had their minds made up before they even looked to see if I had changed. Hell with them. They want me to be bad—I'll *be* bad.[27]

Eventually the notion that he is bad will be a part of his self-concept as he accepts the role and incorporates it into his behavior patterns.

In other words, roles are not incorporated immediately into our self-concepts but only gradually as we learn the meaning of the role and decide whether to accept it. In a study of student nurses, Coe used the TST to measure self-concepts over a nine-month period. He found that there was a significant increase in the proportion of responses referring to nursing situations during the period.[28] The nursing role, like all roles, was only gradually reflected in self-concepts as the students learned the meaning of the role and accepted it for themselves.

THE DEVELOPMENT OF SELF-ESTEEM

As the delinquent boy illustrates, self-concepts can develop in various ways—towards a high degree of self-esteem or towards self-deprecation. High self-esteem is of course preferable. In fact, there is considerable evidence that we all have a basic need for self-esteem. In both the Manis and the Engel experiments referred to above, there was a tendency for increasingly favorable self-concepts over time; and in Engel's study, those who maintained a negative self-concept over the two-year period manifested considerably more personality maladjustment than those who main-

---

[27] Don E. Hamachek, *Encounters with the Self,* Holt, New York, 1971, p. 15.
[28] Rodney M. Coe, "Self Conception and Professional Training," *Nursing Research,* 14 (Winter 1965), 49–52.

tained positive self-concepts. Since self-esteem is tied up with group memberships, we would expect individuals to also be concerned about the status of their groups. And indeed individuals in low-status groups have been found to minimize the status distance between their group and others by enhancing their perceptions of the status of the low-ranked groups.[29]

Self-esteem, as Engel's findings also indicate, is an integral part of emotional well-being. No one can maintain psychic health and a negative self-concept at the same time. A number of clinical psychologists have argued that self-esteem is a prerequisite for mental health and that one of the prime goals of therapy is to build such self-esteem in the patient.[30] In an interesting study of prostitutes, some researchers found that most of the women maintained a consistent self-image through various rationalizations and identification with groups that accepted prostitution or justified it. Subcultural affiliations and the selection of reference groups generally serve this same function as we shall see in the next chapter. Some prostitutes were unable to do this and suffered from various psychic ills.[31] Thus, we all have a need to develop and maintain a positive self-concept, to have a sense of self-esteem. The alternative is various kinds of maladjustment.

This raises the question of how self-esteem does develop, and a number of factors have been identified. One of the most important is the family experience. Loving parents and a suitable family have been found to correlate significantly with self-esteem. With respect to the role of parents, two large studies underscore the significance of the parent-child relationship. Morris Rosenberg used a variety of scales to measure the self-image of adolescents, including one scale on self-esteem.[32] His sample included over five thousand high school students in New York. Among his findings were:

1. Adolescents who reported close relationships with their fathers were much more likely to have high self-esteem than those who reported more distant relationships;
2. Only children have a higher self-esteem than those with siblings (again suggesting a closer relationship with parents);
3. Various indications of parental interest in the adolescent are correlated with higher self-esteem.

[29] C. Norman Alexander, Jr., "Status Perceptions," *American Sociological Review,* 37 (December 1972), 767–773.

[30] See, for example, Carl R. Rogers, *Client-Centered Therapy: Its Current Practice, Implications, and Theory,* Houghton Mifflin, Boston, 1951.

[31] Norman R. Jackman, Richard O'Toole, and Gilbert Geis, "The Self-Image of the Prostitute," *Sociological Quarterly,* 4 (Spring 1963), 150–161.

[32] Morris Rosenberg, *Society and the Adolescent Self-Image,* University Press, Princeton, N.J., 1965.

With respect to the third point, indications of parental interest included: the mother knowing most of the adolescent's friends; parental concern over school grades; and parent-child conversations during meal times.

A few years after Rosenberg's study was published, Coopersmith reported the results of an eight-year project on the antecedents and consequences of self-esteem.[33] Again, parents were found to be important, with parental warmth, respectful treatment of children, and other expressions of concern for the child's well-being all associated with the development of self-esteem. Thus, we can conclude that loving parents—those who support, are interested in, and express warmth towards their children—tend to generate high levels of self-esteem in children.

Stable families also seem to be important in the development of self-esteem, although all children are not affected in the same way by a broken home. Rosenberg found that a larger proportion of children coming from homes where the parents were divorced or separated had low self-esteem than those who were in stable families. But the effects of a broken home varied by religion, age of mother, and whether the mother remarried. Specifically, the broken home was likely to have a negative effect when: the child was Catholic or Jewish rather than Protestant; the mother was very young; or the mother remarried, particularly when the child was four years or older at the time of the divorce or death of the father.[34]

While we cannot enter into a detailed discussion of these interesting findings, we should note that they all support the basic point that the parent-child interaction is crucial to the development of self-esteem. They also remind us of the complexity of social interaction, for the meaning of interaction varies by such things as religious background and age. Nevertheless, it is uniformly true that loving parents, as defined above, are extremely important in the development of self-esteem in children.

Once developed, however, self-esteem is not a permanent possession, and the failure to develop it as a child does not preclude its later appearance. The fate of the individual's self-esteem depends upon his or her group involvements, and particularly upon involvement in primary groups. This accounts for some of the diverse findings on social class, race, and self-concepts. Many studies have noted the negative self-concepts of blacks and of those in the lower class vis-à-vis the middle class. But the results are not clear-cut. Recent studies question the extent to which blacks have low self-esteem,[35] and Trowbridge has reported a study of 116 classrooms

---

[33] Stanley Coopersmith, *The Antecedents of Self-Esteem,* Freeman, San Francisco, 1967.

[34] Rosenberg, pp. 85–105.

[35] See, for example, John D. McCarthy and William L. Yancey, "Uncle Tom and Mr. Charlie: Metaphysical Pathos in the Study of Racism and Personal Disorganization," *American Journal of Sociology,* 76 (January 1971), 648–672.

in Iowa in which children from the lower class had higher self-concepts than those from the middle class.[36]

We suggest that the contradictory findings are related to the fact that primary groups are basic to self-esteem, and that neither black nor lower-class children are uniform in their primary group relationships. There will be a tendency for lower-class individuals to have a lower self-esteem because they are not as anchored in primary groups as are those in the middle class. This is supported by a study by McPartland and Cumming.[37] Using the TST on a sample of 137 middle-class and 36 lower-class subjects, they hypothesized that the former would report more self-identifications in terms of institutional positions, while the latter would report more in terms of "personal characteristics, without reference to positions in groups." The hypothesis was confirmed, but the point is that these were tendencies and not absolute differences. With respect to blacks, we suggest that the black power movement and, indeed, the whole civil rights movement have changed the group position of many blacks. Rather than being the lower stratum of American society, blacks are now part of a group—black people—and of primary subgroups within the larger group, that stress the belongingness and worth of every group member. We should expect, therefore, that more recent studies will find higher levels of self-esteem among blacks than older studies.

This line of interpretation is supported by Rosenberg's findings of the self-esteem of those who live in a dissonant religious context. A "dissonant" context was simply one in which the individual's religion made him or her a member of a minority group in his or her neighborhood. Thus, a Catholic growing up in a non-Catholic neighborhood is more likely to have low self-esteem than one who is raised in a Catholic or at least half-Catholic neighborhood. The point is that the *neighborhood,* not the general society, is the crucial factor. The societal evaluation of the group was not as important as the neighborhood environment. Rosenberg found no clear relationship between the social prestige of groups and the self-esteem of their members. Thus "acceptance or rejection within the neighborhood may be more important than acceptance or rejection within the broader society." [38] It is not necessary, to return to our argument, that blacks be evaluated higher than formerly by the broader society in order for their self-esteem to rise. It is only necessary that the neighborhood experience include primary relationships that support self-worth. And the latter can occur in a black neighborhood, an ethnic neighborhood, or a lower-class neighborhood even though the evaluation of the broader society is still

[36] Norma Trowbridge, "Socioeconomic Status and Self-Concept of Children," *Journal of Teacher Education,* 23 (Spring 1972), 63–65.

[37] Thomas S. McPartland and John H. Cumming, "Self-Conception, Social Class, and Mental Health," *Human Organization,* 17 (Fall 1958), 24–29.

[38] Rosenberg, p. 80.

basically negative. The individual in a low-status group who chooses the broader society—or some part of that society—as his or her reference group, will have low self-esteem (as did some of the prostitutes in the study mentioned above). Whether a part of a minority group or not, we only develop self-esteem through being an integral part of a primary group that conveys and supports our sense of worth.

THE SELF-CONCEPT AS PROCESS

It is not merely self-esteem but the self-concept generally which changes over the course of the individual's life and through various interaction experiences. A number of studies have explored the effects of success and failure on self-regard with respect to ability or competence. Wylie reviewed fifteen of these and concluded that under certain conditions we will change our self-evaluations after experimentally manipulated success or failure:

> These changes are most likely to involve self-ratings on the experimental task itself, or on the characteristic which has been evaluated, and are least likely to involve reports on global self-regard . . . There is some evidence that changes in self-rating upward after success are more frequent than are changes downward after failure.[39]

Changes in self-evaluation are illustrated in a study by Videbeck, who took thirty students, all rated as superior by their speech instructors, and had them participate in a test of oral communication ability.[40] The stated purpose was to evaluate the relative abilities of males and females in the oral reading of poetry. Subjects evaluated themselves both before and after the experiment, which also included an evaluation of the reading by an expert. Videbeck found that subjects who had been positively appraised increased their self-evaluations, while those negatively appraised decreased their self-evaluations. And, as with the experiments reported by Wylie, the changes in self-evaluation were generally with respect to attributes relevant to the task and the appraisal. Contrary to Wylie's subjects, Videbeck's subjects changed most in the negative appraisal situation. However, Videbeck presented evidence that the negative appraisals were stronger than the positive appraisals, and this could account for the difference in degrees of change.

The experiment supports the point that changes are task-specific.[41] We do not alter our whole self-conceptions because we succeed or fail at one particular task. On the other hand, to fail or succeed generally in tasks and interpersonal relationships would result in a generalized positive or negative self-concept. As the experiments also suggest, not all others are

[39] Wylie, p. 198.
[40] Videbeck, pp. 351–359.
[41] See also Martin L. Maehr, Josef Mensing, and Samuel Nafziger, "Concept of Self and the Reaction of Others," *Sociometry,* 25 (December 1962), 353–357.

significant in the process of changing self-concepts. The experiments generally have used experts as evaluators for tasks on which there was a clear
basis for judging success or failure (although the subject had no control
over whether he or she succeeded or failed). Which others and which situations then are most likely to affect our self-evaluations? Gergen identifies
six factors relating to appraisers and their appraisals that are significant.[42]
The appraiser must be defined as credible, and he or she must be personal
rather than impersonal in relating to us if he or she is to have maximum
impact. And his or her appraisal is most likely to influence our self-
evaluations when:

1. there is a moderate rather than great discrepancy between the
   appraisal and prior self-evaluation;
2. there are subsequent confirmations by other appraisers of this
   appraisal;
3. the appraisal is consistent with other information received about
   the self;
4. the appraisal is positive rather than negative.

There is another factor which we emphasized above and which is important here: the individual's group involvements. Appraisers who are
members of groups, or importantly related to groups, which are significant
to the individual are more likely to affect self-concepts. Thus, in Videbeck's
study, the expert was defined as important for the educational group that
was significant for the students. In another study, Sherwood examined
changes in self-concepts of members of human relations training groups.[43]
He found that changes in the individual's self-concept depended upon the
importance of various other group members to that individual and upon
the extent of his or her involvement in the group.

In sum, self-concepts change as a result of ongoing interaction experiences. They are less resistant to change in a positive than a negative
direction.[44] And the impact of others on the change varies by a number of
factors as outlined above.

Behavior and the Self-Concept

Shibutani has pointed out that self-concepts are an important factor in
human behavior. We each attempt to act in ways that are consistent with
our self-concepts; this means that we are able to behave consistently in

[42] Kenneth J. Gergen, *The Concept of Self,* Holt, New York, 1971, pp. 43–49.
[43] John J. Sherwood, "Self Identity and Referent Others," *Sociometry,* 28 (March
1965), 66–81.
[44] Compare Marc Pilisuk, "Cognitive Balance and Self-Relevant Attitudes," *Journal
of Abnormal and Social Psychology,* 65 (August 1962), 95–103. Pilisuk conducted
an experiment in which the subject maintained a favorable estimation of his competence even when he thought he was being adversely criticized by a friend.

spite of a changing environment.[45] This point is underscored by Secord and Backman, who note that when the expectations of others are incon-sistent with the individual's self-concept, the individual will achieve con-gruency by one of three methods: misperceiving the way others see him or her; misinterpreting his or her own behavior; or restructuring the situ-ation.[46] Thus we all strive to act in ways that are consistent with our self-concepts, and we will employ various methods to make our self-concepts consistent with the perceived expectations of others.

The relationships between self-concept and behavior have been investi-gated along a number of lines. Empirical studies have examined the way in which behavior relates to the self-concept, in particular many have focused on self-esteem and on the real-ideal gap in the self-image. A gap between the real (what I am) and ideal (what I would like or ought to be) suggests a low level of self-esteem and, indeed, the studies generally indi-cate the same kind of behavioral manifestations for a real-ideal disparity as for a low level of self-esteem.

ACHIEVEMENT

The bulk of studies relating the self-concept to achievement have focused on academic achievement. They consistently report a relationship between the two, namely, the higher one's conception of one's ability, the higher one's achievement. Thus a 1960 study compared grade-point averages of high school students with their scores on the Primary Mental Abilities Test in order to identify achievers and underachievers; self-concepts of the students were measured by an adjective check list. The researchers found differences in self-concepts between the two groups, with male under-achievers having more negative self-evaluations than male achievers, and female underachievers having ambivalent feelings about themselves.[47]

A considerably more extensive study was carried on by Brookover and his associates, involving 1,050 seventh graders in a midwestern city.[48] Three hypotheses formed the focus of the study:

1. The self-concepts of high achievers among junior high school stu-dents with similar levels of intelligence . . . vary significantly from the self-concepts of low achievers.
2. Students' self-concepts of ability in specific school subjects vary

[45] Tamotsu Shibutani, *Society and Personality,* Prentice-Hall, Englewood Cliffs, N.J., 1961, pp. 260–269.

[46] Paul F. Secord and Carl W. Backman, *Social Psychology,* 2nd ed., McGraw-Hill, New York, 1974, pp. 529–530.

[47] Merville C. Shaw, Kenneth Edson, and Hugh M. Bell, "The Self-Concept of Bright Underachieving High School Students as Revealed by an Adjective Check List," *Personnel and Guidance Journal,* 39 (November 1960), 193–196.

[48] Wilbur B. Brookover, Ann Paterson, and Shailer Thomas, *Self-Concept of Ability and School Achievement,* Office of Reseach and Publications, The Michigan State University Press, East Lansing, 1962.

both from one subject to the other as well as from their general self-concepts of ability.

3. The expectations of significant others as perceived by junior high school students are positively correlated with students' self-concepts as learners.[49]

Self-concept-of-ability scales were developed to measure both a generalized self-concept of ability and one related to specific school subjects. The researchers found all three hypotheses supported by the results. Self-concept of ability was significantly correlated with school achievement, and high achievers had a higher self-concept of ability than low achievers with comparable IQ scores. Self-concepts of ability for specific subjects differed from each other and from generalized self-concepts of ability. And self-concept of ability was positively correlated with the perceived image held by significant others (parents, teachers, and peers).

Self-esteem has also been found to be positively correlated with achievement among students. In his study of adolescents, Rosenberg found that self-esteem was related to participation in extracurricular activities, leadership roles, interest in public affairs, and occupational aspirations.[50] Specifically, low self-esteem is correlated with fewer extracurricular activities and less time spent in those activities; fewer leadership positions in school organizations; lower popularity among peers; less participation in classroom discussions; less participation in, and leadership in, informal interaction with peers; less interest in, knowledge of, and discussion of, public affairs; and a greater anticipation of occupational frustration and failure. In other words, those with low self-esteem are less likely to have those characteristics which our society values in adolescents, and which adolescents themselves deem to be important indicators of their worth and potential.

Finally, the individual with a disparity between his or her real and ideal self does not achieve academically as much as one with less of a disparity. Turner and Vanderlippe tested 175 college students, then compared 25 students with the best match between real and ideal self with 25 students who had the poorest match.[51] They found a significant difference in the grade-point averages of the two groups even though there was not a significant difference in scholastic aptitude scores between them. In a later study in India, Deo and Sharma reported a curvilinear relationship.[52] Students with a middle-range discrepancy achieved more than did those with

---

[49] *Ibid.*, p. 5.

[50] Rosenberg, pp. 201–238.

[51] Ralph H. Turner and Richard H. Vanderlippe, "Self-Ideal Congruence as an Index of Adjustment," *Journal of Abnormal and Social Psychology,* 57 (September 1958), 202–206.

[52] Pratibha Deo and Sagar Sharma, "Self-Ideal Discrepancy and School Achievement," *Adolescence,* 5 (Fall 1970), 353–360.

the lowest and highest gaps. The authors suggest that too high a congruence indicates a lack of anxiety and motivation. Another interpretation is available, however, for a number of studies indicate that extremely high correlations between real and ideal self are probably "defensive self-reports made by the most maladjusted subjects."[53] Thus, those with the lowest gaps may have had as problematic a selfhood as those with the highest, and, in addition, were unable or unwilling to acknowledge it on the test.

The above studies all support the notion that individuals who think of themselves as poor or mediocre achievers will act accordingly, while those whose self-concepts include a positive self-image have higher levels of achievement. But, as noted before, correlation does not tell us causation. The question must be raised of whether the self-concept causes achievement or achievement results in a high self-concept. The two are undoubtedly mutually supporting, but there is evidence that the self-concept brought to school by the young child significantly affects academic achievement. Wattenberg and Clifford studied 128 kindergarten students over a period of two and a half years. They found that the self-attitudes of the students while they were in kindergarten were better predictors of their reading achievement in second grade than were measures of intelligence.[54] Another study involved college freshmen; underachievers were found to have lower self-concepts of themselves as students regardless of whether they initially intended to make high grades.[55] And, finally, a study by Dyson reported a high correlation between self-concept and achievement among seventh graders regardless of the grouping procedures used in the school.[56] Such studies all suggest that various efforts to manipulate students to achieve will fail unless self-concepts are changed in a positive direction.

The way in which changed self-concepts can lift levels of aspiration is illustrated in an experiment involving seventy-two black females who had been unemployed.[57] Half of the women particpated in role-playing and problem-solving groups in an effort to make their adaptation to work more satisfying. The researcher expected the women to develop a more positive self-concept and, at the same time, a more positive attitude toward work. It turned out that self-concepts did improve, but the women left the work

[53] John M. Schlien, "The Self-Concept in Relation to Behavior: Theoretical and Empirical Research," in *Dynamic Social Psychology,* ed. Dwight G. Dean, Random House, New York, 1969, p. 20.

[54] William W. Wattenberg and Clare Clifford, "Relations of Self Concept to Beginning Achievement in Reading," *Child Development,* 35 (June 1964), 461–467.

[55] Bernard Borislow, "Self-Evaluation and Academic Achievement," *Journal of Counseling Psychology,* 9 (Fall 1962), 246–254.

[56] Ernest Dyson, "A Study of Ability Grouping and the Self-Concept," *The Journal of Educational Research,* 60 (May/June 1967), 403–405.

[57] Virginia E. O'Leary, "The Hawthorne Effect in Reverse: Trainee Orientation for the Hard-Core Unemployed Woman," *Journal of Applied Psychology,* 56 (December 1972), 491–494.

environment to seek something better! Their enhanced self-concepts led to an aspiration that had unexpected consequences for the employer.

INTERPERSONAL RELATIONSHIPS

Acceptance of others. As a basis for organizing behavior, the self-concept is important in the nature and quality of interpersonal relationships, including the basic problem of accepting the other. Acceptance means neither approval of all the other does nor acquiescence to all that the other desires, but rather a willingness to interact with the other as a fellow human in a noncondemnatory fashion. Such acceptance has been identified by clinical psychologists as important to individual well-being and growth. How does the self-concept affect our ability to accept others? The evidence indicates that those with positive self-concepts are more willing to accept others.[58] They have less of a need to manipulate others to protect themselves (recall that we all have a basic need for self-esteem). By the same token, those with low self-esteem are less accepting of others. Wylie reviewed twenty-one studies that support the hypothesis that low self-regard is related to the tendency to be less accepting of others and to have lower regard for others.[59]

Choice of friends. When we can choose those with whom we will interact, we will select those who are congruent with our self-concepts and who support a positive self-concept. Thus, sorority girls were found to interact most frequently with others whom they perceived as most supportive of their self-concepts.[60]

Wylie surveyed a number of studies relating to self-concepts and choice of friends and drew a number of conclusions, including: those who are selected as friends are perceived by the chooser as more like him- or herself than those not chosen; those who are selected as friends are perceived to be more like the chooser's ideal self than are those not chosen; and these perceptions do not reflect actual similarities—self-reports among friends are virtually as different as self-reports between nonfriends.[61] Methods used in the various experiments, as Wylie notes, make interpretation of the conclusions problematic. But they do support our basic contention that we act in ways consistent with our self-concepts, for in none of the studies was there a tendency for people to prefer others who would

---

[58] See, for example, Julie Vavrik and Anthony P. Jurich, "Self-Concept and Attitude toward Acceptance of Females: A Note," *Family Coordinator,* 20 (April 1971), 151–152.

[59] Wylie, pp. 235–240.

[60] Secord and Backman, p. 534.

[61] Wylie, pp. 150–151.

challenge their self-concepts or hold expectations incongruous with their self-concepts.

When the interaction is involuntary, of course, an individual may be forced to interact with those whom he or she would not otherwise choose. Even then, however, his or her self-concept will affect the nature of that interaction. Using the TST, Faine studied the impact of imprisonment on 257 male inmates in two prisons.[62] He found that those with a high degree of deviant social anchorage (consensual responses referring to deviant statuses or group memberships) were increasingly "criminalized" during their imprisonment—they increasingly identified with other criminals over the course of confinement. On the other hand, those with a high degree of legitimate social anchorage did not change in the extent to which they identified with fellow inmates and other criminals.

Social influence. Some of the above findings of Rosenberg have already indicated problems in interpersonal relationships for those with low self-esteem: they participate less, and when they do participate they are more likely to be marginal or subordinate members of the group. Similarly, Williams and Cole found that sixth graders with high self-esteem were more likely to be emotionally well adjusted and to have a higher status among their peers.[63] Other research shows that people with high self-esteem manifest social power in interpersonal relationships—they are much more likely to influence others—while those with low self-esteem are more likely to be influenced by others.[64]

In addition to self-esteem, the individual's anchorage in groups will affect the extent to which he or she is influenced by others in any particular situation. Couch used the TST on ninety-six subjects in an experimental situation and found, among other things, that those with a high number of consensual responses were less dependent upon immediate others for evaluating their performance on a task.[65] Presumably, being more firmly anchored in a number of groups, they were able to act more independently of the constraints and pressures of others in the proximate situation. They defined themselves in terms of groups external to the situation and were therefore less subservient to the situation.

Definition of relationships. Some of the above findings may be related to the way in which self-concepts lead people to define interpersonal re-

[62] John R. Faine, "A Self-Consistency Approach to Prisonization," *The Sociological Quarterly,* 14 (Autumn 1973), 576–588.

[63] Robert L. Williams and Spurgeon Cole, "Self-Concept and School Adjustment," *Personnel and Guidance Journal,* 46 (January 1968), 478–481.

[64] Gergen, pp. 74–77.

[65] Carl J. Couch, "Self-Attitudes and Degree of Agreement with Immediate Others," *American Journal of Sociology,* 63 (March 1958), 491–496.

lationships. That is, we not only define specific relationships and situations of interaction in particular ways, but we also define interpersonal relationships generally in particular ways. Thus, in general, those with low self-esteem appear to define interpersonal relationships as threatening. Rosenberg reported that the adolescent with very low self-esteem feels that

> he is more vulnerable in interpersonal relations (deeply hurt by criticism, blame, or scolding); he is relatively awkward with others (finds it hard to make talk, does not initiate contacts, etc.); he assumes others think poorly of him or do not particularly like him; he has low faith in human nature; he tends to put up a "front" to people; and he feels relatively isolated and lonely.[66]

Such a perceived threat explains the relationship which has been found between aggressiveness and self-esteem. Coopersmith found a greater degree of destructive behavior towards objects among children with low self-esteem.[67] And a study of college students reported that those with low self-esteem were more likely to be aggressive in a provoking situation than were those with high self-esteem.[68]

Obviously, those with low self-esteem are easily drawn into a vicious cycle, in which they initially define situations as threatening because of their self-concept, interact with others in a way that elicits behavior that confirms their definition and their self-concept, and thus have no basis for altering their self-esteem or their mode of defining interaction.

DEVIANT BEHAVIOR

In the next chapter we will detail a symbolic interactionist approach to deviance. Here, we want to note that a number of studies have shown the self-concept to be related to delinquency, mental illness, and emotional problems. In general, we would argue that the self-concept develops concurrently with the maladjusted behavior (rather than causing the behavior) and functions to legitimate and perpetuate the behavior.

With respect to delinquency, self-concepts vary not only between delinquents and nondelinquents, but among the former as well. Dorn used the TST to distinguish among institutionalized and noninstitutionalized delinquents and nondelinquents.[69] He found that contradictory or self-deprecating responses were made by 52 percent of the institutionalized

[66] Rosenberg, p. 187.

[67] Coopersmith, p. 137.

[68] Milton E. Rosenbaum and Robert F. Stanners, "Self-Esteem, Manifest Hostility, and Expression of Hostility," *Journal of Abnormal and Social Psychology,* 63 (November 1961), 646–649.

[69] Dean S. Dorn, "Self-Concept, Alienation, and Anxiety in a Contraculture and Subculture: A Research Report," *The Journal of Criminal Law, Criminology and Police Science,* 59 (December 1968), 531–535.

delinquents, 22 percent of the noninstitutionalized delinquents, and only 16 percent of the nondelinquent group.

Dorn's finding of differences among delinquents was also reported by Kinch, who divided a group of delinquent boys into three groups as a result of his study: the prosocial, antisocial, and asocial.[70] The first viewed themselves favorably in accord with middle-class values; the second exhibited lower-class values in their self-concepts; and the third group saw themselves as confused and nervous, but daring and disorderly. Still another study reporting differences among delinquents is that of Clinard and Fannin, who found both similarities and differences between middle-class and lower-class delinquents.[71] Among the differences, the former saw themselves as clever, smart, smooth, bad, and loyal, while the latter saw themselves as tough, fearless, powerful, fierce and dangerous. The latter also committed more violent offenses and were engaged more often in violence.

The important point in the latter study is that there is congruence between self-concept and behavior. The studies show that we cannot lump all delinquents together: delinquent boys have various self-concepts, and these self-concepts are congruent with the type of delinquent behavior involved. Furthermore, we may use the self-concept measures to determine which others are important to the delinquents. This apparently varies by race, as Schwartz and Stryker found in a study of 313 white and 85 black boys.[72] The boys were divided into two groups of high- and low-delinquency risks, based on judgments of their teachers. The whites who were considered high risks made particular use of good friends in their self-definitions, while those judged to be low risks made particular use of teachers and mothers. The black boys showed the reverse pattern in their self-definitions. It should be emphasized that these were not delinquents and nondelinquents, but boys judged to be probable delinquents or nondelinquents by their teachers. Nevertheless, there were behavioral differences between the groups that formed the basis for the teachers' judgments, and the self-concept measures differentiated between these different behavioral groups, and identified the others most significant for their self-definitions.

Likewise, self-concept measures have distinguished between emotionally disturbed and normal populations, and have given us some insight into

[70] John W. Kinch, "Self-Conceptions of Types of Delinquents," *Sociological Inquiry,* 32 (Spring 1962), 228–234.

[71] Marshall B. Clinard and Leon F. Fannin, "Differences in the Conception of Self as a Male among Lower and Middle Class Delinquents," *Social Problems,* 13 (Fall 1965), 205–214.

[72] Michael Schwartz and Sheldon Stryker, *Deviance, Selves and Others,* American Sociological Association, Washington, D.C., 1970.

the cognitive processes and interpersonal relationships of the former. One study, using a check list to measure self-concepts, found: considerable congruence between patient self-concepts and the conceptions of the patients held by significant others; discrepancies between the view patients had of significant others and the view the others had of themselves; and a lack of relationship between patient self-concepts and such factors as age, sex, diagnosis, or length of confinement.[73] In another study, Rosengren studied ten institutionalized boys diagnosed as "passive-aggressive personality—aggressive type." [74] They held views of themselves which were at variance with the views they believed others held of them. Thus, whereas this research showed that the emotionally disturbed individual believed that others viewed him differently than he viewed himself, the other research found the disturbed individual's self-concept to be congruent with the *actual* views of others. We have seen that normal individuals have a self-concept which is congruent with the actual view of others, but which is also congruent with the *perceived* view of others. Thus one difference between the mentally ill and the normal is that the former perceive a disparity between what they really are and what others believe them to be. The meaning of such a disparity is unclear, however, from the evidence we have. It suggests an inadequate role-taking capacity and a definition of others as for some reason ignorant of the true nature of the disturbed individual.

A relationship between self-concept and interpersonal behavior has been found among the emotionally ill by the use of the TST and observations of behavior.[75] The two studies included 136 patients in two psychiatric hospitals. Four different patterns of responses to the TST were found. These patterns were labeled A, B, C, and D, and each refers to a modal pattern of response as follows: the self as a physical entity in time and space (A); the self existing in a social structure (B); the self as a social interactor, though somewhat detached from social structures (C); and the self as an entity detached from physical being, social structure, and social interaction (D). These varied self-conceptions were related to ward behavior, with a preponderant number of "As" being withdrawn or pleasant; "Bs" and "Cs" tending to be pleasant and to socialize well; and "Ds" tending to be restless and extravagant in their behavior. Clearly, whether we are talking about normal or maladjusted individuals, we find significant congruence

[73] Simon Dinitz, A. R. Mangus, and Benjamin Pasamanick, "Integration and Conflict in Self-Other Conceptions as Factors in Mental Illness," *Sociometry,* 22 (March 1959), 44–55.

[74] William R. Rosengren, "The Self in the Emotionally Disturbed," *American Journal of Sociology,* 66 (March 1961), 454–462.

[75] Thomas S. McPartland, John H. Cumming, and Wynona S. Garretson, "Self-Conception and Ward Behavior in Two Psychiatric Hospitals," *Sociometry,* 24 (June 1961), 111–124.

between self-conceptions and patterns of behavior. We all strive to act in those ways which are congruent with our self-concepts, and therefore choose to interact with others, whenever possible, who will support our self-concepts.

Self-concepts are also related to anxiety levels. Those with low self-esteem have been found to exhibit high levels of anxiety. Both Coopersmith and Rosenberg found a correlation between self-esteem and anxiety —the higher the level of self-esteem, the lower the level of anxiety tended to be. The anxiety level can be measured by various overt signs and reported symptoms. Rosenberg notes a considerable list of manifestations of anxiety which are more likely to be found among those with low self-esteem, including trembling of the hands, nervousness, insomnia, pounding of the heart, various kinds of pain, biting of the fingernails, shortness of breath, hand sweating, loss of appetite, and nightmares.[76] Similarly, a large gap between the real and ideal self is associated with anxiety. In a review of studies that investigated the gap between real and ideal selves, McCandless concluded that those with large discrepancies are less well adjusted than those with more moderate discrepancies: "Evidence indicates that highly self-critical children and adults are more anxious, more insecure, and possibly more cynical and depressed than self-accepting people." [77]

Since anxiety is a common aspect of neuroses, it is not surprising that neurotics are low in self-esteem. Wylie summarized nine studies that indicate a significantly lower level of self-esteem among neurotics than among normal people.[78] However, as she notes, psychotics appear to have higher self-esteem than neurotics, even though we usually think of the former as more seriously ill. A possible explanation is provided by a more recent study of self-concepts and the emotially disturbed role.[79] The researchers found support for the hypothesis that the more committed the individual is to the deviant role of being emotionally disturbed, the better and more stable will be his or her self-concept. This hypothesis was based on the premise that humans strive to create and maintain a stable identity. If disturbed behavior is rewarded, it may become a central part of the individual's role-making process, and he or she may develop and value a stable identity as a disturbed person. Consequently, the individual will be highly committed to the disturbed role, and will have a better, more stable self-concept.

[76] Rosenberg, p. 149.

[77] Boyd R. McCandless, *Children: Behavior and Development,* 2nd ed., Holt, New York, 1967, p. 280.

[78] Wylie, p. 216.

[79] Michael Schwartz, Gordon R. N. Fearn, and Sheldon Stryker, "A Note on Self Conception and the Emotionally Disturbed Role," *Sociometry,* 29 (September 1966), 300–305.

Since neurotics are able to function in conventional society to a far greater extent than psychotics, we can speculate that the former are marginal individuals, fully committed to neither the sick nor the well roles, and therefore experiencing anxiety and an unstable and negative self-concept. Psychotics, on the other hand, are committed to a deviant role, that role is stable, and their self-concept is actually better and more stable that that of a neurotic. Considerable more research is required, however, before such a conclusion and its significance can be understood and accepted.

Conclusion

We have not, in this section, begun to examine all the studies relating to the self-concept—that would require a book in itself. We have shown, however, that the self-concept is manifest in such kinds of behavior as achievement, styles of interpersonal relationships, and various kinds of deviance. We must, however, once again emphasize the point that we are not positing a simple causal relationship. That is, it might facilitate our thinking if we could simply say that self-concepts cause achievement or the lack of achievement. But the problem is that the variables interact. Thus, whereas we have shown evidence above that a gap between the real and ideal self can inhibit achievement, there is also evidence that achievement works to diminish the gap between the real and ideal self.[80] The study of human beings and their social life is complex, for a human is a complex creature. As Hermann Hesse said of one of his characters: "Harry consists of a hundred or a thousand selves, not of two. His life oscillates, as everyone's does, not merely between two poles, such as the body and the spirit, the saint and the sinner, but between thousands and thousands." [81]

Suggested Readings

The literature on the self-concept is voluminous. A good short summary is provided by Kenneth J. Gergen, *The Concept of Self* (Holt, New York, 1971). In the symbolic interaction tradition, one of the most readable and insightful of the writers is Charles Horton Cooley; see his *Human Nature and the Social Order* (Scribner, New York, 1902). *The Sociological Quarterly* [7 (Summer 1966)] contains a number of articles on the self and the self-concept, including some empirical work that used the Twenty Statements Test. There have been sufficient studies using the TST so that a bibliographic work is now available: Stephen Spitzer, Carl Couch, and John Stratton, *The Assessment of the Self* (Sernoll, Iowa City, 1971). Any study of the self must of course include the

[80] Florence L. Denmark and Marcia Guttentag, "Dissonance in the Self-Concepts and Educational Concepts of College- and Non-College-Oriented Women," *Journal of Counseling Psychology,* 14, No. 2 (1967), 113–115.
[81] Hermann Hesse, *Steppenwolf,* Bantam Books, New York, 1963, p. 66.

reading of Erving Goffman's *The Presentation of Self in Everyday Life* (Anchor Books, Garden City, N.Y., 1959), which is both provocative and readable. Those who want to study the self-concept in more depth and who are prepared to tackle some more difficult materials will secure Ruth Wylie, *The Self Concept* (University of Nebraska Press, Lincoln, 1961), and Chad Gordon and Kenneth J. Gergen, eds., *The Self in Social Interaction* (Wiley, New York, 1968).

Chapter 6

The Process of Creating Deviants

As we have already seen, human social action is thoroughly normative. It is the result of peoples' definitions and values, expressed in norms of appropriate conduct for particular situations. While these norms may be highly institutionalized and therefore followed mechanically and effectively in some situations, there are other situations in which the norms are flexible and change fairly rapidly. In these situations, the ability of people to adjust their definitions of the situations and their values is crucial to the maintenance of order. Both may have to be compromised in order to negotiate a set of acceptable procedures for coordinating action in a predictable way.

Individual identities develop through one's performance in interaction and are maintained through the responses of others to that performance. The individual's identity is a social product in two senses: (1) the norms against which performance is measured are socially created, and (2) the response of others to particular cases is crucial to its development. In a fully institutionalized system, the response to performance might mechanically follow the well-defined and stable norms that characterize such social situations. However, in less institutionalized systems the responses to action are likely to be more variable and must be studied as important factors in the creation of identities.

Negative identities, those that afford the individual relatively low status and relatively poor treatment by others, are as natural a product of social life as more desirable ones. The deviant identity or "label" is a particular and especially harsh type of social identity. In effect, then, to define who is deviant is to explain the circumstances under which some people receive relatively negative treatment from others, develop a bad reputation or deviant identity, and perhaps a negative self-image.

Deviance as a Negative Identity

DISTINGUISHING RULE-VIOLATORS FROM DEVIANTS

Norms, whether they are rigidly institutionalized or flexible and negotiable, are basically rules. If rules are not made to be broken, they are certainly made so that they can be. Peter Winch suggests that rules are "defined" by the fact that they can be broken. In his view, the crucial contrast is between situations in which any action is regarded as being equally appropriate and situations in which some actions are regarded as more appropriate than others. It is only when some actions are more highly valued than others in a situation that a rule can be said to exist. It is the potential for inappropriate actions and thus the possibility of mistakes or rule violations that defines the rule. This defining characteristic of rules—the fact that they can be broken—applies equally to a set of instructions for adding a column of figures and to instructions for the degree of deference to be shown an employer. The existence of the rule makes it possible to evaluate behavior, and in turn to respond differentially to action on the basis of the evaluation.[1]

[1] Peter Winch, *The Idea of a Social Science,* Humanities Press, New York, 1967, p. 32.

Intuitively, the nature of rules and the observable fact that social rewards are distributed unevenly in society form an attractive pair. It is tempting to believe that the distribution of social rewards is linked directly to the degree to which different people conform to social norms. With respect to deviant action, we might suspect that negative sanctions of all forms are the response to norm violations and only to norm violations. That would be simple and, barring drastic disagreement concerning the legitimacy of the norms, it would be just.

Applying sanctions is a social act. But, for both theoretical and practical methodological reasons, we must distinguish between the process of rule-breaking, on the one hand, and negative sanctioning, on the other. We will begin with the theoretical reasons for this distinction. First, we must remember that we are not talking about the actions of a single individual in this instance, but rather the fitting together of two or more lines of action. In the simplest case, we would be confronted with a single act performed by a person while a second person evaluated the act and responded to it. However, each person responds not only to the other with whom he or she is interacting at a given moment but also to the networks of others with whom he or she deals. The social networks of the two interacting people may overlap only slightly, if at all. Further, the interactants may have different reference groups, different self-concepts, different values, and may occupy different social roles. Because of these routinely encountered conditions, each of the interactants must respond to a different set of social contingencies. One implication of this view of interaction is that each interactant is only one of the many concerns of the other and may not even be an important one. For example, the social pressure brought to bear on a person to avoid a "scene" may be strong enough to lead him to decide not to apply negative sanctions to rule-violating activities, even if the sanctions were legitimate. This occurrence is common when the application of sanctions would be more disruptive than the violation.

Similarly, the decision to violate a rule may be more subject to external social pressures which outweigh the sanctions that might be applied. Even the certainty of punishment, if the punishment is not defined as severe by the potential violator, may be outweighed by either the material gain from rule violation or the social pressures that favor it. Facing virtually certain punishment, a public school classroom invariably produces at least one person willing to blatantly defy the authority of a substitute teacher.

Thus to understand the interaction between a rule-violator and those who sanction his or her actions we must attend to two sets of social relationships and controls: the one to which the rule-breaker responds and the one to which his or her sanctioners respond. The sanctioners' set of relationships affects the form sanctions will take and the more basic decision of whether to utilize sanctions at all.

Second, there will sometimes be a discrepancy between those who have violated the rules and, in that sense, deserve to be sanctioned and those who will actually be sanctioned. Both outright mistakes and the complexity of the social relationships involved contribute to this discrepancy. Howard Becker points out that this discrepancy creates four categories: (1) those who have violated a rule and have been sanctioned; (2) those who have violated a rule but have escaped sanction for the violation; (3) those who have not violated a rule but who have been negatively sanctioned anyway; and (4) those who have neither violated a rule nor been negatively sanctioned.[2] In short, two kinds of mistakes are made in the application of sanctions: some people are unfairly sanctioned, while others misbehave with impunity.

The discrepancy between rule-violators and those who have been sanctioned creates many problems for the study of deviance. One major problem is that if we study only those people who have been sanctioned we cannot be sure that those who escaped sanction for the same acts are similar to those who were caught nor that there are not marked differences in their social circumstances. Any differences between the sanctioned and unsanctioned offenders, or between the mistakenly and the justly sanctioned, would bias studies of deviant motivation, causes of deviance, types of deviants, and so forth, if the study were based only on those who have been sanctioned.[3]

Rule-violators sanctioned by official agencies are unrepresentative. As a practical matter, the official records of the police, courts, psychiatric hospitals, juvenile courts, and other agencies of control are the easiest source of information about deviance. Those records concern only sanctioned people; but several considerations encourage the study of deviance in the setting of official agencies despite the biased view of rule-violating and sanctioning they provide.

Rule-breaking is ubiquitous. It occurs in all groups. However, it is frequently concealed from those who are expected to bring severe sanctions to bear. Thus while we can easily locate groups of people and places in which rules of various kinds are routinely violated, we will not as easily locate instances of sanctions. For example, we could observe in a gay bar that a variety of strongly held social norms are violated. Because of the composition of the bar population, though, we would only rarely witness

[2] Howard Becker. *Outsiders,* Free Press, Glencoe, 1963, p. 19.
[3] *Ibid.,* pp. 19–20.

negative sanctions for the behavior. We could observe also that many groups of people routinely violate the narcotics laws and do so in a variety of surprisingly public places, such as in theaters during concerts. Nonetheless, by remaining in close contact with such groups, we would seldom observe negative sanctions for the behavior. When we turn from violations of law to nonlegal rule violations the problems of study become more severe. People utilize negative sanctions as a routine response to events in their everyday lives. The use of such sanctions is, however, often difficult to observe because of the subtlety of the sanctions, their sporadic occurrence, and the emphemeral character of their effects. While watching a group of ordinary people engaged in routine activity would reveal the use of negative sanctions, only minor sanctions might be observed and those would occur sporadically and with little consequence. The procedure would be inefficient.

The agencies of our society specifically organized to exert social control, such as the police and the courts, do not present these difficulties. These agencies in a routine and organized way apply negative sanctions and engage in the decision of whether to apply those sanctions and how severely. Although such agencies do not represent the entire range of sanctioning activities in the society, they provide an approach to them that is practical. The price for this approach is that the results cannot be generalized easily to the entire range of negative-sanctioning activities in the society, but give, primarily, a picture of serious instances of perceived rule violations. That is, studying the sanctions of such agencies, we will be concerned with events that someone has decided are not only sanctionable but serious enough to warrant the involvement of official agencies. By studying the police and similar agencies, we will not learn much about subtle and ephemeral negative sanctions—curt treatment, sarcasm, sexual withdrawal in marriage, not letting children watch television, and so on. In the long run, a complete understanding of deviance will require evidence from studies in natural settings to be sure that the processes involved are the same.

Egon Bittner has noted that the involvement of the police in family disputes[4] or in the handling of instances of possible mental illness[5] occurs only when the events are more dramatic than the usual behavior of the person and/or exhaust the capabilities of families, friends, members of the clergy, neighbors, and others to cope with them. In a similar vein, Robert Emerson documents the use of the juvenile court as a "dumping ground" for cases that cannot be handled by schools, the juvenile authorities, or

[4] Egon Bittner, "The Police on Skid Row," *American Sociological Review,* 32 (October 1967), 699–715.

[5] Egon Bittner, "Police Discretion in Emergency Apprehension of Mentally Ill Persons," *Social Problems,* 14 (Winter 1967), 278–292.

welfare agencies.[6] Further, he argues that juveniles who reach juvenile court have typically already caused unmanageable trouble for their families and for a variety of agencies.[7] These observations suggest another dimension to the difficulty of studying rule violations. In addition to a bias in favor of serious offenses, there may be a bias toward the type of cases that cause bureaucratic trouble in a variety of agencies. "Bureaucratic troubles" may not be simply related to the seriousness of the offense. One point is clear: by studying the official agencies of social control we are not studying the broad range of rule-violators in the society, nor the broad range of techniques for dealing with them. We are not studying "rule-violators," but rather a group of people who have become involved, for a variety of reasons, with sanctioning agencies.

Value dissensus makes sanctioning political. There is another systematic way in which the population of negatively sanctioned people is distinct from the population of rule-breakers, namely, the well-documented differences between subcultures concerning the exact substance of the appropriate rules to be followed. This value dissensus becomes more apparent when we consider matters of decorum and morality rather than dramatic, almost universally disapproved activities such as rape. Even after the official-sanctioning agencies of the society have become involved and have acted there will often be disputes regarding the legitimacy of the rules and sanctions employed. For example, in some segments of our society the use of marijuana is regarded as a grave offense requiring harsh criminal penalties. Other segments of the society regard the same action as a minor vice, or as behavior less socially and personally dangerous than alcohol use, or as a routine aspect of group relations.

It is in the context of such dissensus that Becker refers to the process by which official sanctions are applied as essentially a political one.[8] Stated boldly, those with political power, whether measured in interpersonal relationships or in terms of the larger social structure, are able to punish violators of those rules which they consider important. Becker sees this political process as occurring in two stages, each reflecting the dominance of a type of "moral entrepreneur." A moral entrepreneur is a person who takes initiative in the process of creating or enforcing rules and through this initiative has an extraordinary influence on the distribution of sanctions.

The first type of moral entrepeneur is the rule creator. Typically, the rule creator is a zealot, a person with a deep concern for morality and for

[6] Robert Emerson, *Judging Delinquents,* Aldine, Chicago, 1969, p. 63.
[7] *Ibid.,* p. 83.
[8] Becker, p. 18.

the content and enforcement of rules concerning some moral issue. Zeal is transformed into a crusade or reform movement, in which support is sought for modifying the existing rules and/or making their enforcement more stringent. Moral entrepeneurs of this type are found leading movements against pornography, prostitution, gambling, drinking, or sexual license, and in favor of conscientious objection to war and the legalization of marijuana.

Once a set of rules has been established, their enforcement is usually entrusted to a professional group, such as the police. These professionals are not so concerned with the content of rules as they are with competent enforcement regardless of content. Competent enforcement of the rules, as we will examine in some detail, entails more than simply following the rules to the letter. Limited resources require that priorities be established that lead to selective rule enforcement. The need to deal with many segments of a community, each with its own values, requires a complex ethical compromise. Regardless of legality, for example, many police departments may simply not enforce the rules concerning drinking by people under the legal age. To do so would create too much conflict in the community as "decent kids" began to routinely accumulate police records. This professional, compromising approach leads to the sort of violation of rules that is fertile ground for the reformer to again be a credible voice in the community. Thus any type of ethical stricture will be influenced alternately by zealous reformers and by professionals who compromise ethics in the process of routinizing their enforcement.[9]

William Chambliss has similarly documented the importance of political power in both a current and a historical perspective. In a discussion of the history of the content and enforcement of the vagrancy laws, he showed that both the written law and the pattern of enforcement change in response to the changing needs of politically and economically powerful groups and their efforts to control the less powerful. The long history of the vagrancy laws shows that they have had the effect of controlling the freedom of movement of desirable laborers and stabilizing the labor supply in geographic locations.[10]

Law enforcement also shows responsiveness to political pressure from powerful members of the community. Chambliss found that the discretionary powers of the municipal bureaucracy with regard to licensing, sanitary codes, fire codes, building ordinances, and so on are used to extort bribes from business owners and to drive uncooperative owners out of business. In a sense, those prosecuted for violations of many municipal

---

[9] *Ibid.,* pp. 147–163.
[10] William Chambliss, "A Sociological Analysis of the Law of Vagrancy," *Social Problems,* 12 (Summer 1964), 67–77.

codes have violated fewer rules than those who are not prosecuted. They have not bribed anyone. Further, this discretion allowed the development of a symbiotic relationship between the police and local suppliers of vice. The police would not enforce the laws against gambling, prostitution, pornography, drug use, and so forth in certain areas of the city or against certain groups, thus granting them a virtual monopoly. In return, the suppliers of vice would limit their activities to certain areas of the city, reduce their visibility to citizens who might object to their presence, and contribute directly and indirectly to the financial support of local politicians.[11] Thus, those officially sanctioned for rule violations are likely to differ with respect to their political and economic power from those who are allowed to violate the same laws with impunity.

One consequence of dissensus is that coupled with differences in political power it leads to a systematic bias in the laws enforced and the people they are enforced against. Another consequence is that unless we affiliate ourselves with the official morality, or the morality of some specific group, we must recognize that everyone is a rule-breaker. That is, even if we are careful to conform to the norms and values of our own group, we will be violating the rules of some other groups. Rule-breakers are not a class of people with distinct needs or unusual motivations or personalities. Rather, everyone breaks rules and the meaningful distinction must be made between those who are observably sanctioned for their violations and those who are not. Becker has suggested that the really important questions concerning deviant behavior do not focus on the reason why people violate rules but rather on why people differ in the degree to which they violate rules for which they are likely to be sanctioned.[12] Phrased in this way the study of deviance is a sociological and political study, rather than one concerned with aberrant psychological drives. The dual focus of study has already been mentioned: the social processes through which sanctioning agencies decide whom to sanction, for which crimes, under which circumstances, and how severely, and the social processes through which individuals become involved in rule violations of the type that invite official sanctions.

A DEVIANT IS ANYONE LABELED AS SUCH

We have gone to considerable pains to illustrate that rule-breakers are not a "special" kind of people and that the group of those who are sanctioned is a biased selection from among the group of rule-violators. In addition, we must recognize that the sanctions may be applied mistakenly or for unusually trivial violations. The severity of the sanction may also vary

[11] William Chambliss, "Vice, Corruption, Bureaucracy and Power," *Wisconsin Law Review, 1971* (1971), 1150–1173.
[12] Becker, p. 26.

from insignificant to extremely severe. The perceived severity of both the offense and the sanction may vary from group to group in the society.[13] However, whatever the reason for applying the sanctions and whatever the severity of the sanctions in each case, a process has occurred that culminates in a decision to sanction and to select a sanction of a particular severity. While all of us have been subject to this process and to at least mild negative sanctions, the application of severe sanctions is relatively rare and creates a distinctive social group. One such sanction is the definition of the offender as a deviant—providing him or her with a deviant identity. We will reserve the term "deviant" for those who, for whatever reason, have developed a deviant identity. Such identities are often referred to as "labels" and the prcoess of conferring them is referred to as "labeling."

Implications of the definition. The deviant label has many characteristics that transcend the particular offense for which the person has been labeled. In certain respects the thief, the juvenile delinquent, the mentally ill, and the prostitute share a common social fate by virtue of being labeled. Before describing the common features of deviant labels or identities, we should briefly consider the implications of defining the deviant as a person who has been so labeled by others in the society. First, this definition completely separates the definition of the deviant from the sociologist's perception of who has violated a rule. If the person has been perceived by others as violating a rule and has been labeled as a deviant, he or she is one. This is true whether or not the person has actually violated the rule and whether or not the sociologist agrees with the perception of the behavior. Those who have not been labeled are not deviants, even if they have violated rules. Thus, the apprehended and imprisoned marijuana smoker is a deviant, while friends who have not been arrested, but who have violated the same laws, are not deviants. Second, regardless of the many differences among them, deviants share a distinctive social role. Thus, the deviant, of whatever type, can be discussed in normal sociological terms—he or she is the holder of a role or identity, is recruited to the role, and is sanctioned for its performance through the same processes as those holding other roles. Third, this definition of who is deviant tends to limit the deviant population to those serious violators who have become involved with official agencies of control. Finally, by being relatively precise and well matched with the methods of study, the limits to generalizing from studies of deviants is made clear. We must remain aware that some people may acquire a deviant identity in a community without coming into contact

[13] Arnold Rose and Arthur Prell, "Does the Punishment Fit the Crime?—A Study of Social Valuation," *American Journal of Sociology,* 61 (November 1955), 247–259.

with any official sanctioning agency. For example, a recognized liar may be a deviant in the full sense of the term without ever encountering official agencies. This danger can only be avoided by studies in other settings to complement those that study official agencies. Although our lives are becoming increasingly bureaucratized and our contact with a variety of government agencies is becoming more frequent, certain types of rule violations may never be handled officially.

Consequences of being labeled. The sanctions employed by the official agencies of control in our society are varied and, in some instances, severe. They include the confinement and regimentation of individuals for long periods of time, forced labor, and the use of drugs to control problem behavior within the institution. In addition, contact with these agencies creates a public and permanent record of the individual as an offender. This record provides the basis on which the status of "offender" or "deviant" becomes the consensually recognized self-characteristic, upon which the individual's social identity and self-concept may be constructed. As such roles as "doctor" or "husband" provide a basis for the many inferences about identity that are included in others' definitions of the situation, the official record of being a "thief" or "homosexual" becomes the core of the identity of a person. It is the achievement of an identity based upon such negative core features that defines deviants and it is the process of applying such an identity to someone that is called labeling.

Applying a negative identity is a special and severe form of social sanction that has many material consequences. These consequences are largely independent of the official sanctions available to the agencies of control. For example, Schwartz and Skolnick found that applicants for unskilled jobs whose records showed that they had been tried and acquitted for assault had more difficulty getting jobs. On the other hand, doctors who were convicted in malpractice suits showed no loss of patients and no sanctioning from their colleagues.[14] The issue for such sanctions is not guilt or innocence in the legal sense, but the establishment of a negative identity with a recognizable rule violation at its core. The fact that a person's identity is transformed in this way carries sanctions of its own, in addition to those officially prescribed and available for the offense which leads to the identity transformation.

The transformation of an individual's identity in a negative direction is called "status degradation." A person has undergone status degradation when the opinions of others are transformed so that he or she comes to be looked upon as, in essence, a "lower" social type. It is not merely that the

[14] Richard Schwartz and Jerome Skolnick, "Two Studies of Legal Stigma," *Social Problems,* 10 (Fall 1962), 133–141.

person has been perceived as doing an immoral or disgraceful thing (a behavioral classification). In addition, he or she must have been perceived as having reprehensible motives.[15] The importance of the motivational classification is that it implies that the person might do the same thing again, that he or she is essentially different from normal people, and is not trustworthy as a normal member of society. The deviant label provides the community with a specific set of expectations about the person's future conduct: the person will repeat the same or other unknown offenses. The individual is not trusted and receives negative treatment based on this mistrust and the expectation that he or she is more likely than others to misbehave. Kai Erikson has observed that degradation rituals, such as conviction for a crime or confinement to a psychiatric institution, are not usually balanced by a reinstatement ritual. This failure to readmit the deviant to a normal social status causes the negative treatment to continue for an extended time, even after other more explicit penalties have stopped.[16]

Status degradation need not occur in a dramatic, easily identifiable event. Rather, it may be regarded as the result of a process that may involve many encounters with official agencies and with members of the community. Status degradation or labeling has occurred when those with whom an individual interacts begin to respond to him or her as a person of degraded status or deviant. This may occur gradually as a number of offenses are committed and a number of preliminary negative sanctions are applied or it may happen suddenly, following a severe offense or the sudden awareness of a history of offenses. The theme that deviants are a lower social type is stressed dramatically by many theorists. Becker used the term "outsiders" to indicate that, in some senses, deviants are outside the normal life of their social group. Erikson argues that it is the decision as to who is deviant that defines the boundaries of acceptable social behavior in groups.[17] This again stresses the insider-outsider division.

Under extreme circumstances, the outsider may be regarded as so alien to the social group that he or she ceases to be regarded as human. When such an extreme inside-outside division is drawn, the outsider may be treated by ordinary people in a way that is shockingly brutal. The enslavement of racial outsiders, with all that it implies about their perceived humanity, and the existence of concentration camps, in which religious or political outsiders are interned, are examples. The status of outsider or deviant can be regarded as a continuum, ranging from exclusion from some

---

[15] Harold Garfinkel, "Conditions of Successful Degradation Ceremonies," *American Journal of Sociology,* 61 (March 1956), 420–424.

[16] Kai Erickson, "Notes on the Sociology of Deviance," *Social Problems,* 9 (Spring 1962), 311–312.

[17] Kai Erikson, *Wayward Puritans,* Wiley, New York, 1966, pp. 10–11.

narrow range of social activities in the group to exclusion from treatment as a human being.

EXAMPLE: SCHEFF'S LABELING THEORY OF INSANITY

The distinction between the rule-violator and the deviant and consideration of the consequences of applying a deviant label form the core of "labeling theory." We have stressed that the label is an identity, specifically a negative one, that is applied in interaction and that has implications for how one will be expected to act in the future. Although they are specifically concerned with negative identities, the processes discussed by labeling theorists are esentially the same as those involved in any interaction. Thomas Scheff has made a clear, propositional statement of labeling theory as it applies to mental illness.[18] We will present his nine propositions and comment about the relationships between mental illness and other deviant labels and the interaction process.

Each culture, in Scheff's view, provides a vocabulary for categorizing rule-violators. Violators of certain rules are called thieves. Other rule-breakers are called perverts, and others are called drunks. However, a large group of fundamental and diverse rules remains to be classified— those concerning "common decency" and acceptance of the reality defined by the social group. These are residual rules, and their violation, if labeled, constitutes mental illness.[19] Insanity is the violation of social norms, although norms of a different type than those violated by thieves. Certain aspects of Scheff's theory apply only to this specific type of rule violation.

An example of a residual rule violation will help to clarify the special quality of this sort of rule. When a male is already seated at a table, a female who is able to choose between several vacant seats will seldom choose to sit down next to him. The reverse is true as well. However, when a male or female is seated at an otherwise empty table, schizophrenic patients of both sexes violate this rule.[20] What can one say about such a

---

[18] Thomas Scheff, *Being Mentally Ill*, Aldine, Chicago, 1966. In addition to the clarity afforded by the propositional statement, another consideration recommends Scheff's statement. A controversy has arisen over his arguments and provides the student with the opportunity to read an explicit exchange of views. See Walter Gove, "Societal Reactions as an Explanation of Mental Illness: An Evaluation," *American Sociological Review*, 35 (October 1970), 873–874; Thomas Scheff, "The Labeling Theory of Mental Illness," *American Sociological Review*, 39 (June 1974), 444–452; Walter Gove, "The Labeling Theory of Mental Illness: A Reply to Scheff," *American Sociological Review*, 40 (April 1975), 242–248; Robert Chauncey, "Comment on 'The Labeling Theory of Mental Illness,'" *American Sociological Review*, 40 (April 1975), 248–252; and Thomas Scheff, "Reply to Chauncey and Gove," *American Sociological Review*, 40 (April 1975), 252–257.

[19] Scheff, *Being Mentally Ill*, pp. 33–34.

[20] Robert Somer, "Studies in Personal Space," *Sociometry*, 22 (September 1959), 247–260.

violation? Very little, except that if a person frequently violates this rule, or others like it, by sitting in the wrong place, talking too loudly or too softly, making too much or too little eye contact, or standing too close or too far away, his or her behavior will make one uncomfortable. And at some point, the breaker of residual rules will be labeled as mentally ill. Insanity is a label of desperation. It denotes behavior that violates rules that we cannot state clearly but which are fundamental to social interaction.

Proposition 1: "Residual rule-breaking arises from fundamentally diverse sources." [21] Scheff discusses four cases of residual rule violations: psychological, organic, external stress, or intentional defiance. He makes no attempt, within the labeling framework, to explain the origins of rule violations. Instead, rule violations are the starting point of labeling theory, which studies the response to these violations and the consequences of the response. Scheff's discussion of mental illness, then, is compatible with many different explanations of the origin of rule violations. This is generally true of labeling theory approaches to any kind of deviant behavior. One parallel with interaction in general is apparent. If we were to reverse the question and ask for the causes of conformity to residual rules, we would have to recognize a similar list of causes. This is appropriate since the distinction between conforming and deviating behavior does not lie in the character of the act, but in the social definition of propriety.

Propositions 2 and 3: "Relative to the rate of treated mental illness, the rate of unrecorded residual rule-breaking is extremely high." [22] "Most residual rule-breaking is denied and is of transitory significance." [23] These two propositions reflect the fact that observers of a deviant act may not notice that it is a rule violation and may not respond to it as such even if they do notice its character. In general, we can expect there to be some proportion of any type of rule violation that goes unnoticed or unpunished. The proposition of rule violations that are responded to as such may vary with the type of rule violation that is considered. For example, lies may be less often sanctioned than assaults. Most residual rule violations have little effect and few people are labeled as insane because of them. In our discussion of interaction we discussed several processes, such as face work and the display of embarrassment, that smooth over difficulties in interaction. These processes are employed in residual rule violations and allow the interaction to proceed without serious disruption. For example, face work is often a response to the simultaneous presentation of two selves through contradictory communication. Such a presentation is in violation of the sort of rule that Scheff calls residual.

---

[21] Scheff, *Being Mentally Ill,* p. 40.
[22] *Ibid.,* p. 47.
[23] *Ibid.,* p. 51.

Propositions 4 and 5: "Stereotyped imagery of mental disorder is learned in early childhood." [24] "The stereotypes of insanity are continually re-affirmed, inadvertently, in ordinary social interaction." [25] Scheff asserts that the role of the insane, like any other role, is learned in interaction and supported and refined in interaction. Once this stereotyped role of insanity is learned, it can be utilized to guide one's behavior and one's response to the behavior of others. In most cases, our imagery of insanity serves as a negative model. Our tendency is to avoid acts that are stereo-typically insane. As observers, the stereotyped role of insanity is used to evaluate the conduct of others. Residual rule violations that conform to the role of insanity are more likely to be perceived as insane and responded to as such. If the term insanity is applied to one's own behavior, the stereo-typed role may function as a positive rather than a negative model in guiding future behavior. Others may begin to characterize one as insane and to treat one accordingly. Part of that treatment is to negatively sanc-tion sane behavior, which, although normally desirable, is unpredictable in the context of insanity. Once this process begins, the stereotyped role of insanity may serve as a guide to correct insane behavior. This treatment of the role of insanity is identical to the analysis of other deviant roles and to the way in which role performance is institutionalized in other, nonde-viant, situations.

Propositions 6, 7, and 8: "Labeled deviants may be rewarded for playing the stereotyped deviant's role." [26] "Labeled deviants are punished when they attempt to return to conventional roles." [27] "In the crisis occurring when a residual rule-breaker is publicly labeled, the deviant is highly sus-ceptible, and may accept the proferred role of the insane as the only al-ternative." [28] Defining the other's identity makes his or her conduct more predictable and, therefore, serves as a basis for coordinating action. While many negative sanctions may accompany a negative identity, incarceration for example, positive sanctions will accompany conformity to it, as they accompany conformity to any norm. Once labeled, the deviant may be rewarded for predictability, perpetuating his or her deviant but predictable behavior. If the deviant revises his or her conduct, even in the direction of normalcy, predictability will be impaired and he or she may be nega-tively sanctioned for his or her improvement. In these ways, the deviant identity is normatively imposed on the individual just as a normal identity is. But why would an individual accept such an identity without an enor-mous protest? Scheff argues that the strained relationships and anxiety

[24] *Ibid.,* p. 64.
[25] *Ibid.,* p. 67.
[26] *Ibid.,* p. 84.
[27] *Ibid.,* p. 87.
[28] *Ibid.,* p. 88.

that accompany chronic residual rule violations and the attempts to classify them may be so severe that *any* basis for order is preferable. Group life may be so disrupted by the breakdown of fundamental shared definitions that even the person who will suffer by being labeled prefers the order that will be achieved at his or her expense to the existing anomic condition.

Proposition 9: "Among residual rule-breakers, labeling is the single most important cause of careers of residual deviance." [29] Most of us violate residual rules from time to time with no lasting effects. The episodes are ignored or smoothed over by others and our normal identities are not discredited. Some, however, become established in the role of an insane person. The causes of the initial deviant acts are diverse, but the major cause of the institutionalization of a pattern of insane behavior is being labeled as insane and becoming enmeshed in the processes that normatively impose that role. Other deviant labels also lead to the institutionalization of deviant roles. However, the importance of the labels, in comparison with other factors, may not be as pronounced as in the case of the label of insanity. For example, the role of the insane is seldom if ever adopted because of the appeal of the subculture of the insane. By contrast, the subculture of the professional thief or of the homosexual is a more important factor in the recruitment of individuals to those roles.

SUMMARY OF THE PROCESS OF BECOMING A DEVIANT

To be a deviant is to have a negative identity. The process of becoming a deviant, in this sense, is similar to that involved in achieving any identity. Thus, the discussion of social interaction applies to deviant identities and to the perceived rule violations that lead to labeling. The primary difference between positive and negative identities and between different types of negative identities, so far as the process of defining and maintaining them are concerned, is the relative importance of different parts of the process.

The Process of Labeling in the Legal System

The bureaucracy is the increasingly dominant mode of social organization in our culture. As more areas of life become bureaucratically regulated, it becomes increasingly important to understand how a bureaucratic system works. Our society authorizes a number of interlocking bureaucratic agencies to make official judgments concerning who and what is deviant and to apply sanctions based on those judgments. The legal system is not a single bureaucracy but a group of them, each with its own internal problems, and each operating in the environment of the others. Among them are the police, other state and federal investigative agencies, the courts,

[29] *Ibid.,* pp. 92–93.

the prosecuting attorney's office, the public defender's office, various social agencies, and the schools. Together, these organizations comprise our legal system and produce guilty and innocent people—deviants and normal citizens.

We will consider the operation of this system as a complex social act, made up of less complex social acts. That is, the system will be regarded as a network of social interactions, each constrained by the occurrence of the others, in the way we suggested in Chapter 3. In that chapter we focused on the internal workings of single interactions. Accordingly, small details of the communication process were discussed at length and the mechanisms that contributed to the smooth flow of the single interaction were of primary significance.

The study of complex systems requires a change in the focus of our attention. In a sense, we will take two steps back from the detailed analysis of communication in particular interactions. We are not abandoning that material. Quite the contrary, we are *assuming* it, and turning our attention to the interrelationships among different interactions. The first step is to consider, in detail, the concerns of participants in the system. We have chosen the police for close attention. The concerns of the participants include both situational (those immediately present in the interaction) and nonsituational ones. Foremost among nonsituational concerns are the pressures put on the individual by others who may not be present in an interaction situation, but with whom he or she must deal on subsequent occasions, and to whom he or she must justify actions. The step back includes a shift from considering the concerns of a particular police officer on a particular occasion to a consideration of the usual concerns of the police—professional, ethical, and practical. Concretely, we will be defining the police officer's role, as it is seen from a variety of other roles— the judge, the prosecutor, the accused, and so on. From these diverse roles the officer fashions a pattern of behavior that synthesizes and balances these demands on his or her time. That is, the police officer acts from the perspective of the generalized other or reference group.

The second step back is to consider not just the one role, but how each of the participants responds to the set of expectations that confronts him or her and fashions a stable line of action. It is from all of these lines of action that the social system emerges. Again, some detail must be sacrificed. While the police officer's role is discussed in some detail, the concerns of the others in the system are treated more quickly. Still, enough detail is presented to indicate that the processes involved are identical to those discussed in the context of the police. Finally, we briefly consider psychiatric diagnoses in the official bureaucratic context. Our intention here is to illustrate that the processes involved are again similar to those of the legal system.

This change of focus is essential to the study of large social systems. It is inconceivable that large systems could be fruitfully studied by analyzing them into single interactions, and analyzing each interaction in fine detail. For the analysis of large systems, a general knowledge of the communication processes that occur within single interactions is sufficient. With that context, it is possible to consider in more detail the typical, stable, practical concerns of the participants rather than the more detailed and ephemeral ones that are found in each interaction. If the stable, practical concerns of the various regular participants in a system are known, we can begin to understand how the complex pattern of behavior that emerges reflects a bargain or collective definition of the situation. To describe this complex bargain is to describe a social system.

In this section, then, we have two concerns. The first is to show how the deviant label is applied in an organizational context. The process of labeling deviants is a complex one, and we will trace many of its steps. The second is to show how the conception of social interaction that we discussed earlier can be used to study larger social systems. We expect that other large social systems could be analyzed in essentially the same way. The practical concerns of the participants and the role requirements would be different, of course, but the interaction process and the development of a complex bargain struck and reaffirmed in interaction would remain.

THE DECISION TO INVOLVE THE AUTHORITIES

The origin of police activity, psychiatric commitments, or juvenile court involvement is often a citizen complaint. In such cases, the response of laymen to offenses becomes a crucial step in the interpretation of the law or psychiatric diagnosis by directing the authorities who must make professional judgments to specific cases. In determining that certain events are worthy of the attention of some official agency, citizens apparently employ a practical criterion: the event or person they report has become a source of trouble that they cannot handle themselves. This practical principle leads to two major types of citizen complaints. First, a major event may occur—one that is extraordinary from the citizen's perspective, and which he or she is not prepared to handle. Being victimized in a serious crime falls in this category as does a sudden encounter with bizarre behavior. Second, the event which precipitates the call for official help may not be dramatic at all. Rather, a person or situation that has been problematic for a period of time becomes, for some reason, intolerable or unmanageable. In such cases, no particular offense motivates the complaint, but a continuing attempt to control a chronic, disruptive factor in social life.

The application of this apparently simple, practical standard is in fact quite complex. Kitsuse has shown that people's interpretations and responses to particular rule violations are quite variable. In a study of the response to homosexuality, he observed that a person may be negatively sanctioned by others and the person's actions interpreted in terms of his or her "homosexuality" purely on the basis of a reputation and without the occurrence of overtly homosexual actions. This is an instance of how being labeled affects one's life. On the other hand, even overt homosexual overtures may be shrugged off with little or no response and no long-term effects.[30] In a similar vein, Scheff reports that the sorts of rule violations that may lead to diagnoses of mental illness may also be ignored and have no, or only transitory, effects on relationships.[31]

Much of the existing evidence indicates that the response to rule-breaking is heavily influenced by the extent of "trouble" perceived by others in the offender's social network. Goffman argues that many people who are eventually labeled mentally ill have a long history of tolerated offenses. Severe action is taken against them when their behavior, perhaps without any change in its character, causes probems for others. A wife may commit her husband to a psychiatric hospital when she finds a boyfriend and her husband becomes a problem. Children who had helped care for a problem parent move away from home and the loss of resources makes the situation unmanageable for those who remain. A promiscuous daughter chooses a too public, too inappropriate affair.[32] In all these cases, it is clearly the trouble caused by the behavior that is the impetus for taking official action, not some quality of the behavior, which may have been stable for long periods of time. In effect, the offender may be acted against because of some change in the social environment rather than the offender's behavior.

Hammer reports that grossly bizarre behavior consistently leads to immediate psychiatric treatment and hospitalization. Over the long term, those close to the offender will take such action if there is a failure of the person to meet social obligations. Irresponsibility is more often responded to in psychiatric terms when it emerges in those with critical roles in the group than when it emerges in more peripheral ones.[33] Similarly, in family

[30] John Kitsuse, "Societal Reaction to Deviant Behavior: Problems of Theory and Method," in *The Mental Patient,* ed. Stephan Spitzer and Norman Denzin, McGraw-Hill, St. Louis, 1968, pp. 40–51.

[31] Thomas Scheff, "The Role of the Mentally Ill and the Dynamics of Mental Disorder," *Sociometry,* 26 (December 1963), 436–453.

[32] Erving Goffman, *Asylums,* Doubleday, Garden City, N.Y., 1961, pp. 134–135.

[33] Muriel Hammer, "Influence of Small Social Networks as Factors on Mental Hospital Admission," in *The Mental Patient,* ed. Stephan Spitzer and Norman Denzin, McGraw-Hill, St. Louis, 1968, p. 250.

units the crisis leading to a call for professional help often seems to involve a breakdown of the family's means of handling problem behavior rather than an abrupt change in the behavior itself.[34]

Juveniles, before they are brought to the attention of the police or juvenile court, have typically already exhausted the abilities of their families, schools, and often welfare agencies to deal with their behavior. For example, school officials generally work with problem students on an unofficial basis. As a result, a labeled truant is not simply a student who will not attend school but one who has not responded to a variety of informal efforts to negotiate the problem.[35]

Thus, for nondramatic offenses, the decision to involve official agencies is more a measure of the community's perception of its own resources than of the behavior of the offender. Hollander has suggested that this pattern of reaction is a general property of social group response. He argues that each person has "idiosyncrasy credit" in his or her social group. That is each person is allowed a certain amount of idiosyncratic or nonconforming behavior before sanctions are applied. Credit, or the right to violate rules without penalty, is earned by conforming to a group's norms over a period of time. The amount of credit may differ for each person.[36] The evidence suggests that the importance of the person's position in the group, variations in group resources, and changes in the situations of other members of the group affect one's freedom to violate norms. Lemert suggests a similar pattern of social responses—the "tolerance quotient." Lemert specifically recognizes that the tolerance quotient varies with the nature of the perceived offense and suggests that certain kinds of nonconformity will more likely lead to negative reactions.[37] This recognition accords with the observation that severe violations are more quickly sanctioned and also suggests that different social groups may respond negatively to different types of violations.

THE PROFESSIONAL CONCERNS OF THE POLICE

The activities of the police must be understood in the context of the social pressures to which they are subject in the course of their duties. The police are subject to pressure from their colleagues, superiors, citizen groups, the courts, and other sources which serve as a stable context for their treatment of particular cases with which they are confronted. In their official capacity, the police come into contact with rule-violators of many types

[34] Sheldon Stryker, "Symbolic Interaction as an Approach to Family Research," in *Symbolic Interaction,* ed. Jerome Manis and Bernard Meltzer, Allyn and Bacon, Boston, 1972, pp. 435–447.

[35] Emerson, p. 53.

[36] E. P. Hollander, "Conformity, Status, and Idiosyncrasy Credit," *Psychological Review,* 65 (March 1958), 117–127.

[37] Edwin Lemert, *Social Pathology,* McGraw-Hill, New York, 1951, p. 57.

and must make judgments in the field as well as in official reports and in court. In addition to violations of the legal statutes, the police also become involved in family disputes, instances of suspected mental illness, violations of civil codes, such as the sanitation or building codes, disturbances of the peace on their beat, runaway and problem children—in short, in anything that may cause trouble for citizens. In their responses to the troubles of others, the police are affected by their own troubles, the career contingencies involved in receiving favorable evaluation of their competence within their own social network, and in advancing professionally through the ranks. Three general groups of career contingencies will be considered: the nontransferability of police skills; the threat of wasted time through waiting; and the nature of bureaucratic evaluation through the clearance rate.

Nontransferability of police skills. The skills needed by the police in the performance of their duties are as diverse as the types of troubles that are encountered in social life. Police must make legal decisions, both as to whether observed or reported activities are illegal and whether their own procedures are legal. In addition, when some behavior is perceived as illegal, they must decide which statute it violates, often an ambiguous matter. These judgments may be challenged by citizens, the prosecutor's office, or in court, and the woman or man's career may be affected. Yet the police officer is *not* permitted to practice law. The officer's legal skills, upon which his or her career depends, are not transferable to work outside the police department. The officer must make preliminary decisions about the sanity of people whose futures hinge on that decision. As a matter of applied psychology, the officer must defuse potentially explosive and violent family disputes, barroom brawls, and so forth. Yet a police officer is in no sense awarded the status of psychologist. The work of the beat officer, comprised primarily of peace-keeping activities, requires a detailed knowledge of the specific beat, its inhabitants, and the normal range of activities. Offenses are recognized against this specific background, which may vary from neighborhood to neighborhood, and is therefore not transferable even to a new assignment within a department.[38] Finally, the officer has means available which are not allowed to others, even if they are equally skillful. The police officer is armed and is entitled to use weapons, is allowed to direct the actions of others, is permitted to make inquiries, and so on, that are not allowed to others. These privileges are contingent upon present employment as a police officer. Ex-officers do not retain these rights, regardless of the level of their skills.[39]

[38] Bittner, "The Police on Skid Row," p. 73.
[39] Egon Bittner, *The Functions of the Police in Modern Society,* Department of Health, Education and Welfare Publication Number 72-9103, Washington, D.C., 1970, p. 73.

As a result of the nontransferability of skills and prerogatives, the police career is typically one of continuous employment, not only in the same profession, but in a single department. One consequence is that, more than in other jobs, a successful career depends on the maintenance of good interpersonal relations with superiors, colleagues, and community.[40] Getting along is essential to the officer's career and suggests that the ability to solve people's troubles and avoid complaints is crucial.

Waiting. When the officer comes into contact with other bureaucratic agencies, it is likely that his or her time will be regarded as expendable by those in the agency. That is, their routine will not take into account the pressures of police responsibilities. As Barry Schwartz has recently pointed out, many bureaucracies organize their standard operations to conserve the time of their most important figures. This practice may not be efficient on an overall basis but it does make the maximum use of the key personnel. This is accomplished if the materials for the next task of the key figures are always fully prepared when they are ready for them, even if they are operating ahead or behind their usual schedule. These materials include other people with whom the central figure must deal and who must be ready to conduct their business when the central figure is ready. In effect, this means they must be ready at the earliest possible time, and wait until the central figure needs them.

In the courts, one of the crucial organizations in the police routine, exactly such a bureaucratic arrangement usually prevails. The judge is the central figure in the court system. The chronic shortage of judges and the unpredictable length of each case contribute to a heavy workload for each, an erratic schedule, and a shortage of time. Therefore, court appointments are not typically scheduled for a particular time as are, for example, dentist appointments. Rather, *all* of those who have business in a particular court session are required to appear at the beginning of the session and wait until their case is called. This may mean a full day of waiting for police, lawyers, probation officers, witnesses, and defendants. During this time, little work is accomplished by these people because the court facilities seldom include work space for paperwork, reading, and so forth; they will probably have to wait in the corridors of the court building or in the courtroom itself while other cases are handled. In the Chicago Gun Court, for example, forty to fifty police officers may be present in court at the beginning of the session. On some days sampled, from twenty to thirty-one were still there at one p.m. In the Narcotics Court, police wait 13,000 man-days a year at a cost of $700,000.[41] Whatever standards are employed

---

[40] *Ibid.*

[41] Barry Schwartz, "Waiting, Exchange and Power: The Distribution of Time in Social Systems," *American Journal of Sociology,* 79 (January 1974), 853–854.

to judge police performance, it is clear that productivity will be negatively affected by frequent appearances in court. Accordingly, we should expect the police to try to minimize the number of their appearances in court.

Bittner has found that the police also regard their encounters with psychiatric institutions as wasteful of their time. This is especially the case when the police are involved in the procedures surrounding involuntary commitment. When called to an emergency situation that might be handled as a psychiatric problem and temporarily solved by the commitment of a person whose behavior has become uncontrollable, the police consider the delays involved in dealing with the institution an important factor in how to handle the case, and they are disposed to use a variety of informal solutions to such behavioral emergencies. For example, they can bring the situation back under control and within the resources of the family group. They might also persuade the person to be voluntarily committed, thus reducing their official contact with the psychiatric institution and their responsibility for the case, which might involve future court appearances. Becoming too frequently involved in the bureaucratic apparatus surrounding the diagnosis and confinement of the mentally ill is regarded as an indication of a lack of professional skills.[42]

These two instances of how the police feel about dealing with bureaucratic agencies suggest a general pattern in good police work. Informal solutions that solve problems to the satisfaction of those involved *without* bureaucratic entanglement are preferable to official action.

Clearance rate. The clearance rate is the primary measure of police efficiency. This rate is the percentage of reported crimes that are solved. Crimes may be solved (in the bureaucratic sense of having them cleared from police responsibility) in a number of ways: the prosecuting attorney may refuse to prosecute, the defendent may plead guilty, the defendent may be found guilty at a trial, or the police may transfer jurisdiction. From the police perspective, the best procedures for clearing a crime must be those that minimize waiting and put the least strain on relationships with colleagues and superiors. Thus, a guilty plea is preferred to a trial and an acquittal is a disaster on all counts: it wastes time and does not clear the crime. In 1962, for example, the national average for clearance rates was 28 percent. The existence of national figures provides a relatively clear standard for rating the efficiency of departments. In addition, changes in a department's clearance rate are easily computed and used.[43] Police options in particular cases are evaluated in terms of their effect on the clearance rate. The result is a preference by police for bargaining for guilty

---

[42] Bittner, "Police Discretion in Emergency Apprehension," pp. 278–292.
[43] Jerome Skolnick, *Justice Without Trial,* Wiley, New York, 1967, pp. 164–181.

pleas, solving problems before they are even reported as crimes, limiting their own jurisdiction, and generally reducing the number of officially reported crimes and the number of unsolved crimes that are reported.

POLICE DISCRETION IN THE FIELD

A police officer's action in the field is a response to two sets of troubles: those encountered among citizens, either by being called to the scene or by direct observation, and those that characterize his or her own career situation. In many cases, the problems that must be solved for others are chronic and have been attacked unsuccessfully by other agencies. The official sanctions of arrest or commitment are only one tool which the officer uses in a practical, problem-solving approach to trouble that is similar to the approach of laymen. In deciding how to handle problematic situations, the police officer considers the presence and severity of a legal offense, personal consequences of any decision, and consequences for the citizens involved.

Police involvement without citizen complaints. First, we will consider cases in which no citizen complaint is involved. Bittner has observed that on skid row beats virtually everyone is subject to arrest on a variety of minor charges at virtually any time the police officer chooses. Many arrests are made for public drunkenness, vagrancy, and the like, but close examination shows that such arrests and the threat of them are used by the officer to handle problems that have little to do with the formal charge. The real reason for arrest may be that a person has publicly challenged the officer's authority, or to remove an aggressive drunk from a situation in which he may harm someone, or to protect someone with a dangerous amount of money from aggressors. The principle followed seems to be that the needs of the situation are assessed and a charge selected that will fill those needs.[44] For example, a drunken husband who appears to be on the verge of beating his wife, but who is acceptably decorous when sober, may be charged with the type of minor offense that will detain him until sober but not cost him his job or remove him from the family. Legally, he may be subject to more severe punishment but to utilize the statutes regarding assault would cause more problems than it solved. The family would incur legal expenses, the man would lose a job, the family would be broken up, and so on. In effect, the officer, in concert with those involved, determines what should be done to the person and then chooses a formal charge that will accomplish that end. Similarly, many who are liable to prosecution for various offenses are simply ignored because they are not defined as a source of trouble.

There is at least one other group of illegal activities commonly observed

[44] Bittner, "The Police on Skid Row," pp. 699–715.

by the police that, because of the variety of pressures on the police, do not lead to arrest, namely those activities collectively referred to as vice: gambling, prostitution, pornography, contraband drugs, homosexuality, and so forth. The laws against such activities present the police with an occasionally explosive political dilemma: while there are often active groups in the community that exert pressure on the police to vigorously enforce such laws, there are other groups (including the customers for these goods and services) that demand that the laws not be enforced or that they be changed. Chambliss argues that a compromise of a highly intricate, political nature evolves out of this common situation. The police enforce the vice laws in such a way that vice is neither eliminated nor seriously threatened with elimination. Rather, vice is controlled by geographical confinement and by reducing its visibility to those who would like to see it eliminated. In turn, the purveyors of vice on the local levels become organized and maintain a degree of self-control by cooperating in the containment and concealment of their enterprises. In addition, the money generated by vice enterprises is used to support the political careers of those in positions of power in the legal system. Bribery is also common, with both the police and higher-ups as recipients. The police maintain discipline through selective arrests and may help to preserve monopoly in the community by arresting newcomers who provide unwanted competition along with troublemakers.[45] The police involvement in the enforcement of vice laws is a paradigmatic instance of "getting along" as a career contingency. With money, political pressure, and competing community groups involved, vice is trouble for everyone and requires the police to accurately assess a delicate, sub rosa policy and conform to it.

Response to citizen complaints. The police also have discretion in cases involving citizen complaints. Both the immediate interaction with the complainant and offender and the network of police responsibilities are reflected in the way police define and respond to troublesome situations. First, we must remember that the citizen complaint is typically made by someone who is not familiar with the law, so that an official decision must be made as to whether the trouble is a legal matter. This decision is initially made by the responding police officer. But it is not strictly a legal judgment: events that could be classified as crimes may not be, and events which have no legal implications may still be dealt with by the police informally.

For serious crimes, the probability is high that the matter will be handled and reported officially as a criminal matter.[46] As the crime becomes less serious, other factors become important. The police are likely to offer the

---

[45] Chambliss, "Vice, Corruption, Bureaucracy and Power," pp. 1150–1173.
[46] Donald Black, "Production of Crime Rates," *American Sociological Review,* 35 (August 1970), 746.

complainant the option of handling the matter as a crime or settling it informally. The complainant's preference is a major factor in the police decision. Many complaints involve offenders known to the victims, and as the social relationship between the victim and offender becomes closer, the police are less likely to handle the problem or officially report it as a crime. Finally, the complainant's attitude in dealing with the police is an important factor in their decision. If the complainant is more deferential to the police, it is more likely that a report will be filed and the matter handled in the way the complainant prefers.[47]

The initial decision of how to handle the complaint is important in terms of later judgments of the police officer's competence. When the matter is handled informally, the incident cannot affect either the clearance rate or the incidence of reported crimes. One way in which the police can, in terms of the official records, prevent crime is to handle matters that could be reported as crimes informally. If we consider that there are a large number of troubles that can be solved informally, then the good officer is one who can effectively handle them in that manner. In such cases resorting to arrest or other official action is a failure not a success of police practice.

The confrontation between police and juvenile offenders usually involves citizen complaints and the sorts of minor legal matters in which police discretion is broadest.[48] In dealing with offenses by juveniles, Emerson argues, the police job is not to solve crimes but to handle complaints. The power of the law is used primarily as a threat in arriving at an informal solution. Satisfaction of the complainant is often the main goal. To this end, the police officer often acts as a negotiating agent between the victim, the offender, and the offender's family, working out a bargain involving cash settlement for damages, coerced apologies, promises of better behavior in the future, and so on. The officer in such cases is often active in lobbying for the complainant to accept an informal solution.[49] Such a solution is obviously to the advantage of the offender and his family. If a juvenile has been a chronic source of trouble, however, the officer's goal in the situation may change drastically. In dealing with a problem juvenile, the officer responds with all available legal sanctions to even minor offenses. In so doing he or she may lobby the victims to officially press charges, act as witnesses, and so on.[50] In such cases the judgment has apparently been made that the immediate troubles caused by the official response are less

[47] *Ibid.*
[48] Donald Black and Albert Reiss, "Police Control of Juveniles," in *Theoretical Perspectives on Deviance,* ed. Robert Scott and Jack Douglas, Basic Books, New York, 1972, p. 135.
[49] Emerson, pp. 42–43.
[50] *Ibid.*

than the future troubles implied by the failure to harshly control the youth. Put another way, the perceived pressures of the community as a whole outweigh the pressures from those immediately involved in the case and the involvement in court and official paperwork.

The format in which official bureaucratic reports are made allows the exercise of the kinds of discretion we have been discussing. Officially, there are five options open to the police for reporting encounters with juveniles. In ascending order of seriousness, the five options are: (1) outright release; (2) release with the submission of a field interrogation report that briefly describes the circumstances of the encounter; (3) official reprimand and release of the juvenile to a parent or guardian; (4) citation to juvenile court; and (5) arrest and confinement.[51] The first two options are informal arrangements. Only the last three options give the youth a record, and only the last involves him or her officially with the police and the clearance rates. The flexibility of the reporting system facilitates the problem-solving approach. However, the police officer is not protected from the consequences of errors in judgment. If an informal solution is effected and the offender repeats the offense or commits worse ones, the initial judgment will be called into question. Concretely, confronted with a broken store window and a set of citizens who will be happy if the window is paid for and the vandal apologizes, the officer must make a judgment about the risk that the offense will be repeated. If the officer thinks it will be, the informal arrangement will appear to be a bad choice for the long run.

Notice that this sort of choice is one regarding the future activities of the people involved, or, in other words, their identities. While it is hard to pinpoint exactly where in the process the label is applied, the decision that a person must be officially sanctioned because he or she is too likely to repeat offenses is a major decision point. The decision to utilize formal solutions to problem behavior is one of the ways in which a label is applied. That act changes a youth into an official juvenile delinquent.

In this context, it is not surprising that the seriousness of the offense and its implication for the future are interpreted in terms of the youth's character and the case is dealt with on the basis of that interpretation. Thus the same offense will be handled differently depending on the perceived character of the offender. The demeanor of the youth is extremely important to this decision. Police assess character from visible signs of group affiliation, age, grooming habits, and dress. Further, the attitude of the youth towards the police is considered. Youths who appear to be contrite, respectful, and visibly afraid of the possible consequences are likely to be treated informally, while those who are stubborn, nonchalant, or fractious are likely

[51] Irving Piliavin and Scott Briar, "Police Encounters with Juveniles," *American Journal of Sociology,* 69 (September 1964), 206–214.

to be arrested.[52] Black and Riess report that unusual demeanor, either overly respectful or overly disrespectful, increases the chances of arrest.[53] (Emerson reports a similar emphasis on demeanor in the juvenile court; he reports that a judge based his decisions on similar character assessments.)[54] Cicourel has extensively documented the importance of official assessment of the character of the entire family unit and its ability to control the juvenile offender in the future. This judgment is based on the demeanor of the family, their resources, their willingness to cooperate with various agencies, and their apparent ability to control the juvenile.[55] (The assessment of the resources of the family and its ability to control the offender is also characteristic of decisions about how to handle apparently mentally ill people.)[56]

The decision of how to handle reported and observed violations, then, is complex. The police utilize the discretion allowed in their bureaucratic and legal duties to take a problem-solving approach when the offense is not serious. They consider the satisfaction of those immediately involved in case, the consequences of their treatment of the case throughout the community and for their own careers, and the "character" and resources of those involved in the problem. From the police perspective the judgment of character is a response to evidence, but the effect of this judgment is to add official weight to a positive or negative identity for the individual. The police judgment about the future behavior of the individual, especially if it is negative, becomes an official label. If others respond to the individual on that basis, it may also become a self-fulfilling prophecy of trouble.

DISCRETION THROUGHOUT THE LEGAL SYSTEM: PLEA-BARGAINING

After a decision has been made to respond formally to an offense, the decision must be legally confirmed in the judicial system. The two most obvious matters to be resolved are the legal guilt or innocence of the accused and the exact legal definition of his or her offense. These two elements form the central commodities in a complex exchange involving all participants in the legal system to some degree: judges, lawyers, prosecutors, victims, and of course the police and defendants.

Defendant's interests. A plea of guilty eliminates all chance of emerging from the situation unscathed. Regardless of the other penalities, a criminal

---

[52] *Ibid.*
[53] Black and Riess, p. 135.
[54] Emerson, pp. 200–201.
[55] Aaron Cicourel, *The Social Organization of Juvenile Justice,* Wiley, New York, 1968. This point is discussed at length and is summarized in Chapter 8.
[56] Bittner, "Police Discretion in Emergency Apprehension," pp. 278–292.

record is created which can be expected to alter the treatment one receives upon returning to the community. With this in mind, it is perhaps surprising that a study by Donald Newman showed that approximately 94 percent of convictions for felonies were not the result of trials but of guilty pleas. Of these, 38 percent originally pled not guilty but changed their pleas before trial. Examination of those who originally pled not guilty provides insight into the nature of the legal-bargaining process and the role of defense counsel. Those who originally pled not guilty retain counsel more often than those who begin with a guilty plea. Among this group, those who do not retain counsel tend to have bad records, to be vulnerable to threats of extreme penalties, and to have prior experience in dealing with the police in similar situations. They tend to bargain for themselves, and change their plea to guilty when they have negotiated legal concessions to avoid the worst penalties. Those who retain counsel typically have no record or bargaining experience. On counsel's advice they hold to the not guilty plea until a similar bargain is struck for them by the attorney. They then change their plea to guilty.[57]

Newman divides the bargains into four major types, each involving different legal considerations in exchange for the guilty plea. The accused may agree to plead guilty if the charge is reduced in gravity; for example, changing a charge of murder to one of manslaughter. The accused may plead guilty in exchange for some guarantee of a lighter sentence. The accused may plead guilty to multiple offenses in exchange for some guarantee that the sentences will be served concurrently rather than consecutively. Finally, the accused may plead guilty to some charges in exchange for immunity from prosecution on other charges to which he also confesses.[58]

Defense counsel's interests. Defense counsel also has a vested interest in striking a bargain in which the client pleads guilty. Because of this, Abraham Blumberg has argued that the bargaining process, despite its apparent benefits, works against the best interests of the accused. He argues that the bureaucratic pressures of the judicial system impose an undesirable set of constraints on the defendant-counsel relationship, for the lawyer becomes an agent or negotiator for the client rather than an advocate and typically influences the client to plead guilty.[59] Blumberg does not argue that the client is hurt materially by peading guilty. Rather, he is concerned

[57] Donald Newman, "Pleading Guilty for Considerations: A Study of Bargain Justice," *Journal of Criminal Law, Criminology and Police Science,* 46 (March/April 1956), 780–790.

[58] *Ibid.*

[59] Abraham Blumberg, "The Practice of Law as Confidence Game," *Law and Society Review,* 1 (1966), 19–20.

by the lawyer's motivations and goals in the bargaining process. When the evaluation of the lawyer is disregarded, Blumberg's evidence has a familiar appearance. He suggests that the lawyer's motives in dealing with a particular client are not limited to the client's interest, but include the lawyer's own interests and the pressures of the legal bureaucracy.

The lawyer must maintain good relations with those in the legal bureaucracy. Two benefits follow from this: the lawyer is more effective in plea-bargaining and receives clients through references.[60] Good relations depend on the lawyer's overall performance and this may adversely affect the handling of particular cases. Aside from interpersonal aspects, good relations are maintained in at least two ways: the lawyer must not bring many cases to court in which the client pleads not guilty but is convicted in a trial; and if a guilty plea is arranged, the lawyer must see that the client does not change his or her mind later and cause trouble. These practices aid the court in the use of time and resources. In a sense, the lawyer is held responsible for predicting the outcome of trials with relative accuracy. To an extent, the lawyer's career is shaped by the ability to fit into the legal bureaucracy and this may lead to a pessimistic evaluation of a client's chances of acquittal. In any event, the lawyer is clearly responding to pressures within his or her own social network. Another aspect of the lawyer's self-interest that may lead to a compromise of the client's interests is the pressure of earning a living. It is in the attorney's interest to handle each case as efficiently and quickly as possible. This too may dispose him or her toward undue preference for the guilty plea.[61]

The role of the lawyer in criminal proceedings appears to follow the same pattern of practicality as those of the other participants. The lawyer acts as an agent or negotiator for the client and the treatment of the client reflects the lawyer's own interests and the pressures of those in his or her social network as well as the pressures exerted by the client and the legally defined role relationship between them. This raises ethical questions and also the practical one of whether the client's material interests are sacrificed by this arrangement. In addition, it confirms our general understanding of how roles are negotiated.

Bureaucratic interests. The nature of these bargains is such that the accused, on the assumption that he or she would be found guilty, will be more quickly returned to freedom. There are advantages to those who work in the legal apparatus as well. The prosecutor eliminates all risk of acquittal, in effect trading a reduced penalty for a guarantee that the accused, who is believed guilty, will not escape completely. The court bene-

[60] *Ibid.,* pp. 20–21.
[61] *Ibid.,* p. 27.

fits from the reduction in its workload.[62] And, as we have seen, the police avoid court appearances.

The police and the prosecuting attorney's office are also important parties to the plea-bargaining. The clearance rate and similar measures of efficiency in the prosecutor's office provide the incentive for their participation in the plea-bargaining process. The plea bargain aids the police clearance rate in two ways. First, the guilty plea obviously clears a case in the most favorable way, without expenditure of time by either the police or the prosecuting attorney in preparing and trying the case. In certain common forms of the plea bargain, the clearance rate is improved in a second way. In these bargains the accused confesses to many offenses, pleads guilty, often to a reduced charge on a small number of them, and receives immunity from prosecution for the others. Skolnick's description of such bargains points out the advantages to both sides in the arrangement. The accused pleads guilty, often to a reduced charge, to offenses for which there is sufficient evidence to convict. In return, the police clear other offenses for which there is not sufficient evidence to convict.[63] Concretely the bargain may proceed in the following way. Many burglaries are reported. When a burglar is apprehended, he or she confesses to many of the crimes in addition to the one for which he or she can be convicted. This clears all of the confessed burglaries, whether the burglar actually committed them or not. In exchange the burglar is allowed to plead guilty to a reduced charge, or a reduced number of charges, or is granted some other consideration.

The widespread existence of plea-bargaining for serious offenses extends the practical problem-solving approach to the treatment of them as well. In police discretion in the field and in the response of citizens to troubles, we saw a pattern in which offenses perceived as serious were handled differently from minor ones; the use of informal solutions and bargaining seemed to be less evident. However, the existence of plea-bargaining indicates that the practical approach is indeed extended to serious offenses, although it appears at a different stage in the process. It is as if the police in the field as well as the citizen are unable to cope with the serious offender using their own resources. The immediate apprehension, without attempts to solve the troubles informally, is equivalent to the citizen's call for help. It involves institutional resources that are unavailable to the individual police officer and passes the problem on to others with more resources. As soon as these resource are brought to bear, the practical approach reappears. The difference between serious and minor offenses may be simply that the serious ones more quickly and finally exhaust the resources of the citizenry

---

[62] *Ibid.*
[63] Skolnick, p. 173.

and the isolated police officer and can only be dealt with by those with broader institutional resources.

The public interest. Plea-bargaining raises the issue of whether the public interest is being sacrificed to bureaucratic expediency. This is a complex issue, indeed, which involves not only the possible earlier release of particular felons, but the effects on the penal and judicial systems if the practice were abandoned. There are indications that plea-bargaining is at least not irresponsible. First, Blumberg's argument that the particular client's interests are sometimes sacrificed to other concerns of the lawyer may be viewed positively as well as negatively. The effect is to balance the interests of the defendant against the need for a smooth-running judicial system so that police and courts are not tied up in hopeless cases. This practice may contradict legal philosophy, but unless innocent defendants are pressured into guilty pleas it may be for the best in a practical sense.

The operation of the public defender's office, as described by Sudnow, lends further support to the view that plea-bargaining is conducted within limits that may exclude outrageous bargains. In bargaining with the police and prosecutor's office on behalf of their clients, the public defender apparently makes an independent judgment of the offense and attempts to reach a standard bargain for offenses of a given type. The standard bargain is guided by the definition of what Sudnow calls "normal crimes." A "normal crime" is an offense for which stereotyped expectations exist about the sort of person involved, the kinds of situations that lead to the offense, the likelihood that the offender will repeat the offense, and the danger posed to the community by the offender's freedom. In short, it is a judgment of the offender's social character based not on detailed knowledge of the particular case but on knowledge of the typical pattern of similar cases. The plea reduction attempted in the bargaining is based on whether an offense is a recognizable, predictable one. The reduction for a particular normal crime is made to a particular lesser charge, even if the lesser charge does not fit the case in question. For example, a case of normal child molesting would be reduced to loitering even if no loitering occurred. This allows the reduced charge to be understood in the future as a sort of code so that a person with a record of seemingly minor offenses can be recognized as having been involved in particular, more serious ones.[64] This allows minor charges and penalties to be used while a record is maintained that can, upon repetition of the offenses, be recognized as serious and taken into account. At least as far as the public defender's office is concerned, plea-bargaining seems to be conducted in the context of character evaluations that are similar to those used informally in earlier stages of the

[64] David Sudnow, "Normal Crimes," *Social Problems,* 12 (Winter 1965), 255–270.

judicial process. In a sense, the reduced plea allows serious action to be taken without applying the worst possible label to the offender.

Plea-bargaining as a social act. Throughout the legal system, from laymen responding to troubles to the securing of convictions, all those involved seem to take a practical approach to the problems they confront. All parties in the procedure appear to consider their own interests and the demands of their social networks in dealing with particular offenders. All parties also appear to utilize informal, less severe means to deal with problems unless their resources are overwhelmed. At that point, the problem is passed along to someone with more resources—from citizens to police to the police bureaucracy to the judicial system. Even in the final stages of the process, the influence of many social pressures is seen in the negotiated definitions and responses to events.

The legal system, then, appears to be not a network of individuals, but a network of smaller networks. Each person involved in the system is subject to a variety of often conflicting expectations from his or her set of role others. In a sense, the performance of any role in the system forces a person to represent the synthesized demands of the entire network of others to each particular person with whom he or she deals. In dealing with a police officer, the prosecutor is dealing indirectly with the sergeant who thinks court appearances are a waste of time, the administrator who is concerned with a clearance rate, the customers for vice, the political figures involved in both moral crusades and the vice industry, and so on. The perspective then is sociological: it leads to an analysis of large social systems into smaller ones, ultimately single interactions, not into psychological mechanisms. And what of the person acting in isolation with no apparent others present? Insofar as the others are represented in action through such mechanisms as the reference group, self, and generalized other, solitary action is still social. The police officer who gives a parking citation on a deserted street is acting in a way that can be analyzed socially.

OFFICIAL PSYCHIATRIC DIAGNOSIS

In discussing the response of laymen and police in the field to troubles, criminal and psychiatric problems were considered together. In addressing the complex arrangements of plea-bargaining, however, psychiatric problems are less involved. We would like to indicate briefly that the process of applying official psychiatric diagnosis is similar to that involved in handling criminal cases. We have already seen that the early stages of the process are indistinguishable from those involving other kinds of problem behavior and we will begin with the later stages of psychiatric labeling.

Psychiatric commitment, whether it is officially voluntary or involuntary, is typically the result of extensive pressure from the family of the committed person and from other agencies as well. Mechanic reports that self-commitment usually follows social pressure after a period of problematic behavior.[65] Bittner reports, as we have noted, that when the police are involved in psychiatric problems they utilize voluntary commitment, if they can arrange it, to avoid becoming enmeshed in hospital bureaucracy.[66] Involuntary commitment with police involvement is usually a result of the inability of the case to be handled by less drastic means. In this context, the screening of cases by the degree of trouble they are causing, the presumption by hospital staff members that illness is present in cases brought to them, appears quite pragmatic. By presuming illness the staff members align themselves with the complainers who, as a rule, will have more social and political resources than the prospective patient. Scheff has reported a similar attitude in the courts, and explicitly links this attitude to political and social pressures on the judge who must order commitment. By the time a case reaches a court proceeding, a third screen is involved—a psychiatric evaluation by an appointed or private physician. Confronted with a negative evaluation and a family willing or eager for commitment, the judge appears to assume insanity rather than to scrupulously apply the legal definition of mental illness. Community pressure also predisposes the judge to this course of action. From the perspective of the community, as it is impressed upon the judge, the danger to the community is far greater if a truly dangerous person is mistakenly released than if one who is not dangerous is occasionally confined.[67] In fact, since the family is usually in favor of commitment and other agencies may also have exhausted their resources in dealing with the patient, all the pressures, except perhaps the wishes of the patient, favor confinement. Thus, in legal commitment proceedings and in the hospitalization process, the pattern of response to troubles in a way that takes broader social factors into account is continued.

More detailed evidence is available about psychiatric diagnoses in the military. Officially, the military uses a very narrow definition of mental illness—limiting that term to psychoses. Arlene Daniels argues that both the narrow definition of mental illness and the way in which diagnoses actually occur are effected by the organizational constraints of the military bureaucracy.

De facto policy may vary between post or hospital commanders, but certain bureaucratic demands provide a context for military psychiatry. First, the strength of units must be preserved and this implies that anyone

[65] David Mechanic, "Some Factors in Identifying and Defining Mental Illness," *Mental Hygiene,* 46 (January 1962), 66–74.

[66] Bittner, "Police Discretion in Emergency Apprehension," pp. 278–292.

[67] Thomas Scheff, *Being Mentally Ill,* pp. 130–155.

who can recover and function acceptably should be retained in the service. Second, if mental illness is conceded, exemption from disciplinary measures is implied and expensive medical compensation may also be required. Finally, the prevailing attitude of the military bureaucracy makes it difficult to justify expensive medical decisions of a psychiatric nature.

It is in the context of these pressures, relayed through the military command, that the psychiatrist must make medical judgments and recommendations. Diagnosis is recognized as a medical matter and also as a means of dealing with problem behavior that is satisfactory to both the bureaucracy and the patient. The psychiatrist's problem is not simply to make a medical diagnosis, but to decide what is best for the patient and how to present an evaluation to achieve the best within the possibilities offered by military regulations. Consequently, the psychiatrist often functions as a negotiating agent for the patient. For example, homosexuality is by regulation nonmedical. In cases of homosexuality, the psychiatrist may destroy the files to prevent their use in disciplinary proceedings, claim that an unspecified disorder existed prior to entry into the service as a pretext for discharge, or arrange a nonprejudicial administrative discharge.[68]

The military psychiatrist functions in much the same way as the police officer or the defense counsel. The psychiatrist makes a decision concerning the case and then uses the regulations to achieve a desirable outcome, whether the actual facts fit the official report or not. In making a decision, the psychiatrist considers medical judgment, the welfare of the patient, and the pressures from the bureaucracy.

Processes Leading to Continued Deviant Behavior

We have argued that becoming a deviant, except when a dramatic offense has been committed, is a complex process in which many members of the community and official agencies may become involved. At each stage of the process, the attempt to reduce the disturbance caused by perceived deviant behavior tends toward the least drastic means available. In a sense, the process by which a person comes to be labeled as a deviant can be characterized as a series of attempts by various concerned parties to stop the problem behavior and avoid serious consequences to the offender. Drastic sanctions, including labeling, appear to be the result of successive failures to stop the problem behavior by less drastic means. In this light, we must consider why a person continues to engage in problem behavior. We will briefly discuss three social processes that contribute to this result: the sense of betrayal that arises from the application of sanctions; acci-

[68] Arlene Daniels, "The Social Construction of Military Psychiatric Diagnosis," in *Recent Sociology No. 2: Patterns of Communicative Behavior,* ed. Hans Peter Dreitzel, Macmillan, New York, 1970, pp. 182–205.

dental socialization into deviant roles by those attempting to prevent such an outcome; and the availability of alternate value systems and sources of support that provide the basis for socialization into subcultures.

THE SENSE OF BETRAYAL

We have suggested that problem behavior is often tolerated without negative sanctions for long periods of time. At some point, the group perceives its resources to be exhausted or altered and begins to respond negatively to a well-established and previously tolerated pattern of behavior. From the perspective of the offender, this sudden change in response to unchanged behavior may appear to be a betrayal at the hands of his or her most intimate social group. This perception of the sudden introduction of negative sanctions has been documented by Goffman in the careers of mental patients. Two additional factors contribute to the sense of betrayal. First, the psychiatric institution to which a person is committed may appear much worse than it was described by family, friends, and others involved in the commitment process. Even if the commitment was legally voluntary, and even if the patient agreed that it was necessary, the persuasion leading to that decision may be reinterpreted as coercion in light of the harshness of institutional conditions. Further, assurances that the institution would be helpful may appear to have been deceitful. Even a person who entered the institution willingly may feel, in retrospect, that he or she was coerced into this decision and that those involved were deceitful about the consequences of the decision. This reaction would be greater for those who were less willingly or involuntarily committed. Second, the commitment may involve official agents outside the intimate social network: the police, doctors, priests, social workers, and so forth. Once patients are committed, they may begin to perceive the cooperation of family and friends with such agents as a conspiracy that excluded them from the decision-making process concerning their own futures.[69] These three factors, then, at least in the case of psychiatric commitment, may lead to a sense of betrayal. This reaction may then lead to at least an initial rejection of further advice and support from friends and family, thereby contributing to the failure of efforts to alter the troublesome behavior patterns.

ACCIDENTAL SOCIALIZATION

By "accidental socialization," we mean that those who disapprove of a pattern of behavior may, through their response to it, encourage its continuation. Scheff, for example, argues that when rule violations are perceived as arising from insanity, those surrounding the individual actually support behaviors that conform to their stereotypes of insanity. These

[69] Goffman, pp. 131–146.

stereotypes are learned through media and social interaction and can form the basis for a predictable and orderly relationship with an individual, even though some components of the stereotype are bothersome. In effect, once insanity is suspected, the offender is socialized into the role of the insane, providing a stable context for responses to the behavior.[70] In a similar vein, those who become labeled as criminals may be rejected when they attempt to conform to normal social roles. For example, they are less likely to be hired, even if their other qualifications are identical to those of their "noncriminal" competition.[71] Even the attempt to seek help for problems may lead to rejection. An individual who is known to have sought psychiatric aid is likely to be rejected and further cut off from normal social life.[72] These responses are illustrative of how social responses to deviance, apparently intended to lessen its occurrence, may actually contribute to its stabilization.

ALTERNATE SUBCULTURES

The third, and most significant, factor in the continuation of deviance is the existence of groups that do not disapprove of the questionable behavior and may, in fact, actively support it. The existence of delinquent subcultures, those that require acts perceived by other groups as deviant, is well established. These groups present individuals with a choice between alternate sets of values as materials and social support.[73] The preference for a delinquent or deviant subculture and conformity to its values increasingly estrange an individual from the larger society and provide positive sanctions and support to counter the negative responses to his or her behavior.

Sometimes the term "deviant subcultures" is applied loosely to include groups with unusual or eccentric lifestyles and values, but whose members have not necessarily undergone the labeling process. Examples of such groups are the jazz musicians and unapprehended marijuana users studied by Becker,[74] the pool hustlers studied by Polsky,[75] and the nudists studied by Weinberg.[76] All of these groups have been shown to have alternate

---

[70] Thomas Scheff, "The Role of the Mentally Ill and the Dynamics of Mental Disorder: A Research Framework," *Sociometry,* 26 (December 1963), 436–453.

[71] Schwartz and Skolnick, pp. 133–141.

[72] Derek Phillips, "Rejection: A Possible Consequence of Seeking Help for Mental Disorders," *American Sociological Review,* 28 (December 1963), 963–972.

[73] Richard Cloward and Lloyd Ohlin, *Delinquency and Opportunity,* Free Press, New York, 1960, pp. 16–20.

[74] Becker, p. 1.

[75] Ned Polsky, *Hustlers, Beats and Others,* Anchor Books, Garden City, N.Y., 1969.

[76] Martin Weinberg, "Becoming a Nudist" and "Sexual Modesty and the Nudist Camp," both in *Deviance: The Interactionist Perspective,* ed. Earl Rubington and Martin Weinberg, Macmillan, New York, 1968.

values and the resources to offer social support to members. Yet, they are not necessarily deviant groups. We will restrict our discussion to two subcultures that are deviant in the full sense: the culture of the skid row derelict and the culture of the professional thief.

Skid row. Skid row derelicts qualify as deviants even if the most stringent definition of that term is applied. In addition to the unconventional and disreputable nature of their lifestyle, they are under constant threat of arrest for a variety of behavior which is a routine part of their lives—public drunkenness, vagrancy, loitering, and so on. From their perspective, the peace-keeping activities of the police constitute an environmental hazard —the constant threat that they will be placed in jail, not so much for a particular offense as for the routine practice of their lifestyle or for their own protection.

Wallace describes three paths by which a person becomes increasingly involved in the skid row community. Each path is characterized by increasing conformity to the norms and values of skid row life and, at the same time, increasing rejection of the norms and values of the larger community.[77] A common entry to skid row involves an initial pattern of sporadic, migrant employment. During periods of unemployment, especially when they occur at some distance from their homes, almost all such itinerant workers come into contact with the permanently unemployed and are exposed to the values of skid row life. After this exposure, some of these itinerant workers find that they are no longer acceptable to their family and friends. Thus, a choice must be made between home and the skid row area during periods of unemployment. Especially in the face of family disapproval or other family problems, skid row may appear to be the more attractive choice. Once committed, the individual increasingly conforms to the values and norms of skid row life, even if the pattern of sporadic work continues.

Welfare clients may also find their way to skid row. Many agencies are located in skid row areas and many clients are skid row residents. Clients from many areas and backgrounds may be brought into contact with skid row residents by these agencies. As a result some of them adopt the skid row life style.

Third, Wallace points out that skid row may serve as a haven for deviants. Having been labeled as a deviant in his or her own community, a person may seek skid row as a place where he or she will be accepted, or at least tolerated. To these people, skid row acts as a relief from nega-

---

[77] Samuel Wallace, "Routes to Skid Row," in *Deviance: The Interactionist Perspective,* ed. Earl Rubington and Martin Weinberg, Macmillan, New York, 1968, pp. 235–236.

tive sanctions. For example, an alcoholic who wants to avoid the continued negative response of the community may go to skid row with the expectation that he or she will not be bothered there.[78]

Spradley discusses still another route to skid row. The routine to which one is subjected after arrest for drunkenness is an extremely degrading one. One is held in a "drunk tank," deloused, paraded through court, and often held in jail for want of money to pay a fine. If this happens repeatedly, as it might to an itinerant worker, the victim begins to feel cut off from his or her identity in the community. Some seek to preserve respectable status by relocating in a new community, but frequently the lack of resources brings them only to a new skid row area. After exposure to the life of traveling from one skid row area to another, the values of the tramp, a particular skid row type, become a viable alternative. The society of tramps and of skid row dwellers becomes a source of acceptance and identity. Further, contact with more experienced citizens of skid row while in jail serves as an instructional period.[79]

These various routes to skid row emphasize an important, if unintended, consequence of negative sanctions. The sanctions are often intended to discourage certain types of behavior and to bring the person into greater conformity with the disapproving group. But if they are severe or degrading, in the view of the offender, they may lead the individual to reject the sanctioning group and affiliate with a group in which social support is available without changing the behavior.

Professional thieves. Like the skid row subculture, the subculture of professional thieves offers its members technical and material support as well as social support and a sense of identity. In addition to learning a set of values and norms during early exposure to the culture, prospective thieves are instructed in technical skills and in ways of dealing with legal troubles that might arise. Maurer reports that professional thieves serve an apprenticeship during which they learn technical skills and demonstrate their competence and commitment to the value system of the thieves. The commitment to the group's values is expressed in a variety of ways. The apprentice performs menial tasks for more accomplished thieves, shows enthusiasm for the values and rewards characteristic of the group, and shares the sexual style of the thieves. Further, the novice thief can expect to be arrested for minor offenses and must exemplify a professional, non-whining attitude toward arrest as an occupational hazard.[80]

The professional criminal, as part of the necessary career skills, becomes

[78] *Ibid.*, pp. 237–238.
[79] James Spradley, *You Owe Yourself a Drunk,* Little Brown, Boston, 1970, p. 224.
[80] David Maurer, *Whiz Mob,* College and University Press, New Haven, 1964, pp. 153–172.

an expert of sorts on the operation of the legal system. The ability of those accused felons with prior records to bargain for themselves is an instance of this expertise. These negotiating skills are learned from criminal colleagues, often while in prison. Prison inmates also exhibit a highly developed, unofficial moral order called the "convict code." This code regulates the relationships among prisoners and between prisoners and guards and, in addition, provides a basis for group solidarity and mutual support.[81] This moral order continues to guide behavior after release.

The legal resources available to professional thieves are not limited to their own bargaining skills. It is not uncommon for the professional thief to retain a lawyer on a permanent basis and to maintain a contingency fund of accessible cash for bail and legal fees.[82] Obviously, the use of legal counsel will be productive only if the counsel is better able to maneuver within the legal system than the client. This is accomplished through a specialized set of legal skills known collectively as the "fix." The "fixer" is an attorney who is utilized only by professional criminals. The fixer's primary skill is pretrial maneuvering, occasionally of an illegal nature, based on personal influence in a particular legal system.[83] In fact, the fixer may be recognized as incompetent in the trial setting and may be replaced by another attorney if a trial becomes necessary. The fixer depends for clients upon a reputation among thieves and must remain relatively honest in estimates of his or her ability to help in a given case. The fixer then sets a fee and employs special skills to bargain on behalf of the client. Among the special skills of the fixer are bribery of the police, prosecutors, judges, or witnesses. The victim also may be bribed by financial restitution in excess of the damages in exchange for dropped charges or refusal to testify. In addition, of course, the fixer is expert in the routine bargaining that characterizes the disposition of criminal cases.[84]

Thus, the subculture of professional thieves offers material and technical benefits as well as social support. Certainly, a moral code different from that of more conventional social groups is the basis for social support and the definition of identities. In addition, though, the professional thief learns the skills necessary for the practice of the trade and gains access to legal services that are essential to anyone who frequently encounters legal difficulty as a career contingency. This suggests that affiliation with deviant subcultures need not be costly in terms of material benefits.

[81] Gresham Sykes and Sheldon Messinger, "Inmate Social Systems," in *Theoretical Studies in the Social Organization of the Prison*, Social Science Research Pamphlet #15, New York, 1960, pp. 5–19.

[82] Bruce Jackson, *Outside the Law*, Transaction, Rutgers, 1972, p. 68.

[83] Anonymous, *The Professional Thief*, annotated and interpreted by Edwin Sutherland, The University of Chicago Press, Chicago, 1937, p. 82.

[84] Harry King, *Box Man: A Professional Thief's Journey*, told to and edited by Bill Chambliss, Harper and Row, New York, 1972, pp. 97–108.

Suggested Readings

Labeling theory has been applied to many types of deviance. A detailed treatment of mental illness from this perspective is presented by Thomas Scheff in *Being Mentally Ill* (Aldine, Chicago, 1966). Scheff's work has the added advantage that it has been criticized in readily available sources and Scheff has responded to his critics. For those interested in labeling theory, the dispute highlights the issues involved and presents opposing viewpoints and interpretations of evidence. The dispute is developed in the following articles: Walter Gove, "Societal Reactions as an Explanation of Mental Illness: An Evaluation" [*American Sociological Review*, 35 (October 1970), 873–874]; Thomas Scheff, "The Labeling Theory of Mental Illness" [*American Sociological Review*, 39 (June 1974), 444–452]; Walter Gove's and Robert Chauncey's responses to Scheff and Scheff's response to them are all found in *American Sociological Review*, 40 (April 1975), 242–257. A more general, easily read exposition of labeling theory is present in Howard Becker, *Outsiders* (Free Press, Glencoe, 1963). The references of this chapter include many studies of police activities, many quite specific. Jerome Skolnick's *Justice Without Trial* (Wiley, New York, 1967) includes a discussion of many aspects of police activities.

Chapter 7

The Study of Everyday Life

The questions we might ask about humans and human life are endless. They range from the broad philosophical question of the nature of human beings and society to empirical questions such as the minimum reaction time under stress or the relationship between societal violence and the stage of socioeconomic development. Moreover, the questions encompass multiple levels of human existence, from the very personal experiences of the individual to broad societal processes. Symbolic interactionists have not begun to investigate all the possible or all the interesting questions, but they have looked at various facets of human life at every level. Thus, in contrast to those who argue that different models must be used for various levels of life, symbolic interactionists apply their perspective to everything from dyadic interaction to broad, societal phenomena. Human life is symbolic and dependent upon interaction whatever the level we are examining.

In this chapter we will discuss analyses that have been made at a variety of levels, beginning with the personal experience of embarrassment and working up to the large-scale processes of collective behavior. We call this the "study of everyday life" because the various phenomena covered in this chapter are part of the lives of all of us—either directly through participation or indirectly through reading or hearing about them. They do not begin to exhaust the common experiences which have been studied, but they illustrate the symbolic interactionist approach and show its utility for a wide range of human phenomena at various levels of existence. They also suggest that symbolic interactionists, perhaps more than other social psychologists, have been aware of the significance of the so-called "ordinary" and "taken-for-granted" happenings of everyday life. A moment of embarrassment may appear to be of little consequence. But to symbolic interactionists it is an object of study which is not only accessible to their methods but which is also important in understanding human behavior.

Embarrassment

Although human emotions have been extensively studied, there are no generally acceptable explanations of them. A common sense notion is that emotions generate certain kinds of behavior: we are frightened and we run; we hate and we fight; and so forth. William James reversed this reasoning and argued that emotions represent reactions to our motor attitudes—we are afraid because of our tendency to run; we tend to fight and consequently we hate. To look at the behavioral basis for emotions rather than the emotional basis for behavior has also been the approach of symbolic interactionists. We shall see this both in our discussion of Strauss' work in Chapter 10 and in the following discussion of embarrassment.

EMBARRASSMENT AND PRESENTATION OF SELF

Goffman related embarrassment to the self presented in interaction, pointing out that whatever else it was, embarrassment "has to do with the figure the individual cuts" in interaction.[1] In our society, any kind of interaction

---

[1] Erving Goffman, *Interaction Ritual,* Anchor Books, Garden City, N.Y., 1967, p. 98.

seems capable of becoming embarrassing to one or more of the actors. Since embarrassment is generally considered a negative experience, its occurrence is unsettling; moreover, its unsettling effects can quickly spread to other participants in the interaction and disrupt the encounter.

Thus embarrassment is not a private, subjective emotional state, but a social phenomenon. It is an outgrowth of interaction. In particular, according to Goffman, embarrassment arises out of social interaction in which something has happened to discredit or threaten the identity of one or more of the participants. Each participant in interaction is expected to acknowledge and honor the self presented by every other participant. If a presented self is somehow threatened or discredited, the assumptions upon which the interaction is proceeding are no longer valid. Thus not only the embarrassed individual but all others are discomfited.

As Goffman notes, an individual is embarrassed not because he or she is maladjusted or lacks social graces, but precisely because he or she is not maladjusted—any other individual with the same set of statuses would also be embarrassed in the situation. In other words, embarrassment may be an indicator of social competence—the embarrassed individual has correctly appraised the situation and responded with the socially appropriate emotion. For example, a student who is successful in presenting himself as a widely read and highly intelligent individual will be quite embarrassed if he pronounces "non sequitur" as "nohn sekee'ter," and clearly misunderstands its meaning while engaged in conversation with a group of professors. The latter will also be embarrassed for they have accepted and honored the self he presented. But the group is not maladjusted; anyone with similar statuses in the situation would be similarly embarrassed. Nor does the one have to do or say something that leads to one's embarrassment. A professor who has presented herself as staid, prestigious, and always able to "keep her cool," may be quite embarrassed when the department chairman castigates her before some of her students.

EMBARRASSMENT AND ROLE PERFORMANCE

The above hypothetical cases of embarrassment are reasonable and they lend support to Goffman's analysis. But we have more than hypothetical illustrations. An extensive study has been made by Edward Gross and Gregory Stone, who gathered and analyzed approximately one thousand cases of embarrassment.[2] Like Goffman, they argue that embarrassment interrupts interaction and inhibits continuing role performance. But they broaden the sources of embarrassment, asserting that it occurs whenever "a *central* assumption in a transaction has been *unexpectedly* and un-

[2] Edward Gross and Gregory P. Stone, "Embarrassment and the Analysis of Role Requirements," *American Journal of Sociology,* 70 (July 1964), 1–15.

qualifiedly discredited for at least one participant." [3] Since such a disruption means that continuing role performance is extremely problematic, if not impossible, a study of embarrassment allows us to determine the conditions for role performance. These conditions are three: maintaining an appropriate identity; maintaining poise; and sustaining confidence in each other.

The failure of such conditions can be easily illustrated. Consider a man who goes into a store, establishes his identity as a customer, makes a purchase, and then discovers he has left his wallet at home. His identity as a paying customer has suddenly collapsed, he is embarrassed, and he can no longer continue functioning in the role. The second condition, the maintenance of poise, was a major source of embarrassment according to Gross and Stone. They identified five ways in which loss of poise commonly occurs. First, people use space to enable them to function in their roles, and the transgression of that space can bring about loss of poise (as the individual who enters a small group at a party and breaks a mood which had developed). Second, props are also used in interaction, and the individual who loses control of the props will be embarrassed (as the woman who stumbles over her own furniture). Third, equipment is normally a part of interaction (equipment is movable, whereas props are generally stationary). The loss of control over equipment also generates embarrassment (as one who drops one's bowling ball). Fourth, interactants must control their clothing; tears, frayed ends, stains, and so forth all indicate loss of control and, therefore, embarrassment. Finally, the individual's body is important in interaction, and any loss of control (stumbling, trembling, and so on) is embarrassing.

The third condition, the maintenance of confidence, means that the assumptions which the interactants hold about each other must not be undermined. Thus an abrupt switching of identity can generate embarrassment as the other interactants are no longer able to function in terms of the assumptions they held and are uncertain of the meaning of the new identity. For example, a group of researchers were making a report to their client when the head researcher suddenly made the unwarranted and surprising claim that the group was about to confirm a hypothesis which would be a major scientific contribution. The other researchers were quite embarrassed. For this represented an abrupt switch from the "truth-seeking scientist" identity to the "wheeler-dealer" identity. Apparently the head researcher defined the situation as one in which a lie was necessary in order to retain the client's support of the research. The other researchers defined the situation in terms of maintaining scientific truth. The disparate definitions led to a breaking of confidence and embarrassment.

[3] *Ibid.,* p. 1.

Although he has made no empirical studies, Michael Argyle added two more sources of embarrassment, the failure of the basic interaction processes of "meshing" and "social skill." [4] The failure to mesh refers to situations in which there are diverse definitions of the situation or dissensus about roles. The disruption of social skills may occur through accidents of various kinds: tripping or stumbling; forgetting the name of, or important facets about, another; or simply not possessing the necessary skill for the situation at hand. Thus, this latter cause overlaps with Gross and Stone's notion of maintenance of poise.

In offering these two causes, Argyle was attempting to present a more inclusive explanation of embarrassment than either Goffman's or Gross and Stone's. The other explanations, he argued, did not cover all the cases. But it seems clear to us that while the failure to mesh *may* result in embarrassment, it doesn't necessarily always do so; it may simply result in anger. Similarly, the disruption of social skills may produce other results, either intended or unintended. For example, an individual may deliberately "forget" the name of another in order to show contempt or superior status.

EMBARRASSMENT AND SOCIAL INTERACTION

We do not yet have a comprehensive explanation of embarrassment. In fact, Gross and Stone pointed out that their categories did not cover all the instances which they studied. Nevertheless, we can draw a number of conclusions. Embarrassment, in the first place, is a function of situations rather than a generalized personality trait. It arises in the course of interaction, including situations where the individual's projected identity is suddenly challenged by his or her behavior or by others, or where there are contradictory definitions of the situation, or where there are contradictory expectations about roles. In any case, embarrassment makes subsequent interaction highly problematic. Consequently, the study of embarrassment provides us with important insights into the conditions necessary for ongoing interaction.

Clothing

The clothes we wear have significance that goes far beyond the physical benefit of protection from the weather. In the mid-nineteenth century, Thoreau wrote that he never lowered his estimation of someone merely because he had patched clothes. Nevertheless, he was "sure that there is a greater anxiety, commonly, to have fashionable, or at least clean unpatched

[4] Michael Argyle, *Social Interaction,* Aldine, Chicago, 1969, pp. 389–390.

clothes, than to have a sound conscience." [5] That the clothes we wear have not become less significant since Thoreau's day is illustrated by the woman who said, "Clothes, personal appearance, can make one's life. There is something about it that gives you courage." [6]

In his study of clothing, Gregory Stone has explored its significance in a systematic way. Whether Thoreau was right in asserting that people commonly prefer proper clothes to a sound conscience is debatable, but unquestionably there is great concern with clothing and Stone's analysis illuminates the basis for that concern. At the same time Stone addresses a neglected area which we noted earlier: the significance of nonverbal elements in interaction.

ESTABLISHING IDENTITY, VALUE, AND MOOD

We have pointed out that actors enter the interaction with practical interests and preliminary definitions of the situation. Their definitions are modified during the course of interaction, but they may be modified prior to any verbal exchange. Through clothing, in part, individuals establish an identity and give indications of their value and mood. [7] In some cases the identity is established by a uniform—the nurse, policeman, or bride. Uniforms can quickly change a definition of the situation when they are unanticipated. Consider, for instance, a professor who is telephoned by a sexy-sounding woman. She makes an appointment with him to discuss a class he is scheduled to teach; his initial definition of the situation will be quickly altered when the young woman turns out to be a nun. It is not only uniforms that establish identity, of course. The upper-middle-class student who dresses like a factory worker is affirming a political identity. The elderly man who dresses "mod" may be trying to establish his youthful attitudes and/or his sexual prowess. Whether the intended identity is actually established is problematic, of course, but it is clear that clothing can play an important part in the effort. Thus, Stone reports that one of his subjects, a real estate operator, was asked if he preferred more or less variety in the clothes he wore while working. The man replied: "A smaller variety so you will look the same everyday. So people will identify you. They look for the same old landmark." [8]

As this suggests, one important identity which is related to our clothing is occupational. And integrally tied up with occupation is the individual's

[5] Henry David Thoreau, *Walden and The Essay on Civil Disobedience,* Lancer Books, New York, 1968, p. 30.

[6] Gregory P. Stone, "Appearance and the Self," in *Social Psychology through Symbolic Interaction,* ed. Gregory P. Stone and Harvey A. Farberman, Ginn-Blaisdell, Waltham, Mass., 1970, p. 405.

[7] *Ibid.,* pp. 397–402.

[8] *Ibid.,* p. 400.

status identity. Thus, a truckdriver said that he would feel "out of my class" with dress clothes; a woman who worked part-time in a restaurant said that she and furs would not mix, since it would be like "someone tryin' to overdo, and make people think they're higher than they are"; and a small-shop operator said that he dressed conservatively because it would appear as if he were stepping out of his class if he went "too far" in his dress.[9] In other words, people believe that there are certain kinds of clothes which are appropriate and other kinds which are inappropriate for their status, position and occupation. In essence, clothes are a basic part of appropriate fulfillment of roles.

Sexual identity is also closely related to clothing in defining identity. Stone notes that there are traditions in clothing which are related to sex roles (blue for boys and pink for girls), and that when we accept the notion of sexually distinctive clothing we are expressing our acceptance of, and commitment to, our social world.[10] One other identity discussed by Stone is age, which he argues is also related to clothing as a factor in defining roles but is not as consistent nor as clear-cut as sex.

In addition to establishing an identity, clothing may be used to convey the value and mood of the individual. These qualify his or her identity, enabling him or her to indicate to others the kind of person he or she is. He is not simply a teacher but a good teacher in a good mood, or she is not merely a working woman but a successful businesswoman who is enthused about a new project. In other words, as Stone points out, value and mood refer to the fact that we appraise and define the moods of others. He found that responses to clothing included such appraisal and appreciation of mood. Subjects evaluated clothing, for example, in terms of the way that it indicated wealth, prestige, or power of the wearer; in terms of the way that it suggested moral character; and in terms of the way that it indicated ease of interaction with the wearer.

Thus, in the presentation of the self, the establishing of one's identity, the attempt to indicate to others the appropriate way to define the situation, appearance as well as discourse is important. In fact, Stone posits a "universe of appearance" which is analogous to the "universe of discourse" discussed by Mead. Appearance establishes the identities of the interactants, while discourse refers to the content of the transaction. Appearance "sets the stage for, permits, sustains, and delimits the possibilities of discourse . . ."[11] Thus, there is a universe of appearance as well as a universe of discourse. Both are shared sets of meanings, and since the

[9] Gregory P. Stone, "The Circumstance and Situation of Social Status," in *Social Psychology through Symbolic Interaction,* ed. Stone and Farberman, p. 250.

[10] Gregory P. Stone, "Sex and Age as Universes of Appearance" in *Social Psychology through Symbolic Interaction,* ed. Stone and Farberman, p. 234.

[11] Stone, "Appearance and the Self," p. 397.

former establishes identities it can be "regarded as the guarantee, foundation, or substrate of the universe of discourse." [12] Clothing, of course,
is one facet of the universe of appearance.

CLOTHING AS INDICATOR OF STATUS

In addition to pointing out that clothing helps to establish identities upon
which the universe of discourse may proceed, Stone pointed out certain
implications of this function of our dress. For one thing, clothing can
substitute for reputation in the large urban areas, where the sheer number
of people and the consequent anonymity force us to evaluate others by
some way other than our personal knowledge of them.[13] A sample of
people were asked how they would recognize others who were "high society," the "middle class," the "working class," and "down-and-outers."
They were also asked about the criteria they would use in deciding whether
to invite anonymous others into commensal and connubial relationships.
Specifically, they were asked what questions they would raise about a
strange young man brought home by their daughter and introduced as the
one she loved, and what they would want to know about a stranger they
met and liked before they would invite him or her to their home. With
respect to identifying people in various social categories, the most frequently mentioned criterion was "style symbolism," which included manner, mode of dress, and conversational style. And the most frequently
mentioned form of style symbolism was mode of dress. With respect to
the other two questions, style was relatively unimportant in deciding how
to respond to the strange young man who loved the daughter, but combined
with identity was of considerable importance in deciding whether to invite
a stranger to one's home. In sum, appearance (including clothing) is an
important factor in ascribing status to a stranger and, thereby, in deciding
whether to pursue more enduring kinds of interaction. For more intimate
kinds of interaction, however, appearance becomes of less importance than
the position and participation of the other in the larger society. The
greater the commitment implied by the interaction (connubial relationships demand maximum commitment), the less important is style as a
criterion for making the commitment.

Another implication pointed out by Stone is the possibility of manipulating our status through our clothing. Although many of his respondents
indicated that clothing should be chosen which is appropriate to status,
it is possible for some to alter their status (recall the upper-middle-class
student who identifies with, and dresses like, factory workers) by "manipu-

[12] Stone, "Sex and Age as Universes of Appearance," p. 231.
[13] William H. Form and Gregory P. Stone, "Urbanism, Anonymity, and Status
Symbolism," *American Journal of Sociology,* 62 (March 1957), 504–514.

lating the apparent symbols available on the consumer market." [14]   Indeed, more than one writer has capitalized on this idea and written a story
about a remarkable transformation in an individual as a consequence of
new clothes. As one of Stone's subjects put it: "My new clothes had put
me instantly into a new world." [15]   That clothes do have this kind of social
significance, and that they elicit positive and negative sanctions, can be
tested by anyone through a simple experiment: try a radical change of
dress, such as wearing "dress" clothes to school when very casual clothing
has been worn before (and is the norm), and observe the reactions.

Obviously, this line of reasoning can be overdone. We do not intend
to slip into a vulgar Freudianism and attribute subtle, spicy meanings to
every item of clothing that is worn. At the same time, appearances are
used in defining situations and in striving to create definitions for the other.
The "universe of appearance" is a useful concept, reminding us of the
importance of nonverbal factors in interaction. To be sure, appearance
is likely to be most significant in the initial phases of interaction. But
appearance can also delimit the nature of the interaction possible. An
older man may be unable to interact in friendly fashion with a young man
who looks like a "hippie" to him regardless of the background, interests,
or education of the young man. Thus, the universe of appearance may
mean that any particular interaction starts off with friendliness, neutrality,
or hostility. The identity, value, and mood of each participant is more
or less established by appearances, including the clothing worn. Thoreau's
lament notwithstanding, there are good reasons for people being concerned
with clothing.

Smoking Marijuana

DEFINING BODILY EXPERIENCES

What is pain? What is anxiety? What is orgasm? We can answer those
questions by describing the physiological processes involved, but we still
have not provided a full answer. As we showed in our discussion of the
definition of the situation in Chapter 2, even such a basic physiological
experience as pain is experienced quite differently by differing people.
The meaning of pain was defined in diverse ways by Jewish, Italian, and
Old American patients. There is no uniform meaning of any experience,
whether pain, sex, fear, or whatever.

This observation underlies Howard Becker's analysis of smoking marijuana. There are no intrinsic and inevitable effects of marijuana which
impose themselves on everyone who smokes it. Rather, the effects will

[14] Stone, "The Circumstance and Situation of Social Status," p. 259.
[15] Stone, "Sex and Age as Universes of Appearance," p. 227.

vary according to how they are defined. And the way they are defined depends upon interaction experiences; defining the effects of smoking marijuana is a learning process.

Experimental evidence for this ambiguity of bodily experiences is provided in a 1962 report by Schachter and Singer.[16] The authors set forth three hypotheses. First, when one experiences some kind of physiological arousal for which one has no immediate explanation, one will label the experience according to cognitions which are available. Thus the same physiological experience might be variously defined as anger, joy, fear, and so forth. Second, if one has a ready explanation of the physiological arousal, one is unlikely to label one's emotions according to alternative cognitions which are available. And third, even under the same cognitive circumstances, one will not label one's experiences as emotional without physiological arousal.

These hypotheses were all supported by the experiment in which some students were given an injection of epinephrine while another group received a placebo. Epinephrine produces a number of physiological effects, which the subject experiences in terms of palpitation, tremor, and perhaps accelerated breathing and a feeling of being flushed. The students were told that the drug was being given to them to ascertain its effects on vision. Some of the students were given no information on side effects of the drug, some were correctly informed, and some were misinformed. While they waited for the effects to take hold and the subsequent "vision test," they were placed in a room with another student, a stooge, who created either a situation of euphoria or one of anger. The results supported the hypotheses and the line of reasoning we have been pursuing. After the injection of epinephrine, subjects who had no explanation for their experience (they were given no information or misinformation) "gave behavioral and self-report indications that they had been readily manipulable into the disparate feeling states of euphoria and anger." [17]

DEFINING DRUG EFFECTS

The same physiological symptoms can mean different, and even contrary, things depending upon how they are defined. This is the point that Becker makes when he notes that a variety of effects are possible from the use of many drugs.[18] The user, therefore, "may single out many of them, one

[16] Stanley Schachter and Jerome E. Singer, "Cognitive, Social, and Physiological Determinants of Emotional State," *Psychological Review,* 69 (September 1962), 379–399.

[17] *Ibid.,* p. 395.

[18] Howard S. Becker, "Social Bases of Drug-Induced Experiences," in *Readings in Social Psychology,* ed. Alfred R. Lindesmith and Anselm L. Strauss, Holt, New York, 1969, pp. 158–159.

of them, or none of them as definite experiences he is undergoing." [19]
As a result, the same drug will be experienced quite differently by different
people, and the way in which any individual user defines the experience
will depend upon the way significant others define the effects of the drug.
Indeed, in some cases it may not be possible to verbalize the experience
without the help of others. Blum reports the following account of the
experience of LSD:

> Really, when I first took LSD, I didn't know how to describe what
> had happened. It was intense and important, very much so, but there
> were no words for it. But after talking with others who had taken it,
> I could see that they were talking about the same thing. They did
> have words for it . . . and so I started using these words myself.[20]

The young man who gave the above account said that his wife had the
same problem; she said little about her experience until she had "learned
to talk about it" from others.

COLLECTIVE DEFINITIONS AND DRUG EFFECTS

The above suggests that the drug experience is the result of a process in
which a collective definition of the effects emerges over time and provides
meaning for users. Becker speculates that such a process is involved in
the historical assimilation of any intoxicating drug in a particular society.[21]
The process begins when someone in the society discovers or invents a
drug with the intoxicating effects. Because the drug produces unusual
subjective states, its use spreads, but the users are initially unable to conceptualize the experience. Individuals gradually seek to communicate the
nature of the experience to each other, and a consensus emerges about the
effects and other pertinent information for users. An interesting sidelight
on this process is the tendency to associate the experience with a psychotic
state in the initial phases of use. Since there is no consensual definition
of the meaning of the experience, it will often be viewed as a psychotic
episode. This has happened of course with LSD, and Becker points out
that there were a number of reports of psychosis associated with the use
of marijuana when that drug was first used in the United States in the
1920s and early 1930s. "Psychosis," of course, was available as a descriptive term of the experience. It was not until a consensual definition of
the effects of marijuana emerged that people stopped having "psychotic
episodes" when they used the drug.

---

[19] *Ibid.*, p. 159.
[20] Richard Blum and associates, *Utopiates: The Use and Users of LSD-25,*
Atherton, New York, 1964, p. 16.
[21] Becker, pp. 167–169.

LEARNING TO DEFINE MARIJUANA

In addition to suggesting the historical process by which a collective definition is built up, Becker raises the question about an individual user. How does the individual come to try marijuana and, once having tried it, to define it as a desirable, pleasurable experience? Both the initial willingness to try the drug and the affirmation of the experience as pleasurable are the result of interaction. Marijuana is variously defined as illegal and immoral in the larger society, and when an individual decides to try it he or she is going counter to the forces of social control. Becker notes that the potential user must be able to explain away or ignore the "morally toned conceptions" about drug use which prevail in the society; this, in turn, is dependent upon his or her participation in a group of users, who become his or her normative reference group and enable the individual to engage in behavior which is generally disapproved in the larger society.[22]

But the fact that an individual tries marijuana does not mean that he or she will automatically find it a gratifying experience. Becker traces the process by which a person defines him- or herself as experiencing pleasure rather than illness.[23] His analysis is based upon fifty interviews with marijuana users from a variety of backgrounds and social positions. First, he points out that quite often the initial attempt does not result in getting "high." There is a technique to smoking marijuana, a technique which differs from the smoking of cigarettes and which is learned by interacting with users. The learning may occur either by observing others or through direct instruction.

Second, having learned the proper technique, the individual may still not get high. He or she must be aware of the effects of the drug; since those effects can come from other causes, a person must associate them with use of the drug. For example, intense hunger is one symptom of being high. But obviously, hunger can reflect other factors, and the user must be aware that his or her experience of hunger is a consequence of smoking marijuana and, moreover, of getting high from smoking marijuana.

Third, once the effects are produced and the user knows that they are the result of smoking marijuana, he or she must define them as pleasurable. Becker points out that the ability to enjoy the effects is the result of social learning. The dizziness, thirst, tingling of the scalp, and so forth, could all be interpreted as illness rather than pleasure, or at least as undesirable rather than desirable. But the pleasurable definition emerges in interaction with other users, who reassure the novice that he or she is not

[22] Howard S. Becker, "Marihuana Use and Social Control," in *Human Behavior and Social Processes: An Interactionist Approach,* ed. Arnold M. Rose, Houghton Mifflin, Boston, 1962, p. 606.

[23] Howard S. Becker, "Becoming a Marihuana User," *American Journal of Sociology,* 59 (November 1953), 235–242.

losing his sanity, that he or she need not be afraid, that others have the same experience, and that this is what they have all been striving for.

Thus, the process of learning to use marijuana in a pleasurable way illustrates the symbolic nature of human existence and the crucial importance of interaction in human behavior. A set of physical symptoms which could be variously interpreted are defined as pleasurable as the individual accepts the collective definitions of the experience offered by the reference group.

Behavior in Organizations

SYMBOLIC INTERACTIONISM AND THE STUDY OF ORGANIZATIONS

An enormous part of modern life is linked up with large-scale organizations. Governmental bureaucracies, corporations, and educational and religious organizations have an impact on our lives even when we are not members of them. And for many of us, a considerable part of our lives will be spent in the context of organizations, from the time we enter school, through our working lives, until we eke out our last days in a nursing home or hospital. The study of behavior in organizations, therefore, encompasses a great deal of all behavior in a modern society.

As with all human phenomena, there are various approaches to the study of organizations. Some researchers have identified various consequences of such structural factors as variations in size, technology, and the pattern of authority. Others have taken a variety of social psychological approaches, looking at such problems as motivation, the nature of decision-making, and the significance of informal interaction. An approach that accords with symbolic interactionism has been set forth by David Silverman, who calls it an "action approach." [24]

Silverman gives seven propositions as the basis for his approach.[25] First, the social and natural sciences deal with different kinds of subjects and cannot therefore employ the same perspectives. Second, sociology seeks to understand action rather than to observe behavior, and action arises from "meanings which define social reality." Third, meanings are social phenomena which are shared and learned. Fourth, there is interaction between the individual and his or her social context, so that meanings can only be sustained by being constantly reaffirmed in everyday actions. Fifth, meanings are also altered as a result of interaction. Sixth, explanations of human action demand an understanding of the meanings of actors. Seventh, positivism, which argues that action is determined by external factors, must be rejected.

[24] David Silverman, *The Theory of Organizations,* Basic Books, New York, 1970.
[25] *Ibid.,* pp. 126–127.

Silverman goes on to suggest six areas in organizations which should be investigated in the following sequence:[26]

1. The system of roles and pattern of interaction which have emerged in the organization, and the extent to which they reflect shared values of the participants.
2. The kind of involvement of participants (such as alienated, instrumental, or other), their personal goals, and the extent to which their involvement and goals reflect extra- and intraorganizational experiences.
3. The way participants define their situation.
4. The typical kinds of action of various participants, including the meaning of that action to them.
5. The intended and unintended consequences of action, including the way those consequences affect actors.
6. Changes in the kind of involvement and in the personal goals of actors, including the extra- and intraorganizational sources of such changes.

Silverman uses a number of empirical studies of organizations to show the utility, indeed the necessity, of his approach. For example, he notes that studies of work satisfaction could not yield satisfactory results as long as they focused on purely objective factors; for what is important is not merely something objective like the reward system, but the meaning which the reward system has for the workers. Silverman argues much along the line which we have pursued above in our discussion of marijuana smoking —there are no universal meanings of phenomena which are imposed upon actors. Rather, actors may define the same objective situation in various ways, and they will respond to their symbolic representation of the situation rather than to the situation as it is somehow "objectively" constituted. In the context of organizations, this means that factors like the reward system, the size of the organization, the technology employed in the organization, and the structure of authority in the organization do not have an inherent, inevitable impact on the participants. Rather, various meanings will be attached to these factors, and only when we identify the meanings as well as the external factors will we understand the behavior.

In other words, since the human is a symbolic creature we can understand neither his or her behavior in general nor his or her behavior in organizations if we ignore such things as subjective meanings of action. In the following paragraphs, this will become clear as we show the utility of symbolic interactionism for understanding organizational processes.

[26] *Ibid.,* p. 154.

We will examine a number of organizational phenomena, most of which have been rather extensively studied and all of which are illuminated by the application of the symbolic interactionist perspective.

ORGANIZATIONAL SOCIALIZATION

We have previously pointed out that socialization is a lifelong process, and that we are socialized each time we enter a new group. As this suggests, one of the important processes in organizations is the socialization of new members. But obviously not all new members are socialized to an equal extent. For example, among new church members, some will be committed and regular while others will remain marginal; or among new students in a university, some will graduate with honors while others will express disenchantment and drop out prior to graduation, and some will adopt the notion that learning is valuable for its own sake while others will never view their education as anything other than an open door to employment.

How can we account for these differing degrees of socialization in organizations? An important part of the answer is found in the research of D. A. Ondrack, who made a comparative study of professional schools.[27] Ondrack hypothesized that the amount of socialization would depend upon the extent to which significant reference others in the organization were consistent in the relevant attitudes and values. The organizations studied were schools of nursing. In one there was high consistency in nursing attitudes among the significant others (teachers, staff nurses, and head nurses), in another there was moderate consensus, and in the third there was low consensus. The attitudes and values measured had to do with dogmatism (degree of open-mindedness), nursing as a career, democratic student-teacher relations, professional ideals, nursing school goals, teacher versus staff nurse as a model, and socio-therapeutic philosophy.

In accord with the hypothesis, Ondrack found that students in the high-consensus school were much more thoroughly socialized than those in the other two schools. Moreover, this was not due to initial similarity between students and staff. The students who entered the high-consensus school were significantly different from their teachers on five of seven scales (measuring the above-mentioned attitudes and values); but the graduating students from that school were different from their teachers on only one of the scales (the one measuring democratic student-teacher relations). As Ondrack points out, this suggests that organizations concerned about socializing new members need to attend to the values and attitudes of those responsible for the socialization as well as to the

[27] D. A. Ondrack, "Socialization in Professional Schools: A Comparative Study," *Administrative Science Quarterly,* 20 (March 1975), 97–103.

mòre typical concern of selecting the "right" kind of trainees or students for the organization.

INTERACTION PATTERNS IN ORGANIZATIONS

It has been known for some time that organizations cannot be understood merely by delineating the formal structure. The so-called "organizational chart" shows us the formal lines of authority and communication, but there is always an informal organization—patterns of interaction—which is as important for organizational behavior as the formal setup (this insight originated with the human relations perspective on organizations). A good example of the importance of interaction patterns in organizations is provided by Turner's study of the navy disbursing officer as a bureaucrat.[28] Turner's analysis, based on his experience during World War Two, shows that the disbursing officer was subjected to contrary roles and expectations. The contradictions arose from the fact that a bureaucracy has a set of rules and a hierarchy of authority. In some cases, the disbursing officer would be told by a superior to do something that conflicted with regulations, so that these two elements of the bureaucracy contradicted each other and left the disbursing officer with a dilemma. In such cases, informal patterns of interaction could determine the course actually taken by the officer.

The informal patterns of interaction took three forms: friendships; "simulated" friendships (such as the officer who treated someone of lower rank as a friend); and exchange relationships (in common terms, "you pat my back and I'll pat yours"). The disbursing officer was in the unfortunate position of being subjected to continuing demands from these informal patterns that were contrary to the formal rules of the organization. Turner found that various disbursing officers responded in differing ways to these contrary demands. One type of response was to go strictly by regulations; few of the officers adopted this response, and some who did adopt it at first later abandoned it. A second type of response was to go strictly by demands of informal patterns of interaction, breaking regulations without hesitation; officers who followed this mode did not last long in the position. A third response, also relatively infrequent, was that of the "sincere type," the individual who thought the conflicts generated by the contrary demands on him were due to his own inadequate understanding of the regulations. The most common response was that of the "realist," the officer who realized the illogical facets of his position and who was able to move back and forth between enforcing regulations and yielding to informal pressures depending upon the situation.

[28] Ralph H. Turner, "The Navy Disbursing Officer as a Bureaucrat," *American Sociological Review,* 12 (June 1947), 342–348.

In sum, Turner shows that the same kind of organizational pressures yield differing responses among different individuals. The only responses one might have predicted from a knowledge of the formal organizational structure—enforcing regulations or yielding to a superior officers's command and filing a grievance (also according to regulations)—were a small proportion of the actual responses. Informal patterns of interaction were as important in the disbursing officer's behavior as the formal bureaucratic structure. And differing definitions of the situation led to diverse kinds of responses in the face of the contradiction between formal and informal demands.

SUBJECTIVE MEANINGS IN ORGANIZATIONAL BEHAVIOR

The importance of understanding subjective meanings can be inferred from Michel Crozier's study of two French bureaucracies.[29] Continuing conflict and power struggles existed in the two bureaucracies; the struggle was primarily between occupational groups: controller-versus-director conflict, assistant director-versus-director conflict, and so forth. There was little or no opportunity for mobility across occupational categories; the only avenue of advancement for the individual was through the enhancement of the position of his or her group with respect to other groups. The conflict therefore was a struggle for power in the context of discrete, homogeneous groups.

In the course of the power struggle, some groups pressed for organizational change, while others opted for the status quo. An interesting finding of Crozier is that the directors pressed for change, although they were socially conservative with regard to the wider society. Their striving for change reflected a situated effort to gain power, not a general liberal attitude; the changes they wanted to effect would have solidified their own power. Again, Crozier points out that the various groups "fight rationalization in their own field while trying to further it in other fields."[30] "Rationalization" here refers to the regulation of behavior by explicit and definite rules. The effort to implement such rationalization in groups other than one's own again reflects a situated struggle rather than a value on rationalization per se.

If we try to explain organizational behavior on the basis of personality variables, the conservative directors' efforts to change the organization make no sense, and those who insisted on rationalizing the organization in one area while resisting it in another area appear as living contradictions. If we try to explain the behavior solely on the basis of the "ideal" bureau-

[29] Michel Crozier, *The Bureaucratic Phenomenon,* The University of Chicago Press, Chicago, 1964.

[30] *Ibid.,* pp. 299–300.

cracy, we again are perplexed. The hierarchy of authority was not working properly, since the directors were resisted by those below them; and rationalization, the essence of bureaucracy, should have been welcomed since increasing it can only benefit everyone. But once we know the meaning of change, the meaning of resisting change, and the meaning of rationalizing or resisting rationalization, the behavior becomes understandable. Once the situation has been defined as a power struggle, the behavior will take forms that seem to contradict basic personality patterns and that run counter to that ideally desired in a bureaucratic organization.

DEFINING THE ORGANIZATIONAL SITUATION

Various bureaucratic rules and policies are defined differently by differing actors, and these differing definitions are important in understanding behavior. This was the basis of Zimmerman's study of "rule use" in a bureaucracy.[31] Zimmerman argues that the meaning of rules, policies, and goals in any particular situation must be taken as problematic rather than as a settled issue; in contrast to those researchers who assume that bureaucratic employees tend to comply with the rules, Zimmerman offers the notion of "competent rule use." His study involved a governmental agency in which aid was administered to people in need. The receptionists in the agency had the task of insuring an "orderly and appropriately paced preprocessing" of clients and the assignment of clients to a caseworker. Zimmerman observed cases in which the receptionist would break the rules by not assigning clients to various caseworkers in the proper order. For example, one caseworker was due to receive a third applicant and the receptionist discovered that the first applicant was still being interviewed. Eventually, the applicant was switched to another caseworker; this required alterations in certain records as well as being a violation of the rules. Nevertheless, the receptionist fulfilled the "spirit" of the rule, which was designed to maximize efficiency in the processing of applications. As Zimmerman notes, from the point of view of the receptionist, the desired outcome was achieved. In breaking the rule, the receptionist was acting in accord with the "competent use" of rules.

It is not difficult to imagine another receptionist who would adhere to the rules regardless of how long a particular applicant had to wait. In such a case, the rules would have a different meaning; the situation would be defined differently, and contrary kinds of behavior would be observed within the context of the same set of rules.

Actual organizational behavior is not as static as the above may suggest. That is, definitions of situations change as a result of interaction in

---

[31] Don Zimmerman, "The Practicalities of Rule Use," in *People and Organizations,* ed. Graeme Salaman and Kenneth Thompson, Longman, London, 1973, pp. 250–263.

the organization. We are not suggesting that the meaning of a situation remains constant for an individual, that his or her definition of a particular situation remains the same over time for all similar situations. There is an interaction process in the organization as well as in other situations, and definitions are altered as a result of that interaction. This is illustrated in Davis' study of polio patients.[32] Davis investigated the changing definitions of two aspects of the situation of children hospitalized with polio—the definition of time and the definition of progress towards recovery.

With respect to the definition of time, the initial expectation of the patient and the family is a short duration of hospital confinement. This must be changed to a long-term perspective which contains uncertainty about the outcome. The shift in parental perspective occurs through interaction with the physician and, in many cases, with other hospital personnel and acquaintances outside the hospital. The child's perspective is altered by loosening his or her ties with home and integrating him or her into the subculture of patients in the hospital. Davis identified a number of mechanisms through which the child's perspective is changed, including: restrictions on the number of parental visits; assumption by hospital personnel of many parental functions; duplication of home activities such as television and comic books; rewards and punishments; and, most importantly, the fact of living where sickness is the norm rather than deviance.

Associated with this changing definition of time is a changing definition of progress. Both parents and child are led to shift their initial definition of rapid recovery to a definition of the situation as one of ambiguity. This facilitates the hospital's work, for it enables the child to think about such goals as moving a particular muscle rather than the goal of running and playing. It also inhibits constant questioning on the part of parents, who accept the uselessness of "pestering" doctors who can tell them very little in any case. Finally, the changed perspective facilitates adjustment of the parents to the situation, giving them time to reorganize their attitudes to their child's condition.

Thus, interaction in the organization resulted in alterations in unrealistic definitions of the situation. But changed definitions are not always unilateral. That is, it is not merely the patient and his family who necessarily do all the changing. Medicine is not an exact science, so that there is some scope for negotiating and bargaining between patient and physician. Roth found considerable negotiation in a tuberculosis hospital, with patient and physician each striving to define the timetable for the patient's treatment. The patients as a whole, he noted, exert continuing pressure to move more quickly along the timetable, particularly if they perceive themselves as

---

[32] Fred Davis, "Definitions of Time and Recovery in Paralytic Polio Convalescence," *American Journal of Sociology,* 61 (May 1956), 582–587.

getting behind in the established schedule. The physicians on the other hand resist the patients' efforts and strive to control the timetable in a way they feel is appropriate for the treatment.

> The result of these opposing pressures is a continual process of bargaining between patients and physicians over the question of when given points on the timetable will be reached. Such bargaining includes the application of pressures for decision or action, threats, deals, manipulation, and compromise as each party strives to reach his goals, but recognizes the limitations imposed by the counter-stance and the bargaining power of the other party . . . The actual timetable of treatment is a resultant of the interaction of such . . . forces.[33]

THE SELF AND THE ORGANIZATION

In each of the above examples we have tried to show the importance of considering the subjective meanings of actors, of getting at the actors' definitions of the situation in organizations, and of recognizing the creative force of interaction. A more fundamental application of symbolic interactionism is Melville Dalton's use of Mead's theory to explain certain phenomena he found among managers in commercial and industrial settings.[34] According to Dalton, managers are engaged in a continuing struggle for power, a struggle which finds expression in the creation and manipulation of cliques and factions. In this context, managers resorted to practices which were contrary to accepted moral standards: they violated rules, manipulated rules, and grievance procedures, and so forth.

Such a situation will contain considerable uncertainty, since decisions will depend on various practices and patterns of interaction which are not accounted for by, and may run counter to, the formal organizational structure. Those who are able to deal with the uncertainty will emerge as official or unofficial leaders in the organization: "Ambiguity thus selects those most able to absorb, or resolve and utilize, conflict for personal and organizational ends." [35]

Thus some managers will advance in the organization because they are able to cope with the ambiguities and use them in a way defined as good by others in the organization. How can we then explain differences in individual capacities for functioning effectively in a climate of uncertainty and conflict? Dalton suggests Mead's theory of the self. We noted earlier that Mead regarded the self as a process with the two phases of "I" and

---

[33] Julius A. Roth, *Timetables: Structuring the Passage of Time in Hospital Treatment and Other Careers,* Bobbs-Merrill, New York, 1963, pp. 61–62.
[34] Melville Dalton, *Men Who Manage,* Wiley, New York, 1959.
[35] *Ibid.,* p. 258.

"me." Dalton notes that one reared in a small community would likely behave predominantly in accord with the "me," the attitudes of the whole community which have been integrated into the self. But where there is uncertainty and change, there will be ambiguity and disputes about what is "right," and the individual's impulses will not be as tightly controlled by the "me." Further, the self will acquire a variety of "me's" over time, as a person becomes more morally complex through interaction in diverse situations. This does not mean that the individual has lost his or her conscience, but that he or she "has become able to consider and deal with all the conflicting interests and values around" him or her.[36]

Consequently, the manager with this kind of self will have a greater range of behavior at his or her disposal within the boundaries of the formal organization and the managerial role. And if those boundaries are too restrictive, he or she may reshape them through his or her influence and manipulation of cliques. In other words, the manager who is successful is less subject to a particular and narrow "me" than others. This line of reasoning also enables us to distinguish between the foremen and the higher managers, for the former have "few and simple 'me's' fashioned by narrow experiences . . . The foremen who are left behind are shaped more by what they have been than by what they anticipate becoming. Using Mead's terms, one can say overneatly that the executives are 'I'-dominated and the foremen 'me'-dominated." [37]

IMPORTANCE OF STUDYING ORGANIZATIONS

In sum, while symbolic interactionism has not been frequently used in the vast organizational literature, it can illuminate organizational processes in a unique way. And since behavior in organizations comprises a significant proportion of all behavior in a modern society, we can greatly enhance our understanding of modern life by investigating symbolic processes in organizations in a systematic way. One symbolic interactionist has attempted to do this in the context of hospitals—Anselm Strauss. We will explore his research in Chapter 10.

Collective Behavior

Everyone has had some personal experience of collective behavior. For all of us have been in crowds, and all of us have been part of the "public" for some issue or other. Collective behavior also includes social movements, and all of us have either participated in, or known a participant, or read about various social movements. Thus collective behavior is a part of the "everyday life" of each of us.

[36] *Ibid.,* p. 254.
[37] *Ibid.,* p. 255.

In contrast to much of this chapter, however, collective behavior specifically focuses on the group, and refers to group rather than individual characteristics. Groups are collectivities, which means that they are more than a number of individuals: "A group always consists of people who are in interaction and whose interaction is affected by some sense that they constitute a unit . . . the operation of some kind of group norms is a crucial feature of interaction."[38] The norms that characterize groups in collective behavior, however, are different from those that characterize established groups like organizations; the former are emergent or spontaneous, while the latter are formalized.

In this section, we will focus on the work of Ralph Turner, who, in his study of collective behavior, has particularly emphasized two concepts which are integral to symbolic interactionism—process and symbolic behavior. Turner has explored the way in which each of these concepts must be applied to the study of collective behavior. We will examine his ideas and supplement them with some supporting evidence from the work of others.

COLLECTIVE BEHAVIOR AS PROCESS

The notion of process is stressed in two ways. First, Turner has suggested that any particular instance of collective behavior can be understood in terms of the "resolution of competing and often contradictory processes which are in continuous operation."[39] For example, in social movements there is an ongoing effort to both maximize the power of the movement vis-à-vis the larger society and enhance the satisfaction of members; such processes may, and often do, contradict each other, so that the characteristics of the movement at any point in time may be understood as an effort to resolve these contrary processes.

The second way in which Turner stresses process is through his notion of "emergent norms." Turner contrasts emergent norm theory with contagion and convergence theories of collective behavior.[40] In contagion theories, collective behavior reflects a process in which emotions and behavior spread rapidly and are accepted uncritically by the members of a collectivity. Convergence theories, on the other hand, argue that collective behavior represents the coming together of people who share certain emotions and behavioral tendencies. By contrast, emergent norm theories emphasize the guidance of behavior in accord with norms that arise through

---

[38] Ralph H. Turner and Lewis M. Killian, *Collective Behavior*, Prentice-Hall, 1957, p. 12.

[39] Ralph H. Turner, "New Theoretical Frameworks," *The Sociological Quarterly*, 5, (Spring 1964), p. 124.

[40] Ralph H. Turner, "Collective Behavior," in *Handbook of Modern Sociology*, ed. Robert E. L. Faris, Rand McNally, Chicago, 1964, pp. 384–392.

interaction in specific situations. The key problem in emergent norm theory is not to explain why "an unnatural unanimity develops," but to explain why crowd members and observers perceive unanimity in the ·face of differing kinds of behavior and experiences.[41] Such a perception occurs because of a social norm that emerges from the interaction in the collectivity, which is specific to the situation, and which results in a "shared conviction of right" that sanctions behavior in accord with the norm.

Obviously, the emergent norm approach does not require a heightening of emotions such as that postulated by contagion theories. "Under contagion people find themselves spontaneously infested with the emotions of others so that they want to behave as others do; under a norm people first experience the social pressure against nonconformity and do not necessarily share the emotion themselves."[42] This is not to say that people in a crowd act wholly rationally, but it is to say that they do not act wholly irrationally under the impact of overwhelming emotions.

One of the problems in the emergent norm theory is to determine the conditions under which a norm will emerge and be accepted as the basis for collective action. Actually, events occur in all societies for which there is no organized way of responding and no existing shared definition (Turner gives the examples of an automobile accident and a class for which the teacher fails to show up). In such cases, responses will not be idiosyncratic, but will vary, if at all, by subgroups within the collectivity. Subgroups in turn form norms through three processes. The first is an effort to determine the rules which should be observed in such a situation. The second is an effort to define the situation in terms of explaining it and perhaps faulting or absolving someone whose behavior has led to the situation. Third, there is an emergence of leadership, and leaders are depended upon to legitimate the rules and initiate appropriate behavior.

The fact that individuals in a group create shared norms through their interaction is not novel in social psychology, of course. One of the classic experiments, Muzafer Sherif's investigation of group influences on the formation of norms, focused on this phenomenon.[43] Sherif used the "autokinetic effect" (a stationary point of light in a totally darkened room will appear to move to the observer) to show that individual norms can be modified by group norms, and that individuals in a group develop norms which are peculiar to their group. In his experiments the subjects were brought into a darkened room. They were told that they would see a point of light after they were seated and that the point of light would move. After the light disappeared, the subjects were to verbally indicate their estimates

---

[41] *Ibid.,* p. 390.

[42] *Ibid.*

[43] Muzafer Sherif, *The Psychology of Social Norms,* Harper, New York, 1936, pp. 89–112.

of the distance the light had moved. Sherif found that estimates of distance tended to converge over a series of trials. Individuals in a group would tend to develop a group norm for the distance, closely agreeing on how far the light moved rather than maintaining their initial, disparate estimates. Furthermore, individuals who were tested alone and developed their own norm, would modify it when brought into a group so that it accorded with that which emerged in the group.

Sherif's experiments illustrate a point we have stressed before—human beings are social creatures and their behavior must be understood in terms of their interaction experiences. An individual's perception of what he or she "sees" depends on his or her interaction as well as on his or her physiology. And the mere fact of interacting with others tends to make a difference in the individual's behavior. This latter point has been demonstrated in experiments investigating bystander intervention in emergencies. For example, in one study Darley and Latané told subjects that they were to participate in discussion groups, the purpose of which was to examine personal problems in college.[44] In the group meeting, each would communicate through an intercom to avoid embarrassment and encourage frankness. The members were to speak in turn, since only one could be heard at a time. Actually, the "others" in the group were taped recordings. One member mentioned a tendency toward seizures. The second time around, the victim sounded as if he were having a seizure. How quickly would the subjects respond to his apparent need for help? Responses depended upon the number of others in the group. When the subject believed that he and the victim were the only ones in the group, he tended to act much more quickly than when he thought there were three or six people in the group. Over eighty percent of those who thought they were alone with the victim reported the emergency before the seizure had ended and the intercom was cut off, but less than one-third of the subjects who believed they were participating in a group of six reported the incident that quickly. In other words, the pattern of responses varied by size of "group," and also varied somewhat between "groups" of the same size. Thus, individuals behave differently when they are interacting, even if the other interactants are part of an imaginary group.

Turner has applied this insight to large-scale collectivities. People's behavior in those collectivities cannot be explained simply on the basis of what "kind" of people they are (as though they would behave the same whether alone or in the collectivity). Furthermore, it is not simply in the small group that norms are created, but in crowds gathered for various

---

[44] John M. Darley and Bibb Latané, "Bystander Intervention in Emergencies: Diffusion of Responsibility," *Journal of Personality and Social Psychology,* 8 (April 1968), 377–383.

purposes. Those who participate in "senseless" kinds of behavior like a lynch mob are not merely doing what they would like to do as individuals and what they receive the courage to do by the crowd, but act in accord with a norm that has emerged through crowd interaction. Consequently, the respectable citizen who joins the lynch mob will become respectable again after the lynching, and may have exerted leadership in a tense situation to create the norm necessary for the act. But beyond that, the bulk of the crowd would probably be ordinary people caught up in a situation where enormous group pressures are exerted to behave in accord with an emergent norm.

COLLECTIVE BEHAVIOR AS SYMBOLIC

In addition to his emphasis on process in collective behavior, Turner has stressed the importance of symbolic behavior. In particular, he has examined the significance of the definition of the situation and shared meanings. In fact, he has identified the role of symbols as a key problem in collective behavior theory.[45] His own efforts to understand the significance of symbols are reflected in an early study of hostile crowd behavior.[46] In 1943 there were "zoot suit riots" in Los Angeles. A number of violent incidents occurred, primarily between naval personnel and Mexicans who had adopted the distinctive style and dress of the "zooter." Turner hypothesized that such hostile acts of crowds require an unambiguously unfavorable symbol which can overshadow any favorable aspects of the object of hostility. The crowd acts as a unit, and shared symbols are essential for uniform action. Therefore, hostile action on the part of a crowd should require some unambiguously unfavorable symbol which can be attached to the object.

Turner tested his thesis by reading a sample of editions of the *Los Angeles Times* for the ten and one-half years preceding the riots. He found that the symbol "Mexican" tended to be displaced by the symbol "zoot-suiter" during the latter part of the period. Turner notes that the zoot suit theme did not even appear until 1940, and when it did appear it had no favorable connotations attached to it as did the symbol "Mexican" (which also had unfavorable connotations, of course). Thus, the "zooter" symbol resolved the ambivalence of the community toward Mexicans, relieved the community of its moral obligations and sanctioned the hostile behavior of the crowds.

Shared meanings—a common definition of the situation—are important, then, for collective behavior. One of the useful functions of rumor in a

[45] Ralph H. Turner, "Needed Research in Collective Behavior," *Sociology and Social Research*, 42 (July/August 1958), 461–465.
[46] Ralph H. Turner and Samuel J. Surace, "Zoot-Suiters and Mexicans: Symbols in Crowd Behavior," *American Journal of Sociology*, 62 (July 1956), 14–20.

crowd is to aid in the formation of a collective definition of the situation, and thereby in the development of a norm that will provide directives for collective action. As Turner put it: "Rumor is a process of referring back to the group for a verified conception of a situation which will enable individuals to act with at least a modicum of confidence."[47] Groups, like individuals, require definitions of the situations for coordinated action. As this suggests, the same "objective" conditions will yield various kinds of behavior depending upon the way the situation is defined. For example, instances of misfortune or deprivation may be viewed as undesirable but inevitable, and charity may be the only ameliorative action defined as possible. On the other hand, when a substantial number of people see the misfortune as an intolerable injustice in the society, a social movement may emerge. "A movement becomes possible when a group of people cease to petition the good will of others for relief of their misery and demand as their right that others ensure the correction of their condition."[48] The way the misfortune is collectively defined will determine whether a movement is even possible.

In addition to the definition of the situation created by the collectivity, the definition of the collectivity by the larger society is an important factor in collective behavior. There is interaction between the collectivity and the larger society and their respective definitions of the situation. This emphasizes the processual nature of all collective behavior; groups engage in an interaction process analogous to that which we have outlined for individuals in Chapter 3.

The definition by the larger society is important for the course of development of the collective behavior. The larger society seeks to exercise control and to redefine the organization and values involved in the collective behavior. This reaction of the larger society is carried out by a "special public" which has the task of defining the collective action. In defining the collective behavior, the public answers a number of crucial questions about the nature and probable future course of the behavior, and about the ways to effect justice in the situation.

The importance of the public definition for collective behavior may be seen in the effects of such definitions on social movements. The public definition influences recruitment to the movement, the means of action available to the movement, and the type of opposition the movement will encounter.[49] For example, if the public defines a movement as "peculiar," members will likely encounter ridicule and ostracism and will have limited access to legitimate means of action. Of course, the public definition may

[47] Turner, "Collective Behavior," p. 405.
[48] Ralph H. Turner, "The Theme of Contemporary Social Movements," *British Journal of Sociology,* 20 (December 1969), 391.
[49] Turner and Killian, pp. 327–329.

change over time through movement-public interaction, and in fact the course of a movement must be seen in terms of ongoing interaction and consequent modifications in both the public definition and various characteristics of the movement.[50]

The importance of public definitions of collective behavior may also be seen in the consequences of those definitions for protest.[51] Any particular instance of a disturbance may or may not be defined as social protest. In 1969, most people questioned in a poll in Los Angeles viewed high school disorders as the work of agitators rather than as social protest, even though Mexican-Americans and blacks were leaders in the disorders. How the disturbance is defined is important, because defining it as a protest "spurs efforts to make legitimate and nonviolent methods for promoting reform more available than they had been previously, while other definitions are followed by even more restricted access to legitimate means for promoting change."[52] It is important, then, to those who intend to engage in social protest that their actions be defined by the public as protest rather than as the work of agitators or delinquents. The fate of all collective behavior is linked up with definitions of situations, and the definitions of both the participants and the public bear upon that fate.

Conclusion

In addition to illuminating various social phenomena, this chapter has shown how symbolic interactionism can be used to make analyses at every level of human life. For whatever the level, we are always dealing with people interacting. People enter that interaction with preliminary definitions of the situation and with practical interests. They present themselves as particular kinds of people, in part through the clothing they wear and the roles they identify. The interaction proceeds from this initial base. But if an individual's self-presentation is somehow discredited, or if there are contradictory definitions of the situation or contradictory expectations about roles, embarrassment may result and interrupt normal interaction.

Barring interruption, the interaction will proceed along the lines we have previously described—whether it is dyadic, organizational, or a large-scale collectivity. Thus, there will be socialization: an individual will learn to define marijuana smoking as a pleasurable experience or he or she will learn to accept as his or her own the attitudes and values common in an organization. Reference others are crucial to the socialization—the nursing

---

[50] See Robert H. Lauer, "Social Movements: An Interactionist Analysis," *The Sociological Quarterly,* 13 (Summer 1972), 315–328.

[51] Ralph H. Turner, "The Public Perception of Protest," *American Sociological Review,* 34 (December 1969), 815–831.

[52] *Ibid.,* p. 817.

student who remains ambivalent about the profession and oriented towards those outside nursing will not be well socialized even in a school with high consensus. Preliminary definitions of the situation will be modified in the course of interaction, as with the parents of a polio victim who redefine their expectations regarding the course of recovery. A certain amount of negotiation and role-bargaining occurs: patients may negotiate with their doctors in some matters.

In all cases we cannot understand the behavior unless we understand what it means to the actors—how they define it. Some people will be embarrassed in a situation, while others will not. Individuals will respond differently in the face of an organizational contradiction (such as that faced by the navy disbursing officer). And people will act differently depending upon the collective definition of the situation; an "unfortunate" situation may be viewed with sympathy, while the same situation, redefined as "intolerable and outrageous," may generate a protest movement. The monk in his cell, the lovers absorbed in each other and oblivious to the world, the groups in schools, offices, and factories, and the masses gathered together for various reasons are all behaving as they are because they are symbolic creatures, and what they do in any particular situation depends upon the way in which they define it.

Suggested Readings

In addition to the areas covered in this chapter, symbolic interactionists have investigated a number of other aspects of everyday life. We have already noted in Chapter 5 a number of studies of deviance and emotional illness. See for example, Thomas S. McPartland and John H. Cumming, "Self-Conception, Social Class, and Mental Health" [*Human Organization,* 17 (Fall 1958), 24–29] and Michael Schwartz, Gordon F. N. Fearn, and Sheldon Stryker, "A Note on Self Conception and the Emotionally Disturbed Role" [*Sociometry,* 29 (September 1966), 300–305]. Work has also been done in the political sphere: Joel Smith and Allan Kornberg, "Self-Concepts of American and Canadian Party Officials: Their Development and Consequences" [*Social Forces,* 49 (December 1970), 210–226]; Richard S. Brooks, "The Self and Political Role: A Symbolic Interactionist Approach to Political Ideology" [*The Sociological Quarterly,* 10 (Winter 1969), 22–31]; and Peter M. Hall, "A Symbolic Interactionist Analysis of Politics" [*Social Inquiry,* 42, No. 3–4 (1972), 35–75]. An interesting analysis of culture change by an anthropologist has employed the symbolic interactionist perspective: Edward M. Bruner, "The Missing Tins of Chicken: A Symbolic Interactionist Approach to Culture Change" [*Ethos,* 1 (Summer 1973), 219–238]. Finally, the last four chapters of this book provide numerous references to substantive areas in which Blumer, Strauss, Shibutani, and Goffman have made contributions.

Chapter 8

Ethnomethodology

Cultures that have not adopted Western science and technology retain "nonscientific" theories about those matters that are addressed by scientists in our culture. Members of such cultures have theories about the plant and animal life around them, the practice of medicine, the apparent movement of the stars, agriculture, engineering techniques, and navigation. To distinguish between these folk theories and their Western scientific counterparts, anthropologists sometimes prefix the native theories with the term "ethno" (or "folk"). Thus, non-Western scientific theories about plants may be called "ethnobotany." Similarly "ethnomedicine," "ethnoastronomy," or "ethnophysics" denote folk theories that deal with similar subject matter as their Western scientific counterparts—medicine, astronomy, and physics.

Harold Garfinkel coined the term "ethnomethodology" for similar reasons. He was involved in a study of the activities of jurors and was struck by their concern with how to decide matters of fact and how to make proper interpretations of the law. In the process of deciding the substantive question of guilt, the jurors made a variety of procedural judgments. What does the law mean? What counts as credible testimony? How can proper inferences of intention and motive be made? How can a convincing description of events, suitable for a clear judgment concerning whether the law was violated, be properly assembled from fragmentary evidence? These procedural issues are distinct from the discussion of the facts themselves and their implications. Although the jurors were from a Western culture, these matters were not discussed in scientific terms nor were the standards and practices developed by the jurors scientific. Within sociology such issues fall in the province of methodology. Hence, to indicate that the concerns of jurors related to the same issues as those of methodology and to indicate that the jurors were not scientific, Garfinkel introduced the term "ethnomethodology." [1]

While there are significant differences among their approaches, ethnomethodologists continue to be concerned with the issues as defined by Garfinkel's original insight. "Ethnomethodology" refers to the study of folk methods and standards for deciding on questions of fact, proper reasoning, proper procedures for investigation, proper application of general rules to specific cases, and proper justifications for actions that are planned, in process, or completed. These "methodological" decisions, undertaken by people in the course of their activities, are part of those activities. For example, "setting standards for investigating matters of fact" is a form of social action. At the same time, other social action is facilitated if it is organized. This is analogous to the way that methodology organizes scientific research. And these methodological practices are part of the social activities they organize, just as scientific methodology is an integral part of science. Ethnomethodologists regard these organizing activities and rules as especially important because they are different from scientific ones and thus suggest that the organization of social life is based on principles that are

---

[1] Richard Hill and Kathleen Crittendon, *Proceedings of the Purdue Symposium on Ethnomethodology,* Institute Monograph Series Number 1, Institute for the Study of Social Change, Purdue Research Foundation, Lafayette, Ind., 1968, pp. 5–9.

currently unknown and different from the principles of scientific investigation and theorizing.

The emergence of ethnomethodology has been the occasion for a highly technical and frequently acrimonious debate over, among other things, the extent to which ethnomethodology is fundamentally different from other approaches, the exact nature of ethnomethodological interests, and the current and potential value of the new approach. While the terminology employed by ethnomethodologists is certainly distinctive, their research interests, methodological techniques, and findings are in many ways similar to those of symbolic interactionists. In fact, some sociologists feel that ethnomethodology is fundamentally the same as symbolic interaction.[2]

The student who pursues symbolic interaction, theoretical sociology, or sociological studies of interaction from any perspective will increasingly come into contact with enthomethodology and the dispute over its character. The terminology of ethnomethodology is derived from phenomenology, from sophisticated information-processing models, from segments of cognitive psychology, and from linguistics. This diverse terminology may be necessary for certain technical discussions, but for the beginning student and for many sociologists in other specialties it is more of a barrier to communication than an aid. Our intention is to provide an introduction to ethnomethodological thought that is comprehensive yet, as much as possible, in ordinary language. We will try to explain the technical terminology itself rather than use it to explain or describe other events. Such an approach will provide interesting insights into the interaction process and social life that complement those of symbolic interaction. In addition, for students who become more deeply involved in any of the related areas, it should provide a basis for further, more technical study.

Ethnomethodology as a Distinctive Approach to Interaction

TWO VIEWS OF THE FUNCTION OF INTERACTION

Symbolic interactionists are concerned in a profound way with people's interpretive practices—their ways of understanding reality and of organizing their responses. Further, they have long recognized that these interpretive practices are an important part of the social scenes they analyze. Despite

[2] For an interesting exchange of views concerning the relationship between symbolic interaction and ethnomethodology see Norman Denzin, "Symbolic Interaction and Ethnomethodology," pp. 261–287, and Don Zimmerman and D. Lawrence Wieder, "Ethnomethodology and the Problem of Order: Comment on Denzin," pp. 287–298, both in *Understanding Everyday Life,* ed. Jack Douglas, Aldine, Chicago, 1970. The following sources should serve as a sample of the tone and content of the response to ethnomethodology: Guy Swanson, Anthony Wallace, and James Coleman, "Review Symposium of Harold Garfinkel, *Studies in Ethnomethodology,*" *American Sociological Review,* 33 (February 1968), 122–130; Edward Tiryakian, "Review of *Studies in Social Interaction,* edited by David Sudnow," *Social Forces,* 52 (June

these commonalities of interest, ethnomethodologists argue that their work is not an extension nor a restatement of symbolic interaction in a new terminology.

The crucial difference between the two approaches lies in the functions attributed to the interpretive process. Ethnomethodologists argue that the characteristics of the perceived world are entirely a product of the interpretive process. The interpretive process has as its function the construction of the world as we experience it. Symbolic interactionists argue that we perceive a world of objects which is creatively defined in response to our goals *and* to conditions imposed by the external world which is there independent of our experience of it. The function of the interpretive process, in this view, is to define a world of objects which allows us to successfully predict the results of our manipulation of the world. In other words, the crucial function is to orient the person toward action that is successful in the practical sense of meeting his goals.

Because the two approaches have many apparent similarities, there has been special interest in the differences between them. Ethnomethodologists, however, have consistently argued that their approach to the study of social life is fundamentally different from *all* of sociology and that their topic has been neglected in sociological theory.[3] They argue that sociology springs from a common sense perspective that obscures the very processes which ethnomethodology attempts to analyze. In fact, Aaron Cicourel has argued that sociology will never transcend the status of formalized common sense unless it deals with the connection between definitions of the situation and the underlying cognitive process by which we define unique individual occasions in terms of normatively recognized, general definitions.[4]

Sociology is often criticized, both from within and without, for being "glorified common sense" or, worse yet, for being less adequate than common sense. "Common sense" here refers to generally known but unsystematic knowledge in use among the populace; such knowledge is considered inferior to scientific knowledge. Thus, the term "common sense" is intended to be, and is, an insult to the discipline. Ethnomethodologists do not use the term in that way. Rather, "common sense" means a well-de-

1974), 567–569; John Touhey, "Review of *Studies in Social Interaction,* edited by David Sudnow," *Contemporary Sociology,* 2 (September 1973), 504–506; Thomas Luckman, "Review of *Understanding Everyday Life,* edited by Jack Douglas," *Contemporary Sociology,* 1 (January 1972), 30–32; and James Wilkins, "Review of Harold Garfinkel, *Studies in Ethnomethodology,*" *American Journal of Sociology,* 73 (March 1968), 642–643.

[3] For example, see Don Zimmerman and Melvin Pollner, "The Everyday World as a Phenomenon," in *Understanding Everyday Life,* ed. Jack Douglas, Aldine, Chicago, 1970, pp. 80–104, and Thomas Wilson, "Conceptions of Interaction and Forms of Sociological Explanation," *American Sociological Review,* 35 (August 1970), 197–210.

[4] Aaron Cicourel, *Cognitive Sociology,* Free Press, New York, 1974, p. 7.

fined set of philosophical presuppositions about reality (see the definition below, p. 282).

Thus the difference between ethnomethodology and other sociological theories is related to fundamental philosophical assumptions. Ultimately, because fundamental philosophical issues are involved, the difference between the ethnomethodological approach to the interpretive process and that of symbolic interaction must be made in abstract terms. Before addressing the issue in that way, however, we will contrast the two approaches in a concrete, simple case.

In our discussion of the interpretive process in interaction we argued that interpretation occurs when actual events contradict expectations based on our existing definition of the situation. Through interpretation we redefine the situation and bring our expectations into agreement with the facts we encounter. The critical factor in precipitating interpretive activity is a factual contradiction, a surprise, a disagreement between what we know and expect and what seems to be occurring. Before characterizing the difference between symbolic interaction and ethnomethodology in abstract, philosophical terms, then, we will consider concretely the analysis of a simple, factual contradiction from each perspective.

FACTUAL CONTRADICTIONS AS ERRORS: THE COMMON SENSE APPROACH

We have all had the experience of filling out forms for the various organizations with which we have contact. Often, what we include in the forms is the only information the organization has about us. In those cases, the information in the form defines us entirely for the purpose of that organization and its treatment of us. For example, in subscribing to a magazine one's name and address as written on the form define these matters for the purpose of delivering the magazine. Too frequently, the name and address used by the magazine are different from the name and address used by the person for other purposes. This may arise through such contingencies as illegible handwriting, the inadequate size of the application form, typing errors, computer errors in printing address labels, or failing to notify the the magazine when we move.

Using common sense, we assume if a person's name is spelled differently by different organizations, if he or she is considered to live at different addresses, to have different social security numbers, to have different ages, to be a male in one organization's files while a female in another's, or to have already paid and not paid the same bill, that an error has been made. Symbolic interactionists are in accord with common sense on this issue. They regard such factual contradictions, whether on paper or arising in interaction, as correctable errors—as the occasion for interpretive effort and individual or collective action to redefine the situation in a consensually acceptable way.

But to talk about factual contradictions as errors one must make assumptions about the "true facts" and the possibility of discovering them. In our discussion of deviance we argued that the existence of a rule is defined by the possibility of error or violation. Accordingly, confronted with something we regard as an error, we should be able to identify the rule that has been violated. In the case of a "misaddressed" magazine the sort of rule that must have been violated is one that determines the "true facts" about one's address. The treatment of factual contradictions as error implies not only that there is some truth to the matter, but also that there is a rule or procedure that will determine the truth.

Let us reconsider the case of an errant magazine subscription. Various magazine employees utilize a series of procedures, about which we could be told or which we could observe. These procedures could be stated as a series of rules which lead to the production of a mailing label. When the procedures used by the magazine to obtain and act upon the subscription request result in a mistake, we respond that the procedures must be flawed. Perhaps a typist was careless. Perhaps coffee was spilled on an application blurring the ink. Perhaps a computer program that prints the address labels is faulty. Perhaps a card was bent, folded, stapled, and mutilated. In each case, the flaw in the procedure can be contrasted to a more adequate procedure for generating correct information. The typist could proofread more carefully, for instance. In some cases the flaw might be a violation of the company's official rules; in others the company's rules may themselves be inadequate. In either event we are confronted with the result of contradictory information. We respond to it as an indication of error. Finally, we locate the error in the rules followed, or procedures employed, to generate the information.

This approach to factual contradictions seems to be more strongly held with regard to some kinds of contradictions than others. For example, we are all probably quite secure in the belief that each of us has a height, weight, age, gender, name, and address that can be determined unambiguously if the correct procedures are employed. Thus, if two scales show that a person has two different weights at the same time we have no doubt that one, or both, of the scales is inaccurate and that a correct scale could be found. On the other hand, we are not typically surprised to find that different people hold different views of our less tangible characteristics, such as personality traits, or different opinions about the propriety of actions. We are all sometimes friendly and sometimes withdrawn, for example. What exactly is the correct procedure for deciding whether a person is basically friendly but occasionally withdrawn, or basically withdrawn but occasionally friendly? Although the exact procedures for deciding such questions are not as clearly formulated, we ordinarily regard this sort of contradiction in the same way as the apparently clear ones. We suggest criteria such as "knowing the person better" or being a "better judge of character" or being "more insightful." These criteria, while they may not be as clearly defined, act as the equivalent of our belief in an accurate scale which is able to resolve contradictions.

Redefining a situation results in either a correct application of this sort of rule, when it has been applied incorrectly, or the adoption of a new rule. The analogy is simple. As a mailing label is created by following a set of rules, a social relationship is created by following a set of rules. Either set of rules could be faulty or misapplied. Another person can be wrongly defined, with negative consequences resulting, either by making a mistake in applying one's rules for defining people or by having an inadequate set of rules.

ETHNOMETHODOLOGY: A NON-COMMONSENSICAL PROGRAM

As intuitively attractive as the equation of factual contradiction with error is, it has one serious flaw. It divides our attention between what people actually do—how they actually produce factual information—and other procedures which do not exist, but which we think would be an improvement. This dual concern is beautifully suited to practical situations in which we have an interest in the outcome. For example, it directs the attention of magazine publishers to revised procedures to reduce the number of subscriptions that are mailed to the wrong address. For sociological theory, however, ethnomethodologists perceive this practical advantage to be a liability. Sociological theory should be directed to what actually happens in society; it should explain and describe actual events. A misaddressed magazine subscription may be an inconvenience to the subscriber and an expense to the publisher and postal service. To the sociologist, however, it is a phenomenon that must be explained. Ethnomethodologists believe that the practical response to these factual contradictions should be abandoned for the purposes of sociological theory. That is, while attempting to generate theory, we should not employ the ordinary standards that lead us to treat factual contradictions as errors. Rather, we should deal with exactly the information-producing procedures that we find, whatever they are, without concern for their "adequacy" in practical terms. People's ways of producing factual information are to be studied, not judged. Both Garfinkel [5] and Alfred Schutz [6] have suggested that common sense and scientific reasoning are fundamentally different and not appropriate to the same situation.

This view leads to a distinctive approach to the nature of factual knowledge. Ethnomethodologists recognize that people act on the basis of their

[5] Harold Garfinkel, *Studies in Ethnomethodology,* Prentice-Hall, Englewood Cliffs, N.J., 1967, pp. 262–284.

[6] See Schutz's essay, "Common-Sense and Scientific Interpretation of Human Action," in Alfred Schutz, *Collected Papers I: The Problem of Social Reality,* edited and introduced by Maurice Natanson, with a preface by H. L. van Breda, Martinus Nijhoff, The Hague, 1967, pp. 3–47.

own interpretations and definitions of the situation. That is people respond to events and to each other entirely on the basis of the procedures they employ to decide on matters of fact and not on the basis of some ideal but unutilized procedure. While practical interests may lead us to regard some facts as more accurate than others, the sociologically relevant characteristics of people and events are those they are perceived to have. Contradictions that the sociologist observes between situations, or between what is actually done and what the sociologist thinks ought to be done, are not regarded as signs of error. Rather, whatever interpretations and investigative practices are employed in a social situation define events and people *for that occasion.* Thus, for purposes of theorizing, we must recognize that a person may really have different characteristics on different occasions. The only standard of truth is that standard employed in a given situation. That standard is not be contrasted with or evaluated in comparison to other standards used in other situations.

A final consideration of the magazine subscription should help to clarify this difficult invitation to abandon intuition. Let us consider the case of a man who receives his magazine without inconvenience to himself, even though the address label shows different information than those on other documents. Commonsensically, that label is in error, independent of his response to it. Ethnomethodologists would not agree with that judgment. If he decides to try to bring the label into conformity with other documents and his beliefs, ethnomethodologists would agree that the label does not meet the standards used to establish factual knowledge in that situation. (Notice, in order to be delivered it must have passed the standards for factual knowledge employed by the postal service.) If, however, the man ignores the contradiction, ethnomethodologists would consider the address label as accurate enough for the situation in which it is evaluated. In either case, the inquiry is directed to the actual procedures that lead to the information on the label and to the actual practices employed by the subscriber to decide whether the label is "close enough" to the truth to be ignored. The ethnomethodologist makes no independent judgment of the truth of the facts or the adequacy of the decision-making process.

An early study of the relationship between the verbal expression of attitudes and the associated behavior illustrates this problem. Richard La-Piere was investigating racial prejudice against orientals. He called a large number of motels and hotels and asked whether they accepted orientals as guests. The overwhelming majority of them said they did not. Subsequently, LaPiere and a young oriental couple made an extended automobile tour and attempted to register in the same motels that had expressed a discriminatory policy. They were accepted as guests in most of them.[7] The racial discrim-

---

[7] Richard LaPiere, "Attitudes vs. Actions," *Social Forces,* 13 (1934), 230–237.

ination policy of the hotels, it appears, was different on the phone than in person and may have varied in response to other factors as well.

At its current stage of development, ethnomethodology can be fairly conceived as a program or invitation to direct sociological investigation in a particular direction. First, we are invited to suspend the intuitive attractive belief that there are procedures that can be used to resolve factual disputes finally and with validity that transcends particular situations. Second, we are invited to consider that events are not finally or really one particular thing. Rather, events may be really different things when examined on different occasions using different procedures. They are defined, for each occasion, entirely by the procedures utilized to make factual judgments on that occasion. The truth is relative to the purposes for which it is sought and to the procedures through which it is sought. Third, we are invited to follow through the implication of this program in sociological research and theory.

THE ATTITUDES OF COMMON SENSE AND SCIENTIFIC THEORIZING

Common sense. The term "common sense" is used by ethnomethodologists in essentially the way that it was defined by Alfred Schutz, a phenomenologically oriented social philosopher.[8] The "attitude of common sense," as Schutz defined it, has as its central component the belief in the existence of the world as a reality independent of our experience of it. The world is believed to have existed before one's birth, to continue after one's death, and to have characteristics which are independent of our knowledge and beliefs. Particular doubts may be raised: we may believe that certain events are confusing or ambiguous, but only in the context of a general belief that some set of facts prevails and can be determined. Specific questions about the nature of events are raised, but reality is never questioned as a whole.

The unquestioned world is approached with a practical interest—it is the arena in which our goals must be accomplished. The world is considered to be a condition of action. Its features are the obstacles we must overcome and the resources with which to overcome them. Other individuals exist in this world, with their own knowledge and practical interests. Their activities and plans are further conditions that must be considered in formulating our own plans and which can serve as either obstacles or resources for them.

The reality of the world and its possession of real features that are unalterable conditions of action in no way denies the importance of the interpretive process. We remain free to define the world in any way that we want. However, we must be aware that only some definitions, if acted upon, will produce the desired results. Thus, the function of interpretation,

[8] Schutz, pp. 3–47.

of defining objects in one way rather than another, is to orient the individual in a particular way to the world. The pragmatic tradition, like Schutz's common sense attitude, includes a practical orientation to the world. Interpretation is an attempt to orient oneself successfully to the world. One attempts to define objects in such a way that if the definitions are acted upon the world will respond to our action as the definition predicts.

A successful definition of the situation cannot be regarded as the "true" one. Other definitions may work as well. In the practical approach, however, the criterion is success in practical endeavors rather than final or absolute truth. Interpretation is, then, in the symbolic interactionist tradition, a way of orienting oneself for successful action in the world. Interpretation may define and redefine particular features of the world, but the reality of the world and our need to take it into account in action are never questioned.

If one adopts this view of reality as a premise for scientific theory, certain types of problems are suggested. Some definitions of events are perceived to be more successful than others in achieving desired ends. The scientist's attention is directed to the formulation of increasingly successful definitions and to educating the public at large in order to enhance its success. Thus, the scientist must incorporate values, a definition of success, into his or her work and to set his or her own knowledge into competition with that of the general public as well as his or her colleagues. Scientific knowledge, then, is valued in large part because it has practical utility. Biological research is expected to help medicine and agriculture; physical research is expected to help engineering; sociological research is expected to ameliorate social problems.

Defined in this way, the attitude of common sense is a set of beliefs about the reality of the world and the relationship of perception and the acting person to it. This set of ontological beliefs is held by most social scientists, including most symbolic interactionists. It is virtually identical to the expressed position of the pragmatist philosophers, including Mead, from which many scientists and philosophers continue to draw insight. Most important, defined in this way, common sense is not a fighting word but a formulation of philosophical presuppositions.

Scientific theorizing. The ethnomethodologists do not share this ontological position as a basis for their work. When Schutz defined the attitude which he called "common sense," he did so to contrast it with other ontological positions, other attitudes about the reality and nature of the world that could be adopted. Schutz argued that the view that the world is a condition of action independent of our experience, reflects a particular attitude toward it. Other attitudes suggest a world with different characteristics, both in terms of particular features and fundamental characteristics. Other realities exist in experience that do not resemble the reality associated with the common sense orientation to everyday life. These include the reality of dreams and the reality of the theater. These realities are experienced quite frequently. They are not exceptional or bizarre, and yet they do not have the same characteristics of objectivity as does the reality of common sense. In short, human experience is varied. We may take different attitudes and in so doing create different worlds, worlds that are experienced to have different internal logic, and different types of reality.

Schutz argued that the common sense world is the paramount reality, the world in which most of our experience and social life occurs. To study this world, he thought, means more than to describe the particular factual features of the world as it is seen from within this attitude. In addition, Schutz suggested that we should study the common sense attitude itself. But to do so, Schutz argued, we would have to adopt a different attitude, one in which the attitude of common sense appeared as an object to be studied. This is the attitude of scientific theorizing. When this attitude is taken, the attitude of common sense becomes an object that can be studied. However, the objectivity of the world as it appears to common sense experience is lost. The world and its objectivity are seen as products of common sense assumptions and the investigations based upon them.

An example may help to clarify what happens to our experience when we adopt the attitude of scientific theorizing. In the attitude of common sense, we assume that the world is there and exists as a set of conditions which we must take into account. When we perceive that a car is moving toward us, we perceive it as a danger that cannot be defined away. We perceive that we *must* get out of its way or be struck. In the attitude of scientific theorizing, we continue to perceive the car. However, we perceive that our perception of the car as a "real" object, as a danger, as existing outside of our experience, is a product of our initial assumptions concerning reality and our places in it. We also perceive that, with different assumptions, the car might be seen in other ways. It might be seen as a dream or fantasy. Or, it might be seen as a product of our ontological assumptions.

Clearly, this is no way to cross a street. A radical separation is suggested between the world of theory and the common sense world. Rather than integrating the two, as scientists who accept the common sense view of reality do, the ethnomethodologists propose that *while doing scientific theorizing* we adopt the special attitude which makes the fundamental assumptions of everyday life perceptible and available as an object to study. Attention is not directed to studying the objects of the common sense world, the tangible objects that are studied in the other sciences; rather, attention is directed to studying the basic assumptions upon which that world rests. This redirection of attention is called "reduction": suspending belief in the world of common sense.

Interpretation is transformed in function by adopting this scientific-theorizing attitude. The experience of the world as an externally existing reality is seen as a consequence of the common sense attitude. Interpretation creates that world totally. However, this is not to say that defining things in a given way we can make them real in the practical sense of the term "real." The world that is created is a world of "experience." The common sense attitude creates one such experience totally, through its characteristic process of interpretation. From the scientific theorist's attitude, we can see how the world of experience, any world of experience, is constructed. However, the accuracy of facts within these worlds cannot be judged from that perspective. By seeing the world as the product of an attitude, we become unable to see what characteristics it might have independent of that attitude. Only by readopting the common sense attitude can we make judgments of what is real and what is mistaken, in the practical sense, but to do so we must assume the reality of the world as a whole and lose sight of the assumptions which have created our experience of the world.

The difference between the two approaches to interpretation is a fundamental one, having to do with ontological assumption. The symbolic interactionist studies interpretation from within the real world and sees it as a process of orientation to the objective, unavoidable conditions imposed by the world and its reality. The ethnomethodologist attempts to adopt a different ontological position—the attitude of scientific theorizing. From this perspective, the world does not have the objective character that it does in common sense thinking. Instead, the world is perceived to be a particular kind of experience that is defined and supported by a particular attitude. It has no reality, except as an experience, when the attitude is altered. Thus, the symbolic interactionist theorizes about interpretation as a human device for guiding action successfully in the world while the ethnomethodologist theorizes about interpretation as the construction of experiences of the world. The two approaches agree on the nature of the everyday world and the orientation of people to and in it. They disagree on whether to share this orientation as a basis for science, and therefore propose very different topics for study, although the term "interpretation" is used by both approaches.

Illustrative Ethnomethodological Studies

To illustrate the ethnomethodological perspective, we have chosen to select a few studies and discuss them in some detail. Ethnomethodological studies are characterized by intense attention to the details of social organization, and this approach will allow us to retain that flavor. Also, by concentrating on a few studies we have been able to select those that are paradigmatic in the sense that the findings are extremely difficult to explain in terms of other theoretical approaches.

AGNES

The anomaly. "Agnes" is the pseudonym for an intersexed person who applied for a sex-change operation at the Medical Center of the University of California, Los Angeles.[9] She was born with a normal penis and scrotum, and, accordingly, was named, registered, and raised as a male child. However, by the age of nineteen when she came to the medical center, she had developed large well-developed breasts, rounded, feminine hips, and displayed no facial hair. In addition, she had elected to live as a female and was wearing feminine clothes and affecting feminine mannerisms. In short, Agnes had the appearance of a normal female when clothed and behaved appropriately for a female in our culture. However, Agnes had a fully developed penis and scrotum.

Garfinkel's case study of Agnes is a paradigmatic illustration of ethnomethodological interests. First, human sexuality is usually considered to divide the population into unambiguous males and unambiguous females. Further, the supposed "best test" of gender involves the nature or the primary and secondary physiological sexual characteristics. This test, though, founders on Agnes' anomalous physiology. She is not, by this usually unapplied test, either a normal male or a normal female: she has male primary sexual characteristics and female secondary sexual characteristics. Second, the confounding of this test of gender has little, if any, sociological relevance. Agnes was not treated in her daily life as a "freak" or physiological anomaly. She was treated as a *female* by her employer, by her female roommate, by her friends, and by her fiancé until she told him about her condition. In terms of serving as the basis for social relationships, there are very few occasions in which the physiological test of gender is relevant, appropriate, or applied. Rather, other procedures are employed to determine gender and the physiological characteristics that nominally define gender are assumed to be in line with the results of these other procedures.

Because gender is one of the sociological variables usually regarded as subject to objective measurement, the existence of ambiguous cases is interesting in itself. But Agnes' ability to pass as a normal female is more important as a source of insight into the ways in which gender is established as a social characteristic under more typical conditions. It is hard to believe that there are a surfeit of anomalous cases, such as Agnes, among our social contacts. Nonetheless, we must recognize that there are relatively few people of whose physiological normalcy we can be sure, and few situations in which this matters. Agnes' ability to be defined and treated as a female by other people serves as a reminder that most practical social purposes do not require physiological proof for gender to be determined. Her case indicates

---

[9] The details of the case history of Agnes are taken from Garfinkel's report (Garfinkel, pp. 116–185). We will not make specific page citations within the report.

that, in addition, one need not even be able to pass such a physiological test in order to be defined and treated as a female in many situations. Finally, her case indicates strongly that some other procedure for assigning gender is actually employed. At least as far as the word "female" is concerned, Agnes' case indicates that meaning is not based on objective or ideal ways of categorizing people but on some other practical procedures. To say that someone is a female is to say only that some practical procedure for determining that fact has been applied and the meaning of the statement is relative to the nature of that test.

Being a female. Being a female was undoubtedly a more complicated task for Agnes than for most others who attempted it. In most situations her physiological peculiarities probably caused few problems. However, in those situations in which her physical characteristics were potentially visible she had to be especially careful to maintain her female identity. The ability to pass, or conceal those characteristics, is aided by one feature of the way in which facts are established in social interaction: the procedures for establishing facts are self-concealing. Once established, facts are treated as objective and the exact way in which they were established is ignored. Consider our tendency to define gender in terms of physiological characteristics. Every time we decide a person's gender without a rigorous application of the definition, we remain unaware of exactly how we did decide. Garfinkel has argued that people are uninterested in investigating the procedures of their own investigation. To do so, he argues, would disrupt the practical use of those procedures.[10] The nonintuitive character of ethnomethodology and the distinction between scientific and common sense reasoning are both related to ethnomethodologists' interest in issues that are not of interest in practical situations.

The fact that Agnes learned suitably female behavior in an unusual way highlights other features of the way in which facts are established in practical situations. Because she was raised as a male and became a female abruptly, aided by a new hairstyle and clothes, Agnes was denied the usual long socialization period associated with sex roles. Instead, she had to learn the details of the female role at the same time that she was performing it. To this end she regarded the remarks, suggestions, and responses of others as lessons, as part of a compressed and delayed apprenticeship. For example, she began to learn to cook, to select appropriate clothes, to shop, and to manage a home late in her adolescence. She learned from her fiancé's responses how he liked women to behave. For example, he regarded sunbathing in front of other men as immodest.

The important issue is that prior experience and detailed knowledge of

[10] Garfinkel, pp. 7–9.

the appropriate female response to situations is not essential to maintaining a female identity. Apparently we possess the ability to behave in a way that is acceptable to others by responding to the cues immediately available in interaction. Agnes' skill in this regard should not be regarded as greater than anyone else's nor as related to her physical peculiarities. If any of us wanted to do what Agnes did, we could. In more common situations this skill makes it possible for us to successfully fulfill the expectations of others even if they are unexpected and unfamiliar to us. If the various situations we encounter require it, we could, using this skill, appear to be fundamentally different people on different occasions.

In some situations, Agnes felt threatened by the literal exposure of her physical secret and took preventative steps to protect it. Her female roommate presented a constant threat to discovery that was countered by consistent insistence on privacy and by always remaining dressed in her presence. Bathhouses at the beach required similar precautions and her choice of swimsuits was restricted to old-fashioned types with skirts. On dates Agnes had to be especially careful about sexual activities and maintained an absolute rule of "no petting below the waist," even against the insistence of her fiancé. When employment depended on a physical examination she refused to undress below the waist, precluding gynecological examination, and expressed an intention to leave if a more thorough physical examination was required. In one very subtle instance she became afraid that the examination of a urine sample would reveal her ambiguous sexuality to the doctor. Claiming to have a kidney infection that would prevent her from being hired, she borrowed a urine sample from her roommate and brought it to the physical examination she took in connection with a job.

In conjunction with our knowledge about her physical condition, each of these devices can be seen as a direct attempt to conceal particular anatomical facts. However, none of the devices was perceived that way by those people with whom she dealt. This discrepancy indicates the importance of assumed background knowledge in the determination of particular facts. Since we make typical assumptions about human sexuality, the same activities that serve as passing, protective, or concealing devices are seen as well within the range of usual behavior, perhaps expressive of extreme modesty. In the context of different assumptions, the same action will be perceived to have fundamentally different meanings. Further, Agnes was clearly able to anticipate more or less how her actions would be perceived. She was able to provide background information that made even the request to borrow urine seem reasonable. Above all, Agnes clearly oriented herself to anticipated practical investigations of her gender, not to an idealized one.

Summary of implications of Agnes' case. We are now in a position to consider what one needs and what one does not need to be accepted as a woman in social situations. One does not need to be a physically normal female. Choice of clothes and other devices can conceal even extreme irregularities. One does not need extensive preparatory practice and experience in the female role. Apparently, one can learn and perform the role at the same time. One must be able to anticipate the sorts of background information and practical investigative procedures that will be employed in various settings, or at least fulfill the expectations they lead to in social settings. In short, to be a female one needs only to be competent in the use of interpretive skills, including reasonable assessments of relevant background knowledge and the nature of the reasoning others will use. If this conclusion applies even to fundamental, physically based characteristics, such as gender, it is difficult to deny that it applies to other less pervasive ones.

USE OF RULES IN THE BUREAUCRATIC SETTING

Sociologists commonly regard bureaucratic rules to be more explicit and coherent than the norms found in other social settings. Bureaucratic rules are written and are oriented toward the efficient achievement of organizational goals. Attempts are made to avoid contradictions and to make the rules as explicit as possible so that they can be followed reliably by any employee to whom they are relevant. These characteristics are in contrast to the implicit, unwritten character of other norms, which may be in contradiction and which are not organized around a clear objective.

This contrast has led sociologists to regard the bureaucracy as a virtual laboratory for the study of the nature of rules and how they are used. In bureaucracies, the researcher is able to determine exactly what rules are supposed to be operative and what purposes are supposed to be achieved. Thus, relatively clear judgments may be made about the degree of conformity to rules, the effects on known purposes of nonconformity, and the conditions under which conformity is increased and decreased. Finally, sociologists have been able to study functions of rules other than that of serving as standards of behavior. Our discussion of the operations of the legal system illustrated a variety of functions served by bureaucratic rules in the interpretive activity of assigning labels.

Ethnomethodologists have also used the bureaucracy as a sort of laboratory. For them, the crucial issue has been whether rules are ever followed habitually or whether they are used in the context of continuous interpretive activity. We considered Agnes' case and concluded that if she could be a woman, anyone could. Her circumstances allowed us to distinguish between what is necessary and what is merely common to maintaining a female identity. We will address the bureaucratic rule with an analogous approach: if a simple, direct, clear, written rule is not followed habitually, we can reasonably conclude that *no* rule is. That, then, is the nature of our experiment: to locate a bureaucratic rule that is so simple and clear that if it is not followed habitually and if violating it is not regarded as inappropriate, then our belief that any rule is ever followed habitually will be challenged.

Practical use of a simple rule. Don Zimmerman's study of the receptionists' tasks in a public assistance agency [11] includes a discussion of a suitably simple rule that was intended to govern the assignment of applicants for assistance to caseworkers. Each day the order in which caseworkers would be assigned clients was determined. Then each incoming client was assigned to the next caseworker in the rotation. A visual device reduced this rule to a simple, mechanical procedure. A calendar of appointments was constructed each day by listing the caseworkers, in the proper order, in a column on the left of the calendar. Then the calendar was divided into squares with the first column indicating the first client assigned to each caseworker, the second indicating the second client assigned to each caseworker, and so on. The receptionist, using this chart, could reduce her task to writing the name of each client immediately below the name of the preceding one on her chart. When each column was filled the receptionist could start at the top of the column immediately to its right. Thus, writing clients' names from top to bottom and from left to right on the blocked-off chart would result in following the rule. This rule matches the most repetitive assembly line routine in simplicity. It is incredible that a receptionist could fail to understand the rule or be unable to determine what the rule demanded on any given occasion.

Zimmerman observed that the proper procedure for receptionists is not always to observe the rule. That is, the requirements of the rule were not always met and violating the rule was, on some occasions, an indication of the competence of the receptionist, not of error or willful deviance. For example, in one instance, a caseworker was taking an unusually long time interviewing her first client of the day. The third applicant who had been assigned to her expressed anxiety about being able to keep an appointment with her doctor if she was forced to wait much longer. The applicant was reassigned to another caseworker. This was both a violation of the rule-defined procedure and the cause of additional paperwork, including revising the appointment chart. Yet this suspension of the rule as an ad hoc response to an unusual circumstance was a proper performance of the receptionist's task.

In order to understand organizational behavior, the relevant question does not seem to be "What is the rule?" Rather, we should apparently be concerned with "What has to be done?" The rule does not appear to gov-

---

[11] Don Zimmerman, "The Practicalities of Rule Use," in *Understanding Everyday Life,* ed. Jack Douglas, Aldine, Chicago, 1970, pp. 221–238.

ern action, but appears to be only one among a group of contingencies including in this case: an overall goal of providing rapid service to clients; the anticipation of troubles arising for both clients and caseworkers; competent performance of one's job (avoiding complaints); and the fair distribution of work among the caseworkers. The procedure defined by the rule appears to be used when it is appropriate in the context of all practical contingencies considered. In other cases, the rule is suspended and alternate procedures are developed to do the work.

Suggesting that rules are not "followed" does not imply that they are meaningless or serve no function. It does compel us to try to understand what functions rules do serve. When the contingencies of the immediate situation result in a practice that was not in accord with the rule, Zimmerman observed that the receptionists verbalize the contingencies that justify their departure from the rule. They announce, for example, that the pressing concern of a medical appointment makes the rearrangement of scheduling reasonable and proper, even if it violates the rule. When the routine action is appropriate, the rule itself accounts for or justifies the action taken.

Thus, existing rules serve to justify actions undertaken for a range of practical reasons. Following a rule means, on any occasion, responding to the particular set of practical contingencies that are confronted on that occasion. The rule does not have a particular meaning, but provides a convenient justification for responses to a wide variety of contingencies.

The kinship between the standardized rule and the ad hoc justifications that are offered when the rule is broken is close indeed. Each time we decide to act we must assess whether the practical contingencies we confront can be competently handled by conforming to the applicable rule. Further, we have to decide whether our action is close enough to conformity to the rule so that others will not challenge it. Finally, we must decide what sort of ad hoc justification, if one is necessary, will be accepted as a reasonable explanation of our actions by others. Thus, no matter how frequently actions are "close enough" to appear to be in conformity to the rule, and in need of no further explanation, those involved must be employing interpretive devices to establish the applicability and reasonableness of the rule to their situation and their possible need for additional explanation. In this view, the repetitive behavior that characterizes institutionalization must result from relatively stable contingencies, not from habitual conformity. In fact, Robert Merton has identified the following of rules in the face of contingencies that should override them as a form of deviance.[12]

Informal organization as an alternative explanation. The violation of rules accompanied by justifications is an extremely well-documented and

---

[12] Robert Merton, *Social Theory and Social Structure,* rev. ed., Free Press, New York, 1968, pp. 238–241.

long-recognized fact of organizational behavior. Ordinarily, a quite different interpretation arises from such observations. An informal organization with rules that are unwritten and that arises from the interaction and community ties of organization members is believed to exist alongside the formal organization. These rules are enforced by a set of informal sanctions and, in many cases, influence the distribution of official sanctions as well. When deviance occurs, it is often attributed to following the informal rather than the formal rules, or to effecting a compromise between the two sets of rules. In fact, Chester Barnard's classic statement of organizational theory, which preceded much of the empirical work in this area, included the informal organization as an essential part of every organization and argued that it would serve exactly that purpose, among others.[13] To many, results such as Zimmerman's are an indication that Barnard and others were largely correct about informal organizations.

In this context, D. Lawrence Wieder's study of a rehabilitation halfway house for drug addicts is a critical and necessary study in support of the ethnomethodological position.[14] A group of unofficial norms called the "convict code" are regularly observed to emerge in prisons and similar institutions and constitute one of the most widely documented informal organizations. Wieder's study shows that the convict code is used as a justification for action in the same way as the formal rules of the halfway house. For example, when a halfway house resident was asked to provide information about another resident he or she might answer that "snitching" is against the code. Citing the code as a reason for behavior, even when that behavior appears to violate official rules, is accepted by the guards as a reasonable justification of action. The informal rules are not followed either. They provide a second set of preformulated justifications for behavior, allowing the inmate to justify behavior in terms of two different sets of norms, or to provide ad hoc explanations that do not fit either. Notice that the two sets of norms are in partial contradiction and by judiciously selecting between the formal and informal norms one could justify contradictory actions. Thus the informal and formal norms are shown to have the same functions in their actual use. Using the existence of one set of norms to explain behavior that cannot be explained by the other still leaves the fundamental processes that underlie the use of both unexplored.

Organizational behavior as a skilled endeavor. The picture of the organization member that emerges from these studies is that of a skilled actor rather than a rule follower. One acts in the service of practical interests.

---

[13] Chester Barnard, *The Functions of the Executive,* Harvard, Cambridge, 1938.
[14] D. Lawrence Wieder, "Telling the Code," in *Ethnomethodology,* ed. Roy Turner, Penguin, Baltimore, 1974, pp. 144–172.

One is able to anticipate the emergence of problems for oneself and others from one's action. One is able to justify either deviance or conformity by citation of appropriate norms or by creating ad hoc explanations that uniquely fit one's circumstances. One is able to behave in ways that others will recognize as reasonable without explanation, and anticipate, with some success, both when one needs an excuse for one's action and what sort of excuse will be accepted. These skills are similar, it should be noted, to those discussed in Agnes' case.

Egon Bittner discusses three types of organizational skills that assume a set of rules exists as a resource in organizing and justifying behavior.[15] He calls these three skills the "gambit of compliance," "stylistic unity," and "corroborative reference." These are not intended as an exhaustive list, but as a preliminary statement of the skills employed in organizational settings to use rules in the construction of reality.

The "gambit of compliance" makes use of the general belief in the existence of known rules as a resource in organizing and justifying behavior. By anticipating that others will interpret our actions in the context of their prior background knowledge, we can organize our behavior so that they will interpret it as complying with a common, applicable rule. For example, the use of a turn signal makes slowing down, or even stopping, in an intersection appear reasonable to others as following a routine procedure. The nonverbal compliance allows others to interpret what we are doing and to predict, more or less accurately, what we will be doing in the future. It is made possible by anticipation of the background knowledge that others will apply in interpreting our actions, including the applicable rules. The successful use of the gambit of compliance does not require that a more careful analysis would uphold the sense of conformity to a rule. Agnes' efforts are an instance of employing the gambit of compliance with respect to the rule that everyone is either a male or a female. Verbally, compliance consists of convincing others that whatever you are doing is in conformity to some applicable rule.

We have already observed that a variety of possibly conflicting rules are available to justify action in an organization. "Stylistic unity" refers to the preference of organization members for behavior that is in compliance with particular rules, rather than others which are possible. For example, the receptionists preferred behavior that was reasonable and that avoided anticipated troubles rather than behavior that was strictly in accord with the rules. A rule could be cited to justify either course of action, but actors have preferences. In this case, the implicit rule to avoid trouble is preferred to a formal rule that requires the mechanical assignment of work

---

[15] Egon Bittner, "The Concept of Organization," *Social Research,* 32 (Winter 1965), 239–255.

according to a predetermined formula. Organizational skill includes anticipating the preferences of others.

"Corroborative reference" takes into account the fact that, on some occasions, specific rules are not sufficient to justify one's actions. In that case, the overall significance of the behavior for the organization, rather than its isolated merits, can be used to justify action. Citation of the organization's overall policies, purpose, and so on, corroborates that some action that may appear senseless or foolish is indeed meaningful. That is, the behavior is justified by reference to the overall pattern, not some more specific rule. In an organization, this device could be used by executives to justify the toleration of theft by employees that drains a specific budget but contributes to overall morale and output.

Important Concepts

THE DOCUMENTARY METHOD OF INTERPRETATION

The "documentary method of interpretation" [16] is one of the terms used by Garfinkel to denote the process by which matters of fact are established. The term originated in the work of Karl Mannheim, a major figure in what is now called the "sociology of knowledge." Mannheim was concerned with his observation that each generation of historians presents a new view of what happened in earlier eras. In addition, during a given era, historians with different economic and social positions had different opinions regarding the nature of prior historical events, current social structure and trends, and the prospects for future developments. These differences included both matters of fact and values.

Mannheim argued that the historian has a world view or global outlook *(Weltanschauung)* determined by his educational experiences, his position in the social structure, and the historical era in which he lived. The global outlook cannot be eradicated; it is an essential part of social scientific knowledge. The implications of this ineluctable world view as an influence on knowledge are profound. First, in contrast to knowledge in the natural sciences, social scientific knowledge cannot be cumulative or objective or correct in any final sense. Instead, it is regarded as correct only during a particular era and for a particular social and economic group. That is, its truth is dependent on a shared world view. Second, the procedure for arriving at such knowledge, and defending it from critics, is not a direct logical inference from evidence. The global outlook influences both the selection and interpretation of data, which in turn are the evidence used to support the world view. Evidence is searched to find a coherent and mean-

---

[16] Garfinkel, pp. 76–103.

ingful pattern, but, at the same time, existing general beliefs affect both what information we will regard as relevant and how it will be interpreted. Mannheim called this process of evaluating data in the context of an underlying, coherent world view to discover other, less general patterns, "the documentary method of interpretation." [17]

Garfinkel recognized that this process of interpretation applies to the establishing of facts in social interaction as well as to the interpretation of events of historic scale and duration. In interaction, the background knowledge used to interpret particular events serves the same functions as the world view does in the study of historical events. The various skills we have mentioned in the discussion of Agnes and of the use of bureaucratic rules are specifications of how the documentary method of interpretation occurs in interaction. Unfortunately, it is impossible to provide a concise definition of the documentary method. In fact, the task of ethnomethodology can be defined as the study of the documentary method of interpretation; only the accumulation of studies and refinement of the theoretical concepts will make a concise definition possible.

The practical orientation of the documentary method should be emphasized. The interpretation of events, we have observed, is undertaken in the service of the individual's ongoing plans and in the context of various practical contingencies. These plans provide a context that influences what will be regarded as relevant and set a standard for the termination of inquiry. When the investigation is complete enough for the purposes at hand, the inquiry stops, the facts are treated as objective, and the adequacy of the process of inquiry is accepted. Agnes' ability to maintain a female identity depended on this practical character of inquiry, especially the fact that inquiry is terminated whenever matters are clear enough for the current situation. Given typical background knowledge (that everyone is either a male or a female) and most purposes (excepting, for example, medical examinations and sexual encounters), particular physical characteristics are not necessary to determining gender.

Earlier we discussed the nonintuitive character of ethnomethodology's interests. The self-concealing characteristics of the documentary method of interpretation makes it necessary to adopt this nonintuitive approach. The reasoning employed in practical situations is such that one is prevented from observing the *processes* of inquiry and reasoning and is limited to observing their *results*. It is only by a theoretical nonintuitive approach that the details of the interpretive process (practical reasoning or documentary method) can be studied.

---

[17] See Mannheim's essay, "On the Interpretation of Weltanschauung," in Karl Mannheim, *Essays on the Sociology of Knowledge,* ed. Paul Kecskemeti, Routledge, London, 1952, pp. 33–84.

INDEXICALITY

"Indexicality" has been recognized as a characteristic of some linguistic communication (both verbal and written) since the beginning of Western philosophy. Ordinarily, "indexical communication" is contrasted with "objective communication" and treated as inferior. Attempts are made to avoid indexicality and to correct it when it occurs.[18] Bar-Hillel has located the difference between objective and indexical communication in the degree to which one must know the contextual background in which the statement was made to understand its meaning. Objective statements will be understood in the same way by almost anyone who speaks the language, even without knowledge of the context in which the statement was made. Indexical communication cannot be understood without contextual knowledge: when the statement was made, under what circumstances, and by whom.[19]

For example, "Officers in the United States army are called 'sir' by those who hold lower ranks" is a statement that is objective in this sense. All of the important terms are generally known, and knowing the names and order of military ranks is not necessary to understanding the statement. Thus, whether the statement is true or false, any of us will understand the statement in essentially the same way. On the other hand, "They salute me" is an indexical expression. Who are "they"? Who is "me"? The words cannot be understood clearly without this knowledge. Verbal expressions are often accompanied by the contextual knowledge needed to understand them. In such cases, they can be understood and can be used to communicate effectively.

Garfinkel has argued that indexicality is a characteristic of *all* communication in two important senses. First, understanding *always* requires contextual knowledge.[20] Using the term "indexicality" allows a more formal restatement of our earlier discussion in which we observed that the meaning of rules, for example, is relative to background knowledge, the investigative procedures employed in the particular situation, practical contingencies, and the plans and interests of the people involved. All of these matters serve as the context for particular indexical communications, the rules.

Second, Garfinkel has extended the concept from linguistic communications to any means of communication that is employed. This includes paralinguistic and nonlinguistic behavior and physical objects and events that have symbolic significance. Thus, tone of voice or posture are indexi-

---

[18] Harold Garfinkel and Harvey Sacks, "On Formal Structures of Practical Actions," in *Theoretical Sociology,* ed. John McKinney and Edward Tiryakian, Appleton-Century-Crofts, New York, pp. 334–338.

[19] Yehoshua Bar-Hillel, "Indexical Expressions," *Mind,* 63 (July 1954), 359.

[20] Garfinkel, pp. 4–7.

cal communications to be understood in reference to their context. They may also serve as the context for linguistic communication. We have discussed one extreme instance of what might serve as an indexical communication: Agnes' urine sample. In the context of her knowledge of her own physical peculiarities, Agnes regarded the urine sample in the context of her knowledge and expected doctors to do the same in the context of their specialized medical knowledge.

Indexicality and the documentary method of interpretation are closely related. Indexicality refers to the fact that the meaning of a particular statement or event is relative to its context. The documentary method of interpretation is the process through which this meaning is understood. The difference lies in whether the process of interpretation or the structure of knowledge is being emphasized.

REFLEXIVITY

The term "reflexivity" is used extensively in the ethnomethodological literature, but without a clear definition. It is used to characterize a variety of relationships whose common theme is that the practices and assumptions (or the interpretive process) involved in the construction of an experience are part of the experience they construct. Thus, when doing research from the common sense perspective, one's research practices, or methodology, for studying the world are also part of the world. Similarly, any person who attempts to decide factual questions uses methods that are part of the common sense world he or she wishes to study.

A paradox is involved here and is, perhaps, the reason why the term "reflexivity" has a "sense" rather than a definition. Even if one studies the procedures one uses for studying, as scientists do when they consider methodology, some procedures are still in use, and assumed, for studying other procedures. And if the sequence is pushed one step further back or infinitely further back, to studying the procedures used to study the procedures used to study the procedures used to study the procedures . . . a set of assumptions and procedures will always be *employed* rather than studied.

Solving this paradox is another formulation of the ethnomethodological program. One solution has been suggested which helps to illustrate the sense of reflexivity and the paradox it suggests. Cicourel has suggested a procedure which he calls "indefinite triangulation." A video or sound tape recording is the most appropriate data for this procedure. The tape recording is played, and sometimes replayed, for the participants and for the researchers. In each instance, a commentary is appended to the tape, concerning what the participants really meant. It is expected that each appendix will be different, even if provided by the same person on two different occasions. At this point, the various "meanings" of the taped interaction are not combined into a single authoritative version of what really happened.

(That procedure would be within the common sense world.) Rather, the differences among the various versions are combed to see if they reveal interpretive practices that are common to all of them. For example, one might discover how the context is used to interpret indexical utterances. Notice that the topic of interest is not the meaning of the original interaction. Rather, it is the basic practices that support *any* meaning of the interaction in the common sense world.[21]

Suggested Readings

Because ethnomethodology is a new approach, much of the writing in this area is still programmatic in character. In addition it is eclectic, reflecting the fact that the approach is still borrowing from others and still developing its own character. Three collections of readings provide a good overview of the kinds of work that are characterized as ethnomethodology. Roy Turner's collection, *Ethnomethodology* (Penguin, Baltimore, 1974), has the distinctive feature of including excerpts from longer, earlier studies by Cicourel and Garfinkel. Jack Douglas' collection, *Understanding Everyday Life* (Aldine, Chicago, 1970), includes several papers that characterize the ethnomethodological program and its relationship to the rest of the discipline of sociology. David Sudnow's collection, *Studies in Social Interaction* (Free Press, New York, 1972), emphasizes conversational analysis, an approach that is becoming increasingly important among ethnomethodologists. Harold Garfinkel's statement, *Studies in Ethnomethodology* (Prentice-Hall, Englewood Cliffs, N.J., 1967), is essential to a systematic study of this approach. Aaron Cicourel's essays (collected in *Cognitive Sociology,* Free Press, New York, 1974) explore the relationship of ethnomethodology to linguistics, socialization, and cognitive psychology.

[21] Cicourel, p. 124.

PART 3

SOME MAJOR

CONTRIBUTORS

The pioneers of symbolic interactionism, such as Mead and Cooley, have received extensive treatment in various works, including the present one. The individuals whose work we will examine in this part have not been systematically treated in secondary sources, although their productivity has been sufficiently large to warrant detailed consideration. Each one has conducted research, exerts contemporary influence, and is likely to grow in that influence. Although we have referred to their work throughout the preceding chapters, we need to look at each one systematically.

All four of the scholars examined in this part are still living and all received their doctorates from the University of Chicago. Herbert Blumer was a student of George Herbert Mead and received his Ph.D. in 1929.

He has taught at the Universities of Missouri, Chicago, and California, and is now professor emeritus at the University of California, Berkeley. His influence has been considerable—through his writings, his numerous students, and his professional activities. Included in the latter are service as editor of the *American Journal of Sociology* (1940–1952), editor of the Sociology Series of Prentice-Hall (1936–1967), and director of the Institute of Social Sciences at the University of California, Berkeley (1959–1965).

Anselm Strauss received his Ph.D. in 1945. He has taught at the Universities of Indiana, Chicago, and California, Berkeley; he is presently professor of sociology at the latter school. Strauss has extensive experience in research projects, including the directorship of a six-and-a-half-year Public Health Service study entitled "Hospital Personnel, Nursing Care, and Dying Patients."

Tamotsu Shibutani obtained his Ph.D. in 1948. He has taught at the Universities of Chicago, California, Berkeley, and California, Santa Barbara, where he is currently professor of sociology. He studied with Blumer, and has done research in a variety of areas, including collective behavior, ethnic relationships, and the relationship between society and personality. His primary concern has been the development of a general theory of social control based on the principles of cybernetics.

Erving Goffman obtained his Ph.D. in 1953. His teaching experience includes the University of California, Berkeley, and the University of Pennsylvania, where he is currently Benjamin Franklin Professor of Anthropology and Sociology. He has also served as a visiting scientist at the National Institute of Mental Health (1954–1957). He has developed his own distinctive approach, including the well-known dramaturgical model of analysis. Goffman's work is characterized by detailed attention to the normative structure of small social systems, especially the self-defining implications of appearances and their use in interaction-based strategy.

As the following chapters will show, each of these four contributors has made a distinctive contribution to sociological analysis. The intellectual tradition within which these works developed is not monolithic. As thought developed in different substantive areas, diverse vocabularies and insights emerged—still within a common tradition, but reflecting the creativity and interests of different thinkers. By presenting these bodies of work as distinctive coherent units and retaining the specific character of each, the applicability of the tradition of thought to many sociological problems is highlighted.

Chapter 9

Herbert Blumer

It is fitting that we begin our study of major contributors with the man who coined the name "symbolic interactionism"—Herbert Blumer.[1] Early in his career, Blumer established himself as a formidable critic, but used his

---

[1] Since the bulk of citations in this chapter is to involve the works of Blumer, we will refer to them by date only in the footnotes. For the titles of the works and complete publication information see the list at the end of the chapter.

critical works to expand and systematize symbolic interactionist theory. His concern from the first was to show how symbolic interactionism could greatly enlarge our understanding of social life and human behavior. In other words, he has not been critical merely in order to reject the work of others, but in order to offer a better alternative.

Critic and Advocate

In 1937, the Social Science Research Council considered a charge that it had drifted from critical and scientific activities toward promotional and administrative concerns. The result was the formation of a committee which was to plan appraisals of completed research projects. The first appraisal was Blumer's critique of William I. Thomas and Florian Znaniecki's monumental and influential work, *The Polish Peasant*. Thomas offered a rejoinder, and the two pieces of work were the focus of a special conference held in 1938.

The Polish Peasant was a study that grew out of the massive Polish emigration of the early twentieth century. The authors analyzed the structural and social psychological changes of the Polish peasant community which had migrated to America. According to Thomas and Znaniecki, one significant consequence of the migration was the conflict of attitudes with rules; the attitudes of the Polish immigrants conflicted with the established rules of American society. This meant that the immigrants existed in a state of social disorganization—the rules by which they had formerly lived were no longer appropriate.

Blumer's critique made a number of points. One of the more important was that the materials used by the authors were inadequate for their theoretical generalizations. Extensive use was made of human documents, and such documents "seem to lend themselves readily to diverse interpretations." [2] Documents may provide us with "hunches, insights, questions suitable for reflection, new perspectives, and new understandings," [3] but this is far different from using documents to validate theoretical statements. Blumer argued that documents are valuable only in terms of the theory used to interpret them, that the validity of any theory cannot be established by the use of documents. [4] Thus, early in his career Blumer made a point that recurs throughout his work—the necessity of making sociological generalizations congruent with the empirical world.

Among the other subjects of Blumer's criticism are: social psychological uses of the concept of "attitude" and the imprecision and ambiguity of

[2] Blumer, 1939a, p. 77.
[3] *Ibid.*, p. 76.
[4] *Ibid.*, p. 79.

concepts in general; sociological views of the nature of human society; views of the nature of human association; the use of variable analysis; social theory; analyses of race relations; analyses of industrial relations and of the effect of industrialization; public opinion research; and the analysis of social problems and collective behavior. However, as noted above, these varied critical efforts were not made simply to attack the work of others, but to affirm symbolic interactionism. By juxtaposing the symbolic interactionist approach with others, Blumer has brought the former into sharper focus and demonstrated its unique features.

We will outline Blumer's exposition of the theory and methods of symbolic interactionism, using a number of the critical works to show how he has consistently explicated his position and contrasted it with others.[5] We will then point out certain emphases which recur throughout his work, and show how certain criticisms can be addressed. Finally, we will note his contributions to a number of substantive areas.

The Theory of Symbolic Interactionism

BASIC PREMISES

Blumer begins with three premises. First, humans behave on the basis of meaning. Human behavior cannot be understood as merely the response to stimuli that are external to the individual or as merely the reflection of an overarching and overwhelming system of culture. Rather, in contrast to the infrahuman world and to the view of humans set forth by other theoretical perspectives, behavior at the human level is a function of the meaning attributed to objects, situations, and the anticipated consequences of the behavior.

Second, meaning arises out of interaction. The meaning of an object or situation is not inherent; meaning is not an external phenomenon which is imposed upon the individual. Rather, meaning emerges from the interaction process. For instance, if a young man encounters a young woman on a lonely stretch of beach, the situation itself may suggest certain lines of action to him. But there is no automatic meaning to the situation; rather, the meaning will depend upon the way in which the young woman acts toward him and/or responds to his behavior. Thus, the young man's behavior will depend not merely upon the situation, but upon the meaning that arises out of his interaction with the young woman in the situation.

Third, the use of meanings for guiding behavior occurs through a process of interpretation. Blumer posits two steps in the interpretive process. In the first, one makes indications to oneself regarding the possible courses

[5] Our outline follows Blumer's own. See Blumer, 1969b, pp. 1–60.

of one's action in a particular situation. In other words one interacts with oneself, indicating to oneself the relevant meanings. The second step involves the selective and creative use of the various meanings which one has indicated. Interpretation, then, "becomes a matter of handling meanings." [6] This stresses the processual, emergent nature of human behavior; interpretation is not a matter of mechanically applying preformed meanings from an existing repertoire, but of selecting and revising meanings. In our example, the young man may have seen a motion picture in which a similar situation led to a love affair. His initial tendency to apply this meaning to his own situation may be quickly changed, however, if the young woman treats his overtures with contempt.

Blumer points out that most analysts of human behavior would agree with the first premise above, even though they may generally ignore it in practice. It is the second and third premises which really distinguish symbolic interactionism. The derivation of meanings from interaction, and the use of meanings through an interpretive process to guide behavior are two crucial premises, and they apply to human life at every level. That is, these premises do not simply underlie dyadic interaction such as the above illustration, but are the foundation for all analyses of social reality. If, for example, we go beyond the dyad and look at larger groups, symbolic interactionism again stresses the necessity of discovering processes of interaction, meanings, and interpretation. An analysis based upon the assumption that the group is nothing more than a cultural organization comprised of a network of social positions will yield partial understanding at best. People do not behave simply on the basis of playing out roles in an organized network of positions; rather, the formal, sociocultural organization is the framework within which the crucial interpretive processes are carried on.[7]

BASIC IMAGES

The distinctive nature of symbolic interactionism comes into sharper focus when we look at some of the basic ideas or images, all of which have the above three premises as their foundation. All theoretical perspectives have such images, which may be implicit or explicit. For example, there is an image of human beings in all perspectives, whether or not the perspective explicitly addressed itself to the issue. Humans may be viewed in Hobbesian terms as base creatures who must be constrained, or in Marxian terms as creatures whose nature reflects the productive structure, or in cultural terms as creatures fashioned by a transcendent system in which they necessarily have their being, and so forth. Such images have important consequences for sociological analysis; thus, Bendix asserted in 1961

[6] *Ibid.*, p. 5.
[7] Blumer, 1953.

that "no more important task faces the social sciences today than to determine by which 'image of man' they are to be led." [8]

Human society. What, then, are the images that prevail in symbolic interactionism? Blumer identifies six that are particularly important. The first is the image of human society, which must be seen in terms of action rather than culture or the social structure. It is not that we can ignore the latter two, but that they are essentially "derivations from the complex of ongoing activity that constitutes group life." [9] The most basic fact about any society is that it consists of people in action, and the culture and social structure are both the framework for and the consequence of that action. Thus, we can study a phenomenon such as industrial relations in a number of ways. One approach treats industrial relations as though they were cultural in nature—"expressions of a body of established regulations or definitions." [10] Another approach views them as a structure of hierarchical relationships. Along with other approaches, these are deficient in that they ignore the dynamics of industrial relations, the fact that workers and management are engaged in an ongoing struggle, with consequent adjustments and modifications in the relationship. To set up a relatively inflexible system in which invariant patterns of behavior are presumed to recur through time is to distort the nature of the industrial organization. Industrial relations "are either moving, or if not moving, in tenuous accommodation poised to move." [11]

Social interaction. The second important image is that relating to social interaction. In symbolic interactionism, interaction is a formative process, rather than a mere arena in which behavior occurs. That is, interaction is not simply the *expression* of behavior; it is a *creator* of behavior. Social interaction is a creative process rather than an expression of a priori factors such as culture, personality, or social structure. There are two types of interaction, however—nonsymbolic and symbolic. This follows Mead's formulation, although Mead identified nonsymbolic interaction in terms of the "conversation of gestures." "Nonsymbolic interaction" occurs when people respond to each other without interpretation. An individual may respond directly to the action of another—to the other's raised hand or some facet of the other's appearance that generates certain emotions, for

---

[8] Reinhard Bendix, "The Image of Man in the Social Sciences: The Basic Assumptions of Present-Day Research," in *Sociology: The Progress of a Decade,* eds. Seymour Martin Lipset and Neil Smelser, Prentice-Hall, Englewood Cliffs, N.J., 1961, p. 31.

[9] Blumer, 1969b, p. 6.

[10] Blumer, 1947, p. 274.

[11] *Ibid.,* p. 273.

example—without the process of interpretation. But the typical mode of interacting is symbolic, which always involves an interpretation of the action of the other.

In "symbolic interaction," actors "take each other into account." [12] This means that the relationship is one of *"subject to subject,* not of object to object, nor even of subject to object. Each person has to view the conduct of the other in some degree from the standpoint of the other." [13] In fact, there is a threefold structure of meaning to each gesture; every gesture indicates what the other is to do, what the one making the gesture intends to do, and what the joint action arising out of this situation should be. As is evident, this is a process involving role-taking. Each individual must apprehend the attitude of the other so as to anticipate the attitude of the other and thereby direct his or her behavior. But his or her behavior takes into account the line of action of the other, so that we may speak of joint action rather than simply individual behavior. To reiterate the point above, symbolic interaction is always a relationship of subject to subject. Consequently, interaction is always a formative process, and we cannot understand human behavior by treating the individual as a subject who acts vis-à-vis an object or a plexus of objects. An example of the latter would be an analysis of behavior on the basis of personality. The individual is viewed as a subject whose behavior takes place in a plexus of objects, and whose behavior can be accounted for solely in terms of factors within the acting subject. By contrast, symbolic interactionism views the individual as a subject whose behavior occurs in interaction with other subjects, and the person's behavior must be understood in terms of the formative process of interaction.

Objects. The third basic image involves the nature of objects. The world in which humans must act is comprised of various objects. Three types of objects are found in the human environment: physical, social, and abstract. "Physical objects" include such things as desks, automobiles, and lakes. "Social objects" refer to people in their varied roles. And "abstract objects" include such things as the various ideologies, and ethical and philosophical systems which characterize all human groups.

But while we may differentiate objects along these three lines, the nature of any object is a function of the meaning it has for an individual. Objects do not possess intrinsic meaning which is imposed upon actors; rather, actors impose meanings upon objects through the same processes of interaction and interpretation identified above. This is similar to Holzner's argument that the more we reflect upon our experience of reality the more

[12] Blumer, 1953, p. 194.
[13] *Ibid.*

we recognize that even our perception of the physical world is "influenced by our mapping of time and space, our symbolic patterns, our values, and our communicative links." [14] Even an object like a chair may have completely different meaning to differing actors and may enter into the behavior of differing actors in diverse fashion. For one actor, the chair is a resting place for a weary body. For another, it is part of an acrobatic act. For a third, it is an example—good or bad—of craftsmanship. For another, it is aesthetically pleasing or offensive in the context of a particular decor. And so forth. No object has an intrinsic meaning that imposes itself on all individuals. The meaning of any object, whether physical, social, or abstract, is a consequence of human interaction and interpretive processes.

Human actors. A fourth basic image in symbolic interactionism posits humans as actors. Here we must understand "actor" in contrast to "reactor." The human is impelled by neither internal nor external factors which determine a priori the behavior in interaction. One of the problems of attitude research, for example, has been its tendency to conceptualize the attitude in terms of a cognitive state that virtually predetermines behavior.[15] This conceives interaction in the terms argued against above: as an arena in which behavior occurs rather than as a formative process.

But again we must emphasize the interpretive process that characterizes human behavior. Human beings do not merely react to external stimuli, nor do they merely behave in accord with prior attitudes. Humans are actors, creatures who interpret situations and whose behavior is subject to modification and to alternative courses as a result of creative participation with others in situations. A human is able to interpret, furthermore, because he or she has a self, which means that he or she has "a mechanism of self-interaction with which to meet the world—a mechanism that is used in forming and guiding . . . conduct." [16] This insistence on the self clearly differentiates symbolic interactionism from those perspectives which treat humans as "merely responding organisms" and action as a "mere response to factors playing on human beings." [17] There is always a process of self-interaction between the initial thrusts toward behavior and the subsequent action. Through this self-interaction one interprets the situation and organizes one's behavior accordingly. Self-interaction means that one makes indications to oneself and responds to those indications.

Thus, as an actor a human does not engage in mechanical or automatic

[14] Burkhart Holzner, *Reality Construction in Society,* rev. ed., Schenkman, Cambridge, Mass., 1972, p. 14.
[15] Blumer, 1955a.
[16] Blumer, 1966a, p. 535.
[17] *Ibid.,* p. 542.

responses to impinging stimuli. In making indications to him- or herself, a process which is only possible because the human possesses a self, the individual endows objects with meaning. Consequently, his or her behavior "is constructed or built up instead of being a mere release." [18]

Human action. The fifth important image has already been touched upon—the nature of human action. Since human beings must interpret situations in order to act, the social scientist must know how people define situations in order to understand why they behave as they do. Human behavior cannot be understood if we neglect subjective meanings. "Process is the becoming of experience," wrote Whitehead.[19] And it is not difficult to show both theoretically and empirically that subjective meanings are necessary for sociological explanation. For example, in commenting on studies by the Yale Labor-Management Center, Matson points out that the only way to understand the behavior of the workers is to recognize it as a rational adaptation to the situation *as defined by the workers.*[20] For human action is not merely a function of hierarchical relationships, but of processes of interaction and interpretation.

Blumer indicated the importance of subjective meanings for understanding action in his first empirical work: the study of the effects of motion pictures on viewers. The study was based primarily on personal accounts of experiences with motion pictures:

> The study assumes that one way to find out about the experiences of people is to inquire into those experiences . . . chief reliance was placed on the use of the written life history or the motion-picture autobiography. The subjects . . . were asked to write in narrative form their motion-picture experiences.[21]

Human action is an interpretive process not only in terms of the behavior of the individual, but also in terms of collective action. In collectivities, people indicate their interpretations of a situation to each other and not simply to themselves. The result is the emergence of collective definitions of situations which are employed to direct individual behavior. For instance, social problems must be viewed as the consequence of a "process of collective definition" rather than "a set of objective social arrangements with an intrinsic makeup." [22] This is not to say that the objective arrange-

---

[18] Blumer, 1962, p. 182.

[19] Alfred North Whitehead, *Process and Reality,* Free Press, New York, 1929, p. 193.

[20] Floyd W. Matson, *The Broken Image: Man, Science and Society,* George Braziller, New York, 1964, pp. 248–249.

[21] Blumer, 1933a, p. 3.

[22] Blumer, 1971, p. 298.

ments are irrelevant, for such arrangements may enter into the process of collective definition. Nevertheless, social problems only emerge as a result of a collective definition of certain social arrangements as problematic.

For example, child labor was not considered a social problem during a considerable part of the time that children were subjected to oppressive labor. "Only when a considerable number of people decided that child labor was harmful and began saying, 'Isn't it awful!'—only then did child labor become a social problem." [23] While this statement simplifies the matter, it does illustrate the fact that whether certain social arrangements are a problem depends upon how they are socially defined. And, as Blumer notes, that definition will emerge as the collective product of processes of interaction and interpretation.

Joint action. The sixth and final important image in symbolic interactionism involves the interlinkage of action. Blumer notes that social life is composed of developing lines of actions of various individuals which are articulated together. And in this case, the whole is more than the sum of its parts. For joint action, "while made up of diverse component acts that enter into its formation, is different from any one of them and from their mere aggregation." [24] Again, this stresses the point that human action must be understood in terms of interaction, and that interaction is processual and formative. To use a simple example, a politician might rehearse a speech at home prior to giving it before a mass gathering. The resulting mass situation would be different from the rehearsal and from the behavior of any of the individuals in the audience. As a consequence of audience reaction, for instance, the politician might bring in spontaneous remarks or delete portions of the prepared speech. Furthermore, certain meanings would be attributed to the situation and certain conclusions drawn by the participants which emerged from the interaction and which could not be explained as simply the sum of individual acts. Various participants might draw differing and contradictory conclusions about the politician's prospects on the basis of the meeting; none of these conclusions would reflect the net positive and negative responses of the individuals present.

Again, however, we must recognize that this image refers not simply to dyadic relationships but to intergroup relations. In industrial relations, for example, we must look at the ongoing relationships between union and management, recognizing that we are dealing with "a moving pattern of accommodative adjustments largely between organized parties." [25] The

---

[23] Paul B. Horton and Gerald R. Leslie, *The Sociology of Social Problems*, 4th ed., Appleton-Century-Crofts, New York, 1970, p. 4.

[24] Blumer, 1969b, p. 17.

[25] Blumer, 1947, p. 277.

resulting action is not simply the total of the acts of union leaders and management leaders, but is something qualitatively new and different which emerges from the intergroup relationships. In other words, we cannot understand what goes on in a union by simply looking at the union, for the union is an organization involved in ongoing interaction with management. There has been an unfortunate tendency in organizational studies generally to analyze organizations as though they existed in a vacuum, as though what goes on in the organization could be understood purely in terms of organizational variables. More recently, there is increasing awareness of the importance of the organization's environment, of the fact that the organization necessarily functions in the context of an interorganizational network.[26] Such an emphasis is congruent with Blumer's point about the significance of the interlinkage of action on the group as well as the individual level.

One other facet of the interlinkage of action must be noted—the interlinkage is in time as well as space. That is, "joint action" refers not simply to the articulation of various lines of action with each in a particular situation, but also to the articulation of the present with the past. Thus, "any instance of joint action, whether newly formed or long established, has necessarily arisen out of a background of previous actions of the participants."[27] There is historical continuity in human action as well as interdependence among individuals and groups. Consequently, although the emphasis is on process and emergence, social reality is not conceived in terms so fluid that analysis is impossible. Reality is process, but that does not imply a lack of continuities, stable factors, and persistence in social life. A politician approaches a particular crowd in a certain way because of his or her experience with crowds. And he or she will approach future crowds in a certain way which is different from the present because of new experiences. A politician's interaction with the citizenry changes over time, but there is continuity in the sense that the new has arisen out of the past as well as the present.

The Methods of Symbolic Interactionism

The theoretical perspective outlined above has a number of methodological implications. One implication which might be drawn, however, is untenable, as Blumer is quick to point out: the fact that social reality necessarily involves subjective meanings does *not* mean that reality is only in the sphere of images and conceptions. By "social reality," Blumer always

---

[26] See, for example, Merlin B. Brinkerhoff and Phillip R. Kunz, eds., *Complex Organizations and Their Environments,* Wm. C. Brown, Dubuque, Iowa, 1972.

[27] Blumer, 1969b, p. 20.

means the empirical world. To reduce that world to pure subjectivity is a serious error, for the empirical world has the character of being able to challenge and resist the images and conceptions which we form of it. "This resistance gives the empirical world an obdurate character that is the mark of reality." [28] Having made this point, Blumer proceeds to offer us three important methodological principles which follow from the theoretical perspective.

RESEARCH AS SYMBOLIC INTERACTION

First, methodology applies to every facet of scientific research from the prior theoretical orientation of the researcher to the interpretation which the researcher makes of his or her findings. Research itself is a process of symbolic interaction. We noted this in Chapter 4 when we discussed Friedman's critique of psychological research. To reiterate, any experiment involving humans is a symbolic interaction process. Contrary to the experimental ideal, the laboratory does not provide us with virtually total control over the stimuli that impinge upon the subject. In fact, the subjects are subjects in the sense noted above: they are actors who enter the experimental situation with their own definitions of the situation and who interpret and ascribe meanings during the course of interacting with others in the experiment.

In other words, any interaction between humans involves processes of interpretation and the fitting together of developing lines of action. The fact that such interaction occurs in a laboratory setting where a social psychologist is attempting to expose individuals to particular stimuli does not change the nature of humans or of human action. The task of methodology is to address social scientific research in the light of these facts.

RESEARCH AND EMPIRICAL TESTING

A second methodological principle is that all facets of research are subject to and must be validated through empirical testing. Again and again, Blumer directs us to the empirical world, continually emphasizing the importance both of testing hypotheses and generalizations through empirical studies and of working closely with the empirical world in generating knowledge. We must make a "meticulous examination" of the empirical world in order to ascertain whether our premises, images, data, concepts, and interpretations are valid. In fact, the empirical world always takes precedence over methods. There is no method which is *the* tool of the social scientist. To idealize a method leads us to accept what has been called the "law of the tool," the tendency to define problems in precisely

[28] *Ibid.*, p. 22.

those terms which can be solved by the methods we already possess and desire to use. Methods themselves, therefore, must be subject to examination in the light of the empirical world.

As an example of what it means to subject methods, concepts, and so forth to the scrutiny of the empirical world, we may consider the problem of "attitude" as a scientific concept.

> The concept of attitude as currently held fails to meet any of these three simple requirements: it has no clear and fixed empirical reference, its class of objects cannot be distinguished effectively from related classes of objects, and it does not enable the enlargement of knowledge of the class of objects to which it presumably refers.[29]

Thus, Blumer argued in 1955, attitude research had yielded little insight into the nature of human behavior. The concept was, he said, empirically ambiguous, just as concepts in general tended to be. In fact, social theory itself poses problems at this point: "Its divorcement from the empirical world is glaring." [30] Social theorists, according to Blumer, tend to shape the empirical world into their theoretical molds rather than systematically test their theories by empirical research.

This was, in part, the basis for Blumer's first critical work. In his analysis of *The Polish Peasant,* Blumer noted that the authors were guilty of a serious disjunction between their theoretical generalizations and their empirical evidence. Their interpretations went far beyond their data. "The authors have shown surprising liberality in making generalizations—generalizations which seem to be very good, but for which there are few if any data in the materials." [31]

Blumer's insistence that every facet of research be rigorously subjected to empirical testing is worthy of continued emphasis. The history of the social sciences is replete with examples of conclusions made from inadequate data. For instance, the classic "Yankee City" series of W. Lloyd Warner has been faulted by the historian Stephan Thernstrom for its failure to probe into history. Among the resulting errors were the propagation of the notion of blocked mobility and a misinterpretation of the shoe factory strike. The former is the idea that America had a much more open class system in the nineteenth century than in the twentieth and that mobility has become increasingly difficult for the lower strata. This thought dominated American sociology for a decade,[32] though it is now known to be false.

---

[29] Blumer, 1955a, p. 59.
[30] Blumer, 1954a, p. 3.
[31] Blumer, 1939a, p. 75.
[32] Otis Dudley Duncan, "Social Stratification and Mobility: Problems in the Measurement of Trend," in *Indicators of Social Change,* eds. Eleanor Bernert Sheldon and Wilbert E. Moore, Russell Sage, New York, 1968, p. 678.

With respect to the shoe factory strike, Warner identified the strike as a radical departure from community tradition. But historical research shows that strikes were not that uncommon. Furthermore, the "craft order" and "simple folk community" of the past were largely myths in the minds of the inhabitants. In essence, Warner and his associates accepted without criticism, "the community's legends about itself." [33] They then used those legends as history in order to explain the processes of change.

A community's legends about itself are not unimportant, but they cannot be substituted for historical research that will yield a more accurate knowledge of the past. Unfortunately, too little attention has been given to the notion which pervades symbolic interactionism: reality is process. To make processual conclusions from cross-sectional data is always hazardous. An interesting example of the problem is provided by the fate of the concentric zone theory of city ecology which was developed by Burgess. The theory was originally conceived as a process, and has been consistently faulted on the basis of cross-sectional data. More recently, Haggerty used Markov chain analysis and found a trend towards a direct relationship between socioeconomic status and distance from the center of the city.[34] In other words, when the theory is treated and analyzed as a process—as Burgess formulated it—it appears to validly describe the nature of urban growth.

The above examples serve to stress the importance of the researcher keeping in intimate contact with the empirical world. In particular, they emphasize the fact that keeping in intimate contact means to recognize the processual nature of the empirical world. Again and again, Blumer reminds us that we are not dealing with a mechanical structure, but with a continually shifting phenomenon. As the above examples show, the failure to empirically investigate the process, or to be satisfied with making processual inferences on the basis of cross-sectional data, can lead to wrong conclusions about the social world.

RESEARCH AS EXPLORATION AND INSPECTION

The third methodological principle stressed by Blumer is that the empirical world rather than some model of scientific inquiry is the ultimate criterion of all social scientific work. This means that the researcher must know that world and not simply a theoretical framework or a set of research procedures. And the way to know the empirical world is through the two processes of exploration and inspection.

[33] Stephan Thernstrom, *Poverty and Progress: Social Mobility in a Nineteenth Century City*, Harvard, Cambridge, 1964, p. 230.

[34] Lee J. Haggerty, "Another Look at the Burgess Hypothesis: Time as an Important Variable," *American Journal of Sociology*, 76 (May 1971), 1084–1093.

Exploration. Exploration is research that is flexible and that involves a progressive sharpening of focus as the research proceeds. A variety of techniques may be needed to achieve this. If Warner had used historical research along with his field research, he would have arrived at more valid conclusions. In his own work on movies, Blumer used five different methods, though the bulk of information came from autobiographical data.[35] The other four methods were personal interviews, a collection of conversations about movies, direct questionnaires, and direct observation of children. The various data collected through the differing methods served as corrective checks on possible misinterpretations of the data of any single method.

The aim of exploration is to provide a comprehensive description of the phenomenon under study. But how can one be both comprehensive and flexible? Blumer's answer is "sensitizing" concepts. Sensitizing concepts are not meant to be precise; as noted earlier, they offer us guidelines rather than rigid directives. But this does not mean that they are ambiguous. Indeed, one of Blumer's criticisms of *The Polish Peasant* was the ambiguity of the conceptualizations. In particular, two crucial concepts in the work, "attitude" and "value," were found to be "vague, ambiguous, and confused."[36] Blumer pointed out that the authors often referred to the same thing when using the two concepts; in some places one could substitute either concept for the other without altering the meaning. Thus flexibility does not mean ambiguity.

Exploration and concepts. Blumer's critique of social scientific concepts and his advocacy of sensitizing concepts are of sufficient importance to warrant a more detailed discussion. Therefore, we will look at the progressive development of his ideas regarding concepts. In 1931, he pointed out that concepts have three important aspects.[37] First, they shape our perception and thereby facilitate action. Without concepts, human behavior would be equivalent to animal behavior. Second, concepts have a conceived content, thereby permitting us "to catch and hold some content of experience and make common property of it. Through abstraction one can isolate and arrest a certain experience which would never have emerged in mere perception."[38] Thus, concepts enable us to investigate the content. And third, concepts have a symbolic character, which means that they can be shared.

Because of these aspects, concepts perform three important functions in

---

[35] Blumer, 1933a, pp. 3–11.
[36] Blumer, 1939a, p. 24.
[37] Blumer, 1931.
[38] *Ibid.,* p. 520.

social science. First, they provide us with an orientation. One does not approach research with a blank mind. And contrary to what we might call a vulgar empiricism, the facts never speak for themselves. We necessarily approach any study with a perspective; concepts provide us with a particular perspective, and hopefully with a scientific rather than common sense perspective.

Second, concepts are tools for dealing with the environment. Concepts facilitate and direct action. At this point, we see the germ of the notion of sensitizing concepts, for Blumer points out that initially, as with any tool, a concept "may be crude and may be used quite experimentally; later, like perfect tools, it may become refined and its use quite standardized." [39] Third, the concept opens the way to deductive reasoning. We can use concepts as a basis for further thinking about some phenomenon by drawing out implications of the concept other than those which are immediately evident.

In 1940, Blumer continued his criticism of the vagueness of social psychological concepts. Because of this vagueness, he argued, there is a disjunction between conceptualizing and empirical work. The problem cannot be solved merely by creating a new set of concepts, for they will present us with the same difficulty. Nor can operational definitions resolve the issue, for they distort reality by limiting meanings, or by attempting to reduce complex social phenomena to a particular quantity, or by disregarding the processual nature of social reality. Suppose, for instance, that we define poverty in terms of an income of $5,000 per year for a family of four. Any family above that figure (adjusted for number of people in the family) would be considered nonpoor. But this ignores the meaning of income to various families; many families of four with incomes of $6,000 in 1976 would consider themselves in the midst of financial disaster. If a particular quantity is our only way of defining poverty, we are simply creating a disjunction between our concept and the realities of the empirical world.

The problem with concepts, then, must be approached in terms of the root causes of our difficulties. And that means that the problem must be seen in terms of the nature of scientific observation, which is a form of human behavior in which inferences are made about the observed phenomena. Observation has been divorced too much from empirical reality. Thus in 1940 Blumer suggested that we must improve our observation, which means "the need for an enrichening of experience which will make it possible for observers to form more dependable judgments in those observations which give us our trouble." [40] Again Blumer emphasizes the necessity of involvement with the empirical world.

[39] *Ibid.*, p. 529.
[40] Blumer, 1940, p. 718.

Thus far, then, Blumer has emphasized the problem of concepts—their vagueness and questionable relationship with the empirical world—and has suggested that concepts should be flexible tools of inquiry that must be tested by intimate study of the empirical world. These notions were crystallized in 1954, when Blumer again identified conceptual ambiguity as the "crucial deficiency" of social theory. What we need, he argued, are not definitive concepts, but "sensitizing" concepts which suggest directions rather than compel specifics. In fact, social psychological concepts are inherently sensitizing rather than definitive. The processual nature of social reality and the nature of social scientific research—making inferences from observation—both demonstrate the true nature of our concepts. For "since what we infer does not express itself in the same fixed way, we are not able to rely on fixed objective expressions to make the inference." [41]

This does not mean that our concepts are so flexible as to preclude any consensus among social scientists as to their meaning. Sensitizing concepts may be "tested, improved, and refined." And if their use makes the researcher uncomfortable, he must recognize that the alternative is to abandon the reality of the empirical world and to ignore the nature of scientific observation.

Inspection. To return to the main line of reasoning above, one aspect of knowing the empirical world is exploration, and exploration demands the use of sensitizing concepts. The other aspect is inspection, an analysis of the accounts of the empirical world which have been constructed through exploration. Such analysis demands a careful study of various "analytical elements" used (integration, social mobility, attitudes) in the light of the empirical materials. The analytical elements must be viewed from different angles and must be subjected to diverse questions. In other words, like exploration, "inspection is flexible, imaginative, creative, and free to take new directions." [42]

Together, exploration and inspection offer the necessary processes for empirically valid research. They comprise a "naturalistic" type of research in that the empirical world is studied in its ongoing reality rather than in a presumed reconstruction in a laboratory. They enable the researcher to gain what Blumer called in 1947 an "intimate familiarity and broad imaginative grasp" of the empirical world.[43] The failure to gain such "intimate familiarity" can result in wrong generalizations and misconceptions of the empirical world. A somewhat trivial but amusing example is

[41] Blumer, 1954a, p. 8.
[42] Blumer, 1969b, p. 44.
[43] Blumer, 1947, p. 277.

the "case of the Bulgarian Pigs." [44] The number of pigs in Bulgaria on January 1, 1910 and January 1, 1920 was reported as 527,311 and 1,089,699, respectively. It was concluded that the pig population had doubled in the decade; but the inference was wrong, and a greater familiarity with the situation would have precluded such a conclusion. For during the decade, the Gregorian calendar replaced the Julian and the peasants thereafter celebrated Christmas in January. Half of the pigs were always slaughtered just before Christmas, so that the extra pigs reported in January 1920 were simply waiting for the imminent Christmas kill.

Summary of Blumer's Views on Theory and Methods

Blumer has consistently emphasized a number of points. One is that we must remain in contact with the empirical world throughout the research process. This point has been affirmed, but not necessarily observed, since the beginning of sociology. Auguste Comte rejected armchair theorizing and advocated observation directed by theory as one appropriate method for sociology. [45]

Second, Blumer has consistently argued that social reality is a process. Beginning at the individual level, the self is a process. [46] Group relations are also processual; for example, the relations between workers and management are "dynamic, uncrystallized and changing." [47] Society itself is "an ongoing process of action" rather than "a posited structure of relations." [48] Any social research must account for the processual nature of the phenomenon being studied. For instance, in studying social problems we must examine the emergence and career of the problem. Social problems pass through five stages: emergence, legitimation, mobilization of action, development of a plan of action, and modifications in that plan during the course of its implementation. [49]

Third, Blumer continually reminds us of the importance of interaction. Any kind of human association may be analyzed in terms of symbolic interaction, including "cooperation, conflict, domination, exploitation, consensus, disagreement, closely knit identification, and indifferent concern for one another." [50] Interaction includes intergroup as well as interindividual

[44] Jerome R. Ravetz, *Scientific Knowledge and Its Social Problems,* Oxford, New York, 1971, p. 86.

[45] Auguste Comte, *The Positive Philosophy,* trans. Harriet Martineau, Calvin Blanchard, New York, 1858, pp. 473f.

[46] Blumer, 1966a, pp. 535–536.

[47] Blumer, 1947, p. 272.

[48] Blumer, 1966a, p. 541.

[49] Blumer, 1971, p. 301.

[50] Blumer, 1966a, p. 538.

relationships; during the course of interaction collective definitions are formed that transcend any particular individual but affect his or her behavior.

Fourth, social analysis must always investigate meanings, the interpretation by actors of their situation. Much social analysis has involved variables and their relations. Such analysis is inadequate because it tends to ignore the process of interpretation. A researcher takes a factor which, he or she presumes, affects group life and correlates this factor with some type of group activity. But this ignores the interpretive process which always intervenes between the external factor and the group activity.[51] For instance, mass media effects have been studied by identifying a particular influence, the group subject to that influence, and the consequences of the influence. This ignores the inevitable variations in the influence, the variable reactions of the subject group because of the process of interpretation, and the fact that other media than those studied bring other perspectives to the group.[52]

Finally, our methods and the process of research must be appropriate to the above points. From the critique of *The Polish Peasant* to the analysis of social problems in 1971, Blumer has consistently suggested approaches to research that take into account the nature of social reality. This stresses the fact that Blumer's numerous critiques have not been made simply to identify flaws, but have always included alternatives that express and demonstrate the utility of symbolic interactionism.

Criticisms and Deficiencies

Blumer's work can be—and has been—criticized along a number of lines. In this section, we will examine some of these criticisms. Essentially, they fall into two areas. One criticism relates to the meaning of the image of human beings presented by the perspective. The other criticism involves certain deficiencies in the perspective, deficiencies which are identified on the very basis Blumer emphasizes—our knowledge of the empirical world. We will deal with this latter criticism first.

APPARENT DEFICIENCIES

As we examine the apparent deficiencies, two points will become clear. First, Blumer has addressed himself to them, though he has not elaborated or focused upon them. And, second, this means that they are deficiencies only in the sense that Blumer has chosen to focus on other matters, not in the sense that the perspective is incapable of handling them.

[51] Blumer, 1956b.
[52] Blumer, 1959b.

Stability in interaction. The first deficiency involves stable forms of inter-action. We know from our involvement in the empirical world that there are stabilities in interaction. Blumer has continually reminded us of the processual nature of the empirical world, however; can the perspective account for those stable situations which we know exist? Blumer is well aware of such situations: "In most situations in which people act toward one another they have in advance a firm understanding of how to act and of how other people will act." [53] Nevertheless, this does not mean that such situations involve mechanical responses, for even when the joint action is of a repetitive nature it has to be "formed anew" each time. The reason that joint action can be repetitive and relatively stable in spite of being continually formed anew is found in the controls that constrain human action. The very fact that one must take other individuals into account means that a control is exercised over one's developing line of action. [54]

One type of stable interaction is what Blumer calls "codified relations." [55] Such relations follow rules and expectations which are both shared and observed by actors. Blumer contrasts these relations with power and sympathetic relations, and notes that codified relations have been the primary interest of sociologists and anthropologists. In other words, Blumer recognizes the existence of stable relations, and is able to account for them, but stresses the most important but neglected kind of relation—the relation characterized by movement and development.

Impact of the social structure. A second apparent deficiency involves the social structure. We are aware that there are forces which transcend the individual, but which bear upon his or her behavior. For example, a Marxist would point out that the organization of production in any society is crucial for every other aspect of that society; if people relate to others in an exploitative way, it is because they must function within a capitalist system that impels them to so behave. Or an organizational analyst might point out that individuals within an industrial organization enter into conflict because their relationships are structured by organizational rules in a way that virtually insures conflict. Conflict in some plastics firms occurred because of the differing degrees of bureaucratization and diverse time perspectives of the production, marketing, and research and development units. [56] To what extent can symbolic interaction account for such effects? It cannot, according to Irving Zeitlin. Or at least, Blumer's symbolic inter-

[53] Blumer, 1969b. p. 17.
[54] Blumer, 1953, p. 195.
[55] Blumer, 1954b, p. 234.
[56] Charles Perrow, *Organizational Analysis: A Sociological View,* Brooks/Cole, Belmont, Calif., 1970, p. 70.

action cannot, because it offers us a society which is "nothing more than a plurality of disembodied selves interacting in structureless situations." [57]

Such criticisms misinterpret the perspective. For one thing, Blumer does not deny the existence of social structures but only the assertion that structural factors have some kind of automatic impact upon individuals. He would argue that in the examples above the impact is not uniform. All executives do not exploit workers; all individuals in the plastics firms who might have conflict on the basis of their location in the structure do not in fact enter into conflict. For there is an interpretive process between the external factors and the actual interaction which results in diverse behavioral patterns.

Furthermore, Blumer nowhere offers us "structureless situations." In Chapter 4 we pointed out that race relations must be understood in terms of group relations rather than individual prejudice; the latter reflects the former. Intergroup relations, then, are one type of structural factor that Blumer identifies as significant. Racial prejudice arises out of the sense of group position, which "refers to the position of group to group, not to that of individual to individual." [58] Similarly, in trying to account for something like public opinion we must recognize that "the diversified interaction which gives rise to public opinion is in large measure between functional groups and not merely between disparate individuals." [59]

Such analyses stress the fact that social life cannot be understood merely in terms of individual factors. On the contrary, individual factors must be accounted for in terms of social factors. Consider, for instance, the various kinds of individual disorganization. Some psychiatric approaches argue that the outcome of individual disorganization is social disorganization. On the contrary, Blumer has argued, we must see individual disorganization as a consequence and not a cause of social disorganization. This is illustrated by those apparently well-adjusted individuals who "become quite disorganized under certain social conditions." [60]

Quite often, those concerned with structural effects are concerned with the distribution and exercise of power. Indeed, structural power is of great significance in social life, and a considerable amount of sociological research has probed the question of power. It may be that criticisms of Blumer as providing us with "structureless situations" reflect, in part, the notion that symbolic interaction ignores the distribution and exercise of power. But Blumer has written that our entire society is "caught up in the

---

[57] Irving M. Zeitlin, *Rethinking Sociology: A Critique of Contemporary Theory,* Appleton-Century-Crofts, New York, 1973, p. 217.
[58] Blumer, 1958a, p. 5.
[59] Blumer, 1948, p. 545.
[60] Blumer, 1937, p. 876.

play of power," and may be conceived in terms of "innumerable groups and organizations relying on the exercise of power at innumerable points in seeking to maintain position, to achieve goals, and to ward off threats." [61] This power struggle among various groups is particularly evident in the industrial sector of society in such things as competition among businesses, conflict between workers and management, and so on.

Blumer goes on to identify three characteristics of power relations. First, the groups are marked by contrary "interests, intentions, and goals." Second, various sources of strength are used in the pursuit of goals; traditional and sympathetic considerations give way to the exercise of force. And third, "because of the freedom of action thus provided, there is elbow room for scheming, maneuvering, the devising of strategy and tactics, and the marshaling and manipulations of resources." [62]

Power relations enter into social problems as well as the industrial sector. Blumer addressed the question of segregation by pointing out that the problem could only be resolved by controlling the decisions of those responsible for executing various forms of segregation. It is not a matter of changing people's attitudes or feelings or values, but of bringing pressure on "centrally placed functionaries" through the use of "transcending prestige, authority, and power." [63] This, in turn, demands the building of a strong organization. Thus, Blumer advised those who oppose segregation to build an organizational base and use it to exert power on those in strategic positions. This is a far cry from acting in a structureless situation.

Clearly, Blumer has not ignored power. He would deny that a particular distribution of power leads directly and automatically to a particular consequence. For if it is true that power is differentially distributed and exercised in the pursuit of group goals, it is also true that the consequences of a particular distribution must be understood in terms of interaction and the process of interpretation among those involved in the power relations. If there is no collective definition of racism as a problem, the power distribution will maintain a segregated society. But once the collective definition emerges, the power distribution may be altered through the action of those accepting the new definition.

Nonsymbolic interaction. A final criticism of deficiency in Blumer's work relates to a subject we dicussed in Chapter 4: the role of affects, ignorance, and nonverbal interaction. As we noted there, Blumer did deal with the question of affects in an early paper, noting their importance in sustaining attitudes. In the same paper, he pointed out the significance of various

[61] Blumer, 1954b, p. 232.
[62] *Ibid.,* p. 235.
[63] Blumer, 1956a, p. 141.

kinds of expressive behavior—"quality of the voice—tone, pitch, volume," facial expressions, eye movements, posture, and so on.[64] In one of his latest papers, he points out that fashion virtually always occurs "without awareness on the part of those who are caught in its operation." [65] Thus, again, it is not that Blumer is unaware of or incapable of dealing with such phenomena as affects, ignorance, and nonverbal interaction, but rather that he has chosen to stress what he considers the most crucial facet of human life—symbolic interaction. The importance of human emotions, the extensiveness of interaction involving ignorance, and the effects of nonverbal factors in interaction all probably merit more attention than Blumer has given them. Nevertheless, they can all be incorporated into the perspective, for all have been acknowledged as a part of social reality.

IMAGE OF HUMAN BEINGS

The second area of criticism mentioned above related to the meaning of the image of human beings presented by symbolic interactionism. Zeitlin has characterized Blumer's image as one of "disembodied, unconstrained selves floating about in amorphous situations." [66] Fichter has criticized Mead as offering us a picture of humans that requires us to "abandon the concept of innate human dignity, natural rights of man, freedom, and all other values that men hold dear." [67] But we would argue that in symbolic interactionism we have a humanistic perspective, one that exalts rather than degrades humans. It is true that in much modern thought there has been a strain of despair that has included a denigration of the human being. But in Blumer's thought, a man or a woman is an *actor*. He or she is to be thought of in terms of a creative process. A human being actively creates as well as responds to his or her situations. This endows a person with far more meaning and dignity and other values that we "hold dear" than does a view that conceives of a human as a creature who is only the plaything of vast impersonal forces or who is buffeted about by external stimuli like a mindless puppet. As Matson has rightly argued, a view that denies that an individual can be a subject, that makes his or her reason for being something wholly external from the individual, is dehumanizing.[68]

In sum, while there have been facets of the empirical world which have received minimal attention from Blumer, his perspective is not incapable

---

[64] Blumer, 1936, p. 520.
[65] Blumer, 1969a, p. 286.
[66] Zeitlin, p. 218.
[67] Joseph H. Fichter, "The Concept of Man in Social Science: Freedom, Values and Second Nature," *Journal for the Scientific Study of Religion,* 11 (June 1972), 114.
[68] Matson, p. 68.

of handling them. And while Blumer has not explicitly addressed the humanistic meaning of his image of humankind, that image clearly exalts rather than degrades human beings; the human that emerges from Blumer's writings is active, creative, concrete, rather than shapeless or pitiable.

We have now examined the substance of the theoretical and methodological position of Blumer and have briefly noted some points of criticism. In the remainder of the chapter, we will give an overview of substantive contributions made by Blumer. These substantive areas reflect the perspective which we have just delineated.

Substantive Contributions

MOTION PICTURES

Blumer's first research was part of a series of studies involving psychologists and sociologists and financed by the Payne Fund. The studies were published in 1933 and 1935, and relatively little has been done since with specific reference to motion pictures (there is, of course, a vast literature on the mass media generally); however, there has been sufficient research on motion pictures to make some interesting comparisons with Blumer's work.

Blumer drew a number of conclusions about the effects of motion pictures on youthful audiences.[69] In the first place, young children played at the roles which they observed in the movies. Boys played at being policemen, gangsters, pirates, aviators, and other roles, while girls played at being society ladies, dancers, singers, and other roles regarded as typically female. Whatever the role, one of the primary influences of motion pictures on young children was with respect to their play.

The particular roles chosen by young children were not related to socioeconomic status. Rather, there was "an essential uniformity in the kinds of movie-inspired play among children regardless of their social status." [70] Since children of every status played at the same kind of roles, what precisely were the effects of playing at those roles? Blumer said that he had insufficient data to answer the question.

Similarly, adolescents imitated various kinds of conduct which they observed in motion pictures. They would imitate such things as dress and beautification patterns. Thus, their response went beyond the make-believe of play to everyday conduct. Furthermore, both young children and adolescents experienced a variety of emotions in watching motion pictures.

[69] The various methods used by Blumer to secure these data were noted earlier.
[70] Blumer, 1933a, p. 21.

Fear, terror, sorrow, love, and excitement were among the emotions generated by various pictures.

Blumer's data did not permit much beyond describing the consequences just noted. He could draw no larger conclusions. Subsequent studies, however, help fill in this picture and confirm the influence of movies on behavior. In particular, a number of studies have investigated the way in which motion pictures affect aggressive behavior. A 1957 study by Albert concluded that conventional cowboy films tend to decrease aggression.[71] But studies of other kinds of films come up with contrary findings. Lövaas let children choose between playing with a ball and aggressive dolls. Those who had watched an aggressive cartoon prior to their choice had a greater tendency to play with the hitting dolls.[72]

Other studies support the finding of Lövaas. Bandura and his associates have conducted a number of experiments that show that children behave more aggressively after watching aggression on film.[73] Berkowitz has come to similar conclusions; contrary to one line of argument, fantasy aggression through watching violent films does not reduce the likelihood of aggressive behavior. In one experiment, Berkowitz and Rawlings had a male graduate student insult one group of students and treat another group neutrally. A female student then gave a summary of a plot which either did or did not justify the severe beating received by one of the combatants in a filmed prize fight. The fight was then shown. All the subjects were then asked to rate the male graduate student. Instead of reducing hostility, those in the justified fantasy aggression group exhibited a heightened overt hostility towards the male graduate student.[74]

In other words, most of the evidence indicates that the audience does not release aggression through watching a violent film; on the contrary, the film may only facilitate later aggression by individuals in the audience. Blumer was quite correct in concluding that motion pictures have significant effects upon behavior, even though he could not be specific about those effects with the data he had.

Blumer also found that a considerable number of adolescents fantasize as a result of watching movies. Again, he was unable to specify the significance of this behavior. Perhaps fantasy serves as an escape and has no

[71] Robert S. Albert, "The Role of Mass Media and the Effect of Aggressive Film Content Upon Children's Aggressive Responses and Identification Choices," *Genetic Psychology Monographs,* 55 (February 1957), 221–285.

[72] O. Ivar Lövaas, "Effect of Exposure to Symbolic Aggression on Aggressive Behavior," *Child Development,* 32 (March 1961), 37–44.

[73] See, for example, Albert Bandura, Dorothea Ross, and Sheila A. Ross, "Imitation of Film-Mediated Aggressive Models," *Journal of Abnormal and Social Psychology,* 66, No. 1 (1963), 3–11.

[74] Leonard Berkowitz and Edna Rawlings, "Effect of Film Violence on Inhibition Against Subsequent Aggression," *Journal of Abnormal and Social Psychology,* 66, No. 5 (1963), 405–412.

further function; we know that for certain individuals the mass media do serve as an escape.[75] On the other hand, we must be cautious about drawing such a conclusion, since it can imply a catharsis, a releasing of tensions and frustrations. And as we have seen, this is certainly not true with respect to aggression. Further research must be undertaken before the significance of fantasizing can be known.

A more important finding relates to the framework of thought. Blumer concluded that motion pictures provide children with "both specific ideas and a general framework of thought. A large part of the average child's imagery used for interpretation of experiences in everyday life has its source in motion pictures." [76] Movies also facilitate the development of stereotypes and various conceptions of life and love. This shaping of the framework of thought is critical, since it means that motion pictures would have an effect on virtually the totality of the individual's life. Unfortunately, the relationship between movies and cognitive processes has not been explored sufficiently to draw firm conclusions; however, a 1960 study by Catton supports Blumer's point that films can affect cognitive processes.[77]

These effects of motion pictures are not uniform in their impact. Blumer noted that films are apparently less influential on the highly educated, and more influential where the family, school, church, and neighborhood relationships are weak.[78] The latter point suggests that movies may be related to crime and delinquency; indeed, the Payne Fund Studies were a response to a rising concern about the moral impact of films. Blumer investigated possible relationships between films and crime and delinquency, and found that—according to self-reports—movies were important in the careers of about 10 percent of male and 25 percent of female offenders in his sample. On the other hand, he argued that films have little if any value in rehabilitation: "Both inmates and institutional heads rank motion pictures as markedly inferior in reformatory value to such activities as training for a job, shop or outdoor work, outdoor athletics, chapel service, and school work." [79]

Apart from the various findings, it is interesting to note the way in which Blumer applied the symbolic interactionist perspective to his analysis. Whenever explanations were offered, they were given in symbolic interactionist terms. Thus, differential emotional responses to a particular movie were explained on the basis of role-taking and appropriating the

[75] Lotte Bailyn, "Mass Media and Children: A Study of Exposure Habits and Cognitive Effects," *Psychological Monographs,* 73, No. 1 (1959), 1–48.

[76] Blumer, 1933a, p. 142.

[77] William R. Catton, "Changing Cognitive Structure as a Basis for the Sleeper Effect," *Social Forces,* 38 (May 1960), 348–354.

[78] Blumer, 1933a, p. 193, and 1933b, p. 202.

[79] Blumer, 1933b, pp. 200–201.

attitudes of one's group: "Apparently the chief source of emotional de-
tachment lies in the effort to respond to the attitude of one's group." [80]
Also, the human is clearly an actor rather than reactor. In explaining imitation, Blumer notes that when "an individual sees some form of conduct
which promises to aid the realization of one of his aims, it is likely to be
chosen." [81] And the influence of a picture depends not simply on the
picture's content, but on the "sensitivity and disposition" of the observer.

Furthermore, in this first research we see human action depicted in
terms of an interpretive process. In order to understand the impact of a
picture, we must know "something of the interests and experience" of the
individuals in the audience. For films may exert contradictory kinds of
influence on different people. The social background of an individual is
"the basis for the selection and interpretation of motion picture themes and
patterns of behavior." [82] In particular, group position provides a basis for
the individual's interpretation; the latter will reflect to some extent the
interests of one's group.[83]

In sum, while not yet fully developed, Blumer's first research already
shows the mode of analysis of symbolic interactionism. Whether studying
films or any other phenomena, we must get at the subjective meanings of
actors, the influence of interaction on actors' developing attitudes and
behavior, and the impact of group memberships and intergroup relations
on the overall process.

INDUSTRIALIZATION AND INDUSTRIALISM

Blumer's concern with the processual nature of social life and with the
significance of people's interpretation of their social context clearly
emerges in his treatment of industrial society. His contributions here can
be summed up in three points: industrial phenomena must be seen in processual terms; the consequences of industrialization must be seen in terms
of the interpretive nature of human action; and the industrial sector must
be viewed in terms of power relations. We will look briefly at each of
these.

First, industrialization and industrialism must be seen in processual
terms. To stress process in industrialization is to stress history and, in
particular, the fact that the process is not identical at various historical
periods. Thus, in writing about the broad process of social development,
he denied the common notion that contemporary development would necessarily reflect the historical pattern of the West. The historical settings

[80] Blumer, 1933a, p. 134.
[81] *Ibid.*, p. 57.
[82] Blumer, 1933b, p. 202.
[83] Blumer, 1933a, p. 186.

are different, so that interpretations of Western development cannot be used as valid models for the current scene.[84] Most scholars are coming to accept this position.

To stress process in industrialism is to look at intergroup relations in the industrial sector of a modern society in terms of a "moving pattern." Blumer argued that we may liken industrial relations "to a vast, confused game evolving without the benefit of fixed rules and frequently without the benefit of any rules." [85] Moreover, the setting of the game is also changing; we face a process within a process! For instance, the focus has changed from local worker-management contacts to union-management organizational contacts; worker-management relations have become similar to those between "vast opposing armies" and decisions are made by large-scale organizations which are far removed from the individual worker and manager. There are other facets to the processual nature of industrialism, but the point is that industrial relations cannot be adequately studied as though they were either a stable set of practices and routines or a stable structure of hierarchical relationships.

Second, the consequences of industrialization must be seen in terms of the interpretive nature of human action. As with other phenomena, industrialization does not have a single, uniform impact on people; its actual consequences are the result of the way in which it is interpreted by various individuals and groups. Industrialization provides a "neutral framework" within which various consequences may follow (note that it *does* provide a framework; thus, only a finite number of consequences may follow). The actual consequences depend on four factors: "the composition of the class; the milieu encountered in industrial establishments; the conditions of life to which workers are subject outside of industrial establishments; and the schemes or definitions which the workers use to interpret their experience." [86] Blumer actually identifies five different responses which have been made in traditional societies. Industrialization may be: rejected outright; tolerated as a separate and disjunctive part of the society; assimilated into the traditional patterns; used to strengthen tradition; and accepted in a way that leads to the disruption of the traditional order.[87] Research supports this argument about the differential consequences of industrialization and leads us to reject what has been called the "myth of unidirectionality and utopia apprehended." [88]

---

[84] Blumer, 1966b, pp. 9–10. For further discussion and corroborating evidence, see Robert H. Lauer, *Perspectives on Social Change,* Allyn and Bacon, Boston, 1973, pp. 216–217.

[85] Blumer, 1947, p. 277.

[86] Blumer, 1960, p. 10.

[87] Blumer, 1964.

[88] Lauer, pp. 9–14.

Third, Blumer stresses the fact that the industrial sector must be seen in terms of power relations. Labor-management relations clearly illustrate a power struggle and the three characteristics of power relations discussed above. While this point has been more widely accepted than the above two, we should point out that at least one school of organizational thought —the human relations school—has emphasized the cooperative nature of industrial relations and the congruence of labor-management interests. By contrast, Blumer has argued that the two groups have inherently conflicting interests which result in an ongoing power struggle.

RACE RELATIONS

Blumer's contributions to this area have been well stated by Killian.[89] However, he focused on the way Blumer's views contrasted with other perspectives. We shall focus on the way in which Blumer's contributions reflect the symbolic interactionist perspective.

First, what is the meaning of race? The question has been much debated, for race is a matter of social definition as well as biological characteristics. Race may be defined as "a class or group of human beings who are regarded and treated in social life as a distinctive biological group with a common ancestry." [90] The definition of any particular group as a race is the result of a historical process in which factors such as biological appearance and distinctive cultural and behavioral patterns are important.

These observations are not trivial. For to define a group as a racial group has significant consequences for intergroup relations. Yet, while the definition is normally based on skin color, we could use other biological factors. People might be categorized on the basis of blood type, for example; there is no biological reason for preferring skin color to other possible characteristics. Race is a socially defined phenomenon, and it has important consequences for the people so defined as well as for intergroup relations.

One important consequence is prejudice, which, as pointed out in Chapter 4, is rooted in group position rather than individual personality traits. Prejudice is "fundamentally a matter of relationship between racial groups." [91] Although prejudice is a group rather than individual phenomenon, there are certain feelings involved. Members of the dominant group tend to: feel superior; ascribe inherent differences from themselves to the subordinate group; feel justified in possessing advantages and privileges; and both fear and suspect that the subordinate group would like to dis-

---

[89] Lewis M. Killian, "Herbert Blumer's Contributions to Race Relations," in *Human Nature and Collective Behavior,* ed. Tamotsu Shibutani, Prentice-Hall, Englewood Cliffs, N.J., 1970, pp. 183–190.

[90] Blumer, 1955b, p. 5.

[91] Blumer, 1958b, p. 3.

place them and appropriate their advantages and privileges. The point is, however, that we have not explained prejudice when we identify such feelings, for the feelings themselves derive from membership in the dominant group.

Consequently, while prejudice is important, it does not explain the relationships between the races. Race relations are not the result of the prejudice of many individuals (where prejudice is understood as an attitude reflecting personality and individual experiences). This has important implications for policy. For if we argue that prejudice leads to discrimination, and discrimination leads to segregation and a consequent racial problem in a society, then we must rightly assume that the racial problem can be resolved by attacking the problem of prejudice. Blumer explicitly denied this, and argued that only by the exercise of power over the decisions of centrally placed functionaries could undesirable racial practices like segregation be eliminated.[92] In fact, we may make "massive change" in race relations "without a prior effort to change individual feelings or group mores." [93] Although Blumer does not explicitly state this, we would presume that the interruption of the undesirable process by the exercise of power alters group positions in a society. In turn, this modifies the interpretive processes and behavioral patterns of group members. For the interpretive process is a function of group membership and collective definitions rather than individual preferences or tendencies, while the behavioral pattern reflects the nature of the interpretive process.

Even without the intervention of change agents, of course, we must understand race relations as a process. Like all relations, those between the races are not stable or rigid over time. Blumer identified seven different types of relations in which we may trace changes between the races: formal economic (represented by differences between groups in such matters as occupation, wealth, economic control, and standard of living); formal status (represented by group differences in socioeconomic standing and the associated prestige and privileges); preferential (represented by "the selection of associates" in various situations); ideological (represented by differing images which groups have of each other); attitudinal or feeling (represented by various sentiments such as affection, hatred, fear, and respect); orderly or discordant overt (represented by cooperation and harmony or conflict between people); and organized manipulative relations (represented by efforts of one group to control another in some way).[94] These seven types represent both intergroup and interindividual contacts, and cover a broad range—perhaps the great majority—of race relations.

[92] Blumer, 1956a, pp. 140–143.
[93] Blumer, 1958b, p. 438.
[94] Blumer, 1955b, pp. 9–11.

But while there are modifications and shifts among a broad range of relationships, there is also an identifiable pattern involved. First, race relations involve a vertical relationship—the dominant-subordinate ordering. This does not deny the processual nature of race relations, for the nature of dominance and subordination can vary even while the vertical ordering remains. The economic situation of blacks vis-à-vis whites is vastly different in the 1970s from what it was in the 1930s; but blacks are still subordinate. The subordination of one group by another occurs through a historical process, and continues to be a shifting relationship over time; nevertheless, the dominance-subordination tends to remain even while its nature varies.

The vertical metaphor is not sufficient to capture the nature of discriminatory race relations, however. Blumer also employs a horizontal metaphor in defining the "color line" as "a series of ramparts, like the 'Maginot Line,' extending from outer breastworks to inner bastions." [95] As blacks gain access to the outer circle from which they had been previously excluded (such as eating at a public restaurant) they encounter inner circles from which they are still excluded (such as equal access to economic opportunities) and with an even greater hostility than that with which they were barred from the outer circles. And as they seek to penetrate into the innermost circles of private association, blacks will find intense resistance, because the inner circles are defined as crucial to the maintenance of values. In other words, the inner circles represent those areas of social life which are defined by groups as particularly important in maintaining their rights and their preferred lifestyle.

In sum, race relations must be studied as a historical process which involves the development of dominant-subordinate relations between racial groups. Collective definitions arise out of the intergroup relations which help shape certain feelings and behavior patterns of individuals. Thus, interaction among individuals is a function of intergroup relations rather than the reverse.

COLLECTIVE BEHAVIOR

The meaning of collective behavior may be gained by comparing it with small-group behavior and culturally defined behavior. [96] In contrast to small groups, collective behavior involves relatively large numbers. Fads, crazes, revivals, and so forth, are not found in the small group apart from a larger manifestation in the society. And in contrast to culturally defined behavior, "collective behavior" reflects "a forging process of interaction" rather than the expression of established cultural rules. As such, to study

[95] Blumer, 1965, p, 323.
[96] Blumer, 1959a, pp. 128–130.

collective behavior is to study the way in which social order comes into existence. This kind of behavior, Blumer pointed out, is becoming more extensive and more significant in contemporary society; we are becoming a people more and more characterized by both large-scale organization and activity which is not directed by established prescriptions.

A number of phenomena, therefore, fit into the area of collective behavior; included are crowds, various forms of mass behavior, public opinion, propaganda, and social movements. Blumer has made a number of important contributions to the concept of collective behavior:

1. he provided the field with its first and most influential definition both in terms of its nature and as an area of sociological study;
2. he identified certain kinds of interaction which comprise the mechanisms of "elementary collective behavior"—milling, collective excitement, and social contagion;
3. he provided a classification of social movements as "general" (e.g., labor, youth, and women's movements), "specific" (e.g., particular revolutionary movements), and "expressive" (e.g., a religious or fashion movement);
4. he proposed a number of heuristic concepts and distinctions that gave direction to subsequent work in the field.

Rather than examine the various manifestations of collective behavior per se, we shall look at Blumer's work in this area in the light of the symbolic interactionist framework and the emphases which we have noted appear throughout Blumer's writings. As will be clear, collective behavior involves a considerable degree of nonsymbolic behavior.

First, collective behavior is processual. This is well illustrated by Blumer's insightful discussion of fashion.[97] Others have analyzed fashion in psychological terms (self-enhancement through being fashionable), or in terms of social status (those things are fashionable that characterize the elite). But Blumer argued that fashion is "a collective groping for the proximate future." [98] Fashion itself is a process and it reflects the processual nature of the social world. For in a changing world, fashion represents the effort to secure "new congenial social forms." Fashion thereby becomes a form of control in a changing society, just as custom is a form of control in a stable society. That is, fashion prevents change from becoming chaos. The new, congenial social form which is chosen is not the result of an individual choice, but represents a collective selection. Thus, fashion facilitates "collective adjustment to and in a moving world of divergent possibilities." [99] Although our society continually changes, fash-

[97] Blumer, 1968 and 1969a.
[98] Blumer, 1969a, p. 281.
[99] *Ibid.*, p. 289.

ions insure that there is some collective direction to the change, that two hundred million people will not change in fifty million different directions.

Fashion is an important process to study because it involves more than such things as dress and beautification. Blumer noted that fashion is an important part of modern civilization in general, and the number of areas in which fashion is operative is increasing. As Crane has shown, Blumer's analysis of fashion may be profitably applied to the sciences, and to the physical as well as the social sciences.[100]

Other kinds of collective behavior must also be understood as processual. A social movement, for instance, cannot be explained merely by trying to locate the causes of the movement. For the movement must be constructed and it "has to carve out a career in what is practically always an opposed, resistant, or at least indifferent world." [101] To fully understand a movement, its process of development must be studied. That development depends upon a number of factors. Specifically, Blumer discusses five important "mechanisms" that enable a movement to grow and become organized: agitation, esprit de corps, morale, ideology, and operating tactics.

"Agitation" is particularly important during the early phases of a movement. It refers to the process of arousing people, generating dissatisfaction, and offering new directions. Once people are aroused, it is important for "esprit de corps," a sense of unity in a cause, to develop. This can be achieved through stressing the solidarity of the movement in the face of its "enemy," through informal interaction in which members relate to each other personally, and through formal ceremonies or rituals. The enthusiasm created by esprit de corps must be supplemented by "persistency and determination." The latter come through "morale," which enables members to remain unified and committed in the face of adversity. Like the esprit de corps, however, morale must be developed, and a useful method is to give the movement a sectarian or religious flavor (which does not necessarily mean a religious movement—*Das Kapital* is the "bible" of the communist movement). An "ideology" must also be developed if the movement is to survive and grow. The ideology is the set of beliefs and myths that provide the movement with both its philosophy and its psychology. That is, the ideology furnishes members with such things as values, weapons of attack and defense against outsiders, and motivation. Finally, the "operating tactics" are important for the development of the movement, for they can cause the movement either to achieve some of its objectives or to fail.

---

[100] Diana Crane, "Fashion in Science, Does It Exist?" *Social Problems,* 16 (Spring 1969), 433–441.
[101] Blumer, 1959a, p. 147.

Social movements, then, are dynamic phenomena. A movement develops and changes over time, in part because of its own internal dynamics and in part because of its interaction with the larger society. Research has shown that the genesis of a movement, the development of its ideology and program, and motivational factors involved in the recruitment of members are all processes that are a function of interaction between the movement and the larger society.[102]

In addition to process, Blumer has described the kinds of interaction that characterize collective behavior. As in interaction generally, collective behavior is always a formative process rather than an arena for the playing out of prefabricated behavior. But much of the interaction is non-symbolic. "Circular reaction" is contrasted with interpretative interaction; the former is a process which tends to make people alike by stimulating states of feeling and intensifying the feeling among all of the participants. Circular reaction leads to collective behavior which is not based on shared understandings or rules; as such, it underlies much of the interaction which Blumer has characterized as the "mechanisms of elementary collective behavior."

One such mechanism is "milling," a form of interaction in which people become "more sensitive and responsible to one another, so that they become increasingly preoccupied with one another and decreasingly responsive to ordinary objects of stimulation." [103] A second mechanism is "collective excitement," which is intensified milling. In collective excitement, people "become more emotionally aroused and more likely to be carried away by impulses and feelings; hence rendered more unstable and irresponsible." [104] Finally, "social contagion" is a more intense and extensive form of collective excitement; it is a "relatively rapid, unwitting, and nonrational dissemination of a mood, impulse, or form of conduct." [105] It can bring in what were initially detached observers and lead them to behave like the others involved.

As this suggests, another emphasis of Blumer is minimized in the area of collective behavior—the interpretive process. Emotions are more significant than interpretation in collective behavior. This does not mean that such behavior is mindless or purposeless. Blumer argues that an "acting crowd" has its attention focused on a shared objective or goal, while an "expressive crowd" is concerned only with expressing impulses and feel-

[102] Robert H. Lauer, "Social Movements: An Interactionist Analysis," *The Sociological Quarterly,* 13 (Summer 1972), 315–328. For a more detailed discussion, see Robert H. Lauer, ed., *Social Movements and Social Change,* Southern Illinois University Press, Carbondale, Ill., 1976.

[103] Blumer, 1939b, p. 75.

[104] *Ibid.,* p. 76.

[105] *Ibid.*

ings, usually in physical movements. Nevertheless, the emotional element prevails in the "crowd."

In other kinds of collective behavior, the interpretive process remains important. The "public" is a group of people who face an issue, have contrary opinions about the issue, and debate the issue. Thus, the interaction of the public is far different from that of the crowd. In contrast to the emotion-laden uniformity of the crowd, the public "interacts on the basis of interpretation, enters into dispute, and consequently is characterized by conflict relations." [106] While much collective behavior is non-symbolic and lacks the interpretive process, therefore, at least some forms still involve symbolic interaction.

Berk has criticized Blumer for this emphasis on the emotional and non-rational in collective behavior. He argues that there is far more rationality to crowd behavior than Blumer acknowledges. In fact, he offers a gaming theory approach in which collective behavior is the "consequence of *Collective Decision-Making* involving compromises among participants. Each crowd member tries to make the most of the situation while constrained by the need for support from others." [107] This "making the most" of situations demands a certain amount of rational assessment, and Berk offers numerous illustrations of how such assessment can occur in collective behavior. For instance, during urban riots black-owned stores were less often vandalized than white-owned stores. This, argues Berk, reflects a rational assessment and conscious decision on the part of rioters.

Berk's position seems to reflect his desire to make such things as anti-war demonstrations rational acts. But while the planning may be rational, it would be hard to maintain that rationality prevails throughout the execution. Individuals behave in crowds in ways which they themselves cannot justify afterwards. Far from conceiving of their behavior as the result of rational decisions, they perceive themselves as having been caught up in a tide of emotion or lurching forward in spontaneous acts. However, Berk is right in calling our attention to the fact that at least some individuals seem to be able to "keep their heads" and avoid succumbing to social contagion. But at this point, we simply lack the necessary research to explore these points.

Our final observation about Blumer's analysis of collective behavior is that the group relations which have been prominent in his other analyses are also of less importance here. The "mass" for instance is represented by people who are not directly interacting, who are merely "an aggregation of individuals who are separate, detached, anonymous, and thus,

---

[106] *Ibid.*, p. 90.
[107] Richard A. Berk, *Collective Behavior,* Wm. C. Brown, Dubuque, Iowa, 1974, p. 73.

homogeneous as far as mass behavior is concerned." [108] The mass may be those who are disturbed by a national event or those interested in a certain sporting event, or those speculating in land at a particular time. In any case, the behavior of the mass is not explicable in terms of group relations. On the other hand, the public is normally composed of interest groups as well as detached individuals. The issue over which the public emerges is usually a point of conflict between interest groups. Thus, group relations are significant for some kinds of collective behavior, but not for all.

In sum, while some of the elements of social life that have been stressed by Blumer may be lacking in certain kinds of collective behavior, the same approach has been used. Any analysis must take into account the processual nature of social reality, the importance of interaction, the significance of interpretation (even if that significance is overshadowed by other factors), and the role of groups in formulating collective definitions. Such considerations are the foundation of symbolic interactionist analyses.

Conclusion

In Chapter 7 we showed how a variety of symbolic interactionists have analyzed different levels of social life. In this chapter, we have seen how a single scholar has systematized the perspective and applied it to a variety of phenomena at different levels. Blumer has consistently explored social phenomena in terms of their processual nature, the formative nature of interaction, and the interpretive activity of the actors involved. All social life is processual: there are changes over time in labor-management relationships, relationships between racial groups, the rules that regulate intergroup relationships, and the characteristics of groups and movements. All social life involves the interpretive activity of actors. For this reason, there are no inevitable consequences of any social structure on people: a particular movie will have contradictory effects on different people; an industrial structure will provide various alternatives to people; interracial contacts will vary depending upon collective definitions; the public will be composed of conflicting groups that interpret an issue in differing ways.

All of this does not mean that social life is totally fluid. There are certain continuities and points of stability. In the midst of change, labor-management relationships continue to be a power struggle; relationships between racial groups continue to be ones of dominance-subordination and concentric circles of areas of exclusion; and social movements are invariably characterized by such mechanisms as agitation, esprit de corps, morale, ideology, and operating tactics. Blumer has made a serious effort

[108] Blumer, 1939b, p. 87.

to come to terms with both the processes and the stable facets of social life.

Suggested Readings

As noted in the introduction to Part 3, the four authors treated in this section have not been analyzed to any great extent in the literature. There are therefore few analyses of any depth or length available. A particularly negative critique of Blumer has been made by Irving M. Zeitlin, *Rethinking Sociology* (Prentice-Hall, Englewood Cliffs, N.J., 1973, pp. 215–218), and an exposition and critique of some of Blumer's ideas may be found in Jonathan H. Turner, *The Structure of Sociological Theory* (Dorsey, Homewood, Ill., 1974, pp. 180–207, 316–317). Blumer has engaged in a number of exchanges in the journals, and these provide insight both into his own thought and into the kinds of criticisms which have been directed against him. See: his exchange regarding certain aspects of Mead's thought with Robert F. Bales, Joseph Woelfel, and Gregory P. Stone and Harvey A. Farberman in the *American Journal of Sociology* [71 (March 1966), 535–548, and 72 (January 1967), 409–412]; his exchange about public opinion and polling with Theodore M. Newcomb and Julian Woodward in the *American Sociological Review* [13 (October 1948), 542–554]; his exchange about the meaning of morale with Henry Zentner in the *American Sociological Review* [16 (June 1951), 297–310]; and his exchange about similarities and differences between symbolic interactionism and Parsons' structural-functionalism with Jonathan H. Turner in the *Sociological Inquiry* [45, No. 1 (1975), 59–68].

References to Blumer's Works

1931   "Science Without Concepts," *American Journal of Sociology* 36 (January), 515–533.

1933a *Movies and Conduct*, Macmillan, New York.

1933b *Movies, Delinquency, and Crime*, Macmillan, New York (coauthored with Philip M. Hauser).

1936   "Social Attitudes and Non-Symbolic Interaction," *Journal of Educational Sociology*, 9, 515–523.

1937   "Social Disorganization and Personal Disorganization," *American Journal of Sociology*, 42 (May), 871–877.

1939a *Critiques of Research in the Social Sciences: I. An Appraisal of Thomas and Znaniecki's* The Polish Peasant in Europe and America, Social Science Research Council, New York.

1939b "Collective Behavior," in *Principles of Sociology*, ed. Alfred McClung Lee, Barnes & Noble, New York, pp. 67–121. (Our quotes are all from the 1969 edition.)

1940   "The Problem of the Concept in Social Psychology," *American Journal of Sociology*, 45 (March), 707–719.

1947   "Sociological Theory in Industrial Relations," *American Sociological Review*, 12 (June), 271–278.

1948   "Public Opinion and Public Opinion Polling," *American Sociological Review*, 13, 542–554.

1953   "Psychological Import of the Human Group," in *Group Relations at the*

Crossroads, ed. Muzafer Sherif and M. O. Wilson, Harper, New York, pp. 185–202.

1954a "What is Wrong with Social Theory?" *American Sociological Review,* 19 (February), 3–10.

1954b "Social Structure and Power Conflict," in *Industrial Conflict,* eds. Arthur Kornhauser, Robert Dubin, and Arthur M. Ross, McGraw-Hill, New York, pp. 232–239.

1955a "Attitudes and the Social Act," *Social Problems,* 3, No. 2, 59–65.

1955b "Reflections on Theory of Race Relations," in *Race Relations in World Perspective,* ed. Andrew W. Lind, University of Hawaii Press, Honolulu, pp. 3–21.

1956a "Social Science and the Desegregation Process," *The Annals of the American Academy of Political and Social Science,* 304 (March), 137–143.

1956b "Sociological Analysis and the 'Variable,'" *American Sociological Review,* 21 (December), 683–690.

1958a "Race Prejudice as a Sense of Group Position," *Pacific Sociological Review,* 1 (Spring), 3–7.

1958b "Research on Race Relations: United States of America," *International Bulletin of Social Science,* 10, 403–447.

1959a "Collective Behavior," in *Review of Sociology: Analysis of a Decade,* ed. Joseph B. Gittler, Wiley, New York, pp. 127–158.

1959b "Suggestions for the Study of Mass-Media Effects," in *American Voting Behavior,* eds. Eugene Burdick and Arthur J. Brodbeck, Free Press, Glencoe, Ill., pp. 197–208.

1960 "Early Industrialization and the Laboring Class," *The Sociological Quarterly,* 1 (January), 5–14.

1962 "Society as Symbolic Interaction," in *Human Behavior and Social Processes,* ed. Arnold Rose, Houghton Mifflin, Boston, pp. 179–192.

1964 "Industrialization and the Traditional Order," *Sociology and Social Research,* 48 (January), 129–138.

1965 "The Future of the Color Line," in *The South in Continuity and Change,* eds. John C. McKinney and Edgar T. Thompson, Duke, Durham, pp. 322–336.

1966a "Sociological Implications of the Thought of George Herbert Mead," *American Journal of Sociology,* 71 (March), 535–544.

1966b "The Ideal of Social Development," *Studies in Comparative International Development,* 2, No. 1, Social Science Institute, Washington University, St. Louis, pp. 3–11.

1968 "Fashion," *International Encyclopedia of the Social Sciences,* Macmillan, New York, V, 341–345.

1969a "Fashion: From Class Differentiation to Collective Selection," *The Sociological Quarterly,* 10 (Summer), 275–291.

1969b *Symbolic Interactionism: Perspective and Method,* Prentice-Hall, Englewood Cliffs, N.J.

1971 "Social Problems as Collective Behavior," *Social Problems,* 18 (Winter), 298–306.

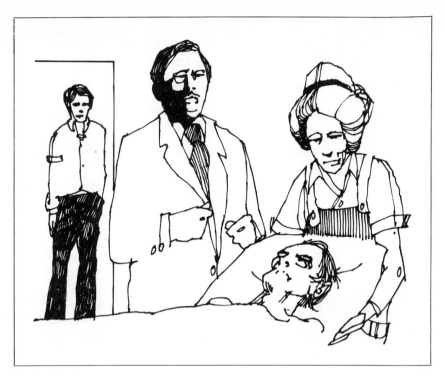

Chapter 10

Anselm Strauss

Lawrence Durrell had a fictional character stop all the clocks in his house when his brother came to visit him. This, wrote Durrell, was his way of saying to his brother: "Your stay with us is so brief, let us not be reminded of the flight of the hours. God made eternity. Let us escape from the despotism of time altogether." [1] But whether time is seen as "despotism" or

[1] Lawrence Durrell, *Balthazar,* Dutton, New York, 1958, p. 79.

opportunity, it is an ineluctable fact of human existence; reality, as symbolic interactionism emphasizes, is process, and stopping clocks can only temporarily mask the relentless process of human existence.

George Herbert Mead addressed himself to the question of time and process in various ways. Blumer, a student of Mead's, continued the emphasis on the processual nature of reality. And Strauss, a student of Blumer's, has rooted all of his work, from methodology to theorizing to critiques, within a processual perspective.[2] We shall begin this chapter, therefore, with an overview of Strauss' thinking on process in human life. We shall then look at some other emphases which appear in his work and, finally, at some substantive areas to which he has contributed.

Social Reality as Process

PROCESS AND CHANGE

Strauss' emphasis on process has important implications for sociological understanding and research. To affirm process is to assume change as the essence of social reality. Indeed, "it is not change that needs to be explained but its specific directions; and it is not lack of change that needs to be taken for granted, but change itself." [3] Thus, in a study of psychiatric ideologies and hospitals, there is an *assumption* of "organizational and ideological change" and the task of the researchers includes that of "explaining the directions of such change." [4] In this respect, symbolic interactionism takes the same stance as Marxism. All phenomena must be understood in terms of their movement, their development; to do less is to have deficient understanding. The subject matter of social psychology must be seen in "creative, emergent terms: it is neither fixed nor finite, nor independent of human conception and subsequent redefinition . . ." [5]

This processual orientation has characterized Strauss' work throughout his career. Some of his earliest papers involved critiques of work that assumed too much stability in human life. For example, he noted that some social psychological studies were deficient because they assumed that attitudes have "always a rather fixed and settled character. They ignore so completely the possibility of rapid change of attitudes that stability is made to appear an essential feature of all attitudes." [6] Similarly, culture-person-

[2] Although a considerable number of Strauss' works have been coauthored, we we shall for convenience refer to them in the footnotes by Strauss' name and the date of publication. For the titles, publication information, and the coauthors where applicable see the list at the end of the chapter.

[3] Strauss, 1959a, p. 43.

[4] Strauss, 1964a, p. 17.

[5] Strauss, 1973, p. 7.

[6] Strauss, 1945, p. 332.

ality writings often make the mistaken assertion or assumption that personality patterns are established early in the individual's life, and that basic patterns either do not change thereafter or only change in relatively unimportant ways.[7]

On the contrary, Strauss argues that the essence of human life is change, development, growth. Individual life is a process, and that process involves the most fundamental kind of change—the change in identity as individuals "move in and out of, and up and down within, social structures." [8] To be concerned with identity is to be concerned with changes that occur in adulthood, and those changes reflect the individual's passage through the social structure, that is, through various statuses: "central to any account of adult identity is the relation of change in identity to change in social position; for it is characteristic of adult life to afford and force frequent and momentous passages from status to status." [9] Even the very last experience of a human life—death—must be seen as a process rather than simply as an event.[10] As we shall see below, viewing death as a process sheds new light on organizational functioning (the hospital) and on interaction patterns (between the dying patient, his or her relatives, and the hospital personnel).

THE PROCESS OF CONCEPTUAL DEVELOPMENT

All human phenomena, then, may and must be studied as processes. For, in looking at concepts and meanings, Strauss looked at them as developmental phenomena. The development of conceptual meanings was not unique with Strauss, of course; rather, he was concerned to employ "a more rigorous method" than had been used by such researchers as Piaget.[11] He also examined a concept that had not been previously studied—money. Using a number of different coins, a variety of questions, and a complex system of scoring weights for children's responses to the questions, Strauss drew a number of conclusions about the development of concepts in children. First, similar to Piaget's conclusions, he found that conceptual learning progressed "from simple responses to complex ones, from concrete to abstract, from discrete to systematic, from undifferentiated to differentiated, from rigid to flexible, from egocentric to non-egocentric." [12] Children do not at first grasp concepts in their entirety; rather, there is a slow process of development along the lines just suggested. Furthermore, the process is the same for both sexes and for samples of children from the working class

[7] Strauss, 1950a, p. 598.
[8] Strauss, 1959a, p. 89.
[9] Strauss, 1956, p. 263.
[10] Strauss, 1968c.
[11] Strauss, 1950b, p. 753.
[12] *Ibid.*, p. 762.

and the business class. All children pass through stages of learning, and these stages are cumulative in the sense that the appearance of a new stage is dependent upon the learning of the preceding one. Finally, chronological age is more important than mental age in children's differential ability to grasp conceptual meanings; at least in terms of understanding the meaning of money, the number of years a child has lived is more important than his or her mental age as measured by the Stanford Binet Test. Children simply cannot learn some materials before they reach a certain age.[13]

Strauss attempted to refine our understanding of the developmental process by specifying nine different stages and the age range encompassed by each stage.[14] For example, stage one occurs at a median age of five years and four months. The child can distinguish some but not all coins. He or she cannot yet consistently match pairs of coins according to color and size, and the child prefers coins on the basis of size rather than value. He or she understands that money is related to buying, but tends to believe that any money buys anything. Such understandings keep developing until stage nine, which occurs at a median age of eleven years and two months, and which involves moral as well as fiscal understandings of money. All these stages, as noted above, are cumulative. "Later meanings are not only built upon but absorb earlier and simpler ones." [15]

In addition to the nine stages, Strauss identified a "substage" which occurs some months prior to stage one; the substage is the point at which meanings about money first begin to emerge. It is questionable whether such an elaborate description of stages is applicable to all concepts, however. More important is the notion of development itself, the fact that such development is cumulative, and the variations in rate of development among children.[16] Meanings are not static phenomena; they emerge over time as a result of interaction and, in the case of children, they develop by a cumulative process.

PROCESS IN PROFESSIONS, ORGANIZATIONS, AND CITIES

Strauss' primary contribution to the study of conceptual development was the use of a rigorous, quantitative method. Piaget had already delineated a sequence of intellectual growth from "sensory-motor intelligence" to the point at which the child can deal with abstract relationships (conceiving of the form of an argument independently of its content). But Strauss applied his processual perspective (though not his rigorous method of inquiry) to human phenomena at every level. For example, in studying

---

[13] Strauss, 1951, p. 523.

[14] Strauss, 1952.

[15] *Ibid.,* p. 285.

[16] The same cumulative process applies to the development of conceptions of rules in children. See Strauss, 1954.

the professions, Strauss emphasized the existence of diverse, competing, and conflicting groups within each profession; such groups, or "segments" as he called them, insure that professions will change. In fact, the segments themselves "tend to be more or less continually undergoing change," so that one could initially analyze a profession as a kind of social movement.[17] Interaction between segments, and between segments and the larger society, insure all professions of change in organization and ideology.

Likewise, in studying organizations we might opt for various approaches and focus on various phenomena such as goals, structure, or technology; but again, Strauss sees organizations as processes. This is well illustrated by the notion of the hospital as a "negotiated order," a notion we shall examine in detail below. One final illustration of Strauss' consistent processual perspective is provided by his analysis of urban areas. As we shall discuss below, the city is a complex place, and Strauss argues that individuals manage their existence in it by symbolizing it to themselves in terms that simplify and that evoke particular images and sentiments. "All such symbolic representations of an urban milieu, however, are inherently unstable. Cities change, forcing those who live in them to face the inadequacies of what once were tried and true conceptions."[18]

PROCESS AND INTERACTION

Thus, Strauss has consistently applied the concept of process to his analyses, whether the analysis has been at the micro level of individual development or the macro level of urban life. We must go a step further now and point out that the emphasis on process is complex; process is more than simple development. Process involves interaction, including the interaction of diverse processes. That is, the process that characterizes social life differs from the common differentiation model, which assumes that the "primitive" social unit contains within itself the germs of all that appears in the mature unit.[19] Like Blumer, Strauss affirms emergence in social life, the appearance of novelty out of interaction; moreover, such novelty cannot be predicted on the basis of what we know about the structure of the interacting units, for interaction is a creative process. In the course of interaction, novel situations appear that demand redefinitions. Indeed, even diverse opinions and arguments between members of a group "make for the emergence of new perspectives, meanings, values, etc."[20] Moreover, the personal histories of individuals interact with the social histories of groups;

[17] Strauss, 1961 and 1966a.
[18] Strauss, 1958, p. 532.
[19] See Amitai Etzioni, "The Epigenesis of Political Communities at the International Level," *American Journal of Sociology,* 68 (January 1963), 408–409.
[20] Strauss, 1953, pp. 117–118.

both the process of the individual's own life and those of the groups of which he or she is a part must be studied if we are to understand behavior.

Likewise, social units larger than the individual change over time as a result of various interacting processes, and not simply as a consequence of the unit's own internal dynamics. A profession, for instance, develops as a result of at least five different processes.[21] In the case of psychiatry, these five processes include: ongoing modifications in the psychiatric hospital which result from conflict and negotiation; segmentation of the organization and ideology of psychiatry itself; changing public views of psychiatry; historical and socio-cultural forces that impinge upon psychiatry; and institutional forms that affect the careers and practice of psychiatrists. Obviously, according to Strauss, neither psychiatry nor an individual nor any other social unit can be understood if that unit is studied as an isolated entity.

PROCESS AND STRUCTURE

To be sure, the emphasis on process and on emergence means that the social sciences will not duplicate the methods of the natural sciences. The social structure which is the object of much sociological study is undergoing continual change, and a structure might assume a new form even before "highly rigorous research can be accomplished." [22] This clearly represents a shift from Strauss' initial emphasis on a strongly quantitative methodology. But it also represents a full acceptance of symbolic interactionism's conception of the processual nature of reality. And our understanding of social reality must not be surrendered to an apparent rigor of method.

On the other hand, this does not imply either a rejection of quantitative methods or an affirmation of total fluidity in social life. With respect to the former, quantitative methods may be useful for some purposes, but their limitations for understanding the complexity of social life must be recognized. And as for the latter, we noted in the last chapter that Blumer has been wrongly accused of having a totally fluid view of social life; Strauss might also be open to such criticism, but he clearly is concerned with structure as well as process. His purpose in writing *Mirrors and Masks* applies to all of his work: "to juxtapose and fuse symbolic interactional and social organizational perspectives into a workable, suggestive social psychology." [23] Thus, individuals must be understood in terms of the groups in which they participate, so that we may view interaction "as both structure, in the sense that the participants represent social positions; and at the same time as not quite so structured." [24]

[21] Strauss, 1966a, p. 15.
[22] Strauss, 1966b, p. 61.
[23] Strauss, 1959a, p. 11.
[24] *Ibid.,* p. 71.

Where does this leave us in the problem of the relationship between structure and process? Strauss' answer is that we must try to see social reality in terms of structures in process. To pose the problem as one of structure *versus* process is to suggest a false dichotomy. For social life involves changing structures. For example, when we examine the process of dying, we find the hospital's structure in continual change in order to cope with the various phases in the dying process. "Its structure, then, is in process," [25] and only by recognizing and identifying the structural process can we properly understand this social phenomenon. (We should note that Strauss includes in the concept "structure" various phenomena, some of which are not normally considered as structure—e.g., the sentimental "order" of a ward, the personnel working on the ward at any particular time, and outside experts brought into a work area for a particular task.) In sum, neither Blumer nor Strauss ignore the importance of structure, but both argue that structures have no inherent, automatic effects and that structures themselves are in a more-or-less continual process of change.

Social Process as Symbolic Interaction

TYPES OF INTERACTION

As noted above, the social process assumes a direction which is determined by interaction. But interaction must not be understood solely in the narrow sense of two or more individuals in a particular setting. Strauss pointed out that there is: "personal interaction," in which each individual takes the other(s) into account and adjusts his or her own behavior accordingly; "vicarious interaction," in which the taking of the roles of others is implicit or covert; and "parasocial interaction," in which the course of action is controlled by one performer who, nevertheless, appears to directly address others and adjust his or her own behavior accordingly.[26] The latter is the type of interaction characteristic of the mass media and a situation with a large audience. Thus interaction may occur between individuals in a face-to-face situation and between individuals who are separated but influenced by each other (such as policy makers in an organization and those affected by the policies).[27]

In addition, interaction does not necessarily involve awareness of the true attitudes of others; there are nonrational acts and erroneous judgments which are made by interactants.[28] Finally, there are variations in the extent to which interaction involves change. Some institutionalized kinds of inter-

---

[25] Strauss, 1968c, p. 239.
[26] Strauss, 1957, p. 580.
[27] Strauss, 1959b, p. 99.
[28] Strauss, 1959a, pp. 58–59.

action, like those occurring in a court of law, may be quite stable and repetitive. Other kinds of interaction are more likely to be fluid. But all
kinds "are somewhat indeterminate or open-ended, leaving the way open
for bargaining, compromise, negotiation, and improvisation." [29] Thus there
is some stability, some regularities, in social life as well as some fluidity;
but social life is never immobile and never totally fluid. The social process
is characterized by complex and diverse kinds of interaction, providing social life with both its regularities and its fluidity.

INTERACTION AND LANGUAGE

Above all, the interaction that characterizes the social process is symbolic.
No one has paid greater attention to the symbolic nature of human existence than Strauss. Even nonverbal interaction involves meanings that depend upon symbols. In essence, human existence occurs in a symbolic
environment in a twofold sense: the individual responds directly to symbols
and his or her "relationships to the external world are mediated through
symbols." [30] These symbols are not idiosyncratic, of course; they are social
phenomena, shared meanings which emerge through interaction and which
influence the course of subsequent interaction.

Language then is crucial, giving human life its distinctive nature. This is
well illustrated by cases where there is a lack or loss of language. For instance, children who never learn a language because of isolation or physical
incapacity "fail to become socialized human beings; they exhibit . . . behavioral disabilities . . ." [31] There are only a few known cases of this. The
evidence, therefore, is subject to various interpretations, but the conclusion
is congruent with what we have previously said about the significance of
language.

Strauss has particularly emphasized two broad functions of language:
first, language is the cohesive factor for human groups, and second, language is the means of organizing individual cognition, emotions, and behavior. We will look at each of these in turn.

Language and cohesiveness. Language is the cohesive factor for human
groups because each social unit has its own peculiar mode for communication; even in small groups, individuals "develop jargon and special vocabularies which serve instrumental or ritualistic ends." [32] Consequently, a
human group is a symbolic rather than a physical phenomenon; an individual can be a member of a group in a formal sense, but be marginal in the
sense of not sharing in the group's symbolic milieu. We cannot fully par-

[29] Strauss, 1968a, p. 312.
[30] *Ibid.,* p. 53.
[31] *Ibid.,* p. 110.
[32] Strauss, 1953, p. 110.

ticipate in groups when we lack the symbolic meanings shared in those groups. A member of a Baptist church who finds terms like "immersion," "trinity," and "eternal life" meaningless or pointless may be "in" the church but he or she is not really "of" it.

On the other hand, where symbols are shared, the group is cohesive even though the members may differ along many lines. Chemists, for instance, have many different kinds of work, ranging from basic research to testing sewage for harmful bacteria. But membership in the American Chemical Society has a symbolic significance, indicating certain shared experiences and values. The ACS member is a professional, and even if he or she does nothing more than test sewage the member has "a general status above and away from ordinary men. The apparatus of the Society, the mere formal membership, revives within him the knowledge that he is different from and superior to most men of his community." [33] Each member identifies with others, for all are professional chemists; the group is cohesive even though the professional lives of the members are quite diverse.

Language as organizing mechanism. Language is also the means of organizing cognition, emotions, and behavior. The precise nature of the influence of language upon thought has been the subject of much controversy. Strauss' position is that while language does not rigidly determine thought, it "so thoroughly interpenetrates the modes of experiencing that at the very least it limits the possibilities of perception and of thinking." [34] Thus, young children cannot reason as adults because they lack the necessary concepts; abstract thinking is independent upon the acquistion of language. This is corroborated by the extensive work on cognitive development carried on by Jerome Bruner and his associates. Bruner has argued that cognitive growth proceeds by "a series of technological advances in the use of the mind. Growth depends upon the mastery of techniques." [35] These techniques are various skills; one of the most important is language, which enables the individual to represent the world in symbolic form. This makes possible intellectual activities which go significantly beyond those available through either the "enactive" (involving motor responses) or "iconic" (organization of percepts and images) modes of representation. The use of language gives the individual a "progressive release from immediacy." [36]

Thus, the way we think about anything depends upon the language which is available to us, and the particular symbols we apply. Even the meaning of the individual's life may be seen as a "symbolic ordering," which will differ according to the particular concepts applied to past events.

[33] Strauss, 1962, p. 197.
[34] Strauss, 1968a, 137.
[35] Jerome S. Bruner, "The Course of Cognitive Growth," *American Psychologist,* 19 (January 1964), 1.
[36] *Ibid.,* p. 14.

Language is also important for emotions. Emotions are not autonomous, and emotional behavior is not a distinct type of behavior per se. Rather, emotional behavior is the result of the interaction of an emotion-provoking situation with the individual's values. That is, the individual responds to a particular situation by defining it and responding to his or her symbolic representation; the emotion is then a response "not to a raw stimulus as such but to a defined, classified and interpreted stimulus . . ." [37] The stimulus for the emotion is the individual's definition of the situation rather than something which is external to the individual. We are not afraid unless we define the situation as a frightening one. Indeed the same overt experience can arouse very different emotions, depending upon the individual's interpretation. A tap on the shoulder by a defined opponent arouses anger; the same tap by a defined lover arouses passion; and the same tap by a defined threatening stranger may arouse fear. Moreover, different individuals in the same situattion may experience differing emotions; a lover's tap may be defined by one as a cold and inappropriate invitation, while another may define it as subtle and flattering.

Finally, language provides directives for action. When an object is a given name, the individual is given directives for behavior with respect to the object. Concepts give discrimination, selectivity, and intelligence to our behavior. Furthermore, when our concepts change, our behavior also changes. An individual who adopts a new set of concepts to explain the world begins to live in a different world and to behave differently than he or she did in the past. Thus, the young man who rejects the conception of the world as a place where everyone can make it if he tries, and accepts a conception of the world as a "dog-eat-dog" place, may shift from ambitious, hard-working behavior to passivity and cynicism. It is not the world that changed, however; rather, it was the individual's conceptualization of the world. Likewise, the woman who experiences religious conversion will explain the world with a new set of concepts and her behavior will change accordingly; her aspirations, values, understanding, and actions may all shift as she sees the world as God's work place rather than as a fighting ring for human beings.

Thus, different conceptual systems necessarily involve differing patterns of cognition, emotions, and behavior. This is illustrated by a study of communities that were struck by tornadoes. [38] The respondents, all residents of the communities, were categorized by social class according to income and education. Significant differences were found between middle-class and lower-class respondents in terms of such things as ability to take the listener's role. Lower-class respondents tended to give descriptions as seen through their own eyes, with apparently little ability to understand or

[37] Strauss, 1968a, p. 179.
[38] Strauss, 1955.

communicate alternative perspectives. Middle-class respondents were more sensitive to the problem of adequately informing the interviewers, and used far more imagery and greater complexity of detail. Finally, the middle-class respondents used a greater number of concepts; the lower-class respondents tended to be particularistic or concrete in their descriptions. All of this accords with what we know about language differences between the social classes,[39] and illustrates the way in which differing conceptual systems affect interaction.

Some of the points made in this section are also illustrated in Strauss' work on the "symbolic management" of the city. A city is a complex entity and "complexity forces us to analogize . . . The city may be termed or compared with a factory, a madhouse, a frontier, a woman." [40] By thus symbolizing the city, we are able to organize our behavior and respond to it. The symbol indicates the significance of the urban milieu for our behavior, and provides directives for that behavior. For instance, John Steinbeck has related the way in which New York City changed from something monstrous the first time he visited it, to a "Temptation" on his second visit, to his "village" when he returned to live there. Strauss comments:

> Each Steinbeck who came to the city was, in some sense, a different man; and each time he perceived, and therefore used, the city quite differently . . . The urban milieu . . . is responded to not merely as physical terrain, a bit of geography, but as symbolic space filled with meaning and peopled with significant persons, artifacts, and institutions.[41]

Thus, whether we deal with face-to-face interaction or behavior in the urban milieu, individuals respond to and act on the basis of the symbols with which they interpret their environment.

Theory and Research in Symbolic Interactionism

In any scientific perspective, theory, methods, and standards comprise an "inextricable mixture." [42] Thus far we have focused on Strauss' theoretical emphases. In this section, we will see the way in which his theory and research blend together in an "inextricable mixture."

---

[39] See, for example, Martin Deutsch and associates, *The Disadvantaged Child,* Basic Books, New York, 1967; Robert D. Hess and Virginia C. Shipman, "Early Experience and the Socialization of Cognitive Modes in Children," *Child Development,* 36, No. 4 (1965), 869–886; Vera P. John, "The Intellectual Development of Slum Children: Some Preliminary Findings," *American Journal of Orthopsychiatry,* 33 (October 1963), 813–822.
[40] Strauss, 1958, p. 529.
[41] Strauss, 1968b, p. 5.
[42] Thomas S. Kuhn, *The Structure of Scientific Revolutions,* The University of Chicago Press, Chicago, 1962, p. 108.

THEORETICAL DIRECTIVES FOR RESEARCH

One of the problems with attitude research, wrote Strauss in 1945, is that it "is not effectively guided by attitude theory." [43] Such a divorce of theory and research obscures our understanding. For the two go hand in hand, with theory providing guidelines for research and research providing the matrix out of which theory develops. We shall discuss both points in their respective order. In this part, we want to see the kinds of things the theory leads us to look for in research.

First, the researcher must try to see the processes involved in what he or she studies. In researching a profession, for example, one approach would be to see the profession in terms of shared identity, values, roles, and interests; actually, however, there is considerable diversity, so that it is more useful to examine professions "as loose amalgamations of segments pursuing different objectives in different manners and more or less delicately held together under a common name at a particular period in history." [44] As this suggests, the processes of any phenomenon will likely be marked by conflict, competition, negotiation, and bargaining. Symbolic interaction theory directs the researcher, therefore, to look for change, diversity, conflict, and so forth.

Second, all phenomena must be examined from the perspectives of the actors involved. While this is fundamental to any phenomenological approach, no one else seems to have applied it to such massive, complex things as the city. The urban milieu has been studied in many different ways; Strauss examined it in terms of the image of the city held by urban dwellers. In all of his research, in fact, it is the perspective of the actors that is prominent. In the study of chemists, the scientists' own conceptions of a "successful" career were elicited; a definition of success was not imposed upon them. Furthermore, the researchers investigated the way chemists see themselves and the meaning of membership in the ACS for chemists. Similarly, in studying dying patients, the dying "trajectory" was defined in terms of "perceived courses of dying rather than the actual courses." [45] Examining phenomena from the actors' point of view has been a consistent aspect of Strauss' research.

Third, the researcher must examine him- or herself and the process of his or her research. He or she must be careful to regard his or her presuppositions as tentative and to watch for data that may direct him or her to shift the focus of the research. To study a fluid social reality demands that the researcher be flexible. In studying psychiatric institutions, an initial as-

[43] Strauss, 1945, p. 333.
[44] Strauss, 1961, p. 326. See also Strauss, 1967a, which argues that deviance is the result of a social definition which is the outcome of conflict between diverse groups. As a result, "the defining of deviancy is a continual, never-ending process" (p. 265).
[45] Strauss, 1968c, p. 6.

sumption was that psychiatrists tend toward one of three ideological positions—the somatic, the psychotherapeutic, and milieu therapy. "From the start of our research, however, we assumed that these enumerated positions were only crude concepts, useful only as beginning tools for analyzing the complex totality of contemporary psychiatric belief" [46] (compare this with Blumer's notion of "sensitizing concepts"). The researcher does not go into the field to study social phenomena without first formulating a problem, of course. But the researcher must realize that there is a process of discovery which may "lead [him] to his problem *after* it has led him through much of the substance in his field." [47]

RESEARCH METHODS

What kind of methods are appropriate for studying social processes? Initially, Strauss employed rigorous, quantitative methods. This was an expression of his early concern with methodological adequacy; as with Blumer, some of Strauss' first writings are primarily methodological critiques. But "adequacy" must be defined in terms of the object of study, and not in terms of a preconceived bias toward quantitative methods. The bulk of Strauss' research, therefore, has involved qualitative methods rather than complex statistical analyses.

Qualitative research usually takes place in the field rather than in the laboratory. Much of Strauss' research has occurred in medical settings. Depending upon one's purposes, of course, a variety of methods might still be employed. Both questionnaires and interviews were used in the study of chemists. But such methods run the risk of missing the process and the emergent phenomena. A combination of interviewing, discussion, and observation in natural settings is best for grasping the reality of a particular social phenomenon.

The actual tactics used in fieldwork were detailed in *Psychiatric Ideologies and Institutions*.[48] The researcher must make a number of decisions about observing and interviewing, namely, who, when, where, and what. Timing is important because any social entity has its own processual pattern, including recurring events. For the psychiatric study, both continuous observation and time samples were used ("time samples" involve the selection of blocks of time so that the researcher ultimately observes all types of situations).

The researcher's location is also important because the information available to him or her will vary from one location (such as the nurses' station) to another (a conference room). One option is to stay with someone who acts as a "tracer," bringing the researcher into contact with diverse people

[46] Strauss, 1964a, p. 9.
[47] Strauss, 1973, p. 3.
[48] Strauss, 1964a, pp. 22–29.

and situations and locations. Another option is to observe particular situations, such as admissions or regular meetings. A third option is to observe various status levels in sequence (from patients up to hospital administrators, for instance).

Having decided what and when to observe, the researcher must also attend to how to observe. One may remain external to that which one is observing, or one may be in the group but remain passive. One may also choose to interact only when necessary to clarify matters for oneself, or one may more actively talk with others in order to provide particular kinds of information. Finally, one may fully participate in activities, either disguising oneself as part of the group (as a patient or a minor staff member) or identifying oneself as a researcher while sharing fully in the group life. Neither extreme was employed in Strauss' psychiatric study; the researchers participated as researchers, asking questions and securing interviews as they felt it appropriate and necessary. The interviews were carried on without a schedule of specific questions, however.

This kind of research raises questions, particularly to those who feel that the true scientific methods are quantitative. Indeed, Strauss' published works on field methods have been strongly criticized in reviews. There are checks that the researcher can impose on his or her work, of course. One is the use of comparison groups. Nevertheless, the use of qualitative data always raises questions which go beyond the validity of interpretation to the issue of the validity of the data themselves. How can we be certain that the researcher has not omitted important data because of his or her perspective? All perception is selective; how can the researcher avoid selecting just those data which support his or her theoretical perspective?

A number of responses can be made. First, the questions make an unwarranted assumption about the validity of quantitative data. The use of quantitative methods does not eliminate the problem of bias in the selection of problems, the choice of variables, or the interpretation of results.[49] Second, some of the more important variables in social life may not be subject to quantification; the qualitative researcher could argue that the insistence on quantitative methods leads many researchers to collect nothing but mountains of trivial data.

Third, then, the qualitative researcher employs checks, such as the use of comparison groups mentioned above, just as does the quantitative researcher. Ultimately, researchers must trust the credibility of the knowledge they have gained through their research. A researcher has lived with and studied a particular phenomenon, testing his or her tentative hypotheses, remaining flexible for shifts in his or her focus, and learning the subject by living with it as well as observing it and interviewing others about

[49] For a devastating critique of survey research, see Derek L. Phillips, *Knowledge From What?*, Rand McNally, Chicago, 1972.

it. Moreover, if the researcher works with a team, he or she has the check of his colleagues. Consequently, the qualitative researcher should be able to trust the knowledge which has emerged from his or her own hard work and his or her "own ability to know or reason." [50]

THEORY CONSTRUCTION

Research does not merely test theory; as Merton put it, it also *"initiates, it reformulates, it deflects* and it *clarifies* theory."* [51] Strauss particularly stresses the point that research does not merely modify theory, but generates it. Theory not only guides research but emerges from it. There is an inter-action between research and theory, with each stimulating and being stimu-lated by the other. We pointed out above how symbolic interaction theory gives direction to research; but research also is the basis for theory con-struction. Here we refer to so-called "middle-range" theories which can be derived within the context of the broader theory of symbolic interactionism. For instance, in the study of psychiatric hospitals, the data gathered by the researchers led them to conclude that existing organizational theory was simply not adequate for understanding the hospital; rather, a theory is re-quired that allows for the "continual reconstitution of bases of work through negotiation." [52]

Grounded theory. Such theory, theory that is generated from research, is called "grounded theory." [53] The grounded theory approach stresses the generation of concepts and theory and describes this generation of theory as a process of interaction between theoretical activity and research activity. Research begins with a general theoretical perspective and a particular problem, but the accumulation of data soon allows the development of con-cepts and an incipient theory. The data, incidentally, may be either qualita-tive or quantitative. Our remarks above about the value of qualitative data should not lead to the conclusion that quantitative data are useless. In fact, Strauss argues that there is "no fundamental clash between the purposes and capacities of qualitative and quantitative methods or data. What clash there is concerns the primacy of emphasis on verification or generation of theory. . . ." [54] Those who take the quantitative approach tend to stress verification rather than generation of theory (and sometimes disparage qualitative research). But both kinds of data can be used for generating theory.

[50] Strauss, 1966b, p. 59.
[51] Robert K. Merton, *Social Theory and Social Structure,* revised and enlarged edition, Free Press, New York, 1957, p. 103.
[52] Strauss, 1964a, p. 375.
[53] Strauss, 1967c.
[54] *Ibid.,* p. 17.

Theoretical sampling. The concepts that are developed through research, along with the emerging theory, provide guidelines for further collection of data, which further refines the concepts and develops the theory. This further collection of data proceeds by "theoretical sampling," which means that data collection is directed by the emerging theory. No data collection can be planned beyond the initial collection until the theory has been developed sufficiently to provide additional directives. The emerging theory answers the questions as to what groups are to be studied next and for what purpose.

Obviously, theoretical sampling differs from probability sampling. In the former, the researcher is concerned to saturate his or her theoretical categories; in the latter the researcher is concerned to randomize his or her subjects. Theoretical sampling aims at understanding concepts and the relationships between concepts; thus, theoretical sampling focuses on the nature of a relationship, while statistical sampling focuses on the magnitude of a relationship (that is, the extent to which the relationship holds in a population).

Comparison groups. In this process of developing theory, the use of comparison groups is important. Comparative analysis can involve social units of any size, from individuals to nations. But such analysis is an integral part of the generation of theory for a number of reasons. First, comparative analysis is a useful check on initial evidence; do the findings from one ward of a hospital hold when we study another ward? Or do the data gathered for a professional organization reflect the reality of an industrial organization? Comparative analysis supports or refutes the evidence gathered initially. Secondly, comparative analysis helps us to estimate the magnitude of a relationship, to see to what extent we may generalize on findings. Third, comparative data help clarify concepts used in research by contrasting one concept with others which are similar yet different in some important way. Fourth, comparative studies are useful in testing hypotheses; the verification of a theory is greatly aided by the support of comparative data. Finally, and most importantly, comparative analysis aids in the generation of theory. The researcher can be much more confident about his or her emerging theory and much more precise about his or her concepts, when he or she works from comparative data.

Practical strategies. In addition to the use of theoretical sampling and comparison groups, researchers can generate theory through various practical strategies. Strauss suggested three such strategies for the development of urban theory.[55] First, we can "study the unstudied." This rests on the

[55] Strauss, 1967b.

assumption that we still do not know which topics will be most fruitful for developing theory. It is an invitation, then, to search for unexplored but valuable topics. Second, we should "study the unusual." This could include topics which appear trivial on the surface, or odd in some sense, or simply something which is unlikely to be chosen by others, such as Chinese laundries and laundry workers (the topic of a master's thesis which Strauss found to be "one of the most informative" papers he has seen on the urban area). The third strategy is to minimize ideological commitments in the topics studied. This reflects again the need for flexibility and the willingness to shift directions in one's research.

Obviously, all three strategies can be applied to areas other than the urban milieu. There is some risk in pursuing them, however. It may turn out, for instance, that what appears to be trivial on the surface is trivial in fact. Nevertheless Strauss has suggested, in effect, that we take bold steps in order to pursue the task of generating theory. And those who hesitate to examine the unstudied and the unusual might recall that Georg Simmel wrote some intriguing essays on such things as handles.

Substantive versus formal theory. We noted above that the theories about which we are talking are "middle-range." But Strauss makes a further distinction between substantive and formal theories.[56] Both types are grounded, and comparative analysis can be used to generate both. Substantive theory is, however, more concrete than formal theory. The former applies to substantive or empirical areas such as patient care, while the latter applies to conceptual areas such as stigma. A substantive theory might focus on the social loss of dying patients; a formal theory would deal with the social value of people.

An example offered by Strauss of formal theory which is also grounded theory is the work on "status passage."[57] The notion of status passage itself is not new. The French ethnographer Arnold van Gennep talked about it in a 1908 work in terms of "rites of passage." And Strauss wrote about it some fifteen years before the formal theory was elaborated in print. Simply put, "status passage" refers to important transitions from one social position to another which occur in all of our lives. The passage may either be inevitable—from infancy to childhood or life to death—or voluntary— the assumption of a new job or marriage. Strauss tried to develop a formal theory about these passages, in order to show both how formal theory may be developed and stimulate further research in status passages.

Actually, the "theory" of status passage is primarily a detailed discussion of the concept itself, focusing on certain properties of status passages.

---

[56] Strauss, 1967c, pp. 32–35.
[57] Strauss, 1971a.

Fourteen possible properties are offered, but the analysis is carried out around six of them: reversibility, temporality, shape, desirability, circumstantiality, and multiplicity.[58] "Reversibility" refers to such things as "direction, repeatability, arrestability, inevitability, and preventability." "Temporality" deals with such things as "schedule, regularity, prescribed steps, speed and pace." "Shape" has to do with such things as "periods, plateaus, and the like, along with the crucial issue of 'control' over the passage." "Desirability" refers to such matters as how desirable, how central, and how voluntary the passage is. "Circumstantiality" deals with whether passages are made alone or in a group. And "multiplicity" refers to the fact that all individuals are engaged in a number of status passages simultaneously.

The way these properties are treated may be illustrated by a brief consideration of one aspect of temporality, namely, that there are temporal expectations and legitimacy attached to any status passage. In the case of serious illness, for instance, the doctor communicates expectations to the patient about the length of time the patient is expected to cooperate with the doctor's directives. Such expectations vary in degree of certainty. The doctor may be vague, while the expectations of a student about the date of his or her graduation and the time of his or her availability for a job may be very precise. All such expectations, of course, are social phenomena in the sense that someone has the legitimacy to determine them; in the case of illness the physician has the legitimacy, while in the case of marriage the couple normally has the legitimacy.

Those who legitimate the timing of the status passage are important to those engaged in the passage, though they are not as theoretically important. This is particularly true where the passage follows a regular schedule (such as school graduation) and the legitimator simply makes the public announcement (such as the registrar). On the other hand, when there is ambiguity or ignorance about the schedule, the legitimator and his or her announcement take on theoretical significance. In such cases, the legitimator may have the power to establish certain temporal expectations and thereby influence the behavior and the organization that follow. Physicians may have this power vis-à-vis their patients. Influential political figures may have this power vis-à-vis the public; the continuing public assertions during the Vietnam war that we were approaching the end may have dulled the edge of protest for many years.

These are the kind of considerations developed and discussed in *Status Passage*. The categories, to be sure, are interrelated; for example, the desirability of a passage bears upon the motivation to control shape, to attempt a single or multiple passages, and to go alone or with others. But we do not have a set of logically related propositions that cohere and that com-

[58] *Ibid.*, p. 12.

prise a theory of status passage. This is not to deny either the utility of generating formal theory or the insights into the nature of status passage which are found in the book. But we do not have a theory; we have, rather, a rich development of a concept, a concept that inherently deals with processes. Even though the "theory" of status passage falls short as theory, then, the work demonstrates the nature of theory construction, namely, that theory must flow from research; that the theory is then used to guide further research, which modifies the theory, and so forth; that an important aspect of theoretical development is a richness of conceptual content; that theory must address itself to social processes and to changing social structures; and that the definitions of actors are an integral part of the direction of the social process.

Substantive Concerns

Strauss' early published works reflected a concern with factors related to marital choice.[59] This was not a lasting concern, however. In this section, we will look at five substantive areas to which he has contributed: careers and occupations, social mobility, the urban milieu, organizations, and health care. These areas often overlap; the theory of organizations ("negotiated order") arose out of work in health care, and the study of careers is obviously related to organizations, to social mobility, and to personnel in the field of health care.

CAREERS AND OCCUPATIONS

The study of careers and occupations is important for a number of reasons, one of the most important being the integral relationship between career and identity. The question of adult identity cannot be addressed adequately merely by looking at the childhood experiences; "central to any account of adult identity is the relation of change in identity to change in social position," [60] and one of the most important changes of social position is that related to one's occupation. We have previously noted that one of the more frequent and salient responses on the Twenty Statements Test is the individual's occupation, indicating the importance of work for the individual's self-concept. There is, in addition, an enormous amount of evidence on the importance of work for various psychological processes.[61] But Strauss has made an even profounder assertion—the very selfhood, the identity, of the individual is tied up with his or her career, and as the individual moves along various stages of his or her career, his or her identity

---

[59] Strauss, 1946 and 1947.

[60] Strauss, 1956, p. 263.

[61] See, for example, Melvin L. Kohn and Carmi Schooler, "Occupational Experience and Psychological Functioning: An Assessment of Reciprocal Effects," *American Sociological Review,* 38 (February 1973), 97–118.

is changing accordingly. The importance of career for identity underlies the fact that great psychological stress may occur during the critical periods of the career.

In studying careers, we are studying processes; it is appropriate, therefore, to speak about the "career line." In fact, focusing on the career line rather than simply on the career may aid us in keeping the processual perspective foremost. But what is involved in the study of career lines? Essentially, we must try to identify the movement involved, the characteristics of various phases of the movement, and the important variables along the way. The movement itself includes both horizontal and vertical moves; a horizontal move is illustrated by the change from head of one department to head of another, while a vertical move is illustrated by the change from department head to division head. Certain positions in this matrix will be critical ones in the sense that they test the individual and determine whether he or she will continue to move vertically or remain at that level for the remainder of his or her career. There is a tendency, particularly during the early part of a career, for the movement to be from less to more desirable kinds of positions.

The movement is not exhausted by the foregoing considerations, however. We must also study such phenomena as switching directions (choosing a new career) and variations in rates (which is an example of a temporal aspect of status passage). In some cases, rates may be fairly standardized, as with the university that has a well-defined schedule for promotions. In other cases, rates may be highly variable, such as the industry that allows a few individuals to make rapid advancement in the management hierarchy; in fact there is evidence that those who do reach the higher levels "tend to move rapidly along specific career lines leading to the top." [62]

In line with his emphasis on social organizational factors, Strauss has also pointed out the importance of considering the context in which careers take place. For one thing, the individual's career occurs within a particular broader work group. A physician carves out a career within the context of the profession itself. And, as we have noted, the profession is also in process. Thus, we have movement (individual career) within movement (process of the profession). Indeed, this would occur with respect to most kinds of careers: "The occupations and organizations within which careers are made change in structure and direction of activity, expand or contract, transform purposes. Old functions and positions disappear, and new ones arise." [63]

This latter statement directs us to another social organizational aspect of

[62] Strauss, 1959b, p. 89.
[63] Strauss, 1956, p. 262.

careers—the organization within which the career takes place. Any particular organization may have only a short-term impact; a particular psychiatric institution, for instance, is likely to be a "way station" for the professional's career. Nevertheless, even a way station can have a significant impact, and the overall significance of organizations for careers opens up numerous possibilities for fruitful research.

Finally, in the study of careers we must be careful to determine the actors' own perspectives. For instance, if we want to determine the consequences for the individual of achieving more or less success in his or her career, we must first ascertain how he or she defines success. In the case of chemists, the signs of success are successful research and colleague esteem for academicians, and promotion, position, and salary for others; moreover, most chemists believe that the individual can know whether one will be a success or not by the time one is thirty-five.[64] It is such definitions that must be taken into account rather than those constructed by the researcher and imposed on the actors. That is, the researcher cannot arbitrarily decide that money is an important indication of success for academic chemists when they themselves have not so defined it. The researcher cannot arbitrarily decide that the chemist who tests sewage for bacteria is not truly a professional; chemists define themselves as professionals, and the sewage tester's definition of him- or herself will have consequences for his or her behavior whether or not an observer agrees with that definition. The study of careers, like all sociological study, must always include the perspectives of the actors themselves.

SOCIAL MOBILITY

Mobility is also an inherently processual topic for analysis. Strauss has attended somewhat to traditional concerns of students of social mobility in looking at questions of direction and distance of mobility (that is, whether the mobility is upward or downward and how far people are mobile through the stratification system). But his basic approach to mobility parallels his work on status passages. He is interested in the context in which mobility occurs and the experiences of the mobile, including the way in which they perceive the process. He is interested, then, in again bringing social organizational and social psychological variables to bear upon the study of an important social process.

The basic scheme is straightforward:

> There are, first of all, various *"objective" conditions* (geographic, economic, climatic, political, social) which characterize frontiers, cities, countrysides, flows of immigration and the like . . . These partly, if not wholly, account for the *processual* and *ideational* variables . . .

[64] Strauss, 1962, pp. 86–87.

Those variables operate as conditions for various *mobility perspectives* . . . The perspectives give rise to various *behavioral and institutional consequences*.[65]

The italicized words are the major variables of the analysis. The way they are used may be illustrated by briefly considering one objective condition and its corresponding imagery—the frontier. For the way in which the frontier has been symbolized is reflected in certain symbolic representations of social mobility, particularly the idea of the frontier as a place for advancement and betterment. There were, of course, failures on the frontier, but the dominant emphasis was on the possibility of success, and this dominant image found expression in a dominant theme in American mobility imagery—the possibility of success for all who have the courage to try and the determination to persist.

Other images arose when the frontier became settled. The most powerful was the image of the honest yeoman working on his family farm in the context of agrarian democracy. This image persisted in fiction after the frontier and the small family farm were mainly a part of history; and perhaps it finds contemporary expression in the continuing idealization of rural life and the flight of the well-to-do to second homes or weekend homes outside of the cities.

Thus, the way in which the frontier has been symbolized has been incorporated into mobility imagery, with corresponding consequences for behavior and institutions. Strauss' concern is not simply with the usual variables looked at in mobility studies—occupation, income, education, and so forth of fathers and sons—but with the way in which the process itself is symbolized, and the consequences this has for behavior and social organization. He is also interested in developing a theory of mobility, and his theory derives from the theory of status passage. Thus, questions of temporality, shape, direction, and distance are examined. For instance, among the temporal aspects of mobility, three issues are quite important: "the *amount of time* committed to achieving or preventing mobility; the *rate* of movement, whether up or down; and the *temporal articulation* of actions pertaining to mobility." [66] "Temporal articulation" refers to such problems as the timing of actions in order to achieve mobility goals; a woman who opts for a professional career may have to make some difficult decisions about marriage or the raising of children (difficult in the context of social expectations in American society).

In sum, Strauss pursues a unique route in his study of mobility, a route which is congruent with his general approach but which is different from most studies. He reminds us that an individual's mobility is not merely a

---

[65] Strauss, 1971b, pp. 16–17.
[66] *Ibid.,* p. 197.

matter of probability based on such things as occupation of father and education; rather, mobility must be understood in terms of the way in which the process is symbolized and in terms of the various characteristics of the process.

THE URBAN MILIEU

The urban milieu presents us with still another area of study in which symbolic processes are of paramount importance. As already discussed, cities are complex places, and an individual can organize his or her behavior in one only by organizing that complexity into some meaningful symbols. Such symbols give the city a unity and enable the individual to act in the context of massive amounts of stimuli.

The symbols used to organize the meaning of the city are not idiosyncratic and, therefore, unlimited. Rather, Americans symbolize the urban milieu in a number of typical ways. It is important to know these various symbolizations because we can then understand how different people behave differently and employ diverse ways of coping with the city. Furthermore, we may pursue such questions as which groups use which symbols and why, and the nature of the ongoing interaction between people, symbols, and the physical layout and social relationships of the city.

Strauss suggests that a fruitful source of urban imagery is the American novel, and from the work of novelists writing about New York City he identifies six different themes or images.[67] The first is that of the heterogeneity of the city; the urban milieu embodies diversity, and diversity is applauded because it results in a cosmopolitan atmosphere. Second, there is the image of the city as a "feast," a place of exciting objects, events, and scenery where people can be free to pursue their interests. Third, the city is contrasted with the rural scene, and the small town and countryside are a human being's true home and the place of his or her true fulfillment (obviously, the various images are not compatible with each other). Fourth, the city is seen as dehumanizing, an impersonal, artificial, and purposeless place that is inimical to the realization of human values. Fifth, the city is a place of change, and particularly a place where families are prone to break up, important relationships are likely to deteriorate, and neighborhood stability is always precarious. Finally, the city is a place of important social class relationships, including the upwardly and downwardly mobile, the decadent rich, and, sometimes, certain good qualities which are possessed by both the upper and lower classes.

Such images are not necessarily held individually by one person for an extended period of time. An individual might apply differing images to different parts of the city. An individual might shift over time in his or her

[67] Strauss, 1968b, pp. 6–18.

dominant imagery (as noted earlier with respect to Steinbeck). But in any case the images are important for behavior. The urban dweller is not a creature buffeted about by complex, irresistible forces in the city; rather, he or she is an actor who copes with the complexity by defining the city in meaningful symbols and responding to those symbolizations.

COMPLEX ORGANIZATIONS

While the very term "organization" implies stability and static relationships, Strauss continues to show the processual nature of all social phenomena in treating a particular organization, the hospital, as a "negotiated order." [68] He suggests that other organizations may also be so treated, but his own analyses focus on the hospital. The negotiated order model attends not only to organizational processes, but also to a variable neglected by other researchers—interactional features of organizational life.

First, then, organizations are processual phenomena. Work is a process, and the organization's functioning is integrally linked up with the temporal characteristics of the work carried on in the organization. Organizations do have a structure, of course, but in the negotiated order model that structure is loose and pluralistic. There are a number of goals, and the goals are diverse. There may even be contradictory goals in the organization. There is no single basis of legitimacy and no single hierarchy of authority. The various subunits of the organization are heterogeneous, have a certain autonomy, and differ in terms of their goals and the power they possess.

The central problem in a negotiated order is how order is maintained in the face of inevitable change. All shared understandings lack permanence and must be continually reconstituted. Indeed, rules that apply to the behavior of various professionals in the organization are neither extensive nor unambiguous. This means that continual negotiation is required. In one psychiatric hospital, the researchers found that "hardly anyone knows all the extant rules, much less exactly what situations they apply to, for whom, and with what sanctions." [69] The negotiations are complex because the participants may share only a single, vague goal, such as the recovery of the patient (vague because of differing treatment ideologies and different notions of what is "best" for the particular patient). Moreover, the participants often face unique problems, and they operate in the context of continual changes which have resulted from past negotiations. This means that shared understandings, roles, norms, rules, and so forth all emerge from the interaction as well as give a certain preliminary shape to the interaction.

This is not to say that the negotiations are chaotic, or that there are no regularities in the hospital. The negotiations follow a pattern at least "in

[68] Strauss, 1963.
[69] *Ibid.*, p. 151.

the sense that certain amounts, kinds, *and* participants of negotiation recur predictably." [70] This predictability reflects the fact that status in the organization is important in defining who will negotiate on what matters and to what extent. In addition, two structural factors affect negotiations. The first is the number and kinds of professionals who must work together, and the second is the extent to which the professional team is fluid in terms of personnel composition.

Some of these points are well illustrated in a study of negotiation in a state mental hospital.[71] Prior to the actual study, a new superintendent had assumed office and sought to attract psychiatrists to the hospital by giving each a single ward with a team of professionals and the freedom to establish his or her own mode of treatment. The researchers studied five wards, each of which had a different treatment philosophy. These philosophies varied from a radical patient-government system in which each patient was expected to understand him- or herself and assume increasing responsibility for his or her progress to a medical authority system in which considerable use was made of electroshock and drug therapy. One ward had an "unresolved" system because the professional team was divided in its purposes: the psychiatrist viewed himself as an expert whose authority should be supreme; the physician had a somatic orientation; and the psychologist and social worker were committed to the notion of group therapy.

All of the chiefs of the teams were younger men with little or no experience in a state hospital, increasing the necessity of coming to terms with other professionals by negotiating about methods of treatment and task assignments. Moreover, the teams were relatively fluid, increasing the importance of negotiation.

The result was that virtually any task assumed or advocated by a professional was subject to alteration or denial through negotiation. Even when a claim was established, it could be lost in subsequent negotiations. The kind of claim a particular individual might set forth depended on his or her profession, the ideology he or she and others on the team held, and the ward's division of labor. In addition, knowledge was important in negotiating. None of the professionals deferred to others, so no one had an inviolable status that insured their own triumph. But the professional who knew, or who appeared to know, what he or she was saying was more likely to have his or her claim accepted.

In such a context one could say that for practical purposes we cannot know "what the hospital 'is' on any given day" unless we have "a comprehensive grasp of what combination of rules and policies, along with agree-

---

[70] Strauss, 1964a, p. 374.

[71] Leonard Schatzman and Rue Bucher, "Negotiating a Division of Labor among Professionals and in the State Mental Hospital," *Psychiatry,* 27 (August 1964), 266–277.

ments, understandings, pacts, contracts, and other working arrangements, currently obtains." [72] The social order of the hospital is created anew each day. There is no long-term stable structure that determines the interaction of personnel and patients; rather, the structure provides a context for the interaction of personnel and patients that, in turn, continually forges the changing structure. Structure and process interact in the ongoing development of a social situation.

The extent to which the negotiated order model is applicable to other organizations is a matter for research. In any case, Strauss has brought to bear upon the study of organizations an important and useful perspective. Nevertheless, the model is not without its problems. A good many studies of organizations have shown such variables as size and technology to be important; these variables impose certain inherent limitations on behavior in the organization. Other studies have focused upon the question of power in the organization, and while Strauss deals with the question, his model does not allow for the possibility of stable centers of power which make negotiations either nonexistent or moot. In sum, the model is useful and is a corrective to others which have neglected interactional features of organizations, but it does not embrace all the important and interesting organizational phenomena.

THE SOCIOLOGY OF HEALTH CARE

Thus far, we have seen the consistency of Strauss' theoretical, methodological, and substantive concerns. There is a constant emphasis on process, on the symbolic interactionist nature of that process, on securing the perspectives of the actors themselves, and on the social organizational context of behavior. The last substantive area of concern, health care, reveals the same consistent approach. In essence, health care is a process of symbolic interaction that occurs in particular social organizational contexts and the understanding of which demands that we secure the perspectives of the actors involved.

Thus, dying is not merely an event, but a process, and the care of the dying patient has important temporal characteristics.[73] At the most basic level, the patient has a schedule of feeding, bathing, being turned in bed, and receiving drugs. In addition, just as we may speak profitably of a career "line," we may usefully think of the dying "trajectory." There are various kinds of trajectories (long or short duration, moving continually in one direction or vacillating, moving in spurts or steadily downward towards death), and these trajectories are perceived as well as objective phenomena. That is, the parties involved have expectations regarding the trajectory, and

[72] Strauss, 1963, p. 165.
[73] Strauss, 1968c, pp. 2ff.

their behavior is based on these expectations; physicians, nurses, family members, and the patient all relate to each other on the basis of their perception of the trajectory.

For example, when a patient first enters the hospital, the staff make initial definitions of the patient's trajectory. They expect him or her to die quickly or to linger; they are certain or uncertain about his or her death; they have expectations about how the patient will fare in the last days and hours. Such definitions are crucial determinants of how the staff will relate to the patient. The initial definitions change as the staff redefine the patient's trajectory during the course of care. Occasionally, however, the trajectory may be wrongly defined by the staff, with unsettling consequences for the organization of the hospital. To put it crudely, patients are expected to move toward death in a particular way and to die "on time," and when the expectations are suddenly or radically thwarted, the hospital is forced to make adjustments; particularly disconcerting is the patient who vacillates between life and death, and whose death is greeted by a sense of relief.[74] The organization is geared to care for patients in accord with its own needs as well as the needs of patients, so that the loss of a patient who has disrupted the hospital's expectations and schedules creates more relief than sorrow.

The interaction process between patient, relatives, and hospital personnel is affected not only by the definitions made of the dying trajectory but also by the "awareness context." [75] This refers to the fact that each actor may or may not know the identity of the other and the other's view of his or her identity. That is, we are reminded again that interaction may involve ignorance and nonrational aspects; furthermore, we are given a scheme for studying such interaction. There are four kinds of awareness contexts: the open, closed, suspicion, and pretense. With respect to dying patients, an "open context" is one in which all the actors know of the coming death and all know that the others know. In a "closed context," an individual is ignorant either of the other's identity or the other's view of his or her identity; thus, the dying patient may be unaware of his or her fate while the staff knows about it. A "suspicion awareness context" occurs when one individual suspects the true identity of the other or the other's view of his or her identity; a patient may suspect that the physician defines him or her as dying even though the physician has not directly informed the patient and believes that he or she is ignorant of his diagnosis. Finally, a "pretense awareness context" occurs when the interactants are aware of identities but pretend not to be; patient, relatives, and staff may all know of the impending death and may with unspoken consensus all pretend that neither they nor

[74] Strauss, 1970, p. 137.
[75] Strauss, 1964b; Strauss, 1965.

the others know. Since the awareness context may differ for the various individuals involved, we must ascertain it for each of the interactants in order to fully understand the course of the interaction.

A similar approach illuminates the question of the care of psychiatric patients. We have already noted that the psychiatric hospital itself must be understood as a negotiated order. The negotiation includes the patients as well as the staff, however. Patients "negotiate their fates" in the hospital: ". . . patient and professional careers develop in arenas characterized by confrontation and negotiation, with the patient actively bargaining on his own behalf, but also influencing professional decisions and careers." [76] In this context, professional ideologies provide the basis for the definition of the patient's illness and the appropriate treatment, providing a kind of framework within which negotiation may take place. The patient's career occurs in interaction with various other processes, including the interprofessional negotiation of the therapeutic team, the various professions represented in the care, professions which themselves are in flux, and the ongoing alterations in the organization, the psychiatric hospital.

In general, then, we have a portrait of health care as a problematic process, with any individual's fate dependent upon the particular perspectives and the particular context in which treatment occurs as well as his or her definition of the situation. Health care is not the application of a precise science; it is a variable process of interaction. Like all of human life, it must be understood in interactional terms, in terms of symbolic processes. That may not be altogether comforting to a prospective patient, but reality cannot be sacrificed to comfort.

Conclusion

As in the case of Blumer, Strauss has consistently applied a symbolic interactionist perspective to phenomena at various levels of social life. Whether it is the urban milieu or a hospital ward or an individual's career, he has made his analyses in terms of process, the symbolic interactionist nature of the process, the perspectives of the actors involved, and the social organizational context. Humans are symbolic creatures whose behavior must be understood in terms of interaction at whatever level we observe. And humans behave in the context of structures which are in process. Since human life is a matter of symbolic interaction processes, appropriate methods of study must be found. Strauss' response was to move away from complex statistical analyses and advocate a "grounded" approach, in which the research itself would be a process of interaction between theory and concepts on the one hand and participation, observation, and interpretation on the

---

[76] Strauss, 1966a, p. 11.

other hand. Thus, the question raised in Chapter 4 about how we can study processes has been neatly answered by making the research act itself as a process of discovery.

Suggested Readings

Unlike Blumer, Strauss has not engaged in exchanges in the journals. One exception is a brief debate with Mark Abrahamson on awareness contexts; see the *American Sociological Review* [30 (October 1965), 779–780]. Criticisms of Strauss' works appear rather frequently, however, in reviews of his books. Although some very good reviews have been written, quite a number have been negative. See, for example, the reviews of: *Awareness of Dying* in the *Annals of the American Academy* [336 (June 1966), 202]; *The Discovery of Grounded Theory* in the *American Journal of Sociology* [73 (May 1968), 773]; *The Contexts of Social Mobility* in *Choice* [8 (September 1971), 921]; and *Status Passage* in the *American Anthropologist* [75 (April 1973), 477]. For a brief exposition of some of Strauss' ideas in *Mirrors and Masks,* see his chapter, "Transformations of Identity," in *Human Behavior and Social Processes* (ed. Arnold M. Rose, Houghton Mifflin, Boston, 1962, pp. 63–85). A short, readable explanation of "grounded theory" may be found in Strauss' chapter, "Discovering New Theory from Previous Theory," in *Human Nature and Collective Behavior* (ed. Tamotsu Shibutani, Prentice-Hall, Englewood Cliffs, N.J., 1970, pp. 46–53).

References to Strauss' Works

1945   "The Concept of Attitude in Social Psychology," *The Journal of Psychology,* 19 (April), 329–339.

1946   "The Influence of Parent-Images upon Marital Choice," *American Sociological Review,* 11 (October), 554–559.

1947   "Personality Needs and Marital Choice," *Social Forces,* 25 (March), 332–335.

1950a "A Critique of Culture-Personality Writings," *American Sociological Review,* 15 (October), 587–600 (with Alfred R. Lindesmith).

1950b "A Study of Concept Learning by Scale Analysis," *American Sociological Review,* 15 (December), 753–762 (with Karl Schuessler).

1951   "Socialization, Logical Reasoning, and Concept Development in the Child," *American Sociological Review,* 16 (August), 514–523 (with Karl Schuessler).

1952   "The Development and Transformation of Monetary Meanings in the Child," *American Sociological Review,* 17 (June), 275–286.

1953   "Concepts, Communication, and Groups," in *Group Relations at the Crossroads,* ed. Muzafer Sherif and M. O. Wilson, Harper, New York, pp. 99–119.

1954   "The Development of Conceptions of Rules in Children," *Child Development,* 25 (September), 193–208.

1955   "Social Class and Modes of Communication," *American Journal of Sociology,* 60 (January), 329–338 (with Leonard Schatzman).

1956   "Careers, Personality, and Adult Socialization," *American Journal of Sociology,* 62 (November), 253–263 (with Howard S. Becker).

1957   "Interaction in Audience-Participation Shows," *American Journal of Sociology,* 62 (May), 579–587 (with Donald Horton).

1958 "Symbolic Representation and the Urban Milieu," *American Journal of Sociology,* 63 (March), 523–532 (with R. Richard Wohl).

1959a *Mirrors and Masks,* Free Press, Glencoe, Ill.

1959b "Patterns of Mobility Within Industrial Organizations," in *Industrial Man: Businessmen and Business Organizations,* ed. W. Lloyd Warner and Norman H. Martin, Harper, New York, pp. 85–101.

1961 "Professions in Process," *American Journal of Sociology,* 66 (January), 325–334 (with Rue Bucher).

1962 *The Professional Scientist: A Study of American Chemists,* Aldine, Chicago (with Lee Rainwater).

1963 "The Hospital and Its Negotiated Order," in *The Hospital in Modern Society,* ed. Eliot Friedson, Free Press, New York, pp. 147–169 (with Leonard Schatzman, Danuta Ehrlich, Rue Bucher, and Melvin Sabshin).

1964a *Psychiatric Ideologies and Institutions,* Free Press, New York (with Leonard Schatzman, Rue Bucher, Danuta Ehrlich, and Melvin Sabshin).

1964b "Awareness Contexts and Social Interaction," *American Sociological Review,* 29 (October), 669–679 (with Barney G. Glaser).

1965 *Awareness of Dying,* Aldine, Chicago (with Barney G. Glaser).

1966a "A Sociology of Psychiatry: A Perspective and Some Organizing Foci," *Social Problems,* 14 (Summer), 3–16 (with Leonard Schatzman).

1966b "The Purpose and Credibility of Qualitative Research," *Nursing Research,* 15 (Winter), 56–61 (with Barney G. Glaser).

1967a "A Sociological View of Normality," *Archives of General Psychiatry,* 17 (September), 265–270.

1967b "Strategies for Discovering Urban Theory," in *Urban Research and Policy Planning, Vol. 1,* ed. Leo F. Schnore and Henry Fagin, Sage Publications, Beverly Hills, Calif.

1967c *The Discovery of Grounded Theory: Strategies for Qualitative Research,* Aldine, Chicago (with Barney G. Glaser).

1968a *Social Psychology,* 3rd ed., Holt, (with Alfred R. Lindesmith).

1968b *The American City: A Sourcebook of Urban Imagery,* Aldine, Chicago.

1968c *Time for Dying,* Aldine, Chicago (with Barney G. Glaser).

1970 *Where Medicine Fails,* Trans-action Books, Chicago.

1971a *Status Passage,* Aldine, Chicago (with Barney G. Glaser).

1971b *The Contexts of Social Mobility: Ideology and Theory,* Aldine, Chicago.

1973 *Field Research: Strategies for a Natural Sociology,* Prentice-Hall, Englewood Cliffs, N.J. (with Leonard Schatzman).

Chapter 11

Tamotsu Shibutani

In examining the work of Blumer and Strauss, we have noted that a few
themes pervade their work, appearing again and again in the context of
diverse substantive interests. In the work of Tamotsu Shibutani there is a
single theoretical theme that unites a variety of diverse topics: the nature
of social control in modern mass society. Shibutani pursues this theme
through several substantive topics: the development of self-concepts

among infantrymen in basic training; rumor; social stratification based on ethnic identification; reference groups; intergroup conflict; and the relationship of the psychoanalytic insights about human personality to social control.[1] In this chapter we will show how these various topics are united by the theme of social control in mass society, treating each substantive topic (as Shibutani does) as a vehicle for understanding and clarifying the important theoretical issue represented by the theme.

We have used the term "social act," following Mead, to refer to the coordination of individual acts, or lines of action, in the achievement of a cooperative end. Social control refers to any process that helps achieve this coordination. Social control may be informal, such as the communication among strangers that transforms a group of people waiting to enter a theater into an orderly line. Social control may also involve the explicit and socially legitimized use of sanctions by designated authorities. The legal bueraucracy and, on a smaller scale, the enforcement of proper behavior by teachers in classrooms are examples.

Social control should not be equated with one individual's attempts to maintain others' conformity, however. The process of social control is a social act—its "product," coordination of lines of action, arises from multiple efforts. Some may not even be aware of their participation in that endeavor. For example, the process of social control that results in the stable pattern of illegal drug production, use, and law enforcement involves state, federal, and international law enforcement agencies, the economic situation of peasant farmers in several nations of the world, consumer demand, the American scofflaw, pioneer spirit and sense of individual rights, youthful rebellion, the politically treacherous emotional climate surrounding the issue, the ability of middle-class parents to affect the political and legal apparatus to protect their children, and our consumer- and advertising-oriented culture which exploits the psychedelic market. Notice that the efforts of many of the agencies and individuals involved in this complex pattern of action may be at cross-purposes. While some may act in opposition to what others would like, it is the combined efforts of all of them that produce the resulting social order.

The Issue of Social Control

MODERN MASS SOCIETY AND AMBIGUITY

The term "modern mass society," used frequently in Shibutani's work, obviously refers to an enormously complex and poorly understood reality. While we cannot concisely define this reality or indicate all of the ways in

---

[1] Since the bulk of the citations in this chapter will be to the work of Shibutani, we will refer to them in the footnotes by date only. For the titles of the works and complete publication information see the list at the end of the chapter.

which it differs from other social arrangements, we can, as does Shibutani, indicate several of its characteristics that affect the process of social control. The most crucial characteristics are the ambiguity of the situations which people must confront and the variety of communication channels in which they participate. In their daily lives men and women face frequent ambiguous situations which must be clarified in order for effective, concerted action to be undertaken.[2] In many ways, the communication channels used to provide clarifying information can also be regarded as sources of this pervasive ambiguity of modern life.

Ambiguity from complex role relationships. The first of these sources of ambiguity is the involvement of citizens in complex societies in a large, and increasing, number of role relationships. As our social structures become more differentiated, and the roles within them become more narrow and specialized, we become increasingly involved with, and dependent upon, our fellow citizens. For example, when furniture was made by relatively small groups of cooperating craftsmen in a combined area, the degree of social cooperation necessary to produce a chair was relatively small. Certainly raw materials had to be supplied and refuse removed, but these ends could be met by contacts with a few people. Within the shop itself, virtually all tasks, from sweeping the floor to highly skilled woodcarving could be done by a few craftsmen and apprentices in a collegial relationship. In the extreme, a single owner (master craftsman) and an apprentice might perform all aspects of the trade.

A brief look at a modern chair will indicate that this is no longer the case. Very possibly, the legs unscrew. They are made by machine in large factories to standardized sizes and distributed to other factories where chairs are assembled by attaching legs, and other prefabricated components, in a relatively unskilled assembly line operation. Even the cushion covers and the cushions themselves, especially if they are foam, may be made in separate locations and assembled at a central point.

The quality of chairs is not the issue. Sociologically, the making of chairs in this way requires that all participants in the process become enmeshed in a complex web of role relationsips involving not only those with whom one works in the shop or factory, but also with those at other locations where prefabricated parts are produced, and with a wide array of suppliers, unions, government regulators, and so on. In purchasing materials, the perspectives of the suppliers must be taken; in arranging for a work force, the perspectives of the available pool of laborers must be taken; and to design the product, the perspectives of consumers and a variety of regulatory agencies must be taken. Nor can these perspectives be adopted singly. To successfully manufacture and sell the product, the perspectives

---

[2] Shibutani, 1966, p. v.

of all must be taken at once and integrated into an acceptable, profitable judgment concerning design, quality, wages, working conditions, costs, and prices. This explosion of the role relationships involved in social life is not limited to manufacturing but is generally characteristic of our social life in complex societies.

As Shibutani points out, involvement in multiple role relationships requires one to adopt different perspectives, different ways of defining situations, in one's dealings with others. Often this multiplicity of perspectives is unnoticed and we lead compartmentalized lives—defining and redefining events without recognition that we have done so. In extreme cases, where the role relationships in which we are involved are both numerous and incongruous, the behavior patterns of the individual and, therefore, the self may become fragmented. Even when this extreme is not reached, one is faced with frequent, if unrecognized, choices between different ways of defining events, each appropriate in only some of one's role relationships. The necessity for choice among perspectives and the attendant lack of coherence in the lives of individuals is a characteristic of modern mass societies and suggests a unique problem for social control.[3] We can provisionally state the problem as one of maintaining orderly social arrangements among a group of people whose individual lives are, to varying degrees, fragmented.

This problem has received considerable, if implicit, attention in earlier chapters. Our discussion of interaction processes recognized the importance of poorly institutionalized situations in which individuals with varying perspectives must develop a joint perspective to interact successfully. The development of this joint perspective, in each situation, must respect the perspectives imposed on the participants by other relationships. Our discussion of deviance provided an example of this constraint on perspectives by indicating that the various participants in the legal system orient their actions to the often contradictory perspectives of a variety of others with whom they interact. In Shibutani's work, we find both indications of the sources of these different perspectives and an analysis of their effects on social control beyond the level of single interactions.

Ambiguity from diverse perspectives. The second source of ambiguity in mass society is the frequent use of the perspectives of groups in which a person is not a member, with which he or she is not in direct contact and interaction, or which may exist only in his or her imagination. The importance of such groups is highlighted by the following considerations. Ordinarily, we might conceive of one's "best interests" as the sum of the sanctions, positive and negative, that one's action will precipitate from one's environment, and from the various people with whom one interacts.

[3] Shibutani, 1955, p. 567.

The social sanctions could include intangible ones, such as approval or affection, as well as material ones. When "best interests" are defined in this way, it is frequently the case that people are not responsive to them, even when the consequences of their actions are known to them.[4] Once the importance of such intangible sanctions as approval is recognized, however, we must also recognize that the sources of the sanctions are crucial. Affection or respect from the immediately present group may be, then, worthless and the individual may be concerned with other groups that are not immediately present or with groups that do not even exist, such as "posterity," or the judgment of "history." To understand human action, we must specify the group towards which the individual is oriented and what the perspective of that group dictates in particular situations. The way in which success is measured may be so different in different groups that people located in the same geographically defined community may become mutually incomprehensible by responding to the perspectives of different groups.[5]

The primary example of such misunderstandings, in Shibutani's work, is the division and stratification of communities by ethnic group identification. By strong identification with an ethnic group people may exhibit its culture, rather than that of their geographical neighbors. The behavior, habits of dress, style of communication, preferred food, morals, and social relationships that comprise the culture may estrange them from those with whom they are physically close. Reciprocally, neighbors may be excluded from many avenues of contact on the basis of real or imagined ethnic differences. These two processes, which limit communication, are reciprocally reinforcing and tend to reify the differences and misunderstandings between groups. This feature of life in mass societies adds another source of choice or ambiguity to both choosing a course of action and understanding the actions of others. In addition, it points immediately to the crucial role of sentiments, especially the attitude toward various groups, in social control.

Ambiguity from diverse communication networks. The third source of ambiguity in mass society is the nature of the communication patterns that have developed. In mass societies, information is, of course, still transmitted by direct social contact with other individuals and this information remains extremely important. Shibutani's discussion of rumor shows how this form of communication is shaped and sustained by mass society and how it contributes to social control. In addition, however, mass societies are characterized by mass media. Through their technology and their

---

[4] *Ibid.,* pp. 562–565.
[5] Shibutani, 1962, pp. 137–138.

social arrangements, the mass media act as a source of both ambiguity and information in modern societies.

Perspectives emerge from, and are maintained by, participation in communication channels. In some cases, these channels are characterized not only by access to information, but also by the use of special symbols or jargon known only to insiders.[6] Further, especially in situations of intergroup conflict and high levels of group solidarity, information that is contrary to the accepted interpretation of the group may be discredited and omitted from the communication channels of the group.[7] Generally, networks of social communication are not merely sources of information but are regulated by understandings concerning *"who may address whom, about what subject, under what circumstances, and with what degree of confidence."* [8] Such regulation of communication between individuals in particular role relationships varies greatly. At one extreme, there are the exceptionally informal boundaries governing the exchange of pleasantries and gossip in brief encounters, such as waiting to receive change while boarding a bus. On the other extreme are highly formalized chains of command, like those in many bureaucracies, which regulate to whom one must and can report, what information, and in what format, in great detail.

Involvement in multiple role relationships, each with its own understandings of propriety in communication, confronts people with contradictions in the information they receive, in standards for judging information, in evaluations of their sources' credibility, and in the propriety of using additional sources of information. Thus, our involvement in multiple role relationships results in multiple communication networks and the ambiguity arising from contradictory communication.

In fact, multiple role relationships and multiple communication channels are so closely intertwined that the two may have been identical before the development of mass media, a form of communication unique to our mass societies. Mass media, by definition, are utilized by an enormous audience, usually geographically dispersed. These communication channels are generally accessible to individuals whatever their group affiliation. For example, anyone can read *Fortune* in a public library, even if one cannot afford to buy the magazine oneself. Television or radio shows can be received by anyone with access to a television or radio receiver. The economics of mass media dictate that they appeal to a large audience. This constraint on the broadcaster or publisher usually translates into the need to appeal to a relatively broad or diverse audience in order to achieve large distribution. Thus, the content of the media is shaped by the interests of the broad audience, which can be conceived as a variety of social groups

[6] Shibutani, 1955, pp. 565–567.
[7] Shibutani, 1973, pp. 227–228.
[8] Shibutani, 1966, p. 21.

with varying interests who share the mass media outlets, both in the sense that they all have access to them, and in the sense that the content is manipulated to appeal to as many of them as possible. This sharing of the mass media by a variety of social groups, each using them as part of their communication channels, implies that each group will sometimes be confronted with information that is contrary to that transmitted by its other channels; such information may be offensive, and may heighten ambiguity by providing contradictory information. That is, the mass media, through their accessibility, allow us to "eavesdrop" on part of the communication of other groups to which we would not otherwise have access. While this may provide understanding of these groups and their perspectives, it also serves to generate confusion and occasional outrage at the sort of information that is available and the form of its presentation.

A number of specific implications can be drawn from the "sharing" of mass media. Many topics addressed by mass media will be regarded as irrelevant and simply ignored by many of those who have access to the information. The overall credibility of the mass media may be affected as well. Although a mass medium source may be regarded as a generally reliable one, every selection of content may be regarded by some groups who utilize the outlet as irrelevant, inappropriate, or incorrectly presented. That is, the content will not conform to the group's beliefs or norms. Some groups will regard the information presented by mass media as slanted to give a certain erroneous impression.[9] Whether a presentation is slanted or not is clearly and unavoidably a judgment that is made in the context of group affiliation, and cannot be understood as an objective characteristic of the presentation itself. In fact, as Warren Breed has pointed out, even those responsible for assembling the information in mass media may be in sharp disagreement concerning what constitutes slanting. He observed that staff members of newspapers are in conflict with publishers over the "policy" concerning what should be reported, with what degree of prominence, and with what degree of detail. Two important factors in these disputes were the differences in political orientation between the staffs and the publishers and the conflict between the publishers' desire to control the news and the norms of the journalistic profession— in short, group affiliation.[10]

Thus, while the mass media may be important channels of communication for many social groups, they are likely to be sources of discomfort to each of them. The same content may be experienced by different groups as accurate or inaccurate, as relevant or irrelevant, as normatively acceptable or outrageous, or as properly or improperly accessible to segments of the group. (For example, certain content may be deemed inappropriate

[9] *Ibid.,* pp. 41–44.
[10] Warren Breed, "Social Control in the Newsroom," *Social Forces* 33 (May 1955), 326–335.

for children in some groups and therefore improperly shown when children are awake, although acceptable at other times.) These characteristics of the mass media imply that they will be more or less inadequate for the needs of all groups that utilize them. This creates the need for what Shibutani calls "auxiliary channels," which transmit information of specific group interest that is either not available or improperly presented through formal channels.[11]

Finally, we must mention the ambiguity produced by the technology of mass communication, especially the development of the electronic media. Through electronic technology, communication has become virtually instantaneous, virtually unaffected by distance. Through the use of electronic supplements such as teletype machines and telephones even the print media have become immeasurably faster in the dissemination of information. Marshall McLuhan has suggested that the speed of electronic communication has transformed the mode of human interdependence and welded the population of the entire planet into a single tribal community.[12] By this, he means that through electronic media we are as swiftly and as intimately in touch with events all over the world as are the inhabitants of small tribal communities with each other.

Instantaneous access to information on a global scale, however, does not guarantee its relevance. While there may be many topics that are relevant to the concerns of groups throughout the world, other topics are of little interest, regardless of their inclusion in mass media presentations. With the availability of enormous amounts of information, in great detail, at great speed, we are quite possibly faced with an overload of information —a volume of information, relevant or not, that exceeds our capacity to consider it and act rationally upon it. The sheer volume and speed of communication compounds the problems caused by the sharing of channels. For example, throughout this country, undated information concerning the prices of stocks on the various exchanges is continuously available from several media sources. Even for a person concerned with investment, but not intimately involved with other channels of economic information, stock prices in such profusion may be a distraction and a hindrance to decisions. In addition, the sheer variety and speed of communication allows individuals to come into contact with esoteric values and perspectives and to "keep up with them" although the adherents are geographically dispersed. While this is welcome in many ways, such as the dissemination of art forms, entertainment, fashion, and so on, it also has some negative consequences. For the ability to respond to events from the perspective of a widely dispersed group fractures the geographic basis of com-

[11] Shibutani, 1966, p. 44.
[12] Marshall McLuhan, *The Gutenberg Galaxy,* University of Toronto Press, Toronto, 1962, pp. 3–8.

munity and contributes to misunderstanding among those who are in direct contact, but who respond to the values of dispersed groups, as represented by the media. That is, we have not become a single global village, but a number of global villages whose members are geographically intermingled and frequently in conflict. Social control, too, loses its geographic base—and individuals living side by side may have little understanding or influence on one another's conduct.

MEAD'S SOCIAL BEHAVIORISM AS A POINT OF DEPARTURE

Shibutani's work on the problem of social control has its basis in the social behavioristic framework developed by George Herbert Mead more than fifty years ago. Mead's work was in many ways abstract and general. In addition it was often speculative, offering suggestions about social life that were not yet supported by concrete research (usually a reflection of the limited research technology of the period; Mead's use of the existing empirical knowledge of his day was extensive). Subsequent empirical efforts have borne out Mead's speculations in many areas and have been consistent with his general approach to an astonishing degree. Thus Mead's work itself, as well as that of his many students and followers, remains a viable source of insight and a reasonable starting point for current research.

Shibutani is forthright in this regard, explicitly acknowledging both the continuing value of Mead's work and its inadequacies. In his discussion of Mead's use of the cybernetic principle of feedback to explain goal-oriented behavior, Shibutani acknowledges that this contribution is crucial to the understanding of purposive behavior. At the same time he recognizes that Mead's approach was "crude and represents only a beginning." He rejects the notion of social psychologists retreating to "speculative schemes developed more than a half century ago. Using some of these basic principles as a point of departure they should be able to construct far more sophisticated statements." [13]

It is this goal, then, that characterizes Shibutani's work: to provide a more sophisticated analysis of social control than that of Mead. At the same time, the general "cybernetic" framework suggested by Mead (although he did not employ that term) is retained. Thus, Shibutani's discussion of social control in mass society must be set in the context of Mead's use of the cybernetic principle of feedback and its application to social control. Shibutani's work can then be seen as an attempt to adjust our understanding of social control to the realities of the mass society which was barely forming at the time of Mead's death, and to our increased knowledge of the principles of cybernetics.

[13] Shibutani, 1968a, pp. 330–336.

Feedback and purpose. One of the recent trends in psychology is the use of cybernetic models, especially the concept of negative feedback, to try to explain purposive behavior in a scientific way. "Purpose" has always posed a problem for scientific explanation because the goal is a future state of affairs. Explaining behavior in terms of its goal has seemed to violate the principle that the cause must always precede its effect. The concept of feedback, however, avoids this difficulty. The goal or purpose can be defined as a model, existing in the present, that is used to evaluate all incoming information. When the incoming information does not "fit" the model, action is taken, based, not on the goal itself, but on the difference between the goal and the existing state of affairs. This difference between the goal and the state of affairs is negative feedback. Thus, behavior is caused by a condition that is measurable in the present, one that precedes behavior, but one that includes the concept of a goal or purpose.

A simple example of this process is found in the thermostat, a purposive machine. A temperature is selected as the goal (setting the thermostat). A thermometer measures the actual temperature. When the actual temperature and the desired temperature are different a switch is connected (behavior) which activates a device to correct the difference (furnace or air conditioner). The behavior is clearly goal oriented. But, at each instant, it is controlled not by the future state of events, or goals, but by the existing state of events: the measurable difference between the actual and desired temperature.

The rapidly developing techniques for employing bio-feedback are based on our ability to respond to feedback. Many clinical problems such as anxiety and inability to sleep are consistently accompanied by physiological symptoms. These physiological correlates are difficult to discern, apparently because of our lack of practice at recognizing our internal responses. For example, few of us can recognize small changes in our blood pressure, brain wave pattern, pulse rate, or galvanic skin response, and still fewer can internally control these behavioral events. However, machines can respond to these changes and represent them visually on a screen. This visual information can be used as feedback to train people to bring these physiological processes under control. By "watching" the pattern of brain waves, for example, a person can learn to produce the desired pattern, even after the machine is removed. People are literally taught to reduce blood pressure, and to relax in the physiological sense. Often, this produces the psychological sense of relaxation as well. Grosser behaviors, such as a baseball player's batting stance and swing have long been corrected through the use of films, another type of feedback. While more complicated, these human behaviors, are regulated by essentially the same principle as the simple home thermostat.

The cybernetic or feedback model has been in use for many years among engineers and physical and biological scientists. It is now being increasingly used by social scientists in a variety of applications. For our purposes, it is important to note that this feedback model has been recently proposed as a general explanation for goal-oriented human behavior that is based on the operation of the central nervous system.[14]

This is exactly the explanatory task that Mead set for himself, and the cybernetic solution is the one he proposed. Mead argued that the meaning of events are ultimately defined by configurations of neurons in the central nervous system. He felt that the ongoing act of an individual is organized by the purposive operation of the nervous system and its successive modification of the muscles toward the achievement of a goal.[15] For Mead, then, the goal of action is defined by connections between groups of neurons. The nervous system operates to achieve goals, using the object as a standard against which to evaluate existing conditions. The act is not regarded by Mead as an unvarying sequence of behaviors that is carried out automatically once initiated. Neither is the "stimulus" merely a switch or trigger for such an unvarying sequence. Rather, Mead suggested that the object of an act may remain constant throughout, but as the act proceeds, its progress changes the "distance values" between the existing state of affairs and the desired achievement of the goal. These continually changing distance values define a continually changing series of adjustments or modifications of the ongoing act until it is completed.[16]

Thus, human conduct can be goal directed, but it is controlled by changing distance values to the goal, not by the goal itself. Mead's work of some fifty years ago employs the same cybernetic principle as is currently coming into vogue, and to the same explanatory end. Shibutani suggests that perhaps Mead's failure to coin a striking term for this process accounts for the failure of social scientists to have recognized its use by Mead and his fellow pragmatists.[17]

Mead's approach to social control. Purpose or goal orientation, then, can be scientifically explained as the control of ongoing action by the changing relationship between the actual state of affairs and a model of the desired state of affairs or goal. Mead distinguishes a special class of conduct which he calls the "social act." Social acts are defined, as we pointed out in Chapter 3, by a division of labor among participants and by

[14] For example, see William Powers, *Behavior: The Control of Behavior,* Aldine, Chicago, 1973.

[15] George Herbert Mead, *Mind, Self, and Society,* ed. Charles Morris, The University of Chicago Press, Chicago, 1934, pp. 11–12.

[16] George Herbert Mead, "The Genesis of the Self and Social Control," in *Selected Writings: George Herbert Mead,* ed. Andrew J. Reck, Bobbs-Merrill, Indianapolis, 1964, p. 289.

[17] Shibutani, 1968a, p. 333.

the fact that the object of the act is not achieved in the behavior of any single individual, but in the collaborative process of the group. For Mead, social control brings the "act of the individual into relation with this social object." Mead meant by this that the action of the individual contributes to the achievement of the collective goal.

Mead recognized that social control could be achieved in different ways, and illustrated this possibility by contrasting social control of insect societies with that of human society. Mead argued that the distinctive form of social control that characterizes human group life was made possible by the evolutionary development of our complex central nervous system. This development has increased our capacity to analyze information sufficiently so that we can store in our memories not only our own objects and procedures for achieveing them, but also the objects and procedures of the others with whom we cooperate. In short, the social object, achieved in the activities of many individuals, becomes internalized and becomes the model which controls our individual behavior.

The anatomical detail of the central nervous system was too minute to allow direct examination of the process. Thus, the mechanism of social control, ideally defined in terms of nervous system function, was addressed behaviorally by Mead. He recognized that each of us does not internalize a model containing all of the complete, technical, specialized knowledge necessary to perform all parts of the social act. Rather, each of us has a sufficiently detailed model to allow us to recognize, anticipate, and call forth the appropriate components of the social act in ourselves and others.[18]

Concretely, to participate in a social act, such as getting dry cleaning done, we do not need to know how to perform all aspects of the dry cleaning process. Rather, we need to know how we must behave to enlist the cooperation of those who *do* know other aspects of the social act in detail. In the cybernetic terms we discussed before, the difference between the actual and desired state of our laundry is an object or goal that we can achieve only through cooperative social action. This discrepancy serves as the stimulus for a succession of actions—choosing a dry cleaning establishment, going to it, handing in the laundry, returning to retrieve it, paying for the service—that is modified as the "distance value" between the actual and desired states changes as a result of our ongoing action. In this process, we control our own behavior by anticipating the response of others to it and bring their behavior under the control of the same social object as our own. In a sense, we each bring the behavior of others under the control of our own goals.

The objects that control human conduct are not provided genetically in

[18] Mead, "Genesis of the Self."

the form of "instincts." They are learned through communication with others. Since human communication occurs in the context of social groups, human conduct must be explained in terms of the organized social group in which one participates. Society explains individual conduct, rather than individual conduct serving as an explanation and basis for society.[19] Thus, the process of social control is not fully understood until the communicative processes by which we internalize objects are specified.

Mead's work specifies only one such process. Through the imitative process of "play" the child learns to take up the role of each of the others with whom he or she interacts. Later, in the stage of development characterized by "games," the child abstracts the common elements of these various roles and synthesizes a "generalized other" from them. By taking the role of the generalized other, rather than a particular other, the child can define objects in his or her environment from the organized perspective of his or her group and anticipate the responses of others in the group. That is, the child is able to use the social act of all the others and its collective object as an object of his or her own conduct.

Perhaps the most important object defined by taking the position of the generalized other is the self, which is an organized synthesis of the reactions of the group to the individual in each of his or her roles within it. Through taking the role of the generalized other, one can respond to oneself as part of a group and anticipate how others in the group will respond to one. That is, one can see one as an object that acts and is acted upon in a given way.

To call forth the desired response from others requires another element. Each person must be able to indicate the nature of the object to which he or she wants others to respond. Defining the object is equivalent to defining one's goal or purpose. Even when events are perceivable, the purposes of others (their objects) may not be. Mead argues that human beings utilize gestures to accomplish this purpose. A gesture is a behavior which indicates to others the nature of objects in the environment, and thereby indicates the proper model for the control of behavior. Words are gestures in this sense. The word "eyesore" defines a different object for the control of behavior than the word "billboard," even when the two words are used to refer to the same physical reality.

Our ability to take the role of the generalized other makes it possible for humans to use a special form of gesture. By taking the role of the generalized other, we are able to anticipate how others will react to our gestures. That is, the gesture creates the same object for the individual using it as it does for others. That object is the social act, synthesized from the acts of the various participants. While each participant does not, and may not be able to, perform each component of the social act, the

[19] Mead, *Mind, Self, and Society,* p. 7.

entire act is defined by such gestures. This allows us not only to elicit a response from others by indicating an object or goal to them, but to share an understanding of that object with them. Mead called these gestures "significant symbols." [20]

MULTIPLE FORMS OF SOCIAL CONTROL

The cybernetic control of action by models of desirable objects remains a viable explanation of purposive human behavior. The use of social objects in the control of human conduct is supported by extensive behavioral evidence. Thus, the skeleton of Mead's position—that human conduct is controlled by organized perspectives learned in communication with others —is a sound basis for social psychological theorizing. Mead's more specific analysis is restricted, however, to a single kind of communication situation (interaction with the group of which one is a member) and to the kinds of objects that are constructed by such communicative activities (the generalized other and the self).

Mead recognized that overcoming the barriers of distance and time, of language and convention, and of social status would have a significant impact on the process of social control and that this was becoming possible in the modern world. He also recognized that conflict between groups affects the process of social control within them.[21] However, Mead died before the implications of changing modes of communication were realized and before he could work out further implications of his cybernetic model.

Shibutani has attempted to improve upon Mead's analysis by explicating the effects of different modes of communication upon social control. Each distinctive kind of communication network, in defining the propriety of subject matter, the form of presentation, and the audience, creates a different form of social control. The differences may lie in the nature of the objects constructed, in the boundaries of proper response, or both. Shibutani has focused on three forms of social control, and in the remainder of this chapter, we will discuss each: social control through reference groups; social control through the development of contrast conceptions; and social control through rumor.

Social Control Through Reference Groups

REFERENCE GROUPS AND THE "GENERALIZED OTHER"

In Mead's work, the generalized other provided the perspective from which the individual defined the objects in his or her environment. The "generalized other," or organized perspective, was conceived to be shared

---

[20] Mead, "Genesis of the Self."
[21] *Ibid.*, pp. 292–293.

by the members of the group, allowing each of them to organize their action with reference to common social objects. As Shibutani interprets this concept, the generalized other provides a stable perspective. Once incorporated by one, it serves as the perspective from which to define objects even when one is separated from the group and thus gives continuity to one's actions in the variety of situations one encounters. Shibutani is explicit in his view that the generalized other is a perspective that develops through communication in a social group in which one is a member.[22]

Shibutani defines the "reference group" as "*that group whose presumed perspective is used by an actor as the frame of reference in the organization of his perceptual field.*"[23] This definition does not limit reference groups by the actor's standing in them, nor by the type of communication networks through which the perspective is developed, nor by the accuracy with which the perspective is perceived. Thus, the generalized other can be conceived as one type of reference group, defined by the participation of the person in the group whose perspective he shares. Other kinds of reference groups may be "real or imagined, envied or despised." Even in those cases in which one adopts a perspective from a real group, the group may not be one to which one belongs or in which one participates. Thus "reference group" is a generic term for organized perspectives developed through communication of some kind with some group.

Defined in this way, the reference group concept would have more utility than the concept of the generalized other only if it were common for people to adopt the perspectives of groups in which they did not participate directly or which are imagined. As we observed in our discussion of communication in mass society, Shibutani believes that this *is* a common occurrence and defines the utility of the reference group concept on that basis. He points out that in mass societies people often develop their perspectives from groups in which they are not members and which may not, in fact, actually exist.[24] And the possibility of these occurrences is increased by the nature of modern communication.

An example will clarify how imaginary groups may serve as the basis for shared social perspectives. Insofar as we are sensitive to advertising we gain our definition of certain objects in the world from a fictional group, created for a specific purpose but similar to characters and groups in other types of fiction. The group of characters in commercials has many shared characteristics and values that transcend their separate obsessions with different products. Its members are relatively prosperous and generally attractive or, at least, interesting in appearance. They are oriented to material consumption and displays of prosperity. They are

[22] Shibutani, 1955, p. 565.
[23] Shibutani, 1962, p. 132.
[24] Shibutani, 1955, pp. 563–565.

generally concerned about appearance and responsive to products that enhance it. They are minutely and explicitly aware of the differences between products, the implications of a product for status and identity, and the role of particular products in helping satisfy their own needs and the needs of those around them. They are responsive to whatever new products or services become technologically possible (from deodorants to fabric softeners that also whiten to electrically operated car windows).

Any of us would probably take offense at the suggestion that we are overly affected by advertisements. Yet in many ways our personal values and perspectives are drawn from our contact with this group. To the extent that we wear clothes that this imaginary group defines as fashionable, we have adopted their perspective. To the extent that we share their views about how to care for our hair, how we shall smell, and so on, we have adopted their perspective.

Similarly, we respond to a variety of fictional or imaginary groups. (How many of us learn about law by watching the parade of fictional police, lawyers, criminals, and even cowboys on television?) Other imaginary groups, such as "posterity," leave us free to imagine that any view we hold will be shared by others who are significant to us. In short, through mass media our access to imaginary groups has greatly increased and has affected the development of our perspectives.

Mass media of communication may also allow sufficient contact with real groups and individuals for us to share their perspectives without further contact. For many years, information about the views and habits of politicians and statesmen have been available for use. Increasingly, however, mass media exposure has been extended to many kinds of people throughout the world—spokesmen for protest groups, subjects of human interest stories, sports figures, literary and entertainment celebrities, victims of personal and massive tragedies, victims of crimes, convicts, religious leaders, and so on. These people are all quite real and members of real groups. Technology has made communication with them possible, unhampered by distance or by absence of other forms of more direct contact. Mass communication media provide us with sufficient information to adopt the perspective of any of these groups and to utilize it in defining objects in our own environments. However, the paucity of information and our inability to confirm its accuracy through other channels may lead to faulty understanding of the perspectives expressed.

MULTIPLICITY OF PERSPECTIVES

Shared perspectives arise and are maintained through participation in communication channels. In modern societies, we observed, each person has access to many such channels. Each of his or her various role relationships defines a communication channel with a set of others. Further, the mass media, because they are shared and accessible, put each of us in partial contact with communication channels that would otherwise be unavailable to us. Our participation in these multiple channels of communication, each defining a reference group with its own organized perspective, makes it possible for us to internalize a variety of these perspectives.[25]

The internationalization of multiple perspectives from which to define objects creates additional complexities for social control. In any situation, one may have more than one way to define objects, each suggested by one's participation in a communication channel and one's sharing of its perspective. Thus, to understand behavior in a particular situation we need to know which reference group or perspective serves as the basis for the definition of the objects that control behavior.[26] In addition, one's choices may not be consistent—one may act from different perspectives in different situations. Thus, people's participation in multiple communication channels in modern societies suggest two additional problems for social control: the basis of choice among available perspectives in a given situation and the implications of inconsistency among these choices in various situations.

Sentiments as a basis of choice among perspectives. Before examining the connection between "sentiments" and the choice among available, internalized perspectives, we must clearly define this term. In common usage, a "sentiment" is usually regarded as a feeling, existing within a person's experience and uniquely available to him or her. In using the term "sentiments," Shibutani refers to a "stable relationship between individuals." The feeling or experience often regarded as the totality of the sentiment is regarded by Shibutani as a reflection of one person's definition of another. Like other definitions, the sentiment guides our conduct toward the other person, but it differs from other defining characteristics, such as the socially defined role, in an important respect. People assume many roles, and the definition and treatment of a person varies as the role and other defining characteristics change. The sentiment one feels for another, however, defines the other as a total, particular person. It guides our conduct in many situations, providing a stable orientation that transcends changes in role or immediate goals. Thus, sentiments toward a particular person will guide our conduct in ways that it will not be guided toward others in the same role relationship to us. The sentiment, then, provides a stable basis for conduct toward a particular person. That is, it defines a personal relationship between individuals.

[25] *Ibid.*
[26] Shibutani, 1962, p. 129.

This use of the term does not deny that people have feelings. Rather, it recognizes the complexity of the expression of sentiments and the difficulty of accurately determining others' sentiments. Another's sentiment cannot be identified by observing a single act, *including a single, direct, verbal report of one's feeling.* The sentiment can only be accurately identified by observing the configuration of multiple acts by the person toward the object. Through these multiple acts, the value placed on the object can be assessed.[27]

This restriction recognizes that one must define another person as an object that controls one's behavior each time one responds to that other. One person's sentiment toward another cannot be determined by observing any one action, but only by observing the pattern of actions in different circumstances, which taken together express the sentiment or value consistently placed on the other person. Thus, it is by acting toward a person as if he or she had certain characteristics and value that consistently control our action in a variety of situations that a sentiment is expressed.

Shibutani illustrates this procedure for understanding others' sentiments with the hypothetical problem of recognizing the love of a girl for a boy. One aspect of expressing love at young ages is heated denial of the sentiment. In itself, this behavior would indicate the absence of love. This graphically illustrates the importance of evaluating multiple actions in an attempt to infer the characteristics attributed to the person. The girl may blush when she accidently brushes against the boy. She ignores the attention paid her by other boys. She becomes irritable when another girl holds his attention. Here we must note that one's response to the relationship between two others may express our sentiments about either of them.[28]

In short, love is expressed and recognized in various responses to the beloved in different situations: in responses to his or her relationhips to others; in differences between the response to him or her and to others; and in the verbal expression of sentiments to third parties. Each of the expressive acts might be ambiguous in isolation. For example, the negative response to some boys may indicate distaste of them as well as love for another. But in each case, conduct is controlled by the definition of a person as an object with particular characteristics and values. The configuration of various instances of conduct define the characteristics of the person, our sentiments toward him or her.

Shibutani points out that conformity to group norms is often motivated by a desire for approval from the group. As we mentioned earlier, approval and other social sanctions are only valued when received from

[27] Shibutani, 1964, p. 147.
[28] *Ibid.,* p. 148.

particular individuals. Thus our sentiments, the values we place on other people or groups, determine the extent to which we will utilize their perspectives as our own, and the extent to which we will be controlled in our conduct by the objects and norms defined by the group's perspective. Sentiments, therefore, are crucial to social control.[29] The sentiment provides a link between identifying or defining others and identifying with them, orienting oneself to their perspectives (either positively or negatively).

Our primary concern is with situations in which the individual has internalized a variety of perspectives that suggest contradictory definitions of objects, and, therefore, of proper responses. This contradiction presents one with the need to choose among one's various reference groups before one can undertake action—a choice that may depend on one's higher degree of loyalty (a sentiment) to the members of a particular group.[30] Shibutani argues that when one cannot make up one's mind about the nature of events and one's proper response to them, the decision about which set of norms, which perspective, to assume, will be based largely on one's relative sentiments toward the people one associates with the alternative perspectives.[31] One's sentiments transform some others into "significant others," people whose perspectives are important to the framing of one's own. Negative sentiments may create significant others as well as positive ones. We may model our thinking in opposition to the perspective of a disliked person or group as well as in conformity to an admired one.

These sentiments may, of course, be either positive or negative in varying degrees. On the one hand, we observe soldiers in combat who prefer to risk death rather than have their comrades regard them as cowards. Their commitment to the shared perspective of the group is so great that they risk death rather than contradict the group's definition of the characteristics they ought to possess. On the other hand, the temptation to violate group norms may be reinforced by negative sentiments toward group members.[32]

We can now summarize the relationship between sentiments and the adoption of a group's perspective. If we think of sentiments in the non-technical, common usage as our "feelings" toward others, a simple proposition emerges: we will more readily adopt the perspective of a group for which we have positive sentiments than the perspective of a group for which we have negative sentiments, even when the group's perspective requires us to make great personal sacrifices. However, single acts are

[29] Shibutani, 1971, p. 149.
[30] Shibutani, 1955, p. 568.
[31] Shibutani, 1964, p. 152.
[32] *Ibid.*, pp. 152–153.

often misleading evidence about sentiments. We must recognize that judgments of sentiments are unreliable unless they are based on observation of a configuration of responses in varying situations. Thus, to utilize this proposition to understand and predict human behavior we must have extensive evidence to support our assessment of sentiments.

Inconsistency in the choice of reference groups. Participation in multiple reference groups implies that a person may utilize the perspective of different groups on different occasions. As the different perspectives are adopted, events are redefined and behavior is controlled by different objects. People become aware of these differences in outlook only when they are caught in a situation in which conflicting demands are made upon them and some difficult decision must be made. For the most part, people in complex societies lead compartmentalized lives. They change from one perspective to another in response to the contingencies of the various situations they encounter.[33]

Whether these changes in perspective are recognized, or whether our ability to keep the parts of our lives separate conceals them from us, one implication remains: since one's self is defined by the organized attitude of one's group toward one, one's self becomes inconsistent, or disintegrated. As one responds from the perspective of each reference group, one's own characteristics change along with the characteristics of other objects in the environment. Each group will define the person according to the behavior they observe, so that a person may have different selves in different groups. At the same time, one will define oneself differently from each perspective—behaving toward oneself in the appropriate way for the perspective one is employing. In this sense, the self-concept is a way of acting toward oneself as an object of a particular kind, a person with particular characteristics.[34]

It is clear that the self is expressed in behavior and evaluated by others in essentially the same way as sentiments. A person exhibits his self-concept by acting towards him- or herself as if he or she had certain characteristics—by demanding certain treatment from others, by relating to objects in certain ways, by responding to certain sanctions, by maintaining certain levels of demeanor, and so forth. Others define one's self from these same actions and treat one accordingly. If one frequently changes the perspective that controls one's action, others, who perceive only part of one's actions, may hold different opinions of one's characteristics, different definitions of one's self. If, in addition, one is observed by particular others when acting from different perspectives, they may evaluate one

[33] Shibutani, 1962, p. 139.
[34] Shibutani, 1961, p. 227.

as inconsistent, as not having a coherent self. If, in addition, one becomes aware of the inconsistencies in one's own behavior, one's own self-concept may also become inconsistent; in effect, one may lose the sense that one is a coherent person with stable characteristics. The degree of consistency among observers concerning a person's characteristics, single observers' estimates of the degree of a person's consistency, and the degree of the sense of one's own consistency, or self-concept, all vary.[35]

An example should help to clarify this point. Consider an attorney who earns his or her living practicing law for corporate clients and donates time and legal services to indigent clients. As a corporate employee and as a lawyer with a client, he or she is held responsible by relatively inflexible norms to advocate the position of the client as strenuously and competently as he or she can, independent of his or her own sentiments. The corporate clients will call upon the attorney to design standardized contracts, to influence the courts' interpretation of the law, and perhaps to influence legislators to write laws that benefit those corporations. The corporation's gain may be the loss of the indigent. For example, a request for a zoning variance to allow commercial development in a poor residential neighborhood pits corporate interests against those of the indigent. While he or she cannot be involved in both sides of the same case (another relatively inflexible norm), the lawyer who divides his or her activities in this way will display different self-characteristics in his or her different professional activities, though in each case he or she will be acting from the perspective of a client who serves as the reference group for the case.

If the lawyer segregates his or her activities so that each type of client perceives only activities consistent with the client's perspective, each client may evaluate the lawyer differently, but each will feel that the lawyer is a consistent person with clearly defined characteristics. If, however, the different types of clients are able to observe the lawyer's activities with other types of clients as well as with themselves, they will regard his or her behavior as inconsistent. If the attorney becomes aware of the different self-defining effects of his or her different activities, he or she too will possibly begin to regard him- or herself as inconsistent.

In mass societies, characterized by the frequent occurrence of this incoherence of selves, the individual person sustains an integrated character by virtue of his or he unique personality. Shibutani argues that a unique and relatively stable set of personal values underlies the variety of perspectives we assume and the activities we perform.[36] These values are our personal preferences (sentiments) and may not be exhibited by our action in particular situations. They can be inferred from the con-

---

[35] *Ibid.*, p. 231.
[36] *Ibid.*, pp. 287–288.

figuration of our actions, however, even though many of our actions will contradict our preferences. For example, the voluntary character of the lawyer's association with indigent clients may lead us to infer that this work represents a personal preference. At the same time, the lawyer's corporate work may indicate a value on financial measures of success. This complex of personal values, or personality, can be inferred from the configuration of behaviors, although it may be submerged or contradicted in some of them.

Another effect of social control based on multiple reference groups is to reduce the occasions when our personal values are in accord with the organized perspective which we must adopt. If we had only one perspective (the situation discussed by Mead) our personal preferences and the perspectives of our group would be the same—our personalities and our socially derived perspectives would be in harmony. But in mass society, the multiplicity of conflicting perspectives reduces this harmony in various degrees. Thus, the personality of a person may not be an accurate indication of what he or she will do in a given situation. It is an accurate indication of what the person *would do* if he or she were given the opportunity to act in relative freedom from social constraints.[37]

Thus the multiplicity of perspectives and the inconsistency of choices among them that is necessitated by the conditions of mass society tend to alienate our action from our personal preferences. The personality exists, but it will frequently be less important in guiding our behavior than the shared perspectives of groups with whom we must cooperate. The personality can be inferred, a person's own values and preferences estimated, by considering the configuration of his or her actions in various situations. When one has discretion in one's actions, the direction of that discretion is an indication of personal preference. Consistent use of discretion in the same direction indicates a person's values or sentiments. Also, in situations that are relatively free from social constraints action may be controlled by, and indicative of, personal values. Personal values, once learned in this way, explain action in similar situations. In other situations, the persistence of personal values may explain the feelings of alienation or incoherence that are common in mass society.

In many ways, this conception of the relationship between individual preferences or impulses is similar to that proposed in psychoanalytic theory. In both views, action springs from impulses which can be satisfied in a variety of ways and which, ultimately, are biologically based. Also in both views social norms may block the immediate and direct satisfaction of impulses, requiring people to develop new means that are socially acceptable or to frustrate the impulse.

[37] *Ibid.,* pp. 318–319.

However, in relating personality to the discretion allowed by social norms, Shibutani has suggested an important modification of the psychoanalytic approach. The psychoanalytic tradition is clinical and mentalistic, being concerned primarily with the psychic organization of the troubled individual. In analyzing personality, it uses personal imagery based on verbal reports of dreams, experiences, wishes, and projective tests. In addition, behavior patterns that are abnormal enough to be regarded as symptoms are analyzed closely for their symbolic content. Patterns of forgetfulness, slips of the tongue, psychosomatic or hysterical symptoms, and fears that are so unreasonable that they suggest that the "real" feared object is being symbolically disguised are examples. Although the personality is still treated as an organization of impulses in Shibutani's presentation, it is expressed in terms of normal, unregulated behavior. Personality has a behavioral and normal rather than clinical and mentalistic cast.

Personality characteristics refer ultimately, in this view, to consistencies in behavior that are observed in the use of discretion. Thus, personality traits, like sentiments, become more concrete—they are defined directly in terms of behavior rather than in terms of personal symbolism. For example, generosity does not refer to a state of mind, but to a pattern of consistently offering more than the socially required amount of time, effort, or materials in a variety of situations. Abnormal behavior can also be defined behaviorally, as a pattern of exceeding the socially prescribed limits of discretion.

Knowledge of a person's personality becomes a powerful tool in understanding individual behavior in detail without resorting to mentalistic approaches. Considered alone it does not predict action well for too many impulses are blocked or diverted. However it predicts the use of discretion, adding greatly to the accuracy and detail of our understanding of that phenomenon. (In Chapter 12, we will discuss how knowledge of the appropriate social norms is used to recognize discretionary behavior.)

IMPORTANCE OF THE CONCEPT "REFERENCE GROUP"

"Reference group" is a generic term for any social group whose perspective controls an individual's action. In a sense, we could regard all social control as involving reference groups of different kinds. The utility of the concept lies chiefly in its applicability to the multiple and contradictory communication networks in which people in mass societies become involved. Each communication channel may lead to the internalization of an organized perspective. Confronted with particular situations, one must select an appropriate perspective from which to define objects. This may be done on the basis of one's sentiments for the members of one's various reference groups. This way of conceiving social control allows us to explain the many inconsistencies of behavior in mass society and, given sufficient information about sentiments, to predict which perspective a person will select and how he or she will behave. The constraints on choice imposed by the need to cooperate and by the multiple norms governing behavior in particular situations imply varying degrees of alienation between one's preferences and actions. This is a consequence of social control under the circumstances imposed by mass societies.

Social Control Through Contrast Conceptions

A "contrast conception" is a negative and stereotyped perception of the members of a social group with whom one's own group is in conflict. The contrast conception is a defined object that controls one's behavior toward members of the opposing group through the same cybernetic process that applies to other objects. The contrast conception is a distinctive basis for social control in two important ways. First, the social situation in which the contrast conception is formed—intergroup conflict—includes extreme limitations on the content and channels of communication that are permitted. In a sense, when contrast conceptions develop, the purpose of communication and perception are altered. Ideas are not tested against events and corrected when they prove erroneous; information is controlled to *support* whatever perceptions exist in the group. Second, the contrast conception tends to become increasingly severe; as conflict continues, it is used to justify harsh, often brutal, treatment of members of the opposing group. Thus, social control of action by contrast conceptions is characterized by distinctive limitations of the communication process within the group and by the emergence of brutal treatment of humans who are not members of one's own social group.

Shibutani points out that individual human actions can be interpreted in many ways.[38] This is a consequence of the fact that sentiments and values are not exhibited in single actions, but only in the configuration of many separate and different acts. Since we are unable to observe the many activities of an individual, those activities that *can* be observed must be utilized to make judgments, even though they are inadequate data. Thus, reasonable people, making reasonable inferences, may disagree about the meaning of the observed conduct of others.

Frequently, people are unsure of how to define the behavior of others, and, at the same time, forced to come to some definition of it. This dilemma is resolved by utilizing a simplified perspective that limits the

[38] Shibutani, 1973, p. 225.

range of plausible interpretations. (Shibutani is careful to distinguish between the plausibility of an interpretation and its truth. The truth may not be found among the interpretations believed to be plausible.)[39] Utilizing such a perspective, evidence is selected that is in accord with our expectations. Remaining ambiguities are resolved by assuming that the correct choice is the one that best fits our expectations. Contrary evidence can be recognized and can serve as the basis for revising our perspectives, but the perspective resists revision, to some extent, by imposing standards of plausibility that interfere with the evaluation, or even recognition, of contrary information. The boundaries of plausibility are part of the organized perspective of the group and are necessary to insure effective social control.

In conflict situations as the boundaries of plausibility or stereotypes are altered to form contrast conceptions, negative consequences emerge. The stereotype, or plausible interpretation of the enemy's conduct, becomes increasingly restricted to "foul motives." Every activity of the enemy tends to be interpreted in as negative a manner as possible. With each negative interpretation we provide ourselves with another instance of the enemy's evil character. If the conflict is prolonged, we define the enemy in an increasingly negative way and the contrast between our conceptions of the enemy and ourselves becomes increasingly stark and rigid.

The conditions imposed on communication during intergroup conflict contribute to this process. First, differences among those in one's own group are temporarily disregarded as the group unites against a common enemy. This creates a tendency to interpret the acts of members of one's own group in an unusually positive way. Continuing positive interpretations generate an idealized interpretation of the group and its members. This process occurs at the same time as an increasingly negative definition of the opposing group is developing, and the concurrence of the two processes maximizes the contrast between the perceptions of the two groups. Members of the two groups are defined as increasingly unlike each other —one group as increasingly good, the other as increasingly evil—as the conflict continues.

Second, any information originating from the enemy group comes to be regarded as propaganda. Even the attempt to communicate is interpreted negatively, independent of the content of the message. Thus, whenever possible, information from the enemy is censored so that it cannot have its pernicious effect on the population. If the information cannot be censored, it is still discredited as false or as part of some evil design.

[39] Shibutani, 1966, p. 7.

Finally, information that is inconsistent with the prevailing contrast conception may be discredited, even if it originates within one's own group. Certain content comes to be distrusted, as well as certain sources. This further limits the possibility of receiving information that might challenge and modify the contrast conception. The source of such contrary news may also be discredited—in the extreme case, regarded as a traitor to his or her group.

All of these processes contribute to the views that the enemy is both extremely evil, an embodiment of the worst characteristics our culture can define, and that he or she is strikingly different from one's own group, which has been idealized. Ultimately, if the contrast becomes sufficiently extreme, the enemy may be defined as literally "less than human." This qualitative change in our perception of other people is accompanied by a change in the morality that is appropriate for dealing with them. An inhuman enemy can be treated in ways that no human enemy could be. Aside from its manifest horrors, this mutual inhuman treatment provides further proof to each side that the enemy is, indeed, inhuman. This justifies further atrocities on each side, which provide further evidence of inhumanity, and so forth. The atrocities that occur when contrast conceptions control behavior provide support to the processes that are necessary for contrast conceptions to develop and be maintained.

The self-reinforcing character of contrast conceptions and the behavior associated with them may result in this type of social control continuing after the desire for conflict or even the conflict itself has ended. It is difficult to adopt a stance of reconciliation or negotiation toward a dehumanized enemy. Those members of each group who expressed less extreme views are also likely to have been discredited within their own group and considered unsuitable as its representatives. Even mutually desirable outcomes are difficult to achieve because there is insufficient trust in those who propose them.

The revision of contrast conceptions, then, requires a realignment of trust and opening of communication channels, both in terms of content and in terms of who may use them credibly. This process may be aided by defeat, especially if the group has become disillusioned with its leaders and is willing or eager to find new ones unassociated with the prior policies. Sometimes the situation of the antagonistic groups may change so that former adversaries must work together in some common endeavor. The communication necessary to common efforts helps to overcome the contrast conception. Often, however, the conflicting groups are beyond direct communication and third parties must act as mediators.[40]

It is likely that this process is associated in all our minds with the acts

---

[40] Shibutani, 1973, pp. 225–232.

of people in nations at war. Certainly wartime provides many illustrations of the formation and consequences of contrast conceptions. However, contrast conceptions are the basis for social control in other situations as well; they may be maintained against one group within a community by another group within the same community, and based on any characteristic that could serve to differentiate them, real or imagined.

The development of contrast conceptions by conflicting groups within a community is characteristic of the way in which ethnic or racial distinctions are developed and maintained. Shibutani points out that the scientific categories of race are merely categories for convenience of reference. No clear lines of demarcation can be drawn between the races. The actual, measurable genetic differences between humans are often irrelevant to daily life. However, the differences that are *believed* to exist, independent of the truth of the beliefs, are often crucial. The belief in the importance of hereditary ties is a strong, mystical one that has survived the evidence that cultural characteristics are unrelated to heredity.[41]

The ethnic categories used in daily life are more clearly defined than those that are used in making scientific distinctions. In addition, racial categories are considered to have great explanatory power and many behavioral patterns are attributed to them. These racial categories are developed within patterns of communication that reify the categories, providing people with a sense of social identity based on their own ethnic background and a sense that members of other ethnic groups are alien. Once these ethnic boundaries have developed, norms emerge which restrict communication between groups and encourage solidarity within them. These norms may also control the occupations of members of different groups, patterns of friendship, and the suitability of marriage between groups.[42]

If conflict occurs between such groups, the racial or ethnic categories may become the basis for contrast conceptions. Members of the other race come to be regarded as less than human, as embodying the negative characteristics of the culture. The fullness of the analogy between this form of intergroup conflict and political conflict between nations can, perhaps, best be exemplified by the existence of "traitors" in ethnic conflict—in our country, the "nigger lover" and the "Uncle Tom" or "Oreo cookie." (There are no polite words to describe traitors.)

Shibutani argues that the treatment of the black person in the United States and in South Africa, of the Jew in Nazi Germany, and the long-lasting enmity between Jews and Moslems in the Middle East are ex-

---

[41] Shibutani, 1965, pp. 39–41.
[42] *Ibid.,* p. 223.

amples of social control by variously severe and rigid contrast conceptions.[43]

Contrast conceptions exist along a continuum of severity and the severity of the conduct they permit. In the extreme cases, such as when nations are at war or racial antagonisms result in policies such as apartheid or slavery, the opposing group is regarded as clearly less than human, and treated as such. Atrocities occur. In less severe cases the opposing group may be perceived as "different" and only mildly distasteful or inferior. Discrimination in various degrees accompany such contrast conceptions and are a common part of our everyday life.

In the definition of the problem lies the definition of the solution; namely, the solution demands changes in the comunication patterns that result in such perspectives. This solution is suggested by both Mead[44] and Shibutani.[45] Both men argue that increased communication through more open channels would inevitably result in the development of shared perspectives.

Social Control Through Rumor

COMMUNICATION PROCESSES PRODUCING RUMORS:
RUMOR AS AN ONGOING SOCIAL ACT

Laboratory studies of rumor. In common usage, a "rumor" is considered to be a story or report circulated orally among a group of people. In addition, a rumor is usually differentiated from other forms of information by its actual or suspected falsity.[46] Most studies of rumor have proceeded from that definition. The spreading of a rumor was characterized as the unsuccessful attempt to repeat, without alteration, the specific content of a story or report. Rumors were thought to be false, or at least suspect, because people were thought to be unable to accurately repeat what they had been told.

This definition of the rumor and the mode of its transmission made it possible to study rumors in the laboratory. An experimental subject could be given visual or oral information by the experimenter. The subject could be instructed to transmit the information orally to a second, who was instructed to transmit it to a third, and so on. The experimenters could observe the process in detail and study the content of the rumor at each step in its transmission.

The results of such studies have been consistent and unambiguous. Many of the results have been summarized by Allport and Postman in

43 *Ibid.,* pp. 383–389.
44 Mead, "Genesis of the Self," pp. 292–293.
45 Shibutani, 1965, p. 589.
46 Shibutani, 1966, p. 3.

terms of three concepts.[47] The content of rumors becomes increasingly "leveled" as it is transmitted serially from one person to another; it becomes more concise and shorter. Rumors are "sharpened." The selection of significant details becomes more pronounced with successive repetition. Finally, rumors become "assimilated." The content becomes more coherently organized and more consistent with the presuppositions of the experimental subjects.[48] The experimental facts are clear: the attempt to serially transmit a rumor, to repeat its content, consistently results in alterations in that content.

The relevance of these results to events outside the laboratory depends upon the resemblance of the laboratory task to the social situations in which rumors occur naturally. Shibutani has studied a wide variety of rumors that occurred spontaneously in a variety of natural settings and he concludes that the experimental situation we have described does *not* resemble the situations in which rumors occur naturally.

Differences in the impetus for rumors. Shibutani's studies have led him to regard rumors as a distinctive pattern of communication that develops in ambiguous situations. That pattern of communication is different from the attempt to achieve rote transmission of specific contents in a number of ways. Rumors do not develop in an attempt to disseminate a predefined message orally. Rather, the development of rumors is a collaborative effort to respond to ambiguity by developing a collective definition of the situation. The definition of a previously ambiguous situation, of course, has the value of providing objects that may serve as models for the control of behavior in response to the situation.

The content of the rumor is, in a sense, never complete and never defined in a single communication. The achievement of a satisfactory definition of the situation is the end result of the rumor process, existing not in one person's report, but in the organized perspective that the group forms in response to ambiguity. The content that is often specified as "the rumor" is usually a shorthand summary of the general sense of many different statements.[49] This content is the definition of objects from the organized perspective of the group in which the rumor occurs and it does not exist when the rumor process begins, but is rather the result of the rumor process. Technically, the development of the rumor is controlled by the difference between the existing and desired levels of ambiguity. The development of a suitable definition of the situation is one means that can reduce that difference. This is fundamentally different from the

---

[47] Gordon Allport and Leo Postman, *The Psychology of Rumor,* Henry Holt, New York, 1945.
[48] Shibutani, 1966, pp. 3–9.
[49] *Ibid.,* pp. 16–17.

laboratory situation in which the rumor *begins* with an unambiguous content.

Motivational differences. The fact that naturally occurring rumors originate in ambiguity while laboratory rumors originate in clarity suggests that participants in the two settings may be motivated to different ends. In the laboratory, each participant is *told* to try to repeat some specific content as accurately as possible. These instructions define the object controlling his or her behavior. In naturally occurring rumors, one is motivated to reduce ambiguity for oneself and for others. Thus, one's controlling interests do not require that one repeat everything that one is told. Rather, one can be expected to select only the plausible, relevant information for one's own use and for repetition.

While the reduction of ambiguity is the general purpose in the development of rumors in natural settings, the participants in the process may have different practical interests. Various interests may result in varying standards for judging the relevance and adequacy of the information that is available. These differences should be reflected in which information a participant will share, with whom, and when each participant will feel sufficiently informed to begin acting on the available information.

Those involved in developing a definition of the situation may lose interest in concert or may cease participating in the collective defining effort at various times. The sudden cessation of interest in a topic throughout an entire group is illustrated by Shibutani with reference to a rumor developed among infantrymen undergoing basic training during World War Two. Early in the training cycle, which was scheduled to last seventeen weeks, the German army began an advance which suggested that the need for reinforcements was increased and immediate. A variety of clues led to rumors that the group's training period or post-training furlough or both would be shortened. Evidence included reports that other training groups had already undergone this curtailment of their training or furloughs. Many reports were regarded as incredible because the full training period, or one close to completion, was necessary to adequately train infantrymen. The German advance was halted while training was still in progress, and interest in the subject faded quickly in the group.[50]

In other situations, participants may have different standards for the adequacy and relevance of information. Consider the common situation in which many people are interested in the outcome of a particular athletic event, but do not have immediate access to radios or other sources of official information. This situation can be observed in work settings dur-

[50] *Ibid.,* pp. 10–13.

ing major athletic events. Many people are merely interested in the results of these contests. Others may be very interested in the exact score. Many wagers are based on a "point spread" or handicap, and simply knowing which team won would not necessarily be sufficient to determine the outcome of one's wager. In such a situation, some people could be expected to be unconcerned and imprecise about exact scores and satisfied with knowledge of which team won. Others would be extremely interested in the precise score and unsatisfied until they were reasonably sure that they knew those facts accurately. Thus different people would request, remember, and repeat different information, and would become satisfied with different amounts of available information.

The motivation of subjects in laboratory studies of rumor, then, differs from that of contributors to naturally occurring rumors in several ways. First, the general orientation of participants in naturally occurring rumors is to collectively create unambiguous information, rather than to preserve and repeat information that is already clear. Second, while laboratory subjects are instructed to maintain uniform standards of accuracy, participants in naturally occurring rumors may have different standards for the adequacy and relevance of information. These differences reflect the differences in their practical concerns. Thus, the problem confronting those involved in a naturally occurring rumor is to develop a jointly satisfactory definition of an ambiguous situation despite a diversity of motives.[51]

Differences in the restrictions on communication. In the laboratory task, all communication is dyadic and each participant is allowed one, and only one, uninterrupted recitation of information to one other person. There is no dialogue, no chance to clarify ambiguity through questioning or other means, and no chance for a person to participate repeatedly.

These restrictions do no obtain in natural settings. The speech of any interactant may be interrupted by others, as it is in any situation. Information may be challenged, sources questioned, clarifications requested, and so on, by those with whom each person talks. Information may be shared in gatherings of different sizes and many, or all, of the participants may contribute information. Thus, the version of the content in each small group may never be stated by any one person, but exist instead as a synthesis of the group's discussion. Finally, each participant is not restricted to one contribution: he or she can speak more than once in a particular interaction, and he or she can participate in more than one interaction. The mode of communication that exists within the laboratory does not resemble the patterns of communication that occur without it.

[51] *Ibid.,* p. 15.

A reconceptualization of the rumor. Taken together, these differences between the laboratory task and naturally occurring rumors suggest that a different definition of rumor is necessary as a starting point for research. Shibutani has suggested that the rumor is not a particular report or story that is transmitted. Instead, he regards a rumor as a distinctive mode of communication. "Rumor" is a collective transaction, in which different participants make different contributions to achieve a joint definition of an ambiguous situation. The final content is a collective product, found not in the explicit statement of any one individual but in a synthesis of statements made throughout the group.[52] Rumors, then, should not be regarded merely as content, but as communicative efforts to reduce ambiguity.

Thus a rumor is a form of social action, involving a division of labor among participants and a product that is not found in the contribution of any individual but in the collaborative efforts of the group. The final content is a collective definition of a previously ambiguous situation. These definitions, because they are social objects, serve as a basis for social control. Interestingly, the rumor itself is socially controlled action. Reduction of ambiguity is a goal which can cybernetically control behavior through the changing difference between the existing and desired degree of certainty about the environment.

PUBLICS AND NEWS

Singly and collectively, people respond to the world in terms of their organized perception of it. So long as the environment remains unchanged, existing information and definitions of objects remain adequate to control action. However, an unanticipated change in the environment requires a redefinition of objects so that behavior can be adoped to the new circumstances. "News" is information that is relevant to redefining an environment which is perceived to have changed. Since the changes in the environment may be more or less disruptive or established definitions and routines, news may be more or less urgently needed. In modern society, characterized by ambiguity and by a multiplicity of often conflicting sources of information, accurate news has become extremely valuable.[53]

All information is not news. Information is news only if it is helpful in the reduction of ambiguity caused by unanticipated events. Newsworthiness is a characteristic of information that is relative to practical interests and existing information. If an event does not contradict existing perceptions, information about it will not be regarded as news. If an

[52] *Ibid.,* pp. 13–16.
[53] *Ibid.,* p. 40.

event does not disrupt existing routines of behavior, information about it will not be regarded as news. Existing information and practical interests vary from group to group, and within each group from person to person.

Information about an event will be regarded as news by some people but not by others. Those people who perceive that they will be affected by an event and are sufficiently interested in it to seek news so that they can more fully define and control it are called a "public." A public is defined only by the common interest of its members in the consequences of an event, and its members may have no other shared affiliation.[54] For example, a group of co-workers who enjoy, seek, and repeat office gossip are a public for that gossip. Others who are not interested in the gossip are not part of the public, although they may work alongside its members, be discussed by them, and share other relationships with them.

Each person will be a comember of many publics with those in his or her important reference groups. This is guaranteed by the common perspective of reference group members. At the same time, each person will be involved in publics that do not include others from those reference groups. Membership in publics is not restricted by our social role relationships either. We are simultaneously in as many publics as there are events about which we seek news. While the membership of these various publics may overlap considerably, each is a separate entity.

INSTITUTIONAL AND AUXILIARY CHANNELS AS SOURCES OF NEWS

Publics vary with respect to the nature of other relationships in which their members are involved. Thus, they also vary with respect to the nature and degree of formalization of communication networks that already exist among their members. For example, if we are co-members of a public with members of our important reference groups, the established patterns of communication of those reference groups may serve to structure our communication within the public as well. Concretely, one's communication concerning the event that defines the public may be governed by the perspective of one's reference group. On other occasions, people may find that they share no, or very few, other social bonds with their co-members in a public. They have no pre-existing relationships with others with whom they share an interest in some event. In that event, there will be little initial structure to the communication network available within the public. The utility of recognizing the public as a distinct type of group lies largely in the fact that communication channels can develop within a public, even when other types of social relationship are not present.

[54] *Ibid.*, pp. 37–38.

The stable, well-regulated communication channels that develop in and maintain social relationships are called "institutional channels." The use of these channels is governed by well-defined norms concerning the propriety of subject matter, communication between different types of people, standards of evidence, and form of address. Within institutional channels, accountability for the information one contributes is well established. This tends to reduce irresponsibility and the effects of personal preference in communication and to make these channels relatively reliable. Institutional channels are used by members of a public, but publics are often too short lived to develop and maintain them.

While institutional channels may prove adequate with regard to any particular topic, they are always supplemented by "auxiliary channels." The roles governing communication in these auxiliary channels are not clearly fixed. Responsibility for one's accuracy and the propriety of one's contribution is less formally defined than in institutional channels. However, each participant has a personal stake whenever he or she participates. Auxiliary channels may become partially routinized and governed by shared understandings, but to a lesser extent than institutional channels.

For instance, the officially designated information desk in a department store is the major institutional channel available to the customer. The attendant not only provides information about such matters as prices, refund policies, and the location of items in the store, but also directs customers to the official sources of information they cannot provide, for example, the availability of jobs. A common auxiliary channel of information in department stores is to approach any employee with one's question. This procedure is more informal and the chances of receiving no or inaccurate information are increased. However, unofficial but desirable advice about products may be obtained in this fashion, or bureaucratic shortcuts may be suggested, or the need to stand in line may be averted. As this example illustrates the unofficial and official channels have their own virtues and shortcomings.

The circulation of news in auxiliary channels of communication is called "rumor." Relative to the circulation of news through institutional channels, it is governed by relatively relaxed rules. Whenever possible, the news circulated in auxiliary channels, which are supplementary by nature, will be checked for accuracy against the news circulated in institutional channels.[55]

The demand for news within a public will vary with the perceived importance of the ambiguous events. At least in theory, this demand is a variable that can be measured, although no precise indicator is now available. Similarly, the amount of news available in institutional chan-

---

[55] *Ibid.,* pp. 21–23.

nels about the event could be measured. Rumors are likely to occur, that is auxiliary channels of communication are likely to be employed, when the demand for news on a topic exceeds the supply of news available through institutional channels.[56]

Auxiliary channels are clearly supplementary. They are utilized only when a public is not satisfied by the news available in institutional channels. While auxiliary channels are less formalized than institutional ones, they vary in the degree to which normal cultural standards of accuracy and propriety in communication are maintained. The purely supplementary use of auxiliary channels implies that rumors, developed under more relaxed understandings concerning communication, are less desirable as news than that found in institutional channels.

Several apparently diverse conditions may lead to a discrepancy between the demand for news and the supply made available through institutional channels. First, the public may be so heterogeneous that there is little consensus concerning the proper modes of communication. In such cases communication channels may develop ad hoc. This situation characterizes crowds with a common focus of attention such as a fire. Second, information channels are often shared by a variety of groups and the interest in an issue may be insufficiently broad to be included in the shared communication channels. Third, an event may disrupt the communication networks that would ordinarily have provided information. Natural disasters or wartime destruction lead to this situation. Rumors develop in all of these cases, where news conveyed by the usual, socially regulated channels is inadequate and auxiliary sources of news are employed even though they are considered less reliable.

THE RUMOR CONTINUUM: FROM DELIBERATION TO EXTEMPORANEOUS EXCHANGE

The degree of the discrepancy between the demand for news and the supply of it in institutional channels is a crucial variable in the rumor process. As the discrepancy becomes greater, the deviation from normal cultural standards for evaluating news also becomes greater. And such discrepancy is the condition for the type of social action we call constructing a rumor. As this discrepancy becomes larger, the social act becomes more drastic in its efforts to correct the discrepancy and the usual standards that govern our communicative activity become increasingly disregarded. Shibutani defines this continuum in terms of two polar types of rumor: "deliberative" and "extempory." The characteristics of rumors vary between these extremes.

[56] *Ibid.*, p. 57.

Deliberative rumors. If the discrepancy between the demand for news and the supply in institutional channels is not great, the use of auxiliary channels is deliberative. People maintain relatively normal standards of plausibility, refusing to believe reports that contradict cultural expectation. Contacts among members of the public are repeated, providing the opportunity to evaluate sources of information. People whose contributions to the collective supply of news proves to be unreliable are more or less ignored in subsequent contacts. As this information about sources becomes known, the auxiliary channels become increasingly reliable. Reputations for reliability are built and the public develops a degree of structure, based on the relative reliability of its members. The normal cultural standards of plausibility become increasingly important during the process.[57]

Deliberative rumors are an extremely common mechanism for gathering information. Because they are generally reliable and there is little concern for their accuracy, they are generally not recognized as rumors at all. Shibutani suggests that most of the information on which we base decisions in daily life is gathered through the use of auxiliary channels from deliberative rumors, and that most rumors are of the deliberative type.[58] When the membership in publics overlaps, as it does, for example, among people who work together and are therefore often concerned with the same events, the reliability of sources is remembered after a public dissolves. When auxiliary channels are again employed, these reputations provide a degree of existing structure for a new topic. Almost all of our daily conversation is participation in deliberative rumor construction. The objects defined through such efforts are obviously adequate for social control in most circumstances.

Extemporaneous rumors. Occasionally, the unsatisfied demand for news is both urgent and lasting. This is especially likely to occur when events are drastic and the normal channels of communication are disrupted, such as wartime or disasters. In such circumstances, the news that is available to help define the new situation may be inadequate; ideas that would normally be dismissed as incredible become acceptable because they are the only ones available. The development of rumors may introduce drastically new ideas—ideas that may be inconceivable by normally accepted cultural standards.

The crucial mechanism in the development of these extemporaneous rumors is collective tension or excitement, generated by the unsatisfied demand for news. This tension produces important changes in the patterns

[57] *Ibid.*, pp. 74–77.
[58] *Ibid.*, p. 94.

of communication that are employed. First, spontaneous interchanges may occur between individuals who would not interact under normal circumstances. Second, attention may become so focused on the main topic that self-consciousness is lessened or eliminated. Evaluation of ideas within our organized perspectives is disrupted and the new information is accepted less critically. Ideas that would have seemed implausible from any existing perspective may now seem plausible. If the demand for news remains severe, people may relax the standards by which they evaluate sources. People who would ordinarily be regarded as unreliable are treated as credible sources. In extreme cases virtually no criteria for plausibility remain and any information is accepted.[59]

In these cases, definitions of situations may be accepted that are bizarre by normal standards. Kenya in the early 1950s was the scene of a native African rebellion against the colonial government that became known as the Mau Mau uprising. During the entire emergency period only 32 Europeans were killed by the terrorists in contrast to 1,826 Africans who cooperated with the government and were regarded by the Mau Maus as "stooges." During the period of the terrorist attacks rumors emerged about the nature of the terrorist activities. The terrorists were said to invariably split open the stomachs of pregnant women. They were believed to take a series of oaths of loyalty, each involving some disgusting ritual—drinking from a concoction made of such ingredients as putrefying human flesh, the warm brains of murder victims, or the products of menstruation or masturbation. Copulation with a variety of animals was believed to be part of the initiation ceremony.[60] Thus the terror produced by guerilla activities, combined with the secrecy of the rebel group resulted in the development of a contrast conception of the terrorists. The contrast conception, with its ascription of inhuman activities, stands as an example of the bizarreness of beliefs that may be held during crisis periods.

It is crucial to recognize, however, that this is not a breakdown of social control or of communication. Rather, it is the result of temporary changes in people's standards.[61] The process of social control that operates during the construction of even the most bizarre extemporaneous rumors is the same as that which operates during the construction of the deliberative rumors through which we gather most of the information upon which we base our routine actions. The difference between the two types of rumor is that the unsatisfied demand for news varies. We are forced to utilize and act upon whatever news is available. Faced with inadequate news in

---

[59] *Ibid.,* pp. 96–102.
[60] *Ibid.,* pp. 52–55.
[61] *Ibid.,* p. 114.

institutional channels, people resort to less formal auxiliary channels for information. As the unsatisfied demands for news increases, the standards governing communication in the auxiliary channels are increasingly relaxed. As a result, increasingly bizarre ideas, by usual standards, are accepted. But if these bizarre ideas were not accepted, if we retained our normal standards when the supply of information was severely inadequate, the situation would remain ambiguous and no action could be taken.

Conclusion

Shibutani's contributions to sociology must be considered in two ways. First, he has added greatly to our substantive understanding of several phenomena. His reconceptualization of the nature of rumors is now widely accepted and, along with his discussion of reference groups, stands as a major substantive contribution to sociological understanding. The second contribution is less concrete, lying in the integrative character of Shibutani's work. By analyzing the communication networks that produce and support various phenomena, Shibutani has integrated routine common sense knowledge with the most bizarre and excited rumors in a single framework. He has shown how the normal selectivity with which we approach information can become exaggerated and produce vicious behavior that is an exaggeration of our everyday practices rather than an incomprehensible occurrence. He has shown that a single mechanism of social control, the cybernetic control of behavior, underlies a great many aspects of behavior that were previously regarded as reflections of different processes. His work has incorporated a wide range of phenomena, including such mentalistic ones as sentiments and personality, into a coherent behavioral and sociological analysis based on cybernetic self-control. In doing this, he has extended Mead's work in a creative, distinctive way, although he shares many features with other symbolic interactionists.

Finally, he has suggested one possibility for an integration of social psychology with the sociological analysis of large social systems: the cybernetic model. Ordinarily, social psychology and the rest of the sociological discipline are somewhat estranged. Although each draws insight from the other, it is difficult to coherently integrate the two. By stating a social psychology in terms of the cybernetic model, Shibutani has provided a framework in which the study of social psychology can be conducted in the same terms as the study of large social systems.

Suggested Readings

Shibutani's work is characterized by the application of a cybernetic model to the process of the development of meaning in interaction. The work of William

Powers provides an excellent introduction to cybernetic models. His short paper, "Feedback: Beyond Behaviorism," [*Science,* 170 (26 January 1973), 351–356], can serve as a relatively nontechnical introduction to the concept of cybernetic control and its application to behavior. Powers' book, *Behavior: The Control of Perception* (Aldine, Chicago, 1973), represents a more thorough, more technical attempt to develop the model. Cybernetic models have been applied to many aspects of human conduct. The range of the applications is indicated in Walter Buckley's collection, *Modern Systems Research for the Behavioral Scientist* (Aldine, Chicago, 1968). Buckley has shown the utility of cybernetic principles for understanding a variety of sociological and social psychological theories and placing them in a more general conceptual context (Walter Buckley, *Sociology and Modern Systems Theory,* Aldine, Chicago, 1967). Shibutani's own work, fortunately, is clearly written and comprehensible to nonspecialists. *Improvised News* (Bobbs-Merrill, Indianapolis, 1966) is an application of this approach to an interesting empirical phenomenon, and illustrates as well the political implications of studies of small-scale phenomena.

References to Shibutani's Works

1946   "The Making of the Infantryman," *American Journal of Sociology* 51 (March), 376–379.

1955   "Reference Groups as Perspectives," *American Journal of Sociology* 60 (May), 562–569.

1961   *Society and Personality,* Prentice-Hall, Englewood Cliffs, N.J.

1962   "Reference Groups and Social Control," in *Human Behavior and Social Processes: An Interactionist Approach,* ed. Arnold Rose, Houghton Mifflin, Boston, pp. 128–147.

1964   "The Sentimental Basis of Group Solidarity," *Sociological Inquiry* 34 (Spring), 144–155.

1965   *Ethnic Stratification,* Macmillan, New York (coauthored with Kian Kwan).

1966   *Improvised News: A Sociological Study of Rumor,* Bobbs-Merrill, Indianapolis.

1968a "A Cybernetic Approach to Motivation," in *Modern Systems Research for the Behavioral Scientist,* ed. Walter Buckley, Aldine, Chicago, pp. 330–336.

1968b "George Herbert Mead," in *International Encyclopedia of the Social Sciences,* ed. David Shils, Macmillan, New York, X, 83–87.

1968c "Rumor," in *International Encyclopedia of the Social Sciences,* ed. David Shils, Macmillan, New York, XIII, 576–580.

1971   "On Sentiments and Social Control," in *Institutions and Social Exchange,* ed. Herman Turk and Richard Simpson, Bobbs-Merrill, Indianapolis, pp. 145–162.

1973   "On the Personification of Adversaries," in *Human Nature and Collective Behavior: Papers in Honor of Herbert Blumer,* ed. Tamotsu Shibutani, Transaction Press, New Brunswick, N.J., 223–233.

Chapter **12**

Erving Goffman

Of all the contributors studied in this section, Erving Goffman is unquestionably the most controversial. His works cover a variety of topics and use diverse conceptual resources.[1] While his analyses are generally

---

[1] Since the bulk of the citations in this chapter will be to the work of Goffman, we will refer to his works by date only in the footnotes. A list of the titles of the works and complete publication information appears at the back of the chapter.

regarded as brilliant, even by his critics, they are also frequently regarded as eccentric and idiosyncratic, and out of the mainstream of sociological thought. Several characteristics of his work encourage critics to qualify their praise. First, although his work shows a strikingly broad command of the existing literature in sociology, anthropology, and psychiatry, he suggests frequent, original interpretations of their import. His work, therefore, often contrasts sharply with prominent thinkers in a variety of fields. Second, when Goffman does not modify the definitions of standard terms he frequently coins new ones. While his lively original vocabulary gives him an engaging writing style, it is often criticized for needlessly creating new terms when old ones will do, further adding to the burdensome jargon of the social sciences. Finally, Goffman's concern with the control of self-expressing information in interaction is often criticized for suggesting an excessively manipulative view of human beings. Yet this view of humans has become one of the most frequently used in social psychology, even in recent years, among experimentalists.

Controversy aside, no defense is needed for strikingly original interpretations of social life. Even if our science were more advanced and secure than it is, eccentricity combined with brilliance and creativity would have to be regarded as a virtue. Goffman himself has commented on his terminological difficulties and has often suggested alternate terms that, although slightly different in connotation, can be used interchangeably.[2] We will consider the reason for Goffman's use of original terms in the context of his distinctive substantive interest.

Goffman's "ultimate interest is to develop the study of face-to-face interaction as a naturally bounded, analytically coherent field—a sub-area of sociology."[3] Each of his studies reflects that interest and we will consider each in terms of its contribution to our understanding of interaction. We do not intend to minimize Goffman's contribution to other fields, such as the study of mental illness. Rather, we will consider his work in light of his own stated priorities.

Studying the Neglected Situation

Goffman has argued that the topic of face-to-face interaction has been neglected, perhaps even abused, by sociologists, who have utilized practices observed in interaction to illustrate other matters while neglecting to study the structure of interaction itself. He suggests that face-to-face interaction warrants investigation in its own right—that interactions "constitute a reality *sui generis*."[4]

[2] For example, see Goffman, 1961a, p. 8; and 1971, p. ix.
[3] Goffman, 1969, p. ix.
[4] This point is made in several places. For example, see Goffman, 1961a, p. 7; 1963a, p. 4; 1964; and 1971, p. ix.

Goffman's terminological difficulties arise from his attempt to study interaction in a way that is relatively unprecedented—as a reality distinct from other forms of social organization. Existing theoretical resources were developed in the context of other approaches to interaction and must be modified to suit this new approach. At the same time, the lack of precedent has left the subject matter poorly defined, contributing to Goffman's difficulty in developing a precisely apt terminology. In many respects, Goffman's work is unfinished; he is defining a field of study that will require many more contributions before it takes precise form.

CONCRETE BOUNDARIES OF THE SITUATION

In defining an area for study, it is important to specify as clearly as possible the range of phenomena that are to be included. The concrete boundaries defining the area of interest are easy to specify in this case: face-to-face interaction occurs whenever people are mutually accessible to one another's naked senses.[5] This possibility of mutual monitoring through the unaided senses leads people to "modify their conduct in many normatively guided ways." Goffman calls these norms situational proprieties. He suggests that their influence is present whenever people are open to mutual observation by the unaided senses, producing, if they are observed, a characteristic social order. These situational proprieties, and the social order characteristic of interaction, can be studied in the same ways as other forms of social organization.[6]

Goffman says that mutual openness to observation by the unaided senses might also be called "public life" or "public behavior" or a "situation."[7] In his work, the term "interaction" must always be understood as referring to face-to-face interaction. Telephone conversations are not face-to-face interaction, and neither is "asymetrical observability"—some participants able to perceive the others but not be perceived. A "situation," or face-to-face interaction, begins when two or more people come into the range of one another's senses and ends when there are no longer two people within this range.

ANALYTIC BOUNDARIES OF THE SITUATION

Concretely, observable conduct is a "situation" if the people involved are within range of one another's senses. This concrete definition of a situation abstracts sequences of conduct from their social and biographical context. For example, a person might be sitting in an office alone, working. Another person enters the room, beginning a situation, and then leaves,

[5] Goffman, 1964, p. 135.
[6] Goffman, 1963a, p. 243.
[7] Goffman, 1971, p. 9.

ending the situation. But whereas we can study the face-to-face interaction that occurs as a phenomenon in its own right, we cannot ignore the determinants and consequences of that interaction that are beyond the boundaries of the situation. Thus, to define the analytic boundary of the study of situations is to distinguish between the determinants and consequences of situated conduct that are concretely within and without the situation. Situational proprieties, physical characteristics of the setting, and the focus of the interaction, if one exists, fall analytically within the situation. Stable social relationships, normative systems other than those of situational propriety, and the lasting effects of events in the situation are analytically beyond its boundaries.

Goffman's discussion of embarrassment illustrates these points. In order to fulfill their role requirements, in many organizations people are obliged to display different and contradictory self-characteristics in different situations. For example, a person is obliged to display leadership and be forceful in the presence of his or her subordinates, but deferential in the presence of his or her superiors. Ordinarily, these contradictory characteristics are displayed in the presence of different people.[8] But sometimes face-to-face interaction takes place in a group with contradictory expectations concerning a person's behavior. The person must, in order to function effectively on subsequent occasions, maintain his or her credibility as a person who can meet each set of expectations. In such situations, embarrassment often occurs, the result of contradictory expectations that can neither all be met nor be disregarded. The embarrassment expressed by the individual reflects his or her recognition of the dilemma and his or her sensitivity to all the demands. In a sense, by displaying and experiencing embarrassment, the individual accepts the blame and consequences for an imperfection of the normative structure.[9]

Concretely, embarrassment only occurs in a situation. Further, it has situational determinants—the simultaneous expression of contradictory expectations. Embarrassment also has consequences within the situation —activity is temporarily disrupted and effort is expended to re-establish the smoothness of the interaction. All of these matters are *within* the analytic boundaries of the study of situations. But embarrassment also has determinants that are outside the situation—organizational norms and routines influence which people will assemble in situations and with what degree of consensus. Finally, embarrassment has consequences beyond the situation—embarrassing incidents may call into question the

[8] Robert Merton provides a classic discussion of mechanisms that articulate the often conflicting expectations of different role others. Robert Merton, "The Role Set: Problems in Sociological Theory," *British Journal of Sociology* 8 (June 1957), 106–120.

[9] Goffman, "Embarrassment and Social Organization," in 1967, pp. 97–112.

expectations that precipitated them. Thus there are factors that affect or are affected by situational events that are analytically outside of the situations. To understand situations fully we must include concepts and observations that are extrinsic to them.

DUAL CONCERNS: THE STUDY OF SITUATIONS AND DEFINING
THE FIELD OF INQUIRY

Goffman's work shows evidence of self-conscious attention to two intertwined projects. The first is to study face-to-face interaction (or situated behavior, or public life). The second is to define such study as a distinctive sub-area in sociology by locating its concrete and analytic boundaries. Thus, on the one hand, Goffman studies the structure and processes of face-to-face interaction in fine detail, and with unsurpassed insight into the significance of even small expressive behaviors. On the other hand, he discusses the limits of his chosen substantive domain— specifying the external matters that impinge upon observed situated conduct (and that hopefully will improve our understanding of interaction itself).

Our discussion of Goffman's work will retain these dual concerns. After discussing some concepts that provide a necessary background for understanding Goffman's work, we will examine four major aspects of situated conduct: layers of situated order, ritual exchange, self-presentation, and identity. In each case we will identify the boundaries of situated conduct.

It is important to emphasize that the analytic boundaries of the study of situations do not include all that is interesting about those situations. The connection between interactions, and their enmeshment in broader social structures, for example, are beyond the analytic boundaries of interaction. Although our discussion of interaction in Chapter 3 utilized Goffman's work extensively, our overall approach was quite different. We emphasized the connections between interaction and broader social structures while Goffman focuses on the properties of interaction that are distinct from this connection. The two approaches are complementary, increasing the clarity of our understanding of both interaction and its relationship to the social order.

Goffman's Distinctive Approach to Self and the Construction of Experience

Throughout his career Goffman has been concerned with the sociological analysis of self and the construction of experience. His approach to these topics has been consistent, quite unusual, and essential to understanding his analyses of other aspects of situated conduct.

SELF

The "self," in Mead's view, is the person defined as an object from the perspective of the generalized other. Mead equated the generalized other with a group that was both in face-to-face contact with the person and involved in a system of role relationships with him or her. One characteristic of "role" is the interchangeability of incumbents. The obligations and rights associated with the role remain relatively stable as different people assume it. Thus, the perspective of the generalized other towards the various incumbents of a given role should be similar, and similar selves should be attributed to the various incumbents in a role.

The self is attributed to a person, then, not on the basis of his or her unique characteristics but by virtue of the person's incumbency in a role. In a sense the self is a property of the role, not of the person. Goffman has observed that incumbents in a role find a self virtually awaiting them and that incumbents of a role are obligated to accept that self and express appropriate characteristics.[10]

A further refinement of the locus of the self is necessary. The social situation is itself a social system with its own normative order. This normative order imposes a role on each participant regardless of his or her commitment to other roles. This role implies, as do others, a self—one based on one's competence or demeanor in interaction. Thus, even when no other role relationships are relevant in a situation, mere participation in interaction imposes a self and the normative obligation to express its characteristics. When other role relationships are relevant, the requirements of each will be modified by those imposed by the situated role, just as the requirements of the situated role are modified by other social obligations. Goffman refers to the situated self as the self imposed on a person by virtue of his or her presence in a situation with a particular set of normative requirements.[11] The self a person is normatively obliged to maintain may vary with the relevance of his or her various roles and with the demands of the particular situation.

Two features of this conception of self must be kept in mind to understand Goffman's work. First, although it is attributed to a person, the self is an attribute of the social role or combination of social roles in which that person is involved within a given situation. Second, the possession of appropriate self-characteristics, in effect the expression of those characteristics, is a normative obligation of role incumbency.

THE CONSTRUCTION OF EXPERIENCE

Often, when the terms "construction of experience," "construction of reality," or "defining the situation" are employed they refer to a process

---

[10] For example, Goffman, 1961a, pp. 86–88; 1961b, pp. 173–175.
[11] Goffman, 1961a, pp. 95–99.

through which people in a situation, singly or collectively, create the meanings of events. Often, too, there is a tendency to assume that the definition created is a major determinant of events. Goffman's use of these terms modifies these premises. First, he argues that the definition of the situation is not so much created as arrived at or discovered. It is not that events have intrinsic meaning, but rather that one's culture provides conventional interpretations of events. Thus, the individual does not create the definition, but to a large extent his or her social group, through the establishment of conventions, does. This approach gives relatively more emphasis to group norms and a discovery process and relatively less to creation and the negotiation process than most symbolic interactionists. Second, Goffman's main concern is with cases in which the definition of the situation or construction of experience is accomplished by action rather than by cognitive interpretation. For example, a rock becomes a weapon by virtue of its having been thrown as well as by virtue of our cognition of it as such. The two matters may be separate. A person may be hit by a rock that he or she does not perceive to be thrown by a passing child. From an observer's point of view, the rock that struck the person is a weapon, regardless of the target's awareness of that fact. Third, many aspects of events are not affected by our definitions of them. In the physical world we cannot define away the effects of gravity and fly unaided. In the social world we cannot define away many consequences of our acts. For example, a person cannot by thinking it is so transform what another perceives as an insult into a compliment.[12]

Framework. We can begin to understand how experience is constructed in Goffman's view by considering how social norms and observed conduct considered together express social meaning. Social norms, Goffman argues, transform conduct into expression, that is, make it possible for conduct to serve an expressive function.[13] First consider those cases in which the appropriate norms are known—the participants are aware of what ought to occur in the situation. Observed conduct can be compared to normatively prescribed conduct providing information about the state of the social system and the selves of its participants. In other instances, exactly which norms apply may not be known. Observed behavior in such situations can be examined to see which norms are being followed, and by inference which sets of norms are applicable. For example, whether interaction at a party is to be relatively formal or informal may become apparent only from observation of whether norms appropriate to formality or informality are being followed. By observing which terms of address are employed, the distance maintained between interactants,

[12] Goffman, 1974, pp. 1–2 and 247.
[13] Goffman, "The Nature of Deference and Demeanor," in 1967, p. 51.

or the topics discussed, a person can judge which system of norms is in effect and the appropriate selves for those present, including him- or herself. Many social situations are characterized by at least partial normative ambiguity and participants will seek and express information of both types through acting and observing action.

Thus, social norms and action in situations in which they apply are specific instances of what Goffman calls "frames" or "frameworks." A "framework" is a scheme of interpretation that renders observed events meaningful. Frameworks may be primary or secondary. "Primary frameworks," which may be physical or social, suggest meanings for events that are not subject to further analysis. These are the basic meanings of events as defined by the appropriate social group. Primary frameworks vary in their degree of complexity from neat systems of postulates and rules, such as physical theory, to relatively inarticulate bodies of lore, such as the mores of a society. Taken together, the primary frameworks constitute an important element of culture. "Secondary frameworks" suggest transformations of the meaning of events that also have meaning within one of these primary frameworks.[14] For example, a rock traveling through the air can be understood within a primary physical framework as merely a physical object whose trajectory can be anticipated or, if the rock has been thrown in one's direction, as a weapon. If the thrower is a friend and the rock misses by more than the error of a carefully aimed throw, a secondary social framework can transform the rock into a joke. The appropriate secondary framework can be suggested by the thrower through such actions as laughing when the "target" jumps.

In this view, conduct has different meanings depending upon the framework which is provided by accompanying conduct and which is cognitively discovered and applied. The transition from primary to secondary frameworks is conventional or normative. A "key" is a convention that transforms the meaning of events from those they have within a primary framework. "Keying" refers both to the cognitive act of reinterpretation and to observable acts or meanings that transform conventional meanings. Participants know when events have been keyed and acknowledge this transformation. Ordinarily, the applicability of the keyed interpretation is marked by cues that define the beginning and end of the secondary framework.

Two illustrations should serve to clarify this widespread phenomenon. "Practice" is one function served by the keying of events. Participants engage in activities that may be virtually indistinguishable from the real thing. However, the consequences of the events are different, the aims of the participants are different, and the standards for judging participants are altered. Consider a dress rehearsal for a wedding: it is conducted in

[14] Goffman, 1974, pp. 21–27.

clothing that would be appropriate for an actual wedding, in the chapel, and by clergy. At its conclusion, the couple is not married. Instead they have achieved, and only intended to achieve, some expertise in the conduct appropriate for the real ceremony. Finally, mistakes or jokes, such as answering "I don't," have different implications about the selves and abilities of the participants than they would during the unkeyed real wedding, conducted under a primary framework. Acts may also be keyed to indicate that the motives or intentions of the participants are unusual. Goffman calls this "regrounding." Occasionally, for example, prominent people may perform menial services as a way of publicizing a charitable event. The implications for their selves are quite different from those that normally attend such activities, and yet the menial services are actually performed.[15]

Fabrication. The primary framework and the secondary framework suggested by keys provide comprehensible expression in a situation. But they also make experience vulnerable to manipulation. Interactants may be misled about the meaning of events in three ways: keys may be absent; keys may be provided when the primary framework still applies; or false keys may be provided to mask the appropriate framework. For example, an undercover narcotics agent will deliberately withhold keys that make his or her purchase different from that of a typical user. Or a researcher may say that a conversation is "off the record" and then use the information gained in his or her report. And, as a final example, con men earn their living through their ability to provide false keys.

Goffman refers to the intentional misleading of some participants in a situation by others as "fabrication." [16] The conventional understandings concerning the interpretation of meanings are employed to construct an appearance that will mislead some participants. Fabrications are not necessarily harmful to their victims, but it is fabrication that poses the greatest potential for harm.

While our experience of reality is vulnerable, we are not helpless. Our expressive behavior can be controlled to a considerable extent. But we are not able to control all of the fine details of our appearance and conduct that convey meaning to others. Conduct that is intended to convey a particular meaning to others is called "communicative" rather than "expressive." Relatively greater trust is placed on the aspects of conduct that are believed to be uncontrolled, and hence more revealing of the true nature of the selves of the participants and their norms. Of course people may try to control exactly those aspects of conduct that are ordinarily spontaneous, but, Goffman argues, people's ability to detect manipulation

---

[15] *Ibid.,* pp. 45–77.
[16] *Ibid.,* p. 83.

is normally greater than the ability to manipulate and maintain the appearance of spontaneity. In most cases we are able to distinguish between spontaneous and controlled behavior and interpret events accordingly.[17]

Successful fabrication of experience is often made possible by special communicative competence, developed through practice. Typically, for example, a waiter or waitress deals with more diners than a single diner deals with waiters or waitresses. The waiter or waitress has more practice and can usually communicate an air of unaffected respect that we cannot "see through" regardless of his or her real attitudes. Fabrication may also be aided by privileged access to information or by control over the physical setting and materials used in situations. The waiter or waitress's show of deference is aided by the privacy of areas, inaccessible to the diner, in which other attitudes may be expressed. A waiter or waitress's ability to prepare the scene for face-to-face interaction—by cleaning ashtrays and table surfaces, arranging silverware and centerpieces, or lighting candles—also contributes to the smooth contrivance of meaning. Any difference in expertise or access to information contributes to the ability of fabrication to be successfully accomplished.

In checking to be sure that one is utilizing the appropriate framework in a situation, conduct, especially perceivedly spontaneous conduct, is analyzed in a special way. Events are interpreted using the framework believed appropriate to the situation, but at the same time events are sought that are inappropriate to that frame. For instance, we interpret the conduct of a physician and respond to him or her in the context of the framework of a doctor's presumed competence. At the same time, we are sensitive to events that cannot be made meaningful within that framework—a gross misdiagnosis, failure to inquire about allergies to medicines, or inordinate ease in getting appointments (indicating a small practice). Such events lead us to reconsider or rekey the activities of the physician and to establish a framework that will make those discrepancies meaningful.

The inability to understand any events within the framework one has adopted has potentially severe consequences. It is the framework that makes events meaningful. If the framework is inadequate to provide meaning to certain events, its general adequacy becomes suspect. The meaning of events previously understood in the context of the framework may be also called into doubt.

The extreme case of mental illness illustrates this process. Goffman argues that one way in which people come to be regarded as mentally ill is to persistently express assumptions about themselves and the relevant

[17] Goffman, 1959, pp. 1–10.

social organization that are incompatible with those held by others and which, if accepted and acted upon by others, would disrupt the system. From the point of view of the others, the meaning of the person's conduct will fall outside the bounds of the appropriate framework. And behavior which is outside of the appropriate framework calls into doubt or disrupts people's views of themselves and their ability to maintain normal cooperative activities within the system. In short, organizational havoc results from the persistent application of an inappropriate framework.[18] The individual who cleaves to such a framework is likely to be labeled as mentally ill. In less extreme cases, of course, both the organizational disruption and the disruption of one's sense of meaningfulness will be less pronounced.

Summary of Goffman's approach to the construction of experience. The relevance of social norms in a situation transforms conduct into the expression of meaning, independent of whether expression is intended. Definitions of the situation are discovered by observing the actions of others. Any specific set of observed events has a conventional meaning within the primary frameworks of the culture. However, these same events may have different meanings provided by secondary frameworks which may be applied. The relevance of any given framework is determined by the nature of other events that provide the context for the ones being interpreted. The transformation of meaning occurs through adopting secondary frameworks, but all participants may not be equally informed. When they are not, manipulation or fabrication of experience occurs, and one team of participants misleads another concerning the meaning of events by intentionally inducing them to use an inappropriate framework. Participants continuously test the appropriateness of the framework they have adopted by seeking events that are inappropriate within that frame and which can indicate what framework would be more appropriate. Special attention is paid to events that are believed to be uncontrolled and therefore to provide a "truer" insight into events. The failure of events to conform to the appropriate frame leads to confusion and in extreme cases to organizational havoc or anomie.

Layers of Situated Order

Goffman defines a "social order" as "the consequences of any set of moral norms that regulates the way in which persons pursue objectives." The order that results from these norms is not dictated by the norms themselves. Rather, the norms dictate the means by which individuals may

---

[18] Goffman, 1971, p. 356.

legitimately seek their ends; social order emerges as a consequence of the influence of norms upon conduct. Any particular act, or sequence of acts, may be regulated by multiple sets of norms.[19]

Orderly traffic patterns serve as an illustration of the relationship between norms and social order. The norms governing driving specify how the end of getting from one location to another can legitimately be achieved. On the other hand, such decisions as whether to pass another vehicle and the choice of destination are not specified in those norms. Thus certain aspects of driving are normatively regulated but the exact distribution of traffic is not. Automobile drivers are simultaneously influenced by multiple sets of norms. A driver carrying car pool passengers will simultaneously be influenced by traffic regulations, the rules governing interaction among automobile passengers, the rules governing the driver's appearance before those in other cars, and the rules of the economic system that induce large numbers of people to ride at the same time.

Situated conduct may be oriented to multiple systems of norms and the resulting order is the product of their combined influences. To understand face-to-face interaction as a distinctive phenomenon we must be able to analyze the normative bases of social order. After introducing the necessary terminology, we will discuss the layers of social norms that apply to interaction. The imagery of layers has been adopted explicitly by Goffman,[20] and the discussion of his terminology should clarify the sense in which the norms governing situations are layered.

THE TERMINOLOGY OF SITUATED ORDER

Face-to-face interaction exists whenever people are copresent, exposed to one another's unaided senses. Goffman divides face-to-face interaction into two categories: "focused" and "unfocused."

"Unfocused interaction" occurs whenever people who are copresent mutually modify their appearance and demeanor in response to that copresence. Each one observes the other and, at the same time, modifies one's own demeanor because one knows that one is under observation. "Focused interaction" occurs only when a joint topic or focus of attention is maintained within the situation. Those involved in focused interaction will be involved in unfocused interaction as well, but the reverse is not true.[21] In a sense, then, the matters essential to unfocused interaction are essential to every interaction while those found only in focused interaction are "added on" (or "layered").

[19] Goffman, 1963a, p. 8.
[20] Goffman, 1974.
[21] Goffman, 1961a, p. 7.

Situations ordinarily occur in the context of a broader social occasion —an event, undertaking, or affair. An occasion, which may range from a party to participation in some business or work enterprise, provides context for most situations.[22] By providing context, the occasion brings people into some normative social relationship beyond mere copresence. Thus, the focus of an interaction is an occasion. But the occasion is most interesting when it involves matters beyond the interaction itself. Usually, being contained in an occasion links the situation to a broader social context—relationships and systems of norms that apply beyond the concrete boundaries of the situation. The nature of the occasion, of course, modifies situational proprieties and, if it has extreme consequences, constitutes another layer of normative regulation in face-to-face interaction.

A situation may involve the norms appropriate to multiple occasions. An example is the copresence of maintenance or repair workers and the regular office staff, pursuing their different ends in an office setting. The two groups of workers dress differently, talk differently, maintain different noise levels, and have different foci of attention. They are, although together in a situation, participating in separate occasions. From the point of view of the participants in each occasion, the actions of the others produce a disorganizing effect.[23]

A relatively simple situation, an audience watching a movie, illustrates the relationships among the layers of normative order. The movie audience is open to communication and its members are likely to check out one another's clothing, style of hair, and other social characteristics and to be sensitive to the monitoring by others. In addition, the movie provides a focus for interaction. This focus modifies the monitoring possibilities—most of the time is spent in the dark with all participants facing in the same direction. The need to hear the movie alters the legitimacy of talking or other noise-making. Thus, the focus affects both the ability to monitor and the nature of the situational proprieties. Ordinarily, the audience will contain smaller groups such as pairs of people on "dates." Thus, while the attendance of the movie is one occasion, many will simultaneously be involved in "dating," another occasion. Dating defines additional matters that must be focused upon, and transforms the situational proprieties relating those on the date both to each other and to the others in the audience. Each set of norms is imposed upon the others and modifies them.

Situated order, then, involves two systems of norms. First, we will discuss the norms governing copresence. The applicability of particular norms varies from situation to situation, but certain aspects of conduct

[22] Goffman, 1963a, pp. 18f.
[23] *Ibid.*, pp. 17–24.

are normatively governed in every situation, including both such minimal interaction as routine sidewalk traffic and also such closely regulated conduct as that of participants in total institutions. Second, we will consider the order imposed on situations by the maintenance of a focus of attention. Again, the exact normative requirements will vary as the focus of attention changes, but the maintenance of *any* focus of attention has characteristic normative consequences.

Paradoxically, these layers of situated order exclude the aspects of social order most interesting to the majority of sociologists and laymen— the normative order imposed by social occasions. While this layer of order is outside the analytic boundaries of the situation, its effects upon situations are profound. Those effects will be discussed later in the chapter when we examine ritual exchange, self-presentation, and the expression of identity.

NORMS GOVERNING COPRESENCE

Face-to-face interaction occurs, by definition, in every instance of copresence. However, as we have already indicated, both the addition of a focus and the presence and nature of the occasion in which most interactions are embedded alter the norms that govern conduct. In what sense, then, are there norms that are essential to interaction; that are present whenever interaction occurs; and that justify the treatment of interaction as a social system distinct from others? Goffman's answer to this question is that there are matters that are governed by norms in every interaction in which they occur—focused or unfocused, occasioned or unoccasioned. Other aspects of conduct, however, are not always regulated. Only if there is jointly sustained visual focus of attention will norms exist that regulate proper attention to it, and the rights of others with respect to seeing it. Thus the theater stage, as a visual focus, is accompanied by norms governing falling asleep (improper attention to the legitimate focus) and standing up (blocking the view of others). There are also sanctions to enforce these norms. The right to wake a sleeping person and, if one knows the person, to berate him or her later, or to say to a stranger "Down in front," are examples.

The defining characteristic of face-to-face interaction is the mutual modification of appearance or demeanor in response to mutual observability. It is matters that are invariably involved in this mutual adjustment to copresence that are always normatively regulated. In particular, the matters that are always regulated relate to aspects of "expressive behavior," which is behavior that imparts information to others. Goffman distinguishes such behavior from "communication," which is behavior that is intended to impart particular information. Expression always occurs in interaction; communication does not. Goffman discusses two aspects of expressive behavior: "involvement" and "openness."

Involvement. Although there is not always a mutual focus of attention, people who are copresent are required to express their attentiveness to, or involvement with, something. In addition, some aspects of involvement are always regulated. First, each participant is always normatively required to maintain an appropriate appearance or demeanor, although the definition of appropriateness will vary. At the same time, the person must be alert to the demeanor of those around him or her. A minimal social relationship is thus defined.

In addition to appearance, there are normative standards for the extent to which one should attend to the adequacy of others' performance of their obligations,[24] and for the degree to which one should be involved with the immediate situation. Thus, there will be norms regarding such matters as daydreaming and absent-mindedness.

Taken together, the standards for appropriate involvement define adequate self-expression. That is, every situation implies a self for each participant and provides norms regarding self-expression. To be properly involved in a situation is to express a self appropriate to the social role or roles that one assumes in the situation. Those who violate the norms governing self-expression are presenting "inapproprite" selves and are out of place in the situation.

Copresence does not imply that conversation will occur. Goffman argues that involvement is expressed through a normative body idiom. The details of dress, posture, facial expression, and task-oriented activity all have conventional meaning and express one's degree of involvement. Consequently, a person can express a degree of involvement that he or she does not feel. In fact, regardless of feelings, a person cannot avoid expressing some degree of involvement. One is always dressed in some particular way; one always maintains some particular posture; one always has some particular facial expression, and so on. Regardless of one's intentions and true feelings, when these things are observable to others, they will express a degree of involvement. Specific norms governing dress, facial expressions, or the degree to which one should appear busily engaged in some task define the degree of involvement appropriate to a situation and provide a standard by which the actual expressions of participants can be judged.[25]

The degree of self-involvement in a situation is regulated in several ways. The requirement that proper appearance be maintained is, of

[24] *Ibid.*, pp. 24–30.
[25] *Ibid.*, pp. 34–38.

course, the most obvious, including norms governing both over- and underdressing. For example, just as one does not attend a formal party in a T-shirt, one does not attend the laundromat in a tuxedo. Each appearance is equally out of place, is equally an example of bad grooming. Similarly, while extreme slouching may be an inapproprite posture in some settings, the rigid posture and march that characterizes the military would be inappropriate in others.

Many aspects of our appearance can only be maintained by specific grooming activities. Combing the hair, applying make-up, and rearranging one's clothing are examples. In order to accomplish any of these operations successfully a mirror may be necessary. The degree to which such activities are permissible is a second dimension of regulated self-involvement in situations. Very few places allow the adjustment of a girdle, a thorough effort to tuck in a shirt, the application of make-up, or a more-than-casual rearrangement of hair. The details of such norms may be quite fine. For instance, the use of a store window as a mirror may be allowed only if the use is brief and covert while the use of a clearly visible hand-held mirror is not. One may rearrange hair casually, using the hand, but the use of a comb or brush may not be allowed. One may apply lipstick, if it is done quickly, in many places, while eye shadow or liner may not be applied.

Bodily functions not usually associated with appearance are also normatively regulated. Most situations have regulations that prohibit flatulence, loud belching, yawning, and scratching. Even more or less involuntary functions such as sneezing or coughing may be normatively regulated. Sneezing and coughing require an apology as much as stepping on another's foot. A compromise is often effected by covering one's mouth while yawning, muffling a cough, or sneezing into a handkerchief. These activities do not cancel the violation nor do they conceal it, but they do seem to mitigate the extent of the violation; an unchecked, open-mouthed cough is not only less sanitary than a hand-muffled one, but is also a greater violation of norms.

The applicability of norms governing proper appearance in a situation and others limiting the degree to which those appearances may be corrected may put people in a bind. Discovering that they have violated a norm governing appearance, they may be normatively forbidden, in many cases, from correcting that appearance. In other cases, there are places in which such repairs are allowed. Foremost among them, perhaps, are "rest rooms." The use of terms such at "rest room" or "powder room" or "men's room" is as much an accurate functional description as a euphemism. In such places, the situations created by copresence— the literal use of powder, and normative guarantees of sex segregation— permit relaxation from situations outside their boundaries. It is noteworthy that these rest areas do not simply "allow" repairs or other attention to bodily functions. Often such activities are "required" in the setting. Such normative requirements allow homosexuals in public rest rooms to identify one another and initiate contact by ignoring the officially defined purpose for the facilities.[26] Generally, failure to engage in repair work in such settings may be regarded as strange.

Finally, the expression of involvement in the appearance of others is normatively regulated. A person is responsible to pay neither too much nor too little attention to others. Among strangers, the limits of permissible attention may allow very little contact. Looking at the other for any length of time or eavesdropping on others' conversations is normatively prohibited. Among those with closer relationships, too much intimacy for the situation may also be expressed. Couples who embrace in cars while stopped for traffic signals are near, or have crossed, the bounds of appropriateness. Too little attention to others may also be expressed. Among strangers, we must attend to others at least enough to avoid such things as bumping them, separating them from people they are with, and intruding on their conversation. With people in closer relationships, we may be obligated to notice and comment on their appearance—either expressing a compliment or a friendly hint about disarray.[27]

We may easily illustrate the utility of extending the concept of self-expression to such minimal social interactions as that represented by strangers passing one another on a public street. While the exact norms involved will vary from place to place and with the time of day, certain behavior will generally lead to a negative or unwanted response from others on the street. For example, walking in the street while playing a radio loudly, running faster than the general flow of pedestrians, moving so slowly that others will have to stop or move around you, walking erratically from side to side so that you either bump into people or force them to change direction frequently to avoid contact, or walking so close to another group of people that you can obviously hear what they are saying are all instances of improper involvement. All are likely to be followed by disapproving looks, comments made to the offender, or comments exchanged among offended passers-by. Clothing may be judged in a similar way. Women in see-through or scanty tops or in exceptionally short dresses or shorts are likely to be the object of appraising remarks or offensive invitations. Men who wear clothes that are exceptionally colorful, platform shoes, unbuttoned shirts, silk-like fabrics, or exotic jewelry are also likely to be appraised offensively and aloud by others. Occasionally verbal exchanges or even violence can erupt.

[26] Laud Humphreys, *Tearoom Trade*, Aldine, Chicago, 1970.
[27] Goffman, 1963a, pp. 64–69.

We can understand why people bother to respond to such matters if we consider the self-implications of failing to sanction an offense. Norms regulate our attention to others. A person who disapproves of a particular kind of behavior may be socially required to express that belief by sanctioning those who violate a norm. That is, failure to call a long-haired male a "hippie" may compromise one's self-conception as a person who opposes hippie values. Sexual advances, apparently made with little hope or expectation of favorable response, may have the same character. They may be necessary to support one's self-concept as a male who is sexually aggresive, recognizes attractiveness, and is glib and bold with women. Many long-haired males invite and welcome such casual disapproval. They define their selves as rebellious, as out of the ordinary, as liberated from traditional values. For them, the negative response is a ratification of their desired self-expression. Others, of course, are annoyed at such attention, frequently because they reject the idea that these matters of appearance have such importance. Women are not universally offended by casual sexual appraisal. For some these occasions are harmless and ratify their attractiveness; for others they are very offensive. Again, the issue is the self defined by the action. Women object to being treated casually as objects in the attempts of men to establish their own identities, especially when the woman's own self is reduced to a part of the man's plans.

Thus, the casual evaluation of strangers and the response to their appearance and "involvement" in unfocused public situations are quite important. We can understand now why people bother to respond to strangers in the first place. We also understand how the self-implications of involvement may lead to the expression and defense of fundamental values. Finally, we are led to predict that in a pluralistic society, with a variety of values and lifestyles, the expression of commitment to each style may serve to create conflict with those committed to another, even over small matters, and in the absence of other contact.

Goffman refers to inappropriate lack of involvement as being "away." People who are distracted or attending to matters removed from the situation do not have the presence of mind to deal appropriately with the contingencies of the situation.[28] For example, a card player who is away may not be aware when his or her turn to play comes, may bid out of turn, or play a card out of turn. While walking in the street, a person who is away is more likely to bump into others or to block traffic with erratic movement. Ordinarily, when a person is away he or she is easily brought back to the situation and able to resume properly involved conduct. After jostling one person on the street, a pedestrian's expressed

---

[28] *Ibid.*, pp. 69–75.

involvement is likely to increase. A card player who bids out of turn and is sanctioned for it is likely to pay more attention in the future. Also, upon returning to proper levels of involvement, the person is likely to express some apology or account, verbally or nonverbally. This functions to assure one's fellow participants that one's deviance was temporary and that one has not abandoned the norms of the situation.

When a person is away and others are unable to redirect his or her attention appropriately his or her external involvement is called "occult." It is an extreme form of being away characterized by a failure of the person to become reinvolved. This failure to respond to the requirements of the situation put the person beyond the ordinary means of sanctioning. Occult involvement is cited by Goffman as a common impetus for the initiation of psychiatric proceedings against a person.[29]

Openness. A second way in which situations are always normatively regulated is the openness of its participants to focused interaction (especially conversation). The lack of a joint focus of attention in certain situations is normatively guaranteed to those present. A classic example is the impropriety of engaging strangers whom one passes on the street in conversations. Even if focused interaction is already occurring the openness of each participant to each of the others will be normatively regulated. In card games involving bidding many matters may be discussed, but not those relating to information about the hand being played. The substance of proper conversation is thus regulated. Also, especially when status differences or other asymmetrical relationships exist among the interactants, some participants may be more properly addressed than others. In the extreme case of reigning monarchs, all conversation may be passed through an intermediary even though the monarch is physically present. In the normative sense, no one but this intermediary is recognized as present by the monarch. Thus whether the situation is focused or not, norms exist that regulate who may speak to whom and about what subjects.

Goffman's discussion of openness is confined to public places, such as the streets or cafeterias, in which the participants do not sustain a joint focus. He has observed that in such places there are "exposed positions," whose incumbents are open to legitimate approach by strangers. For example, the need to secure directions is common for both pedestrians and drivers. It is a justification for approaching others and initiating a conversation. The police, news vendors, uniformed clergy, or gas station attendants are regarded as more properly open to requests of this kind than others. In fact, Goffman notes, the police and uniformed

[29] *Ibid.,* pp. 75–81.

clergy are open to polite greetings and the initiation of conversation on virtually any subject.

Openness may be permanent or temporary. In our culture, both the very young and very old are permanently exposed to the conversational whims of others. Others are temporarily opened by their extraordinary appearance—a person who is obviously drunk but does not appear to be a drunkard, a person in costume, or a person who has slipped and fallen or bumped into a person or object. Finally, one can become exposed by virtue of the action of others. If one rushes through a crowd one exposes all those one passes to brief proper exchanges. This action opens others to one's right to excuse oneself or to warn them that they are about to be inconvenienced.

People with ulterior motives of various kinds may create a situation which allows them to initiate a conversation that can then be turned to other purposes. Dropping a handkerchief is a cliché for this strategy. Tripping, coughing, jostling another person, or any impropriety that justifies an apology can serve this same strategic purpose.

Just as every situation defines open positions—those whose incumbents may be approached—it also defines opening positions—those whose incumbents may approach others. The police and clergy are entitled to approach others as well as being open to being approached. In addition, anyone who is temporarily out of role—who has committed a situated offense of some kind—has temporary license to initiate apologetic conversations.

Particular people, by virtue of some observable personal characteristic, may be mutually open to each other although not to others. Motorcycle riders who exchange greetings as they pass one another on the street are an example. Another common instance is the mutual openness of people away from home who encounter others from the same place. Americans meeting in Europe, New Yorkers meeting in California, or common speakers of a language in a place where another language is spoken may approach one another, at least for greetings, although they have little else in common and would not approach one another in other circumstances. Signs of membership in a particular subculture may also serve this function. For example, people with long hair and beards, meeting in a place where this style is unusual, may become mutually open.

Certain places, such as cocktail lounges or singles bars, may be defined as places in which anyone may approach anyone else and engage in conversation. Other places may become open only under special circumstances. For example, copresence in an elevator usually does not open people to one another. If the elevator becomes crowded, however, the people in it may become so physically close that to feign unawareness of one another would become rude. Physical proximity creates a situation in which the failue to engage the other in conversation requires an act of avoidance and is offensive. Thus, a bus or train or plane may become socially more open as it becomes full.[30]

MAINTAINING A FOCUS OF ATTENTION

The agreement to sustain a joint topic of attention or focus imposes norms concerning the relevance of events to that situation. These rules define the appropriate involvement and openness in the situation. In addition, agreement on a topic or primary focus makes it possible for secondary involvements to be recognized. Thus, in focused interactions, a new function for norms emerges—the regulation of conduct governing second-ary involvements and the distribution of attention between the agreed-upon focus of attention and other matters.

Involvement is regulated in focused encounters by rules of irrelevance, which lead the participants to ignore many events that are not related to the main focus of attention. For example, a group of adults attempt-ing to play bridge will ignore, as fully as possible, the attempts of a child to divert their attention to a discussion of events in school. Similarly, having decided to investigate events at school, adults will ignore the attempts of a child to divert their attention to a game or television show.

At the same time, of course, attention is diverted to those matters that are relevant. More than simply directing attention, the focus of an inter-action provides a framework for interpreting events. One who attempts to hang a picture high on the wall will interpret physical objects in terms of their suitability as ladders. A chair may be judged in terms of its sturdiness, possible damage to its upholstery if stood upon, the ease with which it can be moved, and its height. All of these matters are suggested by the focus of attention as important criteria. The focus of attention also gives a special meaning to the actions of people in the situation. For example, moving small wooden figures around a checkered surface may be "playing chess" or "dusting," depending on the focus of attention. The physical setting, objects in it, and actions, then, are all transformed by the focus of attention into resources or objects expressed in terms of that focus.

This transformation of normative meanings affects both the expression of involvement and openness. One must not only be involved in the situation, but one must be involved in terms of the jointly sustained meaning. Openness is affected by the limitation of topics that can be

---

[30] *Ibid.*, pp. 124–139.

introduced and the terms in which events must be perceived and responded to. People are relatively more open to engagement concerning the agreed-upon focus and relatively less open to matters not related to it.[31]

Goffman points out that the main focus of an interaction will seldom exhaust the interests of the participants. For example, the externally based social status of participants may cause them to modify the way in which they address others present, although this modification is not dictated by the immediate focus. When one's employer makes a social visit, socializing is not the only concern. While the employee is expected to show deference and to respect this secondary involvement, he or she will also be expected not to disrupt the main focus of attention by doing so. Similarly, a couple attending a movie may express affection unrelated to the main topic of the gathering, but may not become excessive in this involvement. Even in work situations, people maintain secondary involvements. For example, workers often listen to transistor radios while on duty.

The major expressive function of secondary involvements is to allow the participants to express multiple social relationships and multiple selves at the same time. On the one hand, the primary focus is maintained. On the other, a secondary focus of attention may be maintained and expressed in contrast to the normatively prevailing focus. We will discuss this function in some detail when we examine the expression of identity.

Ritual Exchange

SITUATED CONDUCT AS RITUAL SANCTION

We have already observed that the existence of norms allows conduct to serve an expressive function. Norms also allow the same conduct to serve a sanctioning function. Social norms generally specify both the obligations and privileges associated with a position in a social system. Some of these normatively required acts have a reciprocal character: they simultaneously define an obligation of one position and a privilege or expectation of another. The military requirement that superior officers be addressed with the title "sir" is both an obligation to the subordinate and a privilege for the superior.

When a rule that prescribes conduct with this reciprocal character applies to situated action, that action may, in itself, sanction those present. Fulfilling the normative requirements of one's role will, at the same time, provide to others present conduct that they expect to occur. Failure to fulfill those same requirements will deny others' expectations. The links between the expressive and sanctioning functions of conduct are

[31] Goffman, 1961a, pp. 19–30.

intimate. By conforming to one's own role within the system each person will provide others with whatever the system entitles them to receive. For example rules, often supported by name tags, encourage us to address a dentist as "Doctor" and surname but to address a dental receptionist or technician by first name.

Goffman distinguishes between substantive and ceremonial rules. "Substantive rules" relate to matters that are considered significant in their own right. Rules governing property rights, contractual arrangements, and bodily violence fall within this group. "Ceremonial" or "ritual rules" relate to matters that are considered to have little intrinsic significance. The major function of ceremonial or ritual rules is to govern the conduct through which one expresses one's self-regard, one's regard for the others in the immediate situation, and the systems of rules governing their conduct. That is, these are rules governing self-expression and the expression of one's place in social systems. These ceremonial norms govern the aspect of behavior that is often called "etiquette." [32]

SITUATED ORDER AS RITUAL EXCHANGE

The normative order that is intrinsic to interaction governs conduct that is ceremonial or ritual in character. Other substantively significant rules may also apply in situations, but situated order is always ceremonial, whatever the substantive matters may be. Goffman's term for the value of ceremonial exchange is "deference." One is entitled to a degree of deference from others by virtue of one's place in the social system—one's self. The expression of deference by others serves to modify and control one's conduct. Deference is defined and given its value only by participation in a social order governed by normative rules. [33] Face-to-face interaction can be regarded as an order maintained by the exchange of deference among its participants. Other sanctions may be exchanged, but deference is intrinsic to situations, and is always a factor in their order.

Self-expression occurs whether the person intends his or her conduct to serve that function or not. Each person's expectations concerning the degree of deference he or she is owed and owes to others will often be initially defined by the nature of the ongoing social occasion. Adjustments are made in response to the self-expression of others. This process has been discussed in Chapter 3; only two additional points will be noted here.

First, in Goffman's view, whatever other functions may be served, mutual adjustment of responses in interaction ratifies the normative system itself and the selves of the participants. This is particularly clear when these modifications are extensive, as they are in "facework"

[32] Goffman, "The Nature of Deference and Demeanor," in 1967, pp. 47–56.
[33] *Ibid.*, pp. 56–76.

or "remedial rituals." Through participation in facework or remedial ritual, the participants recognize that an infraction of the ceremonial order has occurred. Through ritual exchange they express to one another that such deviations are not appropriate. Accounts, apologies, and requests all serve to reaffirm the respect of participants for the system.[34]

Second, there are occasions on which a person *must* respond negatively to ritual violations, even if his or her material interests are threatened by doing so. Ceremonial violations express the selves of both the offending and offended parties. The absence of remedial rituals following a ceremonial violation implies that the offended party, and all present, find the treatment acceptable. Failure to respond to perceived offenses against a self may lead to downgrading of the self and affect the deference one can claim through the situation. Failure to respond negatively to ceremonial violations also expresses the fact that one is not conforming to one's obligations to sanction others. This expression, another rule violation, may further compromise one's self-definition. Self-maintenance, therefore, must take precedence over material gain.[35]

EXTRA-SITUATIONAL RELEVANCE OF CEREMONIAL EXCHANGE

The analytic boundary of exchange in situations is termed the "consequentiality" of situational events. "Consequentiality" refers to the effects of a sanction in situations following the one in which the sanction originally occurs.[36] Substantive sanctions clearly have consequences in this sense. Money earned in one situation is spent and enjoyed in another. The effects of physical harm may continue after the social situation in which it is inflicted has ended. Ritual sanctions may also have such extended consequences. A person who is discredited as a liar in one situation may not be trusted in subsequent ones.

Those involved in a situation will orient their conduct toward the multiple relationships that exist among them.[37] In doing so, people may consider one's conduct in one situation as relevant to their treatment of one in subsequent situations. One may be required to live up to, or with, the self that one has accepted in other situations. One who allows oneself to be treated poorly may find that one will not be able to confine that treatment to the original situation in which it occurs. These ceremonial consequences of situated actions in subsequent situations impose, in effect, a rule governing the expression of a consistent self. Unless contrary evidence is observed, one will be treated as if one always expresses

[34] Goffman, 1971, pp. 163–165 and 1967.
[35] Goffman, 1969, pp. 134–135.
[36] Goffman, "Where the Action Is," in 1967, pp. 159–160.
[37] Goffman, "The Nature of Deference and Demeanor," in 1967, pp. 61–62.

the same self and will be expected to always express the self appropriate to the treatment one received in other situations.

Goffman argues that a high regard for maintaining a consistent self is essential to the maintenance of social order. Without this concern, people would become purely strategic in their conduct, manipulating the ceremonial order for material gains. Among such people, there would be no grounds for trust. People could not count on one another to fulfill the terms of relationships or places in social systems once they were no longer under mutual scrutiny. There would be no means for the coordination of actions across time and space.[38]

Presentation of Self

"Self-presentation" was originally discussed by Goffman in terms of a theatrical or dramaturgical metaphor. The normative obligation to express the self-characteristics appropriate to one's position in the social system was described as the "obligation to give a performance." The performance consisted of any activity that influenced others in a situation.[39]

As people moved from situation to situation, assuming different places in social systems, they could be observed to drastically alter their self-expression. Goffman illustrated this phenomenon by describing the changes of waiters' expressive behavior as they moved from the dining room to the kitchen. By doing so, they moved out of view of the customers and into a drastically altered social situation. The major variable utilized to account for these changes in self-expression was the nature of the relationships among the people in different situations. In theatrical terms, the others in a situation act as an audience for one's performance, evaluating and responding to its adequacy. As the nature of the audience changes, so does the performance. Finally, situations were observed in which the performance given in other situations was openly and knowingly contradicted. These regions were referred to as "backstage" relative to the performance.[40] The kitchen of a restaurant is backstage relative to the waiters' servile performance in the frontstage dining room. In the kitchen, the waiters openly flaunt the servility they must perform for the diners and, in addition, store their equipment, rehearse for the performance, and arrange for cues, activites similar to those that take place in theater backstages.

The theatrical metaphor directs attention to one extremely important

[38] Goffman, 1969, pp. 135–136.
[39] Goffman, 1959, pp. 1–15.
[40] *Ibid.*, p. 112.

aspect of self-presentation—its often intentional, controlled, nonspontaneous character. The credibility of the self is linked to the degree to which it appears to others to be expressed unintentionally. Close observation indicates, however, that self-presentation is frequently contrived, prepared in advance, and sustained through planned cooperation among members of a performance team. "Self-presentation" refers to observable techniques that foster a particular definition of oneself whether they are intentional or not. Distinguishing between expression and communication remains important.

Recently, Goffman has not utilized this dramaturgical metaphor in discussing self-presentation. In a remark made more significant by his earlier approach, he has observed that "all the world is not a stage—certainly the theater isn't entirely." [41] Goffman has done more than simply drop the metaphor. He has taken considerable pains to indicate the pitfalls of the metaphor.[42] Accordingly, we have discussed expression and will discuss self-presentation as much as possible in nondramaturgical terms. We will, however, indicate the appropriate dramaturgical terms when they apply.

Self-presentation is a situated activity. However, our selves often ratify social relationships that are embedded in broader social occasions. We will discuss three important aspects of self-presentation: the ratification of relationships that do not extend beyond the situation in which they are expressed; the ratification of relationships that extend beyond the boundaries of the situation; and aspects of self-presentation that occur outside the situation, such as preparations and team-cooperation.

RATIFICATION OF SITUATED RELATIONSHIPS

Evolutionary perspective on the role of interactant. The norms governing any situation require that individuals express, through conformity to ceremonial rules, that they are competent interactants. We have discussed this aspect of self-presentation in some detail already. However, the comparison of human conduct with that of other species suggests some additional insights.

Goffman argues that one's immediate environment is either in a normal condition or is alarming. When the environment is perceived as normal, the individual feels that he or she can handle the contingencies that it presents. When alarmed, the individual becomes physiologically aroused and mobilizes his or her efforts toward self-preservation.[43] The effects of alarming conditions among other species are easily observed. They in-

[41] Goffman, 1974, p. 1.
[42] This discussion constitutes one of the major themes of *Frame Analysis* (1974). For our purposes, many of the details have been omitted.
[43] Goffman, 1971, pp. 238ff.

clude the flight of herd animals when a predator's scent is perceived or when loud, unusual noises are heard.

Many conditions can precipitate alarm among people. The failure to conform to ceremonial norms produces alarm among one's fellow participants. Their responses are self-preserving—consisting in cases of mild alarm of "remedial rituals" or "facework." In more extreme cases, the interaction may be terminated, a form of social flight or retreat that recognizes the inability to preserve oneself in the situation.

The use of this concept, derived from studies of animal behavior, is not metaphorical. Within an evolutionary framework, we must expect to find continuities among the behaviors of different species. The functional correspondence of some aspects of our social behavior to the behavior of other species supports the evolutionary perspective. The uniqueness of our mechanisms for recognizing and reacting to alarm corresponds to our unique characteristics as a species—our uniquely extensive use of symbols and the mediation of our social conduct through the mechanism of the self.

This functional correspondence of our conduct to that of other species is also found in territorial behavior. Animals of many species stake out territories, geographical areas, as off-limits to other members of their own species. A variety of territorial markers are used, including scents and vocalizations. Humans apparently maintain territorial boundaries among each other as well, often through self-expression. Humans expect a certain distance to be kept between themselves and others—a personal space. In addition, we maintain territorial preserves that are symbolic. For example, a place in line is not a geographical location but a claim about the proper chronological ordering of events. In addition, our claimed right to be shown deference, including the right not to be approached by others for conversation, is territorial in nature. Perceiving the norms regarding openness and involvement as territorial norms puts our conduct into evolutionary perspective.[44]

Withs. During an interaction, some of the participants may express through their conduct that they form a "with," that the individuals involved are to be treated as a single unit during the interaction. The "with" is a situated relationship that does not necessarily have implications for other situations in which the individuals participate. In the massive audience attending some event in a stadium, each group that operates as a smaller unit than the entire crowd but bigger than one individual (for example, a family) is a with.

The with is expressed in an alteration of the territorial claims made

[44] *Ibid.,* pp. 28ff.

by its members, both among themselves and with regard to outsiders. Members of a with generally: stand closer together; are relatively more open to each other than to outsiders; look at one another more frequently; and are more likely to make intentional physical contact—to guide one another, hold hands, or put an arm around one another's shoulders or waists. Exceptional liberties may be taken, such as mutual grooming (as when people straighten one another's hair), utilizing intimate forms of address, or casually claiming favors as rights (such as holding a package or opening a door).

People who are not part of a with must respect its territorial claims. For example, the members of a with should not be separated by people passing between them. Also, nongeographical territory, such as a place in line, may be shared by all members of a with. Even if only one of the members physically remains in the line, he or she may buy tickets for all the members. Members of a with also assume some responsibility for one another's conduct. A mother with her child is judged not only by her own conduct, but also by that of the child. In general all members of the with may be embarrassed or honored by the conduct of any one of its members.

RELATIONSHIPS EXTENDING BEYOND THE SITUATION

In any situation that is part of a broader social occasion, the relationships of all individuals within the situation will be defined by their place in the occasion. For example, the obligations defined by one's job create relationships with anyone else who is involved in the system of which the job is a part. The significance of these broader relationships, and of the expression of selves appropriate to them, has already been discussed in terms of membership in collectivities and commitment to their norms. In addition, personal relationships may exist between individuals, and these too require expression.

When personal relationships exist between people, they may express the existence and nature of the relationship through a form of situated conduct called "tie signs." "Tie signs" are conduct that is only appropriate between individuals who share a particular kind of social relationship. For example, only relatively intimate relationships allow a male and female to maintain physical contact while engaging in conversation with a third party. By the tie sign more than a with is expressed—a relationship that transcends the interaction is implied.

Tie signs inform third parties about the nature of claimed relationships and impose special normative constraints on interaction conduct that might violate the terms of the relationship, either within the setting or at subsequent times. For example when the tie signs appropriate to marriage are displayed, others are normatively constrained from initiating any action that violates the marriage relationship.

Parties involved in relationships may insist upon the public expression of its terms through tie signs. When the relationship is in flux, tie signs may serve to inform each party of the perceived nature of the relationship. The first public use of intimate forms of address or nicknames may inform one person that the relationship is being regarded as closer by another.

Tie signs are employed in very casual relationships as well. The openness of one person to a greeting from another is the sign of a very slight relationship. As the relationship becomes more intimate, the length and form of the greeting may be altered. Failure to greet someone to whom greetings are "owed" may be regarded as a serious offense. This indicates that the tie sign has functions parallel to those of other forms of expressive behavior.[45]

NONSITUATED ASPECTS OF SELF-PRESENTATION

Self-presentational conduct always occurs in situations, in the presence of others. However, many aspects of self-presentation could not be effectively accomplished without the cooperation of others and the utilization of private regions in which to prepare for anticipated situations. Self-*expression* can occur with no preparations or planning. However, creating a belief in others that a particular, appropriate self has been expressed may require prior effort and the intentional manipulation of conduct. In short, the presentation or communication of a particular self may require preparatory activities that must not be witnessed by those expected to trust the implications of the performance. If seen, these activities would discredit the presented self.

In effect, our selves are regulated in two ways by norms. First, they are expected to be appropriate. Norms governing the self-characteristics appropriate to incumbents of a place in a social system and norms governing consistency between situations impose this requirement. Second, selves must be *expressed*. Norms demanding a negative response upon the discovery of covert control of expressive conduct impose this requirement. People are frequently caught in a bind created by these two different types of constraints. They may be required to exhibit characteristics that demand preparation and intentional effort. At the same time, they are required not to engage in controlled communication. The result is concealment of activities which, if known to the relevant audience, would reframe or discredit the self presented to them. One of the primary mechanisms of concealment is to conduct these activities outside the situation—when the relevant audience is not present to observe them. This can be accomplished by geographic or temporal isolation (assuming no one "snitches").

In Merton's terms, such acts of concealment, such as the use of a

45 *Ibid.*, pp. 200–210.

private room, constitute barriers to perception. That is, they prevent certain members of the role-set from observing activities that if observed would be disapproved.[46] Goffman has added a dimension to barriers of perception—the possibility that they may be intentionally erected. The perception that a barrier has been erected, even if what is concealed is unknown or known not to be threatening, is in itself discrediting.

Goffman illustrates these points by reference to physical disabilities, such as being deaf, which may lower one's ritual status. This can result in reduced levels of trust by others and constraints upon participation in social systems. To avoid these consequences, the deaf often utilize techniques to conceal their disability from others. For example, they read lips and always arrange to be facing the speaker. In addition they may learn to utilize nonverbal cues to know when it is appropriate for them to respond, by laughing or interjecting, even if they do not know exactly what has been said. If there is a better ear, they may keep it in the direction of the speaker.

To some people, however, the very techniques that conceal deficient hearing are recognizable for what they are. That is, instead of concealing the deficiency, their presence is an indication that the deficiency exists. This more accurate frame is generally available to those who either have similar deficiences or those who have had considerable experience with the problem. The concealing actions, the attempts to pass, are as discreditable as the deficiency itself. Both the self-characteristics and the means for concealing them (or, in general, for controlling conduct that ought to be spontaneous) are normatively regulated.[47]

Teams. A "team" is a group of people who cooperate in maintaining a given definition of some situation. Of course, the selves of the participants are major constituents of that definition. Members of a team may have other social connections such as role obligations in an organization. However this need not be the case. Strangers who engage in remedial rituals or facework to maintain their self-definitions after an incident constitute a short-lived team. While team activities are numerous, here we are primarily concerned with cooperation of team members that extends beyond the situation in which the definition is maintained by the team's efforts. This extended cooperation falls outside the analytic boundaries of the situation.

First, we will consider team activities that do not involve other organizational responsibilities in the situation. A tailor who corrects the way in which one's clothes fit is involved in team cooperation with his or her customer; every situation in which the clothes are worn is a collaborative effort, even though the teamwork is not observed in any of them. Team-

[46] Merton, "The Role Set."
[47] Goffman, 1963b, pp. 1–31.

work need not be deceptive, nor need its results compromise the audience.

Sometimes, however, both of these conditions occur. For example, cosmetic surgery, special training to eliminate a regional accent, or legal action to change an ethnically identifiable name all involve teamwork and all have consequences for self-presentation on subsequent situations. In contrast to the altering of clothes, however, which is generally assumed to be necessary, these activities if known would partly discredit the self that they are intended to present. In such cases discovery of the teamwork amounts to the discovery of a fabrication and to discreditation.

When teamwork is acknowledged, activities are reframed, but not necessarily in a negative way. Acknowledgment of diction training, for example, while revealing that one has not come by one's accent naturally also reveals commitment to the requirements of one's role. Often it is normatively required that team activities be concealed to avoid discrediting a self which must be present through a single person's efforts, and yet cannot be. Teams may act as a secret society, cooperating to fabricate situations and to conceal the fabrication.

Team members may also be involved in sustained relationships which include normative obligations. This occurs, for example, when the team members are employees in business and have team responsibilities as part of their work. An employer who calls his or her receptionist by his or her first name but refers to him or her more formally when others are present is engaging in teamwork with the receptionist. The employer is cooperating to maintain the employee's control over his or her openness to others. The employer's use of informal address in others' presence might lead to a definition of the receptionist as open to informal address from anyone in the situation.

Teamwork may also be involved in preparing the scene or defining selves of non-teammates. Goffman points out that bellboys are able to mark the doors of guests who are regarded as suspicious in a way that is easily observable by hotel staff but not likely to be noticed by guests. This mark serves to define the guests for the staff in any situation, making them especially alert to alarming events such as loud noises in the room. In such cases, the teamwork consists of varied and coordinated activities by different people. Each, in pursuing one's other role obligations, maintains a frame of reference known only by team members. Many members of the staff may not be on such a team (such as maintenance personnel, who do not work where such a mark is present).[48]

Backstage activities. In discussing the dramaturgical metaphor we suggested that backstage areas are often utilized for activities which contradict but also contribute to successful self-presentation. The backstage

[48] Goffman, 1959, pp. 77–105.

extends self-presentation beyond the boundaries of the situation in which it occurs. Unlike teamwork, which can occur both within and without a situation, backstage activities always occur without the situation. To reveal them within the situation, whether it is disruptive or not, is to bring them into the front stage. The teamwork between a plastic surgeon and his or her client, then, is backstage if it is not acknowledged in a subsequent situation but front stage if it is. Thus, the definition of the backstage is concerned primarily with the distribution and concealment of contradictory information that, if known front stage, would discredit the performance.

There is considerable variation in the degree to which the details of a performance are rehearsed. When a couple agrees in advance to keep the door to a messy room in their home closed during a party, they are engaging in a minimal rehearsal. But to observe even this rehearsal could reframe the closed door as well as the perceived cleanliness of the couple and perhaps their standing as relaxed, casual hosts. More detailed rehearsals occur when, for example, waitresses are coached in the exact nature of their responsibility to customers. The greeting, the number of trips made to the table, what is to be accomplished on each trip, and the time to be expended may all be standardized through training. In some cases it is obvious to customers that this has been done, but in others the standardization of treatment remains backstage.

Many performances are so detailed and complex that they cannot be carried out without rehearsal. In such cases, even if the rehearsal is not observed and its exact nature is not known, it is not backstage to the performance. Diplomatic protocol provides an illustration of this. Protocol is defined in tortuously detailed codes that have been developed and standardized over centuries of use. It is assumed that everyone rehearses and studies these conventions in preparation for any diplomatic encounter. Consequently, rehearsals of protocol are not backstage, although they may occur outside of the situation in which protocol is employed. Only rehearsals that contradict the front stage performance are backstage.

In addition to rehearsing their performances, participants in an anticipated situation may prepare the scene or props for it. Again, some preparations are not backstage. Washing dishes in the kitchen of a restaurant, although not observed by the customers, is assumed to occur and is consistent with the impression fostered in the front stage area. Other preparations are backstage. The customer will not be shown the dirty surroundings in which his or her food is cooked, or the way in which a dirty spoon is simply wiped off and returned to him or her, or the combination of ingredients which the chef regards as "secret" for a particular dish. The customer might be appalled or delighted by information which would be available backstage, but in neither case does he or she have access to such information.

Finally, the self presented in the front stage area may be openly disavowed backstage. Role requirements may require the presentation of undesired characteristics. Often people in such roles will mock or downgrade those characteristics in other situations. A waiter who must show extreme deference to the customers may burlesque their appearance and mannerisms once he moves out of their sight. A television performer who must smilingly endorse a product may downgrade its merits off camera.[49] Such disavowals may also occur in the front stage area, perhaps with disruptive effects. For example, a waiter may break frame and insult a customer. Such disavowals are crucial to the expression of identity.

It is important to remember that the various functions served by backstage activities may also be served in front regions. When collusive communication occurs, using coded signals known to only some of those present, concealment may occur in the front stage. An area is backstage relative to a performance if, *and only if,* activities actually occur in it that contradict the impression fostered in that performance.

Identity

The term "self," as Goffman uses it, refers to the characteristics that are normatively associated with a particular place in the social order. In any situation, several normative orders may be relevant governing conduct with reference to a multiplicity of social relationships and membership in collectivities. Any person in a given situation, then, would be expected to have and exhibit the same self-characteristics as any other person. The self is social, more linked to social systems than to individuals, and reasonably conceived as loaned to people temporarily for the duration of their particular participation in a social system. Empirically, however, self-expression is not that standardized. At least, as we have frequently observed, inappropriate expressions occur and must be mitigated through ceremonial ritual. In addition, people risk being discredited by attempting to pass, by concealing information that could discredit them and the frame in which their activity had been interpreted.

The characteristics that distinguish one from others in similar socially defined situations, those that mark one as a unique individual, are one's "identity." Clearly identity can only be expressed through contrast with normatively governed self-characteristics. If the two are identical, if one is what one is expected to be, the properties will be attributed to one's social

[49] *Ibid.,* pp. 106–140.

situation, not one's individual characteristics. For example, the normative requirement that dentists express cleanliness by washing hands frequently, changing their linen often, and having clean offices makes it virtually impossible for a dentist to express cleanliness as his or her own characteristic. Almost any degree of extreme cleanliness will be attributed to him or her as a *dentist,* not as a unique person. Only by violating the norms governing cleanliness, either by being sloppy or obsessed with dirt in some demonstrable way, can his or her own attitude toward cleanliness be observed. The presence of normative regulations governing expressive conduct confounds the interpretation of such conduct as information about the individual.

Identity, then, is expressed in the distance between actual expressive behavior and the normative requirements of the situation. Distance can be expressed in a number of ways. First, relationships may be expressed and ratification of them required from others that are not normatively required. For example, keeping a family portrait on one's desk expressively indicates that the normative requirements of the situation do not exhaust the interest or obligations of the person. Sports trophies, an aquarium, or a selection of magazines may serve essentially the same function. Second, a person may sustain secondary involvements. These introduce the pursuit of personal interests into the situation. They may also express an attitude toward the situation. For example, a person may do needlepoint during a business meeting. At the least this indicates that he or she has personal interests and that the immediate situation does not merit or require his or her full attention. As the secondary involvement becomes more attention consuming, the attitude expressed toward the situation becomes increasingly negative. Third, the person may simply violate the rules—either substantive or ceremonial—that govern the situation.

There is a close relationship between the activities through which people express identity and those which cause organizational chaos and lead to the application of psychiatric labels. If the expression of identity, of personal characteristics, becomes pronounced, social order may be disrupted. Distance-expressing activities will be comprehensible as expressions but will also be normatively inappropriate. The more personalized one's activities become, the more they will interfere with the ability of others to predict and orient themselves to one's actions. Goffman remarks that "our sense of personal dignity often resides in the cracks" of organizational structure.[50]

Identity is expressed in the same conduct and interpreted in terms of the same conventional idiom as self. In addition, the techniques available for presenting an identity and for preparing for the presentation are

[50] Goffman, 1961b, p. 320.

identical. Because the expression of self and identity are identical in every respect except that selves are normatively prescribed, we need not present an analysis of expression of identity.

Having already emphasized that the expression of identity is not a normative requirement of role incumbency we will consider the evidence that identity *is* expressed, and even under extremely discouraging conditions. By inference from extreme cases, Goffman suggests that identity is always expressed. Also, we will consider how the expression of identity can, at the same time, contravene norms and contribute to the smooth functioning of a social order.

Expression of identity will be considered in two very different social settings. The expression of identity is discouraged in each but expressed nonetheless in both. First, consider the expression of identity by inmates in state psychiatric wards.[51] Expressions of identity are discouraged by the close regulation of activities, extreme surveillance, institutional ownership and control of facilities, and severe sanctions. Second, we will discuss the expression of identity by surgeons during surgery.[52] Here, such expression is discouraged by the highly inflexible technical requirements of surgery, the seriousness of the occasion, and, especially for the chief surgeon, the extreme attractiveness of the normatively prescribed self.

IDENTITY IN PSYCHIATRIC WARDS

Any organization specifies appropriate standards of welfare, values that ought to be shared, incentives for adequate compliance with organizational rules, and penalties for their violation. Participation in an organization implies acceptance of these definitions, indicating that one is responsive to the incentives and penalties to which one subjects oneself and that one accepts the standard of welfare that applies to one. That is, participation ratifies the implied self.[53]

Participation in organizations may not be limited to activities that conform to the regulations of the organization. There may be a routine use of unauthorized means, the achievement of unauthorized ends, or both. These secondary adjustments, violations of organizational rules or intent, are ways in which the individual stands apart from his or her role, especially the implications it holds for his or her self-characteristics.[54] As conformity to organizational rules ratifies its definition of one's self, secondary adjustments express a separate identity.

A psychiatric hospital is an example of what Goffman calls a "total institution." A "total institution" is an organization which encompasses

[51] *Ibid.,* pp. 173–320.
[52] Goffman, 1961a, pp. 85–152.
[53] Goffman, 1961b, pp. 177–179.
[54] *Ibid.,* p. 189.

the entire lives of its members, usually cutting them off physically as well as socially from outside contact. In our society, recreation, work, and sleeping activities are generally conducted in different places, with different groups of people, and without an overall plan. Total institutions break down the barriers between these realms of life, confining a group of people in a physical location and scheduling all their activities. Further, the facilities are usually standardized, owned, and distributed primarily by the organization, facilitating the degree to which their use can be scheduled and controlled.[55] In psychiatric hospitals, for medical reasons, the inmates are also under drastically more surveillance than is normal. This surveillance is necessary for diagnostic reasons, and to prevent self-destructive or aggressive acts. It also serves to gather the information required for close social control. The inmate role, and the self attributed to it, are highly undesirable. The inmate is usually unable to leave the institution at will. These conditions suggest that secondary adjustments would be desirable in the setting.

The conditions imposed by the total institution drastically reduce the opportunity for secondary adjustments, but they flourish nonetheless. We will discuss only a few of the common secondary adjustments to illustrate that they are employed and that identities are expressed even under severely restrictive conditions. It is important to note that the negative sanctions available to the psychiatric staff are harsh, even if medically sound. They include the right to move patients to back wards in which the facilities are even more impoverished, the ability to extend the time for which the patient is held in the institution against his or her will, and the right to use drugs, physical restraint, or shock treatments to control the patient's behavior. Control of the duration and terms of incarceration provide attractive positive sanctions for conformity. Furthermore, the expression of distance may have symptomatic significance in a psychiatric frame: identity expression may be framed as a symptom and treatment undertaken.

What kind of secondary adjustments are found in such settings? One example involves the schedule by which clothing and linen are washed, and by which the institution imposes a standard of cleanliness on the inmates. Many inmates wash their clothes by hand and dry them on exposed radiators, thus maintaining a personally chosen level of cleanliness. Again, institutional meals are scheduled and the menu is planned without reference to the desires of the inmates. But several devices reduce institutional control over this portion of life. Second helpings of food could be obtained and eaten later, especially if the food is portable or suitable for sandwiches. Such food could also be eaten in a chosen

[55] *Ibid.,* pp. 1–7.

place, such as outdoors in nice weather. Thus, institutional control of the quantity, scheduling, and location of meals can be mitigated to some extent by simple secondary adjustments. Notice that these activities result in secreting food on one's person and withdrawal from social activities. These could easily have symptomatic significance.

Many of the secondary adjustments employed in psychiatric hospitals are cooperative in nature. Often patients are not allowed razors; and shaves, as well as haircuts, are scheduled by the institution. The frequency of shaves and haircuts might not be acceptable to some inmates, who may exchange cigarettes, candy, or other rare items for an extra shave or haircut. Often, too, inmates are able to exchange the special advantages of a work assignment with others. For example, the librarian could exchange early access to new magazines, before they became soiled or ripped, for extra food, well-fitted clothes, shaves, or haircuts.

Secondary adjustments are not limited to such material matters, nor is cooperation restricted to the inmate group. Ceremonial rewards are relatively more valuable if administered by the staff. However, the staff members are neither confined to the institution nor subject to the level of material comfort imposed on inmates: a few cigarettes are not an adequate bribe to staff members. But inmates can often offer desirable material services. For example, an inmate can wash a staff member's car, arrange for his or her laundry to be done at institutional expense, or perhaps repair shoes, tailor, or do carpentry work. In exchange, the inmate can claim the right to intimacies with the staff that are not permitted by the institutional definition of the inmate role. Intimate greetings, public expressions of thanks, or occasional favors such as recognition of one's birthday all ratify the ceremonial status of the inmate at a higher level than that suggested by the institution.

In addition to tangible services, the inmates have another commodity at their disposal—the ability to disrupt the situation and cause trouble for staff members. For example, "acting up" when visitors are on the ward embarrasses the staff. Thus, the willingness of staff to step out of their institutionally defined roles by increasing the ceremonial status of inmates may be essential to the maintenance of order in the wards.[56] In effect, even though the inmates have been diagnosed as having psychiatric problems, they must be treated as more than just patients. If not, they will, whether they appreciate the irony or not, act "crazy" when it is most inconvenient for staff members. Identities, like selves, have a reciprocal character. If the staff member refuses to express distance from the self suggested for him or her by the institution, the inmates will not be able to successfully sustain distance from the self suggested for them.

[56] *Ibid.*, pp. 207–320.

IDENTITY IN SURGERY

In surgery, Goffman points out, irrelevant expressions, even those that contradict the normatively dictated selves of the participants, may increase the efficiency of the proceedings. The success of the surgical procedure is more important to the chief surgeon than his or her maintenance of professional dignity, expression of rank, or insistence upon the expression of deference by others on the surgical team. The overall goal of the situation takes precedence and leads even the surgeon, a person in a highly desirable role, to express distance from it. Goffman suggests that the expression of role distance by surgeons during surgery is a strong indication that distance is always expressed.[57]

Role distance may be utilized in several ways during surgery. All members of the surgical team must remain poised to perform their assigned tasks. Occasionally, members of the team may make an error. After all, interns are involved in on-the-job training. The surgeon is responsible to correct those errors, and by virtue of rank is entitled to be relatively formal and harsh in the correction. However, if this right is exercised, the anxiety of participants may be increased and, thereby, the threat of further errors. Thus, the surgeon may combine his or her sanctions with jokes, reducing his or her claims regarding his or her place in order to increase overall effectiveness. Making orders into requests by the use of politeness may also reduce tension and defuse any resentments about the distribution of ceremonial status. For example, an experienced surgical nurse may resent his or her subordination to a young, inexperienced intern. Through courtesy to the nurse, the chief surgeon may prevent disruptive attention to the details of occupational status. When distractions are likely to ease tension, the chief surgeon may introduce them him- or herself, using nonmedical terminology or dramatic gestures to prevent tension from becoming too severe.[58] The expression of identity not only affirms the surgeon's uniqueness as an individual, but also has the function of maximizing efficiency and effectiveness during surgery.

Integrating Goffman's Work with Other Approaches to Symbolic Interaction

Clearly, in Goffman's work the social situation consists primarily of the existence of social norms, symbols, and conventions (generically, frameworks) as objective conditions of interaction. This treatment contrasts rather sharply with the view of norms, symbols, and conventions as a product of interaction, achieved through a collective negotiating process.

[57] Goffman, 1961a, pp. 120–121.
[58] *Ibid.*, pp. 121–127.

The two approaches can be integrated by considering the consequences of varying degrees of institutionalization upon the meanings, including norms, utilized by a social group.

In highly institutionalized settings interaction proceeds smoothly, with the prior expectations of participants serving to successfully guide their conduct without significant revision. While information is continually gathered and evaluated in light of expectations, the collective negotiating process is a relatively unimportant factor in highly institutionalized situations. Action may be extremely standardized, repetitive, and routine. For example, the ticket-seller at a theater may engage in hundreds of successive interactions with customers. Each is unique in some ways, yet seldom, if ever, are the roles negotiated or redefined.

The collective negotiating process has its greatest importance in situations that are relatively uninstitutionalized. The participants will find, in these situations, a lack of consensus concerning what is going on, what ought to be going on, and what share each should assume of the collective work. The process by which these matters are decided is a central topic of symbolic interactionists.

Institutionalized meanings—norms, symbols, frameworks—have a different character. They define reality and have a coercive power over the actors. So long as they remain institutionalized, these meanings will be enforced with sanctions, and predictions of the flow of events will only be accurate if these meanings are adopted as the basis for planning. Thus these institutionalized meanings constrain the actor to either take them into account or to fail in his or her endeavors. These institutionalized meanings can also be used as a strategic resource. Their predictability makes it possible to plan and, in particular, to manipulate others. Successful, intentional misrepresentation of oneself and one's activities are only possible under those conditions in which the interpretation others will place on action can be reliably predicted.

In brief, meanings are established and maintained in interaction. Once established, they have a real, coercive character. They become a condition of action. When they are not well established, the coordination of action is accomplished by a negotiating process which results in the development of new institutionalized meanings. That is, meanings have the real, coercive character discussed by Goffman or the fluid negotiated character we have discussed at length depending on the degree to which they are institutionalized. The two approaches complement one another by being most fruitful in different types of situations.

Suggested Readings

Goffman's writing style is exceptionally good and much of his work is accessible to nonspecialists. Two of his books, *Asylums* (Anchor Books, Garden City, N.Y.,

1961) and *Presentation of Self in Everyday Life* (Anchor Books, Garden City, N.Y., 1959), are especially interesting. *Asylums* consists of four essays on the theme of involuntary confinement in total institutions, primarily psychiatric hospitals. The characteristics of these institutions, the way in which the patient enters them, adaptation to the institutional setting, and a sociological analysis of the medical model in psychiatry are discussed. *Presentation of Self in Everyday Life,* which has already been recommended in other contexts, is Goffman's most influential book. *Frame Analysis* (Colophon Books, New York, 1974) is more difficult but includes a comprehensive statement of Goffman's views; for students who wish to pursue Goffman's work in detail it is an essential supplement to his earlier theoretical statements.

References to Goffman's Works

1952 "On Cooling the Mark Out," *Psychiatry* 15 (November), 451–463.

1959 *The Presentation of Self in Everyday Life,* Doubleday Anchor Books, Garden City, N.Y.

1961a *Encounters,* Bobbs-Merrill, Indianapolis.

1961b *Asylums,* Anchor Books, Garden City, N.Y.

1963a *Behavior in the Public Places,* Free Press, New York.

1963b *Stigma,* Prentice-Hall, Englewood Cliffs, N.J.

1964 "The Neglected Situation," *American Anthropologist* 66, No. 6, Part 2 (December), Special Publication, *The Ethnography of Communication,* edited by John Gumperz and Dell Humes, 133–136.

1967 *Interaction Ritual,* Anchor Books, Garden City, N.Y.

1969 *Strategic Interaction,* University of Pennsylvania Press, Philadelphia.

1971 *Relations in Public,* Basic Books, New York.

1974 *Frame Analysis,* Colophon Books, New York.

Name Index

Subject Index